Y0-BSM-582

1·25·79

The Complete
Gourmet
Nutrition
Cookbook

The Joy of Eating Well and Right

The Complete Gourmet Nutrition Cookbook

*How To Change Your Eating
For the Better - and Enjoy it!*

By
Margaret C. Dean, M.S., R.N.

Illustrations
created by
Elaine Hay

With the report on
Dietary Goals from the U.S. Senate
Select Committee on Nutrition

Published by **ACROPOLIS BOOKS Ltd.** ● Washington D.C. 20009

ACROPOLIS BOOKS LTD.
Colortone Building, 2400 17th St., N.W., Washington, D.C. 20009

Printed in the United States of America by
COLORTONE PRESS Creative Graphics, Inc.
Washington, D.C. 20009

Acropolis Books are distributed in

Canada
by Carlton House, Ontario, Canada

Europe and the British Commonwealth by
by Paul Maitland, Ltd., Kent, England

Japan
by Atlantic Book Service, Tokyo

Pakistan
by SASI Ltd., Karachi

Elsewhere in Asia and Australia
by ICTO PTE Ltd., Singapore

Library of Congress Cataloging in Publication Data

Dean, Margaret C.   1919–
    The complete gourmet nutrition cookbook.

    Bibliography: p.
    Includes index.
    1. Cookery.   2. Nutrition.   I. Title.
TX715.D282   641.5′632   78-6749
ISBN 0-87491-215-6
ISBN 0-87491-195-8 pbk.

This book is dedicated to

My good parents who allowed me
freedom of thought and
decision

A good husband who has been
patient, understanding and
cooperative in helping me
with home, family, career
and this book

Three children, H. A., Jr., John
Carter and Margarae, who have
been encouraging, and have
helped in family projects
that enabled me to continue
my career, and during the
writing of this book

and

The future of our grandchildren
and to all children that good
nutrition may be promoted through
the teaching of wise eating habits

CONTENTS

ACKNOWLEDGEMENTS

The Complete Gourmet Nutrition Cookbook is like a living plant. It grew from my research and the personal experiences of my family. Its philosophy comes from my conviction that food is a basic force in the life of every person. Its content comes from years of experience working as a dietitian, consulting nutritionist, college and university teacher, director of dietetics and designing nutrition education programs for various community groups of different cultures, throughout the United States and abroad.

It is my pleasure to express appreciation to my many friends, colleagues and family members who have encouraged me. The U.S. Department of Agriculture, the U.S. Department of Health, Education and Welfare, the Senate Select Committee for Human Needs, and Acropolis Books have been very helpful. The American National Red Cross has provided me many opportunities to be of service to humanity through programs that required the adapting of technical knowledge to meet the needs of people—for all of these I am most grateful.

Grateful acknowledgement and thanks are given to the families who contributed their favorite menus and recipes, and to the American Dietetic Association, American Home Economics Association, American Medical Association, and to the Virginia Historical Society for their help and suggestions.

Margaret C. Dean

Washington, D.C.

PREFACE

AS A NATION WE ARE LITERALLY killing ourselves through our poor eating habits.

America produces food—good food—in abundance. There is no lack of information in this country about what constitutes sound dietary habits, and consequently good health, but we ignore it. We have instead chosen to go along with what seems easier in this decade on the go: "fast food," nutritionally empty food, meals on the run, fad diets. The result, of course, is that we are living shorter and less vigorous lives than all reason and available knowledge says we should.

I wrote this book because of my deep and continuing concern with the sociological and psychological influences on individuals and on families which are contributing to poor diet and poor health. In so doing I have drawn principally upon two sources: my experiences as a career nutritionist and the Dietary Goals newly established by the United States Senate Select Committee for Nutrition and Human Needs.

As a food and nutrition consultant for the American National Red Cross, I have had opportunities to work extensively in this country and abroad. I have helped develop community nutrition programs. As a Red Cross team member I have helped to bandage the wounds—physical, mental and emotional—of people caught up in calamity. During disasters I have gained firsthand knowledge of the problems that confront American families today, thereby broadening my personal experience with contemporary lifestyles, food habits and nutritional awareness.

The Red Cross helped me to add flexibility—an essential quality in meeting the needs of people—to my science background. Additionally, I have continued to update this background with further studies of sociology, psychology and anthropology; each of these specialized fields is essential in understanding man's dietary habits.

My research led me to careful scrutiny of our government's conclusions about the current state of America's nutritional health. The importance of what, how, and when to eat was considered by the Senate Committee.

What, therefore, I have tried to do in this book is to offer practical applications to these findings and to accepted theory of what is sound dietary practice. I have combined my own experience with the considerations and conclusions of the Senate report. The menus and recipes I suggest are intended as simple to follow and healthful to eat.

This book is based on my own studies and observations. It does not reflect the policies of the American National Red Cross or any other agency. It represents, rather, a personal effort to give the reader an understanding of our need to return to, and to maintain good food habits.

I am concerned about American families and the pressures exerted on them. I am concerned about American children growing up without adequate nutrition. I am concerned with the loss of a sense of basic values in our lifestyles and dining habits.

I discuss in this book such practical matters as shared dining, proper dieting, the contribution of the marketplace to promoting good food selection, even the healthful atmosphere for healthful dining—which means joy.

Eating right means more than eating enough. It also means eating in an environment which will promote good digestion. It especially means eating good foods which the body can use in the best possible way.

Now is the time to incorporate the pertinent information of the social and biological sciences into an integrated and meaningful whole—the science of eating right as a means toward eating well. In *The Complete Gourmet Nutrition Cookbook* I have tried to take a step forward in accomplishing just that.

Margaret Carter Dean, M.S., R.D.

INTRODUCTION

MORE THAN 200 YEARS AGO Benjamin Franklin wrote in *Poor Richard's Almanac:* "In general, mankind, since the improvement of cookery, eats twice as much as nature requires." This might have been written today. Not only do most of us eat twice as much as nature requires, but also we often select foods of marginal nutritional value.

And, while medical care has improved our general health and well-being, we still cannot prevent serious illness; we have a long way to go. A poor diet certainly contributes to illness. Food consumed in unbalanced quantities, eaten at the wrong time of day and without the enjoyment of a relaxed environment, all too often results in diseases of malnutrition such as obesity, diabetes and hypertension.

Dr. Dorothy P. Rice, Director of the Health Statistics Center of the United States, believes that a vital part of good medical care is proper diet. In fact, medical treatment may fail unless the patient eats the prescribed foods. The health of an individual upon admission to a hospital will determine, to a large extent, the success of the healing process for non-dietary problems.

There is evidence of general obesity in every age group among men and women throughout the United States, and health officials report that the number one killer is heart disease—both diet-related diseases. Not surprisingly, U.S. government studies show that in one out of every three households someone is on a restricted diet.

The human body is a wonderful and efficient machine that performs many functions. It undergoes the wear and tear of daily

breakdown and build-up of cells; it puts up a round-the-clock battle against disease and deterioration. To keep the machine working properly, we need to fuel it properly.

HOW WE USED TO EAT. There is no "typical" American eating pattern. Rather, that pattern is a combination of many factors. Our society continues to experience increasing diversification of cultures, and consequently we are exposed to many more kinds of foods than were commonly known and available even a generation or two ago. We practice traditional and learned food habits associated with a past living environment. Sometimes we have a desire for an exotic diet in the atmosphere of luxury. We share concern and fears about unknown or ready-packaged prepared foods. We have a tendency toward misinformation concerning our foods; therefore, we believe that foods containing additives are dangerous and should be avoided.

Generally, the American diet is based on fiction rather than fact. We use emotional responses to our foods instead of exercising the brainpower which is needed to understand the body chemistry and its biological processes.

"Our grandparents got along all right without worrying about balanced menus. They didn't even know about vitamins and minerals and weren't any the worse for it. So why should I fuss about what my family eats, so long as they get filled up?" These comments represent the attitude of many otherwise up-to-date homemakers.

One of the reasons for the frequent nutritional success of grandmother's unscientific method of filling up her family, and letting it go at that, is that in those days folks had bigger appetites. Everyone worked harder—physically harder—than most of us do now. Eighty years ago, 80 percent of the population lived on farms; in those days, men and women, boys and girls, all worked with their hands and it made them hungry. They lived in colder, draftier houses, too, and needed food to keep them warm, as well as to make energy.

Vitamins and minerals are found rather sparingly in most foods, and the smaller the meals we eat the more difficult it is to get these nutrients in sufficient quantities for good health. Our grandparents ate more food and automatically obtained more of these precious food elements.

The food they ate was different from our food, too. They enjoyed far less variety than we have, but since eight out of 10 of them lived on

4

farms, the foods they ate came fresh from field and garden and orchard, with most of the vitamin value intact. In the winter, their root vegetables, cabbages and apples from cellar and pit, and their canned and dried foods tided them over until spring. Even the city folk, who lived in smaller cities, were much nearer to their source of fresh food supply than their counterparts today. Today's city dwellers, unless they happen to have a garden, seldom see in a market fresh food that is less than 24 hours old; most is, in fact, much older. This may mean that a considerable proportion of the vitamin content has disappeared.

Also, many foods of our grandparents' day were less refined than the same foods are now. For example, whole grain cereals and flours were the rule and not the exception a century ago. These were rich in the essential vitamins and minerals which are removed in today's modern refining processes. Only recently have these vitamins and minerals been restored to some refined flours, breads and cereals by "enriching" them.

Therefore, our forefathers got along as well as they did because they ate more fresh, less refined food and had a better chance to supply their nutritional needs. But is should not be overlooked that many of the diseases now proven to be caused by dietary deficiencies were not recognized at that time, even though they did exist. Our forebears may well have blamed on other causes their sufferings from symptoms of vitamin and mineral deficiencies.

Another factor which influences present-day diets to a great extent, both for better and for worse, is that a vastly greater variety of foods is available to us. Grandmother had only a few basic foods at hand, and if her family wanted to fill up enough they had to eat what was set before them. If Johnny didn't like greens, Johnny had no other choice and, therefore, any food disliked by some members of the family could not be exchanged with another food which might be less valuable nutritionally. In contrast, the wide variety of foods which we have available to enjoy today may affect our diet for the worse.

On the other hand, the possibilities of good nutrition are increased today because we have access to many foods which were formerly not available at all in many parts of the country, or were available only for brief seasons. For example, when grandfather was a boy, oranges were a rarity in the north and east and many children saw them only in their Christmas stockings. Today we can drink fresh orange juice every day

of the year. The same is true of canned and frozen foods of all kinds. If we use these foods wisely, we cannot only improve our nutrition, but also make our meals more attractive. Our untrained taste and preference, however, cannot be depended upon as a reliable guide to a wise choice of nutritionally sound meals, even given this abundance. This is where knowledgeably planned menus are needed.

WHY DID WE CHANGE OUR EATING HABITS? The marked change in our eating habits began with the move from rural to urban living. The urban lifestyle placed heavy demands upon transportation, education, and the food market. New technologies have created new types of jobs. Jobs have become more sedentary in nature, and require more commuting time. The move into more sophisticated living has caused housing to take a greater share of income.

Let us look at what modern technology has done to our diets.

Mothers work in increasing numbers to assist, or even to totally support, their families. Family members assume their own individual styles of living at an early age. Children may be placed in day-care situations all day. At the close of the day, mother and father, exhausted from the day's work, rush home and put food upon the table, many times without much thought. Where once there were eager, laughing children clamoring around the empty table in expectation of the meal there is now a gathering of the family around the television and meals consumed informally and in individual silences. Children may often eat whatever is found in the refrigerator. Adults eat hurriedly while driving to the next meeting. The elderly living alone find little pleasure in preparing balanced meals for themselves. Many elderly persons are without food, or are too handicapped or too ill to shop for and prepare meals.

Food costs more today than it did a generation or two ago. Unfortunately, this is particularly true of the "protective" foods—milk, eggs, meat, green vegetables, and fresh fruit—foods that are high in protein and vitamins form a protective layer of fat under the skin for warmth. Even the farm family encounters this problem with foods they do not raise for themselves, and city families are confronted with it at every turn. Because the most money can be saved by cutting down on just these protective foods, the homemaker who is not guided by a definite menu plan for a well-balanced diet may easily use false economy at the expense of the family's health.

THE MISSING INGREDIENT: JOY. All of these drastic changes in our society have made us forget a most special ingredient in dining—joy! It has been forgotten, probably unintentionally, because of the heavy demands on time and energy. But good food cannot be properly utilized unless it is eaten in an environment that is pleasant and free from stress. It cannot be properly utilized in a lonely environment. It cannot be properly utilized in a rushed or tense environment.

If we cannot take the time to plan, prepare, cook and eat balanced meals suited to our lifestyle and free from stress, we will continue to kill ourselves through poor diet and poor metabolism. (Metabolism is the digestion, absorption and utilization of all food nutrients.)

I

BASIC NUTRITION:
Eating for Good Health

79 EASY-TO-PREPARE RECIPES AND MENUS

IN 1977 THE SENATE SELECT COMMITTEE for Nutrition and Human Needs began a national dialogue about America's food habits. It recognized that dietary habits have changed considerably over the past century, and that eating patterns represent as critical a public health concern as any we now face. After much research the Committee set forth new Dietary Goals for the United States. In the establishment of these goals, the Committee recognized a need for changing the food habits to fit the changing lifestyles of the American public.

Our diets have changed radically within the past 50 years—with great and often harmful effects on our health. There is a strong suggestion that dietary changes represent as great a threat to public health as smoking. Too much fat, saturated in particular, cholesterol, sugar and salt and alcohol cause obesity and stroke. Six of the leading causes of death in the United States have been linked to our diet patterns: heart disease, cancer, cerebrovascular disease, diabetes, arteriosclerosis and cirrhosis of the liver.

The Senate Select Committee on Nutrition and Human Needs has made significant achievements in using analyses of patterns of health and disease and applying these to the American population in a rational manner. The concept of the Dietary Goals represents a step forward in health care and treatment by focusing on preventive health care. The new Dietary Goals represent a sensible diet for a sedentary lifestyle. The guidelines may not be applicable to all. There is, however, substantial evidence indicating that they will be generally beneficial.

Graphically illustrated, the changes recommended in the new Dietary Goals are as follows:

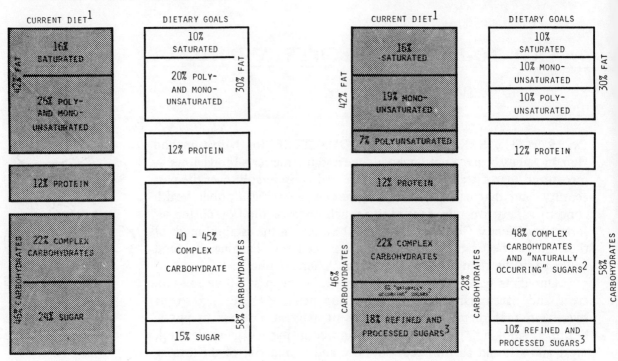

Broken down more completely this means:

* *Reduce overall fat consumption from approximately 40 to 30 percent of energy intake (calories)*

* *Reduce saturated fat consumption to about 10 percent of the total intake*

* *Limit protein consumption to 12 percent of the daily energy intake*

* *Balance that with polyunsaturated and mono-unsaturated fats, which should each account for about 10 percent of energy intake*

* *Increase carbohydrate consumption to account for 55 to 60 percent of the energy intake*

* *Reduce sugar consumption to about 40 percent to account for about 15 percent of total energy intake. See explanation of energy intake (Revision suggests 10 percent)*

* *Reduce cholesterol consumption to about 300 mg. a day*

* *Reduce all salt consumption by about 50-85 percent to approximately 3 grams a day (Revision suggests 5 grams)*

The goals suggest the following changes in food selection and preparation:

* *Decrease consumption of foods high in fat*
* *Substitute polyunsaturated fat for saturated fat whenever possible*
* *Substitute non-fat milk for whole milk*
* *Allow protein to remain at current level, or 1 gram for each kilogram of body weight*
* *Increase consumption of fruits, vegetables and whole grains (complex carbohydrate)*
* *Decrease consumption of butterfat, eggs and other high cholesteral sources*
* *Decrease consumption of salt and foods high in salt content*

The original Dietary Goals were revised one year later; Part II of the Report can be found in the Appendix. To help you understand the revision, energy intake should be explained.

Energy intake means the calorie value of each food we eat. All foods contain a number of total calories. There is no one food which should be considered fattening since we gain or lose weight based on the total of energy intake. The calorie, then, is the measure of energy intake. The quality of energy intake will be determined by our food selection.

To balance energy intake with energy output we need to check body activity. A lower body activity than the energy intake is the cause for overweight.

While energy intake may be more than sufficient, a state of malnutrition can develop if all essential food nutrients are not included.

One year after the release of the first Dietary Goals for the United States the goals were revised. The revisions were made in light of comments received after the original recommendations were published.

The following changes have been made:

(a) A new goal concerning obesity has been added. It reads: "To avoid overweight consume only as much energy (calories) as is expended; if overweight, decrease energy intake and increase energy expenditures."

(b) The recommendation on the consumption of carbohydrates has been changed to: "Increase the consumption of complex carbohydrates and naturally occurring sugars from about 38 percent of energy intake to about 48 percent of energy intake."

(c) A greater reduction in sugar consumption is recommended as follows: "Reduce the consumption of refined and processed sugars by about 45 percent to account for about 10 percent of total energy intake."

(d) Regarding the use of salt, the new recommendation is to: "Limit the intake of sodium by reducing the intake of salt (sodium chloride) to about 5 grams a day." (This is an increase from 3 grams in the original goals.)

Other goals remain the same in the revision.

As in the first release, changes in food selection and preparation are suggested to effect adherence to the goals. In this list of revisions the recommendation concerning meat consumption has been made to read: "Decrease consumption of animal fat, and choose meats, poultry and fish which will reduce saturated fat intake."

Also, the following sentence has been added to the suggestion that consumption of butterfat, eggs, and other high cholesterol sources be decreased: "Some consideration should be given to easing the cholesterol goal for pre-menopausal women, young children and the elderly in order to obtain the nutritional benefits of eggs in the diet."

ENERGY INTAKE. To help you understand what is meant by energy intake further explanation may be necessary.

Energy intake means the caloric value of the foods we consume. Each food contains calories based on the amount of protein, fat content and carbohydrate (starch and sugar). Through physiological fuel factors grams are converted into calories as follows:

1 gram protein = 4 calories
1 gram fat = 9 calories
1 gram carbohydrate = 4 calories

Thus, a slice of white bread made with whole milk contains 2 grams of protein or 8 calories, 6 grams of fat (saturated and unsaturated) or 54 calories and 12 grams of carbohydrate in the form of starch and sugar or 48 calories—for a total of 110 calories.

If your body needs are greater than your energy intake you will lose weight. On the other hand, the only way that you gain weight is to eat more food and increase calories, or energy intake above your requirement for energy.

The Senate report suggests we make fat account for 30 percent of our diet, with 10 percent of that fat total saturated or pure fat. A saturated fat is animal fat found on meats such as beef or lamb or pork. The 20 percent balance would be mono or poly-unsaturated fat. Mono fat would be, for example, animal fat mixed with vegetable fat as found in some oleomargarines. Pure vegetable products such as olive oil or peanut oil would be called a poly-unsaturated fat, or many times unsaturated. There are some oleomargarines on the market made from pure vegetable fat. But most oleomargarines are combined animal and vegetable fats, which can be determined by reading the fine print.

Fats were discussed in the revision of the new goals. The recommendation was that consumption of butterfat, eggs and other high cholesterol sources be decreased.

As with the first report, changes in food selection and preparation are suggested to effect adherence to the goals. A revision in the recommendations concerning meat consumption reads: "Decrease consumption of animal fat, and choose meats, poultry and fish which will reduce saturated fat intake."

The Committee recommendation for reducing fat is based on a study of fat consumption by the United States Department of Agriculture as shown in the chart from 1909 to 1980.

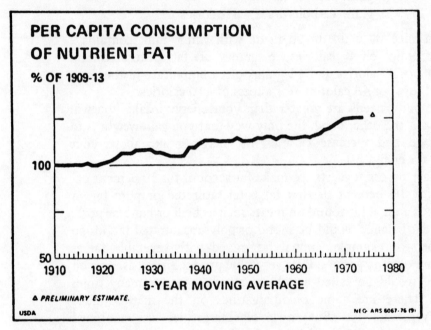

PER CAPITA CONSUMPTION
OF NUTRIENT FAT

Source: Handbook of Agricultural Charts, Agricultural Handbook No. 504, U.S. Department of Agriculture, 1976.

Fat consumption has continuously increased. In consideration of the increasing incident of obesity in the United States, it is timely to consider the percentage of calories from fats in foods as shown.

Percentage of Calories from Fat in Foods

Over 50%

Cream cheese
Weiners
Peanuts and peanut butter
Pork lunch meats
Most cheese and cheese spreads
Tongue
Eggs
Ground beef—regular
Salmon, tuna (canned in oil)
Pork—loin and butt
Granola

50%

Chicken—roasted, flesh & skin
Beef—porterhouse, T-bone, round
        rump, lean ground, kidney
Pork—fresh & cured ham & shoulder
Lamb—shoulder, rib
Salmon—red sockeye, canned

Whole milk
Ice cream
Cream cheese
  sandwich
Peanut butter
  sandwich

40%

Beef—sirloin, arm, flank, heart
Turkey—flesh & skin, dark meat
Lamb—leg, loin
Pork—heart, kidney
Chicken—dark meat, roasted flesh

Creamed cottage
  cheese
Lunch meat or
Cheese spread
  sandwich

30%

Beef—heel of round, pot roast
Liver—pork, chicken, lamb, beef
Fish—bass, ciscoe, oysters, salmon (pink)
Chicken—roasted, light meat broilers—no skin

20%

Fish—haddock, cod, tuna (water pack),
      ocean perch, halibut, smelt, sole
Shellfish—most
Porridge
Bread
Most peas, beans and lentils
Non-fat milk cheese
Uncreamed cottage cheese
Non-fat milk
Most breakfast cereals (other than Granola type)

Under 20%

Concern over the increasing amount of fat being consumed has been caused by the established relationship of fats—in particular, saturated fats—to those diseases which take the most lives. After heart

15

disease are cancer, cerebrovascular disease, diabetes, arteriosclerosis and cirrhosis of the liver, in that order.

The increased consumption of fats and sugars brings little or no added vitamins and minerals to the diet. If a diet reduced to control weight and save money is high in fat and sugar, vitamin and mineral deficiency is likely to occur. Low-income people may be particularly susceptible to inducements to consume high fat/high sugar diets.

To reduce the risk of heart disease, the Committee report suggested that the intake of red meats, which contain high levels of saturated fat and cholesterol, be better balanced with the addition of more chicken, fish and vegetables to the diet. These alternatives would decrease the high saturated fat and cholesterol levels and would still satisfy our need for protein.

By reducing the level of cholesterol in the bloodstream we help protect ourselves from susceptibility to heart disease. There is also evidence that cholesterol is related to fat deposits in arterial lesions in man. We are aware of the increasing cholesterol levels in the bloodstream as man advances in age.

There is, of course, no promise that decreasing saturated fat and cholesterol in the diet will prevent heart disease. But the Committee has pointed out the relationships and the risk, and suggests that across the country we need to reduce the risk.

Intake of dietary fat has been linked not only to obesity but also to cancers of the breast and colon. The high meat consumption countries, of which the United States is one, have a higher mortality rate from colon cancer than those countries which consume far less meat.

The incidence of cancer appears to be related as much to unsaturated fat as to saturated fat. Both types of fat plus cholesterol may caused increased secretion in the breast of the hormone prolactin, and this secretion may induce tumors. A study of the vegetarian diet in a group of American women showed a 40 to 60 percent decrease in prolactin secretion.

We have ample evidence of the problem caused by increasing consumption of fats. We need, therefore, to evaluate our individual diets against our sedentary lifestyle in order to diminish—and eventually eliminate—the risk of heart disease and cancer.

The Senate Committee recommended that the amount of protein in the diet remain at the current level—12 percent—of the total calories.

The 12 percent is based on the total caloric value of a diet adequate in calories. Your individual need for protein may be calculated as 1 gram of protein for each kilogram of body weight. Your body weight, then, divided by 2.2, will require about 60 to 80 grams of protein each day (adult weight). If your total calorie need is 1200 calories a day, then, only 12 percent would come from the protein in your diet.

The Committee suggested that the protein level in the diet remain at the current level because studies have shown that protein calorie consumption has remained stable. The intake has not increased with the increasing consumption of fats and sugar. The stability of the protein intake would indicate that the increase of fats and sugar is due to consumption of food sources lacking in protein.

For our daily diet the Senate report suggests we make carbohydrate 59 percent, of which 43 percent is complex carbohydrate and 15 percent sugar (revised to 10 percent from the earlier figure).

A complex carbohydrate may be better understood by saying starches and sugars. Starch may be called a poly sugar, meaning that it must be ingested before sugar is formed in the body. For example, enzymes found in the mouth, stomach and small intestines break down starch to sucrose and glucose. Table sugar or sucrose when consumed in the form of candy or soft drinks flows more rapidly into the bloodstream because sucrose needs to be broken down by only one enzyme action in order to become glucose, a simple sugar, ready for absorption.

The chart shows how the consumption of carbohydrate in the form of starches and sugars has increased since 1909.

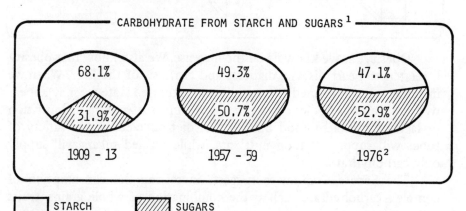

CARBOHYDRATE FROM STARCH AND SUGARS [1]

68.1%	49.3%	47.1%
31.9%	50.7%	52.9%
1909 - 13	1957 - 59	1976[2]

STARCH   SUGARS

[1]SUGARS INCLUDE: 'NATURALLY OCCURRING' (MILK PRODUCTS, VEGETABLES AND FRUIT), SYRUPS, MOLASSES, HONEY, CANE AND BEET.
[2]PRELIMINARY

SOURCE: NUTRITIONAL REVIEW, NATIONAL FOOD SITUATION, CFE (ADM.) 299-9, JANUARY 1975. PRELIMINARY DATA FOR 1976 UNPUBLISHED. AGRICULTURAL RESEARCH SERVICE, U.S. DEPARTMENT OF AGRICULTURE.

The greatest increase has come from the addition of refined sugar to processed food products and beverages. Beverages have increased more than threefold from nearly 20 to 70 pounds, while household purchase has dropped one-half from a little more than 50 to about 25 pounds. Currently, food products and beverages account for more than two-thirds of the refined sugar consumed, according to the U.S. Department of Agriculture.

The largest single business using refined sugar is the beverage industry. The business accounts for more than one-fifth of the total refined sugar in the United States diet. Furthermore, the amount used in beverages has increased nearly sevenfold since early in the century when 3½ pounds were used for each person per year in these products.

The chart showing the increased use of refined sugar will help us understand why we must begin to evaluate our diets to bring all food nutrients back into their important places in the diet.

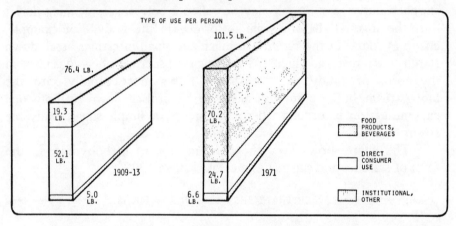

TYPE OF USE PER PERSON

101.5 LB.

76.4 LB.

19.3 LB.

52.1 LB.

1909-13

5.0 LB.

70.2 LB.

24.7 LB.

1971

6.6 LB.

FOOD PRODUCTS, BEVERAGES

DIRECT CONSUMER USE

INSTITUTIONAL, OTHER

Obesity, as we know, is on the increase. We also know that obesity is related to heart disease, diabetes and cirrhosis of the liver. When we increase sugar in refined form and fat in saturated state we may appear well fed. But our bodies can, at the same time, suffer from malnutrition or lack of sufficient food nutrients. A diet selected from a variety of foods will supply all food nutrients, while refined sugars will supply only carbohydrate.

The Senate Committee suggests increasing the consumption of complex carbohydrate such as the combination of whole grains, fruits and vegetables as a possible way to ease the problem of weight control.

In summary, what the Committee is advising is a return to some basics in food habits: Increase consumption of fresh fruits and vegetables; increase whole grain breads and cereals, reduce sugar and salt. In addition, change the type of fat we eat by eating fewer red meats.

All the recommendations are proposed because of real concern among top government authorities of the United States. The Committee members express the concerns of nutritionists and dietitians all over the country.

As a nutritionist and dietitian, I personally feel that we are seeing the increase of malnutrition in a land of plentiful food supply. I believe malnutrition will be a number one problem of the future. My belief is based on our present eating habits—too much food, food eaten too fast, food consumed in an environment of noise and confusion. All of these will prevent proper digestion and the body's proper use of food nutrients.

A change in eating habits begins first with a balance in food nutrients to meet the body's need.

Daily food guide—the basic four food groups

Food group	Main nutrients	Daily amounts*
Milk		
Milk, cheese, ice cream, or other products made with whole or skimmed milk	Calcium Protein Riboflavin	Children under 9: 2 to 3 cups Children 9 to 12: 3 or more cups Teen-agers: 4 or more cups Adults: 2 or more cups Pregnant women: 3 or more cups Nursing mothers: 4 or more cups (1 cup = 8 oz. fluid milk or designated milk equivalent)
Meats		
Beef, veal, lamb, pork, poultry, fish, eggs	Protein Iron Thiamine	2 or more servings Count as one serving: 2 to 3 oz. of lean, boneless, cooked meat, poultry, or fish
Alternate: dry beans, dry peas, nuts, peanut butter	Niacin Riboflavin	1 egg 1 cup cooked dry beans or peas 4 tablespoons peanut butter

Food group	Main nutrients	Daily amounts*

Vegetables and fruits		4 or more servings
		Count as 1 serving:
		  ½ cup of vegetable or fruit, or a portion such
		    as 1 medium apple, banana, orange,
		    potato, or ½ a medium grapefruit, melon

	Vitamin A	Include:
		  A dark-green or deep-yellow vegetable or
		    fruit rich in vitamin A, at least every other day

	Vitamin C (ascorbic acid)	A citrus fruit or other fruit or vegetable rich in vitamin C daily
	Smaller amounts of other vitamins and minerals	Other vegetables and fruits including potatoes
Bread and cereals		4 or more servings of whole grain, enriched or restored Count as 1 serving:
	Thiamine	1 slice of bread
	Niacin	1 cup ready to eat cereal, flake or puff varieties
	Riboflavin	
	Iron	½ to ¾ cup cooked cereal

	Protein	½ to ¾ cup cooked pastes (macaroni,
		  spaghetti, noodles)
		Crackers: 5 saltines, 2 squares graham
		  crackers, etc.

*Use amounts of these foods as desired or needed for your body activity.
†Milk equivalents: 1 ounce cheddar cheese, 3 servings cottage cheese, 1 cup fluid non-fat milk,
  1 cup buttermilk, ¼ cup dry non-fat milk powder, 1 cup ice milk, 1-2/3 cups ice cream, 1/2
  cup evaporated milk.

A WELL-BALANCED DIET. A well-balanced diet should be simple. The more complicated it becomes—with the addition of exotic foods, for example—the more likely the diet will become nutritionally unbalanced.

Many people consider adequate diet to mean grouping foods into "good" or "bad" categories. They are prompted by the fear of too much sugar, salt, fat or fattening foods, along with concerns about the safety and nutritional value of foods which are processed and refined. Judging a food as "natural" is a shortcut that is not usually relevant to a balanced diet.

The Senate report is referring to all foods high in fat, sugar or salt, rather than one group of foods. The total energy intake should be consumed from a variety of foods in a combination to insure an intake of all food nutrients for your specific need. The report is also saying that the American diet has become unbalanced in increasing numbers because foods too high in fat, sugar and salt are favored.

A simple, balanced diet is one in which foods can be easily identified as protein, fat or carbohydrate. The diet should be selected from a variety of foods and should include sufficient intake of protein, fat and carbohydrate for your body's needs and total calories to sustain your activity. The foods need to be prepared in such a way as to preserve the vitamins and minerals. Use of too much water in the cooking of vegetables or pouring off liquid from canned vegetables or juices from canned fruits will destroy valuable vitamins.

The new goal which was added reads: "To avoid overweight, consume only as much energy (calories) as is expended; if overweight, decrease energy intake and increase energy expenditure or exercise more, keeping food intake at same level." This actually means reducing your weight to normal and maintaining body weight.

WHAT IS NUTRITION? What actually does the word "nutrition" mean? It is a word that shows the relationship between food and the body—including digestion, metabolism and utilization. While understanding the "basic four" food groups is important, it does not explain the total meaning of nutrition.

For good nutrition you should select foods from a variety of food sources to suit your individual body needs. You should consider your lifestyle, culture and ability to make the foods you select work for you. And, you should be aware of high stress periods and steer clear of any one fad as being the answer to what is troubling you—including the problem of weight control.

Simplify food preparation. Chew foods thoroughly. Eat in quiet, pleasant surroundings. All these steps will lead to proper digestion and food nutrients in the bloodstream. Eat a variety of foods, divided among three to six meals each day. (A person with a heavy work schedule, for example, requires small amounts of food in the stomach in order to ease digestion.) BEGIN WITH A GOOD BREAKFAST.

Foods undergo chemical changes in the process of digestion. Properly broken down foods prepare food nutrients for absorption through the intestinal wall, and from there they flow into the bloodstream to be transported to all parts of the body.

Food has two major functions in the body: (1) it provides vital building blocks to maintain tissues, and (2) it serves as fuel to supply energy.

Although most foods contain a combination of nutrients, they are classified according to the chief nutrient they provide.

FOOD NUTRIENTS

PROTEIN is the building brick and mortar that enters and tones the muscles, skin and tissues. The body constantly wears out tissues; therefore these nutrients are needed daily and in sufficient quantity to supply all the needed building blocks or all the needed amino acids. Meat, eggs, fish, dairy products and vegetables such as beans, peanuts, dried peaches and rice are the sources of protein.

Specific functions of protein are: (1) to build and repair body tissues, promoting growth; (2) to maintain body structure; (3) to maintain nitrogen balance; (4) to produce essential compounds; (5) to regulate water balance; (6) to maintain blood neutrality, and (7) to provide energy. A constant supply of protein is demanded by the body to maintain health.

Protein supplies four calories per gram. In other words, if a food contains 12 grams protein it supplies 48 calories of the total calorie intake. The average individual needs 1 gram protein for each kilogram of body weight, or 2.2 divided into your body weight. For an adult woman the minimum need would be about 50 to 60 grams or 200 to 240 calories protein out of total calories. The average man would need about 60 to 70 grams or 240 to 280 calories protein as a minimum intake. The protein calories should be spread out over at least three meals each day (this means a diet balanced in food nutrients to meet the needs of your body but not allowing for storage).

During childhood growth the body requires an adequate supply of protein to provide amino acid in sufficient quality and quantity to promote development of new tissues. This is also true during pregnancy. Hospitalized patients often have similar needs for protein in order to build new tissues for wound healing, to recover from surgery, burns and fever and for other conditions in which the body has nitrogen loss.

The Senate Committee recommended that at least 12 percent of our total calories come from protein—a recommendation based on the current amount being consumed. Studies have not shown any relationships between an overdose of protein and disease. It has been found, however, that a low protein intake causes stunted growth, and advanced deficiency associated with low calorie intake causes the horrible and often fatal diseases kwashiorkor and maramus.

If other food nutrients are to perform all their functions in the body, it is essential that amino acids be in sufficient quality and quantity. Also, protein must be balanced with fat and carbohydrate (sugar and starches) in the diet. Insufficient carbohydrate will cause the body to use protein for energy need. Protein is used more slowly in the body because it is usually in combination with fat. Fats delay the emptying time of the stomach and, therefore, prevent hunger. If your breakfast included a good protein source you will be alert all morning and most likely will not feel hunger before lunch.

The quality of protein should be considered, and necessitates three good quality protein sources each day. The number of essential amino acids that your bloodstream will carry to all parts of the body is determined by the quality of the protein you eat. There are 12 essential amino acids to enable protein to perform all its body functions. They are: histidine, lysine, tryptophan, phenylalanine, phenylalanine plus tyrosine, methionine, methionine plus cystine, threonine, leucine, isoleucine and valine.

The Senate report suggests a shift in diet from red meats with excessive fat to chicken and fish supplying the same essential amino acids but providing less saturated fat.

The Dietary Goals warn that the "displacement of complex carbohydrates—fruits, vegetables and whole grains—may be a danger to health for several reasons. First, there is evidence that diets high in complex carbohydrates may reduce the risk of heart disease." The most likely displacement of carbohydrate would mean the diet is unbalanced; therefore, over a period of time "nutrient stress" may cause many illnesses.

One nutrient in deficient amount for body needs will tend to borrow from another nutrient, thereby causing stress of food nutrients. An example is a high protein/low carbohydrate diet. In this type of dieting protein must be used by the body for energy. It cannot, then, perform the necessary functions of building and repairing body tissues. It becomes, then, the most costly source of energy.

CARBOHYDRATES are fuel foods, vital to maintaining the brain and nervous system. They provide the energy to sustain the day's labors.

The sugars and starches found in foods compose carbohydrate. Starches found in potatoes, rice and other cereal grains are considered polysaccharides, or many sugars. Sugars found in fresh fruits are in the form of simple sugars and ready for absorption soon after eating. Table sugar or sugar added to fruits is actually two sugars tied by a chemical bond which must be broken down by the body. It is called sucrose. A starch—for example, a potato—is cooked to break down the starch into sugar to prepare it for digestion. It then becomes sucrose, and later glucose, or simple sugar, ready for absorption into the bloodstream. Refined sugar is pure carbohydrate and contains no other food nutrient.

One gram of carbohydrate supplies four calories. Carbohydrates have a more rapid metabolism by the body than protein because protein is usually in combination with fat. Fat in the diet delays the emptying of the stomach, causing a delay in the digestion of protein. That is why a pancake and syrup breakfast leaves you hungry at 11 A.M., while a ham and egg breakfast with the same total calories will fuel the body until lunchtime.

It would be easy to add up a total day's caloric need with sugar—but don't! Alcohol is in the same class as a potato—it is liquid starch and does not contain other essential food nutrients. It is possible to consume what seems like a normal day's intake of calories—1000 to 1200—entirely in alcohol. While the energy intake will be sufficient, one could develop a state of malnutrition by neglecting the essential food nutrients.

FATS. We know that each day we need some fat, but we do not know the exact need. We do know, however, that there are three essential fatty acids necessary for good health: linoleic acid, linolenic acid and arachidonic acid. Diseases are known to result from the lack of even one of the three. They are essential for certain body functions and there is evidence that the body cannot synthesize them.

Fats are derived from many sources. Saturated fats are found in beef suet, mutton tallow, red meats (beef, pork, lamb, veal), egg yolk, dairy fat and coconut oil. The unsaturated fats come from poultry, seafood and vegetable oils: peanut, soybean, cottonseed, corn, safflower and olive. Fats, then, are divided into two categories—saturated and unsaturated.

Coconut oil, considered to be a plant source of fat, is a notable exception. It is a saturated fat instead of being an unsaturated fat. It is 90 percent saturated. It is an oil because of the arrangement of short and medium chain acids in the chemical composition.

A saturated or unsaturated fat is determined by the amount of carbon in the chemical combination with hydrogen and oxygen in a product. The more carbon the higher the saturation. On the other hand, unsaturated fats contain more hydrogen and oxygen. Incidently, all foods contain carbon, hydrogen and oxygen in varying amounts.

Fats contain the most energy per ounce of all foods in the diet and are the prime source of calories. For each gram of fat consumed 9 calories are provided. Fats should be used sensibly, especially in adulthood. Many foods today contain invisible fat (hidden fat) which may account for the increased fat consumption in the American diet. An example is cottage cheese made from non-fat milk to which cream has been added to give flavor—a common product in the marketplace.

Foods are easier to cook and the product easier to eat when fat is present. Flavor improves with the fat content of food. Fat-free diets are usually test diets used for diagnosis of disease. Low-fat diets, however, need not be dull and monotonous (see menus in Stress chapter).

VITAMINS consist of two types: fat and water soluble. Vitamins are a mixture of chemicals vital to proper nutrition and classified together because each aids the metabolism of protein and carbohydrates. A vitamin-poor diet may cause multiple deficiencies. Let's take a closer look at vitamins.

Water soluble vitamins not stored in the body may be destroyed by air or steam.

Vitamin C (ascorbic acid) is a vitamin with a history. In the early 1700s a naval surgeon described putrid gums and weakness in the knees among sailors who had been long without access to fresh fruits and vegetables. The sailors had scurvy, an occupational hazard of seamen. The medical solution to scurvy was "two oranges and one lemon every day."

Citrus fruits are the best natural source of Vitamin C. Care should be taken to keep fruit juice in covered containers or to eat fruits immediately after cutting them in order to enjoy the maximum Vitamin C content.

The B Vitamins include thiamine, niacin, Vitamin B_6 and Vitamin B_{12}. They appear to help prevent colds.

Deficiencies in thiamine, Vitamins B_6 and B_{12} have plagued people throughout the world for countless centuries. By removing the vitamin-rich outer coat of rice, Southeast Asians on a high rice diet often suffered nerve pain, mental changes and even heart failure. The nervous and mental aberrations of the alcoholic go hand-in-hand with thiamine deficiency. Eggs, wheat germ, liver, pork, green peas, and beans are the best sources of this basic nutrient.

Riboflavin (Vitamin B_2) has been found to prevent scaly skin rash, sores at the corners of lips and colored, sore tongue. The best sources of riboflavin are eggs, pork, beef, spinach, liver, milk and cheese.

Niacin deficiency was known to early Italians and Spaniards as "rough skin." In the early 1900s the disease pellagra was known in the United States as a condition caused by a poor diet of corn and molasses. Lean meat, yeast, milk and fresh vegetables were prescribed as a cure; they are the best sources of niacin.

Vitamin B_6 is found in liver and yeast. Deficiency of it is characterized by anemia, weakness, sores at the corners of the mouth, and neuritis which can be prevented by the administration of pyridoxine.

Vitamin B_{12} helps bring red blood cells to maturity; a shortage produces pernicious anemia. Fatigue, neuritis, psoriasis and hair loss have been treated with this vitamin. A balanced diet of meats, fruits, vegetables and dairy products ensures the presence of Vitamin B_{12}.

Fat soluble vitamins are absorbed with dietary fats and conditions not favorable to normal fat intake will also interfere with the absorption of these vitamins. They can be stored in the body to some extent and are normally excreted in the urine.

Vitamin A can be found in green leafy vegetables, other vegetables such as carrots, and dairy products, eggs and some fish. Fish liver oils are also an excellent source of Vitamin A. Early symptoms of Vitamin A deficiency are night blindness or poor adaptation to darkness. Studies show that truck drivers have improved their night vision by eating carrots.

Vitamin D is the catalyst in calcium metabolism. The calcium necessary for bone and skeletal development and maintenance is not utilized without the presence of Vitamin D. The development of rickets osteomalacis—softening of the bones—is caused by shortage of calcium, phosphorus or Vitamin D, or all three nutrients. Vitamin D is found in fish oil and fortified milk and is extracted from sunlight. Vitamin D shortage usually results from poor absorption which may be a result of insufficient intake or the overuse of laxatives.

Vitamin E has been credited with a host of mystical properties. Partisans claim that Vitamin E reduces arterial blood clots, lowers oxygen needs of muscles and prevents excessive scar tissue formation. Some believe that Vitamin E can alleviate leprosy and sterility. Most American physicians and nutritionists do not agree, however. Vitamin E is known as the anti-sterility vitamin in rat studies and is used for treating gray hair. It is found in alfalfa and green plants.

Vitamin K, extracted from food by bacteria in the intestinal tract, is vital for normal blood clotting, and is an anti-coagulant. It is rare to find a natural Vitamin K deficiency. Shortages of this vitamin may occur, however, as a result of other diseases—liver, prolonged diarrhea and long antibiotic therapy. The food sources of Vitamin K are meat (especially liver), eggs, fruit, leafy vegetables, tomatoes, wheat bran, soybeans and vegetable oil.

MINERALS develop teeth, bone, structure, and maintain the body's development throughout life. They are needed by the body in minute quantities; it is important to include small quantities of them in each day's diet.

The Senate Committee recommends a balanced diet to ensure the inclusion of necessary minerals in the diet. Calcium, phosphorus, iron and iodine are essential minerals. Sources of them are cheese, green leafy vegetables, fish and liver. Iodine is found in few foods but it can be added with the use of iodized salt. Phosphorus is necessary in combination with calcium to make bones and teeth; it is present in good protein foods. About 90 percent of phosphorus is found in combination with calcium.

We do not know enough yet about minerals and those we may need in minute quantity. Copper, for example, helps the body make iron into hemoglobin for the blood. It is present in many foods and therefore we do not need to calculate carefully the necessary amount if we eat a balanced diet.

Flourine helps resist tooth decay. It is present in some, but not all, drinking water sources.

Nutrient	Some Reasons Why We Need It	Foods That Supply Important Amounts
Protein	To build and repair all tissues in the body	Meat, fish, poultry, eggs
	To help form substances called antibodies which help fight infection	Milk, cheese
		Breads, cereals, other grain products
	To supply food energy	Dry beans, dry peas
		Peanut butter, nuts

Nutrient	Some Reasons Why We Need It	Foods That Supply Important Amounts
Fat	To supply a large amount of food energy in a small amount of food To supply substances called essential fatty acids	Butter, margarine, cream Salad oils, oil dressings Cooking fats, oils Peanut butter Bacon, other meat fats
Carbohydrate (starches and sugars)	To supply food energy To help the body use other nutrients	Grain products, including breads, cereals, flours, cornmeal, rice, macaroni, spaghetti, noodles Potatoes, sweetpotatoes, corn Dried fruits, sweetened fruits, bananas Sugar, syrup, jelly, jam, honey
Calcium	To help build the bones and teeth To help blood to clot To help the muscles and nerves react normally	Milk, cheese (especially cheddar-type cheese), ice cream Collards, kale, broccoli, turnip and mustard greens
Iron	To combine with protein to make hemoglobin—the red substance that carries oxygen to the cells	Meat—liver, heart, and kidney are especially good sources Poultry, eggs, shellfish Dark green leafy vegetables, peas, beans Breads, cereals, and other grain products—whole grain, enriched or restored Dried fruits
Vitamin A	To help keep the skin and the mucous membrane (linings) of the nose, mouth, and inner organs healthy and resistant to infection To protect against night blindness	Dark green and deep yellow vegetables: broccoli, chard, collards, kale, spinach, turnip greens, other dark leaves; carrots, pumpkin, sweet potatoes, winter squash Apricots, cantaloupe Liver, eggs, butter, margarine, cream
Thiamine (vitamin B_1)	To keep the appetite and digestion normal To keep the nervous system healthy To help the body change certain substances in the food into energy for work and heat	Breads, cereals, other grain products whole-grain, enriched, or restored Meat, especially pork, liver, heart, and kidney Poultry and eggs Milk Peas, black-eyed peas, lima beans
Riboflavin (vitamin B_2)	To help the cells use oxygen To help keep vision clear To help keep the skin smooth and prevent scaly skin around the mouth and nose or cracking at the corners of the mouth	Milk, cheese, ice cream Meat, especially liver; poultry and eggs, fish Dark green vegetables Enriched bread, cereal products

29

Nutrient	Some Reasons Why We Need It	Foods That Supply Important Amounts
Vitamin C (Ascorbic acid)	To make a cementing substance that helps to hold body cells together and makes the walls of blood vessels firm To help resist infection To help in healing wounds and broken bones	Orange, grapefruit, other citrus fruits and juices, strawberries, cantaloupe Tomatoes and tomato juice, green and red peppers Raw cabbage, broccoli, dark green leafy vegetables Potatoes and sweet potatoes, cooked in their jackets—especially new potatoes
Vitamin D	To help the body absorb calcium from the digestive tract To help the body build strong bones and teeth	Milk with vitamin D added, eggs, butter Sardines, salmon, tuna Fish-liver oils

Your mechanism for food preparation, digestion, metabolism and absorption of all foods by your body.

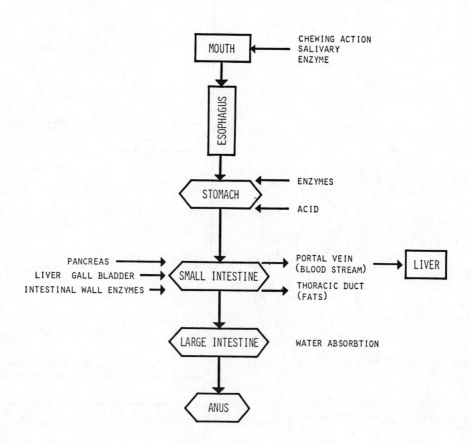

DIGESTION

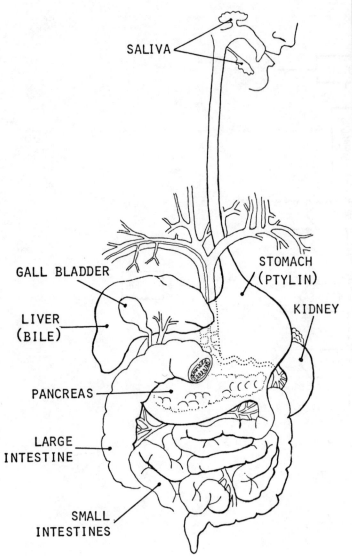

SALIVA

GALL BLADDER

LIVER (BILE)

PANCREAS

LARGE INTESTINE

SMALL INTESTINES

STOMACH (PTYLIN)

KIDNEY

CARBOHYDRATES

	ENZYME	REACT
MOUTH	SALIVARY AMYLASE (PTYALIN)	STARCH → MALTO
STOMACH	RESTS AND SOFTENS MALTOSE AND STARCH	
SMALL INTESTINES		STARCH → MALTO
PANCREATIC JUICE	AMYLOSE (AMYLOPSIN)	
INTESTINAL JUICE	SUCRASE	SUCROSE < GLUCOS FRUCTO
	MALTASE	MALTOSE < GLUCOS GLUCOS
	LACTASE	LACTOSE < GLUCOS GALACT

RENIN AIDS IN DIGESTION OF MIL

PROTEINS

	ENZYMES	REACTION
MOUTH →	NO CHEMICAL ACTION	
STOMACH PROTEASES (PEPSIN)		PROTEIN — PROTEASES AI PEPTONES
SMALL INTESTINES	PROTEASE (THYPSIN)	PROTEIN → AMIN ACID
PANCREATIC JUICE		
INTESTINAL JUICE	PROTEASE (CREPSIN)	PROTEASES — AMINO ACID AND AMMONI

RENIN AIDS IN DIGESTION OF MILK (CASEIN

FATS

	ENZYME	REACTION
MOUTH	NO CHEMICAL ACTION	
STOMACH	LIPASE	EMULSIFIES FAT
	HYDROCHLORIA ACID (NOT AN ENZYMPE)	FATTY ACIDS
		HELPS GLYCEROL BREAK DOWN FAT
	LIPASE	EMULSIFIES FATS
		FATTY ACIDS
SMALL INTESTINES		AND GLYCEROL
PANCREATIC JUICE		
	LIPASE (STEAPSIN)	FATS
		FATTY ACIDS AND GLYCEROL
BILE →	AIDS IN DIGESTION AND ABSORPTION OF FATS BY EMULSIFICATION	

FOOD NUTRIENTS: IS DIET ENOUGH?

The combination of protein, carbohydrate and fat will usually supply us with the vitamins and minerals we need—provided the foods we select are chosen, prepared and served with care. A balanced diet eaten in sufficient quantity and under proper conditions does not require the supplement of vitamin pills or other pharmaceuticals.

Nevertheless, there is a well established psychological need among many people for vitamin pills and the like. The pills give them a feeling of confidence. High-powered advertising of these supplements continues to result in booming sales to these anxious consumers.

This psychological need can be easily understood. Devotees of the "return to nature" philosophy of these times have declared war on those foods they believe are impure, unsafe and non-nutritional because of the addition of chemicals or even machine-handling.

The widely held notion that our soil is depleted of nutrients leads to the belief that plants lack vitamins and minerals. Actually, chemical processes resulting from cooperation of the sun and soil have remained the same. Our green, yellow and red fruits and vegetables supply potentials for our vitamin and mineral needs.

It is up to our body chemistry to make the most of the food potentials. If you doubt that your diet contains sufficient vitamins and minerals, consult your physician or dietition. Don't venture into a drug diet because a friend has.

Remember that overdoses of vitamins and minerals may have an adverse, rather than a beneficial, effect upon health.

How to Implement the Senate Report in Your Home

The Dietary Goals are meant to give advice for learning new eating habits. Proper eating should become as important and as natural a part of each day as brushing your teeth. And—it should be fun!

The human body uses food much like a furnace uses fuel for heating a house. With use of proper fuel and maintenance, a furnace produces long-burning fuel which in turn produces energy in the form of heat. This is true of your body, too.

The proper amount of foods in the right proportions will give your body the energy necessary to carry on your activities. But there should

be a balance of food nutrients in the total number of calories you eat. We do not know everything about food nutrients needed by the body. We have, however, learned enough about carbohydrates, protein and fat and their effects on the body to know that there is extreme importance in balancing these three main nutrients in the diet. The balance will usually provide the vitamins and minerals we need if a variety of foods has been selected.

The Dietary Goals acknowledge that the increase in fat and sugar in the diet will satisfy hunger easily. But, the Senate report pointed out, the increase is not usually in combinations which represent a balanced diet. Fats delay the emptying time of the stomach and consequently may delay hunger longer. But high fat consumption does not represent balance in food nutrients. For example, French fries and hamburger with bread and mustard will allow excess fat but will be absent of necessary vitamins and minerals. Addition of a carbonated beverage means sugar—and sugar only. Calories so far total some 500 to 600 of fat and carbohydrate (starch and sugar)—yet the diet is all unbalanced. A salad in the form of mostly lettuce will add only fiber or bulk to the meal. The excess sugar will add on calories and promote tooth decay. After such a meal you probably won't be hungry. But your body will be. The point is: satisfying hunger is not enough; you must give your body the food nutrients it needs in order to benefit.

Mealtime should be a quiet, relaxed period for eating simple foods that are prepared well for digestion. You will want to prepare foods properly in order for them to be of maximum value. For example, trim excessive fat from meats. If you work under pressure and your body tends toward hypertension, substitute fried meats with meats which are baked, broiled or roasted. Add some fiber or bulk to your diet with fresh vegetables. Make fruits into desserts. Fresh fruits in season, or canned, frozen or dried fruits contain sugars that require less work from the body for digestion than do refined sugar or sucrose desserts. They will also supply Vitamin C.

If you are watching your diet, use non-fat milk. But, by all means drink at least one glass of milk each day to obtain this good source of calcium for building or maintaining strong bones and teeth.

All foods should be chewed thoroughly before swallowing. Salt and fat should be added to foods only when they enhance the flavor. How often salt is sprinkled or even poured on even before the diner tastes the dish! Generally, think carefully about the foods you eat and the quantity and quality of those foods.

Check your living pattern to determine your food needs. Is your environment such that you can eat quietly at least once a day? Do you take time to chew foods thoroughly or do you wolf them down? Do you enjoy the foods you eat? Are you overweight?

The Dietary Goals in the Senate report suggest a decrease in animal fats, sugar and salt. They suggest an increase in fresh fruits, vegetables and whole grain breads and cereals. They go back to the basics in food preparation: good food prepared simply and served in an atmosphere which allows for pleasure in dining.

Some basic principles for good food preparation in line with the new U.S. Dietary Goals are:

* Trim fat from meats.

* Broil, bake or roast meats, rather than fry.

* Serve vegetables raw when possible.

* Use all vegetable shortening for seasoning.

* Add nuts or mushrooms to vegetables to increase protein value and lessen the desire for salt.

* Use fruits for garnish or to chop into salads and desserts.

* Include dried, fresh or canned fruits in whole grain cereals and breads.

* Serve soups which are nutritious because many ingredients are available in one dish.

* If you like desserts, serve heavy ones on days when you and your family are most active.

* Prepare many dishes ahead for the freezer; they will require little or no preparation at mealtime.

* Use lemon juice and herbs to flavor foods when you decrease the salt for seasoning; lemon juice will add Vitamin C to the diet.

All these elements in the recommended proportions should serve as a guide to correct eating for our new technology-dominated lifestyles. While they do not promise that strict adherence will prevent the chronic diseases, they do serve as a basic preventive, based on our present-day scientific facts.

Our habit of fast eating in a noisy environment and other anti-social surroundings is on the increase. Stress is the result—and stress may cancel out all efforts of the Committee recommendations unless we correct eating patterns and raise the level of the dining atmosphere from chaos to quietude.

Americans in all walks of life now live with stress in incredible doses. In applying the new goals, every nutritionist, dietitian and individual will need to consider the stress levels of different lifestyles, cultural influences, dieting programs, and self-image. Our national health is at stake. We can be a vital and vigorous society, as the Senate Committee recommends, or we can continue to ignore the fact that unless we eat right we can never live right.

YOUR DAILY DIET PATTERN
FOR
EATING RIGHT

3-4 servings fresh fruit or fruit juice
3 servings green or yellow vegetables
3 servings meat, fish, eggs, milk, cheese, or substitutes
(beans, peas, peanut butter)
2-3 servings cereal, bread or potato

Larger serving or more servings of each will increase calories. Fewer serving of each or smaller servings will decrease calories. Average serving is 4 ounces for fruits, or 1 small apple or banana.

CALORIC ADJUSTMENT REQUIRED FOR WEIGHT LOSS

To lose 1 pound per week, eat 500 fewer calories daily.

Basic of estimation:

1 pound body fat	=	454 grams
1 gram pure fat	=	9 calories
1 gram body weight	=	7.7 calories (some water in fat cells)
454 grams x 9 calories per gram	=	4,086 calories per pound fat (pure fat)
454 grams x 7.7 calories per gram	=	3,496 calories per pound body fat (or 3,500 calories)
500 calories x 7 days	=	3,500 calories - 1 pound body fat

To help you plan balanced diets, the following menus and recipes may prove helpful to you. These menus have been planned to provide balance in food nutrients and simplicity in food preparation. Notice the visibility of whole grain breads and cereals, fresh fruits and vegetables.

The calories, or energy value, of the menus will depend upon the size serving of each food. The average of 3 to 4 ounces protein source is necessary.

½ cup, or 4 ounces each, for fruits or vegetables

1 slice bread, whole grain

The recipes should be flexible enough to allow for your individual creativity.

Menus and recipes for obesity and special needs will be found in the following chapters.

MENUS FOR BALANCING YOUR FOOD NUTRIENTS / FIRST WEEK

MONDAY

Breakfast

Orange Wedges
Whole Wheat Cereal
Milk†
Peanut Butter Toast Squares
Beverages

Luncheon

Tomato Juice Cocktail
Grilled Cheese-Bacon Sandwich
Pineapple-Cabbage-Raisin Salad
Milk†

Dinner

Polynesian Baked Chicken*
Corn Pudding*   Green Peas
Tossed Salad with Dressing
Fresh Fruit Cup
Beverages

TUESDAY

Breakfast

Grapefruit Juice
Scrambled Egg
Cinnamon Toast
Beverages

Luncheon

Creamed Chipped Beef on Toast
Carrot-Raisin Salad
Brownie
Milk†

Dinner

Baked Virginia Ham Slice
in Pineapple Juice*
Baked Potato   Hot Spiced Beets
Spinach Salad
Whole Wheat Bread
Macedoine of Fruit*
Beverages

*Recipe included in book.
†Milk may be non-fat if desired.

WEDNESDAY

Breakfast

Pineapple Juice with Fresh Strawberry
Ready-to-eat Cereal
Broiled Sausage Patties
Hot Rolls*   Jam
Beverages

Luncheon

Tomato Bouillon*
Paprika Egg Salad over Toast
Sliced Peaches
Milk†

Dinner

Oriental Meatloaf*
Stuffed Sweet Potatoes* with Peanut Butter
Asparagus Tips
Hot Whole Wheat Roll*
Chocolate Ice Cream
Beverages

THURSDAY

Breakfast

Stewed Prunes
Griddle Cakes with Syrup
Beverages

Luncheon

Shrimp Bisque*
Open-faced Sandwich*
(Cheese, Tomato, Bacon Slices)
Cabbage and Green Pepper Salad
Baked Pears with Marshmallows*
Hot Cocoa

Dinner

Braised Liver with Onion Rings
Creamed Potatoes   Vienna Green Beans*
Cranberry Salad*
Whole Wheat Bread   Lemon Pie*
Milk†

*Recipe included in book.
†Milk may be non-fat if desired.

FRIDAY

Breakfast

Tangerine
Ready-to-eat Cereal
Toast, Jelly
Milk†
Beverages

Luncheon

Baked Beans with Frankfurter Cubes*
Indian Cornmeal Muffin*
Cole Slaw*
Fruit Cup   Beverages

Dinner

Split Pea Soup*
Baked Flounder*
Potatoes Au Gratin
Tomato Aspic on Lettuce*
Fresh Orange-Grapefruit Sections
Milk†   Beverages

SATURDAY

Breakfast

Orange Juice
Hot Oatmeal
Peanut Butter on
Toasted Biscuit Half
Beverages

Luncheon

Potato-Carrot Soup*
Crackers
Fish Cake with Almonds*
Tossed Vegetable Salad
Sherbet
Peanut Butter Square*
Beverages

Dinner

Broiled Rib Eye Steak
Baked Potato   Steamed Carrots
Mixed Vegetable Salad
Strawberry Shortcake
Milk†

*Recipe included in book.
†Milk may be non-fat if desired.

SUNDAY

Breakfast

Grapefruit Halves
Hot Cream of Wheat
Scrambled Egg   Bacon
Toast, Jam
Beverages

Dinner

Baked Chicken
Creamed Onions with Peanuts*   Green Peas
Watermelon Pickle
Pineapple Cheese Salad
Whole Wheat Bread
Fruit Ice
Milk†

Supper

Fancy Oyster Soup*
Crackers
Cold Plate
(Cottage Cheese and fruits)
Sweet Potato-Pecan Pie*
Beverages

*Recipe included in book.
†Milk may be non-fat if desired.

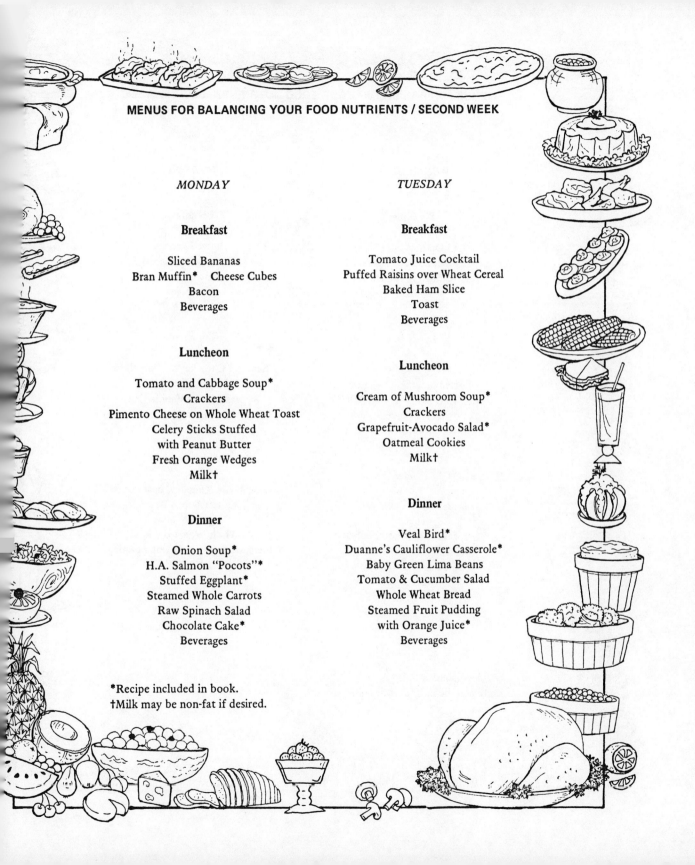

MENUS FOR BALANCING YOUR FOOD NUTRIENTS / SECOND WEEK

MONDAY

Breakfast

Sliced Bananas
Bran Muffin*   Cheese Cubes
Bacon
Beverages

Luncheon

Tomato and Cabbage Soup*
Crackers
Pimento Cheese on Whole Wheat Toast
Celery Sticks Stuffed
with Peanut Butter
Fresh Orange Wedges
Milk†

Dinner

Onion Soup*
H.A. Salmon "Pocots"*
Stuffed Eggplant*
Steamed Whole Carrots
Raw Spinach Salad
Chocolate Cake*
Beverages

TUESDAY

Breakfast

Tomato Juice Cocktail
Puffed Raisins over Wheat Cereal
Baked Ham Slice
Toast
Beverages

Luncheon

Cream of Mushroom Soup*
Crackers
Grapefruit-Avocado Salad*
Oatmeal Cookies
Milk†

Dinner

Veal Bird*
Duanne's Cauliflower Casserole*
Baby Green Lima Beans
Tomato & Cucumber Salad
Whole Wheat Bread
Steamed Fruit Pudding
with Orange Juice*
Beverages

*Recipe included in book.
†Milk may be non-fat if desired.

WEDNESDAY

Breakfast

Orange Juice
Scrambled Egg
Cinnamon Toast
Milk†

Luncheon

Okra Soup*
Potted Meat Sandwiches
Beet, Cheese and Onion Salad
Pears Halves
Beverages

Dinner

Ham-Potato Casserole*
Broccoli
Carrot, Raisin, Pineapple Salad
Whole Wheat Roll
Fruit Cubes in Compote
Beverages

THURSDAY

Breakfast

Stewed Prunes
Ready-to-eat Cereal
Pineapple Muffins*
Beverages

Luncheon

Seafood Chowder*   Crackers
Grapefruit Salad
Applesauce   Vanilla Crisp
Beverages

Dinner

Chicken Ala King on Toast Points*
Viennese Green Beans*
Vegetable Slaw
Whole Wheat Bread
Sliced Bananas with Nut Topping
Milk†

*Recipe included in book.
†Milk may be non-fat if desired.

FRIDAY

Breakfast

Strawberries
Rolled Oats
Fried Egg   Bacon
Milk†

Luncheon

Potato Leek Soup*
Toasted Peanut Butter Sandwiches
Fresh Pineapple
Beverages

Dinner

Baked Macaroni and Cheese*
Seasoned Beets
Tossed Vegetable Salad
Date Nut Bread*
Banana-Peach-Pear Fruit Cup
Beverages

SATURDAY

Breakfast

Grapefruit Juice
French Toast with Syrup
Beverages

Luncheon

Olive and Egg Sandwich
Green Bean Salad
Sliced Bananas in Orange Juice
Beverages

Dinner

Winfrey's Chicken Surprise*
Mashed Potatoes
Asparagus Tips
Waldorf Salad*
Hot Biscuit*
Orange Sections with
Coconut and Cherries
Milk†

*Recipe included in book.
†Milk may be non-fat if desired.

SUNDAY

Breakfast

Fresh Pineapple Cubes
Fried Apples   Sausage Links
John Carter's Blueberry Muffins*
Beverages

Dinner

Turkey Supreme*
Browned Potatoes
Inn-Keeper Spoonbread*
Sliced Tomato Salad
Red Raspberries Juice   Japanese Fruitcake*
Beverages

Supper

Assorted Cold Cuts
Mixed Vegetable Sandwiches (Club Style)
(cucumber, tomato, onion)
on
Date Pecan Bread*
Cantaloupe Slices
Milk†

*Recipe included in book.
†Milk may be non-fat if desired.

RECITES

OUPS . . . .

SEAFOOD CHOWDER

pound white fish filet chunks	1 teaspoon red pepper flakes,
strips bacon	nutmeg or mace
potatoes, diced	1¼ cups celery soup
large onion, diced	1¼ cups condensed clam
tablespoon chopped parsley	chowder (no tomatoes)

ry bacon and set aside. / Sauté potatoes, vegetables and spices, hen add soups and cook until potatoes are done. / Add fish and ook 10 minutes. / Add crumbled bacon and serve. ● Serves 4.

SHRIMP BISQUE

pint non-fat milk	1 tablespoon flour mixed to a
cup milk	paste with a little milk
Juice and grated rind of 1	1 pint of shrimp, cooked and
lemon	broken (not cut) into pieces
2 egg yolks	Dash of salt
¼ cup sherry	

Put non-fat milk in double boiler. / When it comes to a boil, add milk, lemon juice and rind, egg yolks, flour paste and shrimp. / Season with salt, then sherry. ● Serves 2.

OKRA SOUP

1 large beef shank	2 cups tomatoes
1 pound okra sliced across not	1 cup chopped celery
larger than ½ inch	1 cup chopped onions

Boil beef shank in 4 quarts water until meat is tender. / Remove from pot and add vegetables with salt and pepper to taste. / Grind meat from soup bone and add to soup. / If it has very little meat add 1 pound ground beef and 1 quart water. / Soup should cook slowly about 1 hour. ● Serves 4.

ONION SOUP

4 medium onions	1 teaspoon salt
3 tablespoons celery, chopped	1/8 teaspoon pepper
2 tablespoons vegetable fat	2 cups hot chicken stock
(except coconut oil)	2 cups hot non-fat milk
2 tablespoons flour	1 tablespoon parsley chopped

Cook onions and celery until tender. / Drain and sieve. / Melt fat, add flour and seasoning then stock and milk, stirring constantly. / Cook until smooth, about 5 minutes. / Add onion, celery and parsley. / Beat with egg beater until smooth. ● Serves 4.

SPLIT PEA SOUP

1 pound split peas	Celery and tops
Hambone	Salt and pepper
Onion	

Wash the peas and put them in large kettle with three quarts of cold water and hambone, one cut up onion and some chopped up celery tops. / Simmer about three hours. / Remove the bone and put the soup through a strainer. / Chill the soup and remove layer of grease, if any. / Flavor with salt and pepper. / Serve hot. ● Serves 4.

FANCY OYSTER SOUP

1 quart oysters	¼ cup all-purpose flour
1 bay leaf	½ teaspoon salt
2 medium onions, chopped	¼ teaspoon white pepper
and divided	1 pint non-fat milk
2 ribs of celery, chopped and	¼ cup dry sherry
divided	Paprika or parsley
½ cup vegetable fat (except	
coconut oil)	

Drain and chop oysters; reserve. / Add enough water to drained oyster liquor to make 2 quarts. / Add bay leaf, 1 onion, and 1 rib of celery and simmer uncovered for 30 minutes. / Remove from heat and allow to "ripen" at least an hour, then strain. / Melt fat in saucepan and add remaining onion and celery. / Sauté 5 minutes. / Stir in flour but do not brown. / Remove from heat and add part of the oyster stock, stirring constantly. / Return to heat and add remaining stock, stirring until smooth. / Add salt and pepper and cook over low heat 10 minutes. / Add oysters and milk; simmer gently 2 to 3 minutes. / If sherry is to be added, do so just before serving in warm bowls. / Garnish with paprika or chopped parsley. ● Serves 8.

MAIN DISHES ·

POLYNESIAN BAKED CHICKEN

2 frying chickens, cut up
1 cup flour
1½ teaspoons seasoned salt
½ pound vegetable fat (except coconut oil)
1 cup orange juice
2 tablespoons lemon juice
½ cup brown sugar
1 tablespoon soy sauce
1 tablespoon cornstarch
1 fresh pineapple, cubed
1 fresh papaya, cubed
Parsley, chopped
Green pepper, diced, as garnish
Sesame seeds, as garnish

Shake chicken parts in paper bag with flour and seasoned salt. / Melt fat and rub 2 tablespoons of it into a large baking dish. / Put chicken in dish and brush remaining fat over each piece. / Bake 50 minutes at 350°F. or until chicken is brown. / Meanwhile, combine juices, sugar, soy sauce, and cornstarch in a saucepan and bring to a boil, stirring constantly. / Remove from heat when clear and thickened and add fruits. / Pour mixture over chicken, coating each piece, and bake 10 minutes longer. / Serve garnished with chopped parsley or green pepper and sesame seeds. ● Serves 4.

ORIENTAL MEATLOAF

2 pounds lean ground beef
¼ cup dry fine bread crumbs
2 cups can crushed pineapple
½ cup finely chopped green peppers
2 eggs, beaten
2 teaspoons salt
¼ teaspoon pepper
2 cups cooked rice

Sauce

1 cup water chestnuts, halved
2 bouillon cubes
¼ teaspoon salt
6 tablespoons soy sauce
6 tablespoons cornstarch
¼ cup brown sugar

Mix first eight ingredients until thoroughly mixed and pack into 1½ quart ring mold. / Bake in 350°F. oven for one hour. / For sauce, drain water chestnuts, reserve and measure liquid. / Add boiling water to total 2¼ cups liquid, and pour over bouillon cubes, stirring to dissolve. / Add soy sauce and salt. / Combine brown sugar and cornstarch in saucepan. / Stir in combined liquids and cook over low heat, stirring constantly until thickened. / Serve with meatloaf. ● Serves 6.

BAKED VIRGINIA HAM *

Directions are for cooking a ham that has been cured for about 12 months and weighs about 12 to 15 pounds. / Scrub the ham to remove the coating of seasonings, cover it with water and soak for 24 hours. / Place ham, skin side down, in a pan with water to cover; bring to a boil, then reduce heat and simmer, covered, for 20 to 25 minutes per pound. / When done skin the ham and trim off excess fat. / Mix together and top the ham with:

3 tablespoons light brown sugar
1 tablespoon bread crumbs
2 tablespoons pineapple juice
1 teaspoon ground cloves
2 tablespoons dry sherry
2 tablespoons honey

Place in oven and allow top to brown at 350°F. / When cool, cut ham in thin 3 to 4 ounce slices. / Serves 50 3-ounce servings.

*Serve on a day of heavy activity. This recipe should be used only as a special treat.

BAKED STUFFED FLOUNDER

6 baby flounder, boned, or 6 flounder fillets
Seafood dressing (below)
Salt and pepper to taste
3 tablespoons lemon juice
1 cup fine bread crumbs
1/3 pound vegetable fat (except coconut oil), melted

Preheat oven to 375°F. / Grease shallow baking pan. / Stuff each fish with 4 to 6 tablespoons of Seafood Dressing or spread the same amount of dressing over each fillet. / Roll and fasten with toothpicks. / Place in prepared baking pan. / Season with salt, pepper, and lemon juice. / Sprinkle bread crumbs over fish. / Melt fat and pour over fish. / Bake for 25 to 30 minutes or until fish flakes easily when tested with a fork. ● Serves 6.

Seafood Dressing

6 tablespoons vegetable fat (except coconut oil)
¼ cup celery, finely chopped
½ cup onion, finely chopped
¼ cup green pepper, finely chopped
½ pound shrimp, cooked and diced
1 teaspoon parsley, chopped
1 teaspoon pimento, finely chopped
½ teaspoon paprika
1 teaspoon Worcestershire sauce
½ teaspoon seafood seasoning
Salt to taste
1/8 teaspoon cayenne pepper

Mix together all ingredients.

he famous French gastronome Brillat-Savarin wrote a book on
e art of dining. He stated that the turkey was one of the
oblest gifts the Old World received from the New. In early
merica, the turkey was wild; the real prize for catching the bird
found in this Turkey Supreme recipe.

TURKEY SUPREME

cup vegetable fat (except coconut oil)	1 cup milk
cup all-purpose flour	1 pound turkey breast, sliced, and cooked with rice or noodles
cups hot chicken broth	
teaspoon salt	3 tablespoons toasted almonds, chopped
/8 teaspoon white pepper	
cup non-fat milk	

Melt fat and add flour, stirring until smooth. / Pour hot chicken
broth into fat and flour mixture; stir until smooth. / Add salt
nd pepper. / Heat all milk in a separate saucepan. / Pour into
hickened chicken broth and cook over low heat for 10 minutes,
stirring often. / Serve sauce very hot over sliced turkey breast
nd steamed rice or noodles. / Top with toasted almonds. /
Serves 4 to 6.

CHICKEN A LA KING

2 tablespoons vegetable fat (except coconut oil)	1-1/3 cups non-fat milk
1/3 green pepper, cut in strips	1-1/3 cups chicken broth
¼ pound fresh mushrooms, sliced	Salt and pepper to taste
¼ cup flour	2 cups cold diced chicken, free of fat and skin
	½ pimento, cut in strips

Melt fat in top of double boiler over direct heat; / add green
pepper and mushrooms and simmer for 5 minutes, covered. /
Lift out pepper and mushrooms. / Blend flour into fat, add milk,
broth and seasoning and cook, stirring constantly, over direct
heat, until sauce boils and thickens. / Add chicken, pimento,
green pepper, and mushrooms; / place over boiling water, cover,
and cook until chicken is heated through. / Serve hot on toast or
biscuits. ● Serves 5.

H. A.'S SALMON "POCOTS"

2 cups flaked salmon	2 teaspoons lemon-juice
2 cups hot mashed potatoes	1 egg, beaten
Salt (dash)	Bread Crumbs

Add potatoes to salmon. / Season with salt and lemon-juice. /
Add beaten egg and mix. / Shape into 3 inch long balls. / Dip in
bread crumbs and fry in skillet about 5 minutes. ● Serves 6.

VEAL BIRDS

1½ pounds boneless veal steaks or cutlets, sliced thin	3 cups soft bread crumbs
¼ cup flour	1 chicken bouillon cube
1 teaspoon salt	1 cup water
1/8 teaspoon pepper	½ teaspoon salt
1 cup diced celery	Dash pepper
¼ cup vegetable fat (except coconut oil)	¾ teaspoon ground sage

Wipe veal clean with damp cloth; cut into 5 pieces. / Pound with
edge of sturdy saucer or back of heavy knife blade, and dredge
one side in flour mixed with 1 teaspoon salt and 1/8 teaspoon
pepper. / Saute celery in 2 tablespoons fat, / add bread crumbs
and toss together. / Cool. / Dissolve bouillon cube in water and
add ½ cup to stuffing; / add ½ teaspoon salt and dash pepper and
mix well. / Place a portion of stuffing on each piece of veal
(unfloured side up), / roll up with stuffing inside and fasten
securely with toothpicks. / Brown rolls slowly in hot skillet with
remaining fat. / Add remaining bouillon liquid and ¼ cup water;
cover tightly and simmer gently until meat is very tender, about
1 hour. / Gravy may be made if desired. ● Serves 6.

MAIN DISHES . . . .

WINFREY'S CHICKEN SURPRISE

1 frying chicken, about 2½ pounds, quartered	1 clove garlic, minced
¼ cup flour	1 cup water
1½ teaspoons salt	1/3 cup peanut butter
1/8 teaspoon pepper	1 cup tomato sauce
½ cup peanut oil	1 tablespoon sugar
1 medium onion, chopped	1 tablespoon cider vinegar
	1 teaspoon chili powder

Wash chicken and pat dry. / Mix flour, salt, pepper. / Roll chicken in flour mixture. / Shake off excess flour. / Heat oil in large skillet until hot. / Brown chicken quarters on all sides. / Remove chicken when brown and set aside. / Add onion and garlic to pan drippings and cook until lightly browned. / Gradually stir in water and remaining ingredients. / Stir until smooth and bubbly. / Add chicken pieces. / Simmer covered for 45 minutes or until chicken is tender. / Turn chicken in sauce occasionally and add more water from time to time, if necessary, to prevent sticking. / Add salt to taste. / Place chicken on a platter. / Skim excess fat from sauce and spoon sauce over chicken. • Serves 4.

MACARONI AND CHEESE

7 or 8-ounce package macaroni	2 tablespoons flour
1 tablespoon salt	2 cups non-fat milk
3 quarts boiling water	1 teaspoon salt
2 tablespoons vegetable fat (except coconut oil)	½ pound sharp cheese, grated

Add salt to rapidly boiling water in a large saucepan and drop in macaroni. / Cook rapidly for about 20 minutes or until tender; drain. / Run hot water through to rinse well. / Melt fat in top of double boiler over boiling water, blend in flour and add milk gradually, stirring until sauce is smooth and thick. / Add salt and grated cheese, and stir until cheese melts. / Arrange hot macaroni and cheese in layers in a greased casserole and bake in a moderately hot oven 10 to 15 minutes until brown on top. • Serves 5.

VEGETABLES . . . .

There were 37 varieties of vegetables known to Thom[as] Jefferson during the time of his presidency.

Indian Corn was called Roasting-ears. It grew on tall corn stalk[s]. It is probably the favorite way of serving corn today—on t[he] cob. It surely is our favorite. Here's another:

BREADED CORN PUDDING

3 eggs	1 cup bread crumbs
2 cups cream style corn	2 tablespoons vegetable fat
1½ tablespoons sugar	(except coconut oil), melte[d]
½ teaspoon salt	2½ cups non-fat milk

Preheat oven to 350°F. / Grease 1½ quart casserole. / Beat egg[s] until light and fluffy. / Stir in corn, sugar, salt, bread crumbs and fat. / Add milk and mix well. / Pour into prepared casserol[e] and place dish in pan of boiling water. / Bake for 50 to 6[0] minutes or until custard is set. • Serves 6.

CREAMED ONIONS WITH PEANUTS

16 whole small white onions	¼ cup whole salted peanuts
2 tablespoons vegetable fat (except coconut oil)	½ cup bread crumbs
2 tablespoons all-purpose flour	¼ cup salted peanuts, chopped
¼ teaspoon salt	
2 cups non-fat milk	

Cook onions in boiling, salted water until tender; drain. / Melt fat over medium heat; / stir in flour and salt. / Add milk and cook over medium heat, stirring constantly until smooth and slightly thickened. / Put onions in prepared casserole and pour sauce over. / Stir in ¼ cup whole peanuts. / Top with bread crumbs and chopped peanuts. / Bake at 400°F. for 15 minutes, or until casserole is bubbly and lightly browned. • Serves 4-6.

STUFFED EGGPLANT

1 large eggplant, about 1½ pounds	1 tablespoon chopped parsley
1 cup chopped onion	½ teaspoon Worcestershire sauce
1 tablespoon vegetable fat (except coconut oil)	1 cup finely crushed crackers
¼ cup condensed cream of mushroom soup	

Slice off one end of eggplant. / Remove pulp to within ½ inch of skin. / Cook eggplant pulp in a small amount of boiling water until tender, about 10 minutes; / drain thoroughly. / Cook onion in fat until tender but not brown. / Add soup, eggplant pulp, parsley, Worcestershire, and all of the cracker crumbs except 2 tablespoons. / Fill eggplant shell with mixture. / Place in 10x6x2 inch baking dish; / sprinkle reserved crumbs over top. / Carefully pour hot water in bottom of dish to depth of ½ inch. / Bake at 375°F. until heated through, 50 to 60 minutes. ● Serves 4-6.

DUANNE'S CAULIFLOWER CASSEROLE

1 medium cauliflower, separated into flowerettes	1 cup grated cheese
1 cup chopped green pepper	1 cup peanut butter
1 cup sliced onion	½ teaspoon salt
2 tablespoons peanut oil	Dash of pepper
2 tablespoons flour	½ cup chopped roasted peanuts
1½ cups non-fat milk	

Parboil cauliflower flowerettes, green pepper, and onion in salted water just until tender. / Drain and arrange in 1½ quart casserole. / In a skillet over medium heat, blend peanut oil and flour. / Add milk, stirring constantly, and bring to a boil. / Cook for 1 minute, or until smooth and thickened. / Remove from heat, blend in ½ cup grated cheese, peanut butter, salt, and pepper and pour over vegetables. / Top with remaining ½ cup grated cheese. / Bake in 375°F. oven for 30 minutes. ● Serves 6-8.

STUFFED SWEET POTATOES WITH PEANUT BUTTER

4 medium-sized sweet potatoes	¼ teaspoon salt
2/3 cup non-fat milk	Dash pepper
¼ cup peanut butter	1/3 cup chopped, dry roasted peanuts

Bake potatoes in a preheated 325°F. oven until tender, about 1 hour. / Remove from oven, cut each in half, carefully scoop potatoes from skins and mash thoroughly. / Add milk, peanut butter, and seasonings. / Beat until fluffy, then refill skins. / Brown on baking sheet at 425°F. / Sprinkle chopped peanuts on top and return to oven until reheated, 10 to 15 minutes. ● Serves 8.

SALADS . . . .

WALDORF SALAD

1 cup diced apple	French dressing
1 cup diced celery	Lettuce leaves
½ cup raisins	Mayonnaise
½ cup broken walnut-meats	

Fold together the apple, celery, raisins and nuts with French dressing and serve on lettuce with mayonnaise. / Do not allow this to stand long before serving, as the nuts will discolor the fruit. ● Serves 2.

COMBINATIONS FRUITS AND SALADS

Salads may be a combination of fruits, a variety of vegetables, or fruits and vegetables mixed together. Leftover meats, cut into cubes, or fish and poultry make excellent salads. Fruits may be added to vegetables or meat salads. For example—add fresh grapes to your tunafish salad or add fresh apple to a tossed salad.

The choice of salad combinations will be determined by the place of the salad in the menu. Salads may be used as appetizers. Begin the meal with a crisp salad to stimulate digestion. Or, a salad may become the main meal or dessert.

Important Points for Salad Making

Select crisp and green leaves of vegetables for salads. The vitamins are found in the green leaves. Wash carefully and soak in cold water for one-half hour to crisp. Dry on a towel or shake in a wire basket.

The ingredients may be placed in a covered bowl and allowed to remain in refrigerator for several days, if time is limited.

CHILL INGREDIENTS—All ingredients, fruits and/or vegetables, should be chilled. The ingredients should be placed on chilled plates before serving.

ARRANGEMENT OF SALAD—Lettuce leaves should be arranged to avoid all ragged parts hanging over the plate. The leaves should cup the salad.

Place salad on lettuce leaves carefully preventing it from falling apart. No part of the salad should extend over the edge of the plate. Garnish the salad to please yourself. Be creative in using what you have available and make it attractive.

The same ideas should apply to the selection of dressing to use.

Examples of Fruit and Vegetable Salads

- Avocado, grapefruit, romaine
- Avocado, orange and cress
- Avocado, peeled white grapes and chicory
- Avocado, tangerine, pecans and lettuce
- Avocado, tart apple and romaine
- Chicory, shredded cabbage and lettuce
- Escarole, Chinese cabbage and cress
- Chinese cabbage, tomato slices, radishes, olive
- Endive, carrot sticks and grapefruit
- Shredded carrot, Chinese cabbage and romaine
- Orange, Bermuda onion and romaine
- Tomato, cucumber, celery and onion
- Potato cooked and diced, celery, cucumber, green pepper and pimiento
- Green peas, peanuts, mint leaves and lettuce
- Danderlion escarole, pimiento and onion

BREADS . . . .

DATE NUT ROLLS

1 stick vegetable fat (except coconut oil)	1/8 teaspoon salt
1 cup diced dates	1 teaspoon vanilla
1 cup chopped nuts	1½ cups crisp rice cereal
1 cup sugar	1 cup powdered sugar

Mix first 5 ingredients in saucepan and cook 8 minutes at lo heat. / Remove from heat; / add vanilla and crisp rice cereal. Shape into fingersize rolls. / Roll in powdered sugar. • Makes 2 rolls.

JOHN CARTER DEAN'S BLUEBERRY MUFFINS

2 cups all-purpose flour	1 cup non-fat milk
2¼ teaspoons baking powder	3 tablespoons melted
½ teaspoon salt	vegetable fat (except
4 tablespoons sugar	coconut oil)
1 egg	2/3 cup washed, fresh or canned blueberries, drained

Sift flour, measure and resift with baking powder, salt and sugar 3 times, the last time into a mixing bowl. / In another bowl, beat the egg thoroughly, add milk and melted fat. / Pour liquid ingredients all at once into the dry ones. / Stir quickly until flour is just dampened; / then give 4 or 5 more quick stirs. / The batter should be a little lumpy, not smooth. / Fold in the blueberries with the last few stirs of batter. / Dip the batter quickly into greased muffin pans, filling them 2/3 full. / Bake in a moderately hot oven, 425°F., for about 20 minutes until brown. / Makes 12 muffins.

McLean, Virginia's famous place for dining is The Evans Farm Inn. Dining with tradition, one expects traditional foods, and here one gets it. Spoon bread is only one of the favorite foods served in an atmosphere of family dining in the colonial days at Evans Farm Inn. One of my favorite recipes served there by colonial ladies and gentlemen is their spoon bread.

INN KEEPER'S SPOON BREAD

cups non-fat milk	1 tablespoon vegetable fat
cup corn meal	(except coconut oil)
eggs, separated	1 teaspoon salt

cald milk and add corn meal. / Add egg yolks, fat and salt. / Continue to cook until smooth and thick. / Remove from heat and fold in beaten egg whites. / Bake in a well-greased casserole or 45 minutes at 350°F. ● Serves 6-8.

INDIAN CORN MUFFINS

cup corn meal	1 cup non-fat milk
cup sifted all-purpose flour	2 eggs, beaten
1 teaspoon salt	2 tablespoons vegetable fat
2½ teaspoons baking powder	(except coconut oil), melted

Preheat oven to 400°F. / Sift dry ingredients into mixing bowl. / Combine milk with eggs, / add to dry ingredients. / Add fat and stir until blended. / Pour into two-inch muffin tins and bake for about 20 minutes. ● Makes about 12 muffins.

DATE PECAN BREAD

½ cup finely chopped dried dates	2 cups sifted all-purpose flour
1 egg	3 tablespoons baking powder
1 cup sugar	¼ teaspoon baking soda
12 tablespoons vegetable fat (except coconut oil)	¾ teaspoon salt
	½ cup orange juice
	¼ cup water
	1 cup chopped pecans

Soak dates for 2 hours in water, then drain and dry on paper toweling. / In a bowl, mix egg, sugar and fat. / Sift flour with baking powder, baking soda, and salt. / Add dry ingredients alternately with orange juice and water, beginning and ending with dry ingredients. / Stir in dates and pecans and beat until well blended. / Pour mixture into a greased 8½ x 2½ inch loaf pan. / Bake in a preheated 350°F. oven for about two hours, or until bread is done in the center. / Unmold and cool on rack. ● Makes one loaf.

DESSERTS . . . .

PEANUT BUTTER SQUARES—
CHILDREN'S FAVORITE

2 eggs	2 cups sifted self-rising flour
2 cups light brown sugar	1 cup rolled oats
½ cup peanut butter	¼ cup wheat germ

Cream eggs, sugar and peanut butter. / Combine sifted flour slowly with this mixture, using a spatula, then add remaining ingredients and knead. / The batter should be very thick. / Pat into a flanged 10½ x 15½ inch cookie sheet, well coated with peanut oil. / Bake in preheated oven at 325°F. for 20 minutes. / Remove from oven and cut into squares while still hot. / Allow to cool 15 to 20 minutes before removing from pan. ● Makes 36 squares.

JAPANESE FRUITCAKE

1 cup (2 sticks) vegetable fat (except coconut oil) at room temperature
2 cups sugar
4 eggs
3 cups flour
½ teaspoon salt
3 teaspoons baking powder
1 cup non-fat milk
1 tablespoon grated orange rind
1 teaspoon vanilla
1 teaspoon allspice
1 teaspoon ginger
½ cup raisins
½ cup chopped pecans
1 tablespoon flour
Fruit filling (recipe follows)
1½ cups grated coconut
Candied cherries

Preheat oven to 350°F. / Grease and flour three 9-inch layer cake pans. / Cream fat and sugar with electric mixer until soft and fluffy. / Beat eggs until light and add to vegetable fat and sugar mixture. / Sift flour, salt and baking powder together and add alternately with milk to batter. / Stir in orange rind and vanilla; beat well. / Spread 2/3 of batter into two of the three prepared pans. / Add allspice and ginger to remaining batter. / Sprinkle 1 tablespoon flour over the raisins and nuts to coat, then add to batter and mix well. / Spread spiced batter into third pan. / Bake layers for 30 minutes, or until cake tests done and sides shrink from pan. / Invert on wire rack and allow to cool. / When completely cool, spread fruit filling between layers and thinly over the top and side of cake, using a flat knife to spread evenly. / Place the fruit spice layer in the middle when stacking layers. / Cover top and side of cake with the coconut. / Decorate with red and green candied cherries in a wreath design. ● Serves 8-10.

FRUIT FILLING FOR JAPANESE FRUITCAKE

2 tablespoons flour
Juice of three lemons
1 cup sugar
2½ cups crushed pineapple, drained
2 egg yolks
½ cup chopped pecans

Combine all ingredients in the top half of a double boiler over. / Cook, stirring frequently, until mixture thickens. It should be quite thick. / Remove from heat and allow to cool, stirring occasionally.

SWEET POTATO-PECAN PIE

9" pie shell, unbaked
2 cups cooked mashed sweet potatoes
½ cup brown sugar packed
½ cup granulated sugar
3 tablespoons vegetable fat (except coconut oil)
½ teaspoon cinnamon
½ teaspoon vanilla
½ teaspoon salt
1 tablespoon lemon juice
3 eggs
1 cup non-fat milk

Preheat oven to 375°F. / Mix sweet potatoes and sugars. / Add fat, cinnamon, vanilla, salt and lemon juice. / Mix well. / Add eggs and milk and mix until smooth. / Pour mixture into pie shell. / Bake at 375°F. for 30 minutes or until knife inserted in center comes out clean. / Cover top of pie with Pecan Topping. / Bake 20 minutes. ● Serves 8.

Pecan Topping

3 tablespoons melted vegetable fat (except coconut oil)
¼ cup dark brown sugar, packed
1 cup chopped pecans

Combine all ingredients, mix well. / Spoon over pie and bake.

LEMON PIE

1 9" baked pie shell
2½ tablespoons flour
¼ teaspoon salt
2 tablespoons cornstarch
1 cup sugar
1 cup boiling water
2 tablespoons vegetable fat (except coconut oil)
Juice and rind 1 lemon
2 whole eggs, separated
1 extra egg white
4 tablespoons sugar for meringue

Mix flour, salt, cornstarch and sugar, and add boiling water gradually, stirring constantly. / Add melted fat and cook over hot water until very thick and clear, about 30 minutes. / Add lemon juice, rind and the slightly beaten egg yolks. / Cook ten minutes longer. / Cool and turn into a baked pie shell. / Cover with a meringue made from the stiffly beaten whites and 3 tablespoons sugar. / Dust top with remaining sugar and brown in a low oven (300-325°F.). ● Serves 8.

PIE AND PUDDING MERINGUE

Good for topping custard pies and pudding.

2 egg whites
4 tablespoons sugar
Few grains of salt

1/3 teaspoon vanilla or 1/8
teaspoon lemon extract

Beat the egg whites until stiff, then add the sugar gradually, continuing the beating until the mixture is fine grained and will hold its shape. ● Covers one 9" pie.

MACEDOINE OF FRUIT

3 peaches
3 pears
½ cup diced pineapple

½ cup diced watermelon
1 cup raspberries
1/3 cup sugar
Whipped cream (if desired)

Pare and slice peaches and pears, cut pineapple and melon in small pieces. / Mix fruits and sugar, and chill for one hour. / Serve in glasses, adding one tablespoon whipped cream to each glass just before serving, if desired. / A berry or piece of pineapple placed on the cream gives color to the dish. ● Serves 3.

II

SUCCESSFUL DIETING:
Weight Control and Building Self Esteem

46 EASY-TO-PREPARE RECIPES AND MENUS

SELF-IMAGE—AND ESTEEM Self-image is how we feel about ourselves in relation to others and to the world. Our self-esteem is based on whether or not we genuinely like ourselves. Most people need and want positive self-esteem, self-respect, and respect from others. Our image of ourselves may be based on strong values that may override threatened defeat on the superficial bases of money, property or popularity.

It has been found that, when disaster strikes, people need food immediately. This need is not necessarily to satisfy hunger but rather for security, since loss destroys self-esteem. A cup of coffee or hot soup can bring out many hidden qualities—or dormant ones—such as love for neighbors and evident willingness to share any possessions, especially food. Self-worth seems to reappear gradually, bringing back the positive self-image which leads to a determination to rebuild, or begin anew.

When everything else seems wrong, food brings warmth, and shows love, appreciation and recognition of the common human bond, in addition to relieving hunger. Food satisfies deep emotional needs, and is closely related to our feelings of self-esteem.

Obesity is one of the most common results of lack of self-esteem. Abundant statistical evidence attests to the fact that obesity is a health hazard. Excess weight increases the risk of a number of diseases such as coronary atherosclerosis, hypertension, diabetes mellitus, gout and gall bladder disease. It seriously complicates respiratory difficulties such as asthma, chronic bronchitis and emphysema. Obesity is a hazard in

surgery, a complication in pregnancy, a deep embarrassment to the adolescent and a general threat to normal life expectancy.

Numerous studies indicate that there are critical periods in life when obesity is more likely to begin. Early infancy and early adolescence are usually the critical periods for children. For women, it is during the twenties when they change activities without changing their caloric intake, and during menopause when hormone activity changes. For men, the critical periods appear to be in the twenties to forties when the amount of food consumption remains the same even though physical activity may decrease. Both men and women tend to gain weight after fifty because of the decrease in basal metabolism and failure to adjust their caloric intake.

Genetic and cultural inheritance and social and psychological factors related to obesity are a constant concern of the dietitian. Although I recognize that some obesity is inherited and/or organic and must be left to the physician to treat, I believe most obesity is associated with the stresses of society and how a person feels about himself.

Leisure time, with its casual living style and irregular hours, also contributes to more frequent eating of snacks. Often loneliness and a low self-image lead to inferior feelings which cause nibbling and snacking.

Our American society has introduced a "nutrient stress" (disturbance of food nutrient functions) brought on by enforced conformity. We feel, generally, that everyone must be slim to be healthy and that every big person is a victim of poor health. We have simply reversed the thinking of some generations ago when status was associated with size—Mr. Jones, the successful banker, was "portly" and the wealthy dowager, Mrs. Anderson, was "a handsome woman." In other words, the larger, the healthier.

If you think that you should be thinner or heavier, examine your body frame. Is it large, medium or small? Table 1 in the Appendix will show your correct weight in accordance with your height. You may then need to adjust your diet to attain your correct weight, considering the size of your frame.

An obese person should also study the associations between high stress periods and food intake:

—When you are criticized, do you eat? What foods?

—When you fight with your spouse, do you eat? How often?

—If the sudden shock of death or financial loss overwhelms you, what effect does it have on your eating habits?

Forms of obesity caused by organic disorders are rare. It is the so-called simple obesity seen in everyday clinical practice that is most common. It is evident that obesity is not just the simple problem of food intake but a more complex one with a need for more than a prescription for a low-calorie diet.

Obesity is deviation from ideal weight. It is not merely a matter of total weight. The ratio of lean body tissue to body fat must be considered. Obesity beginning in early life is classified as developmental obesity, whereas that associated with loss of self-esteem or emotional strain is called the reactive type.

The types of obesity also have been classified on the basis of differences in body composition. Tests which have been used to measure the variations in body composition include:

- Measurement of body frame
- Skin-fold thickness which measures the surface fat or adipose tissue
- X-ray or shadows measures of fat surrounding organs and fat deposits
- Radioactive potassium count measures of the lean body tissue
- Water displacement measures of the total fat content of the body

Many factors must be considered when studying obesity. Physical factors include the need for food based on energy output. Food need is determined by basal metabolism plus amount of activity. Calories should be adjusted to fill actual body need. It is, therefore, necessary to consider that there are many sedentary persons in our affluent society. Sedentary persons cannot afford to eat as much food as more active persons can.

Although there are numerous weight reduction programs, pills and mechanical exercise machines for sale, studies indicate that most such programs for reducing show only temporary results. One who goes on a

fad diet to lose weight fast usually gains the weight back just as rapidly after the diet is discontinued. Wise eating equalizes the number of calories consumed and the amount of calories used to perform the day's activity. To lose weight, the number of calories consumed must fall below the body's need for calories. But remember, the lower the caloric intake, the harder it is to maintain a nutritionally balanced diet. You are the decision-maker. What you eat, and how much, is all up to you.

Be careful when dieting to watch your Vitamin B, or thiamine, intake. A thiamine deficiency may cause indigestion, severe constipation, gastric atony, deficient hydrochloric acid in the stomach, and loss of appetite. Good sources of thiamine are lean pork, beef, liver, whole or enriched grains. Legumes, eggs, fish and a few vegetables are fair sources. Thiamine is less widely distributed in food than some of the other vitamins such as A and C, and the quantities of thiamine in these foods are less than the naturally available quantities of Vitamins A and C. Therefore, a deficiency of thiamine is a distinct possibility in the average diet, especially when calories are markedly curtailed.

National Research Council allowances for
thiamine in relation to calories

	Age (yrs.)	Calories*	Thiamine (mg.)
Males and females	Birth-0.5	kg. x 117	0.3
	0.5-1	kg. x 108	0.5
	1-3	1,300	0.7
	4-6	1,800	0.9
	7-10	2,400	1.2
Males	11-14	2,800	1.4
	15-18	3,000	1.5
	19-22	3,000	1.5
	23-50	2,700	1.4
	51 +	2,400	1.2
Females	11-14	2,400	1.2
	15-18	2,100	1.1
	19-22	2,100	1.1
	23-50	2,000	1.0
	.51 +	1,800	1.0
Pregnant		+ 300	+0.3
Lactating		+ 500	+0.3

The hypothalamus regulates the amount of food we eat. A cluster of cells in the lateral hypothalamus serves as the appetite center. And another group of cells, located in the bentral medial nucleus of the hypothalamus, functions as a satiety center. What acts directly on these centers to stimulate or depress them is still a matter of theory rather than fact.

One theory, the "thermostat theory," holds that it is the temperature of the blood circulating to the hypothalamus that influences the centers. A moderate decrease in blood temperature produces the opposite effect, a depressed appetite, or anorexia.

Another theory, the "glucostat theory," says that it is the blood glucose concentration and rate of glucose utilization that influences the hypothalamic feeding centers. A low blood glucose concentration or low glucose utilization stimulates the appetite center, whereas a high blood glucose concentration inhibits it.

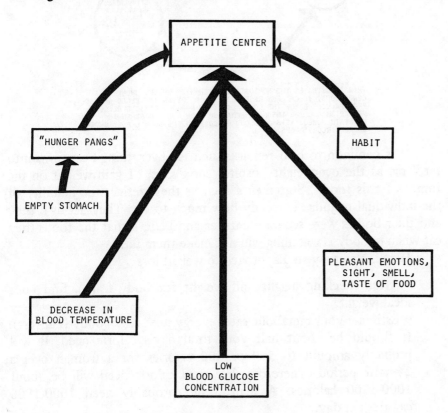

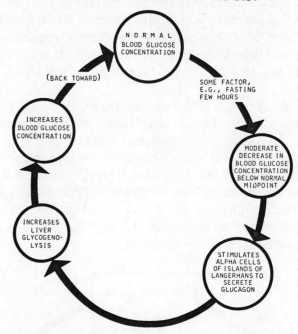

THIS ILLUSTRATES THE HOMEOSTATIC MECHANISM WHICH, UNDER USUAL CONDITIONS, IS CHIEFLY RESPONSIBLE FOR PREVENTING BLOOD GLUCOSE FROM FALLING BELOW THE LOWER LIMIT OF NORMAL. THIS GLUCAGON MECHANISM AND THE INSULIN MECHANISM SHOW WORK TOGETHER TO MAINTAIN HOMEOSTASIS OF BLOOD GLUCOSE IN THE NORMAL BODY UNDER USUAL CIRCUMSTANCES.

It is common to hear remarks such as "Everything I eat turns into fat," or, as the overweight hospital cook says, "I gain weight on the fumes of this food." Statements such as these reflect the inability of the individual to judge correctly how much to eat. They act as if they and their bodies were separate entities and believe that the foods they eat when nobody is watching will not make them fat.

Here is a step-by-step approach to weight loss:

- After checking height and weight for body frame, find your ideal weight.
- Estimate your metabolic rate (energy need when body is at rest). It should be about half your total day's caloric need. It will probably amount to 500 or 600 calories for a woman over a 24-hour period. Therefore, her total caloric need will be about 1000-1200 calories. A man would probably need 1600-1800 calories per day.
- Now, take a look at your activity from the time you arise in the morning until bedtime. Decide if you are an active or inactive person. Active people use more calories than do inactive people.

- See tables II and III in appendix for your food needs.
- You are now ready to begin losing your unnecessary pounds.
- Begin your daily diet pattern.

If you must lose many pounds to reach your ideal weight, see your doctor first. You will then feel more confident in your efforts to lose weight.

Once you have started your weight loss program:

- Divide your food into three meals with three smaller meals or snacks in between.
- Keep the secret to yourself—only you know that you are losing weight.
- Don't skip a meal. Eat at least three meals a day, including breakfast.
- Plan your exercise program carefully.

LOSING WEIGHT. Will power is an important ingredient in losing weight. Select your diet pattern considering your activity, body frame and how your weight compares to ideal weight. The diet patterns shown may be adjusted in calories by selecting larger or smaller servings of foods. The patterns vary from 1000 calories to 1300 calories. If you select a diet plan which contains fewer than 1000 calories, you should consult your physician before beginning it.

A diet should not be too low in calories because it is difficult to supply the body with all of the food nutrients in a very low number of calories. There are times, however, when a physician will prescribe a diet lower than 1000 calories due to some special condition. A starvation diet may also be prescribed. But under these conditions the person is usually hospitalized and under continuous care of the physician. Surely a person partaking in any activity other than complete bed rest is risking his or her life when selecting any diet plan below 1000 calories.

When you have selected your diet pattern, you should be able to remain on that diet schedule for as long as your activity level is maintained. If after two weeks you have not lost two to three pounds, then reduce to the lower number of servings on the 1000 calorie plan. Diet pills cannot be recommended since they are costly, unnecessary, and potentially dangerous. Instead of a diet pill, good substitutes are

broth (bouillon) lemon juice, lime juice, tea or coffee, lettuce, celery and unsweetened pickles. These will supply fiber and give you the same general feeling of no hunger that the diet pill produces. Free foods have practically no calories. You may use the following seasonings:

Paprika	Nutmeg
Garlic	Mustard
Celery salt	Chili powder
Parsley or mint	Vinegar
Horseradish	Cinnamon

Food is one of life's basic necessities, and eating should be one of our greatest pleasures. Dieting needn't change this.

WHAT ABOUT FAD DIETS? Most nutritionists check each new fad diet to keep up with the new deficiency diets on the market. Some general characteristics of fad diets are commonly known. Each one has a new theory on how to force the body's adipose tissue (fat storage) to break down, or fool the body into the feeling of fullness without sufficient food or with a total lack of food.

In recent months a fad diet that has caused a great deal of interest and apparently found a large following is the liquid protein diet. Many reducing diets are low in protein; others are high in protein. When people see the words, "protein diet" many associate it with being a good diet. The rationale for such a diet is the inevitable weight loss that will result from so few calories plus an attempt to counteract the negative nitrogen balance (protein breakdown by the body) that accompanies such severe caloric restriction.

There is nothing magic about a diet that is restricted to 600 or less calories a day. It is a state of fasting for active adults. At the same time there are serious medical consequences which can result from a prolonged negative nitrogen balance. And, unless basic eating patterns are changed, the weight loss from such a diet will be gained back rapidly.

Any permanent weight loss will require a permanent change in eating habits.

We search desperately for fad diets, yet there is only one way to lose weight. The simple scientific fact is that weight loss is a matter of caloric restriction and long-term weight loss means long-term caloric

restriction. So, save your money to spend wisely on good food selections.

After you have reached your desired weight loss, you will want to maintain that same caloric intake. By this time you will have adjusted your food intake to your body's needs and your body will not require additional food. You will be consuming the calories that balance with your body's activity, or "energy balance." To maintain the balance, check your weight on a regular schedule. Compare weight and food intake. See the chart on maintaining metabolism, Appendix.

THE OPPOSITE OF OBESITY. Obesity, however, is not the only diet problem associated with food and self image. The opposite condition, known as anorexia nervosa, or starvation, results from a refusal to eat.

Anorexia nervosa is defined as a feeling of fullness brought about by the person's inability to accept food. Food forced on the person may cause pain or vomiting. It is a state of malnutrition caused by lack of food, and is called enforced malnutrition.

A hunter strike brought on by a determination to lose weight is an example of anorexia nervosa. Fad dieting, depression and mental disorders such as chronic schizophrenia are familiar signs of anorexia nervosa. Other symptoms of enforced malnutrition are tension, self-centered, and self-absorption.

Enforced malnutrition may develop from a feeling of being deprived. Children may blame parents for problems of body shape, or other factors related to their body. For example, a teenage girl may experience feelings about breast development and wish that she could have a flat chest. Often an overconcern with such matters will bring on anorexia nervosa.

Anorexia is actually caused by vitamin deficiency. Vitamin B_1, or thiamine, deficiency is a factor related to anorexia. Thiamine must be present in sufficient amounts to provide the key energizing co-enzyme factor in the cells. The absence of Vitamin B_1 will be reflected in the nervous system, gastrointestinal system and the cardiovascular system.

LONELINESS + SELF ESTEEM. Loneliness has been studied by specialists in some countries, and to our surprise they have found that work, marriage and children are factors related to our health. Some

studies have shown that if we do not live together, we die prematurely.

Those who are lonely may call it "independence," "freedom," "privacy," or "mobility." The rights of individuals in our country have been protected and we do not interfere with each other. Yet loneliness can bring about health problems both physical and mental. Elderly people are particularly prone to loneliness-related disease.

Our society places loneliness on the cafeteria counter of life to be selected like any other commodity. But loneliness is a form of depression and carries with it the same anxieties that other depressed states bear in relation to food. "What's the use of preparing a meal when there's no one here but me to eat?" is a typical complaint of the lonely. On the other hand, the effects of loneliness may be overeating as a possible compensation for the feeling of void. Another effect is stress that will be discussed in the chapter on Stress.

Loneliness and deprivation also may cause other types of behavior. Studies relate that many criminals have been found to suffer from low blood sugar. They have been placed on diets high in protein, fresh fruits and vegetables, to be eaten in a group seating. An improved nutritional diet has resulted in a definite change in attitude and appearance.

Can it be that malnutrition causes violent or criminal behavior? In conducting scientific studies on white rats, I have found that the growth rate of rats beginning with the same weight continues the same even though one may be eating a balanced diet and the other a nutritionally deficient diet. At the adolescent period for each rat, the rat on the nutritionally balanced diet will continue to be healthy and will have a pleasant disposition that allows handling. The rat on the poor diet, however, will become irritable, bites, gain weight more slowly, lose appetite, becomes lesioned (ears and eyes), and begin to eat much less food. The total negative personality finally requires isolation of the rat.

Is there a relationship between the increasingly poor eating habits and crime and violence? We already know that the way a person views himself will determine his eating habits and his behavior patterns. Yet we have only begun to realize the impact society has on the individual, not only in terms of his self-image in relation to his food intake but also the illnesses that may result.

It is, therefore, extremely important that we realize "we are what we eat." We become the results of our eating habits and the quality of the foods that make up the diet.

- Size of serving of food should meet individual needs.
- Standard half-cup serving of vegetables should be maintained.
- Snacks should be checked for calories; they add up quickly.
- Use spices and herbs to make meals more interesting; less salt will be needed.
- Sugar, honey, syrups, fruits canned in heavy syrup, other sweets, flour, and cornstarch should be used sparingly.
- The fat in the diet may be decreased by trimming away the fat from meat.
- Avoid fried foods, nuts, sauces, gravies, and salad dressings.
- All beverages, with the exception of water, plain tea, black coffee, and low-calorie soft drinks, contribute to total caloric intake.
- Chewing foods slowly should be a regular dietary practice. It contributes to a satisfying feeling and the body can use the food better.
- Drink a large glass of water at the beginning of a meal. This helps lessen the desire for food at that meal.
- Meals should be eaten with some regularity. Skipping meals is a poor practice.
- Check your diet weekly for your weight and food consumption.
- EAT A GOOD BREAKFAST EACH DAY. INCLUDE PROTEIN SOURCE AND FRUIT IN EACH MEAL.

The Dietary Goals suggest that an increase in the consumption of complex carbohydrates is likely to ease the problem of weight control. The displacement of fat and sugar reduces the risk of obesity. Furthermore, the high water content and bulk of fruits and vegetables and bulk of whole grain can bring satisfaction of appetite more quickly than do foods high in fats and sugar. To prevent obesity keep calories balanced with activity. Calories reduced below energy need for activity are the only treatment for obesity.

Eat all meals in quiet. Begin with quiet pleasant thoughts. Remember, you must prepare your body, a chemical laboratory, for digestion, metabolism, absorption and utilization of food. Allow time for chewing food thoroughly and rest after each meal for good digestion.

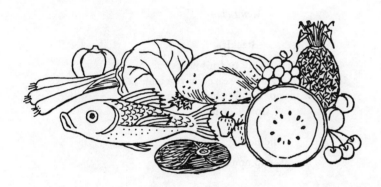

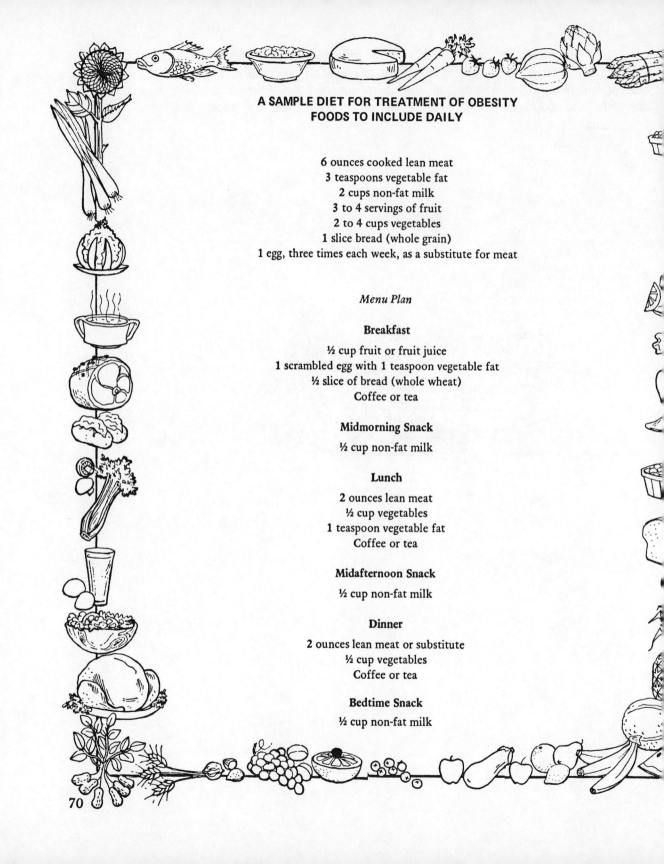

A SAMPLE DIET FOR TREATMENT OF OBESITY
FOODS TO INCLUDE DAILY

6 ounces cooked lean meat
3 teaspoons vegetable fat
2 cups non-fat milk
3 to 4 servings of fruit
2 to 4 cups vegetables
1 slice bread (whole grain)
1 egg, three times each week, as a substitute for meat

Menu Plan

Breakfast

½ cup fruit or fruit juice
1 scrambled egg with 1 teaspoon vegetable fat
½ slice of bread (whole wheat)
Coffee or tea

Midmorning Snack

½ cup non-fat milk

Lunch

2 ounces lean meat
½ cup vegetables
1 teaspoon vegetable fat
Coffee or tea

Midafternoon Snack

½ cup non-fat milk

Dinner

2 ounces lean meat or substitute
½ cup vegetables
Coffee or tea

Bedtime Snack

½ cup non-fat milk

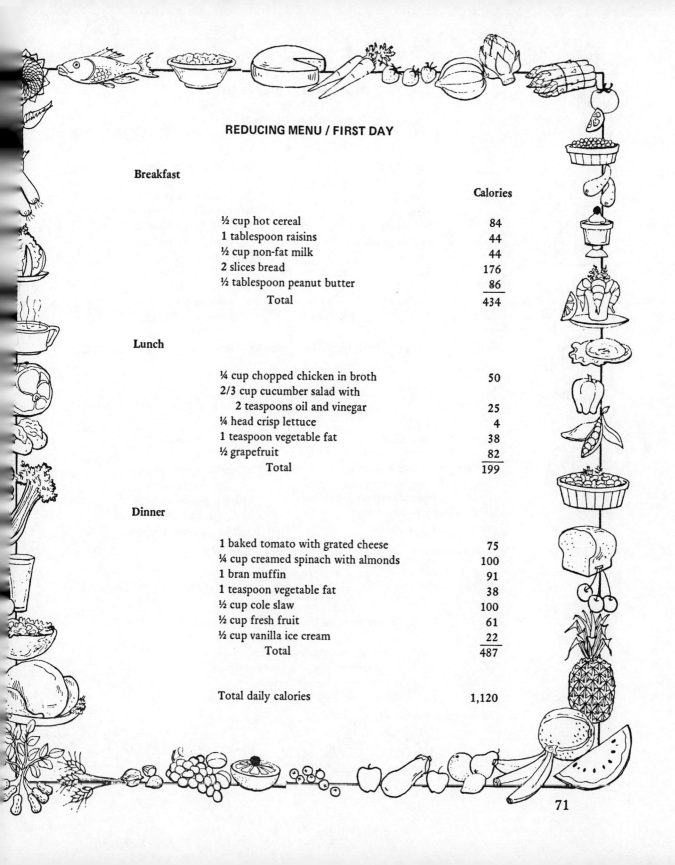

REDUCING MENU / FIRST DAY

Breakfast

	Calories
½ cup hot cereal	84
1 tablespoon raisins	44
½ cup non-fat milk	44
2 slices bread	176
½ tablespoon peanut butter	86
Total	434

Lunch

¼ cup chopped chicken in broth	50
2/3 cup cucumber salad with	
2 teaspoons oil and vinegar	25
¼ head crisp lettuce	4
1 teaspoon vegetable fat	38
½ grapefruit	82
Total	199

Dinner

1 baked tomato with grated cheese	75
¼ cup creamed spinach with almonds	100
1 bran muffin	91
1 teaspoon vegetable fat	38
½ cup cole slaw	100
½ cup fresh fruit	61
½ cup vanilla ice cream	22
Total	487

Total daily calories	1,120

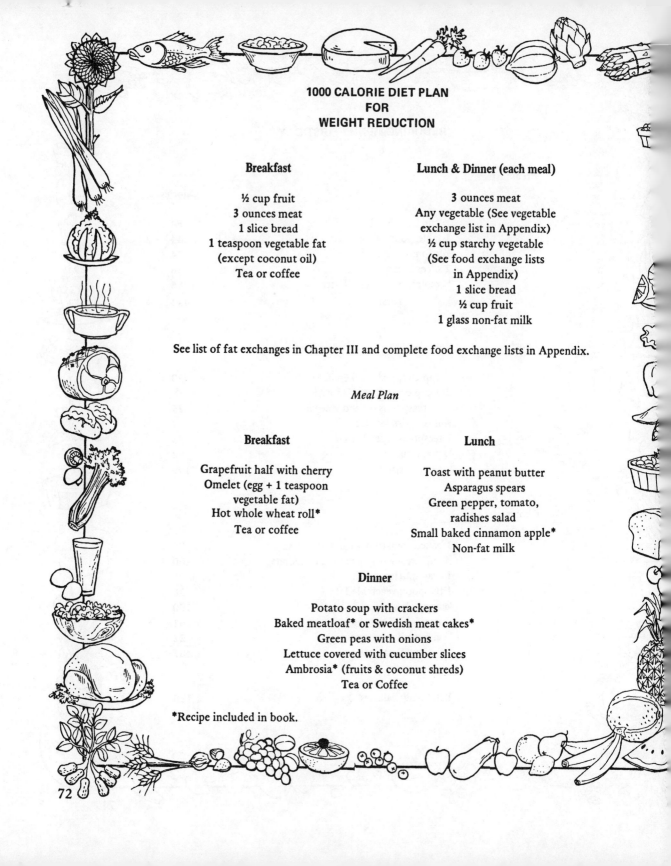

1000 CALORIE DIET PLAN
FOR
WEIGHT REDUCTION

Breakfast

½ cup fruit
3 ounces meat
1 slice bread
1 teaspoon vegetable fat
(except coconut oil)
Tea or coffee

Lunch & Dinner (each meal)

3 ounces meat
Any vegetable (See vegetable
exchange list in Appendix)
½ cup starchy vegetable
(See food exchange lists
in Appendix)
1 slice bread
½ cup fruit
1 glass non-fat milk

See list of fat exchanges in Chapter III and complete food exchange lists in Appendix.

Meal Plan

Breakfast

Grapefruit half with cherry
Omelet (egg + 1 teaspoon
vegetable fat)
Hot whole wheat roll*
Tea or coffee

Lunch

Toast with peanut butter
Asparagus spears
Green pepper, tomato,
radishes salad
Small baked cinnamon apple*
Non-fat milk

Dinner

Potato soup with crackers
Baked meatloaf* or Swedish meat cakes*
Green peas with onions
Lettuce covered with cucumber slices
Ambrosia* (fruits & coconut shreds)
Tea or Coffee

*Recipe included in book.

1800 CALORIE DIET PLAN
FOR
WEIGHT REDUCTION

Breakfast

½ cup fruit
½ cup cereal
3 ounces meat
1 slice bread
½ cup non-fat milk

Lunch & Dinner (for each meal)

3 ounces meat
Any vegetable
(See vegetable exchange list
in Appendix)
½ cup starchy vegetable
(See food exchange lists
in Appendix)
2 slices bread
1 teaspoon vegetable fat
(except coconut oil)
½ cup fruit
1 glass non-fat milk

Menu Plan

Breakfast

Banana over cornflakes
with non-fat milk
Cheese cubes
Whole wheat toast
Tea or Coffee

Lunch

Vegetable soup (1 cup)
Cheese-meat spread sandwich
or baked potato
Fresh pear
Non-fat milk

Dinner

Broiled veal chop
Green beans amondine
Tossed salad* with low-calorie dressing*
Hot biscuit* with vegetable fat
Cherries in natural juice
Hot spiced tea*
Non-fat milk

*Recipe included in book.

A serious dieter should become familiar with the many foods in the market that are packaged without added sugar and salt. With the caloric value clearly marked on packages and cans, it is easier to keep track of your total daily calorie count.

Below are other low calorie recipes for your variety in meal planning. The calorie count has been reduced from that normally found in the individual recipe. The dishes are nourishing and you should lose weight.

SOUPS . . . .

TOMATO BOUILLON

2 tablespoons vegetable fat (except coconut oil)	½ teaspoon dried oregano leaves
¾ cup chopped onion	¼ teaspoon seasoned salt
6 cups tomato juice	1/8 teaspoon pepper
1 bay leaf	
½ cup chopped celery, with leaves	

In hot fat in medium sauce pan, sauté onion, stirring, until golden—3 minutes. / Add other ingredients. / Simmer 15 minutes. / Stir occasionally. / Strain. / Taste for seasoning. / Serve hot or cold. ● Serves 6.

MAIN DISHES . . . .

PLAIN OMELET

2 eggs	2 tablespoons water
¼ teaspoon salt	1 tablespoon vegetable fat
Dash pepper	(except coconut oil)

Beat eggs until well blended. / Add seasonings and liquid. / Melt fat in small frying pan and add egg mixture. / Place over medium heat and lift edges of omelet as it cooks. / Tip frying pan to allow liquid to run under the firm portion. / Shake over heat until slightly brown and fold with spatula from handle of frying pan to outer edge. / Slip onto a hot plate and garnish with parsley. ● Serves 1.

HERB FLAVORED MEAT LOAF

½ cup soft bread crumbs	1 clove garlic, finely chopped
½ cup non-fat milk	1 teaspoon salt
1 pound lean ground beef	¼ teaspoon oregano
1 egg, slightly beaten	1/8 teaspoon rosemary
2 tablespoons grated onion	¼ teaspoon basil
2 tablespoons parsley, finely chopped	½ teaspoon paprika
	¼ teaspoon pepper

Soak bread crumbs in milk. / Combine all ingredients and mix thoroughly. / Place mixture in loaf pan. / Bake for 1 hour in a moderate oven (350°F.). / Serve hot or cold. / When cold, can be sliced thin for cold buffet. ● Serves 4.

SWEDISH MEAT CAKES

¾ pound lean ground beef	2 tablespoons grated onion
1 egg	1 tablespoon chopped capers
¼ cup cooked carrots	1 teaspoon horseradish
¼ cup cooked turnips	1 teaspoon salt
	1/8 teaspoon pepper

Combine ground meat and egg. / Mix well. / Mash cooked carrots and turnips. / Blend with the meat. / Add other ingredients and mix well with hands. / Shape into 4 large patties. / Chill thoroughly in refrigerator for at least 30 minutes. / Preheat broiler and broil meat cakes until brown on both sides. ● Serves 4.

HUNGARIAN GOULASH

pounds top round of beef,
  cut into 1-inch squares
  (trim off all fat)
cup consommé
cup tomato juice
  medium size green pepper,
  diced

2 cloves garlic
1 teaspoon paprika
½ teaspoon salt
½ teaspoon pepper
1 bay leaf
3 medium carrots cut in 1-inch
  lengths

se large iron pot and put in all ingredients except carrots. /
over and simmer for 2½ hours. / Add the carrots and simmer
nother 30 minutes. / If necessary add a little more consommé
r tomato juice. • Serves 6.

PEPPERS STUFFED WITH BEEF
AND WILD RICE

green peppers
cups cooked wild rice (or
  white rice)

¼ teaspoon salt
¼ pound chopped lean beef
  (or lean leftovers)

Cut tops off peppers and remove seeds. / Mix rice, salt and meat.
/ Add small amount of water if rice is very dry. / Fill peppers
and place in baking dish. / Surround peppers with a small
amount of hot water. / Bake in moderate oven (350°F.) until
peppers are tender. • Serves 6.

BAKED CHICKEN A LA PINEAPPLE

1 (3 pound size) broiler fryers,
  cut up
½ tablespoon sage
¼ teaspoon salt
1½ cups bread crumbs
2 teaspoons dried rosemay
  leaves
1 teaspoon ginger
¼ cup finely chopped celery

1 tablespoon orange peel
1 tablespoon vegetable fat,
  melted (except coconut oil)
¼ cup drained crushed
  pineapple
¼ cup orange juice
¼ cups pineapple juice
10 shallots, peeled
½ cup water

Remove skin from chicken. / Rinse the chicken with cold water
and drain. / Dry inside and outside. / Rub cavity of each chicken
piece with sage and salt. / Combine bread crumbs, rosemary,
ginger, celery, orange peel and fat in a bowl. / Toss lightly. /
Place pieces of chicken in baking dish. / Add crushed pineapple,
orange juice, pineapple juice over the chicken. / Add water and
place in oven. / Bake at 375°F. for about 1 hour or until chicken
is tender. • Serves 5 to 6.

VEAL RAGOUT PARIE

1 tablespoon vegetable fat
  (except coconut oil)
1½ pound veal shoulder, cut
  into 2-inch cubes
1 clove garlic, finely chopped
1 tablespoon flour
1½ teaspoons salt
¼ teaspoon pepper

1½ cups boiling water
1½ cups sliced carrots
1 cup sliced celery
2 medium potatoes, pared and
  quartered
1½ cups peas
½ teaspoon dried majoram
  leaves

In hot fat in Dutch oven or heavy skillet, brown veal well on all
sides (in several batches, if necessary). / Add garlic. / Saute 3
minutes. / Sprinkle flour, salt and pepper over veal. / Gradually
stir in boiling water. / Reduce heat. / Simmer, covered, 1 hour,
stirring occasionally. / Add carrots, celery, potatoes, peas and
marjoram. / Simmer, covered, about 25 minutes, or until
vegetables are tender. / (If mixture seems dry, stir in a little
boiling water.) • Serves 6.

SHRIMP IN GARLIC SAUCE

2 tablespoons vegetable oil
  (except coconut oil)
2 pounds of uncooked,
  deveined shrimp
2 small cloves garlic, finely
  chopped

¾ cup tomato paste
2 teaspoon salt
½ teaspoon pepper
½ teaspoon dried basil leaves
1 cup chopped onion

In hot oil in large skillet, over medium heat, saute shrimp,
turning several times, about 5 minutes, or just until they turn
pink. / Remove from heat. / Stir in other ingredients, along with
1 cup water. / Simmer, covered, until heated through. • Serves 6.

TUNA-TOMATO CASSEROLE

1 cup elbow macaroni
¾ cup chopped onion
2 tablespoons chopped parsley
½ cup chopped celery, with tops
1 clove garlic, chopped
2½ cups tomatoes, undrained
1 bay leaf, crumbled
1 teaspoon salt
1/8 teaspoon pepper
½ teaspoon dried basil leaves
½ teaspoon dried oregano leaves
2 tablespoons vegetable fat (except coconut oil), melted
2 tablespoons grated Parmesan cheese
3 tablespoons dry bread crumbs
1 cup tuna, drained (water packed)

Cook macaroni as package label directs. / Drain. / Meanwhile, preheat oven to 375°F. / In 2-quart saucepan, combine onion, parsley, celery, garlic, tomatoes, bay leaf, salt, pepper, basil, oregano. / Bring to boiling, stirring. / Reduce heat; simmer, uncovered, 20 minutes. / Combine fat, cheese, and bread crumbs in small bowl. / Lightly toss macaroni, tomato mixture, and tuna until well combined. / Turn into 6 individual baking dishes. / Top with crumb mixture. / Place on cookie sheet. / Bake 20 minutes, or until crumbs are golden brown. ● Serves 6.

VEGETABLES . . . .

BAKED POTATO

1 baking potato
3 tablespoons cottage cheese
½ tablespoon chopped chives

Wash and dry potato. / Bake at 375°F. one hour, or until done. / Remove slice from top, or make a quarter cut and open potato. / Combine cottage cheese with chopped chives, flavor generously with salt and pepper and pile on top of potato. ● Serves 1.

GLAZED CARROTS OR ONIONS

6 long carrots or 12 to 15 small white onions
2 tablespoons vegetable oil
2 tablespoons sugar, white or brown
2 tablespoons lemon juice
1 tablespoon chopped parsley

Clean vegetables and cook in boiling, salted water until almost done. / Do not cook too soft. / Drain. / In medium sized skillet heat oil, add sugar, lemon juice and parsley and cook over low flame until mixture bubbles. / Add vegetables and cook slowly until browned. / Turn vegetables often, so that glaze will be even. ● Serves 4.

MUSHROOM-GREEN PEPPER HASH

1 tablespoon vegetable oil (except coconut oil)
1 cup sliced onion
3 green peppers (1½ pound), sliced in ½ inch rings
½ cup mushrooms, sliced
1 teaspoon salt
1/8 teaspoon crushed dried red pepper
1/8 teaspoon dried oregano leaves

In hot oil in skillet, saute onion, stirring, until golden—about 5 minutes. / Add remaining ingredients. / Cook, covered, over medium heat, 5 minutes, stirring occasionally. ● Serves 6.

SALADS . . . .

FRUIT AND CHEESE SALAD

2 dried prunes, cooked without sugar
3 medium slices tomato
3 level tablespoons cottage cheese
2 lettuce leaves

Place the three slices of tomato on lettuce leaves. / Top with cottage cheese. / Place pitted prunes on the side. / Garnish with chopped chives, watercress or parsley. / Serve with low calorie dressing. ● Serves 1.

CARROT SALAD MARINADE

cup white vinegar
cup chopped onion
teaspoon salt

1 teaspoon mixed pickling
  spice
9 carrots, quartered lengthwise
  (¾ pound)

medium saucepan, heat vinegar, onion, salt, and pickling spice
boiling. / Add carrots; bring to boiling. / Reduce heat;
mmer, covered, 5 minutes. / Pour into shallow baking dish. /
et cool. / Refrigerate 2 hours. / Drain just before serving. •
erves 6.

GREEN BEAN SALAD MARINADE

½ cups green beans, cut
  (French Style)
tablespoons cider vinegar

1½ tablespoons vegetable oil
  (except coconut oil)
1 teaspoon salt
Dash pepper
½ teaspoon chopped parsley

Cook beans; drain. / Turn into shallow serving dish. / Refrigerate
until well chilled—about 1 hour. / Combine remaining ingredients in jar with tight-fitting lid. / Shake vigorously. / Pour over
beans. / Toss gently, to coat them well. / Refrigerate until ready
to serve. / Then toss once more. • Serves 6.

SALAD DRESSINGS . . . .

LOW-CALORIE SALAD DRESSING

¼ cup sugar
½ teaspoon salt
½ teaspoon dry mustard
1 tablespoon cornstarch

1/3 cup vinegar
2/3 cup water
1 tablespoon minced onion

Mix all ingredients in a saucepan and stir over heat until mixture
boils. / Continue to stir 1 to 2 minutes longer. / Chill before
using. / This is also good with tomato salad and mixed vegetable
salads. • Makes 1 cup.

SALAD DRESSINGS . . . .

BUTTERMILK DRESSING

1 cup buttermilk
½ teaspoon onion juice

¾ teaspoon salt
1½ tablespoon lemon juice

Combine all ingredients in jar with tight-fitting lid. / Shake
vigorously to blend. / Store in refrigerator until ready to use. /
Shake just before using. • Makes 1 cup.

CREAMY CUCUMBER DRESSING

1 cup finely chopped, pared
  cucumber
½ cup chopped green pepper
1 clove garlic, finely chopped
½ teaspoon salt

¼ cup yogurt
¼ cup mayonnaise
¼ cup chili sauce
1 tablespoon prepared
  horseradish

Combine all ingredients in medium bowl. / Mix well. /
Refrigerate 30 minutes, or until well chilled. • Makes 2 cups.

DESSERTS . . . .

FRESH FRUIT CUPS

½ pineapple
1 cup strawberries
3 well-ripened bananas

3 oranges
2 tablespoons lemon juice
Sugar

Peel and dice the pineapple, bananas and oranges. / Wash and
hull the strawberries. / Mix all together, with the lemon juice and
sugar, and set in the refrigerator until very cold.
Peel and slice 3 oranges and arrange in a glass dish alternate
layers of oranges and sugar until all the fruit is used. / Whip some
sweet cream very stiff. / Sweeten and flavor it and spread it over
the oranges. / Serve very cold.
  Crushed pineapple and sliced bananas may be added, if desired.

3 oranges
1 cup diced pineapple
3 well-ripened bananas

Sugar
1 cup moist coconut
Fruit juice

With a sharp knife cut the orange and pineapple into thick slices,
/ then cut them into bits free from seeds and membrane. / Slice
the bananas thin. / Arrange alternate layers of the different fruits
in a deep dish and sprinkle each layer tightly with sugar and
coconut. / Over the whole pour any fruit-juice. / Serve very cold.

BAKED APPLES

Select sound apples; / core them and place from one teaspoon to one tablespoon of sugar in each cavity. / Place the apples in a baking-dish, / add water to cover the bottom of the dish. / Bake in a moderate oven (350°-375°F.) until tender.

Sour apples cook more quickly than sweet ones, and summer or fall apples take less time to cook than winter apples.

Baked apples may be varied by filling the centers with brown sugar and raisins, sections of bananas, red cinnamon candies, marshmallow, marmalade or jelly, honey or corn syrup and lemon juice, nuts, candied orange-peel, candied pineapple, preserved ginger, canned or fresh berries, peaches and other fruits or left-over fruit-juice. / Meringues or custard sauce may be used as garnish.

BAKED STUFFED APPLES

6 large tart red apples	1 cup sugar
1 cup chopped bananas	1 teaspoon cinnamon
1 cup chopped cranberries	Chopped nut meats

Cut off the stem end of the apples, but do not peel them. / Remove all the core and part of the pulp, leaving the walls of the cup about three fourths inch thick. / Mix bananas, cranberries, sugar, and cinnamon. / Fill the cavities in the apples with this mixture, cover with chopped nut-meats. / Bake in the oven (350°-375°F) until tender. / Serve cold. ● Serves 6.

STEAMED APPLES

Core the apples, / fill cavities with sugar and put in a saucepan with hot water about an inch deep. / Cover and cook slowly, turning the apples over once. / This will steam the apples and, if they are red, will preserve their color. These resemble baked apples and the same variations may be used.

BAKED STUFFED PEARS

Pare and core large pears and stuff with seeded dates, raisins or chopped nuts with some tart marmalade or shredded coconut. / Place close together in a baking dish, / cover bottom of pan with water and bake slowly until tender.

MERINGUED PEARS

6 large pears	Candied ginger
6 tablespoons sugar	3 egg whites
Grated lemon rind	¼ cup powdered sugar

Pare and core the pears; / place them in a baking dish and fill the center of each with one tablespoon sugar and a little grated lemon rind or candied ginger. / Add three or four tablespoons of water and bake until tender. / Cover them with a meringue made with stiffly beaten egg whites and the sugar. / Brown quickly. ● Serves 6.

STEWED RHUBARB

Wash, but do not peel, the rhubarb, / and cut it in one-inch pieces. / Add one half as much sugar as rhubarb, / put in a saucepan with just enough water to keep the fruit from burning. / Very little water is needed, as rhubarb provides its own moisture. / Cook rapidly until tender.

BAKED RHUBARB

Prepare as for stewing, using same proportion of sugar and rhubarb. / Bake in a moderate oven (350°-375°F.); /until the rhubarb is reduced to a soft, red pulp.

DRIED FRUITS

If prepared carefully, most dried fruits retain their flavor. / Except for some of the vitamins, none of the food values of the product are lost in drying, for this method of preservation only drives off the moisture of perishable foods through evaporation. / All fruits contain a large amount of water, sometimes as much as ninety percent, which can be restored to the food by soaking in cold water. / The time required for this depends on the kind of fruits; from six to twelve hours is usually sufficient.

ORANGES

Cut oranges in half crosswise. / With a sharp knife, loosen the pulp from the center and from the dividing fiber. / Serve two halves to each person.

An attractive dessert is made by cutting oranges crosswise in quarter-inch slices and laying the slices in an overlapping row on a glass plate, allowing about four slices to each person. / The slices may be sprinkled with sugar and moist coconut or served plain.

STUFFED PEACHES

are large peaches and cut a slice from the top of each. / Remove he pits without breaking the fruit and fill the hollow with nuts r with any chopped fruit, such as apples, citron or raisins. / prinkle with sugar and a little cinnamon or nutmeg. / Pour ustard over the peaches and bake. / Or serve cold soft custard ith the uncooked chilled fruit.

SLICED BANANAS

hill and slice well-ripened bananas, / serve with cream or emon juice and sugar.

MELONS

All melons should be served very cold. They may be laid on chopped ice when served but the ice should never be placed in or on the edible parts of the melon.

CANTALOUPE—Cut the cantaloupe in half and with a spoon remove the seeds without injuring the flesh. / Each half may be served alone or it may be filled with fresh berries or other fruit or with ice cream. / When used as an appetizer at the beginning of a meal, a quarter of a large cantaloupe is enough. / Chilled melon balls are often served.

HONEY DEW AND CASABA MELONS—These are usually cut lengthwise and served in sections two or three inches wide.

WATERMELON—To serve a whole watermelon at the table, cut it in half, crosswise, and cut a slice from each end to make it stand on a platter. / Garnish the platter with green leaves. / The melon may be served in round slices, or in half or quarter slices from which the rind may or may not have been removed; / the pulp may be shaped in balls or dice and served in glasses, / or it may be scooped out in large spoonfuls and served in a watermelon tub shaped from the rind.

HOW TO GAIN WEIGHT?

To gain weight you may first need to check with your physician to determine if you have an over active thyroid gland secreting too much throxine which controls metabolism.

Underweight is due to activity or energy expended above calorie or energy intake. Rapid metabolism will prevent energy storage by rushing foods along the digestive process.

Increase calories by increasing the amount of food, quality of foods and number of meals each day.

Check how you eat. If foods are being consumed rapidly, then it is possible that food is rushing along your digestive system without having been digested and becomes waste rather than allowing absorption of food nutrients to take place.

You may use the planned reducing meals and increase size serving of foods, or the number of meals may be increased to six, using high calorie foods to help you gain weight.

Remember you are able to eat any foods and as much as you like. Fortunately, you are not one of the statistics in the increasing number of obese numbers.

The following recipes may assist with preparing your meals for gaining weight.

HERE ARE SOME RECIPES FOR BEVERAGES TO HELP YOU GAIN WEIGHT. DRINK THEM IN BETWEEN MEALS. ADD ONE ON AT BEDTIME TOO.............

HIGH CALORIC BEVERAGES WITH AN ICE CREAM BASE: BASIC RECIPE

½ cup ice cream   ¾ cup carbonated beverage

Put ice cream in tall glass and pour half the carbonated beverage over it. / Stir till well mixed, / then add remainder of fluid and serve at once. ● Serves 1.
Variations: Many flavor combinations are possible using a variety of ice creams and carbonated beverages.

HIGH CALORIC EGGNOG

1 egg   2 tablespoons cream
1 tablespoon sugar   ½ teaspoon vanilla
¾ cup milk

Beat egg and add sugar. / Combine with milk, cream and vanilla. / Mix thoroughly, chill and serve. ● Serves 1.

HIGH CALORIC BEVERAGES WITH A FRUIT BASE: BASIC RECIPE

¾ cup fruit juice   3 tablespoons lactose
1 tablespoon sugar   1 tablespoon lemon juice

Combine all ingredients and mix thoroughly until sugar is dissolved. / Chill before serving, or pour over cracked ice, strain. / Serve with a sprig of fresh mint or a thin lemon slice garnish. ● Serves 1.

Fresh, frozen reconstituted, or canned orange, pineapple, grape, tomato, prune, apple or mixed fruit juices are suitable.

80

CORN SYRUP LEMONADE

¼ cup corn syrup   ¾ cup water
3 tablespoons lemon juice

Mix corn syrup with lemon juice until thoroughly blended. Add
water and chill. Serve with a sprig of mint. ● Serves 1.

NOTE: This recipe is particularly suitable for raising calories on
low protein diet.

Remember the Dietary Goals are concerned about the total intake of fat and sugar and not just one recipe. Recommend the meals be frequent and low in sugar, salt, and fat to allow for the high calorie beverages. Each meal should be eaten in a quiet environment. Allow time for chewing food thoroughly and rest after each meal for good digestion.

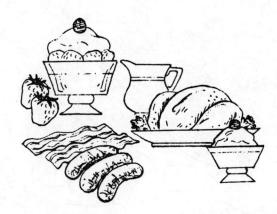

III

STRESS:
Recommended Meal Plans

85 EASY-TO-PREPARE RECIPES AND MENUS

EFFECTS OF STRESS ON YOUR BODY. Stress has always been with us—but in different forms.

To primitive man, stress was a lonely fight to survive each day in a world about which he knew very little. The slaves of Rome two thousand years ago and of the American south little more than a century ago shared in common the stress of lifelong toil for masters who often considered them commodities rather than human beings. The Industrial Revolution brought with it the stress of the sweatshop, where so many children gave up their childhood. The men who staked out homesteads in the Oklahoma Territory or drove railroad ties westward through Appalachia felt the stress of hard physical labor in constant battle with the land and the weather. The stress of the long voyage to America and the long wait at Ellis Island in the early years of this century was a bond among the many thousands of immigrants from many nations.

Today, stress is more sophisticated. In addition to the stresses which have been with us always—personal tragedies, concern about our loved ones, for example—we worry about society as a whole. We feel stress not only within the family unit but about our entire nation. Will the state of our economy improve? How can we resolve the unemployment problem?

And, thanks to the mixed blessing of technology and communications development, we can learn about, and react just as swiftly to news of an earthquake in Japan as to word about a fire down the street. In

short, we cannot be hermits in today's world. We are forced to take on the concerns of our nation and our world as responsible inhabitants thereof, and consequently we experience a tremendous burden of stress.

Our enormously complex social and industrial society has brought about our involvement more and more in mental work and decision-making and less and less in physical labor. We live at a faster pace; we are highly dependent upon other people, machines and devices. We aspire to higher status among our peers—and yet we are afraid of losing security. The man who runs in place, figuratively speaking, is frowned upon; we admire those who are jockeying for position at the head of the line, and we're running right along with him.

It is true that modern technology has removed, or simplified, many of the inconveniences or actual traumas of our forebears. Today it is no big deal for a New Yorker to visit a friend in San Francisco—and he has the luxury as well of watching a good movie while aboard the big jet. (If he can't make the trip he can always phone, anyway.) And today's mother probably takes for granted the vaccines the pediatrician administers to her children; her grandmother may have lost a child to scarlet fever. We have come very far indeed in our knowledge of medicine and in our application of new technology to sophisticated transportation and communications systems. But, we do not lead stress-free lives.

Some tensions, challenges and stresses are good for us, of course, if we are not to live dull lives. Life is empty without change, progress and the richness of personal experience. Our bodies are constructed to react to challenges and dangers, whether physical or mental. Without these mechanisms, the human being certainly would not have evolved this far.

But, how much stress is too much? How does stress relate to the normal functioning of our bodies? Does environment play a part—and does it affect food habits? What role does stress play in understanding and controlling some illnesses? Does a particular kind of stress bring on disease—or is stress significant only when linked with such other elements as diet, smoking and high blood pressure? How dangerous are the stresses of fear, anxiety, anger, frustration, uncertainty, boredom, restlessness, rapid change, time pressures, deadline-chasing, overwork, fatique and lack of sleep?

We do not know the answers to all these questions. But we do know enough to identify the symptoms of stress in today's lifestyle.

To the scientist, stress is defined as any action or situation that places special physical or psychological demands upon a person— anything that can unbalance the equilibrium of an individual. In lay terms, it may be described as a keyed-up feeling.

Research suggests:

- Some distress is necessary; it appears that a certain amount of stress motivates us to action and accomplishment.
- Modern city stress is no greater than stress in the country.
- Stress is related to food intake.
- Stress is related to heart disease.
- Stress is related to obesity.
- Stress causes some serious ailments.
- Stress may be self-induced.
- Stress is related to environment.

Most studies of stress are based on three types of human response: emotional, behavioral and psychological. Emotional stress causes fear or rage tantrums. Behavioral stress can usually be measured by changes in behavioral patterns.

The third type of response to stress—the psychological—has the greatest importance. According to specialists, in the study of psychosomatic medicine, psychologically induced physical illness stress can be a contributing factor in headaches, backaches, ulcers, allergies and heart disease.

Studies further show that physical reaction to stress may be reflected in any strong emotion, and will cause the heart to palpitate, the muscles to tremble, the digestive organs to suspend their functions, and the blood to rush irregularly through the body.

It is difficult to identify the difference between the emotional and the psychological response to stress because it is possible for psychological stress to cause emotional stress. It is also possible for emotional stress to cause psychological stresses. In discussing nutrition we are most interested in emotional stresses. We also will need to keep in mind the possible symptoms of psychological stresses.

From studies of anatomy and physiology, it appears that the primal stress response begins in the very center of the brain, in the hypothalamus. This small bundle of body cells carries on the body

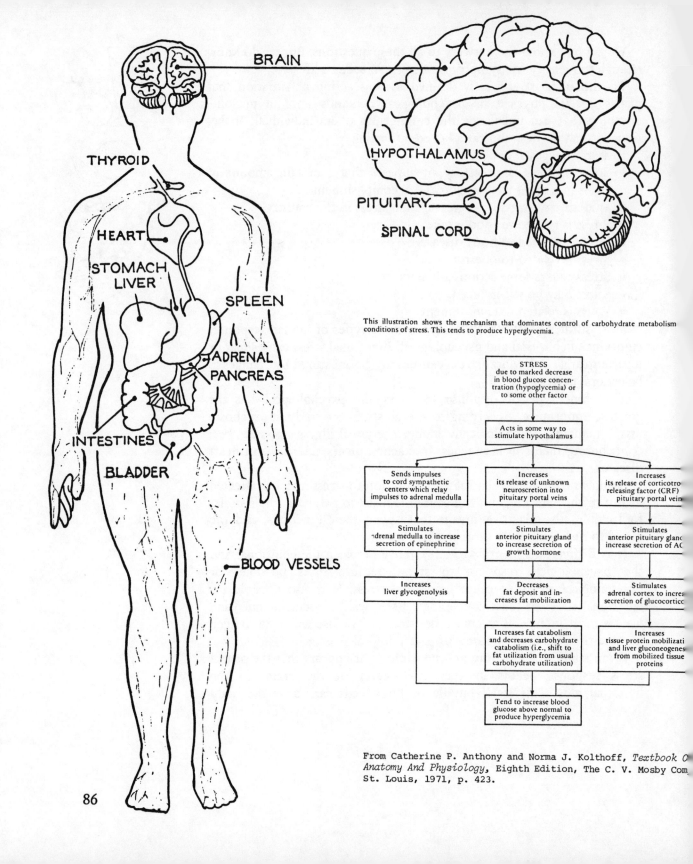

BRAIN

THYROID

HEART

STOMACH
LIVER

SPLEEN

ADRENAL
PANCREAS

INTESTINES

BLADDER

BLOOD VESSELS

HYPOTHALAMUS

PITUITARY

SPINAL CORD

This illustration shows the mechanism that dominates control of carbohydrate metabolism conditions of stress. This tends to produce hyperglycemia.

STRESS
due to marked decrease
in blood glucose concen-
tration (hypoglycemia) or
to some other factor

Acts in some way to
stimulate hypothalamus

Sends impulses to cord sympathetic centers which relay impulses to adrenal medulla	Increases its release of unknown neuroscretion into pituitary portal veins	Increases its release of corticotro releasing factor (CRF) pituitary portal vein
Stimulates adrenal medulla to increase secretion of epinephrine	Stimulates anterior pituitary gland to increase secretion of growth hormone	Stimulates anterior pituitary gland increase secretion of AC
Increases liver glycogenolysis	Decreases fat deposit and in-creases fat mobilization	Stimulates adrenal cortex to increa secretion of glucocortico
	Increases fat catabolism and decreases carbohydrate catabolism (i.e., shift to fat utilization from usual carbohydrate utilization)	Increases tissue protein mobilizati and liver gluconeogenes from mobilized tissue proteins

Tend to increase blood
glucose above normal to
produce hyperglycemia

From Catherine P. Anthony and Norma J. Kolthoff, *Textbook O Anatomy And Physiology*, Eighth Edition, The C. V. Mosby Com St. Louis, 1971, p. 423.

function of regulating growth, sex and reproduction. These body functions are related also to the functions in the diet of protein, the food nutrient responsible for promoting growth and maintaining life, as well as building and repairing body tissues.

In directing the basic physiological changes involved in stress, the hypothalamus acts in two ways: First, it controls the autonomic nervous system, which regulates the involuntary activities of the body's organs; and second, it activates the pituitary gland which, in turn, orders the release of chemical messengers, or hormones, directly into the bloodstream. The two systems, nerves and hormones, reinforce each other to produce powerful, yet unmistakable, signals. They keep each other in balance and keep the body from running out of control. Together, however, they alter the functioning of almost every part of the body. See the illustration for the effects of stress on your body, page 86.

THE PHYSICAL RESPONSE. The *body muscles* become tense at the command of the autonomic nervous system. The effect may be deeper, faster breathing. The heart rate rises and blood vessels constrict, raising the blood pressure and almost completely closing the blood vessels that lie just under the skin. Strong emotion may change muscles in the face while nostrils and throat become open passages. Other muscles suspend their function: the stomach and intestines temporarily halt digestion of food, while muscles controlling the intestines and the bladder will loosen. In other parts of the body, the autonomic nervous system affects other changes such as respiration increases and changes in saliva secretion to a decrease in secretion. A visible sign may be changes in the pupils of the eye, since they become dilated under stress.

The autonomic *nerves* directly affect the adrenal glands. They stimulate the adrenal glands to release hormones. Hormones generate anxiety which is felt when adrenalin is flowing. Hormones affect the circulation of blood, reinforcing the autonomic nervous system's action in elevating heartbeat and blood pressure. They signal the spleen to release more red blood corpuscles, they cause the blood to clot more quickly and the bone marrow to produce more white corpuscles. The red blood cells carry oxygen which consumes food substances to produce energy. This process produces more oxygen and gives oxygen more fuel to burn; the adrenals increase the amount of fat in the blood since body fat is broken down, and the liver is stimulated to produce more sugar.

While all these actions are set in motion by the adrenal glands, the pituitary gland also reacts to the commands of the hypothalamus. The pituitary gland secretes two hormones which play a major role in the basic stress response. The thyrotropic hormone stimulates the thyroid which increases the rate at which the body produces energy. The second is an adrenal hormone which reinforces the signals sent the adrenal glands through the autonomic nervous system. The hormone causes the outer layer of the adrenals to manufacture some 30 hormones that are among the surest signs of stress. For example, in laboratory testing the hormone concentration in the human blood is used for measuring the intensity of stress.

THE STAGES OF STRESS. The body operates an alarm system regardless of the sources of stress: Stage 1—alarm; stage 2—resistance, and stage 3—exhaustion.

In the alarm stage your body recognizes the stress factor and prepares to fight it or to avoid it. Among the signs is a slowed digestion.

In the resistance stage your body repairs any damage caused from the stress. If, however, the stress factor does not go away, the body cannot repair the damage and must remain alert. During this stage food digestion will continue at a slow pace.

This process plunges you into the third stage, exhaustion. If this state continues for a long enough period, you may develop one of the "diseases of stress." Migraine headaches, heart irregularity, or even mental illness may result from prolonged exhaustion. Stress during the exhaustion stage causes the body to run out of energy, and bodily functions may even stop. During these prolonged periods of stress the body tries to compensate as a means of fighting back.

STRESS AND FOOD. One of the ways the body fights against stress is through use of food. Under stress the human body desires more food. Snacking is common. When the digestion of food has slowed, then, frequent eating causes weight gain. Other things we do while fighting stress include smoking and drinking.

CHOLESTEROL AND STRESS. There are many risks related to coronary heart diseases. We know, however, that the single most important risk factor is the amount of cholesterol circulating in the bloodstream at any one period of time. We also know that, when under stress from dieting or otherwise, body fat is broken down, increasing the blood cholesterol level.

What is cholesterol and where does it come from? Cholesterol is an organic, waxy stored compound which is found only in foods of animal origin. This compound is usually synthesized by the human body. It has been found that a level of about 180 milligrams per 100 milliliters of blood serum is considered to be the ideal cholesterol level.

Cholesterol is found in all animal fats. It is an essential constituent of all cell membranes and is a major component of brain and nerve tissues.

Every body cell contains cholesterol and has the enzymes necessary to manufacture it. Some cholesterol is absorbed from the diet, but its major effect is on the liver. This is probably because of the functions of the liver in fat metabolism. A diet high in carbohydrates can cause increased cholesterol formation since carbohydrates contribute to stored body fat, if carbohydrate intake exceeds energy expended. All the things we do under stress contribute to high cholesterol levels.

The pattern of eating large meals containing too much fat and refined carbohydrates can be very dangerous. Other factors that also contribute to high cholesterol levels are cigarette smoking, stress and drinking too much coffee. These cause elevated cholesterol levels by overloading the pathways connecting with the liver.

Have your cholesterol reading taken by your physician. If you are 40 years of age or above, don't be surprised at a reading above 180 milligrams per 100 milliters of blood. It also is possible for young people to have elevated cholesterol readings.

Blood cholesterol levels vary considerably between individuals. If blood cholesterol is abnormally high, fat deposits on walls of blood vessels may result. Such high levels of cholesterol have been associated with atherosclerosis.

The cholesterol content found in foods is shown in the appendix. Keeping the diet low in fat may not be a cure for heart diseases. But, lowering the cholesterol content in the diet is a precaution in reducing the risk of coronary diseases. This is the basic reason for the Senate Committee's recommendation to reduce saturated fats in the diet.

Cholesterol is present in many fat sources of a normal diet and may be manufactured within the body. Individuals undergoing daily tension often show higher levels of cholesterol.

Stress elevates blood pressure, aggravates diabetes, increases the tendency to overeat, and causes elevated blood cholesterol. Emotional stress may contribute to failure to exercise regularly by inducing fatigue.

If you are an average American your body makes more cholesterol than you eat in the normal diet. The saturated fat in the diet tends to make your body produce more serum cholesterol. Top scientists in this country state that saturated fats should account for less than 10 percent of the calories in the diets of all Americans. To change the level of saturated fat in your diet, cut down on the foods in your diet that are high in saturated fat (animal fat). Only about 10 percent of the U.S. adult population reaches the ideal of 180 milligrams cholesterol per 100 milliliters blood serum, considered to be normal level of cholesterol.

An unbalanced diet can cause these problems.

- Too much protein causes protein to be used as energy and contributes to body fat storage.
- Too little protein causes fat and carbohydrate metabolism disturbances since the body is shifting to build and repair body tissues in the absence of sufficient amino acids.
- Excessive carbohydrate intake leads the body to store the excess in the form of fat, bringing about weight gain.
- Too few carbohydrates (starches and sugars) cause protein to be used as energy, an expensive source of fuel.
- Too much fat means excessive storage of body fat and improper liver functioning.
- Too little fat means the body machine lacks oiling of organs and skin.

Become aware of your stress threshold and avoid prolonged stress. It will unbalance the diet. Reduce your food intake when under stress. Any diet required to reduce cholesterol involves a reduction in total calories, a lessening of emotional tension and a substitution of poly unsaturated fat for saturated fat.

If you crave food under stress, however, here are some simple easy to eat snacks and small meals:

- Glass of whole milk with toast cubes (milk toast)
- Hot soups such as cream of chicken, chicken rice, cream of cheddar cheese, cream of carrot, cream of mushroom, and peanut soup

- Hot tea with lemon
- Hot baked potato with vegetable fat (except coconut oil)
- Non-fat milk with iced milk
- Gelatin, any flavor, with whipped topping
- Fruit juice
- Lemonade
- Fruit punch or fruit ice

If you can tolerate a full meal, then a few suggestions are:
- Meal should be very low in fat or fat-free
- Prolonged stress requires a special controlled fat diet
- Soft foods improve ease in food passage along the gastro-intestinal tract
- Whole milk may be preferred to non-fat milk since the fat in milk will coat the lining of the digestive tract and prevent irritation.

It should be noted that alcohol also supplies from five to ten percent of the calories in some people's diet.

The values of energy supplied by food components are:

nine Calories per gram from fat,

four Calories per gram from carbohydrates,

four Calories per gram from protein, and

seven Calories per gram from alcohol.

These values can be used to calculate the caloric value of foods, if the composition is known. For example we see that a steak is 49 percent water, 15 percent protein, 0 percent carbohydrate, 36 percent fat, and 0.7 percent minerals. Thus for a three and one-half ounce piece of meat we have:

water:	49 grams $\times$ 0 Calories =	0
protein:	15 grams $\times$ 4 Calories =	60
carbohydrate:	0 grams $\times$ 4 Calories =	0
fat:	36 grams $\times$ 9 Calories =	324
minerals:	0.7 grams $\times$ 0 Calories =	0
	Total =	384 Calories

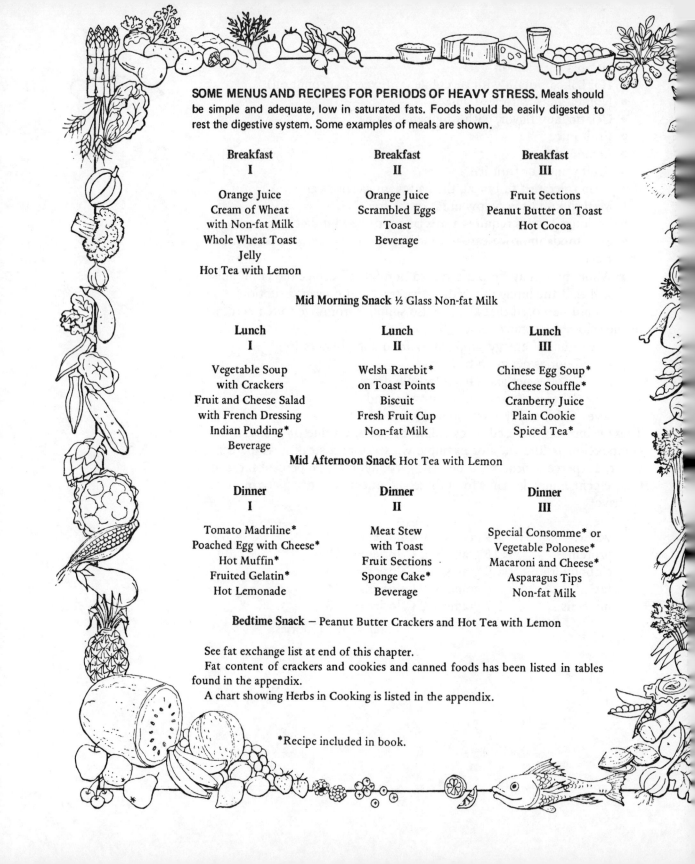

SOME MENUS AND RECIPES FOR PERIODS OF HEAVY STRESS. Meals should be simple and adequate, low in saturated fats. Foods should be easily digested to rest the digestive system. Some examples of meals are shown.

Breakfast I

Orange Juice
Cream of Wheat
with Non-fat Milk
Whole Wheat Toast
Jelly
Hot Tea with Lemon

Breakfast II

Orange Juice
Scrambled Eggs
Toast
Beverage

Breakfast III

Fruit Sections
Peanut Butter on Toast
Hot Cocoa

Mid Morning Snack ½ Glass Non-fat Milk

Lunch I

Vegetable Soup
with Crackers
Fruit and Cheese Salad
with French Dressing
Indian Pudding*
Beverage

Lunch II

Welsh Rarebit*
on Toast Points
Biscuit
Fresh Fruit Cup
Non-fat Milk

Lunch III

Chinese Egg Soup*
Cheese Souffle*
Cranberry Juice
Plain Cookie
Spiced Tea*

Mid Afternoon Snack Hot Tea with Lemon

Dinner I

Tomato Madriline*
Poached Egg with Cheese*
Hot Muffin*
Fruited Gelatin*
Hot Lemonade

Dinner II

Meat Stew
with Toast
Fruit Sections
Sponge Cake*
Beverage

Dinner III

Special Consomme* or
Vegetable Polonese*
Macaroni and Cheese*
Asparagus Tips
Non-fat Milk

Bedtime Snack — Peanut Butter Crackers and Hot Tea with Lemon

See fat exchange list at end of this chapter.

Fat content of crackers and cookies and canned foods has been listed in tables found in the appendix.

A chart showing Herbs in Cooking is listed in the appendix.

*Recipe included in book.

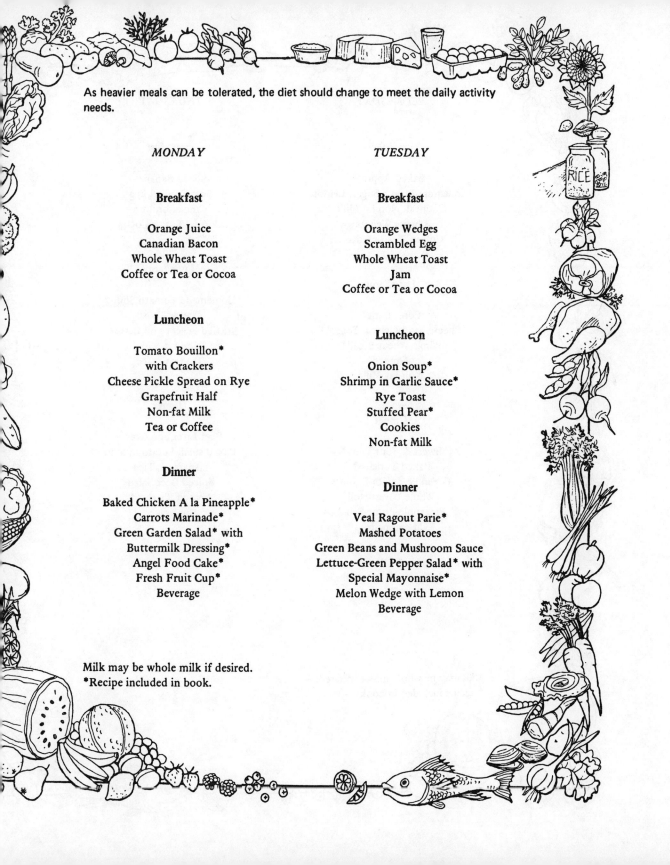

As heavier meals can be tolerated, the diet should change to meet the daily activity needs.

MONDAY

Breakfast

Orange Juice
Canadian Bacon
Whole Wheat Toast
Coffee or Tea or Cocoa

Luncheon

Tomato Bouillon*
with Crackers
Cheese Pickle Spread on Rye
Grapefruit Half
Non-fat Milk
Tea or Coffee

Dinner

Baked Chicken A la Pineapple*
Carrots Marinade*
Green Garden Salad* with
Buttermilk Dressing*
Angel Food Cake*
Fresh Fruit Cup*
Beverage

TUESDAY

Breakfast

Orange Wedges
Scrambled Egg
Whole Wheat Toast
Jam
Coffee or Tea or Cocoa

Luncheon

Onion Soup*
Shrimp in Garlic Sauce*
Rye Toast
Stuffed Pear*
Cookies
Non-fat Milk

Dinner

Veal Ragout Parie*
Mashed Potatoes
Green Beans and Mushroom Sauce
Lettuce-Green Pepper Salad* with
Special Mayonnaise*
Melon Wedge with Lemon
Beverage

Milk may be whole milk if desired.
*Recipe included in book.

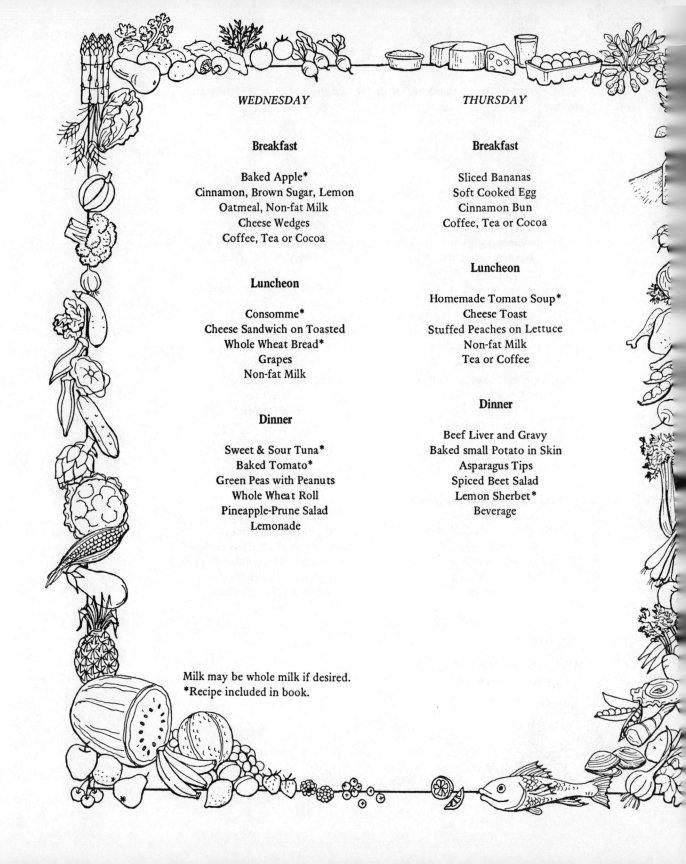

WEDNESDAY

Breakfast

Baked Apple*
Cinnamon, Brown Sugar, Lemon
Oatmeal, Non-fat Milk
Cheese Wedges
Coffee, Tea or Cocoa

Luncheon

Consomme*
Cheese Sandwich on Toasted
Whole Wheat Bread*
Grapes
Non-fat Milk

Dinner

Sweet & Sour Tuna*
Baked Tomato*
Green Peas with Peanuts
Whole Wheat Roll
Pineapple-Prune Salad
Lemonade

THURSDAY

Breakfast

Sliced Bananas
Soft Cooked Egg
Cinnamon Bun
Coffee, Tea or Cocoa

Luncheon

Homemade Tomato Soup*
Cheese Toast
Stuffed Peaches on Lettuce
Non-fat Milk
Tea or Coffee

Dinner

Beef Liver and Gravy
Baked small Potato in Skin
Asparagus Tips
Spiced Beet Salad
Lemon Sherbet*
Beverage

Milk may be whole milk if desired.
*Recipe included in book.

FRIDAY

Breakfast

Cantaloupe
Cream Chipped Beef on
Whole Wheat Bread
Non-fat Milk

Luncheon

Chicken Salad on Whole Wheat*
Sliced Tomato on Lettuce
Meringued Pears*
Hot Lemonade

Dinner

Baked Fish Almondine
Breaded Baked Tomato Half*
Celery-Lettuce Hearts with Vinegar
Baked Stuffed Apple*
Coffee or Tea

SATURDAY

Breakfast

Sliced Tomatoes
Egg Omelet with Mushrooms
Brown Bread*
Coffee, Tea or Cocoa

Luncheon

Vegetable Soup with Crackers
Tuna Fish with Egg Slice on Lettuce
Ambrosia*
Non-fat Milk

Dinner

Swiss Steak
Baked Acorn Squash*
Spinach
Cucumber Marinade*
Cherry Pie with Double Crust*
Hot Tea with Lemon Slice

Milk may be whole milk if desired.
*Recipe included in book.

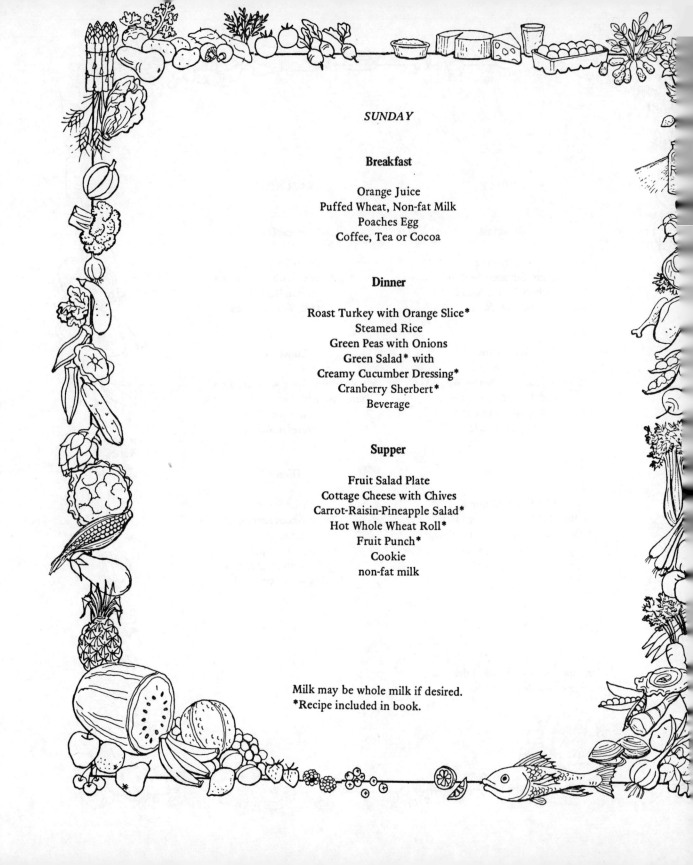

SUNDAY

Breakfast

Orange Juice
Puffed Wheat, Non-fat Milk
Poaches Egg
Coffee, Tea or Cocoa

Dinner

Roast Turkey with Orange Slice*
Steamed Rice
Green Peas with Onions
Green Salad* with
Creamy Cucumber Dressing*
Cranberry Sherbert*
Beverage

Supper

Fruit Salad Plate
Cottage Cheese with Chives
Carrot-Raisin-Pineapple Salad*
Hot Whole Wheat Roll*
Fruit Punch*
Cookie
non-fat milk

Milk may be whole milk if desired.
*Recipe included in book.

RECIPES

KOSHER DILL TOMATOES: These are considerably larger than the tiny cherry tomatoes. Therefore, they are less suitable for serving as tidbits. However, the flavor is good and they can be sliced and used as topping for other hors d'oeuvres.

TINY DILL TOMATOES: One brand carries the name "Tom-olive" because, though actually tiny tomatoes, they resemble olives in appearance.

PICKLES: Artichoke, cauliflower, cucumber, dill, onions, watermelon rind.

DILL PICKLED MIDGET CORN: Eaten whole—cob and all.

97

RECIPES

SOUPS ·

VEGETABLE SOUP

1 cup meat stock or bouillon cube and 1 cup water
½ cup mixed vegetables: carrots, peas
½ small onion, chopped
¼ cup cabbage, shredded
1 stalk celery, diced
¼ cup tomato juice
Salt and pepper

Prepare vegetables and add to broth. / Boil together until vegetables are just tender, about 20 minutes. ● Serves 1 to 2.

SPECIAL CONSOMMÉ

1 tablespoon unflavored gelatin
2 cups well-seasoned soup stock or consommé
Sliced lemon
Minced parsley

Soften gelatin in ¼ cup stock. / Heat remainder of stock and stir into gelatin. / Chill. / When set, beat lightly with a fork and serve in soup cups. / Serve each with slice of lemon dipped in parsley. ● Serves 3 to 4.

TOMATO MADRILENE

Follow directions for jellied consomme, substituting 1 cup tomato juice cocktail for 1 cup stock or consomme. / If a highly seasoned madrilene is desired, add Worchester sauce and Tabasco to taste. / Serve sprinkled with finely cut Pascal celery or green pepper. / Place wedge of lemon on side of plate. ● Serves 3 to 4.

CHINESE EGG SOUP

2 cups clear, seasoned broth (chicken or meat)
1 egg, beaten
1 teaspoon chopped parsley (fresh or dry)

Heat broth; / while boiling, pour in beaten egg slowly, stirring constantly. / Add parsley and serve. ● Serves 2.

SOUP STOCK

3 pounds brisket, shinbone, or other soup meat and bone
1 tablespoon salt
3 quarts cold water
2 cups vegetables
¾ cup tomatoes
½ green pepper

Sprinkle meat and bone with salt. / Let stand for 1 hour. / Add water and soak ½ hour. / Simmer 3½ hours uncovered. / Add remaining ingredients and simmer, covered, ½ hour. / Strain. Chill and remove the fat. / Variations may be made by substituting chicken or veal for beef. / This is a standard method for making soup stock. / The fat content will be negligible if the stock is chilled and the fat removed as directed. ● Makes one gallon.

MAIN DISHES ·

POACHED EGG WITH CHEESE SAUCE

1/8 pound grated cheese (½ cup)
2 tablespoons non-fat milk
1 slice toast
1 egg, poached
Salt and pepper to taste

Melt the cheese over hot water. / Add the milk gradually, stirring constantly. / Add seasonings. / Pour hot cheese sauce on toast, / top with the poached egg. ● Serves 1.

SCRAMBLED EGGS

2 eggs
2 tablespoons non-fat milk
¼ teaspoon salt
Dash pepper
1 tablespoon vegetable fat (except coconut oil)

Beat eggs just enough to mix yolks and whites, / stir in milk and seasonings. / Melt fat in small frying pan and add egg mixture. / Stir over low heat as eggs become firm. / Stir only enough to prevent eggs sticking to pan. / Serve at once.

Scrambled eggs may also be prepared over hot water in a double boiler. They will take longer to cook and need not be stirred as frequently. They will be very delicate and tender when done. ● Serves 1.

MACARONI AND CHEESE A LA BREAD CUBES

¼ pound macaroni	1 to 1½ cups grated or cubed
4 tablespoons vegetable fat	cheese
(except coconut oil)	½ tablespoon vegetable fat
4 tablespoons flour	(except coconut oil)
1 teaspoon salt	½ cup bread crumbs
2 cups non-fat milk	

Cook macaroni in large amount of boiling, salted water until tender. / Drain and place in casserole. / Melt vegetable fat in top of double boiler, / add flour and salt and mix till smooth. / Add milk and cook over low heat until thickened, stirring constantly. / Place over boiling water, / add cheese and stir until melted. / Melt ½ tablespoon vegetable fat and mix with ½ cup of dry bread crumbs. / Pour cheese sauce over macaroni in casserole, / cover with bread crumbs and bake in moderate oven (375° F.) until thoroughly heated and crumbs are brown, about 20 minutes. ● Serves 4.

MEAT STEW

2 or 3 oz. meat, cubed	Salt and pepper to taste
1 teaspoon vegetable fat	½ cup mixed vegetables,
(except coconut oil)	(carrots, peas, onions)
1 cup water	1 small potato

Brown meat in fat. / Add 1 cup water, salt, pepper and a few celery leaves for seasoning. / Simmer slowly until meat is tender. / Add ½ cup vegetables. / Cut potato into quarters and add. / Cook for 30 minutes or until vegetables are done. ● Serves 3 to 4.

CHEESE SOUFFLE

2 tablespoons vegetable fat	¼ pound (1 cup) Cheddar
(except coconut oil)	cheese, grated
2 tablespoons flour	2 egg yolks
¼ teaspoon salt	2 egg whites, stiffly beaten
½ cup non-fat milk	

Melt fat in a small saucepan. / Stir in flour and salt. / When smooth, stir in milk gradually. / Continue stirring until sauce thickens and boils. / Remove from heat, add cheese and stir until melted. / Stir in egg yolks one at a time, beating after each addition. / Fold into the stiffly beaten egg whites. / Pour into greased 1-pint casserole and bake in slow oven (300° F.) 1 hour or in moderately hot oven (425° F.) 25 minutes. ● Serves 2.

WELSH RAREBIT

1 tablespoon vegetable fat	Few grains pepper
(except coconut oil)	1 cup non-fat milk
1 tablespoon flour	¼ to ½ pound Cheddar type
¼ teaspoon dry mustard	cheese
¼ teaspoon salt	4 slices thin, dry toast

Melt fat in top of double boiler over direct heat, / add flour and seasonings and stir till smooth. / Add milk and cook over low heat until thickened, stirring constantly. / Place over hot water, / add the cheese cut into small pieces, and stir till cheese has melted and sauce is smooth. / Pour over toast and serve at once. ● Serves 3 to 4.

BARBECUED FISH

2 pounds haddock or	2 cloves garlic, minced or
flounder fillets	mashed
½ cup soy sauce	1 teaspoon powdered ginger
¾ cup sherry	Lemon wedges
¼ cup lemon juice	

Cut fish into finger-size pieces 1 inch wide, 2 inches long, and 1 inch thick. / Combine soy sauce, sherry, lemon juice, garlic, and ginger. / Marinate fish in this mixture for 2 hours. / Skewer carefully or slip inside a wire toaster and place on the barbecue grill over low coals. / Cook until fish flakes with a fork, about 10 or 15 minutes. / Baste occasionally with the remaining marinade. / Instead of barbecuing, fish may be baked in a very hot oven (450°) for 12 minutes. / Slip the fish under the broiler a minute if you want it browner. Serve with lemon wedges. ● Serves 6.

BAKED FISH IN WINE

2 pounds fish fillets,	1 onion, chopped
fresh or frozen	1 green pepper, chopped
3 medium-sized fresh tomatoes	½ cup dry sherry
finely cut or 1 cup canned	Salt and pepper
tomatoes	

Place fish in a baking dish. / Cover with tomatoes, onion, green pepper, salt and pepper, and sherry wine. / Bake uncovered in a moderate oven (350°) about 20 minutes or until fish is tender. ● Serves 6.

BROILED SCALLOPS

2 pounds fresh or frozen scallops (not breaded)	2 tablespoons chopped onion
1 small clove garlic	½ teaspoon black pepper
½ teaspoon salt	½ teaspoon dried thyme
½ cup lemon juice	¼ cup water

Mash clove garlic with salt in a bowl. / Stir in remaining ingredients. / (If sauce is allowed to stand overnight, the flavors will blend especially well, but this is not necessary.) / Marinade the scallops in this sauce for 1 hour. / Remove the broiler rack and place scallops in broiling pan well down from heat. / Broil slowly for 20 to 25 minutes, basting with remaining marinade. ● Serves 6.

SWEET-SOUR TUNA

1-1/8 cups pineapple tidbits, drained	1 teaspoon soy sauce
½ cup pineapple syrup	1 tablespoon vinegar
1 cup green pepper, cut in ½-inch pieces	½ cup chicken broth (or chicken bouillon)
½ cup water chestnuts, sliced	¼ teaspoon salt
1 tablespoon sugar	Dash pepper
1 tablespoon cornstarch	1 cup tuna, water-pack

Cook pineapple in lightly greased skillet for 5 minutes. / Add pineapple syrup, green pepper, and water chestnuts; / cover and simmer for 10 minutes. / Combine sugar, cornstarch, soy sauce, vinegar, chicken broth, and seasonings; / add to pineapple. / Cook, stirring constantly until thickened. / Add tuna. / Heat through thoroughly. / Serve over boiled rice. ● Serves 6.

TIME TABLE FOR ROASTING POULTRY

Bird	Oven Temperature °F.	Time per Pound, minutes
Chicken, roasting	300	30-45
Duck	325	20-30
Duckling	325	15-20
Turkey:		
8-10 pounds	300	20-25
10-16 pounds	300	18-20
18-25 pounds	300	15-18

PLANTATION CHICKEN

1 2-pound fryer, cut up	Rosemary
Chopped onion	Salt and pepper
Parsley, fresh or dried	

Cut six pieces of aluminum foil. / Place on each a piece chicken sprinkled with onion, parsley, rosemary, salt, an pepper. / Wrap. / Cook on outdoor grill about 30 minute turning once. / Serve and eat from foil packet if desired. / (Th may be cooked in oven, or outdoors.) ● Serves 6.

BARBECUED CHICKEN

1 2-pound fryer, cut up	Dash tobasco
¼ cup vinegar	1 cup water
½ cup catsup	

Place cut-up fryer in baking pan. / Mix together vinegar, catchup tabasco, and water. / Pour over chicken in baking dish. / Bake a 350° about 1 hour. / There will be a small amount of fat in the pan drippings which is not readily removable. / The quantity is so small that it need not be calculated in this recipe. ● Serves 5.

CHICKEN CURRY

1 cup chopped onions	1/8 teaspoon pepper
¾ cup catsup	6 cardamon seeds (remove from pod), crushed
1½ cups buttermilk	2 garlic cloves, minced
2 teaspoons ground tumeric	2½ pounds fryer breasts and legs
1 teaspoon ground ginger	
½ teaspoon ground clove	
½ teaspoon ground cinnamon	

Combine all ingredients in large skillet. / Add chicken. / cover; / simmer 1 hour or until chicken is tender. / Remove cover; cook 15 minutes or until sauce is of desired consistency. / Serve over hot, cooked rice. ● Serves 6.

SWISS STEAK

2 pounds round steak	1/8 teaspoon pepper
Garlic clove	½ cup chopped onion
Flour	2 cups tomatoes heated to
1 teaspoon salt	boiling

Wipe the steak with a damp cloth and trim the fat off the edges. / Rub it with a half clove of garlic. / With the edge of a heavy plate pound into both sides as much flour, combined with the salt and pepper, as the steak will hold. / Cut the steak into pieces or leave it whole. / Pan-brown in a seasoned or salted skillet to prevent it from sticking. / Pour off all drippings. / Place steak in casserole. / Add the chopped onion and tomatoes. / Cover the casserole closely and place it in a slow oven (275°) for 2 hours or more. / Remove the steak to a hot platter. • Serves 6.

SHISHKEBOB

1 pound beef or veal	Tomatoes
Onions	Green peppers

Place on skewers alternate "layers" of 1½-inch cubes of beef or veal from which all excess fat has been cut, thinly sliced onions, tomatoes, green peppers. / Brush with barbecue sauce (recipe below). / Wrap tightly in aluminum wrap and lay on grill or in outdoor oven. / Cook about 30 minutes. / If placed on grill, they must be turned frequently. / These may be cooked in the oven if there are no facilities for outdoor cooking available. • Serves 5.

BARBECUE SAUCE

12-14 ounces catsup	Red and black pepper
½ cup white distilled vinegar	1/8 teaspoon salt
1 teaspoon sugar.	

Combine and mix well. • Makes 2 cups.

VEAL ROLL-UPS IN TOMATO SAUCE

4 tablespoons grated onion	6 thin slices of cooked tongue
1½ cups soft bread crumbs	1 tablespoon vegetable fat
2 tablespoons minced parsley	(except coconut oil)
¼ teaspoon salt	1 cup tomato sauce
Pepper	½ cup water
1 chicken bouillon cube	1 tablespoon chopped parsley
3 tablespoons water	¼ teaspoon thyme
6 slices veal, pounded thin,	½ teaspoon salt
as for scallopini	

To make stuffing, mix grated onion with bread crumbs, / mix parsley, ¼ tsp. salt and a dash of pepper. / Blend well with water in which bouillon cube has been dissolved. / Spread each slice of veal with some of the stuffing. / Cover with a thin slice of cooked tongue, cut the same size as the veal if possible. / Roll and fasten securely. / Saute in a skillet in one tablespoon hot fat until evenly browned. / Remove from pan and roll in paper to absorb fat. / Heat tomato sauce with water and seasonings. / Place veal roll-ups on platter. / Pour on sauce. • Serves 6.

VEGETABLES . . . .

CHESSIE STUFFED EGGPLANT

Medium-sized eggplant	1 teaspoon grated onion
1½ cups cooked rice	¼ cup non-fat milk
¼ clove garlic, minced	Salt
2 tablespoons chopped green	Paprika
pepper	¼ cup bread crumbs
½ pound cooked, cleaned	Sapsago cheese
shrimp	

Cut the top from a medium-sized eggplant. / Scoop out the pulp, drop it into a small quantity of boiling, salted water (1½ teaspoons of salt to the quart) and cook until it is tender. / Drain well and mash. / Combine with the other ingredients. / Fill the eggplant shell. / Cover the top with bread crumbs. / Sprinkle with sapsago cheese. / Place the eggplant in a moderate oven (325°) and bake until the stuffing is well heated, about one hour. • Serves 4.

MASHED POTATOES

6 medium-sized old
   potatoes
4 cups boiling water

½ teaspoon salt
1/3 cup hot liquefied non-fat
   milk

Pare potatoes. / Cook them covered from 20 to 40 minutes in boiling water. / When they are done, drain them well. / Mash the potatoes with a fork or a potato masher, or put them in an electric blender or mixer. / Add salt and hot liquefied non-fat milk. / Chopped parsley, chives, and water cress are all good additions to mashed potatoes. • Serves 6.

SMALL ONIONS BRAISED

Small onions
Beef bouillon cube

Hot water
Salt, paprika

Skin small onions. / Pour over them, to a depth of ½-inch, boiling stock made from bouillon cube and water. / Cook them, covered, over a slow heat. / Permit them to absorb the liquid. / When they are tender, season them with salt and paprika. / Additional stock may be added as required. • Serves 4.

BAKED ACORN SQUASH

Cut acorn squash in half and remove seeds and fibers. Place a tablespoon of consomme and a dash of salt and pepper in the center of each. There are two methods of baking the squash; either with or without wrapping in aluminum foil.

METHOD 1: Place on a shallow pan and bake in 375° oven for about 45 minutes or until tender. / Place a pan containing a little water on the lower grate to keep the oven moist.

METHOD 2: Place prepared half squash on sheet of aluminum foil. / Wrap and seal tightly. / Place on a shallow pan and bake in moderately hot oven (400°) for about 45 minutes. / Larger squash will take an hour or longer. • Serves 2.

PICKLED BEETS

¾ cup vinegar
½ cup water
2 teaspoons dry mustard
½ teaspoon salt
½ cup granulated sugar

½ teaspoon caraway seeds
2 cups sliced cooked beets
   (canned beets may be used)
1 medium-sized onion, chopped
   or sliced

Heat vinegar and water to boiling. / Add mustard, salt, and sugar. / Blend, then heat again to boiling. / Pour over beets, caraway seeds, and onion. / Cover and place in refrigerator to marinate overnight. • Serves 4.

GELATIN CUCUMBER SALAD

2 cups boiling water	1 teaspoon onion juice
3 ounces lime-flavored gelatin	1 tablespoon vinegar
1 large cucumber	½ teaspoon salt

Dissolve gelatin in water. / Grate cucumbers on coarse side of grate. / Press juice from pulp through cheesecloth. / Onion juice may be extracted the same way. / Add cucumber juice, onion juice, vinegar, and salt to dissolved gelatin. / Place in mold and chill. / Serve on lettuce with cottage cheese. ● Serves 6.

GRAPEFRUIT LOBSTER/CRAB SALAD

Fresh or canned lobster or crab meat	Horse-radish
Catsup	Grapefruit sections
Lemon juice	Lettuce

Season catsup to taste with lemon juice and horse-radish. Serve over lobster or crab meat on lettuce bed with grapefruit sections.

CRESS SALAD

1 pint water cress	French dressing
1 onion	

Pick over the leaves of the cress carefully, removing all bruised or wilted ones, wash and drain and with the fingers break the stems into two-inch lengths. / Lay the cress in a salad bowl, chop the onion very fine, strew it over the cress, add French dressing and serve. ● Serves 2.

CRESS AND DANDELION SALAD

1 cup water cress	6 thin slices raw onion
1 cup dandelion greens	French dressing

The dandelion should be fresh and young. Wash the leaves carefully and drain well. Arrange them in a salad bowl with the cress. Add the slices of onion and pour the French dressing over all. ● Serves 2.

CRESS AND WALNUT SALAD

½ cup walnut meats	1 pint water cress
1 lemon	French dressing

Crack walnuts and remove their meats as nearly as possible in halves. / Squeeze over them the juice of the lemon and let them stand for a short time. / Pick over the water cress and wash it carefully. / Drain it on a napkin. / When ready to serve, arrange cress on salad plates, cover with walnut meats, then dressing. ● Serves 2.

CAULIFLOWER AND SHRIMP SALAD

1 cauliflower	Lettuce
Mayonnaise dressing	Cooked Shrimps

Cook the cauliflower in boiling water, drain, and put it head down, into a bowl. / When cold, place it, stem down, on a shallow dish and cover with mayonnaise. / Garnish with lettuce arranged to resemble the leaves of the cauliflower, and add little clusters of shrimps. ● Serves 4.

CELERY SALAD

Strips of pimiento or green pepper and celery curls	2 cups celery
	½ mayonnaise

After thoroughly washing the celery allow it to crisp in cold water. / Then wipe it dry, cut it into inch lengths and these into lengthwise strips. / Place them in a salad bowl, and add sufficient mayonnaise dressing to moisten the whole. / Garnish with the pimiento or pepper and the celery curls. / Serve at once. / Celery salad admits of a wide range of additions; any cold meat, fish or fowl left from a previous meal being palatable served in it. / CELERY CURLS—These are made from the tender inner stalks. / Cut in lengths of two or three inches and slit in narrow strips almost to the end. / Place in water with plenty of ice. / As the slit stalks chill, the ends curl. ● Serves 4.

COCONUT-CELERY-APPLE SALAD

1 cup diced tart apples	4 tablespoons orange juice
½ cup diced celery	Salt
½ cup shredded coconut	Paprika
1 tablespoon lemon juice	Lettuce leaves
4 tablespoons vegetable oil	Currant or plum jelly
(except coconut oil)	

Mix the apples, celery, and coconut. / Sprinkle with the lemon juice. / Add a French dressing made from the oil and orange juice, with salt and paprika to taste. / Line a salad bowl with lettuce leaves and pile chilled salad in center. / Dot with currant or plum jelly. • Serves 2.

FRENCH FRUIT SALAD

1 orange	1 dozen walnuts
1 banana	Lettuce
½ pound Malaga grapes	French dressing

Peel the orange and cut the sections from the membrane with a sharp knife or a pair of shears. / (If the fruit is allowed to stand in cold water after peeling, the bitter white membranes will come off easily.) / Peel the banana and cut in quarter-inch slices. / Remove the skins and seeds from the grapes. / Break walnut meats in small pieces, but do not chop. / Mix these ingredients thoroughly and place on ice. / When ready to serve, place on lettuce leaves or with mint if desired. / Serves 2.

DAISY SALAD

6 hard boiled eggs	½ cup mayonnaise
12 lettuce leaves	

Cut the whites of eggs into rings and mix the yolks with the mayonnaise. / On a platter arrange lettuce leaves to form cups. / On these cups arrange the egg rings to simulate daisy petals and heap the yolks in the center. / Cold string beans, boiled whole, may be used to simulate foilage if desired. • Serves 6.

LETTUCE SALAD

Choosee for this the crisp center of the lettuce. / Wash it, dry it well, pull to pieces or cut it into four or six sections, and add any dressing preferred. / Mayonnaise is frequently used, and Russian dressing is used even more frequently, perhaps, but with a heavy dinner the French dressing is to be preferred to any other. / The following vegetables may be used instead of or with lettuce: endive, peppergrass, water cress, nasturium leaves, spinach, chicory, sorrel, dandelion, escarole, and romaine.

LETTUCE AND ONION SALAD

Strip off the green leaves of lettuce and set aside for some other purpose. / Wash the hearts, pull them to pieces or cut into sections, and drop into ice-water to crisp them. / Peel the spanish onion and cut it into thin shavings. / Shake the lettuce in a colander or wire basket to free it from water or dry on a towel. / Fill the salad bowl with alternate layers of the lettuce and onion slices, sprinkling on each layer a little French dressing. • Serves 4.

SALAD DRESSINGS . . . .

PROTEIN LOW-CALORIE COOKED SALAD DRESSING

1½ cups liquefied non-fat milk	¼ cup vinegar
2 tablespoons cornstarch	2 teaspoons prepared mustard
1 egg yolk	1 teaspoon salt

Mix together in top of double boiler non-fat milk and cornstarch, adding milk gradually to make first a smooth paste and then a smooth liquid. / In small mixing bowl beat together egg yolk, vinegar, mustard, and salt. / Place double boiler top over hot water on low flame and cook milk and cornstarch, stirring constantly, until thick and clear-looking. / (When cornstarch is thoroughly cooked, you should not be able to taste it.) / Add egg mixture and cook until egg has thickened completely. / Pour in jar and refrigerate when cool. • Makes 2 cups.

SPECIAL MAYONNAISE

⸱ teaspoon plain gelatin	2 tablespoons sugar
½ cups evaporated non-fat milk, undiluted	1½ teaspoons dry mustard
	1 teaspoon salt
⸱ egg yolks	¼ cup mild vinegar

⸱oak gelatin in ¼ cup cold milk. / Scald 1¼ cups milk in double ⸱oiler. / Remove from fire and dissolve gelatin in it. / Beat ⸱ogether egg yolks, sugar, dry mustard, and salt. / Stir into egg a ⸱ttle of the hot milk and gelatin mixture. / Blend and add ⸱emainder of milk mixture. / Return these ingredients to the ⸱ouble boiler and cook and stir over a very low flame until they ⸱egin to thicken (about 10 minutes). / Remove from fire. / Add ⸱inegar slowly. / This will still be a comparatively thin mixture. / ⸱t thickens as it cools. / If any lumps of gelatin remain strain ⸱while pouring into jar for storage. / Allow to cool, and then ⸱refrigerate. / This dressing is fine on coleslaw. / If you usually ⸱thin your mayonnaise with vinegar when using it on slaw you ⸱can do so with this dressing.

SPECIAL FRENCH DRESSING

½ teaspoon salt	½ teaspoon paprika
1/8 teaspoon pepper	2 tablespoons vinegar
½ teaspoon sugar	1/3 cup vegetable oil (except coconut oil)
½ teaspoon dry mustard	

Place all ingredients in a jar or in a bottle with a lip. / Store in refrigerator. / Shortly before serving, shake vigorously until the oil and vinegar blend to form a thick emulsion.
Variations: Add herbs or other seasonings singly or in combination: catsup or chili sauce; / crumble Roquefort or blue cheese and add; / or substitute grapefruit juice for vinegar and omit mustard for a fruit salad.

BREADS ....

MUFFINS

2 cups sifted all-purpose flour	1 egg, beaten
2¼ teaspoons baking powder	1 cup non-fat milk
½ teaspoon salt	¼ cup vegetable oil (except coconut oil)
¼ cup sugar	

Heat oven to 400°F. (hot). Lightly oil muffin pans. / Sift dry ingredients together. / Combine egg, milk and vegetable oil. / Stir quickly into flour mixture until dry ingredients are just dampened and batter has lumpy appearance. / Fill muffin pans 2/3 full. / Bake 20 minutes. / Serve hot.
Variations: ½ cup raisins, dates, chopped apple, dried apricots or sliced raw cranberries, or 2 tablespoons grated orange rind may be added to the mixture. ● Makes 12 muffins.

BISCUITS

2 cups sifted flour	1/3 cup vegetable oil (except coconut oil)
3 teaspoons baking powder	
1 teaspoon salt	2/3 cup non-fat milk

Mix and sift dry ingredients together. / Combine oil and milk. / Pour all at once over entire surface of flour mixture. / Mix with fork to make a soft dough. / Shape lightly with hands to make a round ball. / Place on wax paper and knead lightly ten times or until smooth. / Pat out to ½ inch thickness or roll between 2 squares of wax paper (about 12 inches square). / Remove top sheet of paper; cut biscuits with unfloured 2-inch biscuit cutter. / Place biscuits on ungreased cookie sheet. / Bake in hot oven (450°F.) 12 to 15 minutes. / NOTE: For soft biscuits place biscuits close together with sides touching. / For crusty biscuits place well apart. ● Makes 12 biscuits.

DESSERTS ....

FRUIT CUP COMBINATION

Possible combinations of fruits:

Orange, grapefruit, pineapple
Apple, grapefruit, strawberries
Peach, orange, blackberries
Grapes, orange, melon
Melon, grapefruit, banana

One half cup of mixed fruits equals 1 serving. See other variations in Chapter II.

SPONGE CAKE

1/3 cup sugar	½ tablespoon lemon juice
1/3 cup flour	½ teaspoon grated rind of 1
Pinch salt	lemon
3 eggs	

Sift sugar, flour and salt together. / Separate egg whites from yolks and place whites in large bowl. / Beat yolks with lemon juice and rind. / With a rotary beater, beat egg whites until they peak but are not dry. / Alternately fold in the flour and egg yolk mixtures. / Pour into ungreased loaf pan 8½ x 4½ x 2¾ inches. Bake in a slow oven (325°F.) for about an hour. Invert on wire rack and allow to cool. Remove from pan by running the blade of a spatula around the edge. / Serves 12.

BAKED CUSTARD

2 cups non-fat milk, scalded	Few grains salt
3 eggs	½ teaspoon vanilla or
¼ to ½ cup sugar	sprinkling of nutmeg

Beat the eggs slightly; beat in the sugar, salt and vanilla; stir in the hot milk; pour into individual molds of oven glassware or earthenware. / Set the molds into a pan; pour in hot water nearly to the top of the molds. / Bake in a moderate oven (350°F.) for about 45 minutes. / The custard is done when a knife, inserted in the center, comes out clean. ● Serves 6.

APPLE SNOW PUDDING

3 ounces unflavored gelatin	1 tablespoon grated lemon
½ cup water	peel
2 cups unsweetened	3 tablespoons lemon juice
applesauce	¼ teaspoon nutmeg
	2 egg whites

Sprinkle gelatin over ½ cup cold water in small bowl, to soften. Combine applesauce, lemon peel and juice, and spices in saucepan; bring to boiling, stirring. / Add softened gelatin stirring until dissolved. / Pour into bowl; refrigerate 1 hour. Meanwhile, let egg whites warm to room temperature in small bowl. / Beat, with rotary beater, just until stiff peaks form. Gently fold into gelatin mixture; refrigerate until well chilled. ● Serves 6.

BAKED PEARS MELBA

3 fresh pears, halved, cored,	¼ teaspoon ginger
and pared	2 tablespoons red-raspberry
1 cup unsweetened pineapple	preserves
juice	

Preheat oven to 350°F. / Arrange pears in 2 quart casserole. / In small saucepan, heat pineapple juice, and ginger to boiling. / Pour over pears. / Bake, covered, 45 minutes, or until pears are tender. / Spoon warm pear halves, with liquid, into 6 serving dishes. / Top each with 1 teaspoon preserves. ● Serves 6.

COFFEE MOUSSE

3 ounces unflavored gelatin	2 teaspoons almond extract
1 cup non-fat dry milk powder	½ cup ice water
2 tablespoons instant coffee	

Sprinkle gelatin over ½ cup cold water in small saucepan; let stand 5 minutes to soften. / Stir, over low heat, until gelatin is dissolved. / Remove from heat. / Dissolve ½ cup dry milk powder in ¼ cup water. / Add to dissolved gelatin along with coffee, and almond extract; mix well. / Refrigerate until consistency of unbeaten egg white-takes about 30 minutes. / Meanwhile, with rotary beater or portable electric mixer, beat rest of dry milk powder with ice water. / Combine by folding in beaten milk powder and chill. ● Serves 6.

LIME-PINEAPPLE PARFAIT

1½ cups boiling water
6 ounces lime gelatin
1½ cups unsweetened apple
   juice
1 cup unsweetened sliced
   pineapple, drained and diced

½ cup dessert topping mix
¼ cup non-fat milk
¼ cup grated coconut
¼ teaspoon vanilla extract

Pour boiling water over gelatin, stirring to dissolve. / Stir in apple juice; refrigerate until consistency of unbeaten egg white, about 1 hour. / Fold pineapple into gelatin. / Pour into 6 parfait glasses or serving dishes. / Refrigerate until firm. / In small bowl, combine dessert topping mix and milk; beat, with rotary beater, until stiff peaks form. / Fold in coconut and vanilla. / Garnish each with 1 tablespoon topping. • Serves 4.

VANILLA BLANCHMANGE WITH FRUIT SAUCE

6 ounces unflavored gelatin
3 cups non-fat milk
1 tablespoon sugar
¼ teaspoon salt

2 teaspoon vanilla extract
2 cups unsweetened fruit
   cocktail, drained

Sprinkle gelatin over ½ cup milk in medium bowl; / let stand, to soften. / Meanwhile, slowly heat rest of milk just until bubbly around edge of pan. / Pour over gelatin, stirring until dissolved. / Add sugar, salt, and vanilla. / Refrigerate until consistency of unbeaten egg white—about 1 hour. / With rotary beater, beat until very frothy and almost double in bulk. / Pour into 6 individual molds or 8-inch (5½ cup) ring mold. / Refrigerate several hours. / To serve; Loosen edge with sharp knife. / Invert onto serving plates or platter. / Spoon fruit cocktail over molds. / Serves 6.

WARM FRUIT COMPOTE

2 cups unsweetened peach
   halves
2 whole cloves
2 (4-inch) cinnamon sticks

½ cup fresh orange juice
2 cups unsweetened pear
   halves, drained
2 cups packaged cherries,
   drained

Drain peach halves, reserving liquid. / Combine peach liquid, cloves, cinnamon, in 1½ quart saucepan; / bring to boiling. / Reduce heat; simmer, uncovered, 5 minutes. / Quarter peach and pear halves; combine with cherries in medium bowl. / Pour hot syrup over fruit; let stand 15 minutes. / Add fresh orange juice and serve compote warm. • Serves 6.

FRUITED GELATIN

1 tablespoon gelatin
½ cup cold water
¼ to 1/3 cup sugar

¾ cup juice, drained
   from fruit
¼ cup lemon juice
2/3 cup diced mixed fruits

Place gelatin in top of double boiler; add ½ cup cold water; / let stand for 5 to 10 minutes until gelatin has absorbed the water. / Stir over boiling water until gelatin has dissolved. / Add the sugar and stir until it has dissolved. / Remove from stove; add the fruit juice and the lemon juice. / Cool until the jelly is the consistency of an unbeaten egg white. / Stir in the fruit and pour into individual molds rinsed in cold water; or the mixture may be put directly into serving dishes. / Chill for 2 to 4 hours. / Serve plain or with whipped cream or other topping.
NOTE: Fresh pineapple should not be used or the gelatin will not set. • Serves 4.

INDIAN PUDDING

2 cups scalded non-fat milk
2 tablespoons cornmeal
2 to 3 tablespoons molasses

3 to 4 tablespoons sugar
½ teaspoon salt
½ teaspoon ginger

Pour milk slowly over cornmeal and cook in double boiler 20 minutes. / Add remaining ingredients. / Pour into oiled baking dish; / bake at 300°F. for 2 hours. / Serve warm with ice cream or hard sauce. • Serves 3-4.

FAT EXCHANGE LISTS FOR CONTROLLING FAT IN THE DIET

Within each list, any one of the foods may be exchanged for any other food without changing your diet.

List 1—Milk exchanges

Non-fat dried milk	¼ cup
Non-fat milk	1 cup
buttermilk (made from non-fat milk)	1 cup

List 2—Vegetable exchanges

Vegetable A	As desired
Asparagus	
Beans, string, young	
Broccoli	
Brussels sprouts	
Cabbage	
Lettuce	
Mushrooms	
Okra	
Pepper	
Radishes	
Cauliflower	
Celery	
Chicory	
Cucumber	
Escarole	
Eggplant	
Sauerkraut	
Squash, summer	
Tomatoes	
Watercress	
Greens (beet greens, chard, collard)	
Vegetable B	½ cup per serving
Beets	
Carrots	
Onions	
Peas, green	
Pumpkin	
Rutabaga	
Squash, winter	
Turnip	

FAT EXCHANGE LISTS FOR CONTROLLING FAT IN THE DIET

List 3—Fruit exchanges

Apple 2 in. diameter)	1
Applesauce	½ cup
Apricots	
Fresh	2 medium
Dried	4 halves
Banana	½ small
Blackberries	1 cup
Bluberries	2/3 cup
Cantaloupe (6 in. diameter)	¼
Cherries	10 large
Dates	2
Figs	
Fresh	2 large
Dried	2
Grapejuice	½ cup
Grapefruit	½ small
Grapefruit juice	½ cup
Grapes	12
Honeydew melon (7 in. diameter)	1/8
Mango	½ small
Orange	1 small
Orange juice	½ cup
Papaya	1/3 medium
Peach	1 medium
Pear	1 small
Pineapple	½ cup
Pineapple juice	1/3 cup
Plums	2 medium
Prunes, dried	2 medium
Raisins	2 tbsp
Raspberries	1 cup
Strawberries	1 cup
Tangerine	1 large
Watermelon	1 cup

List 4—Bread exchanges

Bread	1 slice
Biscuit, muffin, roll (2 in. diameter)	1

List 4—Bread exchanges—*cont'd*

Bread—*cont'd*

Cornbread (1½ in. cube)	1
Cereal, cooked	1/3 cup
Dry, flake, or puffed	¾ cup
Rice, grits, cooked	½ cup
Spaghetti, noodles, cooked	½ cup
Macaroni, cooked	½ cup
Crackers, graham	2
Saltines	5
Soda	3
Beans, peas, dried, cooked	½ cup
Corn, sweet	1/3 cup
Corn on the cob, medium ear	½
Potatoes, white (2 in. diameter)	1
Potatoes, sweet	½ cup
Parsnips	2/3 cup

List 5—Meat, fish, and poultry exchanges

(Select meat from this group for 3 meals a week)

Beef, eye of round, top and bottom round, lean ground round, lean rump, tenderloin	1 oz.
Lamb, leg only	1 oz.
Pork, lean loin	1 oz.
Ham, lean and well trimmed	1 oz.

(Make selections from this group for 11 meals a week)

Chicken, no skin	1 oz.
Turkey, no skin	1 oz.
Veal	1 oz.
Fish	1 oz.
Shellfish	1 oz.
Meat substitute, cottage cheese, preferably uncreamed	¼ cup

List 6—Eggs

Four eggs per week allowed (as part of meat exchanges) in each diet plan at discretion of physician

FAT EXCHANGE LISTS FOR CONTROLLING FAT IN THE DIET

List 7—Fat exchanges

50% polyunsaturated

Corn oil	1 tsp.
Cottonseed oil	1 tsp.
Safflower oil	1 tsp.
Mayonnaise made with corn or cottonseed oil	1 tsp.
French dressing made with corn or cottonseed oil	2 tsp.

30% to 40% polyunsaturated

Special margarines	1 tsp.
Special shortenings	1 tsp.

List 8—Sugar exchanges

White, brown, or maple sugar	1 tsp.
Corn syrup, honey, molasses	1 tsp.

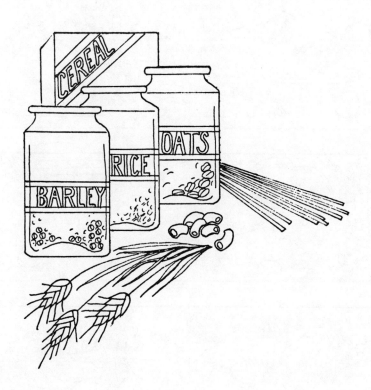

IV

SPECIAL DISEASES:
Food Patterns for Minimizing Diabetes Mellitus, Hypoglycemia, Allergies, Arteriosclerosis and Atherosclerosis, Hypertension, and Cirrhosis of the Liver

89 EASY-TO-PREPARE RECIPES AND MENUS

DIABETES MELLITUS is the fourth leading cause of death by disease in the United States, according to the Senate Committee's Dietary Goals.

Diabetes is an ancient disease. It is traceable as far back as 1500 B.C., when Egyptians are known to have had symptoms. In the first century A.D., a Greek physician wrote of a malady in which the body "ate its own flesh" and gave off large quantities of urine. He gave it the name diabetes.

The mysteries of diabetes have been the subject of study by scientists and physicians for many years. Today we are continuing to learn of new relationships of diabetes to other conditions of the body as we search for the yet unfound cure of the disease.

There are some things we do know about Diabetes Mellitus. It has been found to be a hereditary disease. It is defined in terms of symptoms, which appear as diabetes develops: increased thirst, increased urination, increased hunger, and weight loss. The weight loss may occur early in the progress of the disease even though the person is obese. The other symptoms associated with diabetes may be blurred vision, skin irritation, or infections.

Obesity and other diseases may also cause diabetes. A person who has the symptoms and ignores them for a period of time will show a fluid and electrolyte imbalance, acidosis characterized by acid odor to breath, loss of strength and finally will go into a coma.

Because diabetes symptoms affect the sugar level in the blood, diabetes is called a disease of carbohydrate metabolism. The intimate relationships of carbohydrate metabolism with protein and fat metabolism will impress upon us that diabetes is a disease that causes a

lack of insulin, a secretion of the pancreas. The lack may be only partial, or unavoidable. The problem of insulin affects, more or less, each of the basic food nutrients, especially the interrelated metabolism of the two fuel-supplying nutrients, carbohydrate and fat.

Though its precise role is not entirely clear, insulin has an effect on the body's control mechanisms. It is believed to aid in the transport of glucose through the cell membrane; it enhances the conversion of glucose, a simple sugar, to glycogen and its storage in the liver; it stimulates the conversion of glucose to fat. Primarily, insulin in the diabetic is lacking to facilitate the operation of normal controls of the blood sugar level. Glucose cannot be oxidized properly through the main glycolytic pathway in the cell to furnish energy; it, therefore, builds up in the blood.

This elevation of sugar in the blood is called hyperglycemia. An elevation of blood sugar causes curtailed fat breakdown leading to ketone formation and accumulation (ketosis). The appearance of ketones—acetone—in the urine indicates the development of ketosis. Tissue protein is also broken down in an effort to supply energy, causing loss of weight and nitrogen excretion in the urine.

You should check with your physician if you begin to experience any of these symptoms that have been described.

What is the normal level of blood sugar? It should be 70 to 120 milligrams for each 100 milliters of blood. The absorption of carbohydrate, protein, and fat into the bloodstream in the form of simple sugars, amino acids and fatty acids and from the fat storage in the liver the body maintains a steady supply of blood glucose.

To prevent a continued rise above 120 milligrams per milliters of blood there are several goals desired in treatment of the disease—the conversion of glucose to glycogen for storage in the liver; the conversion of fat and storage in adipose tissue, and the conversion to muscle glycogen and cell oxidation for energy. These goals are accomplished by a regulation diet to balance with the insulin the pancreas is able to secrete. About 40 percent of diabetic patients are able to control the disease by proper diet regulation. Medical treatment objectives are to maintain the best nutrition and maintain ideal weight, keep the patient free of elevated blood sugar, and prevent complications in body tissues.

The need for calories to maintain activity is a first consideration in diet treatment. The carbohydrate should make up 50 to 60 percent of the total calories. The protein should be adequate and will amount to about 60 to 80 grams each day. Fat in the diet is calculated to be about 5 percent of the total number of calories; in a 1500-calorie daily diet, for example, this would amount to about 70 grams of fat. The type of fat should usually be changed from animal to vegetable fat since the diabetic runs a higher risk of diseases related to saturated fat, such as coronary artery disease, than the non-diabetic. The 1500-calorie daily diet would be calculated to include about 150 grams of carbohydrate.

The diet may be divided among three to six meals a day, depending on the type of medical treatment (insulin) that the physician prescribes.

Some of the insulins used in treating diabetes are regular or short acting, medium acting or neutral protamine and lente globin. The long-acting insulin or protamine zinc is now rarely used. The reaction of the insulin will determine the diet division and the amount of food needed.

To give you an understanding of how a diabetic diet is calculated let us look at a 1500 calorie diet, below. Review the food exchanges found in the appendix, then review the diets in Chapters II and III. You will observe that the Diabetic Diet is usually reduced in total calories, therefore sugar, being totally carbohydrate, must of necessity, be eliminated from the diet.

ONE DAY PATTERN

Milk	2 servings
Vegetables	As desired
Fruits, fresh or unsweetened	3 servings
Breads NOTE: Bread exchanges including vegetables (starchy)	6 servings
Meats—baked, broiled or roasted	6 servings
Fats	4 servings

The diabetic is unable to consume carbohydrate in the form of sugar, since the body has a problem in utilizing carbohydrate. Therefore, each food in the diet must provide all the possible food nutrients.

A person with diabetes is able to live a normal life provided the diet is kept under control daily and the physician's advice and medical treatment is followed carefully.

Diabetes appears to be on the increase in the United States. It is safe to predict that the increased consumption of refined sugars, as stated in the Senate report, and the increase of unbalanced diets could most likely be the primary cause.

You have no doubt heard that since sugar, which is a pure carbohydrate, should not be used by the diabetic, he can use honey as a substitute. It is important that we understand sugars and how they relate. Refined sugar is sucrose and composed of glucose and fructose, two simple sugars. In digestion they are ready for absorption. Honey contains fructose which is the same sugar found in fruit. It is known that insulin is not needed for some steps in breaking down fructose in the body. Fructose makes up a little more than half of the sugar in honey; the rest is glucose. After honey is eaten the liver converts most of the fructose into glucose. The insulin, then, is required to convert glucose in order to release energy. You can see that sugar and honey are the same type of carbohydrate. We call carbohydrate foods such as honey "empty calories" because they do not contain other food nutrients, and getting the most nutrition from a low number of calories is highly important.

The diabetic, therefore, should eat a well-balanced diet with the most nutrition from each item. The caloric content should be sufficient for the body's needs, and excess calories should be left off.

What about sugar substitutes? The substitutes for sugar spare calories and serve to curtail sugar intake. They have no food value. The most commonly used sugar substitute is saccharin, which has about 300 times the sweetening power of cane sugar. Cyclamates 30 times the sweetening power compared to cane sugar, have been used as sugar substitutes until the Federal government a few years ago withdrew them from the market because of studies which found them to be substances which could possibly cause cancer.

A Canadian study, released in 1977, of the effect of vert large dosages of saccharin upon laboratory rats, also has pointed to the possibility of the removal of saccharin from the U.S. market. The Canadian study found some of the test rats had incurred bladder cancer. The U.S. government has called for further studies and has, through legislation, held up any ban on saccharin for at least 18 months.

The withdrawal of saccharin would be a tremendous hardship to the diabetic who for years has been able to control the disease through diet, insulin and saccharin. The diabetic can, however, avoid the use of the artificial products by using fresh fruits, fresh vegetables, whole grain cereals, milk, more fish and chicken or baked, broiled or roasted meats. So, if you are a diabetic you may want to begin a change in diet. Your diet may become a better diet for you generally.

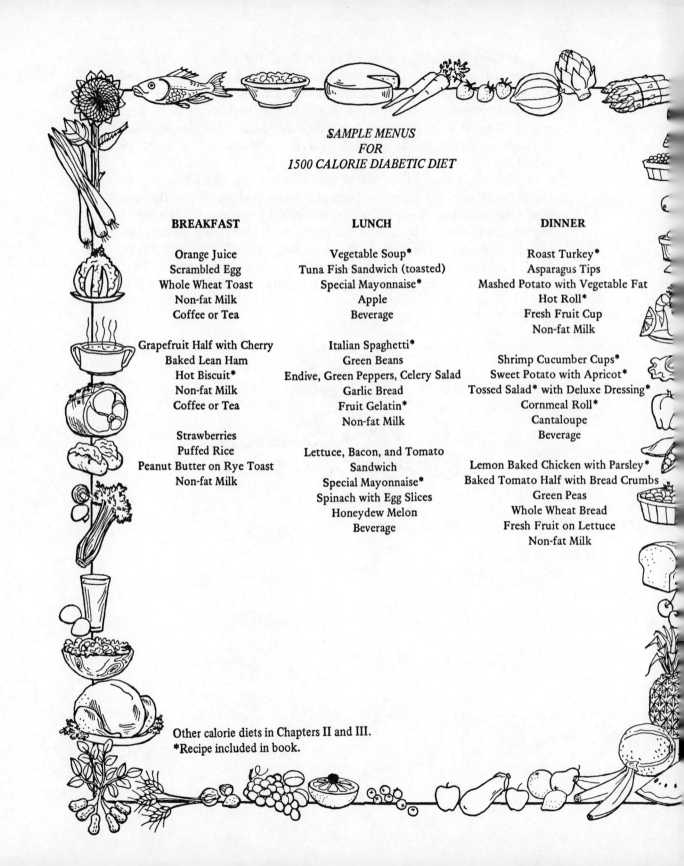

SAMPLE MENUS
FOR
1500 CALORIE DIABETIC DIET

BREAKFAST	LUNCH	DINNER
Orange Juice	Vegetable Soup*	Roast Turkey*
Scrambled Egg	Tuna Fish Sandwich (toasted)	Asparagus Tips
Whole Wheat Toast	Special Mayonnaise*	Mashed Potato with Vegetable Fat
Non-fat Milk	Apple	Hot Roll*
Coffee or Tea	Beverage	Fresh Fruit Cup
		Non-fat Milk
Grapefruit Half with Cherry	Italian Spaghetti*	
Baked Lean Ham	Green Beans	Shrimp Cucumber Cups*
Hot Biscuit*	Endive, Green Peppers, Celery Salad	Sweet Potato with Apricot*
Non-fat Milk	Garlic Bread	Tossed Salad* with Deluxe Dressing*
Coffee or Tea	Fruit Gelatin*	Cornmeal Roll*
	Non-fat Milk	Cantaloupe
		Beverage
Strawberries		
Puffed Rice	Lettuce, Bacon, and Tomato	
Peanut Butter on Rye Toast	Sandwich	Lemon Baked Chicken with Parsley*
Non-fat Milk	Special Mayonnaise*	Baked Tomato Half with Bread Crumbs
	Spinach with Egg Slices	Green Peas
	Honeydew Melon	Whole Wheat Bread
	Beverage	Fresh Fruit on Lettuce
		Non-fat Milk

Other calorie diets in Chapters II and III.
*Recipe included in book.

Sample recipes are shown to assist you if you are a diabetic. The recipes found in Chapters II and III may be used with an adjustment of sugar. Sugar is 100% carbohydrate and, therefore, rapidly becomes glucose in the blood stream. Sugar may be left out of many recipes.

The diabetic must always know the ingredients in any recipe and stay close to basic food preparation by using the whole grain products, decreasing animal fats, sugar and salt. Meats should be baked, broiled or roasted; vegetables and fruits preferably fresh; breads and cereals whole grain.

Unless you are overweight keep the body regulated with a stable food intake.

You may enjoy creating recipes that you find most enjoyable. The following recipes should be helpful.

APPETIZERS . . . .

Use sparingly. One serving should substitute for meat in the meal.

SHRIMP CUCUMBER CUPS

1 large cucumber	Sauce: Catsup or chili sauce
Shrimp	with enough horseradish to
24 ounces (1½ pounds)	make sharp taste. (Or see
Lettuce hearts	recipe below.)
	Parsley flakes

Cut cucumbers into pieces 1½ inch long, removing skin and making striped effect. / Scoop centers out, / put in a little of the sauce and pile the shrimp on top. / Serve on slices of lettuce hearts, / garnish shrimp with more sauce and parsley flakes. ● Serves 12.

SAUCE FOR SHRIMP OR CRAB MEAT

1 cup olive oil	dash tabasco
¼ cup horseradish	½ cup vinegar
1 cup catsup	1 teaspoon paprika
1 teaspoon salt	1 scraped onion, small
½ teaspoon red pepper	1 tablespoon Worcestershire
½ cup lemon juice	sauce

Combine ingredients and serve with cooked shrimp or crab meat.

TUNA FISH CANAPES

Tuna fish	Lemon juice
Special Mayonnaise*	Tomatoes
Celery salt	Toast
Onion salt	Grated cheese

Drain and mash tuna fish and mix with mayonnaise, celery salt, onion salt, and lemon juice. / Slice tomatoes and place on top of rounds of toast, spread tuna fish mixture over tomatoes and sprinkle with grated cheese. / Heat under broiler until brown and serve hot.

MAIN DISHES . . . .

ITALIAN SPAGHETTI

½ small onion, chopped	¼ cup water
1 or 2 ozs. ground meat	Salt, pepper
1 teaspoon vegetable fat	½ cup tomatoes
(except coconut oil)	½ cup cooked spaghetti
2 tablespoons tomato paste	

Brown the onion and ground meat in the fat. / Add the tomato paste, water, tomatoes and seasonings. / Allow to simmer gently 1 hour or more. / If needed, add more water. / Serve on ½ cup cooked spaghetti. / One or 2 teaspoons grated cheese may be used. ● Serves 1.

LEMON BAKED CHICKEN

1 frying chicken (2½ to 3 pounds) cut in serving pieces	1 crushed clove garlic
	½ teaspoon salt
3 tablespoons vegetable oil (except coconut oil)	Dash pepper
	Chopped parsley
3 tablespoons fresh lemon juice	

Arrange chicken in shallow casserole or baking dish. / Mix all other ingredients and pour over chicken. / Cover and bake at 350°F. until tender, about 45 to 50 minutes. / Uncover casserole the last 10 minutes to allow chicken to brown. / Before serving sprinkle with chopped parsley. ● Serves 4.

JIFFY FILLETS

2 pounds rockfish fillets	2 tablespoons lemon juice
¼ cup vegetable oil (except coconut oil)	1 teaspoon salt
	Paprika

Cut the fillets into serving-sized portions. / Combine the oil, lemon juice, salt. / Place the fillets, skin side up, on a well-greased broiler pan and brush with the lemon mixture. / Sprinkle with paprika. / Broil about 3 inches from source of heat for 4 to 5 minutes. / Turn carefully and brush with remaining lemon mixture. / Sprinkle with paprika. / Broil 4 to 5 minutes or until tender. ● Serves 8.

BIRD IN NEST

3 cups cubed cooked chicken	1 apple
1½ cups diced celery	4 marachino cherries
1 teaspoon salt	Lettuce
3 sweet pickles, chopped	1 tomato, sliced
Special Mayonnaise*	1 hard boiled egg, sliced
1 fresh pineapple	

Combine the chicken, celery, salt, and pickles in a bowl. / Add enough mayonnaise to moisten and mix well. / Slice the pineapple in half. / Scoop out pineapple pulp and cut in cubes. / Place back in pineapple shell. / Place the chicken salad on pineapple cubes to form body of birds. / Slice the apple in half and attach an apple half to each pineapple half with toothpick to form head of birds. Attach cherries to apple for eyes. / Form tail of birds with straws. / Place on a bed of lettuce and garnish with tomato and egg slices. ● Serves 2.

SEASONED DRESSING OR MARINADE FOR BEEF, PORK, LAMB OR CHICKEN

1/3 cup tomato sauce	¼ teaspoon pepper
1/3 cup vegetable oil (except coconut oil)	½ teaspoon oregano
	½ teaspoon dry mustard
¼ cup vinegar	¼ teaspoon soy sauce
1 teaspoon salt	

Combine all ingredients and shake well. ● Enough marinade for one to two servings.

Variations:

CHIVE DRESSING: Add 2 tablespoons finely chopped chives or scallions to the above.

ONION DRESSING: To the basic recipe add 1 tablespoon chopped onion, a dash of Tabasco. / Shake well.

SWEET POTATO N' APRICOT BAKE

6 medium sweet potatoes (2 pounds)	2 eggs
1 cup dried apricots	2 teaspoons finely shredded orange peel
½ cup vegetable fat (except coconut oil)	¾ teaspoon salt
	Orange slice

Cook sweet potatoes in boiling salted water about 30 minutes. / Drain and peel. / Meanwhile, cook apricots in a small amount of boiling water about 10 minutes; drain. / In large bowl beat together sweet potatoes, apricots, and fat till fluffy. / Beat in eggs, orange peel, and salt. / Turn into ungreased 1-quart casserole. / Bake covered, in 325° oven 1 hour. / Garnish with orange slice. ● Serves 8.

SPICY BAKED ACORN SQUASH

2 large acorn squash	¼ teaspoon ground cinnamon
2 tablespoons brown sugar	1 tablespoon lemon juice
4 teaspoons vegetable fat (except coconut oil)	1 tablespoon orange juice
½ teaspoon salt	8 whole cloves

Heat oven to 400°F. / Wash squash and cut each in half lengthwise. / Scrape out seeds and stringy portion. / Blend together brown sugar, fat, salt, and cinnamon. / Put one-fourth of the mixture in the center of each squash half. / Sprinkle on lemon juice and orange juice. / Stick a whole clove in the ends of squash. / Bake covered in preheated oven for 45 minutes. / Uncover and continue to bake for 15 minutes, or until squash is tender. ● Serves 4.

CARDINAL SALAD

2 large beets	Special Mayonnaise* made with vinegar from beets
2 tablespoons vinegar	Lettuce
½ cup wax beans	Radishes for a garnish
½ cup peas	
½ cup asparagus tips	

Boil beets until tender, / slice, cover with vinegar and let stand until the following day. / Drain off the vinegar and use it in making a mayonnaise. / Arrange beans, peas, asparagus tips and mayonnaise in little rose-like nests of lettuce leaves placed on sliced beets and garnish with radishes. ● Serves 4.

CARROT SALAD

1 cup grated raw carrot	½ teaspoon salt
1 cup chopped raw cabbage or celery, or cabbage and celery combined	Special Mayonnaise* or cooked dressing*
1 tablespoon lemon juice	Lettuce leaves

Mix the ingredients well and serve on crisp lettuce leaves. / The grated carrot may be served alone on lettuce or may be combined with cold boiled peas, with chopped nuts and apples or with onions and radishes. ● Serves 4.

Use an abundance of fresh vegetables. (See page 00)

DRESSINGS FOR SALADS . . . .

CELERY BUTTERMILK DRESSING

1 cup buttermilk	1 tablespoon minced celery
1 tablespoon minced onion	1 tablespoon catsup
1 tablespoon minced green pepper	1 tablespoon herb vinegar
	Salt to taste

Mix ingredients thoroughly and let stand 1 hour or more to ripen flavor. / A peeled clove of garlic may be placed in the dressing and removed before dressing is used.

DELUXE SALAD DRESSING

½ cup tomato juice
2 tablespoons lemon juice or vinegar
1 tablespoon onion, finely chopped

Salt and pepper
Chopped parsley or green pepper, horseradish or mustard, etc., may be added, if desired.

Combine ingredients in a jar with a tightly fitted top. Shake well before using.

BREADS . . . .

QUICK RAISIN OAT LOAF

1 cup flour
1 teaspoon baking soda
½ teaspoon salt
1 cup quick-cooking oats
1 large egg
¼ cup firmly packed dark brown sugar

1 cup buttermilk
1 cup raisins
½ cup coarsely broken walnuts

Stir together flour, baking soda and salt; add oats. / In a separate mixing bowl beat egg and brown sugar until blended; beat in buttermilk. / Add flour mixture and stir until moistened. / Stir in raisins and walnuts. / Turn into a greased 8 by 4 by 2½ inch loaf pan. / Bake in a preheated 350-degree oven until loaf shrinks from sides of pan and top is browned: 50 to 60 minutes. / Turn out on wire rack. / Turn right side up; cool completely. / When cold, may be sliced about ¼ inch thick. / For easiest slicing wait for top to soften—wrap in plastic film and store in a tightly covered tin box for 6 hours or overnight. / Keep moist, stored this way, for several days; after that, store in refrigerator.

WHOLE WHEAT BISCUITS

1 cup all-purpose flour
2¼ teaspoons baking powder
¾ teaspoon salt

1 cup whole wheat flour
1/3 cup vegetable fat (except coconut oil)
¾ cup non-fat milk

Sift the white flour, measure, and re-sift 3 times with baking powder and salt. / Stir in the unsifted whole wheat flour. / Cut in fat with a pastry blender or 2 knives. / Add milk all at once and stir with a fork until dough just stiffens; then turn out onto a lightly floured board and knead 8 to 10 times. / Roll or pat out to thickness of about 3/8 to 1/2 inch and cut out with floured biscuit cutter. / Place on greased baking sheet and bake in a hot oven 450° F. for about 12 minutes. ● Makes 12 two-inch biscuits.

BOSTON BROWN BREAD

1 cup cornmeal
1 cup whole rye flour
1 cup whole wheat flour
½ teaspoon soda
1 teaspoon baking powder
1 teaspoon salt

¾ cup molasses
2 cups buttermilk
2 tablespoons vegetable fat, melted (except coconut oil)
1 cup raisins, washed and dried

Stir cornmeal, rye flour and whole wheat flour with a spoon to fluff them up before measuring. / Lift lightly into a cup with a spoon to measure. / Sift cornmeal, rye, and whole wheat flour with the soda, baking powder and salt 3 times; / add bran remaining in the sifter to the mixture. / Combine molasses, buttermilk and fat. / Add to dry ingredients and stir until thoroughly mixed. / Stir in raisins. / Spoon batter into 3 well-greased molds, filling them to about 2/3 full. / Cover with lids or double thickness of waxed paper. / Steam 1½ hours or until springy when pressed and no longer sticky. / Cool a few minutes then remove bread from molds. / Serve warm. Improvise a steamer by placing a rack on the bottom of a deep kettle. / Cover the bottom with boiling water and place molds on rack. / Cover tightly. / Add more boiling water as water boils away. / Steam until firm to touch. / NOTE: One pound baking powder cans make very fine molds for the bread. / A small slice will substitute for 1 serving of any other bread.

DESInsERTS . . . .

CHERRY CRUNCH

2 2-inch square graham
  crackers, crushed
1 teaspoon cinnamon
¼ cup vegetable fat, melted
  (except coconut oil)

4 tablespoons flour
2 cups cherries, unsweetened
3 egg whites

Combine the cracker crumbs; cinnamon and vegetable fat in a bowl and mix well. / Reserve ¾ cup for topping and press remaining mixture on bottom and sides of 1½ quart casserole. / Mix flour, cherries and juice in a saucepan and cook over low heat, stirring until thickened. / Pour into crumb-lined casserole. / Beat the egg whites in a bowl until stiff and spread over the cherry mixture. / Sprinkle with reserved crumb mixture. / Bake at 375°F. for 35 minutes. / One half cup should count as a bread slice and fruit. / You will need to adjust diet pattern to allow for this dessert. ● Serves 8.

QUICK APPLESAUCE WHIP

2 cups applesauce
½ teaspoon grated lemon peel
2 teaspoons lemon juice
½ teaspoon ground cinnamon

3 egg whites
1/8 teaspoon salt
Ground nutmeg

Combine applesauce, lemon peel, juice, and cinnamon. / Beat egg whites and salt until frothy. / Continue beating until rounded peaks are formed. / Fold beaten egg whites into applesauce mixture. / Spoon immediately into dessert dishes. / Sprinkle top with nutmeg. / One half cup serving will count as a serving of fruit. ● Serves 6.

PINEAPPLE MANDARIN

1 tablespoon unflavored
  gelatin
¼ cup cold water
1¾ cup pineapple juice
Yellow food coloring

1 cup unsweetened pineapple
  chunks
1 cup mandarin orange
  sections
6 marachino cherries

Soften gelatin in cold water. / Pour 1 cup pineapple juice into a saucepan and bring to a boil. / Add gelatin and stir until dissolved. / Add remaining pineapple juice and mix well. / Add several drops of food coloring and chill until partially set. / Spoon into 6 dessert dishes. / Place 1/6 of pineapple chunks and orange sections in each dish and chill until set. / Top with cherries and serve. ● Serves 4.

HYPOGLYCEMIA. Hypoglycemia is a condition of low blood sugar or glucose. It is a subject of many popular articles. They assert that hypoglycemia is a very serious disease affecting millions of Americans. They cite statistics showing that millions of dollars are spent each year to treat the condition.

Most nutritionists, however, agree that hypoglycemia is an extremely rare disease. Many feel that persons being treated with injections of steroid hormones are being cheated. There is no proof that such injections have any positive effect as treatment for sugar disorders.

Hypoglycemia can be caused by a number of different factors, all of them rare. In some genetic disorders the intestine might not be able to digest the starches or sugars so that carbohydrates cannot enter the body. Low blood sugar can result also from severe intestinal distress. The body, however, may compensate by utilizing fats or protein to raise the level of blood glucose.

In another type of hypoglycemia there is an overproduction of insulin causing a rapid removal of glucose from the bloodstream. The result is an insufficient amount of glucose being supplied to the brain, and the result may be shock and coma. (This is the same response as that of a diabetic given an overdose of insulin.)

Reports show that some tumors that form in the body can produce an insulin-like compound which causes glucose to be removed rapidly from the bloodstream and converted into glycogen or fat. This is an over-supply of insulin. Many believe, also, that overeating sugar causes hypoglycemia, but this is not supported by research and is untrue. If calories expended are less than the intake of energy foods, sweets can cause obesity, however, and this can lead to diabetes.

Mild hypoglycemia may occur when a patient is adjusting to solid foods after having been on intravenous therapy following surgery. The glucose load stimulates an over-production of insulin which in turn leads to a drop in blood sugars below normal fasting levels.

The dietary treatment for hypoglycemia often brings dramatic relief of the symptoms. Carbohydrate intake, especially simple sugars, is kept to a minimum to prevent rapid passage of food. Protein and fat are increased to provide tissue-building material and to delay the emptying of the food mass into the intestine. Meals should be small, frequent and dry, with fluid only in between meals. A sample progression diet pattern may look like this:

124

MILD HYPOGLYCEMIA DIET FOLLOWING SURGERY

I	II	III	IV
Breakfast	**Breakfast**	**Breakfast**	**Breakfast**
Soft cooked egg	Soft cooked egg or	Same as II	Egg, not fried
Salt	poached egg		Cereal
Sugar	Vegetable fat (except		Toast
	coconut oil)		Vegetable Fat (except
	White toast		coconut oil)
	Strained cereal		Canned fruit
	Milk		Milk
10:00 a.m.	**10:00 a.m.**	**10:00 a.m.**	**10:00 a.m.**
Gelatin with cream	Same as I	Same as I	Same as I
Luncheon	**Luncheon**	**Luncheon**	**Luncheon**
Mashed potato with	Sliced turkey or	Roast beef	Tender meat
Vegetable fat (except	plain tender meat	Mashed potatoes	Potato or substitute
coconut oil)	Baked potato with	Pureed vegetable	Whole vegetables
Salt	Vegetable fat (except	White bread	Bread
Sugar	coconut oil)	Vegetable fat (except	Vegetable fat (except
	Salt, sugar	coconut oil)	coconut oil)
		Plain pudding	Dessert (no fresh fruit)
2:00 p.m.	**2:00 p.m.**	**2:00 p.m.**	**2:00 p.m.**
Baked custard	Same as I	Same as I	Same as I
Dinner	**Dinner**	**Dinner**	**Dinner**
Baked potato	Small tender steak	Small tender steak	Tender meat
	Baked potato with	Baked potato	Potato or substitute
	vegetable fat	Pureed vegetable	Whole vegetables
	White toast	White bread	Bread
	Vegetable fat (except	Vegetable fat (except	Vegetable fat
	coconut oil)	coconut oil)	(except coconut oil)
		Vanilla ice cream	Dessert (no fresh fruit)
8:00 p.m.	**8:00 p.m.**	**8:00 p.m.**	**8:00 p.m.**
Plain pudding	Same as I	Plain pudding	Same as III
		with cookie	

NOTE: All meals are small in portions. Fluids, such as soup, milk, fruit juices and other beverages, should be taken in moderation.

We should be aware of the possibility of hypoglycemia that may develop from a starvation diet or fad diet that unbalances the food nutrients. "Nutrient Stress" can cause many diseases; hypoglycemia is only one of them.

Any symptoms you may have that would lead you to think something is wrong should lead you to visit your physician.

125

ALLERGIES. Allergy is a condition of hypersensitivity to a substance, or substances, which do not evoke symptoms in the ordinary individual.

Allergic reactions are caused by a wide variety of substances and conditions, including pollens, dust, cosmetics and animal hair; poisonous plants, serums, vaccines and drugs, and physical agents such as heat, cold and sunlight and a variety of foods.

The symptoms of allergies are as varied as the substances which cause the reaction. Eczema is the most common in infants and children. Rhinitis and asthma occur in children and adults. Hives, physical allergies and angioneurotic edema are common in adults. Drug reactions are directly related to the administration of vaccines and drugs and may occur at any age. A gastrointestinal reaction is disputed as a manifestation of allergy. The extensive surface of the skin and the mucous membranes exposure explain the fact that contact with irritating substances or allergens is either direct or enters through the circulating bloodstream.

We are more concerned in these writings with the relationships of allergies to foods. It should be recognized, however, that an allergy from whatever cause may interfere with the nutrition of the individual. In children the allergy may prevent normal growth and development unless the diet is evaluated and made adequate.

Protein foods are considered to be the cause of most food allergies. Among other allergy-producing foods are oranges, milk, eggs and wheat, and very common food allergens are chocolate, tomatoes, strawberries, fish and shellfish. If oranges will cause an unfavorable reaction, lemons and grapefruits are also likely suspects. If cabbage causes a reaction, then check broccoli, brussels sprouts and cauliflower.

There are other factors that may affect the allergic reactions such as the physical and emotional state of the individual at the time of eating the foods.

The visit to the physician will usually result in a careful history of the patient. If the history reveals no known causes of the allergies, then skin tests will be made. The skin test is really bringing in contact with the skin a suspected allergen. This "patch test" will, upon finding a substance to which the individual is allergic, cause a skin response of redness, welts or wheals.

It appears that many foods give a positive skin test without causing allergic symptoms, however.

When it is not clear as to the definite foods causing a reaction, then the diet is a good test. To the dietitian the allergy diet is common. The diet is designed to eliminate certain foods from the meals for a period of time.

A sample diet plan with typical menus have been presented for your use. You will want to consider the fact that many foods are eliminated for a short period of time and then added back to the diet gradually and in small portions. This is to show that other factors may enter into the body's reactions to foods.

The allergy diet is not recommended except under medical supervision. It should not be used for pregnant and nursing mothers. It is deficient in calcium when milk is eliminated from the diet.

Some reactions to foods have occurred as a result of an imbalance of food nutrients, such as acne or inflammation of the sebaceous glands. This condition may be due to a high carbohydrate diet or a diet too high in fat has been suggested as a cause of the oily skin condition affecting the face, chest, and back.

The best recommendation to adolescents and young adults concerned about the condition is to keep the diet balanced and the body clean.

ALLERGY DIETS

Diet I	Diet II	Diet III	Diet IV
Rice	Corn	Tapioca	Milk† as tolerated
Tapioca	Rye	White potato	Tapioca
Rice biscuit		Breads made of any	Sugar
Rice bread	Corn-rye muffins	combination of soy,	
Lettuce	Rye bread	lima, potato starch	
Chard	Ry-Krisp	and tapioca flours	
Spinach			
Carrot	Beets	Tomato	
Sweet potato or yam	Squash	Carrot	
	Asparagus	Lima beans	
Lamb	Artichoke	String beans	
		Peas	
Lemon	Chicken (no hens)		
Grapefruit	Bacon	Beef	
Pears		Bacon	
Sugar	Pineapple		
Sesame oil	Peach	Lemon	
Olive oil*	Apricot	Grapefruit	
Salt	Prune	Peach	
Gelatin, plain or		Apricot	
flavored with lime	Cane or beet sugar		
or lemon	Corn oil	Sugar	
Maple syrup or syrup	Sesame oil	Sesame oil	
made with cane	Salt	Soybean oil	
sugar flavored	Gelatin, plain or	Gelatin, plain or	
with maple	flavored with	flavored with lime	
Royal baking powder	pineapple	or lemon	
Baking soda	Karo corn syrup	Salt	
Cream of tartar	White vinegar	Maple syrup or syrup	
Vanilla extract	Royal baking powder	made with cane	
Lemon extract	Baking soda	sugar flavored	
	Cream of tartar	with maple	
	Vanilla extract	Royal baking powder	
		Baking soda	
		Cream of tartar	
		Vanilla extract	
		Lemon extract	

*Allergy to it may occur with or without allergy to olive pollen. Corn oil may be used if corn allergy is not present.
†Plain cottage cheese may be used. Tapioca cooked with milk and sugar may be taken.

128

ALLERGY DIETS
Typical Menus Based on Diets I to III

Diet No. I

Breakfast	Dinner	Supper
Half grapefruit	Lamb patties	Lamb stew with carrots
Steamed or Puffed Rice with maple syrup or pear juice	Spinach with lemon	Steamed rice
Lamb chop	Sweet potato, baked	Lettuce and grapefruit salad. Dressing of olive oil, lemon juice, salt
Lemonade	Rye bread or biscuit with grapefruit and lemon marmalade*	Gelatin made with lemon juice sugar and pear
	Stewed fresh pear	Grapefruit juice or lemonade
	Pear and grapefruit juice	

Diet No. II

Breakfast	Dinner	Supper
Stewed prunes or fresh peaches	Roast chicken	Sliced cold chicken
Fried cornmeal mush	Baked squash with bacon	Pickled beets
Bacon	Asparagus vinaigrette, dressed with sesame oil, white vinegar, salt	Ry-Krisp with pineapple jam
Corn and rye muffins*		Stewed apricots with sugar
Apricot and pineapple jam	Rice-Corn Bread with apricot jam*	Pineapple juice
Pineapple juice	Pineapple, fresh or canned	
	Prune juice	

Diet No. III

Breakfast	Dinner	Supper
Half grapefruit	Roast beef	Bacon
Fried potatoes	Boiled potato with pan gravy	Lima bean casserole with tomatoes, seasoned with bacon fat
Bacon	Glazed carrots, using sugar and sesame oil	
Rice muffins, made without eggs	Rice-Barley bread with grapefruit marmalade	Oatmeal-Rice muffins with apricot jam*
Apricot jam	Sliced peaches	Peach tapioca
Tomato juice	Lemonade	Grapefruit juice

SUBSTITUTES FOR 1 CUP WHEAT FLOUR

½ cup barley flour   ¾ cup cornmeal (coarse)

1 cup corn flour   1 scant cup corn meal (fine)

*Recipe included in book.

RECIPES

SOME RECIPES FOR TREATING ALLERGIES

BREADS . . . .

GLUTEN BREAD

2 cups scalded non-fat milk	1½ teaspoon salt
1 yeast cake softened in ½ cup	4 cups gluten flour
lukewarm water	2 egg whites

When the milk is cool, add the softened yeast, the salt, the gluten flour, a little at a time, and finally the slightly beaten whites of eggs. / The mixture should be of consistency to drop from a spoon rather than to pour and should be baked in greased pans filled about half full. / Follow general directions for rising. / When ready, bake one hour in a moderate oven (400° to 350°F.). / If a less moist bread is desired, add enough white flour to make a dough, after beating in the gluten flour, and follow directions for straight dough method of making bread.

CORNMEAL AND RYE MUFFINS

½ cup cornmeal	2 tablespoons raisins
½ cup rye flour	1 tablespoon vegetable fat,
2½ teaspoons baking powder	melted (except coconut
2 tablespoons sugar	oil)
1 teaspoon salt	½ cup water

Sift dry ingredients together. / Add raisins. / Combine fat and water. / Add to dry ingredients. / Stir only enough to mix ingredients slightly. / Batter will be lumpy. / Fill greased muffin tins 2/3 full. / Bake at 400°F. for about 30 minutes. ● Makes 6 muffins.

RYE BREAD

1½ cakes compressed yeast or	3 tablespoons sugar
2 tablespoons active dry	4 tablespoons vegetable fat
yeast	(except coconut oil)
1-1/3 cups water	5 cups rye flour
2 teaspoons salt	

Soften yeast in 1/3 cup lukewarm water. / Add 1 teaspoon sugar. / Measure remaining water, salt, sugar and softened fat into a bowl; / add dissolved yeast mixture. / Pour half of flour into this liquid mixture and beat until well blended. / Add remaining flour; knead on floured board until dough is smooth and will spring back when pressed lightly with finger (about 200 strokes). / Place in well oiled bowl. / Let rise until double in bulk (about 1 hour) at 80°F. / Knead about 100 times and place in two small loaf pans which have been greased only on the bottom. / Let rise again until double in bulk (about 30 minutes) at 80°F. / Bake at 425°F. for 10 to 15 minutes until brown; then at 350°F. for 25 to 35 minutes until done. ● Makes 2 small loaves.

RICE AND CORN BREAD

7/8 cup rice flour	2 eggs
¼ cup sugar	¼ cup vegetable fat (except
4 teaspoons baking powder	coconut oil)
¾ teaspoon salt	1 cup non-fat milk
1 cup yellow cornmeal	

Sift flour with sugar, baking powder and salt. / Stir in the cornmeal. / Add eggs to softened shortening and beat. / Add milk and add liquid mixture to dry ingredients. / Beat about 1 minute. / Pour into greased, hot pan, 9 x 9 inches. / Bake at 425°F. for 20 minutes. / Good when cold.

RICE FLOUR MUFFINS

1 cup unsifted rice flour	2 egg yolks
3 teaspoons baking powder	¾ cup non-fat milk
½ teaspoon salt	2 egg whites
¼ cup vegetable fat (except coconut oil)	½ teaspoon vanilla, lemon or almond flavoring
¼ cup sugar	

Measure rice flour, baking powder, salt and sift together twice. / Cream softened fat, add sugar and cream together. / Stir in egg yolks. / Add flour mixture alternately with milk, beating after each addition. / Fold in well beaten (but not dry) egg whites and flavoring. / Spoon into a well-greased muffin tin. / Bake 30 minutes in a 325°F. (moderate oven) or until lightly browned. ● Makes 6 muffins.

OATMEAL AND RICE MUFFINS

3 tablespoons ground oatmeal	1 tablespoon vegetable fat, melted (except coconut oil)
¾ cup rice flour	
1 tablespoon baking powder	3 tablespoons raisins
½ teaspoon salt	
½ cup water (or enough to make a thin batter)	

Grind oatmeal using a medium coarse blade. / Sift rice flour, baking powder and salt together; / mix with ground oatmeal. / Combine water with fat. / Add liquid to dry ingredients and stir just enough to dampen flour mixture; add raisins. / Fill greased muffin tins 2/3 full. / Bake at 400°F. about 30 minutes. ● Makes 6 muffins.

RICE AND BARLEY FLOUR MUFFINS

1/3 cup rice flour	¼ teaspoon salt
2/3 cup barley flour	¾ cup non-fat milk
3 teaspoons baking powder	1 tablespoon vegetable fat, melted (except coconut oil)
2 tablespoons sugar	

Mix and sift dry ingredients together. / Add liquid and melted fat. / Stir only enough to combine. / Fill greased muffin tins 2/3 full. / Bake at 400°F. for about 35 minutes. ● Makes 5 muffins.

RICE STUFFING

1/3 cup rice	5½ cups crisp rice cereal
½ teaspoon salt	2 tablespoons minced parsley
3 cups boiling water	1 tablespoon poultry seasoning
½ cup diced celery	½ teaspoon salt
¼ cup diced onion	½ cup stock or water
1/3 cup vegetable fat (except coconut oil)	

Wash rice thoroughly in a sieve and drain well. / Add rice to boiling salted water slowly so that water continues to bubble. / Boil rapidly 15 to 20 minutes until rice is tender. / Drain in sieve. / Brown celery and onion in fat. / Stir in rice and mix well. / Crush rice cereal into coarse crumbs. / Add parsley, seasonings and stock. / Combine with rice and mix thoroughly. / Makes 3½ cups stuffing. / NOTE: Stuffing may be baked in a covered casserole in moderate oven (375°F.) for 25 minutes.

DESSERTS . . . .

APPLE STRUDEL

5 cups cornflakes	Cinnamon
3 cups sliced apples	3 tablespoons vegetable oil (except coconut oil)
¾ cup sugar, granulated or brown	

Put layer of cornflakes in greased quart casserole. / Cover with layer of apples, half the sugar, sprinkle with cinnamon and with one third of the oil. / Add another layer cornflakes, remaining apples and sugar. / Sprinkle with cinnamon and dot with more oil. / A layer of cornflakes on top, dot with remaining oil and sprinkle with a little sugar. / Cover casserole and bake in moderate oven (375°F.) Bake 35 minutes, or until apples are soft. / Serve either hot or cold with cream. ● Serves 6.
NOTE: Add about 2 tablespoons water to strudel before baking if apples are not juicy. / Sprinkle few drops lemon juice over apples if they are tart.

RICE FLOUR BROWNIES

2 squares unsweetened chocolate (2 oz.)	2 eggs
1/3 cup vegetable fat (except coconut oil)	2/3 cup rice flour, sifted twice before measuring
1 cup sugar	½ teaspoon baking powder
	½ teaspoon salt

Melt chocolate and fat in a double boiler over hot water. / Remove pan from hot water and beat in sugar and eggs. / Sift rice flour, baking powder and salt together and stir into chocolate mixture. / Spread into a greased 8-inch-square pan. / Allow mixture to stand ½ hour before baking. / Bake in a 350°F. moderate oven for 30 to 35 minutes. / A slight imprint is left when the top is touched. / Cool slightly; / cut into squares. • Makes 16 2-inch squares.

POTATO STARCH SPONGE CAKE

7 eggs	Juice of ½ lemon
1½ cups sugar, sifted	¾ cup potato starch, sifted twice with a dash of salt
Grated rind of ½ lemon	

Separate 6 eggs. / Beat 6 yolks and one whole egg together until frothy. / Gradually add sifted sugar, lemon juice, and grated rind, beating constantly until thick and lemon colored. / (If using an electric mixer, use lower speed for 5 minutes.) / Gradually add sifted potato starch, folding in by hand with a spatula. / Beat 6 egg whites stiff, but not dry, then gently fold into the above mixture. / Pour entire mixture into ungreased regulation tube cake pan. / Bake at 350°F. for about 50 to 55 minutes. / This cake will keep at least a week if wrapped in foil and kept in refrigerator.

PLAIN CAKE

1 cup barley flour	½ cup sugar
3 teaspoons baking powder	½ cup plus 1 tablespoon nonfat milk
¼ teaspoon salt	½ teaspoon vanilla
4 tablespoons vegetable fat (except coconut oil)	

Sift dry ingredients together. / Cream fat, add sugar, mix well. / Add liquid, dry ingredients and vanilla. / Bake in greased pan (9" x 9" x 2") or muffin pans at 375°F. for 25 to 30 minutes. • Makes 1 layer cake or 6 cup cakes.
Variations: Barley, rye, rice or a combination of these flours may be used.

GINGER COOKIES

2¼ cups rice flour	¾ cup vegetable fat (except coconut oil)
2 teaspoons soda	1 cup brown sugar
¼ teaspoon salt	1 egg
½ teaspoon cloves	¼ cup molasses
1 teaspoon ginger	
1 teaspoon cinnamon	

Sift dry ingredients except sugar together. / Cream fat with brown sugar, add egg and molasses. / Add dry ingredients and mix. / Chill dough in refrigerator for 30 minutes. / Roll into small balls, dip the top in sugar. flatten with fork on greased cookie sheet. / Bake at 375°F. for about 10 minutes. • Makes 24 cookies.

RICE FLOUR COOKIES

¼ lb. vegetable fat (except coconut oil)	½ teaspoon vanilla
¼ cup sugar	1 cup rice flour
1 egg yolk	¼ teaspoon salt

Mix fat, sugar and egg yolk well; / add vanilla and flour mixed with salt to make a soft dough. / Divide dough into small balls the size of a walnut. / Place on greased cookie sheet. / Press center with thumb and place dab of jelly in the depression. / Bake at 350°F. until brown. • Makes 18-20 cookies.

ARTERIOSCLEROSIS AND ATHEROSCLEROSIS. What is arteriosclerosis? One definition may be that it is the aging process of the arteries. But, if we stopped there, one could believe that it is impossible to prevent. The Senate Committee has emphasized that the displacement of fruits, vegetables and whole grains may be a danger to health because there is evidence that diets high in these carbohydrate sources may reduce the risk of heart disease.

The over-consumption of fat generally and saturated fat in particular—along with cholesterol, sugar, salt and alcohol—have been related to one of the leading causes of death in the United States, arteriosclerosis.

The term arterosclerosis is derived from a Greek word meaning "hard." The hardening process is known as arteriosclerosis. Lesions which develop in the arterial blood vessels begin a soft deposit and harden with age. The lesions are known as plaque. They grow gradually and thicken the arterial wall, thus narrowing the blood vessels. The plaque is composed of substances such as cholesterol, fatty acids, protein and fat combined, calcium deposits, carbohydrate and blood.

We do not know exactly how and why the plaques form. We do know, however, that the plaques restrict the flow of blood through the blood vessels. If the limited blood supply occurs in the brain, the result is a stroke, or cerebral hemmorhage.

We do not know the cause of atherosclerosis, which is mainly the involvement of the coronary arteries in heart disease. This condition is a number one health problem, the leading cause of disability and death in the United States.

The factors found most associated with coronary heart disease are elevated blood serum cholesterol levels (called hypercholesterolemic hypertension) and excessive smoking. There is usually also evidence of diabetes, obesity, physical inactivity, reduced glucose tolerance, elevated fatty acids, genetic factors, and social and psychological stresses.

A diet plan allowing for flexibility to prevent monotony in the means is presented to help you understand the restriction of fats in treating heart disease. Other fat control diets, menus and recipes have been presented in Chapter III.

The problem of arterosclerosis is the fatty degeneration and thickening that occurs in the arterial wall. The tissue area serviced by the involved artery is deprived of its vital oxygen and nutrients supply and the cells die. The localized area of dying, or dead, tissue is called an infarct.

A search for the cause has focused on lipid metabolism. The artery deposits and plaque formation are largely cholesterol and an elevation of blood cholesterol. There is much unknown about the significance of lowered cholesterol levels in terms of the disease's process.

Some studies have shown that an increase of certain lipoproteins in the blood plasma have been associated with the risk of arterosclerotic heart. Lipoproteins are major forms of lipids in the blood. An increase of these plasma lipoproteins is called hyperlipoproteinemia.

A diet for hyperlipoproteinemia provides foods which may help in the control of levels of cholesterol and triglyceride in the blood. The first step in treatment is the dietary management. All diets are experimental, however, as we await more knowledge.

The diet prescription may vary in types in order to control calories, protein, fat, cholesterol, carboyhdrate and alcohol.

All special medical problems should be taken to your physician. If you should feel uptight, worn, and find that your weight has increased, see your doctor. Keep your body in good condition and have a regular physical examination. Discuss your diet with your physician, since he is aware of your total health needs.

The fat control diets present four patterns, each with a different calorie level, and each with a different percentage of fat. They may prove of benefit to you, when your physician states that you should reduce fat in your diet.

NUTRIENT COMPOSITION OF A 1500-CALORIE FAT-CONTROLLED DIET

Food	Amount	Weight Gm.	Protein Gm.	Total Fat Gm.	Saturated Fat Gm.	Linoleic Fatty Acid Gm.	Cholesterol Gm.	Carbohydrate Gm.	Calories
Milk, Non-fat	1 pt. (2 c.)	480	16	tr	—	—	14	24	160
Vegetables (See appendix)	as desired	varies	—	—	—	—	—	—	—
Vegetables (Starchy) see appendix	1 cup	200	4	—	—	—	—	14	70
Fruit	3 servings	varies	—	—	—	—	—	30	120
Bread and cereal	6 servings	varies	12	3.0	0.6	—	—	90	420
Meat, lean	6 ounces	180	48	12	3.6	0.6	126	—	300
Egg	3/wk. (3/wk.)	21	3	3	0.9	0.2	118	—	35
Fat (veg. oil except coconut oil)	2 tablespoons	28	—	28	4.0	16.0	—	—	250
Fat (Special vegetable margarine)	½ tablespoon	7	—	5.5	1.0	3.1	—	—	50
Sugar (dessert)	1 tablespoon	12	—	—	—	—	—	12	50
Totals			83	51.5	10.1	19.9	258	170	1,455

FAT CONTROLLED DIETS ON THREE CALORIE LEVELS

Diet plans	Total calories from fat	Total day's exchanges		
		1,200 calories	1,800 calories	2,400 calories
I. Modified fatty acid content	40%			
Milk, non-fat		2	2	2
Vegetables (See List in appendix)		As desired	As desired	As desired
Vegetables (Starchy) see appendix		1	1	1
Fruit		3	5	5
Bread and cereals		4	6	8
Meat, fish, poultry		5	6	7
Eggs (if desired, as alternate for a meat exchange)		3 per week	3 per week	3 per week
Fat		5	9	15
Special vegetable fat (except coconut oil)		1		3
Sugar, sweets			9	12
II. Moderate fat reduction	25%			
Milk, non-fat		2	2	2
Vegetables (see List in appendix)		As desired	As desired	As desired
Vegetables (Starchy) see appendix		1	1	1
Fruit		6	8	10
Bread and cereals		3	5	6
Meat, fish, poultry		6	7	9
Eggs (if desired, as alternate for a meat exchange)		3 per week	3 per week	3 per week
Fat, vegetable (except coconut oil)		3	6	8
Sugar, sweets		–	8	22
III. Severe fat reduction	10%			
Milk, non-fat		2	2	2
Vegetables (see list in appendix)		As desired	As desired	As desired
Vegetables (Starchy) see appendix		1	1	1
Fruit		5	8	9
Bread and cereals		4	7	7
Meat, fish, poultry		6	7	9
Eggs (if desired, as alternate for a meat exchange)		3 per week	3 per week	3 per week
Fat, vegetable (except coconut oil)		–	–	–
Sugar, sweets		8	15	36

*Adapted from The regulation of dietary fat, American Medical Association, J.A.M.A. 181:411-429, 1962.

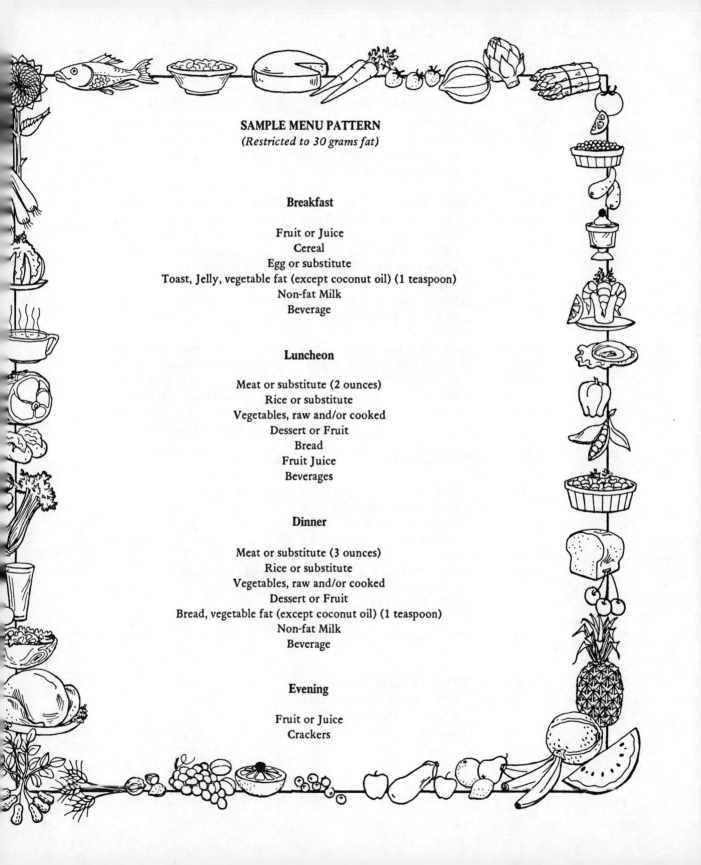

SAMPLE MENU PATTERN
(Restricted to 30 grams fat)

Breakfast

Fruit or Juice
Cereal
Egg or substitute
Toast, Jelly, vegetable fat (except coconut oil) (1 teaspoon)
Non-fat Milk
Beverage

Luncheon

Meat or substitute (2 ounces)
Rice or substitute
Vegetables, raw and/or cooked
Dessert or Fruit
Bread
Fruit Juice
Beverages

Dinner

Meat or substitute (3 ounces)
Rice or substitute
Vegetables, raw and/or cooked
Dessert or Fruit
Bread, vegetable fat (except coconut oil) (1 teaspoon)
Non-fat Milk
Beverage

Evening

Fruit or Juice
Crackers

CONTROLLED FAT DIET—HIGH POLYUNSATURATED FATTY ACIDS DIET

	Foods allowed	Foods not allowed
Soups	Bouillon cubes, vegetables and broths from which fat has been removed. Cream soups made with non-fat milk	Meat soups, commercial cream soups and cream soups made with whole milk or cream
Meat, fish, poultry	One or two servings daily (not to exceed a total of 4 oz.) lean muscle meat, broiled or roasted; beef, veal, lamb, pork, chicken, turkey, lean ham, organ meats (all visible fat should be trimmed from meat); all fish and shell fish	Bacon, pork sausage, luncheon meat, dried meat, and all fatty cuts of meat; weiners, fish roe, duck, goose, skin of poultry, and T.V. dinners
Milk and milk products	At least one pint non-fat milk or non-fat buttermilk daily; non-fat cottage cheese, Sap Sago cheese	Whole milk and cream; all cheeses (except non-fat cottage cheese), ice cream, imitation ice cream (except that containing safflower oil), ice milk, sour cream, commercial yogurt
Eggs	Egg whites only	Egg yolks
Vegetables	All raw or cooked as tolerated (leafy green and yellow vegetables are good sources of vitamin A)	No restrictions
Fruits	All raw, cooked, dried, frozen or canned; use citrus or tomato daily; fruit juices	Avocado and olives
Salads	Any fruit, vegetable, and gelatin salad	
Cereals	All cooked and dry cereals; serve with non-fat milk or fruit; macaroni, noodles, spaghetti, and rice	

	Foods allowed	Foods not allowed
Breads	Whole wheat, rye, enriched white, French bread, English muffins, graham crackers, saltine crackers	Commercial pancakes, waffles, coffee cakes, muffins, doughnuts and all other quick breads made with whole milk and fat; biscuit mixes and other commercial mixes, cheese crackers, pretzels.
Desserts	Fruits, tapioca, cornstarch, rice, Junket puddings all made with non-fat milk and without egg yolks; fruit whips made with egg whites, gelatin desserts, angel food cake, sherbet, water ices, and special imitation ice cream containing vegetable safflower oil; cake and cookies made with non-fat milk, vegetable oil, (except coconut oil) and egg white; fruit pie (pastry made with vegetable oil) (except coconut oil)	Omit desserts and candies made with whole milk, cream, egg yolk, chocolate, cocoa butter, coconut, hydrogenated shortenings, butter and other animal fats
Concentrated fats	Corn oil, soybean oil, cotton seed oil, sesame oil, safflower oil, sunflower oil, walnuts and other nuts except cashew and those commercially fried or roasted Vegetable fat made from above oils Commercial French and Italian salad dressing if not made with olive oil Gravy may be made from bouillon cubes, or fat-free meat stock thickened with flour and add oil if desired	Butter, chocolate, coconut oil, hydrogenated fats and shortenings, cashew nuts; mineral oil, olive oil, vegetable fat, except as specified; commercial salad dressings, except as listed; hydrogenated peanut butter; gravy, except as specified

	Foods allowed	Foods not allowed
	Freshly ground or old fashioned peanut butter	
Sweets	Jelly, jam, honey, hard candy, and sugar	
Beverages	Tea, coffee, or coffee substitutes; tomato juice, fruit juice, cocoa prepared with non-fat milk	Beverages containing chocolate, ice cream, ice milk, eggs, whole milk or cream

If the diet is also to be high in unsaturated fat it should include liberal amounts of:
1. Oils allowed which can be incorporated in salad dressings, or added to soups, to non-fat milk, to cereal, to vegetables
2. Walnuts, almonds, Brazil nuts, Filberts, pecans
3. Extra vegetable fat in or on foods

HYPERTENSION. The elevation of blood pressure is known as hypertension. A very large number of individuals have been found to have a small but steady increase in blood pressure. This disease is on the increase in the United States and may affect 10 to 15 percent of the total population. This disease can result in damage to various organs, such as the kidneys, and hemorrhaging of the blood vessels.

The elevated pressure can cause stroke or death. A heart artery weakened by fat deposits may also rupture under the high pressure. The exact causes of hypertension are unknown, but we know that sodium chloride (table salt) will promote the condition. Salt holds the water in the body tissues. When sodium is present in the bloodstream, water leaves the cells. The result is an increased volume of blood in the circulating system, thus exerting a greater pressure. The elevated pressure causes the heart to pump harder.

The diet is a very important consideration in treating hypertension.

We have described the fat-controlled diets in discussing arterosclerosis.

Saturated fats are known to be high in the bloodstream, so diet and weight control are very important. Saturated fats we have described as animal fats such as fat or red meats. A hydrogenated fat is an emulsified fat such as the cooking shortenings. If you add vegetable shortening to lard it soon becomes easy to work with or soft. The cooking shortenings and oleomargarines are vegetable and animal fat combinations or, totally, vegetable fat.

Obesity or overeating increases the risk of heart disease, especially if the person has hypertension.

The genetic factor should also be considered. If a person has a family history of high level of cholesterol and heart disease, it appears that the children will run a higher risk of having heart disease.

Exercise is probably the most important factor in controlling coronary heart disease. Where people work hard physically there are fewer cases of heart disease. In fact, the high fat intake appears to present no risk to people who exercise regularly.

The Senate report concern is based on high saturated fat intake, heavy smoking, inactivity and excessive calories above the body's need for energy. In addition, we lack sufficient fiber in the diet, and live under heavy emotional stresses in a fast-paced society. So then:

- Eat a prudent diet as a preventive, as the Senate Committee suggests.
- Eat meats and eggs in moderation but do not eliminate them from the diet. Three eggs each week is a good rule of the thumb.
- Unsaturated fats should be increased in the form of fish, chicken and plant fats.
- Increase fiber consumption by eating more fruits and vegetables and whole grain cereals.
- Decrease salt consumption.
- Eat in moderation and reduce to normal weight and eat in an environment suitable for good digestion.
- Exercise some each day.
- Find some time each day to be quiet and relax.

Controlled sodium diets are presented with sample menus and recipes to assist you. If your diet should be also low in fat, refer to Chapter III and reduced calories, Chapter II.

If your physician has recommended a low sodium diet, it is because your body has a tendency to accumulate and retain body fluid when the blood vessels restrict a steady flow of blood to all parts of the body. Sodium or salt (sodium chloride) is responsible for holding the water or fluid in the body tissues.

Here are some of the foods you should avoid if you are placed on a low sodium or sodium restricted diet:

1. Salt at the table (use salt lightly in cooking).
2. Salt-preserved foods such as salted or smoked meat (bacon and bacon fat, bologna, dried or chipped beef, corned beef, frankfurters, ham, kosher meats, luncheon meats, salt pork, sausage, smoked tongue); salted or smoked fish (anchovies, caviar, salted and dried cod, herring, sardines; sauerkraut, olives).
3. Highly salted foods such as crackers, pretzels, potato chips, corn chips, salted nuts, salted popcorn.
4. Spices and condiments such as bouillon cubes, catsup, chili sauce, celery salt, garlic sauce, onion salt, monosodium glutamate, meat sauces, meat tenderizers, pickles, prepared mustard, relishes, Worcestershire sauce, soy sauce.
5. Cheese, peanut butter.

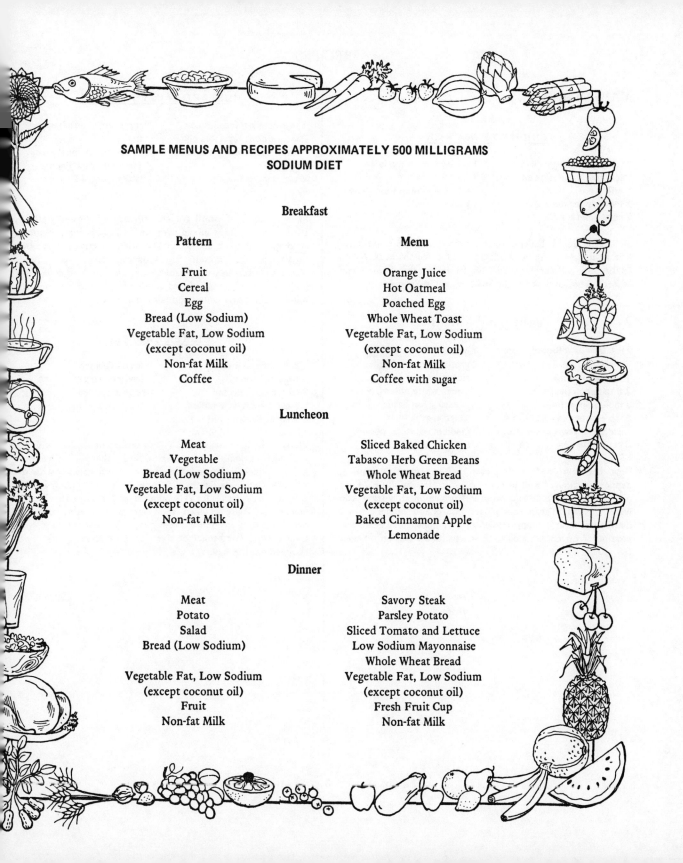

SAMPLE MENUS AND RECIPES APPROXIMATELY 500 MILLIGRAMS SODIUM DIET

Breakfast

Pattern	Menu
Fruit	Orange Juice
Cereal	Hot Oatmeal
Egg	Poached Egg
Bread (Low Sodium)	Whole Wheat Toast
Vegetable Fat, Low Sodium	Vegetable Fat, Low Sodium
(except coconut oil)	(except coconut oil)
Non-fat Milk	Non-fat Milk
Coffee	Coffee with sugar

Luncheon

Meat	Sliced Baked Chicken
Vegetable	Tabasco Herb Green Beans
Bread (Low Sodium)	Whole Wheat Bread
Vegetable Fat, Low Sodium	Vegetable Fat, Low Sodium
(except coconut oil)	(except coconut oil)
Non-fat Milk	Baked Cinnamon Apple
	Lemonade

Dinner

Meat	Savory Steak
Potato	Parsley Potato
Salad	Sliced Tomato and Lettuce
Bread (Low Sodium)	Low Sodium Mayonnaise
	Whole Wheat Bread
Vegetable Fat, Low Sodium	Vegetable Fat, Low Sodium
(except coconut oil)	(except coconut oil)
Fruit	Fresh Fruit Cup
Non-fat Milk	Non-fat Milk

RECIPES

MAIN DISHES . . . .

CURRIED TUNA FISH

3 tablespoons vegetable fat, low sodium (except coconut oil)	1 tablespoon lemon juice
	1-2 teaspoons curry
3 tablespoons flour	1 can low sodium tuna, water packed
2 cups non-fat milk	

Melt fat in double boiler or over low direct heat. / Stir in flour. / Stir in milk and continue stirring until sauce thickens. / Add lemon juice and curry. / Add tuna, flaked but not drained, and reheat. / Serve over rice cooked without salt. ● Serves 4.

BROWN BEEF STEW

2 lbs. lean beaf (boned chuck, round or rump)	1 bay leaf
	2 drops Tabasco
1 teaspoon paprika	4 cloves
1/8 teaspoon pepper	12 small white onions, peeled
3 tablespoons flour	½ pound green beans, cut in short lengths
3 tablespoons vegetable, low sodium (except coconut oil)	
	3 medium potatoes, peeled and halved
3 cups water	

Have beef cut in 1½-inch pieces. / Blend together paprika, pepper and flour. / Roll pieces of meat in flour mixture. / Pour oil in heavy kettle. / Add meat and brown on all sides. / Add water, bay leaf, Tabasco and cloves. / Cover and simmer 2 to 2½ hours until meat is almost tender. / Add onions, green beans and potatoes. / Cover and cook until vegetables are tender. ● Serves 6-8.

MUSTARD SAUCE FOR FISH

1 tablespoon minced onion	1 cup strained unsalted fish stock
2 tablespoons vegetable oil, low sodium (except coconut oil)	
	½ teaspoon dry mustard
	¼ teaspoon black pepper
2 tablespoons flour	2 tablespoons sherry (optional)

Saute onion in oil until golden. / Blend in flour and gradually stir in the fish stock mixed with mustard and pepper. / Simmer, stirring, until thick and smooth. / Stir in sherry. / Serve over unsalted poached or boiled fish. ● Makes 1 cup.
Variations: Add to sauce 1 tablespoon chopped, hard cooked egg yolk and 1 teaspoon minced parsley. / Or add a tablespoon minced chives or a tablespoon minced parsley.

CHICKEN TABASCO

1 2-lb. dressed broiler	Dash of Tabasco
½ lime or lemon	1 teaspoon sugar
2 tablespoons melted vegetable fat, low sodium (except coconut oil)	Chopped parsley

Clean and wipe chicken dry. / Rub surface of chicken with the cut lime or lemon, squeezing to keep the juice flowing. / Combine melted fat and Tabasco and brush chicken with the mixture. / Sprinkle lightly with sugar. / Place in broiler pan, skin side down. / Broil for 10 minutes as far from the heat as possible. / Raise chicken to 4 inches from heat and turn occasionally to ensure even browning. / Allow about 35 minutes total cooking for broiler of this size. / To serve, sprinkle with chopped parsley. ● Serves 2.

SAVORY STEAK

1 flank steak
Flour
Pepper
3 tablespoons vegetable fat,
  low sodium (except coconut
  oil)
2 onions, peeled and sliced
1 small green pepper, seeded
  and sliced
1 bay leaf
3 cloves
2 cups unsalted tomatoes
1 teaspoon sugar

Score steak and pound in the flour and the pepper. / Heat fat in skillet and brown meat on both sides. / Add remaining ingredients, cover and let simmer 1½ to 2 hours until meat is tender. / OR: A stuffing of low sodium bread and low sodium vegetable fat may be made. / After browning, spread the stuffing on the steak, roll it and fasten with string or skewers. / Then proceed as above. ● Serves 4-5.

TUNA AND MUSHROOMS ON MACARONI

2 tablespoons flour
2 teaspoons vegetable fat, low
  sodium (except coconut oil)
1 cup non-fat milk
1 teaspoon grated onion
Dash of white pepper
2 teaspoons chopped pimento
½ cup tuna, water packed
½ cup drained mushrooms,
  water packed
½ cup hot cooked macaroni

Blend flour with fat and part of milk to make smooth paste; / add remaining milk, onion, pepper and pimento. / Cook in small saucepan over low heat until thickened, stirring constantly. / Add tuna and mushrooms. / Heat thoroughly. / Serve over macaroni ● Serves 1.

VEGETABLES . . . .

SWEET POTATO AND APPLE CASSEROLE

1 large sweet potato, boiled,
  unsalted
½ cup applesauce
Sugar
Cinnamon

Place in buttered casserole alternate layers of sliced sweet potato and applesauce. / Top with sugar and cinnamon and heat in moderate oven (350°F.) until hot. / Serve immediately. ● Serves 1-2.

CURRIED CORN

1 cup whole kernel corn,
  cooked
1 tablespoon chopped
  pimento
1/8-1/4 teaspoon curry
  powder
Dash of pepper
1 teaspoon vegetable fat, low
  sodium (except coconut oil)

Drain liquid from corn into small saucepan. / Boil quickly until liquid is reduced to about 1/3 cup (if canned). / Add corn, pimento, fat and seasonings. / Heat thoroughly; toss lightly. ● Serves 1-2.

HERB GREEN BEANS

1 cup cooked fresh or unsalted
  canned green beans
1 teaspoon chopped chives or
  onions
2 tablespoons vegetable fat,
  low sodium (except coconut
  oil)
Dash of thyme
Dash of pepper
Dash of sugar

Drain liquid from beans into small saucepan. / Boil quickly until liquid is reduced to about 1/3 cup. / Add beans, fat and seasonings; / heat thoroughly. ● Serves 1-2.

SWEET AND SOUR WAX BEANS

1 pound yellow wax beans
2 tablespoons vegetable fat,
  low sodium (except coconut
  oil)
1 tablespoon chopped onion
1 tablespoon flour
2 tablespoons brown sugar
2 tablespoons vinegar
Paprika

Cook beans until just tender in boiling water. / Reserve cooking water; make up to 1 cup with boiling water if necessary. / Brown onion in fat, stir in flour, add bean liquid and cook until smooth and thick. / Add sugar and vinegar and cook 2 minutes longer. / Add cooked beans and reheat. / Serve with paprika. ● Serves 4.

SALAD DRESSINGS . . . .

LOW SODIUM MAYONNAISE

1 egg yolk
½ teaspoon dry mustard
1 teaspoon sugar

2 tablespoons lemon juice or
  vinegar
1 cup vegetable oil, low
  sodium (except coconut oil)

Beat together egg yolk, mustard, sugar and 1 tablespoon lemon juice. / Add oil very slowly, beating constantly. / Beat in remaining tablespoon lemon juice. / Chill in refrigerator. ● Makes 1 cup.

LOW SODIUM FRENCH DRESSING

½ cup vegetable oil, low
  sodium (except coconut oil)
¼ cup cider vinegar
¼ cup water

2 teaspoons sugar
1 teaspoon dry mustard
½ teaspoon paprika
Dash of pepper

Combine all ingredients; beat well with rotary beater, or shake well in jar with tight-fitting cover. ● Makes 1 cup.

DESSERTS . . . .

PUFFED RICE BALLS

1 cup sugar
½ cup water

2 teaspoons lemon juice
3 cups puffed rice

Boil the sugar, water and lemon juice to the hard-ball stage (275°F.). Pour the syrup very quickly over the puffed rice in a bowl. Make into small balls, allowing to cool on waxed paper. ● Makes 12.

FRUIT COBBLER

¼ cup softened vegetable fat,
  low sodium (except coconut
  oil)
1 cup sugar
¾ cup sifted all-purpose flour

4 cups sliced apples or 2 cups
  canned or cooked fruit
¼ cup water
1 teaspoon cinnamon

Heat oven to 350°F. / Grease 10 x 6 x 1½-inch baking dish. / Cream fat and sugar together. / Blend in flour, mixing well. / Place fruit in baking dish. / Sprinkle with water and cinnamon. / Spread flour mixture on top of fruit. / Bake in moderate oven (350°F.) 40 to 45 minutes. / Serve warm with or without lemon or spicy sauce. ● Serves 6.

SPICED APPLESAUCE

½ cup fresh or canned
  applesauce
2 teaspoons sugar or honey
Juice from ½ lemon

1/8 teaspoon nutmeg
Dash of cinnamon
Dash of ginger

Combine all ingredients; / heat thoroughly. / Serve hot or cold. / Pour the lemon juice over the applesauce. / Stir and serve. ● Serves 1.

LEMON SAUCE

1 tablespoon cornstarch
½ cup sugar
1 cup boiling water
1 tablespoon vegetable fat,
  low sodium (except coconut
  oil)

Grated rind of ½ lemon
¼ cup lemon juice

Mix cornstarch and sugar in a saucepan; stir in the boiling water. / Stir over direct heat until the mixture boils. / Add fat, lemon rind and lemon juice. ● Serves 4-6.

SPICY SAUCE
Mix ½ teaspoon cinnamon, ¼ teaspoon nutmeg and ¼ teaspoon cloves with 1 tablespoon vinegar; add to Lemon Sauce.

146

LOW SODIUM FOOD EXCHANGE GROUPS

Foods permitted

Foods to avoid

vegetables, low carbohydrate

Raw, cooked or canned without salt or fat; may be eaten as desired; one serving contains little or no calories and 9 mg. sodium

Asparagus
Beans, green
Broccoli
Brussel sprouts
Cauliflower
Celery*
Cabbage, fresh
Chicory
Cucumbers
Eggplant
Endive
Escarole
Lettuce
Mushrooms
Okra
Parsley
Peppers
Radishes
Squash, summer
Spinach*
Tomatoes
Salt-free tomato juice
Watercress

Canned vegetables (unless canned without salt)

The following vegetables are high in natural salt and must be omitted from the diet:

Beet greens
Chard
Swiss kale
Sauerkraut

vegetables, starchy

Only ½ cup of one of the following vegetables may be used per day; contains approximately 9 mg. sodium per serving; 7 gm. carbohydrate, 2 gm. protein and 35 calories.

Beets*
Carrots*
Onions
Peas
Pumpkin
Artichokes
Rutabagas
Winter squash

White turnips
Frozen peas

Fruits

Fresh dried, cooked or canned without added sugar; this list shows the amount of fruit to use for one serving; contains 2 mg. sodium; one serving contains 10 gm. carbohydrate and 40 calories.

*Vegetables allowed once a day if sodium allowance is 1,000 mg.

Foods permitted		Foods to avoid
		Canned tomato juice or vegetable
Apple	1 small	juices.
Applesauce	½ cup	Fruit or fruit products which contain
Apricots, fresh	2 medium	sodium bensoate, maraschino
Apricots, dried	4 halves	cherries; dried fruit sometimes has
Banana	½ small	sodium sulfate added, these should
Blackberries	1 cup	be avoided, read label (use only
Raspberries	1 cup	sundried fruits)
Blueberries	2/3 cup	
Strawberries	1 cup	
Cantaloupe	¼ medium	
Cherries	10 large	
Dates	2	
Figs, fresh	2 large	
Watermelon	1 cup	
Grapefruit juice	½ cup	
Grapes	12	
Grape juice	¼ cup	
Honeydew melon	1/8 medium	
Orange	1 small	
Orange juice	½ cup	
Peach	1 medium	
Pear	1 small	
Pineapple	½ cup	
Pineapple juice	1/3 cup	
Plums	2 medium	
Prunes, dried	2 medium	
Tangerine	1 large	

Bread

One serving contains 15 gm. carbohydrate; 2 gm. protein; 70 calories; 5 mgs. sodium
(substitute the following for one slice salt-free bread)

Salt-free passover		Regular bread and rolls
Matzoth,	½	Biscuit and popovers
Salt-free melba toast,	3	Salted or soda crackers
Low sodium toast		Pastries and cakes
(Nabisco),	2	Prepared muffins, waffles, cakes
Cooked cereals		Pancake and pastry mixes
(without salt),	½ cup	Self-rising flour
Pearl barley,		Cornmeal
rice, noodles,	½ cup	Quick cooking (5 minute) hot cereals
Macaroni, spaghetti,	½ cup	Dry cereals except those listed
Lima beans, fresh	½ cup	Pretzels, potato chips
Navy beans, dried,	½ cup	Salted popcorn
Soybeans, cowpeas,	½ cup	Frozen lima beans

Foods permitted		Foods to avoid

Bread—cont'd

Potato (white),	1 small	
Potato (sweet),	¼ cup	
Parsnips,	2/3 cup	
Corn (fresh, frozen, or canned unsalted or 1 small ear),	2/3 cup	
Puffed Wheat,		
Puffed Rice,	¾ cup	
Shredded Wheat	1 biscuit	
Popcorn, unsalted	1 cup	

Meats

One ounce contains 7 gm. protein; 5 gm. fat; 25 mgs. sodium; 75 calories; substitute the following for one ounce salt-free meat, (baked, broiled, stewed or pan broiled)

Foods permitted		Foods to avoid
Fresh or frozen beef, lamb, liver, pork, rabbit, veal, or tongue	1 ounce	All smoked, processed or canned meats, fish, or fowl, such as anchovies, caviar, herring, salted dry cod, bacon, oysters
Fresh fish (except shellfish)	1 ounce	Cold cuts
		Cornbeef or chipped beef
Fresh or frozen chicken, duck, turkey or quail	1 ounce	Frankfurters or sausages
		Brain, kidney
Canned salt-free tuna or salmon	¼ cup	Ham, smoked tongue, sausage
		All cheese except salt-free cheese
Salt-free peanut butter	1 tbsp.	Frozen fish fillets, clams, crab, lobster, shrimp, sardines, oysters, kosher meats.
Salt-free American cheese	1 ounce	Peanut butter, except salt-free
Salt-free cottage cheese (dry curd)	¼ cup	
Egg (no more than one a day)		

Fats

One serving contains 5 gms. fat; little or no sodium and 45 calories. Substitute the following for 1 teaspoon salt-free vegetable fat

Foods permitted		Foods to avoid
Butter, salt-free	1 tsp.	Salted butter, vegetable fats
Cream, light (sweet or sour)	2 tbsp.	Commercial mayonnaise or french dressing
Cream, heavy	1 tbsp.	Bacon fat and salty meat drippings and olives
Avocado	1/8	
French dressing, salt-free	1 tbsp.	Salted nuts

Foods permitted		Foods to avoid
Fats—cont'd		
Mayonnaise, salt-free	1 tsp.	
Olive or cooking fat	1 tsp.	
Nuts, unsalted	6 small	

NOTE: Seasonings, extracts, herbs and spices may be used to help the foods on your low sodium diet taste better. See list in Appendix.

SEASONINGS, EXTRACTS, HERBS AND SPICES

Low in Sodium May Be Used Freely		High in Sodium Do NOT Use
Allspice	Meat tenderizers, low-sodium dietetic	Vinegar
Almont extract	Mint	Wine if allowed
Anise seed	Mustard, dry, or mustard seed	Walnut extract
Basil	Nutmeg	Bouillon cubes, regular
Bay leaf	Onion, onion juice, or onion powder	Catsup
Bouillon cube, low-sodium dietetic if less than 5 mg. of sodium per cube	Orange extract	Celery flakes, seed, salt
Caraway seed	Oregano	Chili sauce
Cardamon	Paprika	Cyclamate, sodium (sugar substitute)
Catsup, low sodium dietetic	Parsley	Garlic salt
Chili powder	Pepper, fresh green or red	Horseradish, prepared with s
Chives	Pepper, black, red, or white	Meat extracts
Cinnamon	Peppermint extract	Meat sauces
Cloves	Pimiento peppers for garnish	Meat tenderizers
Cocoa (1 to 2 teaspoons)	Poppy seed	Monosodium glutamate
Coconut	Poultry seasoning	Mustard, prepared
Cumin	Purslane	Olives
Curry	Rosemary	Onion salt
Cyclamate, calcium (sugar substitute)	Saccharin, calcium (sugar substitute)	Parsley flakes
Dill	Saffron	Pickles
Fennel	Sage	Relishes
Garlic, garlic juice, or garlic powder	Salt substitutes, if recommended by the physician	Saccharin, sodium (sugar substitute)
Ginger	Savory	SALT
Horseradish root or horseradish prepared without salt	Sesame seeds	Salt substitutes, unless recommended by the physician
Juniper	Sorrel	Soy sauce
Lemon juice or extract	Sugar	Tomato paste
Mace	Tarragon	Worcestershire sauce
Maple extract	Thyme	
Marjoram	Tur rmeric	
Meat extract, low-sodium dietetic	Vanilla extract	

151

SPICES AND HERBS TO FLAVOR UNSALTED FOODS. Certain herbs have been found to blend or contrast better than others with various foods. The following suggestions may be found useful.

BEEF FOR STEAKS AND ROASTS: Season with pepper and mustard, sage, marjoram or thyme before cooking. *Or* after cooking, rub with herb butter flavored with garlic, parsley, thyme, dill or marjoram and a little lemon juice.

FOR HAMBURGER, MEAT LOAF OR STEWS: Add browned onion or mushrooms, chopped green pepper, chopped tomato, or one of the herbs above before cooking. A single stalk of celery or a bay leaf may be added to a pot of stew.

LAMB. FOR ROASTS OR CHOPS: Season with curry, garlic, mint, onion, parsley, rosemary, thyme or marjoram. *Or* use herb butter on chops after cooking.

LIVER. Use any herb butter, or parsley, onion or chives.

PORK. FOR CHOPS AND ROASTS: Rub with garlic, marjoram or lemon juice before cooking. *Or* cook with apples or apple sauce, onion or sage.

VEAL. FOR ROASTS AND CUTLETS: Try summer savory and chervil, or basil and marjoram. *Or* season with bay leaf, curry, garlic, ginger, mushrooms, oregano or paprika.

POULTRY. Choose one or more of these: fresh or dried leaves of celery, basil, marjoram, parsley, rosemary, summer savory, sage or thyme for the many dishes prepared from chicken, turkey or other poultry. Stuffing for poultry may be made with low sodium bread and unsalted butter or margarine.

FISH. Try lemon, garlic, dill or mustard butter on broiled or fried fish. Finely chopped dill, basil or tarragon leaves, or paprika add color and accent.

For boiled fish and chowders, chopped basil leaves, dill, or a dash of powdered thyme is the "right" flavor for some.

EGGS. Add finely minced chives or parsley, or a dash of curry to deviled, creamed or scrambled eggs for special accent.

Enhance omelets by adding one or more of the fine herbs—basil, marjoram, rosemary, tarragon or thyme. Finely chopped onion, green pepper or tomato are favorites for other egg mixtures. Salt-free mayonnaise may be used for egg salads or sandwiches.

VEGETABLES. Season these delicately for best results.
ASPARAGUS: Season with chives, lemon, caraway or herb butter.
CAULIFLOWER: Add nutmeg, herb butter.
CORN: Use chives, parsley, green pepper, onion or tomato.
PEAS: Use chives, mint, parsley, chervil or onion.
POTATOES: Parsley, chives, dill, onion, rosemary or mace may be added.
GREEN BEANS: Add onion, chives, scallion, dill, marjoram, nutmeg, rosemary or lemon.
SQUASH: Try lemon, ginger, mace, basil or chives.
TOMATOES: Use garlic, onion, parsley, basil or sage.

There are many other herbs and spices which will suggest themselves. The addition of oregano, dry mustard, leeks, chili powder, poultry seasoning, mint, sage, curry, cloves or mace will aid in giving variety of flavor and interest to many foods. The housewife who learns to experiment with these may find that the loss of salt as a flavor becomes greatly minimized.

A number of seasonings are either high in natural sodium or else have salt added in their preparation. These should never be used on the salt-restricted diet. See list in Appendix.

SALT SUBSTITUTES. A number of "salt substitutes" which owe their flavor to mineral salts other than sodium chloride are available. The most acceptable of these has a number of spices added as well. They are often a welcome addition to recipes for main dishes and soups. Salt substitutes should not be used without permission of the physician.

SODIUM IN FOODS AND BEVERAGES. SALT. Salt or sodium chloride, commonly used in cooking and preserving food, is approximately 40 percent sodium. Thus, 1 Gm. of salt (1,000 mg.) contains 0.4 Gm. or 400 mg. of sodium. It can readily be seen why salt, added to foods during cooking or at the table, must be omitted or used only in very limited amounts on sodium-restricted diets. Also foods which have had sodium added during processing or preservation are avoided.

Some examples of high sodium foods:

- One olive added to your salad or drink will add 130 milligrams to the diet.

- One ounce of processed cheddar cheese will increase the sodium in the diet 420 milligrams.
- A slice of regular commercial bread contains 150 milligrams sodium.
- One half can of tomato juice (canned) will add to the diet 275 milligrams of sodium.

CIRRHOSIS OF THE LIVER. Cirrohisis of the liver is a final stage of liver injury.

The Senate Committee report lists cirrhosis of the liver as one of the six leading causes of death in the United States. The over-consumption of fat generally and saturated fat in particular—as well as cholesterol sugar, salt and alcohol—have been related to the sixth leading cause of death.

The liver is a very quiet but extremely important organ of the body. Its daily functions in the metabolism of protein carbohydrates and fats. The liver regulates the distribution of the amino acids after protein is digested by the body. The liver converts glucose into glycogen, which is animal fat, and stores it. Energy, then, is regulated by the liver. In fat metabolism the liver oxidizes fatty acids to ketones. It converts excess glucose to fat for storage. The minerals and vitamins are handled by the liver. Iron is stored by the liver and distributed as needed in the synthesis of hemoglobin for the red blood cells. The liver stores Vitamin B_{12} needed for the development of red blood cells in the bone marrow and the liver stores Vitamin A.

Most of the Vitamin A stored in the body is stored in the liver. The conversion of carotene (yellow color in foods) into Vitamin A takes place in the liver. Other vitamins are found in the liver.

The liver produces bile which is important to digestion and absorption of fat. Bile is manufactured in liver cells and stored in the gall bladder. One of the components of bile is cholesterol.

Because of the important part the liver plays in the body's health maintenance it is a primary concern when the liver becomes diseased. A liver disease, hepatitis, is an infection of liver cells as a result of viral or bacterial infections, toxins or drugs. Acute hepatitis is characterized by headache, elevated body temperature, abdominal pain and loss of appetite. Most patients recover completely; however, it can reoccur. Often a patient with acute hepatitis is unable to consume much food due to severe lack of desire to eat, pain and nausea. A diet of high protein, high carbohydrate and moderate fat is usually the diet prescription after the intravenous fluids which have been administered in the early stages.

Hepatitis reoccurring can lead to cirrhosis or a final injury. However, it is thought that most deaths caused from this fatal disease are due to chronic alcoholism. Chronic alcoholism causes a deficiency in food intake over a long period of time. The individual may consume the total caloric need of 1200 to 2000 calories daily just from alcohol. Alcohol yields 7 calories for each 1 gram of alcohol consumed. There is little desire for food since hunger has been satisfied. The lack of protein which is necessary for metabolism of fat causes fat stasis and death of liver tissue. There is finally a replacement of liver cells by scar tissue or hardened tissues. At this same time vitamin and mineral deficiencies occur.

Uncontrolled diabetes can also, lead to cirrhosis of the liver.

Many patients with alcoholic cirrhosis suffer from a severe degree of malnutrition. There are a number of nutritional deficiencies since there has been an intake of "empty calories" over a long period of time.

As with any dietary treatment the meals are planned to help restore the malnourished body. The diet is increased in protein and carbohydrate in an effort to build back body tissues, supply the necessary vitamins and minerals and provide energy. The fat in the diet is restricted to a moderate amount to allow emptying of the stomach and higher intake of food.

A sample diet prescription for cirrhosis of the liver is listed for your better understanding of the recommendations of the Senate Committee.

Once cirrhosis of the liver has been diagnosed, the diet prescription has the objective of stimulating the liver to perform, its regular functions normally.

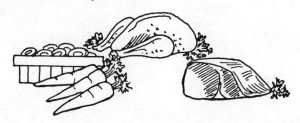

A SUGGESTED MENU CONTAINING 100 GRAMS OF PROTEIN, 120 GRAMS OF FAT, 300 GRAMS OF CARBOHYDRATE AND 2,550 CALORIES[1]

Food	Household Measure	Calories	Protein Gm.	Fat Gm.	Carbohydrate Gm.
Breakfast					
Citrus fruit	1 serving	43	1	–	10
Cereal	1 serving	89	3	1	18
Milk	8 ounces	160	8.5	9	12
Toast	1 slice	63	2	1	12
Vegetable Fat (except coconut oil)	1 teaspoon	34	–	4	–
Jelly	2 teaspoons	34	–	–	10
Coffee	–	–	–	–	–
Sugar	1 tablespoon	46	–	–	12
		469	14.5	15	74
Midmorning					
Milk	8 ounces	160	8.5	9	12
Chocolate syrup	2 tablespoons	98	–	–	26
		258	8.5	9	38
Lunch					
Meat	1 ounce	94	7.5	8	–
Bread	2 slices	126	4	1	24
Vegetable Fat (except coconut oil)	1 teaspoon	34	–	4	–
Egg	one	81	7	6	–
Salad, lettuce, tomatoes	1 serving	45	2	–	10
Mayonnaise	2 teaspoons	62	–	7	–
Milk	8 ounces	160	8.5	9	12
Fruit	1 serving	85	–	–	22
		687	29	35	68
Midafternoon					
As midmorning		258	8.5	9	38
Supper					
Meat	3 ounces	282	22.5	23	–
Potato	1 serving	65	2	–	15
Vegetable	1 serving	27	2	–	6
Vegetable Fat (except coconut oil)	1 teaspoon	34	–	4	–
Ice cream	1/6 quart	173	4	10	19
Tea	–	–	–	–	–
Sugar	2 teaspoons	32	–	–	8
		613	30.5	37	48

A SUGGESTED MENU CONTAINING 100 GRAMS OF PROTEIN, 120 GRAMS OF FAT, 300 GRAMS OF CARBOHYDRATE AND 2,550 CALORIES[1] —cont'd

Food	Household Measure	Calories	Protein Gm.	Fat Gm.	Carbohydrate Gm.
Evening					
Milk	8 ounces	160	8.5	9	12
Cookie	1 3-inch	109	2	3	19
		269	10.5	12	31
	Total Calories	2,554	101.5	117	297

[1]Recipes have not been presented since the diet is liberal enough to allow for increased intakes in protein, fat, carbohydrate. This pattern is a six meal plan. The pattern allows for any food the patient desires.

V

LIFE STYLES:
Nutrition for the Way You Live

202 EASY-TO-PREPARE RECIPES AND MENUS

DR. PAUL C. GLICK AND ARTHUR J. NORTON, specialists in marriage and family statistics at the U.S. Bureau of the Census, said in a recent report that new living patterns reflect significant changes in basic American attitudes about conformity with traditional behavior. They noted that both marriage and divorce rates are high and that the number of unmarried persons living together is increasing. In fact, during the early 1970s, statistics showed that one in every three marriages in the United States ended in divorce.

Such evidence leads many preachers, politicians and social scientists to throw up their hands and lament that the modern family is hopelessly in trouble. As one behavioral expert said recently, "The family has lost its power and sense of direction." And some anthropologists, sociologists and psychiatrists have written extensively of "the decline of the family."

These individuals may be rightly concerned. Times are changing. But the family is still the oldest and toughest of all human institutions. It has already outlasted gods, empires, class struggles, castes, and every manner of political management of society as a whole.

One way to strengthen the family is by eating at least one pleasant, unpressured meal together each day.

It is generally assumed that families perform what the social scientists call an affectionate function, serving as a source of love and providing a sense of belonging. Most people form the deepest and most lasting of their emotional involvements with members of their families,

and it is to the family that they are most likely to turn when disaster strikes. "Home," wrote Robert Frost, "is the place where, when you go there, they have to take you in."

The family provides the child his first lessons in getting along with people. The child learns the food habits and customs of his family as a part of his socialization process. Usually the food likes and dislikes of the family members are transmitted to the child. The child learns to associate foods with many factors. Unpleasant experiences associated with any one food may cause the child to dislike the food in adulthood. Love is transmitted, in part, through sufficient eating habits.

From culture to culture, the process of socialization seems to be different. Everywhere the family is a group of people devoted to bringing up children; yet, each culture has its own version of family life with its own goals, organization, ceremonies, stresses, and strains. Writings on the family say that, indeed, among the vast variety of shapes that family life has taken throughout the world, the 20th century Western family life counts as a special and almost eccentric case.

In three-fourths or more of the societies about which information is available, women are expected to carry out such tasks as grinding grain, carrying water, cooking and preserving food, repairing and making clothes, weaving, gathering food, and making pottery. A distinction in work is still made in the modern suburban family where the husband mows the lawn while the wife washes the dishes and stranghtens up the house. The woman's chores are considered additional tasks to child-bearing and rearing, although these patterns, too, are changing.

Today, in our society, the wife often works and the house at workday's end is as it was left in the morning. "We'll have to eat what's in the refrigerator since I had no time to plan a menu," she says at the end of the day. If she's home first she may have defrosted TV dinners. If not, the family may eat hamburgers or a pizza from the freezer. An empty refrigerator leads to, "Oh, I'm too tired to cook supper. Let's go out to eat." The children are hungry, the husband and wife are tired; they run to fill up against hunger, so often with hamburgers and cokes. The children, when the meal is at home, may want to watch television, rather than review their day around the supper table with their parents, while they eat.

160

Nowadays, often when families eat at home, the jangled nerves of parents combine with hunger, fussy children to create tension and stress, thus preventing proper digestion of the food. The family dinner table may be a place of dread when Dad comes home irritable from a hard day at the office and complains about each dish that Mom has struggled to prepare. Opening the day's mail while eating, he may see unexpected bills, repairs for broken windows Johnny has smashed with an errant football. The evening becomes a frightful experience. Indigestion, leftover (cast-aside would probably be more correct) food, and a kitchen filled with dirty dishes remain.

As we see, the American family lives with great stresses and strains. The pressures appear to be increasing. These pressures may ultimately strengthen family bonds, but their immediate effects are always disturbing.

Under stress the happiest family is unhappy. The imposed pressures of status, self-image, and stress have been observed to be factors directly influencing the family food patterns.

Throughout the human life-cycle, food not only serves to meet nutritional requirements for growth and physical maintenance but it also relates to personal, social and psychological development. In the early years the human cycle begins a phase of living critical to the next phase. Each phase presents a struggle, a great challenge, to be a positive experience. Each development problem at each period in life has a positive ego value with the alternative for a conflicting negative response:

- Infant—trusting or mistrusting.
- Toddler—autonomy or doubt and insecurity.
- Pre-school child—initiative or a feeling of guilt.
- School-age child—motivated or inferiority.
- Adolescent—identity as an individual or frustration and confusion.
- Young adult—feeling of relationship with others or isolated and alone.
- Adult—generativity or standing still.
- Elderly—ego integrity or a feeling of guilt, disappointment or despair.

While we should be aware of the circumstances that affect the human life-cycle throughout phases of living, we are mainly concerned in this chapter with how the lifestyles affect eating patterns.

Let us begin with the first phase.

CHILDREN Children are only tiny human beings—certainly not something fragile to be feared, fed and ignored. It is known today that very small babies understand much more about their surroundings and the personalities of their parents than we thought in the past.

The right food, love, and cleanliness will usually produce a satisfied infant. Love, of course, means so much more than that expressed in cuddling the baby and tucking him in at night. It means also that the parents respect their child as the young human he is and that they take upon themselves the full responsibility for being his first patient teacher.

The first food for the infant is milk. You may want to check on the nutritional value of human milk as compared with cow's milk. If your infant is on a prepared formula, then several suggestions may be helpful:

1. Keep all formula items clean.
2. Measure all ingredients accurately.
3. Remember that sterilizing requires about 25 minutes.
4. Leave the cap on a sterilized bottle loose to allow for steam.
5. After filled bottles have cooled, tighten caps and refrigerate.
6. After each feeding, dispose of all unused formula.

For a look at a sample of the usual progression of the infant diet, you may want to check on the calorie needs for children on a later page in this chapter.

The child loved and well fed has an optimistic future for growth and development into each following phase of the life-cycle.

The well-fed child will follow a feeding schedule that may be flexible, however, the suggested schedule below may serve as a guide.

SUGGESTED FEEDING SCHEDULE ON AN APPROXIMATE FOUR-HOUR BASIS

Age	Ounces per feeding	Number of feedings	Time of feedings
First week	2 to 3	6	6, 10, 2, 6, 10, 2
Two to four weeks	3 to 5	6	6, 10, 2, 6, 10, 2
Second to third months	4 to 6	5	6, 10, 2, 6, 10
Fourth and fifth months	5 to 7	5	6, 10, 2, 6, 10
Sixth and seventh months	7 to 8	4	6, 10, 2, 6
Eighth to twelfth months	8*	3	7, 12, 6

*4 oz. milk may be given midafternoon.

APPROXIMATE DAILY REQUIREMENTS OF CHILDREN FOR CALORIES, PROTEIN, AND WATER

Age in years	Calories		Protein	Water	
	per kg.*	per lb.	Gm. per kg.*	ml. per kg.*	oz. per lb.
Infancy	110	50	2.0 to 3.5	150	2¼
1 to 3	100	45	2.0 to 2.5	125	2.0–
4 to 6	90	41	3.0	100	1½
7 to 9	80	36	2.8	75	1.0
10 to 12	70	32	2.0	75	1.0
13 to 15	60	27	1.7	50	¾
16 to 19	50	23	1.5	50	¾
Adult	40	18	1.0	50	¾

*kg. or kilogram. A kilogram of body weight is 2.2 divided into body weight in pounds.

Note the nutritive value of human milk and cow's milk. The comparison is based on whole milk. You will want to read the label on purchased milk since they vary in quality. Be wary of imitation milks.

COMPARISON OF HUMAN MILK AND COW'S MILK

	Human milk			Whole cow's milk		
Water (%)	87	to	88	83	to	88
Protein (%)	1.0	to	1.5	3.2	to	4.1
Lactalbumin	0.7	to	0.8	0.5		
Casein	0.4	to	0.5	3.0		
Sugar (lactose) (%)	6.5	to	7.5	4.5	to	5.0
Fat (%)	3.5	to	4.0	3.5	to	5.2
	(more oleic acid and fewer of the volatile fatty acids)					
Minerals (%)	0.15	to	0.25	0.7	to	0.75
Calcium	0.034	to	0.045	0.222	to	0.179
Phosphorus	0.015	to	0.04	0.09	to	0.196
Magnesium	0.005	to	0.006	0.013	to	0.019
Sodium	0.011	to	0.019	0.05	to	0.06
Potassium	0.048	to	0.065	0.138	to	0.172
Iron	0.0001			0.00004		
Vitamins (per 100 ml.)						
A (I.U.)	60	to	500	80	to	220
D (I.U.)	0.4	to	10.0	0.3	to	4.4 (+ 400 per qt.)
C (I.U.)	1.2	to	10.8	0.9	to	1.4
Thiamine (mg.)	0.002	to	0.036	0.03	to	0.4
Riboflavin (mg.)	0.015	to	0.080	0.10	to	0.26
Niacin (mg.)	0.10	to	0.20	0.10		
Digestion				Occurs less rapidly		
Emptying of stomach				Occurs less rapidly		
Curd	Soft, flacculent			Hard, large		
Calories per fluid oz.	20			29		

I.U. international units
mg. milligrams (1000 = 1 gram)

As the baby grows from infant stage, solid food will be needed to meet the needs for growth and development.

GUIDELINE FOR ADDITION OF SOLID FOODS TO INFANT'S DIET DURING THE FIRST YEAR

When to start	Foods added	Feeding
First month	Vitamins A, D and C in multi-vitamin preparation (according to prescription)	Once daily at a feeding time.
Second to third month	Cereal and strained cooked fruit; Egg yolk (at first, hard boiled and sieved, soft boiled or poached later)	10:00 a.m. and 6:00 p.m.
Third to fourth month	Strained cooked vegetable and strained meat	2:00 p.m.
Fifth to seventh month	Zwelback or hard toast	At any feeding
Seventh to ninth month	Meats: beef, lamb, or liver (broiled or baked and finely chopped)	10:00 or 6:00 p.m.
	Potato: baked or boiled and mashed or sieved	

Suggested meal plan for age eight months to one year or older		
7:00 a.m.	Milk	8 oz.
	Cereal	2 to 3 tbsp.
	Strained fruit	2 to 3 tbsp.
	Zweiback or dry toast	
12:00 noon	Milk	8 oz.
	Vegetables	2 to 3 tbsp.
	Chopped meat or one whole egg	
	Puddings or cooked fruit	2 to 3 tbsp.
3:00 p.m.	Milk	4 oz.
	Toast, zweiback, or crackers	
6:00 p.m.	Milk	8 oz.
	Whole egg or chopped meat	
	Potato, baked or mashed	2 tbsp.
	Pudding or cooked fruit	2 to 3 tbsp.
	Zweiback or toast	

MENU PATTERN AND SAMPLE MEALS FOR CHILDREN BETWEEN ONE AND SIX YEARS OF AGE
Daily Intake Pattern Based on the Basic Four Food Groups for an Adequate Diet

Milk Group	Meat Group	Fruit and Vegetable Group	Bread-Cereal-Potato-Legume Group	Fats and Sweets
Ages 4-6				
1 quart milk	3 ounces cooked beef, veal, pork, lamb, liver poultry, fish, cheese, or one egg	4 servings A dark green or deep yellow vegetable is important for vitamin A, citrus fruits rich in vitamin C are important	5 servings	Without this group the diet contains 1,355 calories 5 teaspoons fat or oil add 225 calories.
Ages 1-4				
3-4 cups milk	3-4 tablespoons meat or alternate	3 servings or 6 tbsp fruit	5 servings breads-cereals	4 teaspoons sugar, jelly, or honey add 80 calories.

Sample Meals

Breakfast	Lunch	Dinner	Between Meal Snack 10:00 a.m., 3:00 p.m. and Bedtime
Orange juice Enriched farina with sugar Toast with spread 1 glass milk	Broiled ground beef Baked potato Carrot rings Bread with spread Ice cream 1 glass milk	Liver in tomato sauce Shredded lettuce Bread with spread Baked apple* or Apple Betty 1 glass milk	1 glass milk

A bedtime snack is planned to prevent the body from not having enough energy to wake you up early each morning. The child's body should not be without food for long periods of time. Routine intake of the same amounts of food is desirable.
NOTE: The amount of food a child will consume at any age will be determined by body size, height and activity.

RECIPES

To assist you with meal planning.

SOUPS . . . .

MEATBALL SUPPER SOUP

1¼ cups condensed mushroom
  soup, undiluted
1 cup milk
1 teaspoon instant minced
  onions

2 cups of meaballs in beef
  gravy
1 tablespoon finely chopped
  parsley

In medium saucepan, combine all ingredients except parsley.
Bring to boiling, stirring. / Serve in bowls, sprinkled with parsley.
• Serves 6.

MAIN DISHES . . . .

BARBECUE BAKED BEANS

4 cups cooked or canned
  brown beans
1 all-meat frankfurter,
  chopped

¼ cup light molasses
1 teaspoon Worcestershire
  sauce
2 tablespoons prepared
  mustard

Preheat oven to 350°F. In 1½ quart casserole, combine beans
with rest of ingredients, stirring gently to mix well. / Bake,
uncovered, 30 minutes. • Serves 6 to 8.

CHICKEN-CORN PILAF

¼ cup vegetable fat (except
  coconut oil)
1½ cups cooked rice
1 chicken bouillon cube
1 cup boiling water
½ teaspoon salt

½ cup boned chicken,
  coarsely chopped
1 cup whole kernel corn,
  drained
2 tablespoons finely chopped
  pimiento

In medium skillet, saute rice in vegetable fat stirring frequently,
until golden brown. / Add remaining ingredients, mixing well. /
Cook, tightly covered and over low heat, 5 minutes. / Serve with
sliced tomatoes, if desired. • Serves 4.

EASY TUNA CASSEROLE

1½ cups condensed cream of
  mushroom soup, undiluted
½ cup milk
1 cup tuna, drained

1 cup green peas
2 tablespoons sliced
  pimiento-stuffed olives
2 cups corn chips, crushed

Preheat oven to 375°F. In 1½ quart casserole, combine soup
with milk, mixing until smooth. / Add tuna, peas, and olives,
mixing well. / Top with corn chips. / Bake, uncovered, 25
minutes. • Serves 6.

EGGS A LA KING

1½ cup condensed cream of
  mushroom soup, undiluted
½ cup milk

4 hard-cooked eggs, coarsely
  chopped
4 corn muffins, toasted
Chopped parsley

In medium saucepan, combine soup and milk, mixing well. Bring
to boiling, stirring constantly. Carefully stir in eggs; reheat
gently. Serve hot, over corn muffins. Sprinkle with parsley. •
Serves 4.

SLOPPY JOES

½ pound ground beef
2 cups cooked beans
¼ cup barbeque sauce

¼ cup catsup
2 hamburger buns, split and
  toasted

In medium skillet, saute meat, stirring, until it loses its red color.
/ Add beans, barbeque sauce and catsup, mixing well. / Simmer,
uncovered, 5 minutes. / Spoon mixture over buns. • Serves 4.

SPAGHETTI MEAT LOAF

1 pound ground chuck
½ cup finely chopped onion
1 egg, slightly beaten

1 teaspoon seasoned salt
2 cups spaghetti in tomato
  sauce

Preheat oven to 350°F. / Lightly grease an 8 by 8 by 2 inch
baking dish. / Lightly toss chuck with onion, egg, salt, and
spaghetti, to combine. Pack mixture into prepared pan; bake,
uncovered, 1 hour. / To serve, cut into squares. • Serves 8.

EGGS IN A FRAME

1 white bread slice	1 egg
1 tablespoon soft vegetable fat (except coconut oil)	Dash of salt

Spread both sides of bread with fat. / With round 2½ inch cookie cutter, cut out center. / In small skillet with tight-fitting lid, saute bread slice and bread round, uncovered, until golden on both sides. / Remove bread round from skillet; keep warm. / Carefully break egg into center of bread slice; cook, covered, 4 to 5 minutes, or until egg is set. / With pancake turner, remove to serving plate; sprinkle egg lightly with salt. / If desired, spread bread round with deviled ham; place on top of egg. ● Serves 1.

PEANUTBURGERS

1 pound ground chuck	1/8 teaspoon pepper
1/8 teaspoon salt	¼ cup crunchy style peanut butter

Lightly toss chuck with rest of ingredients, in large bowl, to combine. / Gently shape into 6 patties. / Broil, 4 inches from heat, 6 minutes on one side. / Turn. Broil 4 minutes on other side, for medium.
Variations: RELISHBURGERS—Proceed as directed above, omitting peanut butter; / add 2 tablespoons chili sauce and ½ teaspoon instant minced onion. / OLIVEBURGERS—Proceed as directed above, substituting 2 tablespoons chopped stuffed olives for peanut butter. ● Serves 6.

SCRAMBLED EGGS IN TOAST CUPS

4 white bread slices	¼ teaspoon salt
2 tablespoons vegetable fat (except coconut oil) melted	Dash pepper
4 eggs	1 tablespoon vegetable fat (for skillet) (except coconut oil)
¼ cup milk	

Preheat oven to 350°F. / Trim crusts from bread slices. Brush both sides with melted fat. / Press a slice into each of 4 (6 ounce) custard cups or muffin tins. / Place on cookie sheet; / bake until bread is toasted. / Meanwhile, in small bowl, with rotary beater, beat eggs with milk, salt, and pepper until well combined. / Heat fat in medium skillet until a little cold water sizzles when dropped on it. / Pour egg mixture into skillet; cook slowly until eggs start to set. / Then stir constantly with fork until eggs are soft and creamy. / Fill toast cups with egg mixture. / If desired, sprinkle with crumbled, cooked bacon or chopped parsley. ● Serves 4.

SALADS . . . .

PETER RABBIT SALAD

3 ounce cream cheese	Spinach leaves
1/3 cup grated carrot	1 cup pineapple tidbits, drained
3 parsley sprigs	

Divide cream cheese into 3 parts. / With hands, shape each part to resemble a carrot 3 inches long. Roll cream cheese carrots in grated carrot, coating completely. / Insert a parsley sprig in top of each. / Serve on spinach leaves; garnish with pineapple tidbits. / Serve with mayonnaise, if desired. / Grate carrot directly onto paper towel; pat dry with another paper towel. ● Serves 3.

CARROT-RAISIN SALAD

1 cup grated raw carrot	2 tablespoons lemon juice
1 cup shredded cabbage	¼ cup mayonnaise or cooked salad dressing*
¼ cup seedless raisins	
½ teaspoon salt	

Lightly toss carrot, cabbage, raisins, salt, lemon juice, until well combined. / Refrigerate until ready to serve. / Just before serving, toss with mayonnaise.

STUFFED CELERY

For a special treat, stuff chilled crisp celery stalks with one of the following: (Celery stalk should be cut 2 inches long)
●Combine 1 cup creamed cottage cheese with 1 tablespoon chopped stuffed olives. / Makes 1 cup. ●Combine 3 ounces of soft cream cheese with 2 tablespoons drained crushed pineapple. / Makes ½ cup. ●Blend ½ cup pasteurized process cheese spread with 2 teaspoons drained sweet-pickle relish. / Makes ½ cup. ● Use creamy or crunchy-style peanut butter.

SANDWICHES ....

SANDWICH CUTOUTS

3 ounces soft cream cheese
¼ cup orange marmalade
6 white bread slices

6 whole wheat bread slices
3 tablespoons soft vegetable
    fat (except coconut oil)

In small bowl, combine cheese with marmalade, mixing until well combined. / With sharp knife, trim crusts from bread. / With animal shape cookie cutter, cut out center of 3 white bread slices and 3 whole wheat bread slices. / Set cutouts and cutout bread slices aside. / Spread remaining bread slices with fat; then spread with cream cheese mixture. / Top with cutout bread slice; fit in animal cutout of contrasting color bread. ● Serves 6.

VEGETABLE ROLL-UPS

10 fresh white bread slices
½ cup soft vegetable fat
    (except coconut oil)
½ cup grated sharp Cheddar
    cheese

Fillings: 10 (3 inch) carrot
sticks, celery sticks, green
pepper strips, or cooked
asparagus spears

Trim crust from bread; / flatten each slice with rolling pin. / In small bowl, mix fat with cheese. / Spread on bread slices. / Place one of fillings along one side; roll up as for a jelly roll. / Wrap each roll securely in waxed paper. / Place seam side down on tray, and refrigerate at least 1 hour before serving.
TOASTED VEGETABLE ROLL-UPS: Make Vegetable Roll-ups, as directed above. / Run under broiler. 4 inches from heat, until golden-brown. / Serve immediately. ● Serves 10.

BLUSHING PUPPY

1 cup tomato sauce
1½ cups condensed Cheddar
    cheese soup, undiluted

¼ teaspoon dry mustard
4 white bread slices, toasted
4 crisp bacon slices, crumbled

In small saucepan, combine tomato sauce with cheese soup and mustard, mixing well. / Over medium heat, bring to boiling, / stirring constantly. / Serve over toast. / Sprinkle with bacon. ● Serves 4.

BREADS ....

MILK TOAST

2 cups milk

4 white bread slices, toasted
    and spread with vegetable
    fat (except coconut oil)

Heat milk in small saucepan just until bubbles form around edge of pan. / Remove from heat; let cool slightly. / Serve toast slices in individual soup plates with ½ cup warm milk poured over each.
Variations:
CINNAMON-SUGAR MILK TOAST: Combine ¼ cup sugar with ½ teaspoon cinnamon, mixing well. / Proceed as directed for Milk Toast, sprinkling toast slices with cinnamon-sugar mixture.
BANANA MILK TOAST: Proceed as directed for Milk Toast, arranging a few banana slices over each toast slice. ● Serves 4.

DESSERTS ....

DANIELLE MARIE FUDGE COTTAGE PUDDING

1½ cups sifted cake flour
1 cup sugar
1/3 cup sifted unsweetened
    cocoa
1 teaspoon baking soda
¾ teaspoon salt

1/3 cup vegetable oil (except
    coconut oil)
1 teaspoon vanilla extract
1 teaspoon white vinegar
1 cup cold water
1 quart soft vanilla ice cream
    or vanilla ice milk

Preheat oven to 350°F. / Sift flour with sugar, cocoa, baking soda, and salt into ungreased 8 by 8 by 2-inch pan, shake pan to distribute flour mixture evenly. / Make 3 wells in center of flour mixture. / Pour oil into one, vanilla into second, and vinegar into third. / Pour 1 cup cold water over mixture; stir until smooth and well combined. / Batter will be thin. / Bake 30 to 35 minutes, or until cake tester inserted in center comes out clean. / Let cool slightly on wire rack. / Cut into squares while still warm, and serve with ice cream. ● Serves 6.

STUFFED DATES

¾ cup pitted dates
About 21 miniature
  marshmallows or ¼ cup
  walnut or pecan halves, or ¼
  cup creamy peanut butter

Flaked coconut or
  confectioners' sugar

Stuff each date with a marshmallow, a nut, or ½ teaspoon peanut butter. / Then roll in coconut or confectioners' sugar. • Makes about 21.

SPICY APPLE BETTY

2 cups sliced apples
6 tablespoons light-brown
  sugar
salt (dash)
¼ teaspoon cinnamon

2 cups cornflakes, crushed
¼ cup vegetable fat (except
  coconut oil) melted
1½ cups soft vanilla ice cream
  or vanilla iced milk

Preheat oven to 400°F. / In a quart casserole, combine apples with 2 tablespoons sugar, salt, and cinnamon. / Mix cornflakes with remaining sugar and fat and spread over apples. / Bake 20 minutes. / Top with vanilla ice cream or milk. • Serves 4-6.

MICHAEL CHRISTOPHER'S CHOO CHOO SOUFFLE

1 cup sugar
3 tablespoons soft vegetable
  fat (except coconut oil)
3 tablespoons flour
2 egg yolks, slightly beaten

Juice and grated rind of 1
  lemon
1 cup milk
2 egg whites, stiffly beaten

Cream sugar and fat. / Add flour, beaten egg yolks, juice, rind, and milk. / Mix well. / Fold in stiffly beaten egg whites. / Pour into quart casserole. / Put in pan of hot water and bake in moderate oven, 350°F. for one hour. • Serves 6 to 8.

DANIELLE'S MOUSSE IN ORANGE SHELLS

8 medium oranges
¾ cup orange juice
1 teaspoon grated orange peel
1 cup sugar
6 egg yolks

1 pint heavy cream
2 teaspoons vanilla
2 tablespoons lemon juice

Slice off the top of the oranges and scoop out the pulp and meat; dry. / Measure ¾ cup orange juice and combine with sugar. / Cook until mixture is at jelly stage, 220°F. / Place egg yolks in top of double boiler, gradually beating in hot syrup. / Place over cold water, beating until cool. / Whip cream until stiff and fold in vanilla, lemon juice, and lemon and orange peels. / Fold into yolk mixture. / Spoon mousse into orange shells. / Cover and freeze until firm. / Remove from freezer 30 minutes before serving. / Garnish with mint leaves. • Serves 8.
NOTE: This recipe may appear high in saturated fat. Since children expend energy at a high rate, the fat content should not be a concern as an occasional treat.

CHOCOLATE ICE CREAM CONES

¾ cup semisweet chocolate
  pieces or butterscotch pieces
12 ice cream cones

Decorations
3 pint assorted ice cream or
  ice milk

Melt chocolate over hot, not boiling water. / With small spatula, spread 1 tablespoon melted chocolate inside each cone. / Swirl top edge of cone in chocolate; spread to make a ¾ inch deep border. / Decorate as desired. / Refrigerate until serving. / Top with ice cream or ice milk. • Serves 12.

PEANUT BUTTER ICE CREAM CONES

½ cup creamy peanut butter,
  softened
12 ice cream cones

3 pint assorted ice cream or
  ice milk

With small spatula, spread peanut butter around top edge and side of cones to make a border ¾ inch deep. / Decorate or sprinkle with one or more decorations. / Top each with scoop of ice cream or ice milk. • Serve at once.
DECORATIONS FOR ICE CREAM CONES: Chocolate covered peanuts; miniature marshmallows, halved crosswise; miniature chocolate sprinkles; colored sprinkles; chopped walnuts; red and green sugar; chopped coconut or light or dark chopped raisins. •
Variation: ¾ cup semisweet chocolate pieces or butterscotch pieces melted over hot water and spread inside each cone.

CRISPY-CARAMEL LOLLIPOPS

1¾ cups or 25 vanilla caramels   4 cups oven-toasted rice cereal
3 tablespoons water

In top of double boiler, combine caramels with 3 tablespoons water. / Cook, over hot water, stirring occasionally, until caramels are melted. / Pour caramel mixture over cereal in medium bowl; stir with wooden spoon until cereal is well coated. / Pack cereal mixture into 4 small paper cups. / Insert wooden skewer into center of each. / Refrigerate at least 30 minutes. / To serve, gently remove lollipops from paper dishes. ● Serves 4.

HEAVENLY HASH

2 cups cold cooked white rice,   ¼ cup maraschino cherries,
  loosely packed   drained and sliced
1 cup pineapple tidbits,   12 marshmallows, quartered
  drained   (or use 1½ cups miniature
                                       marshmallows
                                     1 cup heavy cream whipped

In medium bowl, lightly toss rice with pineapple, cherries, and marshmallows, to combine. / Refrigerate, covered, 1 hour. / Fold in whipped cream just before serving. / Top with additional cherries, if desired. Use miniature marshmallows. ● Serves 6.

MICHAEL'S RAGGEDY ANN PUDDINGS

2 cups vanilla custard (see   1 maraschino cherry, slivered
  Recipe page 00)   10 seedless raisins
4 chocolate wafers, crushed

Prepare vanilla pudding as recipe directs. / Pour into 4 to 5 shallow, round dessert dishes. / Refrigerate 30 minutes, or until well chilled. To decorate pudding; make a face from tip of spoon, sprinkle some of crushed wafers halfway around edge of each pudding to make hair. / Use cherry sliver for the mouth; two raisins for eyes and one raisin chopped in half for nose. / Serve immediately. ● Serves 4.

HALLOWEEN PARTY No other time of year provides a better opportunity for the colorful decorations children love so well. Halloween cutouts of witches, owls, and black cats may be hung in the living room. Have children help you make decorations; it will be a fun time for them. Use Halloween paper plates and napkins. Fill small paper cups with assorted Halloween candy; set at each plate.

Let your child help make the invitations: orange jack-o-lanterns or round black cats, cut out of construction paper. Make costumes mandatory. Have a prize wrapped for the best costume.

MENU
Sloppy Joes*
Halloween Cake (*Chocolate Cake)
with Fudge Frosting, Decorated
with candy corn
Ice Cream or Ice Milk
Hot Cocoa with Marshmallow

CHILDREN'S THANKSGIVING A table just for children at Thanksgiving is an old custom in many homes. It eliminates a gread deal of confusion at traditionally large family gatherings. The children love helping to make decorations for their own table. Make sure the children's table looks like more fun than the adults.

Set up the table in the same room as the adults' table—or choose an out-of-the-way spot, away from the main kitchen traffic. Also, provide special food surprises for the children: Hollow out orange halves, to make baskets for cranberry sauce. Or with animal-shape cutters, cut out cranberry jelly. Or cut celery stalks into 5-inch pieces; stuff with cheese spread. Spear an olive and radish on a wooden pick; insert into each piece of celery.

CHILDREN'S BIRTHDAY PARTIES A child's introduction to the world of party-going and giving is almost certain to be a birthday party. Make it very gay and very traditional, with ribbon-tied packages, paper hats, bright balloons, and noisy snap crackers.

To make the occasion happily memorable, let the young host or hostess answer the door. Plan plenty of games, in case one or two fail to hold youngsters interest. Sure-fire for preschoolers: Pin the tail on the donkey, musical chairs, a tub of water and floating toys, bubble pipes. If outdoor activities are on the agenda, be sure to have rainy day substitutes. Plan a story to read or coloring books and crayons for everybody.

BIRTHDAY PARTY MENUS

Tiny Chicken-Salad Sandwiches*
Tiny Celery Sticks and Carrot Curls
Strawberry Ice Cream   Pink Posy Cake*
(See Recipe for Lazy Daisy Cake on page 219.
Cover cake with white frosting. Decorate cake
with fresh pink rose buds. Remove as necessary
for serving cake.)
Cranberry Juice with Gingerale

Peanutburgers*
Peter Rabbit Salad*
Wagon-Train Birthday Cake
(Chocolate Cake* decorated
with fresh fruit cut in pieces
and arranged to assemble wagon-train)
Ice Cream or Ice Milk
Fresh Orange Juice with Gingerale

*Recipe included in book.

173

MENU PATTERN AND SAMPLE MEALS FOR CHILDREN BETWEEN SIX AND FIFTEEN YEARS OF AGE

Daily Intake Based on Basic Four Food Group Recommended in Illustration Chapter VI

Milk Group	Meat Group	Fruit and Vegetable Group	Bread-Cereal-Potato-Legume Group	Fats and Sweets
Ages 12-15				
1 quart milk	5-6 ounces of cooked beef, pork, veal, lamb, poultry, or fish	4 servings or more including A dark green or deep yellow vegetable daily for Vitamin A value and A citrus fruit or other fruit rich in Vitamin C daily	7 servings	Without this group the diet contains 1,645 calories. NOTE: 10 teaspoons fat or oil contain 450 calories. 10 teaspoons sugar, jelly, or honey contain 200 calories.
Ages 6-12				
3-4 cups	3-4 ounces	3-4 servings	5-6 servings	4-5 servings

Sample Menu Pattern

Breakfast	Lunch	Dinner	Bedtime Snack
1 citrus fruit or ½ cup juice ½ cup cereal 1 slice toast with spread 1 glass milk (non-fat may be substituted) if overweight)	2 ounces meat, poultry, fish, cheese, or eggs ½ cup potato or substitute Dark green or deep yellow vegetable 1 slice enriched or whole grain bread with spread Dessert (see examples throughout book) 1 glass milk (non-fat may be substituted if overweight)	1 egg or 1 ounce cheese, meat, poultry, or fish Vegetable, raw or cooked 1 slice enriched or whole wheat bread with spread Fruit (any) 1 glass milk (non-fat may be substituted if overweight)	1 glass milk (non-fat may be substituted if overweight) Sandwich Whole wheat bread Lean ham Tomato, lettuce, mayonnaise (special mayonnaise may be substituted for regular if overweight (See Recipe page 00)

Milk may be non-fat, buttermilk or whole milk, if weight is a problem decrease fat, and sugar, therefore, reducing calories. The body size, height-weight and activity will determine the individual needs of the adolescent.

STUDENT

Check signs for good and poor nutritional status during the young person's student years, page 00. It is apparent that nutritional resources to meet physical growth are conditioned by the food habits and feeding practices that are psychologically and culturally derived. Large numbers of growing children have these resources and arrive at adulthood vigorous and happy. Many other children do not.

Studies show that adolescent boys are better off than the girls when it comes to pressures influencing eating habits. They require a large amount of food, which usually assures them adequate nutrients. The adolescent girl may be less fortunate. She may become weight-conscious, eat less food and consume less than required food nutrients.

A check on the recommended daily dietary allowances for growth in the Appendix may help you compare the prescribed need compared with actual intake. See food intake chart.

Students usually have the opportunity to eat a pre-planned meal at school if they are away from home. It has been found, however, that many students use the snatch-and-grab method of eating because of schedule pressures.

The menus and recipes for ages 12 to 15 and fat students have been presented to help you eat right through these days on the go. You will want to make the most of the food intake. You will not want to pay tomorrow for today's poor eating habits.

CLINICAL SIGNS OF NUTRITIONAL STATUS

	Good	Poor
General appearance	Alert, responsive	Listless, apathetic, cachexic
Hair	Shiny, lustrous; healthy scalp	Stringy, dull, brittle, dry, depigmented
Neck (glands)	No enlargement	Thyroid enlarged
Skin (face and neck)	Smooth, slightly moist, good color, reddish-pink mucous membranes	Greasy, discolored, scaly
Eyes	Bright, clear; no fatigue circles beneath	Dryness, signs of infection, increased vascularity, glassiness, thickened conjunctiva
Lips	Good color, moist	Dry, scaly, swollen; angular lesions (stomatitis)
Tongue	Good pink color, surface papillae present, no lesions	Papillary atrophy, smooth appearance; swollen, red, beefy (glossitis)
Gums	Good pink color; no swelling or bleeding, firm	Marginal redness or swelling, receding, spongy
Teeth	Straight, no crowding, well-shaped jaw, clean, no discoloration	Unfilled caries, absent teeth, worn surfaces, mottled, malposition
Skin (general)	Smooth, slightly moist, good color	Rough, dry, scaly, pale, pigmented, irritated, petechia, bruises
Abdomen	Flat	Swollen
Legs, feet	No tenderness, weakness, or swelling; good color	Edema, tender calf, tingling, weakness
Skeleton	No malformations	Bowlegs, knock-knees, chest deformity at diaphragm, beaded ribs, prominent scapulae
Weight	Normal for height, age, body build	Overweight or underweight
Posture	Erect, arms and legs straight, abdomen in, chest out	Sagging shoulders, sunken chest, humped back
Muscles	Well-developed, firm	Flaccid, poor tone; undeveloped, tender
Nervouc control	Good attention span for age; does not cry easily, not irritable or restless	Inattentive, irritable
Gastrointestinal function	Good appetite and digestion; normal, regular elimination	Anorexia, indigestion, constipation or diarrhea
General vitality	Endurance, energetic, sleeps well at night; vigorous	Easily fatigued, no energy, falls asleep in school, looks tired, apathetic

RECOMMENDED DAILY DIETARY ALLOWANCES FOR GROWTH (NATIONAL RESEARCH COUNCIL 1968 AND 1974 REVIEWS)

	Age	Weight		Height		Energy	Protein	Fat-soluble vitamins				Water-soluble vitamins							Minerals					
								Vit. A		Vit. D	Vit. E	Vit. C	Fola-cin	Nia-cin	Ribo-flavin	Thia-mine	Vit. B6	Vit. B12	Cal-cium	Phos-phorus	Iodine	Iron	Mag-nesium	Zinc
	yrs.	kg.	lbs.	cm.	in.	kcal.	Gm.	R.E.	I.U.	I.U.	I.U.	mg.	µg.	mg.	mg.	mg.	mg.	µg.	mg.	mg.	µg.	mg.	mg.	mg.
Infants	Birth-0.5	6	14	60	24	kg x 117 (770)	kg x 2.2 (14)	420	1,400 (1,500)	400	4	35	50	5	0.4 (0.6)	0.3 (0.5)	0.3	0.3	360 (500)	240	35	10	60	3
	0.5-1	9	20	71	28	kg x 108 (900)	kg x 2.0 (16)	400	2,000 (1,500)	400	5	35	50	8	0.6 (0.8)	0.5	0.4	0.3	540 (600)	400	45	15	70	5
Children	1-3	13	28	86	34	1,300 (1,250)	23 (25)	400	2,000	400	7	40	100	9 (8)	0.8 (0.7)	0.7 (0.6)	0.6	1.0	800	800	60	15	150	10
	4-6	20	44	110	44	1,800 (1,600)	30	500	2,500	400	9	40	200	12 (11)	1.1 (0.9)	0.9 (0.8)	0.9	1.5	800	800	80	10	200	10
	7-10	30	66	135	54	2,400 (2,200)	36 (40)	700	3,300 (3,500)	400	10	40	300	16 (15)	1.2	1.2 (1.1)	1.2	2.0	800	800	110	10	250	10
Males	11-14	44	97	158	63	2,800 (2,700)	44 (50)	1,000	5,000	400	12	45	400	18	1.5 (1.4)	1.4	1.6	3.0	1,200 (1,400)	1,200	130	18	350	15
	15-18	61	134	172	69	3,000	54 (60)	1,000	5,000	400	15	45 (55)	400	20	1.8 (1.5)	1.5 (1.4)	2.0	3.0	1,200 (1,400)	1,200	150	18	400	15
Females	11-14	44	97	155	62	2,400 (2,300)	44 (50)	800	4,000 (5,000)	400	12	45	400	16 (15)	1.3 (1.4)	1.2	1.6	3.0	1,200 (1,300)	1,200	115	18	300	15
	15-18	54	119	162	65	2,100 (2,300)	48 (55)	800	4,000 (5,000)	400	12	45 (50)	400	14 (15)	1.4 (1.5)	1.1 (1.2)	2.0	3.0	1,200 (1,300)	1,200	115	18	300	15

*The 1974 recommendation is listed first with the previous 1968 recommendation in parentheses under . . . .

FOOD INTAKE FOR GOOD NUTRITION ACCORDING TO FOOD GROUPS AND THE AVERAGE SIZE OF SERVINGS AT DIFFERENT AGE LEVELS

Food group	Servings per day	Average size of servings at each age level					
		1 year	2 to 3 years	4 to 5 years	6 to 9 years	10 to 12 years	13 to 15 years
Milk and cheese (1.5 oz. cheese = 1 cup milk)	4	½ cup	½ to ¾ cups	¾ cup	¾ to 1 cup	1 cup	1 cup
Meat group (protein foods)	At least 3						
Egg		1 egg	1 egg	1 egg	1 egg	1 egg	1 or more
Lean meat, fish, poultry (liver once a week)		2 tbsp.	2 tbsp.	4 tbsp.	2-3 oz. (4-6 tbsp.)	3-4 oz.	4 oz. or more
Peanut butter			1 tbsp.	2 tbsp.	2-3 tbsp.	3 tbsp.	3 tbsp.
Fruits and vegetables	At least 4, including:						
Vitamin C source (citrus fruit, berries, tomato, cabbage, cantaloupe)	1 or more (twice as much tomato as citrus)	1/3 cup citrus	½ cup	½ cup	1 med. orange	1 med. orange	1 med. orange
Vitamin A source (green or yellow fruits and vegetables)	1 or more	2 tbsp.	3 tbsp.	4 tbsp. (¼ cup)	¼ cup	1/3 cup	¾ cup
Other vegetables (potato, legumes) or	2 or more	2 tbsp.	3 tbsp.	4 tbsp.	1/3 cup	½ cup	¾ cup
Other fruits (apple, banana)		¼ cup	1/3 cup	½ cup	1 medium	1 medium	1 medium
Cereals (whole grain or enriched)	At least 4						
Bread		½ slice	1 slice	1½ slices	1-2 slices	2 slices	2 slices
Ready-to-eat cereals		½ oz.	¾ oz.	1 oz.	1 oz.	1 oz.	1 oz.
Cooked cereal (including pastes, rice, etc.)		¼ cup	1/3 cup	½ cup	½ cup	¾ cup	1 cup or more
Fats and carbohydrates							
Butter, margarine, mayonnaise, oils: 1 tbsp. = 100 calories	To meet caloric needs	1 tbsp.	1 tbsp.	1 tbsp.	2 tbsp.	2 tbsp.	2-4 tbsp.
Desserts and sweets 100 calorie portions: 1/3 cup pudding or ice cream, 2 3" cookies, 1 oz. cake, 1-1/3 oz. pie, 2 tbsp. jelly, jam, honey, sugar		1 portion	1½ portions	1½ portions	3 portions	3 portions	3 to 6 portions

RECIPES

Vary The Menu to Make Dining Fun

SOUP . . . .

HEARTY VEGETABLE SOUP

2 pounds of cubed lean beef	1½ cups lima beans
Large soupbone	1½ cups green beans
1 tablespoon salt	1½ cups green peas
1½ cup chopped onion	1½ cups whole-kernel corn,
6 carrots (½ pound, pared, cut	drained
in 3-inch pieces	1 cup cubed potato
1 cup shredded cabbage	2 tablespoons chopped parsley
¾ cup chopped celery	¾ cup tomato paste
1 medium-size onion	½ teaspoon cloves
¼ cup chopped green pepper	1 teaspoon sugar
1½ cups drained canned	2 teaspoons salt
tomatoes	½ teaspoon pepper

Place beef, soupbone, salt, and 4 quarts water in very large kettle. / Cover; bring to boiling. / Skim surface. / Add cabbage, onion, carrots, celery, green pepper, and tomatoes. / Bring to boiling; simmer covered, 30 minutes. / Add other ingredients; simmer, covered, 3½ hours. / Remove meat and bone; discard bone. / Let meat cool. / Refrigerate several hours. / Just before serving soup, skim fat from surface. / Slowly heat soup to boiling. / Store leftover soup, covered, in refrigerator.

MAIN DISHES . . . .

"BILL" CARTER'S BRUNSWICK STEW

This stew was a favorite of hunters and is thought to have originated in Brunswick County, Virginia. It was served at tobacco curings. The stew is named for "Bill" Carter because of his love for the outdoors and hunters.

1 stewing hen (6 pounds), or 2 broiler-fryers (3 pounds each)	2 cups lima beans
	3 medium potatoes, diced
	4 cups corn freshly cut from
2 large onions, sliced	cob or canned
2 cups okra, cut (optional)	3 teaspoons salt
4 cups fresh tomatoes or two	1 teaspoon pepper
1-pound cans tomatoes	1 tablespoon sugar

Cut chickens in pieces and simmer in 3 quarts water for thin stew, or 2 quarts water for a thick stew, about 2½ hours. / Remove chicken meat from bones. / Add raw vegetables to broth and simmer, uncovered, until beans and potatoes are tender. / Stir occasionally to prevent scorching. / Add chicken, boned and diced if desired, and the seasonings. ● Serves 8-10.
NOTE: If canned vegetables are used, include juices and reduce water to 2 quarts for a thin stew, 1 quart for a thick stew. It is thought, by most that Brunswick stew is better the next day after being made. Standing overnight improves flavor. Store leftover in refrigerator.

CHICKEN WAIKIKI BEACH

2 whole chicken legs
2 whole chicken breasts
½ cup flour
1/3 cup vegetable oil (except coconut oil)

1 teaspoon salt
¼ teaspoon pepper

SAUCE

2½ cups sliced pineapple
1 cup sugar
2 tablespoons cornstarch
¾ cup cider vinegar
1 tablespoon soy sauce

¼ teaspoon ginger
1 chicken bouillon cube
1 large green pepper, cut crosswise in ¼-inch circles.

Wash chicken: pat dry with paper towels. / Coat chicken with flour. / Heat oil in large skillet. / Add chicken, a few pieces at a time, and brown on all sides. / Remove as browned to shallow roasting pan, arranging pieces skin side up. / Sprinkle with salt and pepper. / Preheat oven to 350°F. / Make sauce: Drain pineapple pouring syrup into 2-cup measure. / Add water to make 1¼ cups. / In medium saucepan, combine sugar, cornstarch, pineapple syrup, vinegar, soy sauce, ginger and bouillon cube: bring to boiling, stirring constantly. / Boil 2 minutes. / Pour over chicken. / Bake uncovered 30 minutes. / Add pineapple slices and green pepper: / bake 30 minutes longer or until chicken is tender. / Serve with fluffy white rice. • Serves 4.

BRAISED SWISS STEAK

¼ cup packaged dry bread crumbs
2 teaspoons salt
¼ teaspoon pepper
2 pound round steak
2 tablespoons vegetable fat (except coconut oil)

2 cups canned tomatoes
2 medium onions, thinly sliced
¼ cup chopped celery
1 clove garlic, finely chopped
1 tablespoon Worcestershire sauce

Combine bread crumbs, salt, and pepper. / Trim fat from steak; wipe meat with damp cloth. / Sprinkle one side with half of crumb mixture; pound into steak, using rim of saucer. / Repeat on other side. / Brush both sides with fat; place under broiler, turning once, until browned on both sides. / Meanwhile, in Dutch oven or heavy skillet with tight-fitting cover, combine remaining ingredients. / Add steak; simmer, covered, 2 hours, or until meat is tender. • Serves 4.

ISLAND SUKIYAKI

2 teaspoons vegetable oil (except coconut oil)
1½ pounds sirloin or tenderloin steak, sliced "bacon" thin, 2 inches long
½ cup sugar
¾ cup soy sauce
¼ cup water, mushroom stock or white wine
2 medium onions, thin sliced lengthwise

1 green pepper, sliced thin
1 cup celery, sliced diagonally into ½-inch strips
1-12 ounce can bamboo shoots, sliced thin
1 cup fresh mushrooms (or canned) sliced thin
1 bunch green onions cut in 1-inch lengths

Heat oil in heavy skillet, add meat and brown lightly. / Mix sugar, soy sauce and mushroom stock (water or wine) and add half the mixture to the meat. / Stir and push meat to one side of pan. / Add onion, celery and pepper; cook a few minutes. / Add remaining soy sauce liquid, bamboo shoots and mushrooms. / Cook 3 to 5 minutes. / Add green onion tops and cook about 1 minute. / Stir well and serve with fluffy rice. • Serves 6.

HAMBURGERS A'LA CARTE

2½ pound chuck
2 teaspoons salt
1 egg
1 cup bread crumbs
1 tablespoon sugar
1 tablespoon Worcestershire sauce

1 cup tomato paste
1 medium size onion, diced
3 tablespoons vegetable fat (except coconut oil)

Combine ingredients. / Shape into balls and flatten. / Place in greased baking dish and broil until brown. / Place on split hamburger buns and serve with topping.

TOPPINGS

BLUE-CHEESE SPREAD: Combine ¼ cup crumbled blue cheese, 4 tablespoons soft vegetable fat (except coconut oil), and ½ teaspoon Worcestershire sauce.
OLIVE BUTTER: Combine 4 tablespoons chopped pimiento-stuffed olives and ½ cup soft vegetable fat (except coconut oil)
Sliced tomato, sliced cumcumber, lettuce, mayonnaise.• Serves 6.

BEEF CREOLE WITH POTATO PUFFS

1 pound ground chuck	1½ teaspoon chili powder
¼ cup chopped onion	1 teaspoon salt
½ cup chopped green pepper	1/8 teaspoon pepper
½ cup chopped celery	1 cup catsup
1½ cups frozen peas, partially thawed	1 tablespoon Worcestershire sauce
1 tablespoon flour	

POTATO PUFFS:

1½ cups mashed potatoes	1 tablespoon parsley flakes
1 egg, beaten	1/3 cup bread crumbs
½ teaspoon salt	¼ cup unsifted all-purpose flour
1 teaspoon grated onion	½ teaspoon baking powder

Preheat oven to 375°F. / In large skillet, over medium heat, slowly brown chuck, leaving it in large chunks. / Add onion, green pepper and celery; cook, stirring until tender-crisp about 5 minutes. / Add peas. / Blend flour with chili powder, salt, and pepper. / Stir quickly into meat mixture. / Add catsup and Worcestershire. / Cover; simmer 5 minutes. / Meanwhile, make Potato Puffs; / in medium bowl, combine all ingredients, beat to blend. / Turn meat mixture into 2-quart casserole. / Drop potato puffs by tablespoonfuls onto hot meat mixture. / Cover and bake 30 minutes. • Serves 4 to 6.

HEARTY POT ROAST WITH VEGETABLES

3½ to 4 pounds chuck for pot roasting, bone in	1 bay leaf
2 tablespoons flour	6 medium carrots, pared
1 teaspoon flour	6 medium potatoes, pared
1 teaspoon salt	6 medium onions, peeled
1 tablespoon vegetable fat (except coconut oil)	2 cups tomatoes, stewed
6 whole black peppers	2 cups fresh green beans, cut in 1-inch pieces
	2 green peppers, quartered

GRAVY

Pan liquid	Salt
½ cup unsifted all-purpose flour	Pepper

Wipe roast well with damp paper towels. / Combine flour and salt; rub into surface. / Slowly heat large Dutch oven. / Add vegetable fat. / In it, brown roast well on all sides, turning with tongs. / Add black peppers and bay leaf along with 1 cup water; simmer, covered, 1 hour (add more water, as necessary, to keep ½ to 1 inch liquid in bottom of Dutch oven during cooking period). / Turn roast. / Add vegetables; simmer, covered, 45 minutes to 1 hour. • Serves 8 to 10.

ORIENTAL EGG ROLLS

1 large egg, beaten	½ teaspoon salt
1 cup lukewarm water	¼ teaspoon almond extract
1 cup plus 2 tablespoons flour	½ teaspoon sugar
¼ cup cornstarch	

Combine ingredients and beat smooth. / Heat a lightly greased 10-inch skillet over low heat, pour and spread about 2 tablespoons of batter to make a 5-inch square tissue-thin pancake. / Use pastry brush to spread batter. / Fill in holes by brushing more batter in the opposite direction. / Fry on one side only. / Repeat until all of the batter is used. / Set aside pancakes and make the following:

1 cup chopped cooked chicken or flaked tuna	1 teaspoon grated ginger root (or ginger juice)
½ cup chopped bean sprouts	¼ cup ground almonds
½ cup chopped bamboo shoots	2 teaspoon soy sauce
¼ cup chopped green pepper	

Mix all ingredients well. / Spread a thin layer down the center of each pancake. / Fold side edges over filling—roll carefully in jelly roll fashion. / Seal open edge with batter or egg. / Allow to dry. / Fry in deep fat at 360°F., until brown, about 10 minutes. / Slice in 1½-inch pieces, and serve hot. • Serves 10.

HAMBURGER AND NOODLES STROGANOFF

½ package (4 ounce) noodles	1 tablespoon flour
¼ cup vegetable fat (except coconut oil)	1 cup tomato sauce
½ cup finely chopped onion	¼ cup Burgundy
1 clove garlic, finely chopped	1¼ cups beef bouillon, undiluted
½ pound mushrooms, thickly sliced; or 1 can (6 ounce) sliced mushrooms drained	1 teaspoon salt
	¼ teaspoon pepper
1 pound ground chuck	1 cup dairy sour cream
	½ cup grated Parmesan cheese

Preheat oven to 375°F. / Cook noodles until tender. / Drain. / Meanwhile, in hot fat in large skillet, saute onion, garlic, and mushrooms until onion is golden—about 5 minutes. / Add beef; cook, stirring, until it is browned. / Remove from heat. / Stir in flour, tomato sauce, Burgundy, bouillon, salt, and pepper. / Simmer 10 minutes, stirring occasionally. / Blend in sour cream. / In lightly greased 2-quart casserole, layer a third of the noodles, then a third of the meat mixture. / Repeat twice. / Sprinkle with cheese. / Bake, uncovered, 25 minutes. ● Serves 6.

VEGETABLES . . . .

BROWN-RICE PILAF

1¼ cups boiling water	1 teaspoon salt
1 chicken bouillon cube	¼ teaspoon pepper
½ cup raw brown rice, cooked	Dash dried thyme leaves
½ cup chopped onion	½ cup thinly sliced celery
1 can (3 ounce) sliced mushrooms, drained	

Preheat oven to 350°F. / Add water to bouillon cube in 1 quart casserole, stirring until dissolved. / Add remaining ingredients, except celery. / Bake, covered, 1 hour and 10 minutes. / Stir in celery, with fork; bake 10 minutes. / Just before serving, fluff up rice with fork. ● Serves 6.

STUFFED POTATOES CREOLE

6 baking potatoes	2 teaspoons salt
1 medium green pepper, diced	¼ teaspoon ground pepper
1/3 cup vegetable fat (except coconut oil)	1 teaspoon paprika
2 tablespoons instant minced onion	¼ teaspoon crumbled whole rosemary leaves
1 medium tomato, diced	Paprika for garnish
1 to 2 tablespoons non-fat milk	

Wash potatoes. Dry. / Bake in a preheated oven (450°F.) 1 hour or until done. / In the meantime, saute green pepper in 3 tablespoons of the fat until limp. / Add onion and tomato and cook 1 minute longer. / Cut potatoes in half length-wise and scoop out centers, leaving shells intact. / Add milk and seasoning to potato centers and mash well. / Blend in sauted vegetables. / Fill shells with mixture and dot tops with remaining fat. / Bake in a preheated oven (400°F.) 20 minutes. / Serve at once, garnish with paprika. ● Serves 6.

PARSLEY POTATOES

½ cup vegetable fat (except coconut oil)	2 tablespoons finely cut parsley
4 medium size potatoes, peeled and cooked	

Melt the fat and pour over hot potatoes. / Sprinkle with parsley. ● Serves 4.

CABBAGE WITH CARAWAY SEED

1 medium head of cabbage	3 tablespoons vegetable fat (except coconut oil)
¼ cup water	
½ teaspoon salt	1 teaspoon caraway seed
¾ teaspoon crushed marjoram leaves	

Shred entire head of cabbage. / Place in a saucepan with boiling water and salt. / Cover with a tight-fitting lid and cook quickly until the cabbage is tender (approximately 10 minutes). / Stir once or twice. / Meanwhile, blend together the marjoram leaves, fat and caraway seed and add to cabbage. / Serve hot. ● Serves 6.

MINTED CARROTS

1 bunch or (5 or 6) carrots
2 teaspoons finely chopped
  fresh mint

1½ tablespoons vegetable fat
  (except coconut oil)
1/3 teaspoon salt

Slice carrots 1/8" thick. / Cook covered in boiling salted water until almost tender. / Remove cover and cook rapidly until all liquid is absorbed. / Add fat and heat until fat melts. / Add mint mix lightly. / Serve in hot dish at once. / One-fourth teaspoon dried mint may be used, but flavor is much better when fresh mint is used. ● Serves 6.

SANDWICHES . . . .

MONTO CRISTO SANDWICH

Sandwich:
2 tablespoons soft vegetable
  fat (except coconut oil)
½ teaspoon prepared mustard
3 slices bread
3 slices turkey, cut thin
3 slices baked ham, cut thin
vegetable oil (except coconut
  oil) for deep frying

Batter:
1 egg white
1 egg, whole
2 tablespoons non-fat milk
Dash pepper
Dash salt
Currant jelly

In small bowl, blend fat with mustard. / Spread on both sides of bread. / Arrange turkey on one slice of bread; top. / Cut sandwich in half diagonally, and secure with wooden picks. / In deep skillet or deep fat fryer, heat vegetable fat (about 2 inches deep) to 400°F. on deep frying thermometer. / Meanwhile, make batter: / in small bowl, with rotary beater, beat egg white until stiff peaks form. / In another bowl, beat remaining batter ingredients. / Gently fold in egg white. / Dip sandwich halves into batter, coating thoroughly. / Fry in hot fat until golden-about 2 minutes. / Serve with tart currant jelly.

FRANKFURTERS CON CARNE

1 tablespoon melted vegetable
  fat (except coconut oil)
1 1/3 cups finely chopped
  onion
½ pound ground chuck
1 can (8 ounce) tomato sauce
1 teaspoon salt

1 teaspoon chili powder
½ teaspoon light brown sugar
6 frankfurters
6 split frankfurter
  rolls

Slowly heat fat in large skillet. / Add onion, and saute until tender—about 5 minutes. / Add chuck to skillet, cook, stirring occasionally, until meat loses its red color. / Add tomato sauce, salt, chili powder, and sugar. / Mix well. / Cook, uncovered, over low heat and stirring occasionally, 20 minutes or until most of liquid is absorbed. / Meanwhile, broil frankfurters, 4 inches from heat, 3 minutes; turn once. / Place rolls, cut side up, on broiler rack; broil 30 seconds, or just until toasted. / To serve, place a frankfurter inside each roll; top each with some of chili mixture. ● Serves 6.

CRABMEAT-SALAD SANDWICHES

1 cup crabmeat
¼ cup dairy sour cream
1 tablespoon capers, drained
½ teaspoon Worcestershire
  sauce

½ teaspoon seasoned salt
3 tomato slices, ¼ inch thick
3 bread slices
¾ cup grated sharp Cheddar
  cheese

Into small saucepan, separate crabmeat pieces removing membrane. / Add sour cream, capers, Worcestershire, ¼ teaspoon seasoned salt, mix well. / Heat the mixture, stirring occasionally. / Meanwhile, place tomato slices on bread slices; sprinkle tomato with remaining seasoned salt. / Run under broiler, 6 inches from heat, 1 minute. / Spread one third hot crabmeat mixture over each sandwich; / sprinkle each with ¼ cup cheese. / Run under broiler, 6 inches from heat, until cheese is bubbly and melted. / Serve hot. ● Serves 3.

H. A.'S DENVERS

¼ pound cooked ham, ground
2 tablespoons chopped green pepper
2 tablespoons chopped onion
Dash salt
1/8 teaspoon seasoned pepper

¼ teaspoon celery seed
3 eggs, beaten
2 tablespoons vegetable fat (except coconut oil)
4 corn muffins, toasted

In medium bowl, toss ham with green pepper, onion, salt, pepper, and celery seed. / Add eggs; mix well. / Heat fat in large skillet. / Use 1/3 cup ham-egg mixture for each sandwich. / Cook until nicely browned on underside; turn; cook until other side is browned. / Serve on corn muffins. ● Serves 4.

MARGE'S GRILLED TUNA SANDWICHES

1 cup tuna, drained and flaked
¼ cup stuffed olives, coarsely chopped
¼ cup celery
1/3 cup mayonnaise or cooked salad dressing*

2½ teaspoon lemon juice
6 bread slices
¼ cup soft vegetable fat (except coconut oil)

Preheat griddle to 350°. / In medium bowl, combine tuna with olives, celery, mayonnaise, and 1 teaspoon lemon juice, tossing until well mixed. / Spread filling on 3 bread slices; top with rest of slices. / In small bowl, gradually add remaining lemon juice to vegetable fat, mixing well. / Spread on both sides of sandwiches. / Grill sandwich about 5 minutes, or until nicely browned on underside. / Turn; grill about 5 minutes longer, or until they are browned on other side. ● Serves 3.

SUPPER SANDWICHES

You'd call these hearty, hot sandwiches a meal in one. Of course, you could serve a tossed green salad and a simple dessert with them.

CARTER'S STEAK SANDWICH

1 tablespoon vegetable fat (except coconut oil)
1 teaspoon chopped parsley
½ teaspoon lemon juice
½ pound eye of sirloin (½ inch thick)
Salt

Pepper
2 toast slices spread with vegetable fat or special mayonnaise
3 tomato wedges
3 thin large onion slices
Spinach or Watercress sprigs

Saute steak in vegetable fat, lemon juice, salt and pepper. / Serve on toast slices with parsley, watercress or spinach. ● Serves 2.

HAMBURGER ITALIANO

¼ cup vegetable fat (except coconut oil)
½ cup chopped onion
½ cup chopped green pepper
1½ pound ground chuck
1½ teaspoons salt
½ teaspoon pepper
½ teaspoon dried oregano leaves

2 tablespoons Worcestershire sauce
8 ounces elbow macaroni
1 can (3 ounce) button mushrooms, drained
1¼ cups tomato soup, undiluted
1 medium tomato, chopped
½ cup grated Parmesan cheese

Preheat oven to 375°F. / In hot fat in large skillet, saute onion and green pepper until tender—5 minutes. / Add beef; cook; stirring, over medium heat until browned—about 5 minutes. / Add salt, pepper, oregano and Worcestershire. / Meanwhile, cook macaroni until tender. / Drain; turn into 2½ quart casserole. / Add beef mixture, mushrooms, tomato soup, and chopped tomato; toss to combine well. / Bake cover, 40 minutes. / Remove cover; sprinkle with cheese. / Bake 5 minutes longer, or until browned. ● Serves 6 to 8.

184

SALADS . . . .

Salads should be fun and enjoyable. Choose a variety of fruits and vegetables for salads. Many recipes have been included in other chapters. The three presented below are usual favorites, however, do not provide the vitamin content that the fresh fruits and vegetables will provide.

POTATO SALAD

No. 1

1 quart potatoes	2 tablespoons grated onion
2 tablespoons chopped parsley	½ teaspoon salt
2 tablespoons mustard	Mayonnaise*

Cook potatoes with skins on and allow them to cool before peeling, as it is considered a good thing to have potatoes waxy rather than mealy for salad. / Peel potatoes, cut into small cubes and mix with parsley, onion, mustard, salt and mayonnaise. / Set in a cool place for two hours before serving. ● Serves 8 to 10.

No. 2

1 quart new potatoes	1 tablespoon capers
1 tablespoon vegetable oil	1 tablespoon chopped parsley
(except coconut oil)	1 teaspoon salt
2 tablespoons sugar	Thin mayonnaise or cooked
2 tablespoons vinegar or	dressing
mustard	Lettuce
1 onion	Lemon
2 stalks celery	Paprika

Boil potatoes until done, but not too soft, cut them into cubes. / When cooled add oil and vinegar or mustard. / Chop onion and celery very fine, and add, with capers, parsley, salt and sugar. / Pour a thin mayonnaise over all, mixing thoroughly with a wooden spoon and fork. / Garnish with lettuce and a few pieces of lemon. / Sprinkle top with paprika. ● Serves 8 to 10.

POTATO AND PEA SALAD

2 cups boiled potatoes, diced	½ cup French dressing
1 cup boiled peas	Lettuce
	Mayonnaise

Pour two-thirds of the French dressing over the diced potatoes, and the other third over the cold peas, and set where they will be chilled. / After an hour, combine them and arrange on lettuce leaves. / Garnish with mayonnaise. ● Serves 6.

See other salad recipes throughout the book.

SINGLES

Singles—many of them young students who have moved away from home on their own have particular nutritional considerations. A tight budget may be a factor in the arena of school pressures and they also might find loneliness, a stress factor. Poor eating patterns; eating on the run, an inadequate diet, stress periods and a living pattern of confusion will deprive one of health during the years on the eve of adulthood.

Mealtime should be enjoyable, free from stress, and well balanced. The single person may want to consider some good simple basic habits of eating such as a few extra minutes for an adequate breakfast in the morning. *Eat Breakfast Every Day.*

The menus and recipes presented for you are low in calories. Prepare your own food and know the nutrients added. Tips:

- Know good nutrition
- Tell your friends about it
- Plan special juice breaks
- Start a fad of your own—a good nutrition fad
- Eat a mixed salad a day
- Eat a whole grain cereal every day
- Eat fresh fruit at least three times a day
- Eat a whole grain bread 2-3 times each day
- Drink one glass of milk each day
- Eat 2 to 3 vegetables each day, preferably fresh
- Eat protein source three times each day

Above all eat wisely. It is the same as money in the bank for tomorrow.

Make every food you eat the most nutrition you can get for your money. Add to your eating time quietness even though short periods. Think of fun things and laugh while you eat.

Remember that joy in eating is an essential ingredient if the food nutrients arrive at their work station—to make your hair shiny and your skin smooth and glow.

Eat a variety of food, especially fruits, vegetables, lean meats, whole grain cereals and breads.

THE PREGNANT YOUNG WOMAN Pregnancy is considered to be a normal experience in the human life cycle of the young woman. It

186

should be pointed out, however, that pregnancy can become a problem to the young woman whose body has not completely matured, income may be limited and the diet may have been poor in the past. Immediately we should understand that the earlier the physician is the advisor the better prepared she will be to adjust to the new experiences.

As a dietitian and nutritionist there are several recommendations which may prove to be helpful:

- See a good physician.
- Eat wisely and remember that you are living normal days keeping your body in good maintenance. You are not, however, eating for two.
- Follow the normal diet and adjust your diet to three or six meals. The menus and recipes in Chapter II and III may also be helpful.
- Get plenty of rest.
- Visit with good friends, daily.
- It is especially important that you enjoy eating and make mealtime a special time. Eat with others.
- Eat plenty of fresh fruits and vegetables. Drink at least 1 quart of milk, may be non-fat.
- Drink plenty of water.
- Keep your weight gain within 16 to 20 pounds.

Many young women need additional iron. The need may be especially real during pregnancy. Remember that any supplement of vitamins or minerals should have the approval of your physician.

MENUS

I

Breakfast

Grapefruit half
Peanut butter toast squares
Cereal (whole grain)
Non-fat milk or 2%

Luncheon

Cornbeef and hot
slaw* on rye
Orange wedges
Lemonade

Dinner

Watercress soup*
Chicken-fruit salad*
Baked potato with cheese*
Wholewheat rolls*
Beverages

II

Breakfast

Fresh strawberries
Scrambled eggs on
crispy toast
Non-fat milk

Luncheon

Marge's chicken
salad* sandwich
Carrot sticks
Celery hearts
Fresh fruit cup*
Non-fat milk or 2%

Dinner

French onion soup*
Hamburger with chili beans*
Diced cabbage
Green pepper salad*
Red grapes
Beverage

III

Breakfast

Orange juice
Cornflakes
Baked ham slice
Wholewheat toast
Non-fat milk or 2%

Luncheon

Quick potato soup*
Crackers
Shrimp salad*
Baked tomato half*
Lemon sherbert*
Beverage

Dinner

Daily special*
Broccoli in cheese sauce
with almonds
Toss salad*
Cantaloupe
Hot Tea with Lemon

Milk may be whole, nonfat, 2% or buttermilk

*Recipe included in book.

RECIPES

To add Variety to your Menu

SOUPS ....

WATER CRESS SOUP

4 medium sized potatoes	Pepper
1 tablespoon vegetable fat	Mace if desired
(except coconut oil)	1 cup non-fat milk
Salt	1 large bunch watercress

Boil potatoes in jackets, then skin and beat well with vegetable fat and seasoning. / Add milk; smooth to the consistency of heavy cream. / Chop fine the watercress without mashing. / It must remain crisp. / Now heat soup. / Just before serving throw in watercress. / Stir a moment until it is very hot but do not cook the watercress. / Whatever is left over may be served cold in cups with a spoonfull of sour cream on top. / This soup is very nourishing and particularly good for a sick student. ● Serves 4.

QUICK POTATO SOUP

2 cups thinly sliced raw potatoes	1 tablespoon vegetable fat (except coconut oil)
¼ cup finely chopped onion	¼ teaspoon Worcestershire sauce
1¼ cups boiling water	1 teaspoon salt
1½ cups non-fat milk	Pepper

Add potatoes and onion to the boiling water. / Cover and cook for 15 to 20 minutes, or until potatoes are tender. / Mash the potatoes slightly with a fork to thicken the soup a little if desired. / Add milk, fat and seasonings. / Heat. / For a touch of color, garnish each serving with chopped parsley, grated cheese, croutons, diced crisp bacon, or finely cut watercress or chives. ● Serves 4.

CLAM CHOWDER

1 quart clams	3 cups potatoes, diced
1 1/3 cups onion, chopped	Salt and white pepper to taste
1/3 cup vegetable fat (except coconut oil)	

Clean and chop clams to desired size. / Add onions to clams. / Cover with water (or clam juice), add fat and cook 30 minutes or until tender. / Then add potatoes; let come to boil. / Cook until potatoes are creamy. / Season to taste. ● Serves 6.

LEEK SOUP

2 medium sized potatoes thinly sliced	1 stalk celery, diced
2 pints water	2 tablespoons vegetable fat (except coconut oil)
2 chicken bouillon cubes*	
4 good sized leeks cut in 1-inch pieces	

Melt fat in pan. / Add potatoes, leek and celery and stir thoroughly for a few minutes, but do not brown. / Add two bouillon cubes and water and simmer for one hour. / Serve soup with grated cheese. / *Canned bouillon may be used if desired. ● Serves 2.

MUSHROOM SOUP

2 cups diced veal	½ onion
1 cup mushrooms	1 pint non-fat milk

Cover veal with water and simmer the day before using until water boils down to one quart of liquid / Next day chop mushrooms and onions sliced very fine. / Simmer in stock and add milk before serving. ● Serves 2.

NAVY BEAN SOUP

½ pound dry navy beans
  water to cover (cold)
1 pint boiling water
1 strip bacon
2 teaspoons chopped onions

2/3 cup tomatoes
1 teaspoon sugar
¼ teaspoon dry mustard
Salt and pepper to taste

Wash beans thoroughly. / Soak in cold water about six hours. / Do not drain. / Add boiling water to cover and heat to boiling temperature. / Simmer about one hour until tender, but not mushy. / Cut bacon in small pieces and fry together with onions until lightly browned. / Add tomatoes, sugar, mustard, salt and pepper to bacon mixture. / Combine tomato-bacon mixtures with beans, cook for 20 to 30 minutes more and serve. • Serves 4.

FRENCH ONION SOUP

4 medium onions
1 tablespoon vegetable fat
  (except coconut oil)
1 quart brown stock
  (concentrated, or four
  bouillion cubes)

½ teaspoon Worcestershire
  sauce
Salt and pepper
Rounds of toast
Grated Parmesan cheese

Slice onions thin and brown in fat. / Add broth, Worcestershire sauce, salt and pepper; / simmer until onions are tender. / Pour soup into a casserole. / Rub casserole or toast with cut clove of garlic. / Arrange toast on top, sprinkle with grated cheese. • Serves 4.

KIDNEY SOUP

1 beef kidney
1 pound beef for stock
Flour
Pepper
Salt
1 large onion

2 stalks celery
2 carrots, grated
2 quarts water
2 tablespoons vegetable fat
  (except coconut oil)

Soak kidney in cold, slightly salted, water for ½ hour. / Make stock with celery, onion and beef, salt, and pepper. / Cut kidney into small pieces and roll in the flour. / Put 2 tablespoons fat into a pan and brown kidney. / Add this to stock together with the grated carrots and cook until tender. / Remove beef stock and celery. / If a thicker soup is desired, mix some flour into water, add to soup. / Serve hot. • Serves 4.

SANDWICHES ....

JAY'S SATURDAY NIGHT SPECIAL

6 crisp cooked bacon slices
½ pound mild Cheddar cheese
1 small onion, peeled
1 medium green pepper
½ cup pitted ripe olives,
  drained

Dash pepper
1/8 teaspoon garlic powder
¼ teaspoon catsup
1 tablespoon prepared
  mustard
10 hamburger buns, split

Put bacon, cheese, onion, green pepper, olives, through coarse blade of food chopper. / Turn bowl. / Add pepper, garlic powder, catsup, and mustard. / Spread onto bottom halves of buns, place on cookie sheet. / Broil 4 inches from heat, until cheese begins to melt—about 1 minute. / Top with other halves of buns. / Serve hot. • Serves 10.

CORNED BEEF AND HOT SLAW ON RYE

Hot Slaw:
1½ cups shredded cabbage
¼ cup white vinegar
½ teaspoon caraway seed
½ teaspoon salt
Dash pepper
½ cup water

Horseradish Sauce:
1/3 cup dairy sour cream
1 teaspoon prepared
  horseradish, drained
Dash Worcestershire sauce
Dash salt
¼ pound hot sliced corned
  beef
4 seedless rye bread slices

Make Hot Slaw: In medium skillet, combine cabbage, vinegar, caraway seed, salt, and pepper with ½ cup water. / Bring to boiling; reduce heat, and simmer, covered, 5 minutes, stirring occasionally. / Drain. / Meanwhile, make Horseradish Sauce: In small bowl, combine sour cream with horseradish, Worcestershire sauce and salt; mix well. / Place half of the corned beef on one bread slice, half on another. / Top each with half of slaw and sauce, / cover with other bread slice. • Serves 2.

HAMBURGERS WITH CHILI BEANS

Hamburgers:
1 pound ground chuck
3 tablespoons hot catsup
3 tablespoons finely chopped
  onion
½ teaspoon salt
¼ teaspoon Worcestershire
  sauce
1/8 teaspoon pepper

Chili Beans:
2 cups Kidney beans cooked
  and drained
1/3 cup tomato relish
¼ cup hot catsup
½ teaspoon chili powder

4 hamburger buns, split
3 tablespoons vegetable fat
  (except coconut oil) melted
Dried thyme leaves

Make Hamburgers: Toss all ingredients in medium bowl until well combined. / Lightly shape into 4 patties about ½ inch thick. / Broil hamburgers, 4 inches from heat, 5 minutes longer. / Meanwhile make Chili Beans: Combine all ingredients in medium saucepan; heat thoroughly. / Brush buns with melted fat, sprinkle with thyme. / Broil 30 seconds, or until golden. / Place hamburgers in buns. / Serve beans along with hamburgers. ● Serves 4.

BROILED CHICKEN-AND-HAM
SANDWICH A'LA RITIE

¾ cup boned chicken, diced
1 cup deviled ham
¼ cup mayonnaise or cooked
  salad dressing*

½ teaspoon Worcestershire
  sauce

TOPPING:

2 egg whites
Dash cream of tartar
2 tablespoons mayonnaise or
  cooked salad dressing

2 tablespoons prepared
  mustard
2 English muffins, split
Melted vegetable fat (except
  coconut oil)

In medium saucepan, heat chicken, ham, mayonnaise, and Worcestershire. / Keep hot. / Make topping: In small bowl, with rotary beater, beat egg whites with cream of tartar until stiff peaks form when beater is raised. / Combine mayonnaise and mustard. / Gently fold into egg-white mixture. / Brush muffins with fat; / broil four inches from heat, until nicely browned. / Spoon hot chicken mixture on muffins, mounding high in center. / Cover with egg-white mixture. / Run under broiler 2 to 3 minutes, or until topping is golden. ● Serves 4.

LUNCH-BOX SANDWICHES

The lunch you carry can and should be as appealing and satisfying as the lunch you eat at home. And if you're the one to pack a lunch box you'll be interested in the next group of sandwiches.

APPLE-PEANUT BUTTER SANDWICHES

8 wholewheat bread slices
Soft vegetable fat (except
  coconut oil)
2/3 cup creamy-style peanut
  butter
1/3 cup applesauce

¼ cup finely chopped unpared
  red apple
4 crisp-cooked bacon slices,
  crumbled
Lettuce

Lightly spread bread with fat. / In small bowl, combine peanut butter and applesauce, mixing until smooth. / Stir in apple and bacon. / Spread 4 bread slices with filling. / Top with lettuce and remaining bread. / NOTE: Or make sandwiches, omitting lettuce. Then wrap; with freezer paper and label; / freeze until ready to use, no longer than 3 to 4 weeks. ● Serves 4.

MARGE'S CHICKEN-SALAD SANDWICHES

1½ cups cut-up cooked
  chicken
1 hard cooked egg, finely
  chopped
1 tablespoon finely chopped
  onion
2 tablespoon finely chopped
  celery
2 tablespoons finely chopped
  stuffed olives

1 tablespoon sweet-pickle
  relish
1 teaspoon lemon juice
1/8 teaspoon salt
Dash pepper
¼ cup mayonnaise or cooked
  salad dressing
12 white bread slices
Soft vegetable fat (except
  coconut oil)

In medium bowl, combine all ingredients, except bread and fat. / Toss with fork until well mixed. / Spread bread lightly with fats. / Put slices together with chicken-salad filling. ● Serves 6.

DAILY SPECIAL

1 cup chunk style tuna,
  drained
1/3 cup finely chopped celery
¼ cup mayonnaise or cooked
  salad dressing*
3 tablespoons finely chopped
  ripe olives

2 teaspoons lemon juice
1 teaspoon grated onion
Dash of pepper
10 bread slices
Soft vegetable fat (except
  coconut oil)

In small bowl, combine all ingredients, except bread and fat. /
Toss to combine well. / Spread bread lightly with fat. / Put
together with filling. / Cut in half diagonally. / If desired, wrap
for freezer (2 halves together); label, and freeze until ready to
use. (Not longer than 3 to 4 weeks) ● Serves 5.

ZESTY PEANUT BUTTER SANDWICHES

8 white bread slices
8 teaspoons vegetable fat
  (except coconut oil)
½ cup peanut butter

6 tablespoons sweet-pickle
  relish, drained
4 lettuce leaves

Spread each bread slice with 1 teaspoon fat. / Spread each of 4
slices with 2 tablespoons peanut butter and 1½ tablespoons
pickle relish. / Top each with lettuce and bread slice. ● Serves 4.

DEVILED-EGG SANDWICHES

10 bread slices
Soft vegetable fat (except
  coconut oil)
5 hard cooked eggs, finely
  chopped
1 teaspoon prepared mustard
¼ teaspoon onion salt
1/8 teaspoon bottled steak
  sauce

1 tablespoon chopped parsley
2 tablespoons chopped
  pimiento
2 teaspoons cider vinegar
¼ cup mayonnaise or cooked
  salad dressing*

Spread bread lightly with fat. / Combine eggs and rest of
ingredients, tossing with fork until well mixed. / Assemble
sandwiches. ● Serves 5.

PEANUT BUTTER 'N' BACON SANDWICHES

½ cup creamy or chunk style
  peanut butter
½ cup chopped crisp cooked
  bacon
3 tablespoons sweet-pickle
  relish, drained

2 tablespoons chopped
  stuffed olives
2 tablespoons mayonnaise or
  cooked salad dressing*
12 slices bread

Combine all ingredients, except bread; mix well. / Use to fill 6
sandwiches. / Cut in quarters; put in sandwich bags. / Keep
refrigerated until ready for lunch box. ● Serves 4.

SPICY HAM-AND-CHEESE SANDWICHES

½ cup deviled ham
3 cups grated Cheddar cheese
¼ cup chili sauce
¼ cup chopped green pepper

¼ cup sweet pickle relish,
  drained
2 teaspoons grated onion
16 bread slices

Combine ham and cheese, stirring until smooth. / Stir in chili
sauce, green pepper, relish, and onion; mix thoroughly. / Spread
on 8 slices of bread and top with other 8 slices. / Cut in half. /
Wrap individually; label, and freeze. / Remove from freezer just
in time to pack lunch box (sandwiches will be thawed by
lunchtime). ● Serves 8.

TUNA ROLLS

1 cup chunk style tuna,
  drained
½ cup chopped celery
¼ cup sweet pickle relish,
  drained
2 tablespoons chopped onion
2 tablespoons chopped parsley

1 hard cooked egg, chopped
1 tablespoon lemon juice
½ teaspoon salt
1/8 teaspoon pepper
½ cup mayonnaise or cooked
  salad dressing*
4 frankfurter rolls

In medium bowl, combine all ingredients, except rolls; mix well.
/ Fill rolls with tuna mixture. ● Serves 4.

192

SALADS ·

SHRIMP SALAD

1 cup elbow macaroni, that
   has been cooked in salt
   water & drained
2 cups cooked, peeled, and
   drained shrimp
1 teaspoon celery salt
2 teaspoon salt

5 green onions, chopped
1 cup mayonnaise
2 tablespoons parsley flakes
½ teaspoon dillweed
2 hard-cooked eggs, diced
Lettuce

Combine all ingredients mixing well. Chill for about 1 hour. /
Serve on bed of crisp lettuce. ● Serves 6 to 8.

HAM AND ORANGE SALAD

2 cups cooked ham
1 clove garlic
1½ cups drained orange
   sections
1 cup diced celery
½ cup chopped walnuts

½ cup minced onion
1/3 cup mayonnaise
1 to 2 teaspoons vinegar
½ teaspoon salt
Dash of pepper

Rub garlic in salad bowl; discard garlic. / Place ham, orange
sections, celery, walnuts and onion in salad bowl and mix well. /
Combine mayonnaise, vinegar, salt and pepper and mix. / Pour
over ham mixture and toss gently or until dressing has coated
ham mixture. / Chill and serve on lettuce. ● Serves 4.

CHICKEN-FRUIT SALAD

2 cups pineapple chunks
1 apple, cored and sliced
1 cup seedless grapes
3 cups diced cooked chicken
Whipped Cream Fruit Dressing
   (see next in order)

1/3 cup toasted slivered
   almonds
Lettuce

Drain pineapple chunks reserving juice. / Dip apple slices in
pineapple juice. / Combine fruit and chicken; chill. / Add
Whipped Cream Fruit Dressing and toss lightly. / Service on
lettuce, and top with almonds. ● Serves 4.

WHIPPED CREAM FRUIT DRESSING

3 tablespoons vegetable fat
   (except coconut oil)
3 tablespoons all-purpose flour
¼ cup sugar
1 teaspoon salt

1/3 cup lemon juice
1/3 cup pineapple juice
2 egg yolks, slightly beaten
½ cup whipped cream

Melt fat in a small sauce pan over low heat; blend in flour. / Add
sugar, salt, lemon juice, and pineapple juice; cook until
thickened, stirring constantly. / Stir a small amount of hot
mixture into egg yolks; stir into remaining hot mixture. / Cook
about 2 minutes, stirring constantly. / Chill. / Fold in whipped
cream. ● Makes 1 cup.

193

DIVORCED

Studies show that divorce is on the increase in the United States. Many thousands of young people—as well as middle-aged couples—are suddenly thrust into a new lifestyle. The trauma of divorce brings on a heavy stress period. However long that period lasts depends upon the individual—but in all cases there can be very great damage to the divorced person's nutritional needs.

As with all tremendous life changes (and divorce ranks near the top of all depression-inducing situations), there will likely be a period of lack of appetite. Nevertheless, the body's food needs, the emotions notwithstanding, remain. If you have recently suffered the trauma of divorce, you will want to sustain your nutritional needs by eating six light meals daily, rather than following the pattern of three heavy meals. Check the meals under the stress section in Chapter III for menus and recipes if you have a problem eating.

Some divorced persons, instead of losing their appetites, instead try to overeat to compensate for their loss. See the menus and recipes in Chapter II on Self Image—Esteem for guidance.

If you are a mother or father left alone with children after a divorce it is essential that you do not neglect their nutritional needs. Meals should be simple and nutritious. Remember that the emotional shock of divorce is severe upon the children as well and, therefore, it is more important than ever to provide for their future health through today's good nutrition.

It is certainly understandable that at the time following divorce the parent left with children to care for is less than enthusiastic about preparing grand meals. The secret then is simplicity—carefully planned, simplicity which can mean good nutrition.

THE SANDWICH, OR ONE DISH MEALS, CAN BE PREPARED TO SUPPLY GOOD NUTRITION. The Earl of Sandwich, a notorious gambler so dedicated to the gambling table that he would not leave it for a meal, came up with one of the easiest and simplest solutions to his (and possibly your) problem. He conceived the idea of filling two pieces of bread with a full meal of filling inbetween. He could then munch his meal without disrupting his game. Nearly two hundred years later, the "sandwich," still the basic two slices of bread with a filling, is a handy staple.

Today, the Earl of Sandwich would probably not recognize his brainchild, however. Our sandwiches may be made with a combination of desired ingredients and served on a luscious bun, toasted or plain. Sandwiches may be hot, grilled, toasted, open-faced, club, canapes, and made into fancy styles.

Sandwiches should provide more than prevention against hunger, of course; excellent nutrition should be the aim and is certainly possible. If children have been taught to like all foods, or most anyway, then sandwiches can be made using a variety of breads and fillings. Many kids persist in favorites and they will laugh about them as adults. Sandwiches, therefore, can be highly imaginative.

The recipes which follow are excellent nutritionally for the busy parent when children need good but simply prepared meals. You will want to join the children at mealtime.

The young children may enjoy recipes found in the children's part of this chapter. Teenagers may find recipes that appeal to them in this chapter as well.

Mothers and fathers may wish to post favorite menus and recipes in a special place of the kitchen in order to whet appetites and save time in planning. (See Chapter III for overall meal planning ideas during stress periods.)

Casserole menus and recipes presented in this chapter may, also, prove helpful to the busy parent.

ONE MEAL SANDWICHES ....

WASHINGTON REUBEN

2 slices rye bread toasted
6 slices kosher corned beef
 (about 3 ounces)
Cole slaw
2 slices Swiss cheese

½ sweet green pepper, sliced
 seeded, ribs removed
1 cherry tomato split
French Dressing

Place the slices of rye toast, overlapping, on a ovenproof serving plate. / Cover with corned beef, then coat with cole slaw, spreading it evenly. / Add the Swiss cheese. / Place in the preheated oven at 325°F. until cheese melts. / Remove from oven and garnish with pepper slices and cherry tomato. / Add a serving of French dressing. ● Serves 1.

VIRGINIA BARBECUE

½ cup barbecued pork
1 soft enriched egg roll, split,
 and toasted or 1 hamburger
 bun split and toasted
½ cup cole slaw

Sweet green pepper sticks,
 seeded, ribs removed, cut
 into sticks
1 cherry tomato, split
Barbecue sauce

Scoop up the pork and shape into a ball. / Wrap in saran or waxed paper. / Place in the microwave oven for 45 seconds or in a preheated 325° oven until warm. / Spread on the bottom half of the roll. / Cover with other half roll. / Slice diagonally. / Arrange on serving plate with scoop of cole slaw a garnish of green pepper sticks and cherry tomato. / Add a serving of barbecue sauce in individual cup. ● Serves 1.

NEW YORKER CLUB

3 slices rye bread
3 slices baked ham
3 slices cheese (your favorite
 cheese)
½ teaspoon crumbled bacon (1
 slice)

½ cup cole slaw
3 slices turkey breast
Kosher half-sour pickles
Parsley
*Russian Dressing See Recipe
 page 207.

Place 1 piece of the rye bread on a serving plate with the sliced ham on top of it, then add the cheese and sprinkle with bacon bits. / Cover with the second slice of rye. / Spread with the cole slaw and top with the sliced turkey. / Add the third piece of bread. / Cut sandwich in two and arrange somewhat apart. / Between the pieces place the pickle and parsley garnish. / Add a serving of Russian Dressing in individual cup. ● Serves 1.

The "Peaks of Otter" are the highest peaks located on the Blueridge Parkway of Virginia. Any foods served there are a special treat. This is a favorite—

"PEAKS OF OTTER" CLUB SANDWICH

3 slices of rye or whole wheat
 bread cut and arranged on a
 serving plate
3 slices tender white turkey
 meat
2 slices American or Swiss
 cheese

3 tomato slices
Slices of 1 hard-cooked egg
2 slices crisp bacon strips
 garnish with pickle slices

Layer and serve with separate container of Special Russian Dressing. / See Recipe page 207. ● Serves 1.
To make a complete meal serve with a fruit salad and milk.

OREGON'S CRAB 'N CHEESE SANDWICH

3 tablespoons vegetable fat (except coconut oil)	1¾ cups non-fat milk
3 tablespoons all-purpose flour	1 cup shredded sharp cheddar cheese
1 tablespoon chicken-flavored gravy base	3 English muffins, split, & toasted
¾ teaspoon dry mustard	1¾ cups fresh frozen crab, cooked
¼ teaspoon salt	

Melt fat in saucepan over low heat. / Blend in flour, chicken-flavored gravy base, dry mustard, and salt. / Stir in milk all at once. / Cook, stirring constantly, till mixture bubbles; / cook 2 minutes more. / Remove sauce from heat; add shredded sharp cheddar cheese, / stirring to melt. / Arrange toasted English muffin halves on platter; top each muffin with crab. / Cover with cheese sauce. / Broil 4 to 5 inches from heat until hot and bubbly, but not browned. / Serve immediately. ● Serves 5 to 6.
Serve with fresh vegetable salad.

TUNA CUCUMBER SANDWICH

¾ cup light chunk tuna	2 tablespoons softened vegetable fat (except coconut oil)
2 tablespoons lemon juice	
¼ cups finely chopped celery	
2 teaspoon chopped green pepper	1 large cucumber peeled and sliced ¼ inch thick slices (marinate in wine vinegar) for 30 minutes.
¼ teaspoon salt	
12 slices rye bread	

Flake the fish in a bowl. / Add next four ingredients and blend well. / Spread on 4 slices of bread, using ¼ cup of tuna mixture to each slice. / Top with bread slice. / Lay marinated cucumber slices on top, / sprinkle lightly with salt and top with remaining bread. / Cut diagonally in quarters, place cut side up on serving plate. ● Serves 4.
NOTE: Bread slices may be plain or toasted. / Serve with fresh red grapes and a glass of milk.

H.A.'s FAVORITE EGG SALAD SANDWICH

6 hard-cooked eggs	1 teaspoon prepared mustard
Salt, dash	Mayonnaise
¼ cup chopped pickle	10 slices bread

Shell the eggs and chop them rather fine. / Mix with salt, pickle, and mustard. / Add just enough mayonnaise to give a good spreading consistency. / Spread on half of the slices of bread; / top with remaining slices. / Cut sandwiches in thirds to obtain finger shapes. ● Serves 5.

SAN JOSE BOLOGNA RIBBONS

MAKE BOLOGNA LAYERS: Use bologna slice layered with cream cheese which has been creamed with pineapple juices. / Add a second slice of bologna layer cream cheese and third bologna slice. / Cut bologna layers into quarters. / Each quarter has three bologna slices filled with cream cheese. / Place on a skewer as follows: / Quarter raisin bread brushed with mayonnaise, then, lettuce, then quarter bologna layers (ribbons) / Repeat four times. / Garnish with cherry tomatoes. / Serve with a favorite fresh fruit cup. ● Serves 4.

MEATS . . . .

SHRIMP CREOLE

4 tablespoons bacon	3 cups tomatoes
2 medium onions	3 tablespoons tomato paste
1 green pepper	Salt and pepper to taste
1½ cups celery	3 cups cooked shrimp

Chop onions, green peppers and celery. / Fry in bacon grease about 15 minutes. / Add tomatoes and tomato paste. / Simmer until thick (30-40 minutes). / Add salt, pepper and shrimp. / Heat thoroughly. / Serve with rice. / This freezes nicely. ● Serves 8.

197

VEGETABLES . . . .

SQUASH CASSEROLE

Cook 6 cups squash sliced, in salted water, until tender. / Drain and mash. / Add to 2 cups bread crumbs:

1½ cups cream chicken soup	2 medium onions chopped
1 cup sour cream	1 cup vegetable fat (except
¼ cup pimento, chopped	coconut oil)
¼ cup sliced water chestnuts	

Combine: Breadcrumbs with ¾ cup vegetable fat. / Grease a 2 quart casserole, and put a layer of bread crumbs on bottom; / alternate squash and bread crumbs. / End with bread crumbs on top. / Dot with the remaining ¼ stick of vegetable fat. / Bake 30 minutes at 350°F. ● Serves 6 to 8.

For other casserole dishes, refer to meals for on the go in this chapter.

CALIFORNIA-STYLE BROCCOLI

1 bunch broccoli	½ teaspoon garlic salt
3 ounces cream cheese,	½ cup sliced pitted ripe olives
softened	2 tomatoes, cut in wedges
3 tablespoons non-fat milk	

Wash broccoli. / Cut tops into flowerets; / slice stems, discarding any tough parts. / In large saucepan cook broccoli, covered in boiling salted water 6 to 8 minutes or till crisp-tender. / Drain well; cover and chill. / Meanwhile, in small mixer bowl beat cream cheese till fluffy; heat milk, and garlic salt. / Fold in olives. / Cover and chill till serving time. / Arrange broccoli and tomato wedges on platter. / Spoon dressing over. ● Makes 8 servings.

SALADS . . . .

GRAPEFRUIT AND GRAPE SALAD

2 cups grapefruit sections	½ cup Malaga grapes, peeled
2 tablespoons grape-juice	and seeded
2 tablespoons French dressing	

Peel fine large grapefruit and separate the sections, removing every particle of the bitter white inner skin. / Peel and seed the grapes and mix with the grapefruit. / Set, covered, in the refrigerator until very cold. / Pour over them the grape juice and French dressing. ● Serves 4.

WHITE GRAPE SALAD

1 pound Malaga grapes	French dressing or mayonnaise
Lettuce	

Peel grapes and remove the seeds by cutting the grapes almost in two, with a thin sharp knife. / Arrange on lettuce leaves and serve with French dressing or mayonnaise. ● Serves 4.

TOMATO JELLY SALAD

3 cups stewed tomatoes (fresh	¼ green pepper
or canned)	1 teaspoon sugar
½ cup chopped onion	Salt
½ cup chopped celery	1 tablespoon gelatin
1 bay leaf	½ cup cold water
1 clove	lettuce
	Mayonnaise

Cook tomatoes with seasonings. / Soak gelatin in cold water, add to boiling tomatoes, strain and pour into cups about the size of a tomato. / Refrigerate until set. / Make a nest of small green lettuce leaves for each mold when serving, and place one tablespoon of mayonnaise on top of each tomato as it is turned from the mold. / Tomato jelly is often molded in a square pan and cut in diamonds or cubes, when it makes an attractive garnish. ● Serves 6.

TOMATO ROSE SALAD

Firm tomatoes
Cream Cheese
Non-fat milk

Hard-cooked egg yolk
Watercress or lettuce
French dressing

Peel tomatoes and chill them. / Slightly soften cream cheese with milk. / Form two rows of petals on each tomato by pressing level teaspoons of the softened cheese against the side of the tomato, then drawing the teaspoon down with a curving motion. / Sprinkle center of each tomato with hard-cooked egg yolk pressed through a strainer. / Serve on crisp watercress or lettuce with French dressing.

FROZEN FRUIT SALAD

1 pint cream
1½ cups cut up fruit (fresh, canned, or candied cherries, peaches, pineapple, etc.
¾ cup mayonnaise

1 teaspoon powdered sugar
1 teaspoon instantaneous gelatin
2 tablespoons cold water
Lettuce

Soak the gelatin in the cold water, / melt it over steam, and beat it into the mayonnaise. / Add the sugar to the cream and whip it, / then combine with the mayonnaise. / Stir in the cut up fruit. / Pack and freeze in refrigerator freezer tray or shallow pan. / The mayonnaise may be omitted and served separately. ● Serves 4-6.

CHERRIES JUBILEE FRUIT SALAD

2 cups pitted dark sweet cherried, halved
1/3 cup cherry-flavored gelatin
½ cup cream sherry
6 pear halves, cooked and drained

3 ounces cream cheese, cut in small cubes
¼ cup chopped pecans
Lettuce leaves

Drain cherries, reserving syrup. / Add water to syrup to make 1½ cups liquid. / In medium saucepan combine gelatin and syrup mixture. / Heat and stir till gelatin dissolves. / Remove from heat; / stir in sherry. / Chill till partially set. / Reserve 2 pear halves; slice and set aside for garnish. / Chop remaining pears; fold into gelatin along with cherries, cheese, and pecans. / Turn into 4½ cups mold. / Chill till firm. / Unmold; garnish with lettuce leaves and pear slices. ● Serves 8.

BREADS ....

PUMPKIN BREAD ROUND ABOUTS

2/3 cup vegetable fat (except coconut oil)
2 3/4 cups sugar
3 eggs
2 cups pumpkin puree
3½ cups flour
1 teaspoon baking soda
1 teaspoon salt

½ teaspoon baking powder
½ teaspoon cloves
½ teaspoon nutmeg
½ teaspoon allspice
½ teaspoon cinnamon
¾ cup chopped walnuts
½ cup chopped maraschino cherries

Cream together fat and sugar. / Add eggs, one at a time mixing in remaining ingredients, tossing walnuts and cherries in flour first. / Grease and flour pans. / Fill each 2/3 full with batter. / Bake at 325° for 1 hour and 10 minutes. / Cool for 10 minutes. / Unmold breads. / Cook. / Slice ¼ inch thick. ● Makes 2 loaves. / See other bread recipes throughout this book.

DESSERTS ....

MOTHER CARTER'S
PECAN PIE RECIPE

FOR A SPECIAL DAY

To save time make pie shells ahead and place in freezer. / Frozen pie shells save time. / This recipe is the filling for an 8-inch frozen shell.

3 eggs
¾ cup granulated sugar
¾ cup dark karo syrup
1/8 teaspoon salt
3 tablespoons melted vegetable fat (except coconut oil)

2 cups chopped pecans
2 frozen, unbaked 8-inch pie shells* (See Recipe page 00)

Preheat oven to 400°F. / Beat eggs until blended, add sugar, syrup, salt, and beat thoroughly. / Stir in fat. / Put 1 cup of pecans in each pie shell. / Pour liquid mixture equally over each. / Place pies on a cookie sheet on middle rack of oven, bake for 10 minutes, then lower temperature to 300°F. and continue to bake until filling is firm, about 30 minutes. / Makes 2-8 inch pies. / For other desserts see examples throughout this book.

CHILDREN ENJOY
SOFT PUDDING (VANILLA)

2 cups non-fat milk	4 tablespoons sugar
2 whole eggs	½ teaspoon vanilla
1/8 teaspoon salt	

Scald milk in top of the double boiler. / Beat together slightly the eggs. / Sugar and salt. / Add the hot milk to the egg mixture, mix thoroughly and return to the top of the double boiler. / Cook over hot water, stirring constantly until the pudding coats the spoon. / Cool. ● Serves 4.

Variations:

CHOCOLATE—Melt one ounce of chocolate and add two tablespoons of sugar dissolved in two tablespoons of boiling water. / Mix thoroughly. / Add the chocolate mixture to two cups of scalded milk and use as the milk in a plain soft custard or pudding.

LEMON—Substitute ½ teaspoon lemon extract for the ½ teaspoon vanilla.

PEANUT BUTTER—Add 1 cup crunchy style peanut butter to warm pudding. / Mix thoroughly. / Cool. / Soft pudding or custard may be served over fresh fruit, cake, gelatin or as the dessert topped with meringue or whipped cream.

BEVERAGES ....

RASPBERRY-MINT CRUSH

½ cup sugar	1½ cup frozen raspberries
½ cup fresh mint leaves	1-6 oz. can frozen pink
1 cup boiling water	lemonade
1½ cup frozen raspberries	

Combine sugar, mint leaves and boiling water. / Let stand 5 minutes. / Add raspberries and lemonade, stirring until thawed. / Strain into chilled pitcher which is half-filled with crushed ice and add 2 cups ice water. / Garnish with fresh mint leaves and berries. ● Serves 9.

MINTED PUNCH

1 quart water	Juice from 6 oranges
1½ cups sugar	Juice from 3 lemons
¾ cup mint leaves, crushed	Mint for garnish

Heat water and sugar together for 5 minutes. / Add mint leaves. / Let stand 30 minutes; strain. / Add juices, pour into tall glasses; garnish with sprigs of mint. / Ginger ale may be added just before serving. ● Serves 8-10.

SPICED CIDER

1 quart cider	½ teaspoon allspice
4 sticks cinnamon	½ teaspoon whole cloves

Bring cider to boil. / Add spices. / Let stand 4 hours. / Strain. / Serve hot or cold.

EVERYONE ON THE GO MEALS

Whatever your schedule keep your meals simple and well-balanced with fresh fruits, fresh vegetables, whole grain cereals and breads. They are the best nutrition for your money. Add on the milk for calcium, the meats (lean, and fish and chicken) for protein. You will want to spread your meals over three to six meals each day. Plan your few minutes of quiet time to eat. A meal plan can be built around the quiet time.

Here are some menus and recipes to help you get started. Check first the amount of foods you need by the Recommended Daily Allowances Table in Appendix. If you are a teenager you need to be especially careful with your diet. You are making your life in later years by whatever you eat or do. You will become what you eat, so take a look at the food intake chart in this chapter. Check foods by group and amount needed for good nutrition.

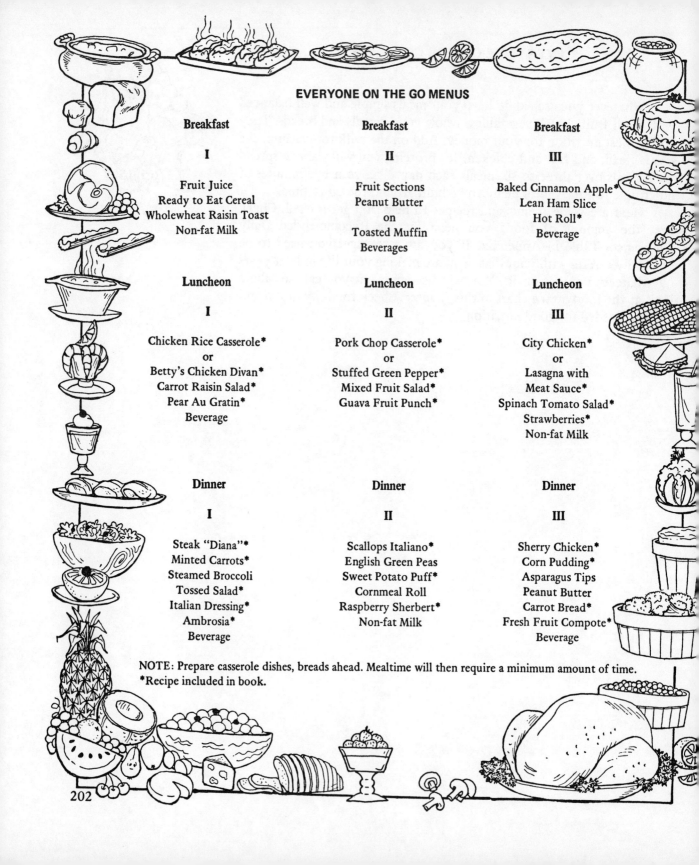

EVERYONE ON THE GO MENUS

Breakfast

I

Fruit Juice
Ready to Eat Cereal
Wholewheat Raisin Toast
Non-fat Milk

Breakfast

II

Fruit Sections
Peanut Butter
on
Toasted Muffin
Beverages

Breakfast

III

Baked Cinnamon Apple*
Lean Ham Slice
Hot Roll*
Beverage

Luncheon

I

Chicken Rice Casserole*
or
Betty's Chicken Divan*
Carrot Raisin Salad*
Pear Au Gratin*
Beverage

Luncheon

II

Pork Chop Casserole*
or
Stuffed Green Pepper*
Mixed Fruit Salad*
Guava Fruit Punch*

Luncheon

III

City Chicken*
or
Lasagna with
Meat Sauce*
Spinach Tomato Salad*
Strawberries*
Non-fat Milk

Dinner

I

Steak "Diana"*
Minted Carrots*
Steamed Broccoli
Tossed Salad*
Italian Dressing*
Ambrosia*
Beverage

Dinner

II

Scallops Italiano*
English Green Peas
Sweet Potato Puff*
Cornmeal Roll
Raspberry Sherbert*
Non-fat Milk

Dinner

III

Sherry Chicken*
Corn Pudding*
Asparagus Tips
Peanut Butter
Carrot Bread*
Fresh Fruit Compote*
Beverage

NOTE: Prepare casserole dishes, breads ahead. Mealtime will then require a minimum amount of time.
*Recipe included in book.

RECURS

RECIPES

MAIN DISHES . . . .

ONE OF HAL'S FAVORITE'S
SHERRY CHICKEN

4 large chicken breasts	¼ to ½ pound fresh
1 1/3 cup mushroom soup	mushrooms
1 cup sour cream	vegetable fat (except coconut
½ cup sherry	oil)

Brown sliced mushrooms in vegetable fat. / Add soup, sour cream and sherry. / Arrange chicken pieces in baking dish, pour mixture over chicken. / Sprinkle with paprika and bake at 350° for 1 to 1½ hours. / Serve with rice (spoon sauce over rice) and lemon buttered broccoli. • Serves 4.

The following recipe was submitted by Elizabeth B. (Mrs. C. Winfred) Carter, Newport News, Virginia:

PORK CHOP CASSEROLE

6 pork chops, lean, fat	½ teaspoon salt
removed	¼ teaspoon pepper
5 medium potatoes, cooked and	1½ cups tomato soup
sliced	½ cup water
½ cup finely chopped onions	

Arrange alternate layers of potatoes and onions in greased casserole. / Then brown pork chops in hot fat in a skillet. / Place chops on top of potatoes and onions. / Season with listed ingredients. / Thin tomato soup with water and pour over chops. / Cover and bake at 350° for about 45 minutes. • Serves 6. A dish for an activity day.

The following recipes were submitted by Heridan (Mrs. John L.) Fox, McLean, Virginia:

CHICKEN IN ORANGE SAUCE

1 chicken quartered	2 tablespoons sherry
¼ cup melted vegetable fat	2 tablespoons brown sugar
(except coconut oil)	pinch salt & paprika
Seasoned flour (flour, salt,	1 tablespoon orange rind
pepper & paprika)	1 tablespoon corn starch
1 medium onion, sliced	½ cup mandarine oranges
½ green pepper	½ cup seedless grapes
1 cup orange juice	

Wash and dry chicken; roll pieces in fat, then in flour. / Arrange chicken in baking dish; top with onions and peppers. / In sauce pan mix orange juice with sherry, sugar, salt and grated rind; dissolve corn starch in little water; stir in orange mixture. / Cook over low heat stirring constantly until mixture thickens. / Pour over chicken. / Bake in 375° F. for 1 hour (uncovered). / In the last 15 minutes of cooking add mandarin oranges and grapes. / Sprinkle on paprika. Serve with wild rice or fluffy white rice. • Serves 4.

STEAK "DIANA"

1½ lbs. round steak, cut ½	1 bay leaf
inch thick	½ teaspoon marjoram
½ cup flour with salt & pepper	2 slices American cheese,
seasoning	halved
1 onion, sliced	Peanut oil for frying

Pound meat and cut into 4 or 5 pieces. / Roll in seasoned flour. / Brown in oil slowly. / Arrange in baking dish. / Add water to skillet in which you fried meat, getting all the flavor. / Pour stock on meat. / Cover with onions, bay leaf and marjoram. / May add more water if needed. / Bake covered for 1 hour & 15 minutes at 325° F. / Top with cheese. / Heat again to melt cheese and serve at once. • Serves 6.

This Recipe has been submitted by Ruth (Mrs. Charles Eastwood, Roanoke, Virginia:

CHICKEN CASSEROLE WITH RICE

1 tbs. vegetable fat (except coconut oil)	1 cup mushroom soup
1 cup uncooked rice (regular)	½ cup dry onion soup mix
6 pieces of chicken, fat removed	1 cup water

Combine and bake 2 hours at 325°F. • Serves 6.

This Recipe was submitted by Mrs. Andrew Keys, Adelphi, Maryland.

"CITY CHICKEN"

(Very popular in Western Pennsylvania)

3 lbs. lean beef	Bread crumbs
3 lbs. lean pork	2 eggs
3 lbs. veal	¼ cup water
1 onion	vegetable fat (except coconut) oil)
Oregano, salt & pepper	
Flour	Wooden skewers—4-5" lengths)

If the butcher cannot supply the wooden skewers, then one can purchase ¼" wooden dowels in a lumber store, cut to size and sharpen one end on a pencil sharpener. / These should be washed in hot, soapy water and then sterilized by boiling in water for 15 minutes—can be used over and over again. / Take a piece of each kind of meat and spear on a skewer; leave about an inch clearance on blunt end of skewer for handling. / Lightly flour each "chicken" then bathe in egg wash (heat eggs and water until foamy) and roll in bread crumbs. / Fry in fat to a golden color and place in baking pan. / Spread sliced onion and touch of oregano over meat. / Salt and pepper to taste. / Cover. / Bake at 375° — 3½ hours. / Let stand 15 minutes before serving. • Serves 12.

This Recipe was submitted by Mary (Mrs. John Carter Dean) Medical College of Virginia, Richmond, Virginia:

LASAGNE WITH MEAT SAUCE

1½ pounds ground beef	¼ teaspoon sugar
1 large onion, chopped	1½ teaspoon oregano
½ cup onion soup mix	2 cups cottage cheese
1½ cups water	¾ pound Mozzarella cheese
2 tablespoons olive oil	½ pound lasagne noodles, cooked
1 cup tomato paste	Parmesan cheese, grated
1 cup tomato sauce	
½ teaspoon salt	

Brown onion and beef in oil. / Stir in soup mix, water, tomato paste, tomato sauce, and seasonings. / Cover; simmer 30 minutes. / Place a thin layer of meat sauce in a 8 x 13 x 2 baking dish; add layers of noodles, mozzarella, cottage cheese and meat sauce. / Sprinkle with Parmesan cheese. / Bake at 350°F. for 45 minutes. • Serves 6-8.

This Recipe was submitted by Mrs. Billy P. Gibson, McLean, Virginia:

BETTY'S CHICKEN DIVAN

5 chicken breasts	2 cups bread crumbs
4 cups broccoli	2 tablespoons lemon juice
2 cups Cream of Chicken soup	¾ teaspoon curry powder
½ cup mayonnaise	1 cup shredded sharp cheese

Cook chicken breasts in water until tender. / Remove from water and drain. / Save the water. / Remove from bone and tear into bite size pieces. / Cook Broccoli in chicken water—drain when tender, lay on a greased baking dish. Add chicken. / Pour over chicken soup, mayonnaise, bread crumbs, curry powder. / Add lemon juice. / Top with shredded cheese. / Bake at 350°F. for 20 minutes. • Serves 5.

204

STUFFED PEPPERS

6 green peppers
1½ cups ham or beef
1 cup peas, or corn, if desired
2 cups cooked rice
2 cups tomatoes
1 large onion, chopped fine

1 teaspoon sugar
salt (dash)
pepper (dash)
½ cup bread crumbs
½ cup grated cheese

Wash green peppers. / Cut in half and remove seeds and place in baking dish. / Grind ham and mix with peas, or corn, add rice, tomatoes, onion, dash of sugar and season with salt and pepper to taste. / Spoon mixture into peppers. / Top the stuffed peppers with bread crumbs and grated cheese. / Baste with the juice from the tomatoes and water to keep moist. / Bake at 350°F. for 1 hour in covered casserole dish. ● Serves 12.

This Recipe was submitted by Mrs. Frank Gerace, Allentown, Pennsylvania.

SCALLOPS—ITALIANO

3 cups scallops
2 tablespoons vegetable fat
   (except coconut oil)
½ lb. fresh mushrooms, sliced
1 cup green pepper, sliced

1 med. onion sliced
2½ cups plum
   tomatoes—chopped
1 teaspoon seasoned salt
1 teaspoon parsley flakes

Thaw scallops if frozen. / Saute mushrooms, green peppers and onions for 5 minutes in hot oil. / Add scallops and continue to saute for about 8 minutes. / Add tomatoes, seasoned salt and parsley. / Cover and simmer for 10 minutes. ● Serves 4.

HAM PUFF CASSEROLE

2 cups non-fat milk
1 tablespoon vegetable fat
   (except coconut oil)
1/3 cup yellow cornmeal
3 eggs, separated

¼ teaspoon salt
¼ teaspoon paprika
1 cup grated cheese
1 cup cooked ground ham

Place the milk and fat in a saucepan and bring to boiling point. / Stir in cornmeal slowly and cook for 5 minutes, stirring constantly. / Remove from heat and stir in the beaten egg yolks, salt and paprika. / Add the cheese and stir until melted. / Add the ham and fold in the stiffly beaten egg whites. / Pour into a greased 2-quart casserole. / Bake at 325° for about 1 hour or until a knife inserted in center comes out clean. ● Serves 6-8.

ISLAND CASSEROLE

2 tablespoons chopped onion
1 tablespoon vegetable fat
   (except coconut oil)
1½ cups cream of celery soup
¼ cup non-fat milk
½ cup shredded mild process
   cheese
2 cups cooked diced potatoes

1 cup cooked cut green beans
1 tablespoon diced pimento
1 cup salmon, drained
2 tablespoons bread crumbs
   mixed with vegetable fat
   (except coconut oil)

Cook the onion in fat until tender. / Combine the soup and milk, stirring until smooth, then add to the onion. / Add the cheese and cook and stir until melted. / Add the potatoes, green beans and pimento. / Pour 1/3 of the potato mixture into a 1-quart casserole. / Break the salmon into chunks with 2 forks, then place half the salmon on top of the potato mixture. / Repeat layers and top with remaining potato mixture. / Sprinkle the crumbs on top. / Bake at 400° for 20 minutes. / Garnish with chopped parsley, if desired. ● Serves 4.

ONION-CRESTED HASH CASSEROLE

4 cups sliced onions
3 tablespoons vegetable oil
   (except coconut oil)
½ teaspoon curry powder
1 teaspoon Worcestershire
   sauce

½ teaspoon salt
1/8 teaspoon pepper
2¼ cups corned beef hash
1/3 cup non-fat milk
½ cup fresh bread crumbs
½ cup grated Cheddar cheese

Preheat oven to 375°. / Saute the onions in oil until golden. / Remove from heat and sprinkle in curry powder. / Mix Worcestershire, salt, pepper and hash and turn into a 1-quart baking dish. / Pour the milk over the hash mixture. / Top with onions. / Toss the crumbs and cheese together and sprinkle over onion layer. / Bake for 30 minutes. ● Serves 6.

BAVARIA KRAUT AND FRANKFURTERS

4 cups undrained sauerkraut	¾ cup non-fat milk
1 cup wine or sherry	1 tablespoon poppy seed
1 medium onion, chopped	½ lb. frankfurters
1 bay leaf	½ lb. bratwurst
1 teaspoon salt	½ lb. bauernwurst
12 peppercorns	
Make soft biscuit dough (see recipe page 00)	

Combine the sauerkraut, wine or sherry, 2 cups water, onion, bay leaf, salt and peppercorns in large kettle or Dutch oven and bring to a boil. / Combine the biscuit dough milk and poppyseed with a fork. / Prick the meats with a fork and add to the kettle. / Spoon the dough by tablespoonfuls on top. / Cook, uncovered over low heat for 10 minutes, then cover and cook for 10 minutes longer. / Serve the meat and dumplings with the sauerkraut, draining the sauerkraut, if desired. • Serves 6.

CHICKEN AND SWEET POTATO

1 fryer, disjointed	Brown sugar
Salt to taste	Vegetable fat (except coconut oil)
2 medium sweet potatoes	
6 to 8 slices pineapple	Cinnamon
½ cup pineapple juice	

Season the chicken with salt and place in a long, shallow, foil-lined casserole. / Cut the sweet potatoes in ¼-inch slices and place over chicken. / Place the pineapple over sweet potatoes. / Pour pineapple juice over top. / Place ½ teaspoon brown sugar in center of each pineapple slice and dot with vegetable fat (except coconut oil). / Sprinkle with cinnamon and seal foil. / Bake at 400°F. for about 1 hour or until chicken is tender. • Serves 6.

Here is a white sauce recipe to assist you with variety in meal preparation.

WHITE SAUCE

White sauce is a useful base for making different cream style dishes. Thin white sauce is blended with puree or strained vegetables to make creamed soups; a medium white sauce is blended with pieces of meat, fish, fowl, or eggs and vegetables to make creamed dishes; a thick white sauce is used as the base for souffles, and a very thick white sauce is blended with other ingredients to make croquettes. To make a white sauce, milk or some other liquid is thickened with flour or some cereal product to the desired consistency.

COOKERY SUGGESTIONS:

1. The purpose of the white sauce influences the proportion of fat to flour to liquid.
2. The melted vegetable fat (except coconut oil) and flour are blended thoroughly to make a smooth sauce.
3. The liquid is added slowly to the blended fat and flour to prevent lumping.
4. The sauce is cooked slowly at a low temperature to prevent scorching.
5. The sauce is seasoned with salt and pepper and, if desired, some herbs or spices, such as paprika or curry, are added for a piquant flavor. Celery salt and garlic salt are substitutes for table salt.
6. White sauce is seldom served alone but is incorporated into a cream style soup, blended with other food into creamed dishes, used as a base to make souffle, and used as the binder to make croquettes.

THIN WHITE SAUCE

1 tablespoon vegetable fat (except coconut oil)	1 cup non-fat milk
1 tablespoon flour	¼ teaspoon salt
	Pepper or paprika, if desired

Melt the fat in a saucepan over low heat. / Stir in the flour and salt, using a wooden spoon, and blend thoroughly. / Add milk slowly, stirring continuously. / Cook sauce for 2 to 3 minutes over low heat, or until thick. / Add pepper or paprika, if desired. / The sauce is ready to blend with pureed vegetables to make cream soups.

MEDIUM WHITE SAUCE

Follow the same procedure, using the proportions of 2 tablespoons vegetable fat (except coconut oil), 2 tablespoons flour, 1 cup milk, and ¼ teaspoon salt.

VEGETABLES . . . .

These Recipes were submitted by Mrs. Glenwood Deacon, Roanoke, Virginia.

CORN PUDDING

2¼ cups cream style sweet corn	¼ cup sugar
1 egg slightly beaten	Salt and pepper to taste
1 cup of non-fat milk	1 tablespoon vegetable fat (except coconut oil)
¼ cup flour	

Mix corn, egg, milk, flour and 1/8 cup sugar. / Add salt and pepper. / Sprinkle on top 1/8 cup sugar and dot on top. / Bake at 450° for 45 minutes or until firm. ● Serves 4.

SWEET POTATOE PUFFS

2 cups sweet potatoes, mashed	1 oz. grated coconut
6 marshmallows	

Roll mashed sweet potatoes into balls. / Push 1 marshmallow down in the center of each ball. / Roll in coconut. / Place under broiler at 450°F. until coconut is brown and marshmallow is slightly melted. ● Serves 4.

SALADS . . . .

TOSSED SALAD

¼ head lettuce	2 radishes
4 leaves spinach	Lemon slices
4 leaves watercress	Bread cubes
2 carrots	2 slices crisp bacon
2 stalks celery	Salad dressing
1 tomato	

Chop lettuce into lettuce lined bowl. / Chop spinach and watercress leaves. / Cube green pepper and celery. / Mix thoroughly. / Slice radishes and place on top. / Quarter tomato for top garnish. / Serve with lemon slices, bread cubes and 2 slices crisp bacon chopped into fine bits. / Add your favorite dressing and enjoy in relaxed atmosphere. ● Serves 1.

See other salads and salad dressings throughout this book.

SALAD DRESSINGS . . . .

RUSSIAN DRESSING

1½ tablespoons lemon juice	1 tablespoon Worcestershire Sauce
2 tablespoons thick chili sauce	½ cup mayonnaise

Mix the lemon juice, chili sauce and Worcestershire thoroughly and add the mayonnaise.

THOUSAND ISLAND DRESSING

1 cup mayonnaise	1 tablespoon chopped green pepper
2 tablespoons chili sauce	
1 tablespoon sweet pickle relish	

Combine ingredients well. / Serve over head lettuce wedges or mixed green salad.

ITALIAN DRESSING

¼ cup olive oil
2 tablespoons lemon juice
1 tablespoon lemon rind grated
Salt (dash)
½ teaspoon oregano or thyme

1 clove garlic, minced
1 tablespoon Parmesan cheese, grated
½ teaspoon black pepper, freshly ground

Combine all ingredients. / Mix well. / Mix shake before using. / Store in covered jar or bottle.

BREADS ....

AUNT NELLIE'S
PEANUT BUTTER-CARROT BREAD

1 cup brown sugar, firmly packed
½ cup chunky-style peanut butter
½ cup peanut oil
2 eggs
2 cups shredded carrots

1 teaspoon vanilla
¾ cups enriched flour
1 teaspoon baking powder
1 teaspoon baking soda
¼ teaspoon salt
¼ teaspoon allspice
¼ teaspoon nutmeg
½ cup non-fat milk

Preheat oven to 350°F. / Grease 1 9 x 3 x 1½ inch loaf pan. / Cream together sugar, peanut butter, peanut oil, and eggs; add carrots and vanilla. / Blend flour, baking powder, baking soda, salt, allspice, and nutmeg. / Alternately add flour mixture and milk to creamed mixture. / Pour into pan and bake 30 minutes. / Cool 10 minutes in pan, remove from pan, and cool on rack. / Makes one loaf. ● Serves 4.

Prepare ahead and store in refrigerator until ready for use. Will keep for 1 week. ● Serves 4.

DESETS ....

This Recipe was submitted by Heridan (Mrs. John L.) Fox, McLean, Virginia:

PEARS "AU GRATIN"

3 or 4 pears sliced, peel and core removed
1 tablespoon softened vegetable fat (except coconut oil)
1/3 cup apricot or peach jam

¼ cup dry vermouth or white wine
3 or 4 macaroons or cookies
2 tablespoons vegetable fat (except coconut oil), cut into dots

Smear baking dish with fat; / arrange pears, sliced to about 3/8 inches thick in dish; / mix jam and wine and pour over pears. / Crumble macaroons or cookies over all and top with fat dots. / Bake at 350° for 25 to 30 minutes or until brown on top. / Serve warm. ● Serves 4.

This Recipe was submitted by Fern (Mrs. George) Heller, Englewood, Colorado.

GUAVA FRUIT PUNCH

2½ cups frozen orange juice concentrate, reconstituted
4½ cups guavanectar, chilled
1¼ cups light rum (optional)
2 oranges, unpeeled but thinly sliced and slices halved

1 fresh pineapple, peeled, cored, and cut into spears
1 large papaya, peeled, seeded, and sliced
2 cups whole strawberries

Combine in a punch bowl the orange juice and chilled guava nectar. / Just before serving pour in the rum, if used. / In a bowl arrange the orange slices, pineapple spears, papaya slices, and strawberries. / Float a few pieces of fruit in the punch. / To serve, spoon fruit into 12 or 14 oz. glasses, fill with punch; offer straws and spoons. ● Serves 14.

ELDERLY

There remains much to be learned about the aging process. We do know that biological changes, conditioned by the experiences that have come before this phase of life, take place. In the later ages there is a cell loss and a reduction in the cell metabolism. We also know, according to studies, that there is a gradual reduction in the performance of most organ systems. The nerve impulse diminishes. Blood flow through the kidneys is reduced. The glucose level of the blood requires longer to return to normal after each meal. The pulse rate and respiration after exercise requires longer to return to normal.

Overall, the elderly experience a gradual reduction in the body's reserve capacity.

Some resulting psychological factors may affect food patterns. There may be a reduction of the digestive juices, a decreased mobility of the gastrointestinal tract, and a decrease in absorption and utilization of food nutrients.

There appears to be an individuality about how rapidly the biological changes take place. Each person bears the results of his experiences with disease, with a direct effect upon his individual aging process. The specific needs of individuals must, therefore, be considered when discussing nutritional needs.

It seems that the greatest influence of nutrition on the aging process takes place in the early years. During the middle years of life nutrition's role in growth and development prepares the individual for the gradual declining of the metabolic processes that occur in old age.

In planning foods for the elderly, changes in metabolism must be considered:

- Calories need to be decreased because of slowed metabolism and decreased activity. For men the need would decrease to about 1800 calories each day, and for women the need would be about 1500 calories each day.
- Carbohydrate intake should be decreased; however, it should amount to more than 60 percent of the total calorie intake.
- Protein need decreases to 0.9 grams per kilogram of body weight. The sources of protein should come from a combination of animal and plant nutrients.

• Vitamins should come from a well-selected variety of foods for normal aging. (The need during illnesses will need to be evaluated individually, with the guidance of a physician.)

• Minerals should be increased in normal aging. Two essential minerals may be lacking in a poor diet—iron and calcium. These should be provided.

• Water should be taken liberally.

The elderly may be more subject than other groups to malnutrition because of poor teeth which make chewing difficult and gastrointestinal problems such as ulcers and indigestion which limit the food supply. There may also be personal factors that prevent good nutrition such as lack of financial resources, lack of knowledge about sound diet, loneliness, boredom, apathy and insecurity. The elderly person who lives alone has lost all the social values related to foods and consequently may have lost the desire to eat. The older person may also be without cooking equipment, food storage facilities, transportation to the market and, sadly, any interest in food. Finally, the elderly person will become ill.

On the other hand, food is often the only interest to the elderly person. How he or she accepts foods will be determined by the feelings about self and the relationship to others. The availability and attractiveness of the meal takes second place. Meals taken once or twice a week, preferably more often, with family and friends can help encourage the elderly person to eat nourishing meals when he is alone the rest of the week at mealtime.

Our knowledge of the elderly needs to be expanded in order to improve their accessibility to the social aspects of good nutrition. The elderly should never be left to malnutrition and despair from loneliness and insecurity. We must consider:

• A preventive disease program to promote good nutrition and general good health.

• Programs that recognize the deep and valuable needs of the elderly in relation to nutrition—focusing on foods to promote social security and a feeling of well-being and importance to self and others.

• A serious evaluation of the many feeding stations designed to satisfy hunger, but promoting nothing else, for the elderly.

- How to stimulate interest in life among the elderly rather than continuing to design institutions where the multiple elderly sit out depressing and purposeless years which should be productive.
- A diet served in an environment of interest and enthusiasm which will be easier digested and used by the elderly body.

Some menus and recipes to help the elderly have been included. These menus and recipes may, also, be helpful ideas for planning programs and meals for the elderly. Elderly people usually have more time to think about what they eat. Food should be as much fun to eat for the elderly as for children. Allow them to participate in the planning of meals.

As you increase in years make life more worthwhile and meaningful by keeping nutrition in its proper place.

DINNER MENUS / FIRST WEEK

Menus for the Elderly Need To Be Especially Attractive And Easy to Eat.

Monday

Baked Macaroni Dinner*
Peach and Cottage Cheese Salad*
Roll with Vegetable Fat*
Raspberry-Pineapple Sherbert
Milk†

Tuesday

Creamed Mushroom Soup*
Country Fried Steak with Gravy
Mashed Potatoes   Peas
Roll with Vegetable Fat
Fresh Fruit Cup*
Milk†

Wednesday

Pea Soup
Meat Loaf*
Baked Rice in Tomato Sauce
Asparagus
Roll with Vegetable Fat
Orange Compote
Milk†

Thursday

Turkey and Noodle Casserole*
Parslied Carrots
Tomato Salad
Roll with Vegetable Fat
Fruit Cup
Milk†

Friday

Pea Soup
Baked Ocean Perch/Lemon
Oven Baked Potatoes
Beets
Cornbread with Vegetable Fat*
Fruit Sherbert
Milk†

Saturday

Spaghetti Sauce and Meat Balls Casserole*
Green Beans
Tossed Salad with French Dressing*
Roll with Vegetable Fat
Apple Sauce
Milk†

Sunday

Sliced Turkey*
Sweet Potatoes
Green Beans
Shredded Lettuce Salad
Roll with Vegetable Fat
Broiled Grapefruit with Cherry
Milk†

*Recipe included in book.
†Milk may be non-fat if desired.

DINNER MENUS / SECOND WEEK

Monday

Tomato Soup
Broiled Mushroom Cubed Steak with Gravy
Mashed Potatoes
Beets
Roll with Vegetable Fat
Pineapple Sponge Cake*
Milk†

Tuesday

Peanut Soup*
Broiled Chicken with Lemon*
Steamed Rice
Carrots
Roll with Vegetable Fat
Peach Half
Milk†

Wednesday

Beef Noodle Soup
Tuna Cakes with Lemon*
Potatoes
Green Beans
Cornbread with Vegetable Fat*
Custard, Baked*
Milk†

Thursday

Breaded Veal Cutlet with Gravy
Baked Grits
Green Peas
Shredded Lettuce Salad*
French Dressing
Roll with Vegetable Fat
Peas
Milk†

Friday

Pea Soup
Tuna Noodle Casserole*
Pineapple Carrots
Roll with Vegetable Fat*
Apple Crisp*
Milk†

Saturday

Broiled Veal Pattie
Corn Pudding*
Spinach
Cranberry Salad*
Roll with Vegetable Fat
Daisy Cake*
Milk†

Sunday

Vegetable Soup
Broiled Chopped Sirloin
Mashed Potatoes
Chopped Kale
Roll with Vegetable Fat
Chocolate Pudding — Milk†

*Recipe included in book.
†Milk may be non-fat if desired.

For the elderly who have difficulty chewing foods or swallowing the foods.

Breakfast
Stewed Prunes
Cream of Wheat
(½ cup) Milk, whole or non-fat
Coffee

10 A.M.
Toast, 2 slices
Jelly or Honey
Non-fat Milk — 1 glass

Luncheon
Cottage Cheese
Toast, 2 slices
Jelly or Honey
Applesauce
Tea

3 P.M.
Junket made with non-fat milk
Crackers
Jelly or Honey

Dinner
Sliced Chicken (diced)
Baked Potato
Soft-cooked String Beans
Apricot Halves in Syrup
Tea

8 P.M.
Crackers
Jelly or Honey
1 glass non-fat milk

RECIPES

MAIN DISHES . . . .

BEEF BAKE

macaroni and cheese (see
  recipe page 00)
1 lb. ground beef
2 tablespoons chopped onion

2 tablespoons vegetable fat
  (except coconut oil)
½ cup cream of mushroom
  soup
½ cup non-fat milk

Prepare macaroni and cheese dinner according to package directions. / Brown the ground beef and onion in fat in a skillet and stir in soup and milk. / Place half the macaroni and cheese in a greased 1½-quart casserole and add half the beef mixture. / Repeat layers. / Bake at 350°F. for 25 minutes. ● Serves 4-6.

GROUND BEEF AND GREEN BEAN CASSEROLE

1 lb. ground beef
1 small onion, diced
½ teaspoon salt

1-1/3 cups tomato soup
2 cups cut green beans
1 cup grated cheese

Cook the beef and onion in a skillet until brown. / Add the salt, soup and beans and mix well. / Place in a casserole and cover with cheese. / Bake at 350°F. for about 30 minutes. ● Serves 5-6.

CHICKEN-CHEESE CASEROLE

1 cup diced celery
2 tablespoons diced onion
2 tablespoons vegetable fat
  (except coconut oil)
2 cups diced cooked chicken
2 cups dry bread crumbs

1 teaspoon salt
½ teaspoon pepper
2 eggs well beaten
¾ cup hot non-fat milk or
  chicken stock
1 cup grated Cheddar cheese

Saute the celery and onion in fat in a saucepan until tender. / Add remaining ingredients except cheese and mix well. / Place in a well-greased 8-inch square casserole and top with cheese. / Bake at 325°F. for 40 minutes. ● Serves 8.

ASPARAGUS-TOMATO-MACARONI BAKE

1 cup cooked macaroni
2 cups green asparagus tips
3 cups whole tomatoes
4 tablespoons melted vegetable
  fat (except coconut oil)

1 tablespoon flour
3/4 cup non-fat milk
1 cup grated American cheese
Salt and pepper to taste
½ cup bread crumbs

Spread the macaroni in a fat greased baking dish. / Drain the asparagus, reserving juice. / Arrange the asparagus on top of the macaroni. / Drain the tomatoes and place over the asparagus. / Place 2 tablespoons fat in a saucepan and blend in the flour. / Add the asparagus juice, milk and cheese, stirring constantly. / Bring to a boil, then sprinkle with salt and pepper. / Pour the sauce over the casserole and sprinkle with crumbs. / Pour remaining fat over crumbs. / Bake in a 350° oven until slightly brown and heated through. / About 1 hour. ● Serves 6 or 8.

GLAZED FRANKFURTER CASSEROLE

2 cups pork and beans with
  tomato sauce
6 frankfurters
2 tablespoon brown sugar

I teaspoon prepared mustard
I teaspoon Worcestershire
  sauce

Pour the beans into a shallow baking dish. / Cut the frankfurters almost in half and arrange on beans, cut side up. / Combine the sugar, mustard and Worcestershire sauce and spread over frankfurters. / Bake at 375° for 20 minutes or until beans are hot and frankfurters are browned. ● Serves 4.

SNOW CAPS

¾ cup chopped onion	1/8 teaspoon pepper
1 tablespoon vegetable fat	2½ cups cooked green beans
(except coconut oil)	1½ cups tomato soup
1½ pound ground beef	2 cups mashed potatoes
1 tablespoon salt	1 egg, beaten

Saute the onion in fat until golden. / Add the ground beef, salt and pepper and cook until brown, then drain. / Drain the green beans and combine with the ground beef mixture and the soup in a 1 1/2-quart casserole. / Combine the mashed potatoes and the egg, mixing well. / Drop mounds of mashed potatoes on top of the ground beef mixture. / Bake at 350° for 30 minutes. ● Serves 6.

VARIEGATED GRITS

6 slices baken, diced	1 teaspoon salt
1 cup diced onions	Dash of pepper
2 cups cooked grits	1 tomato, chopped

Fry the bacon in a skillet until crisp. / Add the onions and cook until tender. / Add the grits, salt and pepper and cook, stirring, for about 1 minute. / Add tomato and pour into a casserole. / Bake at 350° until heated through. About 30 minutes. ● Serves 6-8.

SPAGHETTI CASSEROLE

2 cups spaghetti with 4-6	1½ cups tomatoes
meatballs	½ cup Parmesan cheese
1½ cups mushrooms	

Combine the spaghetti with meatballs, mushrooms and tomatoes in a baking dish and sprinkle with Parmesan cheese. / Bake at 350° for 30 minutes. ● Serves 4.

SWEET POTATO CASSEROLE

1/2 cups (firmly packed)	2 1/2 cups sweet potatoes,
brown sugar	mashed
1/2 cup sugar	1 cup corn flake crumbs
3 eggs beaten	1 cup chopped pecans
1/2 cup vegetable fat melted	
(except coconut oil)	

Combine the sugars, eggs, ¼ cup fat and potatoes. / Mix the crumbs, remaining fat and pecans. / Place the potato mixture in a greased casserole and top with the corn flake mixture. / Bake in 400° oven for 20 to 25 minutes. / Serve hot. ● Serves 6.

SANDWICHES ....

The sandwich is enjoyed by the elderly. It is easy to handle and an easy way to add the nutritional value.

BROWN-DERBY SPECIAL

3 cups finely shredded	12 rye bread slices
cabbage	Vegetable fat (except coconut
2/3 cup mayonnaise	oil
3 tablespoons chili sauce	1 pound thinly sliced ham
1 tablespoon finely chopped	1 pound thinly sliced natural
onion	Swiss cheese
¼ teaspoon salt	6 kosher-style dill pickles

Lightly toss cabbage, mayonnaise, chili sauce, onion, and salt. / Refrigerate about 1 hour, or until well chilled. / For each sandwich, lightly spread 2 slices bread with fat. / On one slice, generously layer ham and cheese slices; then spread with some of cabbage mixture. / Top with second bread slice. / Cut sandwich crosswise into thirds. / Serve with a dill pickle. ● Serves 6.

DEVILED-HAM AND SWISS CHEESE BUNS

4 teaspoons mayonnaise or
  cooked salad dressing*
1/4 cup deviled ham
4 slices Swiss cheese
4 slices thin tomato slices

4 slices thin onion
4 large stuffed olives
4 sweet gherkins
4 hamburger buns

Spread bottom halves of buns with mayonnaise, then with deviled ham. / Top each with cheese slice, tomato slice, onion slice, and other half of bun. / Put olives and gherkins on 4 wooden picks, and stick one in each bun. • Serves 4.

HERO SANDWICHES

2 loaves French bread (about
  8 inches long)
1/4 teaspoon dried oregano
  leaves
1/4 cup soft vegetable fat
  (except coconut oil)

1/4 pound sliced boiled ham
1 tomato, thinly sliced
1/4 pound sliced Swiss cheese
Prepared mustard
Lettuce leaves
Salt

Heat or bake French bread. / Blend oregano into fat. / Cool loaves slightly; slice in half lengthwise. / Spread oregano fat. / On bottom halves, arrange in order ham, tomato, Swiss cheese. / Spread cheese with mustard. / Add lettuce; sprinkle with salt. / Top with upper halves of loaves. • Serves 2.

TUNA-AND-CHEESE CLUB SANDWICHES

1 cup chunk-style tuna,
  drained
1/ cup stuffed olives, chopped
1 hard cooked egg, finely
  chopped
2 teaspoons lemon juice
1/3 cup mayonnaise or cooked
  salad dressing*

16 white bread sliced, toasted
8 whole-wheat bread slices,
  toasted
1/2 cup soft vegetable fat
  (except coconut oil)
Lettuce
16 slices American cheese

Combine tuna, olives, eggs, lemon juice, and mayonnaise, tossing until well mixed. / Spread all toast slices with fat. / Spread 8 white toast slices with tuna mixture. / Top each with 2 slices cheese, then white toast slice. / Cut in half diagonally, garnish with cherry tomatoes and cucumber slices. • Serves 4.

BARBECUED SPOONBURGERS

3 tablespoons vegetable fat
  (except coconut oil)
1/4 cup chopped onion
1/4 cup chopped green pepper
1 pound ground chuck
1 teaspoon salt

1/4 teaspoon pepper
1 cup catsup
2 cups cream style corn
4 hamburger buns, split and
  toasted

Heat fat in large skillet. / Add onion and green pepper; saute, stirring and over medium heat, until golden and tender- about 5 minutes. / Add chuck; cook, stirring, until no longer red. / Stir in salt, pepper, catsup, and corn; heat 5 minutes more, or until mixture is bubbly. / Serve on hamburger buns. • Serves 4.

BUNSTEADS.

1 cup tuna, drained and
  flaked
2 tablespoons finely chopped
  onions
2 tablespoons finely chopped
  green pepper
2 tablespoons finely chopped
  stuffed olives

3 tablespoons sweet pickle
  relish, drained
1/2 pound American cheese,
  cut into 1/2 inch cubes
3 hard cooked eggs, finely
  chopped
3 hamburger buns

To the drained flaked tuna add onion, green pepper, chopped olives, and pickled relish. / Add chopped egg and cheese cubes. / Spread on hamburger buns. / Cut in half or quarters. / Mayonnaise may be used as deisred. • Serves 3.

DESSERTS . . . .

FOUR-FRUIT SHERBET

2 cups mashed bananas (3
  medium bananas)
1/4 cup lemon juice
1/3 cup orange juice
1/2 cup clear syrup
1/8 teaspoon salt

1 egg white
1/3 cup sugar
1 cup non-fat milk
1/4 cup maraschino cherry
Juice

To mashed bananas add sugar, salt, corn syrup. / Mix thoroughly. / Add cherry, lemon and orange juices. / Add milk gradually. / Stir constantly. Beat egg white until peaks are formed. / Fold into fruit mixture. / Place in shallow pan or a freezer tray and freeze. • Serves 2.

RASPBERRY-PINEAPPLE SHERBET

1 1/2 cups frozen raspberries   **1 3/4 cups frozen pineapple**

Break frozen fruit apart with fork. / Put in electric blender a small quantity at a time and blend after each addition. / When smooth and of sherbet consistency serve at once. / If you prefer a firmer sherbet, you may store for a short time in freezing tray of refrigerator. / This sherbet is good served in meringue shells because its tangy flavor contrasts with the sweetness of the meringue. ● Serves 2.

CRANBERRY SHERBET

2 cups cranberries   **¼ cup cold water**
1 1/4 cups water   **Juice of 1 lemon or 2**
1 cup sugar   **tablespoons lemon juice**
1 teaspoon unflavored gelatin

Cook cranberries in 1 1/4 cups water until skins pop. / Press through sieve. / Add sugar and cook until sugar dissolves. / Add gelatin softened in cold water; cool. / Add lemon juice. / Freeze in shallow pan or refrigerator tray 2 to 3 hours, stirring twice. ● Serves 2.

MAPLE BAKED CUSTARD

3 cups liquefied non-fat dry   **3 whole eggs**
** milk**   **5/8 cup maple syrup**
1/8 teaspoon salt

Scald milk and salt. / Stir in maple syrup. / Beat eggs and slowly pour milk, salt, and syrup mixture over them. / Beat the custard until it is well blended. / Pour into baking dish or individual molds. This quantity will fill 8 small custard cups. / Place molds in pan or hot water in moderate oven (325°) for about 3/4 hour or until firm. / To test, insert silver knife. / If custard does not adhere, it is done. ● Serves 3.

ORANGE COMPOTE

Cut the rinds of 4 oranges. Cut rind into thin slices, add to it and boil for 20 minutes:

2 cups water   **1/8 teaspoon salt**
1 1/2 cups sugar

Skin and remove the membrane from the 4 oranges and 5 additional oranges. / Place the sections in a serving bowl or in individual sherbet dishes. / Pour the hot syrup and rind over them. / Chill the compote. / Before serving you may add to the compote any topping. / Pudding or soft custards make good toppings. ● Serves 4.

SCANDINAVIAN PUDDING

1 cup strained fruit (suggested   **1/8 teaspoon allspice**
** fruits: apricots, prunes,**   **1/8 teaspoon cinnamon**
** peaches)**   **2 tablespoons sugar**
3/4 cup water   **1/8 teaspoon salt**
1 teaspoon grated lemon rind   **2 tablestpoons cornstarch**
1 tablespoon lemon juice

Combine all above ingredients. / Cook, stirring until thickened. / Pour into 4 sherbet glasses. / Refrigerate. / To serve, top each dessert with 1 tablespoon vanilla ice cream or ice milk. ● Serves 2.

STEAMED CRANBERRY PUDDING

2 cups coarsely chopped raw   **1/4 teaspoon cinnamon**
** cranberries**   **1/4 teaspoon cloves**
1 1/2 cups flour   **1/4 teaspoon mace**
1/2 teaspoon salt   **1/3 cup hot water**
1 teaspoon soda   **½ cup molasses**

Add cranberries to sifted dry ingredients. / Add water and molasses; mix well. / Fill greased pudding mold, or individual custard cups two-thirds full. / Cover tightly. / Steam about 2 hours. / This pudding freezes satisfactorily but it should be reheated before serving. ● Serves 2.

APPLE SPICE

4 cups fresh or ready-sliced pie
   apples
2/3 cup brown sugar
3 teaspoon lemon juice
1 tablespoon vegetable fat
   (except coconut oil)

1 teaspoon nutmeg
1 teaspon cinnamon
1/2 teaspoon ground cloves
1 cup cornflakes, crumbled

Grease an 8 by 8 by 1 3/4-inch pan, and place in it the drained apples. / Sprinkle with brown sugar and lemon juice. / Dot with fat. / Pour on cornflakes. / Bake for 1 hour in 375° oven. ● Serves 4-6.

BROILED GRAPEFRUIT

Remove seeds and cut around sections of grapefruit halves. / Place 2 tablespoons vanilla ice cream or ice milk on top of each grapefruit half. / Cover entire top of grapefruit half with meringue topping. Brown under broiler. / Serve immediately.

LAZY DAISY CAKE

This is a good cake when you need a quick dessert.

1 cup flour
1 teaspoon baking powder
¼ teaspoon salt
1 tablespoon vegetable fat
   (except coconut oil)

½ cup hot liquefied non-fat
   milk
2 eggs
1 cup sugar
1 teaspoon vanilla

Sift together three times the flour, baking powder, and salt. / Put fat in milk and heat to boiling point. / Fat will then be melted. / Beat eggs; gradually add sugar. / Mix dry ingredients together. / Add dry ingredients and milk to egg mixture, stirring until blended. / Add vanilla. / Bake 20 minutes at 350° in tube pan. ● Serves 4-6.

PINEAPPLE SPONGE

2 tablespoons unflavored
   gelatin
1/4 cup cold water
1/2 cup boiling water
1/2 cup sugar

1/4 teaspoon salt
1 cup crushed pineapple
2 tablespoons lemon juice
2 egg whites
1/8 teaspoon salt

Soak gelatin in cold water; dissolve in boiling water; add remaining ingredients. / Cool until nearly set. / Beat with a wire whisk until frothy. / Whip egg whites and salt until sift and fold them lightly into the gelatin mixture. / Chill until firm. ● Serves 4-6.

VI

ECONOMY:
Making the Most of Your Food Resources

20 EASY-TO-PREPARE RECIPES AND MENUS

WHEN ABRAHAM LINCOLN WAS A CLERK in a country store, his customers had some 900 items from which to choose. Supermarkets today have more than 8,000 items available for selection; the large "specialty" in some cities can boast even more.

Studies of food shopper preferences across the United States show that both low-income and high-income families patronize the same grocery stores, and that the expected amount of money spent on food and shopping patterns is not consistent with income level. The contents of market baskets of low-income shoppers will be similar to those of high-income shoppers.

The big supermarkets, as opposed to the small neighborhood groceries, offer the consumer a vast choice of foods from which to satisfy his or her basic food habits. Cultural factors as well as physiological, psychological and, to some degree, financial differences among shoppers also affect what is purchased.

Adequate income, it seems, does not guarantee selection of good, nourishing food. Evidently, many poor food managers, irrespective of income, patronize the market. With so many items to choose from, lack of time, little interest, inadequate nutritional knowledge, and variations in food prices, the shopper can easily be baffled.

FOOD SHOPPING HABITS Are you making the best of your food money? How much of your income are you spending for food? It is important that your lifestyle be considered along with your budget and food

habit preferences when you shop. If, like most of us you lead a fairly inactive or sedentary life—both at home and at work, then you should check the new Dietary Goals:

- Reduce total calories in your diet.
- Reduce saturated (animal) fats.
- Reduce sugar.
- Reduce salt.
- Change the fats in your diet from animal sources to alternate sources.
- Include more fruits and vegetables.
- Include more whole grain cereals and breads.

How much should you spend for food? There is not, unfortunately, a single dollars-and-cents standard for all. Besides, inflation, so long as it continues, makes such a figure meaningless.

You should spend enough to give your family nutritious meals they enjoy. Many combinations of foods at various costs can provide the nutrients for a well-balanced diet. The less money you have to spend, according to the U.S. Department of Agriculture, the more careful you must be in selecting foods that are economical as well as nutritious. You can be reasonably sure that you are feeding your family wisely if you:

- Prepare menus from a variety of foods, such as fruits and vegetables, whole grain breads and cereals, milk and milk products, meats, beans, and peanut butter, while at the same time considering your family's cultural food habits.
- Choose additional foods such as fruits and vegetables to use as snacks to satisfy appetites.
- Look critically at each food you plan to purchase and compare the price with other foods—be flexible, and get the best buys, in other words.
- Create for yourself a list of recipes that you can easily prepare and that your family likes; be creative in combining foods.
- Prepare a "plan of action"—tentative menus for the next days or week, with a complete or partial shopping list.

Where do you shop: Do you run from one grocery store to another to save a few pennies: This is often a false economy. Instead, it is wiser to check food stores in your community to select one that best meets your needs. Get to know your food store manager and clerks.

Schedule your shopping trips for a time when you have your plans and thoughts together and directed toward your food needs. Try to go shopping when the store is not crowded so that you have time to make wise selections. Avoid food shopping when you are hungry since hunger may lead you to select foods that you don't really need.

Shop alone, if possible, since shopping should be a concentrated adventure in supplying the best nutrition for the dollar. There is no substitute for good food management. The purchase of food is one of the most important expenditures families make. Some household managers spend a high percentage of the dollar on foods, while other families are well-nourished on much less. How you stretch your food dollar to achieve the best economy and nutritional supply is up to you.

Compare prices of similar foods. Check the labels for contents and amounts. You may learn that the price per serving may not be consistent with the overall price. A food-conscious shopper will find the extra attention worth the effort.

Statistics show that the average American shopper spends about 32 minutes on each trip to the supermarket and buys about $18 worth of groceries. Consumers are making fewer trips to the grocery than they were 12 years ago, but they're spending more money each time they shop. These statistics come from a new study of consumer habits conducted by Point of Purchase Advertising Institute and DuPont. Based on interviews with 4,000 consumers in more than 200 supermarkets, the study found that:

- The average shopper spends 121 percent more on a trip to the supermarket now than in 1965 (up to $17.65 from $8.01).

- Only about 35 percent of the supermarket customers make more than two shopping trips a week, whereas in 1965 about 45 percent shopped at the supermarket more than twice a week.

- Shoppers stand in check-out lines for an average of seven minutes.

- Shoppers spend an average of 90 cents for every minute they spend in the supermarket aisles. Obviously, it is to the retailer's advantage to keep the shopper in his store, the study concluded. An extra 10 minutes in the supermarket theoretically will add $9 to a cash register tape.

- About two-thirds of all purchase decisions are made at the store, slightly less than in 1965. The survey called this figure a "dramatic testimonial" to the importance of advertising at the supermarket.
- Today's shoppers are more likely to use shopping lists and to consult newspaper advertising. About 40 percent of the surveyed shoppers prepare shopping lists, up from 37.4 percent in 1965. And, 38.3 percent of shoppers use newspaper advertising, including coupons, while preparing their shopping list—up from 32.2 percent in 1965.

The consumer habits study concluded that produce displays at the supermarket are of growing importance. They create selling environment which flags down the shopper at every aisle.

The report shows that new factors may be influencing our selection of food as well. Shoppers for food may be basing their selections on more superficial reasons (note the booming sales of gimmicky "time-savers" because of the satisfied smile of the hassled TV housewife), instead of using knowledge of food and nutritional needs as a sound guide to food purchases.

Shopping for food in the 1970s demands that the wise buyer prepare for the shopping expedition ahead of time, even though food is usually one of the many chores squeezed into a busy life. It's not sufficient to race off to the market after work to pick up a quick and easy supper. An alert shopper is prepared at all times, knows what the marketplace has to offer and how to purchase the best nutrition for his or her dollar. At this writing, numerous supermarkets are experimenting with the new, lower cost "no advertising" packaging of some foods. The plain boxes may be a boon to the consumer; time will tell.

Within the money allotted for food, consider family income, the number of family members, their ages, their activities and their health. Self-discipline is especially necessary for diet-conscious people when marketing.

The lower the family income, the higher the total percentage of family income is needed for food. Studies generally show that families with lower incomes spend 50 to 60 percent of their total income for food, compared with 30 percent spent by middle-income families.

The following Family Food Budget Guide will help you judge whether you are spending your family's food dollar wisely.

COST PER PERSON FOR ADEQUATE FOOD ON STANDARD BUDGET

Individuals—By Sex and Age	Standard Cost per week	per month
Children—		
Under one year of age	$ 11.00	$ 47.65
1 to 3	11.00	47.65
3 to 6	13.30	57.65
6 to 9	17.50	75.85
Girls—		
9 to 12	21.10	91.45
12 to 15	20.60	89.27
15 to 20	20.60	89.27
Boys—		
9 to 12	22.30	96.65
12 to 15	23.20	100.55
15 to 20	25.90	112.25
Women—		
20 to 35	20.80	90.15
35 to 55	20.80	90.15
55 to 75	18.50	80.15
75 and over	18.50	80.15
Pregnant woman	21.50	93.15
Nursing mother	24.50	106.15
Men—		
20 to 35	26.10	113.10
35 to 55	26.10	113.10
55 to 75	22.70	98.35
75 and over	22.70	98.35
Family of four (2 preschool children)	71.20	308.55
Family of four (2 elementary children)	86.30	373.95
Young couple	51.60	223.60
Elderly couple	45.30	196.30

The Standard Cost Budget Guide represents an adequate allowance for food for each individual in each age and sex group. It allows for food prepared at home. Add on to your budget if you plan to eat out.

The basic figures used for calculating the Standard Cost Budget were provided by the U.S. Department of Agriculture and the Bureau of Labor Statistics, June 1978. They are based on computations of average retail food prices in cities in the United States and the actual cost of food used by families at home to provide a nourishing diet.

Age groups include persons of the first age listed, up to but not including those of the second age listed.

All costs are rounded to the nearest 50.05.

Monthly costs are estimated on the basis of 4-1/3 weeks in a month.

This budget guide is updated each six months to keep pace with inflation.

In some instances, to buy what is "good for" the family may be a waste of food dollars if these foods are ones no one likes and are left in the refrigerator or on the shelf until they spoil and cannot be considered nutritionally good to eat. Only food which is eaten and enjoyed can fulfill nutritional needs.

And, differences of taste within the family also affect food preferences to be considered by the shopper in the overall grocery planning. It requires a creative home manager to stay aware of the family's changing needs and likes to provide good nutrition. Here are some shopping hints.

1. Select variety.

2. Purchase correct size portions (a jumbo size jar may give the illusion of sensible shopping—but not if it cannot be eaten up before it spoils.

3. Allow for second servings.

4. Reduce selection of the extra candies, cookies or potato chips which are poor "fillers-up."

5. Replace the high carbohydrate foods with fruits and vegetables.

The possibilities for good nutrition are increased today because we have access to many foods which were formerly not available at all or were available only for brief seasons. If we use these foods wisely, we can not only improve our nutrition but also make our meals more attractive. Our untrained taste and preference, however, cannot be depended upon as a reliable guide to a wise choice of nutritionally sound meals. This is where knowledgeably planned menus are needed.

Food costs more today than it did a generation or two ago. Unfortunately, this is particularly true of the protective foods—milk, eggs, meat, green vegetables, and fresh fruit—foods that are high in protein and vitamins that form a protective layer of fat under the skin for warmth. Even the farm family encounters this problem with foods they do not raise for themselves, and city families are at a loss. Because the most money can be saved by cutting down on just these protective foods, a homemaker who is not guided by a definite menu plan for a well-balanced diet may easily use false economy at the expense of the family's health.

Thus, the changing conditions of life which have made us an urban instead of a rural nation have added the extra task of meal planning for health. Here are some ways in which carefully worked out menus should help the whole family:

- Menus should be planned for a diet which provides the essential food elements in quantities sufficient to develop and maintain buoyant health. Because of the smaller quantities of food which almost all of us consume nowadays, and because of the smaller vitamin and mineral content of much of that food, it is difficult to do this by haphazard selection of the foods the family happens to fancy.
- Menus should provide for reasonable variety, not only in the foods themselves but also in their methods of preparation. Thus the family may be kept interested in the basic protective foods which must be eaten daily for health.
- Menus should use foods in season. The summer season for fresh fruits and vegetables is so short that it is good practice to serve them very often while they last. Few families would object to strawberry shortcake or strawberries and cream every day during the brief strawberry season. This is also an economy measure; fresh foods in season are usually priced low.
- Menus should make use of inexpensive foods, especially cheaper cuts of meat, with which many people are unfamiliar. These are just as delicious, satisfying and digestible when properly cooked as the more expensive ones. Frequent use of these inexpensive cuts will make it possible to enjoy the choicer ones on special occasions.
- Menus should help the family make use of new recipes, new food combinations, leftovers, and perhaps even foods which have never been tried before. When you build up a recipe repertoire you make for more versatile mealtimes and gain a sense of personal achievement.
- Menus answer that daily recurring question: "What shall I serve today?" that is a nightmare to so many household managers who don't think ahead to the week's and the day's food needs. Relax—through planning ahead.

In short, menus should be designed to help you deal confidently and successfully with our changing world so far as food and nutrition are concerned.

Snacking is an undesirable part of the American cultural system and it plays an increasing role in our nutritional pattern. We eat aimlessly today and it is very difficult to visualize to what extent our nutritional needs are being met, how much of our food dollar is being wasted, and how much we've damaged our long-term health. Items consumed in large proportions include candy, soft drinks, alcoholic beverages, hamburgers, ice cream and sweet baked good. Coffee breaks at work, beer and pretzels around the TV set and a "meal" at the carry-out are questionable nutritional practices, to say the least. The question you should ask yourself is: Are snacks replacing a more nutritional meal?

Another great danger to maintaining your nutritional balance and budget is the escalating practice of eating out. Certainly, good food in a pleasant atmosphere where someone else prepares the food, serves it and does the dishes is a joy to the homemaker—as well as a treat to the whole family—that should not be eliminated. But people who enjoy this luxury should realize the substantial amount of money spent on one meal (if adequate nutritionally) will far exceed the cost of a home-prepared menu of comparable nutritional value. Unless a very wise menu selection is made, it is likely that the amount of money spent will not purchase adequate nutrition. Your food budget should take into account the number of times family members eat out and whether the expense justifies the loss of nutrition (either by way of choosing a menu item deficient in nutrition or throwing off the family food budget because of the high cost of the restaurant meal).

The art of menu-making is the blending of foods into wholesome and satisfying means. Foods for the entire day should be reviewed to determine if all nutritional needs for the day are met. Foods should be of good quality.

Meals should also be planned to meet the needs of the youngest or weakest members of the family first. Foods good for children are equally for adults. We cannot say the opposite is always true.

How long a food can be stored, before and after cooking, and how long it provides energy in the body should be considered. Does the food leave the stomach quickly or slowly? For healthy, active adults working outdoors, large amounts of food which have considerable staying qualities are highly desirable. But for indoor workers and children this may be the wrong choice.

Fats and fat-rich food have staying qualities. Cream sauces, cereals and similar foods have moderate staying qualities. Liquid food and food containing meat juices or fruit acids are likely to encourage the quick passage of food along the digestive tract. (This is one reason for beginning a meal with soup or fruit.)

For food digestion and utilization, generous amounts of bulky, moist food such as fruits, vegetables, whole grain cereals and water should be planned. Too much sweet food should not be included, since it may result in excessive fermentation in the digestive tract and add unnecessary calories. Too much meat and eggs should not be included because they may result in excessive purification in the digestive tract and raise the cholesterol level.

The texture of food plays an important part in its attractiveness. This has always, it seems, been understood in the Japanese, Chinese and other Oriental diets; these diets basically are healthful—the individual foods, in addition, are crispy, crunchy and aesthetically pleasing. Crisp foods should be associated with soft foods. Variations in texture, even in a simple dish, are always appealing. Oatmeal with a sprinkle of sugar, rice pudding with raisins, ice cream with cake, crackers with cheese, and crisp salad with a moist dressing are good combinations.

The appearance of food plays an important part in whetting the appetite. Too often, however, food is selected only on the basis of good taste. The main background of a meal should be of bland, mild colored food such as bread, cereal, vegetables and milk—and the accent should come from more highly flavored foods such as fruits, meats, meat alternates, sugar, herbs, and condiments.

If you throw away the juices in canned fruits and vegetables you are also throwing away very valuable vitamins released from these foods.

If you have planned an adequate menu and the best food has been selected for your money and the health of your family, then you are prepared to prepare the food. The kitchen should be the cleanest room in the house to insure that food will not be contaminated. The stove should be cleaned after every meal preparation. The refrigerator should be free from food odors and checked carefully to see that foods are free from spoilage. The food storage areas should be checked for dryness and canned food should be clean and free from bulge. Bulging,

banged-up canned foods are no bargain at the market—their contents can, in fact, harbor serious disease.

Make certain that the foods you eat are clean. The shiny apple on the produce shelf needs a good water rinse. However carefully packed the chicken legs may be, wash them off with water before cooking. Pat excess blood off beef before cooking. Wipe off the gelatin in which the canned ham is packed.

KNOW YOUR FOOD

Because of convenience foods, microwave ovens, pressure cookers and food processors, simple yet creative meals can often be prepared in a short time. However, you should think carefully about the ingredients you combine. You may carefully plan for low-calorie meals but when combining all the ingredients you may add calories you thought had been eliminated. For example, cooking with oil or sherry adds calories.

Herbs and spices have been used throughout history for seasoning. They may contain small amounts of sodium since they are dried leaves of plants. They should, however, present no concern when used in such small amounts for seasoning and they do not contain sodium chloride (table salt). A list of herbs and spices, identifying their uses, has been included in the appendix.

Know the milk that you purchase. Always look for fortified milk even though you are buying low fat milk. Fortified milk will contain the necessary Vitamin D which is generally otherwise absent in the diet.

HANDBOOK FOR STRETCHING THE FOOD DOLLAR

There are various ways to stretch the budget allowance for food. By putting them into action you may be able to shave a dollar or two (or more) from your estimated weekly food budget.

MAKE IT YOURSELF

Commercially made relishes and fruit jellies are usually more expensive than the homemade product; however, if these products are used only in small quantities it may be more practical and economical to buy rather than to make them. Generally it is more economical to make foods yourself. But some ready-to-eat foods and packaged mixes can be lifesavers on a very busy day and in those unforeseen emergencies that arise in every family—but they are more expensive.

Some things that are less expensive to make than to buy are macaroni and cheese, muffins and breads, and if you do make a lot of things from scratch you can buy the staples to make them in bulk.

A loaf of bread made at home will cost about 25 to 30 cents, compared with 35 to 40 cents when purchased in the market.

Our family purchases all-purpose flour in 25-pound bags. It makes good bread, cakes and pastries. Yeast is purchased in the 12-cake per package size, and sugar in 10-pound bags. On cold, rainy days or in our free time on weekends, breads are made and frozen. We can then enjoy homemade toast for breakfast or hot rolls for dinner. What a joy to have a loaf of homemade bread on the table in minutes! Here is a wonderful, wholesome bread:

EASY MIXED GRAIN BREAD

2 cups whole wheat flour
¼ cup sugar
2 teaspoons salt
2 packets active dry yeast
2½ cups non-fat milk

3 tablespoons vegetable oil (except coconut oil)
1 egg
¾ cup quick oats, uncooked
1/3 cup white or yellow corn meal
3 to 4 cups unbleached flour

Combine whole wheat flour, sugar, salt, and yeast in a large mixing bowl. / Heat milk and oil in saucepan over low heat until liquid is almost hot to the touch (120 to 130 degrees). / Gradually add the milk mixture to dry ingredients, beating at low speed, then add the egg. / Beat mixture 3 minutes at medium speed. / By hand, stir in oats and corn meal. / Begin adding white flour, stirring, until soft dough is formed. / Knead on very lightly floured board for about one minute. / When the dough is smooth and pliable, put it in a well-greased 2½ or 3 quart bowl. / Grease surface of dough, cover with a damp cloth, and set in a warm place (80 to 85 degrees). / Let rise until light and doubled in bulk, about 50 to 60 minutes. / Punch dough down and divide in half. / Shape the portions into loaves and place each in a well-greased 9 by 5 inch loaf pan. ● Makes two loaves.

Determine the purpose for the foods being purchased. The purpose will determine the grade of foods you will select. For example, if you are selecting canned tomatoes for salads, then the top grades are those canned most perfect in shape, color, size and flavor. For soups and stews a lower grade may meet the need and will save you money. You will not want to purchase whole fruits for salads necessarily; chopped fruits are fine for gelatin salads. The top grades are no more nutritious or wholesome than the lower grades.

All the grades have their places. The highest grades are for special occasions where perfect appearance and the highest quality are desired. The medium grades are for everyday use. The lower grades are for thrift—when appearance is not important such as when making soups and stews. It is unwise to buy the highest grade, whole, solid-packed canned tomatoes at a high price for use in a tomato sauce when the lower-priced, cut tomatoes will serve as well. The same reasoning applies to all foods—it is extravagant to buy choice quality when the lower quality will serve the same purchase.

You can save considerably by learning the differences between the various government grades of foods, and then choosing them wisely.

If you buy in bulk you can save money. You know that a 10-pound bag of sugar costs less per pound than 10 pounds bought one at a time. In buying the one pound you are paying not only for the food itself but also for the same amount of labor in packing and labeling that went into the larger bag. Whenever you are choosing between the various sizes of packed foods, compare the weights, and figure out the most economical size. The same principle applies to fresh foods, such as apples and potatoes. If you buy a whole sack of potatoes, rather than two or three pounds every day, it saves a lot of handling by the retailer and you may save several cents per sack.

Form the habit of ordering bulk foods by weight, rather than by volume or number, whenever possible. It is simpler to compare the price of lemons in two different stores, for example, when the price is given by the pound rather than by the dozen, since a dozen lemons may include fruit ranging widely in size.

Many homes today have storage facilities for purchasing canned food by the case. Your yearly savings will make a tidy sum to spend on the occasional extras which make living more joyous.

A caution, however: if you cannot use food in bulk, you will save nothing by purchasing it only to have it go to waste. And remember that foods cannot last forever. For instance, it's an unnerving experience for the homemaker who rarely bakes to get in the mood one rainy day only to find the months-old flour she bought has become the property of the weevils. The same is true of canned goods; learn the shelf life. Only you can determine the best purchase of food in bulk because you know of your family's food habits.

BUDGET YOUR INCOME

Quantity-buying is frequently difficult because a larger amount of cash is needed to pay for the food all at once. The only way to meet this problem is by a system of budgeting, firmly followed.

GARDENING FOR FUN AND PROFIT

Not everyone is fortunate enough to have a large sunny backyard or a convenient spot for a big garden. But many people can locate a place for a small kitchen garden. There, with a minimal expense of a few seeds, some good outdoor exercise, and a lot of fun, the family can raise many of their own vegetables and fruits.

The victory gardens of wartime have proven to thousands of families the advantages, even in a large city, of having a small garden. What was a necessity then is remembered by many as a pleasant and delicious learning experience. The window sill or patio garden or apartment garden are becoming once again popular. These small-time farmers have experienced the thrill of eating perfectly fresh vegetables all summer and have learned the economy of wisely preserving any excess by freezing, canning or drying.

Any family in a suitable location, with a little experience and managing ability (remember the library is full of do-it-yourself gardening books), can plant vegetables. They will grow and be as delightful as flowers—in addition, you can eat them! Each summer we have found that tomatoes, squash, cucumbers and green peppers add to our flower borders. We build menus to include those items and can also share them with our neighbors. A gift from the home garden is so much appreciated.

MAKE USE OF LEFTOVERS AND AVOID WASTE

"Waste makes want." "A penny saved is a penny earned." Those old proverbs apply to food as well as to money. The intelligent family recognizes that preventing any possible food waste is the best known way of stretching the food dollar. As another old saying puts it: "A woman can throw more out the back door in a spoon than the man can bring in a shovel through the front door."

For example, a small rubber scraper should be used to remove every trace of batter, dough or sauce from bowls and pans before they are washed. Dry breads, rolls and cake should be made into crumbs instead of being discarded or allowed to mold. The good outer green leaves of cabbage and lettuce should be saved and combined with other foods in soups and stews. Chicken feet and necks, as well as other parts of the animal's carcass, even though they may contain little visible meat, may also be used for preparing delicious soups.

Food leftovers may be regarded as clear gain or clear loss, according to whether your family has learned to use them gracefully in a new form, or insists that leftovers are only food for the garbage disposal. The way leftovers are presented will usually determine the amount of enthusiasm they can be expected to arouse. An ancient, dried-out morsel of meat or vegetable should rate a cool stare at most, but a well-stored tasty leftover used in the preparation of a new and interesting dish will earn an enthusiastic smile.

Meats are the most generally accepted leftovers, and some people go as far as to choose a larger pot roast, or a larger ham or turkey than the family requires, for use in various casserole dishes the next day. We, too, have found the purchase of a large piece of meat is cost-saving.

The following example will illustrate how a big meat cut can be economically and appetizingly used, even for a small family. Have the butcher saw a whole ham in two and cut two half-inch steaks from the center to be broiled for the first night's dinner. For the next day, roast the butt end, a fine main dish for Sunday dinner. Several days later, prepare a boiled dinner with the shank end, or cut of thin slices to pan broil for breakfast or for sandwiches, then use the bone for making bean or pea soup.

To make the most of your food resources you will find it fun to make the best use of what you have. "Necessity is the mother of invention"—that goes for food, too. You become creative when you lack a few ingredients for a recipe. New dishes (new recipes) are created from having less than exactly what you need. All of us, probably, know someone who seems to be able to go into a practically empty larder and turn out a feast. You can do that too.

The menus and recipes have been presented as examples of economical diet patterns. Economy is saving money through thrift. It should not cost you good nutrition. The best nutrition for the dollar should be the goal for each individual.

The purchase of a big turkey can be economical if you use all of the meat. We usually purchase a 22 to 25 pound bird. (Remember when buying poultry that the bigger bird means more meat; the carcass is more or less about the same in the smaller bird.)

Roast the turkey and stuff with sage-celery dressing (See recipe page 260.) It will keep longer than the delicious but more flamboyant oyster dressing which should be used for only one meal. Then have sliced turkey with dressing, alternating with baked ham or roast beef in a casserole. After the turkey's white meat has been sliced to crumbs of meat we have turkey hash or curried turkey. Our recipe is as follows:

TURKEY HASH

4 strips bacon	1 cup chopped parsley or parsley and
6 tablespoons vegetable fat (except	scallion tops mixed
coconut oil)	2 pounds potatoes, grated
1 medium onion, chopped	¾ pound turkey, chopped in small pieces
	Freshly ground pepper

Fry bacon in a 10-inch pan over moderate heat. Remove bacon, drain, and when firm, crumble the pieces. / Add 2 tablespoons fat and the onion to the drippings. / After 3 minutes add parsley and cook 2 minutes more. / Prepare potatoes and turkey, using a food processor if desired. / Add salt and a generous amount of pepper to the pan, plus crumbled bacon and 2 more tablespoons fat. / When the fat has melted, fold in potatoes and turkey, mixing well to form a cake like mass. / Cover pan and lower heat. / Allow hash to steam for 10 to 20 minutes, using a spatula from time to time to keep mixture from sticking to the pan. / Remove pan from heat, lossen bottom as necessary and invert hash onto a plate. Return pan to heat, melt final 2 tablespoons fat and return hash brown side up. / Remove pan and cook another 15 to 20 minutes.

Serve. / Catsup is the most common accompaniment, although various relishes or chutneys might be offered instead. / Add a salad and a loaf of bread and your leftover meat, is delicious.
● Serves 4-6.

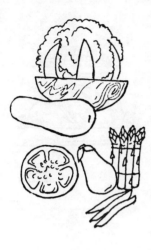

Many times we dice the turkey and place it in sealed plastic containers for the freezer. Then, several months afterwards the leftovers may be used.

Vegetable leftovers are easy to use because usually only small amounts are left. Two or more kinds may be combined to be served hot as a vegetable or in a soup, or chilled for a salad. When leftover vegetables must be reheated, some of their pot liquor should be left on them and they should be heated in it. If there is none, add a little milk and butter.

Leftovers should be cooled and placed in closed containers, as air-tight as possible, to prevent the absorption of any foreign odors and flavors and to prevent drying out. Be sure that the food goes straight into the refrigerator and is used as soon as possible. If care is given to the food while it is stored, it will remain in good condition until the next day. Remember that part of the vitamin content will lessen during storage.

Make it a habit to check the refrigerator daily for leftovers that can be incorporated into the day's meals, and never allow these leftovers to deteriorate unused. Avoid any excess chopping or cutting of leftovers. Let the pieces be large enought to be readily identifiable. Do your distinguishing in some other way, creating a new dish in which the leftover is the star or contributor.

Casserole dishes are also excellent leftover dishes. Children will have fun in identifying ingredients. They can help name a new dish—perhaps for a favorite place or person.

VALUES

The foods you buy will be determined largely by your values. Our value is the satisfaction we get from buying what we like—strawberries out of season, fresh milk instead of canned, and steak instead of ground meat. Each of our preferences usually costs more. The additional cost does not buy extra nutritional value, but life would be a monotonous gastronomic journey indeed if we planned and selected every food we purchased just on the basis of nutritional value.

We know that we buy much more than vitamins and minerals when we buy foods. We buy satisfaction. We buy security. The value of food as security in time of crisis is explained in a previous chapter. But we also buy food for the security of having well-stacked cabinets of foods for use when we need and want them.

Security may be as simple as the receiving of a cup of coffee from a neighbor when your possessions have been lost in a fire. Insecurity is the natural emotional result of loss, and food fills an important gap. The supplying of foods has helped bereaved or traumatized people to build back personal or family security. This building back can be in evidence even as soon as the first hot foods have been served to those stricken.

Some of us are prestige-conscious and buy foods that satisfy an ego feeling. The extras may become conversation foods. We may like to have the image of eating out in a certain romantic place or purchasing exotic foods. We should keep in mind, however, that we are spending money for extras which meet needs other than those of nutrition.

Selecting good, nutritious foods for the best nutritional value requires an understanding of simple ways to prepare them. Such foods need no elaborate methods of perparation. The Senate Committee recommends the easy nutrition way of fresh fruits, fresh vegetables, whole grains products, meats baked, broiled or roasted, or fish and chicken. Sugar and salt are reduced. When you shop, remember the simple, good meal is your priority.

ECONOMICAL FAMILY MENUS AND RECIPES

DINNER I

Buddy's Oven Barbecued Chicken *
Harvard Beets*   Parsleyed Potatoes
Cole Slaw*
Mixed Fruit in Orange Cup
Beverage

DINNER II

Potatoe Soup*
Jellied Fish Salad*
Or
Tomatoe Aspic Seafood Salad*
Low Calorie Dressing*
Fresh Carrot Sticks on Lettuce
Red Grapes
Beverage

DINNER III

Quick Meatloaf with Tomatoe Sauce*
Steamed Kale or Spinach
Lime-Pineapple Mold*
Clare's Banana Pudding*
Beverage

DINNER IV

Fish in Skillet*
Tropicana Salad*
or
Pineapple-Nut Salad in Tomato Basket*
Peanut Butter-Carrot Bread*
Ruth's Peach Sunrise Sherbert*
Beverage

Recipe included in book.

SOUPS ....

POTATO SOUP

3 large potatoes, pealed and
   sliced thin
6 leeks, sliced thin
1/4 cup chopped onions
2 tablespoons flour
4 cups boullion, heated (beef
   is best)

2 cups non-fat milk
1 tablespoon minced parsley
1 tablespoon minced chervil or
   1/2 teaspoon dry chervil

Cook potatoes until tender in small amount of water. / Add
leeks and onions. / Make paste of flour and milk. / Stir in
potatoe mixture slowly. / Add hot bouillon a little at a time,
stirring. / Simmer 8 to 10 minutes, stirring constantly. / Add
parsley and chervil. / Serve with toasted rolls. ● Serves 2.

MAIN DISHES ....

BUDDY'S OVEN BARBECUED CHICKEN

1 frying chicken, 2 1/2 to 3
   pounds, cut into serving
   pieces
1/4 cup water
3/4 cup vinegar
3 tablespoons vegetable oil
   (except coconut oil)

1/2 cup chili sauce or catsup
3 tablespoons Worcestershire
   sauce
1 teaspoon salt
1/2 teaspoon pepper
2 tablespoons chopped onion

Preheat oven to 350°F. / Combine all ingredients except chicken
in saucepan, place over heat, and simmer for 5 to 10 minutes. /
Place chicken, skin side up, in large baking pan. / Pour half the
barbecue sauce over chicken and bake, uncovered, at 350° for
about 45-60 minutes. / Baste with remaining barbecue sauce
every 15 minutes during cooking. / Dieters should remove skin
from chicken. ● Serves 4.

QUICK CASSEROLE

1 pound hamburger, browned
2 potatoes, sliced
1/2 onion, sliced
2 stalks celery, diced
1 green pepper

1 1/2 cups cream of chicken
   soup
1 1/2 cups cream of
   mushroom soup
1/2 cup water

Place first five ingredients in casserole. / Pour the remaining
ingredients on top. / Bake at 350°F. until potatoes are done. ●
Serves 6.

FISH IN SKILLET

1 pound fish fillets or steaks
3 tablespoons vegetable oil
   (except coconut oil)
1 chopped onion
3 tablespoons chopped green
   pepper
2 tablespoons chopped parsley

2 medium tomatoes, cut in
   pieces
1/2 cup water or tomato juice
1/2 teaspoon salt
1/2 teaspoon basil or oregano
Dash pepper

If fish is frozen, thaw it enough to separate pieces. / Heat oil in
skillet. / Add chopped onion, green pepper and parsley; cook
until soft. / Add tomatoes, water and tomato juice, and
seasonings; cook until tomatoes are soft. / Add fish. Cover and
cook gently about 10 minutes, or until fish is done. ● Serves 4.

VEGETABLES ....

HARVARD BEETS

1 cup cooked beets
2 teaspoons sugar
2 tablespoons water

1 teaspoon cornstarch
1/4 teaspoon salt
2 tablespoons cider vinegar.

Dice or slice beets. / Allow sugar to dissolve in water. / Combine
cornstarch, salt, vinegar, and sugar water; cook over low heat
until thickened, stirring constantly. / Add beets, heat until beets
are hot. Serve at once.

SALADS . . . .

JELLIED FISH SALAD

1 tablespoon unflavored gelatin
1/4 cup cold water
1/2 teaspoon salt
1/2 teaspoon celery seed

1/4 cup vinegar
1/4 cup water
2 eggs, beaten
2 cups flaked, cooked, or canned fish, without oil

Sprinkle gelatin on top of 1/4 cup cold water, until it softens. / Combine seasonings, vinegar, and 1/4 cup water with eggs. / Cook in double boiler over boiling water until thickened, stirring constantly. / Add gelatin and stir until dissolved. / Add fish and mix. / Pour into large ring mold and chill. ● Serves 4.

COLE SLAW

1/2 cup shredded cabbage
2 tablespoons low calorie salad dressing

1/2 cup shredded carrots
1 tablespoon finely cut celery
1 teaspoon finely cut parsley

Combine all ingredients well. / Chill before serving. ● Serves 1.

TROPICANA SALAD

1 cup cantaloup balls
6 slices tomato
Garnish of red pepper

Any desired salad dressing
Lettuce leaves

With a vegetable cutter, cut small balls from a cantaloup that is fairly firm in texture. / Arrange several balls on a slice of tomato which has been placed on a nest of lettuce leaves. / Garnish with pieces of red pepper or green pepper cut in diamond shapes. / Serve with salad dressing. ● Serves 3.

PINEAPPLE-NUT SALAD IN TOMATO BASKETS

1 cup crushed pineapple
1 cup broken nutmeats
French dressing*

6 tomatoes
6 teaspoons mayonnaise*

Mix pineapple with nutmeats and marinate in French dressing in the refrigerator. / Peel and cut off the top of each tomato leaving a strip to form a handle. / Carefully scoop out the center and fill with the pineapple and nuts. / Place one teaspoon of mayonnaise on top of each basket. ● Serves 6.

LIME-PINEAPPLE MOLD

3 ounces lime flavored gelatin
1 cup hot water
1 cup pineapple juice

1/8 teaspoon salt
1 egg white

Dissolve gelatin in hot water. / Add the pineapple juice and salt. / Chill until slightly thickened. / Place in bowl of ice and water. / Add the egg white, and whip with egg beater until fluffy and thick. / Pile lightly in sherbet glasses. / Chill until firm. ● Serves 6.

TOMATO ASPIC SEAFOOD SALAD

Aspic:
2 tablespoons plain gelatin
1/2 cup cold water
2 1/2 cups tomato juice
1 teaspoon chopped onion
1/2 teaspoon salt
1/2 teaspoon celery salt
2 tablespoons vinegar
2 teaspoons sugar

Salad:
1 cup tuna fish, flaked
1 cup diced celery
1 cup diced green pepper
1/2 teaspoon salt
Dash white pepper
1/4 cup low calorie dressing*
1 tablespoon juice
Section of one grapefruit
Watercress

For aspic, soften gelatin in cold water. / Combine tomato juice, onion, salt, celery salt, sugar, vinegar in saucepan; bring to boiling point. / Add to gelatin, stirring until gelatin is dissolved. / Cool mixture and pour into one quart ring mold, chill until firm. For salad, lightly toss together tuna fish, celery, green pepper, salt, and pepper. / Combine salad dressing and lemon juice. / Add to tuna fish mixture and blend carefully. / Unmold aspic and fill center of ring mold with tuna fish salad. / Arrange garnish of grapefruit sections and watercress around outer edge of aspic ring. ● Serves 6.

240

SALAD DRESSING ....

SPECIAL LOW CALORIE DRESSING

1/2 teaspoon gelatin
1 tablespoon water
1/4 cup boiling water
1/2 teaspoon prepared
  mustard
1/2 teaspoon sweet pickle
  juice
1 teaspoon salt

1 teaspoon grated lemon rind.
1/2 cup lemon juice
1/4 teaspoon onion juice
1/4 teaspoon paprika
1/8 teaspoon curry powder
1 pinch black pepper
1 pinch cayenne pepper

In a half pint jar, soften gelatin in tablespoon of water. / Add remaining ingredients and stir until dissolved. / Shake well. / Chill. / Makes about 1 cup.

DESSERTS ....

CLARE'S BANANA PUDDING

2 cups non-fat milk
3/4 cup sugar
1/3 cup flour
2 egg youlks and 2 egg whites
  (separated into 2 separate
  dishes)

1/8 teaspoon salt
1 teaspoon vanilla
4 medium-size ripe bananas,
  sliced
Vanilla wafers (35-40)

Blend sugar, flour, salt together thoroughly in top of double boiler. / Add 1/2 cup milk, stirring to make smooth. / Add remaining milk. / Cook over boiling water, stirring frequently until thickened. / Cover and allow to cook about 10 to 15 minutes. / Beat egg yolks slightly; add hot custard slowly to yolks. / Return to double boiler, cook 2 minutes. / Remove from heat and add vanilla. / Preheat oven to 325°. / Line bottom of a 2-quart casserole dish with vanilla wafers. / Arrange the sliced bananas on top of vinalla wafers. / Pour custard over bananas and repeat with layers of vanilla wafers, sliced bananas, custard until casserole dish is full. / Beat egg whites stiff but not day, add remaining sugar, beating constantly. / Spread meringue over custard topped dish. / Bake in oven for 10 to 15 minutes or until meringue is brown. ● Serves 8.

RUTH'S PEACH SUNRISE SHERBET

1 quart water
2 cups sugar
1 teaspoon gelatin

2 cups peach pulp
2 oranges
1 lemon

Boil sugar and water together for 5 minutes, add the gelatin softened in cold water. / When the mixture is cold, add the peach pulp, which has been pressed through a sieve, and the juice of oranges and lemon. / Freeze in freezer tray sherbert dishes or shallow pan. / Garnish with peach slices. ● Serves 8.

VII

JOY:
The Essential Ingredient for Every Meal

106 EASY-TO-PREPARE RECIPES AND MENUS

FAMILIES AND INDIVIDUALS WHO REGULARLY prepare good food at home will feel enjoyment in dining and will be considerably better off nutritionally—even when their meal is simple and inexpensive—than they would be dining out.

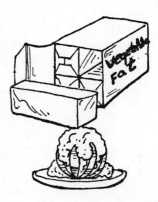

Good nutrition can be achieved by knowing what is right to eat and understanding the effects of the environment upon eating and health. A certain environment with a particular eating pattern forms a lifestyle. That eating pattern may be difficult to change because it is so integral a part of the living pattern. Nevertheless, it is possible to change food habits in order to make the foods you eat as nutritional as possible.

In our family, sharing has been an important family rule. Our ideas may help your family:

- Each member of the family should share responsibility for meal-planning, gathering or selection, preparation and service of foods. Food, in this way, can serve as a tremendous bond for family unity.
- Make family dining a special time for family gatherings at least once each day.
- Family mealtime should include time for individual recognition of each family member.
- Begin the meal with a moment of silence or perhaps a blessing by each family member. The quietness, especially if there is a spiritual moment to start off the meal, will help the emotions to relax and the body to prepare the digestive system for accepting the food.

- Make mealtime simple but attractive. A simple meal, prepared with care, is better accepted by the digestive system than an intricate meal of many courses served amid conflict.
- Educate family members to help with food planning, menu plans, grocery lists, and food selection. (For even the smallest child, food selection can be a happy family project.) Everyone can help in some way with cooking, too.

Very young children can help make rolls, biscuits and muffins. Cutting cookies and counting them can help with arithmetic. As soon as a child is of reading age, he can begin learning the nutritional value of the different foods. Children can understand that milk helps to make teeth and bones; that Vitamin C, from oranges, grapefruits and tomatoes, holds the body cells together; that carrots, green peppers and sweet potatoes make eyes bright and shiny; that meats, eggs, and milk build body skin and help bodies grow; and that cereals, rolls and muffins produce energy for running, jumping and playing. Children can also be taught to fold napkins and set the table.

You can teach your children to enjoy a variety of foods. It is interesting to see that children who have been taught to eat a food variety are likely to select a well-balanced meal when eating out at a restaurant. (When we took H.A. Jr., our first son, to a cafeteria, he selected milk instead of coke or some other soft drink. We felt he had learned something valuable and that our efforts had been worthwhile. In addition, our children were not afraid to try new foods.)

Mealtime at home for the family should be attractive. Why save the candle in a simple candle-holder, or the daisy or fruit centerpiece for guests only? The most important dinner guests are members of the family, certainly.

Make meals a time for discussing pleasant subjects. A troublesome report card or announcements of disciplinary action have no place at the dinner table. Foods themselves should never be used as a tool for disciplining a child. They should be neither reward nor punishment but rather the important and natural part of life from the very beginning.

Remember that the taste buds that lie beneath the tongue must be taught to accept food. A baby desires food soon after birth. The most nutritious and most suitable food for his body is milk—in most cases, mother's milk. After milk, the first food reflects the attitude of the parent; it will determine the attitude of the infant. If mother accepts them, the baby will accept cereal or spinach or liver. It is important, therefore, that the baby learns to eat some of all good foods.

Think of the family dining table as one that is at the same time relaxed but requiring decorum. Acceptable clothing is only one element of good manners which should be brought to the table.

An attractively set table with all family members together, an atmosphere of pleasant conservation, a moment of quiet to begin the meal—all these create an environment lacking only one thing: a simple, well-prepared meal, planned within a budget, shared in all aspects by each family member, and served with care. We must fill this gap.

It is my belief that unless the American diet can meet nutritional needs which are so lacking we will continue to be in bad shape as a nation. We also must work to establish that combination of pleasure, joy and humor to complete the meal. If we do not, our hospitals will continue to increase their patient loads, no matter how hard we try to re-educate Americans about diet habits. The biological processes which take place during food digestion and absorption often relate to factors that cause illness. In children, attention span, motivation and learning are dependent upon the children being well-nourished. The foods you eat, in short, help establish the total you—healthy or unhealthy.

Families must stop and look at what they eat and how they eat and under what circumstances they eat.

The selected menus and recipes in this chapter are suggested by families around the country. They are the favorite foods of families which feel that food served at the family table can contribute greatly to maintaining family unity. The joy of breaking bread together, of making dining a pleasure, is a vital function of these families—and it can and should be of yours.

There are, of course, many people today who are living outside the family group. Individuals who live alone have a problem with loneliness in many cases. They also require a great deal of willpower and determination (to say nothing of self-education) to eat right when alone. The opportunity for sharing is lacking and the desire to eat may be lost as well. The individual who eats alone should evaluate his eating pattern and build toward good nutritional patterns each day within an environment that allows for good digestion. Family and friends—they are often the key for persons living alone to share ways of preparing new dishes and enjoying them.

MONDAY

Breakfast

Sliced Peaches
Pan-broiled Sausage Patties
Raisin Toast*
Marmalade
Beverages

Luncheon

Fresh Corn and Lima-Bean
(Tomato) Casserole
Caesar Salad with Pineapple Cubes*
Milk - Non-fat or 2%

Dinner

Chick A la King*
on
Hot Peanut Butter Biscuit*
Sauteed Summer Squash with Onions*
Tomato Lettuce Salad
Mandarin Orange Freeze*
Beverage

TUESDAY

Breakfast

Orange Juice
Ready-to-Eat Cereal
Egg Poaches on Toast
Milk - Non-fat or 2%

Luncheon

Watercress and Vegetable Salad*
Tomato French Dressing*
Cheese Toasties*
Fresh or Canned Apricots*
Peanut Butter Cookies*
Lemonade*

Dinner

Fish Parmesian*
Green Peas
Stuffed Baked Potato*
Cornmeal Muffin*
Relish   Pickles
Honey Dew Melon with Lemon
Beverages

*Recipe included in book.

EATING TOGETHER—MENUS AND RECIPES / FIRST WEEK

WEDNESDAY

Breakfast

Orange Wedges
Hot Oats
Frizzled Luncheon Ham*
Whole Wheat Toast
Beverages

Luncheon

Stuffed Tomato Salad*
Grilled Cheese Sandwiches
Cinnamon Baked Apple*
with
Lemon Slice
Beverages

Dinner

Watercress Soup*
Stuffed Cabbage Roll,
(Ukranian Style)*
Riced Potatoes
Glazed Carrots
Lettuce
Bread
Fresh Peach Cobbler*
(see Recipe for Bud's Deep Dish
Apple Pie, page 267)
Milk - Non-fat or 2%

*Recipe included in book.

THURSDAY

Breakfast

Stewed Fresh Plums
Fried Eggs
Toast   Jam
Beverages

Luncheon

Cream Carrots and Celery on Toast
Cold Sliced Beef Roast
Sliced Tomatoes
Whole Wheat Muffins*
Lemon Sherbert
Beverages

Dinner

Mandarin Chicken on
Fluffy Rice*
Green Peas   Onion Cucumber Salad
Whole Wheat Bread*
Fruit or Melon Wedges
Milk - Non-fat or 2%

EATING TOGETHER—MENUS AND RECIPES / FIRST WEEK

FRIDAY

Breakfast

Grapes
Broiled Sausage Links
Peg's Blueberry Coffeecake*
Beverages

Luncheon

Ruby Fox Shrimp Jambalaya*
Green Beans with Onions and Almonds
Whole Wheat Bread*
Cheese Wedge
Cole Slaw
Fruit Cubes
Milk - Non-fat or 2%

Dinner

Beef Stew with Carrots and Potatoes*
Peanut Butter-Celery Salad*
Bread Sticks
Apple Crisp*
Beverages

SATURDAY

Breakfast

Orange Juice
Shredded Wheat Biscuits
Toast   Marmalade
Milk non-fat or 2%

Luncheon

Pumpkin Soup*
Baked Ham Slice*
Spinach with Cheese Sauce
Crusty Roll
Grapefruit-Orange Sections
Hot Tea with Lemon

Dinner

"Canja"*
Baked Potato
Spiced Beets
Asparagus Tips Salad
Raisin Bread Toast
Lemon Pie*
Beverages

*Recipe included in book.

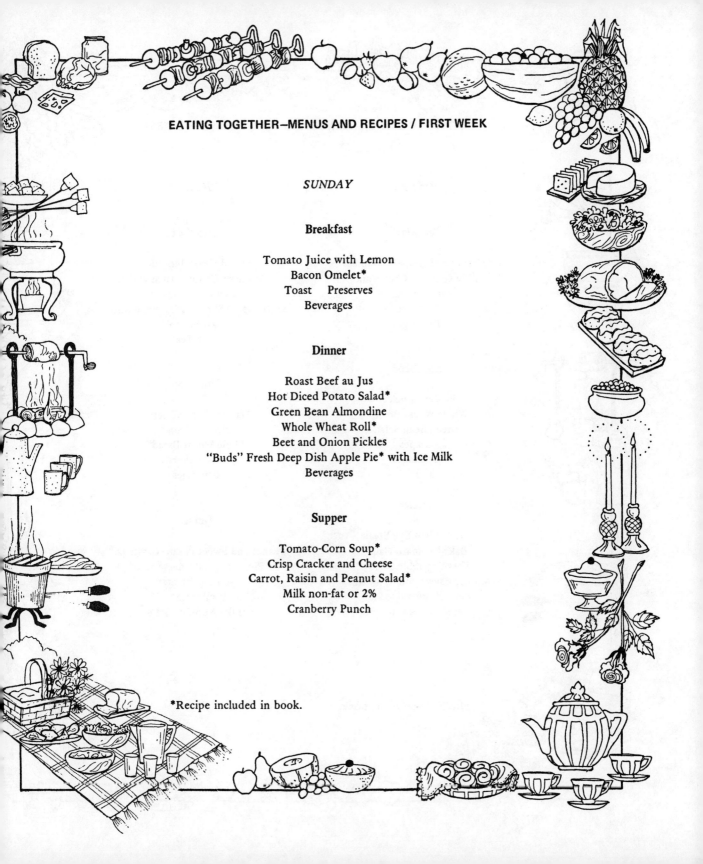

SUNDAY

Breakfast

Tomato Juice with Lemon
Bacon Omelet*
Toast   Preserves
Beverages

Dinner

Roast Beef au Jus
Hot Diced Potato Salad*
Green Bean Almondine
Whole Wheat Roll*
Beet and Onion Pickles
"Buds" Fresh Deep Dish Apple Pie* with Ice Milk
Beverages

Supper

Tomato-Corn Soup*
Crisp Cracker and Cheese
Carrot, Raisin and Peanut Salad*
Milk non-fat or 2%
Cranberry Punch

*Recipe included in book.

MONDAY

Breakfast

Orange and Grapefruit Juice
Billy Gibson's Cheese and
Grit Casserole*
Hot Roll
Beverages

Luncheon

Parsley Omelet*
Whole Wheat Bread*
Green Bean Salad
Grapes
Beverages

Dinner

Broiled Rib Eye Steak
Baked Tomato Half*
Toss Vegetable Salad*
Mother Baleys Potato Muffin*
Fern's Impossible Pie*
Milk - Non-fat or 2%

TUESDAY

Breakfast

Mixed Vegetable Juice
Mother's Country Ham with
Red Eye Gravy*
Baked Apple Slices with Lemon Slice*
Toast Squares
Hot Tea

Luncheon

Macaroni and Cheese*
Pickled Beets*
Whole Wheat Bread*
Red Grapes
Beverages

Dinner

Peanut and Sweet Potato Casserole*
Pineapple and Cheese Salad
Minted Carrots*
Ambrosia*
Milk - Non-fat or 2%

*Recipe included in book.

EATING TOGETHER—MENUS AND RECIPES / SECOND WEEK

WEDNESDAY

Breakfast

Grapefruit Sections
Poached Egg over Toast
Beverages

Luncheon

Tuna Salad in Whole Tomato Cups*
Cheese Cracker
Curried Pecans*
Milk - Non-fat or 2%

Dinner

Chicken Fricassee with Orange Slices*
Steamed Potato
Lemon Spinach
Grapefruit Salad
Whole Wheat Roll*
Beverages

THURSDAY

Breakfast

Sliced Oranges
Whole Wheat Cereal
Cheese Toast
Milk - Non-fat or 2%

Luncheon

Cream of Peanut Soup*
Marvin's Barbecued Kabobs*
Grated Raw Apple
Ripe Olives
Celery
Beverages

Dinner

Sarme*
Celery Stuffed with Peanut Butter*
Turbin Squash Pie*
Green Pepper Rings
Fresh Fruit in Orange Cup*
Lemonade*

*Recipe included in book.

FRIDAY

Breakfast

Grapefruit Half
Rolled Oats
Baked Egg
Raisin Toast
Milk - Non-fat or 2%

Luncheon

Mandarin Orange Sections
Canadian Bacon
Grated Carrot and Green Pepper Salad
Baked Pears* Au Gratin
Beverages

Dinner

Steak Teriyaki*
Fluffy Rice
Tomato-Cucumber Salad*
Carrot Pudding*
Papaya Slices
Hot Tea with Lemon

SATURDAY

Breakfast

French Omelet
Toast
Beverages

Luncheon

Chafin Dish Gourmet*
Whole Wheat Roll*
Cheese Slices
Pineapple-Peanut Salad*
Chocolate Pound Cake*
Milk - Non-fat or 2%

Dinner

Breaded Veal Chop, Broiled
Baked Potato
Stewed Tomatoes
Bread
Spinach and Onion Salad
French Dressing*
Lemon Mousse*
Beverages

*Recipe included in book.

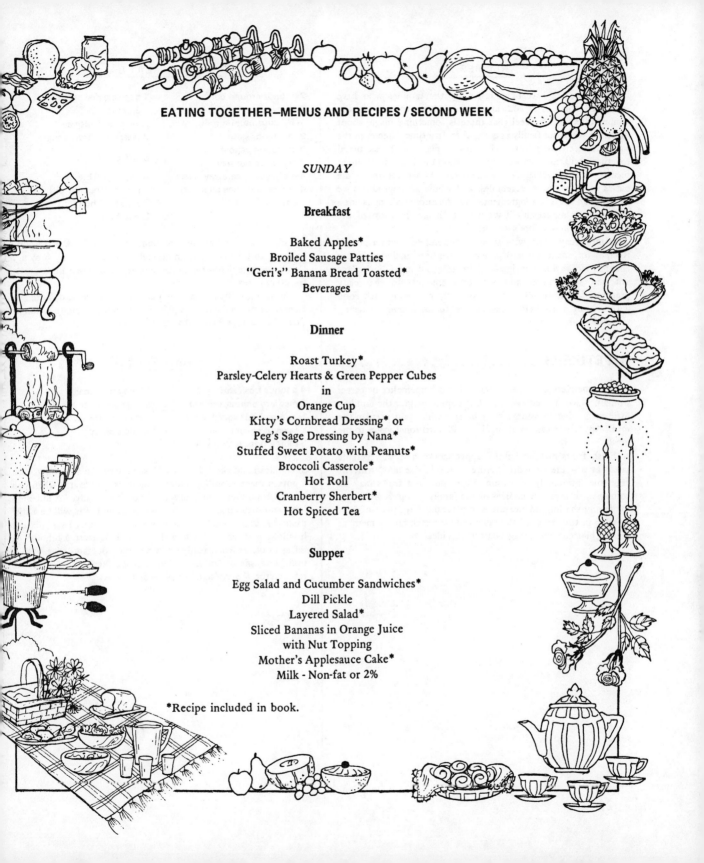

SUNDAY

Breakfast

Baked Apples*
Broiled Sausage Patties
"Geri's" Banana Bread Toasted*
Beverages

Dinner

Roast Turkey*
Parsley-Celery Hearts & Green Pepper Cubes
in
Orange Cup
Kitty's Cornbread Dressing* or
Peg's Sage Dressing by Nana*
Stuffed Sweet Potato with Peanuts*
Broccoli Casserole*
Hot Roll
Cranberry Sherbert*
Hot Spiced Tea

Supper

Egg Salad and Cucumber Sandwiches*
Dill Pickle
Layered Salad*
Sliced Bananas in Orange Juice
with Nut Topping
Mother's Applesauce Cake*
Milk - Non-fat or 2%

*Recipe included in book.

RECIPES

These recipes have been tested by the families who have submitted them. The additional recipes have come from my recipe collection. We feel that there is something magic about digestion when our family eats together. In a time when even the small children have busy schedules, a plan to "break bread together" will not only enhance digestion but build in an inner security for individual family members. As we return to the basics of more fruits, vegetables, and whole grain products we should plan the extra ingredient—Joy. Pleasure in dining is not a luxury; it is a necessity if we want to make the most of the nutritional values in foods we eat.

A meal may begin with an appetizer and end with a punch. Recipes for appetizers and punches have been included in this chapter. Note: Some recipes call for salt and sugar. To reduce salt and sugar never add additional amounts to the ready prepared foods. Increases have come from dashing each food with salt or sugar before tasting the foods. Become a taster, rather than an assumer.

APPETIZERS ....

The appetizers are great friends of the homemaker or career woman. Flavorful and eye-appealing appetizers give the family a little something to assure their hunger while you prepare the meal. Appetizers can be planned to add nutritional value to the meal.

Fresh fruits make delightful appetizers or a fresh vegetable salad assists the appetite before a meal. Use any fruit or vegetable, preferably in season. Vegetables and fruits may be combined to meet the choices of the family group. A great way for family sharing and pleasure is to place one large plate of fruit or salad in the center of the table and have each family member share. Children enjoy being a part of this idea.

COCKTAIL MEAT BALLS

2 pounds ground beef
2 beaten eggs
1-1/3 cups non-fat milk
2 teaspoons salt
½ teaspoon pepper
½ teaspoon nutmeg
4 tablespoons caraway seeds
4 tablespoons fine chopped onions

1 cup fine dry bread crumbs
¼ teaspoon allspice
2 teaspoons brown sugar

SAUCE:

½ cup vegetable fat (except coconut oil)
2 cups beef bouillon
½ cup flour

In large bowl, combine all ingredients. / Mix well. / Use teaspoon to form tiny balls. / Fry in vegetable fat until evenly brown. / Combine ingredients for sauce & heat. / Add meat balls slowly for 20 minutes.

These meat balls may be made in advance and stored in freezer or an immediate supply in the refrigerator (not longer than one week). ● Makes 48 tiny meatballs.

SHRIMP PATE

4 pounds fresh shrimp
2 medium onions, minced
½ cup melted vegetable fat (except coconut oil)
3 tablespoons lemon juice

½ cup mayonnaise
Salt and pepper and dry mustard (to taste)
½ cup brandy

Shell, clean and cook shrimp. / Mash very fine in a big bowl with a potato masher, adding minced onions as you do it. / When you can mash no more, pour in fat, mixing thoroughly. / Add lemon juice and mayonnaise and continue to pound. / It will be a stiff paste. / Add seasoning and brandy and mix again. / Pack mixture in mold and press down well. / Chill at least 12 hours in refrigerator. / When ready to serve, turn out and slice with a thin, hot sharp knife. / This can be kept indefinitely in refrigerator. ●Serve number as needed.

254

PARTY FRANKS

Bread
Frankfurters
Horseradish
Mustard

Vegetable fat (except
  coconut oil)
Olives

Place frankfurters diagonally on slice of bread which has been spread with horseradish and mustard. / Pin opposite corners of bread with toothpick so frank is wrapped in bread. / Brush lightly with vegetable fat, bake 15 minutes in hot oven. / Just before serving, top toothpick with olive. ● Make number needed.

CHEESE BALLS

¾ cup Bacon Cheese Spread
4 tablespoons vegetable fat
  (except coconut oil)
¼ teaspoon of hot sauce

1/8 teaspoon of Worchestershire sauce
¾ cup sifted flour
1 jar of small green olives

Blend cheese and fat until light. / Add seasonings. / Stir in flour until dough. / Using a teaspoon of dough—put one small olive in center and roll until olive is covered. / Place on ungreased baking sheet. / Bake 12-15 minutes at 400°F. ● Makes 15-20.

VIRGINIA HAM STRAWS

2 cups flour
2 level teaspoons baking
  powder
½ teaspoon salt
¼ teaspoon paprika
1/8 teaspoon red pepper

½ cup vegetable fat
  (except coconut oil)
1 egg
½ cup non-fat milk
¾ cup ground Virginia Ham

Sift dry ingredients three or four times, / cut in fat, / add whole egg without beating and stir in, / add milk and ham and mix well. / Roll very thin, / cut in strips about ¼ inch wide and four inches long and lay in rows in greased pan about ¾ inch apart. / Bake in moderate oven until pale brown. / Serve as appetizer or with salads, soups, or breakfast coffee. ● Makes 48.

ANCHOVY ROLL

1 cup of flour
¼ pound vegetable fat
  (except coconut oil)

4 ounces cream cheese
4 ounces anchovy paste

Melt fat and mix with flour and cheese. Roll thin on well floured board, spread with anchovy paste and make into roll about 1¼ inches in diameter, put in refrigerator until firm. To serve slice thin and bake at 400° until golden brown. ● Makes 24.

AVOCADO CANAPE

1 avocado
Onion or chive (chopped)
Salt
Lemon Juice

Chili powder
Celery salt
Pepper
Mayonnaise

Scoop out the pulp of a ripe avocado, / mash, and season with onions or chives, salt, lemon juice, chili powder, celery salt, pepper and enough mayonnaise to make a smooth paste. / Spread on crackers. ● Makes 1 cup.

MUSHROOM ROLL-UPS

20 slices thin sliced bread
1½ cup cream mushroom soup
1 tablespoon minced onion
2 teaspoon Worchestershire
  sauce

3 tablespoons vegetable fat
  (except coconut oil)

Night before, trim crusts from fresh, thin sliced bread. / With rolling pin, roll slices very flat. / Mix undiluted soup with onion and Worcestershire sauce and spread bread with mixture. / Roll jelly-roll fashion and place seam side down, close together on cookie sheet. / Brush with melted fat. / Store in refrigerator until needed. / When ready to serve, toast under broiler. ● Makes 20.

HOT OLIVE CHEESE PUFFS

1 cup grated sharp cheese
3 tablespoons soft vegetable
fat (except coconut oil)
½ cup sifted flour

¼ teaspoon salt
2 dashes red pepper
Stuffed olives (12)

Mix first five ingredients well. / Wrap each stuffed olive in about 1 teaspoon of the cheese dough, completely covering olive, wrap and freeze. / To serve take desired number of frozen puffs, arrange on ungreased pan and bake at 400°F 10 to 15 minutes. / Serve hot. / They do not have to be frozen, but it is easier to have them prepared ahead of time. ● Makes 12.

SHRIMP IN HOT FRENCH DRESSING

4 tablespoons vegetable oil
(except coconut oil)
1 scant tablespoon vinegar
1 teaspoon Worchestershire
sauce

Pepper, salt and mustard
(to taste)
1 pound shrimp, peeled and
cooked

Mix all ingredients well. / Heat, / add cooked medium-sized shrimp. ● Serves 8-10.

CRAB PUFFS

8 ounces cream cheese,
softened
1 teaspoon baking powder
¼ cup vegetable fat, (except
coconut oil) softened

1 cup crab meat
Garlic and onion powder to
taste
1 teaspoon Worcestershire
sauce

Cream together all ingredients, / spread lightly on trimmed bread slices. / Broil until bubbly or bake at 350° until done. / Makes a generous quantity.

SOUPS . . . .

CREAM OF PEANUT SOUP

A specialty of the Hotel Roanoke, Roanoke, Virginia. Their recipe is a secret. This recipe comes nearest to the secret recipe and one that we like.

¼ cup vegetable fat
(except coconut oil)
1 cup thinly sliced celery
½ cup minced green onions
2 tablespoons flour

2 cups chicken stock or
broth
¾ cup creamy peanut butter
1½ cups light cream
6 teaspoons crushed peanuts

Melt fat in large sauce pan over low heat and add celery and onion. / Cook until tender but not browned. / Add flour and stir until mixture is smooth. / Gradually add chicken broth and bring to a boil. / Blend in peanut butter and simmer about 15 minutes. / Stir in cream just before serving. / Add crushed peanuts to the top of each serving. ● Serves 6.

PUMPKIN SOUP

4 cups non-fat milk
1 cup pumpkin
½ teaspoon salt
¼ teaspoon cinnamon

¼ teaspoon nutmeg
1 tablespoon sugar
½ cup rice

Heat the milk in a large saucepan and add the remaining ingredients. / Cook over low heat for about 30 minutes or until rice is well done. ● Serves 4.

CABBAGE-CARROT CHOWDER

4 cups shredded cabbage
2 cups sliced carrots
3 cups diced potatoes
1 tablespoon salt
½ teaspoon pepper

½ teaspoon sugar
2 tablespoons vegetable fat
(except coconut oil)
4 cups non-fat milk

Combine the vegetables, salt, pepper, sugar, and 2 cups water in large saucepan or Dutch oven and cook over low heat until vegetables are done. / Add fat and milk. / Heat thoroughly. ● Serves 8.

TOMATO-CORN SOUP

1 cup non-fat milk
1 cup tomato soup

½ cup cream-style corn
¼ teaspoon curry powder

Add milk gradually to the tomato soup. / Stir in the corn. / Sprinkle the curry powder on top and heat over low heat until very hot. ● Serves 3.

MAIN DISHES . . . .

Recipe submitted by Maria (Mrs. Ralph) Flinchbaugh, Fairfax, Virginia

FISH PARMESAN

2 pounds fish fillet,
  skinned and cut into
  serving size
1 cup sour cream
¼ cup grated Parmesan
  cheese
1 tablespoon grated onion

1 tablespoon fresh lemon
  juice
½ teaspoon salt
Dash liquid hot pepper
  sauce
Dash paprika
Dash chopped parsley

Place fillet in a single layer in a well greased 12 x 8 x 2 baking dish. / Combine remaining ingredients, except paprika and parsley, and spread over the fish. / Sprinkle with paprika. / Bake in a 350° oven for 25-30 minutes. / Garnish with chopped parsley. ● Serves 4 to 5.

Recipe submitted by H. A. Dean, Jr., Sue and Danielle Dean, Charlottesville, Virginia.

MANDARIN CHICKEN

2 chicken breasts
1 stalk celery
1 small onion, sliced
Salt and pepper to taste
4 tablespoons soy sauce
2 cups beef consomme
12 mushrooms, sliced
1 cup snow pea pods or
  green beans
5 scallions, chopped

4 pimentos, slivered
1 cup bamboo shoots
1/3 cup water chestnuts,
  drained and sliced
2 small tomatoes, cut in
  wedges
4 tablespoons cornstarch
2 cups bean sprouts, heated
  and drained

Poach chicken breasts in water until tender, together with celery, onion, salt, salt, and pepper; / cool. / Cut meat from bone into bite-size pieces. / Drain broth; / skim off fat and reserve broth. / Heat soy sauce and consomme; / add mushrooms and pea pods; / simmer until barely crisp. / Add scallions, pimentos, bamboo shoots, water chestnuts, tomatoes, and chicken. / Simmer 5 minutes; / vegetables should be crisp. / Mix cornstarch with enough reserved broth to moisten; / stir into chicken mixture. / Cook until slightly thickened. / Serve on hot bean sprouts. ● Serves 4.

Recipe submitted by Mrs. Billy P. Gibson, McLean, Virginia

CHEESE AND GRIT CASSEROLE

Leftovers of this casserole can be frozen and reheated, with a little extra cheese sprinkled on top.

5 cups boiling water with
  1 teaspoon salt
1 cup grits
½ cup vegetable fat
  (except coconut oil)

1 pound grated cheese
Dash each of Tabasco and
  Worchestershire sauces
5 eggs, separated

Combine water and grits and cook 20-25 minutes. / Remove from heat and stir in fat and cheese. / Stir until melted. / Add sauces. / Beat yolks well and fold into the grits. / Beat egg whites stiff but not dry and gently fold into the grits. / Turn into a large flat greased dish and bake at 350°F for 1 hour. ● Serves 6 to 8.

MOTHER'S OLD-TIME COUNTRY HAM WITH REDEYE GRAVY

Plan to serve on a day of heavy activity.

6 slices country ham, each
  about ½ inch thick
1 cup boiling water

1 tablespoon freshly made
  black coffee

Place ham slices in a large flat pan and cover with cold water. / Let stand 6 to 8 hours; / drain and blot dry. / Remove and discard rind. / Fry ham slices in single layer in an ungreased skillet at 300°-325°. / Fry for 5 to 6 minutes on each side, / then remove to heated platter. / Pour off all but about 2 tablespoons fat. / Add boiling water and let boil up, / scraping bottom to pick up all flavorful bits of ham from the skillet. / Stir in coffee. / Pour over ham slices and serve at once. ● Serves 6.

Recipe submitted by Mrs. Andrew B. Keyes, Adelphi, Maryland

STUFFED CABBAGE ROLLS, UKRAINIAN STYLE

4 pounds ground beef
2 pounds instant rice
½ cup vegetable fat
  (except coconut oil)
1 large onion

4 medium cabbage heads
1¼ cups tomato soup
3¾ cups water
Salt and pepper to taste

Parboil rice, rinse and set aside. / Core cabbage heads, / drop heads one at a time into boiling water to separate leaves. / Stack leaves on a flat baking pan to cool. / Melt down fat and then saute the chopped onion in it. / Mix meat, rice, fat, onion, salt and pepper until blended. / Cut off the rib (or vein) from the center of the cabbage leaf to make it more pliable when rolling. / Put a heaping tablespoon of the meat mixture on the rib end of the cabbage leaf and roll to the other side. / Tuck the sides in. / (The roll will not open while heating.) / Line a roaster or stock pot with the small or broken cabbage leaves. / Place the rolls side by side, on top of one another, until the meat mixture is used. / Cover the rolls with tomato soup and water. / Place remaining cabbage leaves on top of the rolls to keep the steam underneath cover. / Bake at 375°F for 4 hours. / Let stand half hour before serving. ● Serves 12.

Recipe submitted by Iona and Frank Gerace, Harrisburg, Pennsylvania

SARME (CABBAGE ROLLS)

1 large cabbage
1½ pounds ground beef
¾ pound bulk pork sausage
1/3 cup long grain rice,
  cooked
1 medium onion, chopped fine

1 tablespoon salt
½ teaspoon pepper
2½ cups sauerkraut
2 tablespoons flour
2 tablespoons vegetable oil
  (except coconut oil)

Core cabbage. / Put in a large kettle of boiling water and simmer for 5 minutes. / Remove cabbage, drain and let cool for several minutes. / Mix beef, pork, rice, onions, and seasoning. / Remove cabbage leaves. / Fill each leaf with 2 tablespoons of meat mixture. / Roll securely. / Drain sauerkraut. / In large kettle, layer sauerkraut and cabbage rolls alternately. / Dice unused part of cabbage and put on top. / Fill with water and cook for 2 hours. / Brown flour and vegetable oil, add 1 cup of liquid from Sarme to make a gravy. / Drizzle gravy into Sarme and continue to simmer for 5 minutes. ● Serves 6.

RUBY FOX SHRIMP JAMBALAYA

2 teaspoons salt
1 tablespoon hot sauce
1 bay leaf
1 stalk celery with leaves
1 pound shrimp
¼ cup vegetable fat
  (except coconut oil)

½ cup chopped onion
½ cup chopped green pepper
1 garlic clove minced
1 cup rice
4 cups tomatoes in juice
¾ cup bouillon
1½ cup diced cooked ham

Place 3 cups water, 1 teaspoon salt and ½ teaspoon hot sauce in a saucepan and add the bay leaf and celery. / Bring to a boil and add the shrimp. / Bring to a boil again and cook for 5 minutes. / Drain the shrimp and cool quickly. / Shell and devein the shrimp. / Melt the vegetable fat in a large skillet, / then add the onion, green pepper and garlic. / Cook until the onion is tender, but not brown. / Stir in the rice, tomatoes, bouillon, remaining salt and hot sauce. / Bring to a boil over high heat, then reduce the temperature and cover the skillet. / Simmer for 20 minutes. / Add the ham, then cover and cook until the liquid is absorbed. ● Serves 6.

Recipe submitted by Miss L. Margerae Dean, Fairfax, Virginia

STEAK TERIYAKI

1 pound beef round steak or sirloin tips	1 medium onion, finely chopped
½ cup Shoyu sauce	¼ cup water, if desired
3 tablespoons sugar	2 tablespoons peanut oil, if desired
1 tablespoon ginger root, finely chopped or grated, or 2 teaspoons powdered ginger	1 tablespoon sherry, if desired
1 to 2 cloves garlic, crushed	

Slice meat thinly across grain. / Combine remaining ingredients; / soak meat in this sauce for about an hour and broil from 5 to 10 minutes or until brown. / Turn and brown on other side. / When charcoal fire is used, meat may be basted while browning. ● Serves 4-6.

Recipe submitted by Dorothy M. (Mrs. Art) Clanton, Moscow, Idaho

CHAFING DISH GOURMET

This can be made in an electric skillet and transferred to a chafing dish to serve

1 small onion	1 teaspoon Worcestershire sauce
¼ cup mushrooms	
3 tablespoons vegetable fat (except coconut oil)	½ cup of light cream
1½ cup cream of chicken soup	1 cup of crab meat or shrimp
Dash pepper	½ cup sliced ripe olives
Dash tabasco sauce	Sherry
	Slivered almonds

Chop the onion. / Brown with mushrooms in the vegetable fat. / Add soup, pepper, tabasco and Worcestershire sauces; / simmer a few minutes. / Add cream, olives and crab. / Mix gently and cover until heated through (do *not* boil). / Mix gently and pour a small amount of sherry wine over the top, then slivered almonds. / Serve over cooked rice. ● Serves 4 to 5.

Recipe submitted by Heridan (Ms. John L.) Fox, McLean, Virginia

"CANJA"

1 whole chicken, cut up	Salt to taste
½ cup vegetable oil (except coconut oil)	Fresh parsley
½ cup minced ham	1 teaspoon marjoram
1 onion, chopped	Fresh ground pepper
2 cloves of garlic, minced	2 medium tomatoes, seeded, chopped
1 bay leaf	Green onions
1 cup finely diced carrots	½ teaspoon basil
4 bouillon cubes dissolved in 4 cups water or 4 cups fresh chicken stock, if available	1 cup long grain rice

Brown chicken in oil; / then add stock and remaining ingredients. / Simmer for 1 hour, adding more water if needed. / Serve in bowls with chopped onions and parsley sprinkled on top. ● Serves 6 or more.

MARVIN'S BARBECUED KABOB

2 pounds boneless pork shoulder, cut into 1-inch cubes	½ teaspoon salt
	1 teaspoon mixed Italian herbs
¾ cup peanut oil	2 to 3 medium-sized green peppers, seeded and cut into 1-inch squares
¼ cup cider vinegar	
1 clove garlic, peeled and split	2 cups pineapple chunks

Place pork cubes in a non-metal bowl. / Combine oil, vinegar, garlic, salt, and herbs, / blend well, and pour over pork cubes. / Cover and refrigerate for 4 hours or more, overnight if desired. / Drain and reserve. / Alternately thread pork cubes, peppers, and pineapple chunks on a metal skewer. / Brush with marinade and place on barbecue grill as far as possible over glowing coals. / Broil, brushing with marinade and turning often, for 30 to 40 minutes. ● Serves 6.

ROAST TURKEY

1 roasting turkey
Salt
Stuffing

Vegetable fat (except
  coconut oil)
Flour

Wash, singe, and drain the bird, / rub it with salt, inside and out, and stuff with a desired dressing. / Truss and tie the fowl. / Brush skin with melted or softened fat. / Turn breast side down and cover bird with a cloth dipped in fat. / Place in pan large enough for bird. / Place in a moderate oven (325° to 350° F). / Cook uncovered breast side down about one half of total time. / Turn breast side up. / Place any of body fat removed in dressing over breastbone. / Baste with extra vegetable fat. / The cloth may be removed toward the end of the cooking if bird is not well browned. / Allow 30 minutes per pound for small bird or 25 minutes per pound for large bird.

DRESSINGS . . . .

This recipe was submitted by Kathryn B. Wood (Mrs. Robert W.), Roanoke, Virginia

CORNBREAD DRESSING

Toss together about 5 cups crumbled cornbread and 6 cups white bread (not too fresh). / Add 1½ cups onion and 1½ - 2 cups celery chopped and cooked slightly in ½ cup non-fat milk. / Mix in 1 egg slightly beaten and 1 cup stock. / Cook in greased baking dish about 30 minutes at 350° *

The following recipe was submitted by Peggy Taaffe (Mrs. James T.), McLean, Virginia

SAGE DRESSING (NANA'S)

2 large sandwich loaves of
  bread throughly dried
  and ground in grinder
2 cups minced celery
1 cup minced onion
½ pound vegetable fat,
  melted (except coconut
  oil)

1 teaspoon each salt and
  pepper
3 tablespoons sage, ground
  fine

Combine ingredients. / Moisten with water. / Bake in greased baking dish about 350°F. for about 30 minutes. ● Serves 10-12.

VEGETABLES . . . .

This recipe was submitted by Mrs. Glenwood A. Deacon, Roanoke, Virginia

TURBAN SQUASH PIE

8 inch graham cracker pie
  crust
1¼ cups squash, peeled,
  cooked, and mashed
2 tablespoons vegetable fat
  (except coconut oil)
¾ cup non-fat milk

1 teaspoon cinnamon
2 eggs, slightly beaten
½ teaspoon vanilla
¼ teaspoon ginger
2 teaspoons nutmeg
Whipped topping

Mix the squash, vegetable fat, milk, eggs, vanilla, ginger, nutmeg, and cinnamon. / Pour into pie crust and bake at 450°F for 25 minutes or until done. / Top with whipped topping. ● Serves 6-8.

BROCCOLI CASSEROLE

16 stalks of broccoli cooked in unsalted water until just barely tender; / drain and put in greased casserole dish; / cover with the sauce blended in a double boiler.

SAUCE:

½ cup vegetable fat
  (except coconut oil)
4 slices yellow sheese

8 ounce package cream
  cheese
1 cup cream of shrimp soup

Blend sauce ingredients in double boiler. / Pour over broccoli. / Bake at 350 for 20-25 minutes, or until bubbly. ● Serves 8-10.

CARROT PUDDING

The English claim the carrot to be a true native of England.

3 eggs, separated
4 tablespoons sugar
1½ tablespoons cornstarch
1 cup non-fat milk
3 cups (2 pounds) carrots
   cooked and mashed

3 tablespoons vegetable fat
   (except coconut oil)
1 teaspoon salt
1 cup fine bread crumbs
1 cup milk (non-fat)
½ teaspoon nutmeg
¼ cup cream sherry

Preheat oven to 300°F. / Grease 2 quart casserole dish. / Beat egg yolks and sugar until light, / hold aside. / Mix cornstarch with small amount of milk. / Heat remaining milk, add cornstarch mixture and stir until smooth and slightly thickened. / Stir small amount of hot cornstarch mixture into egg yolks and sugar. / Stir and mix, then return to hot milk and cornstarch, / cooking and stirring over medium heat until smooth and thick. / Add carrots, fat, salt, and bread crumbs, blending evenly. / Stir in remaining milk, / add sherry, mix well. / Beat egg whites until they stand in firm peaks, / then fold into carrot mixture. / Pour into casserole. / Place casserole in pan of hot water and bake for about 30 minutes. / Increase heat to 350°F. and bake for an additional 45 minutes. / If knife inserted in mixture comes out clean, the carrot pudding is ready to serve. ● Serves 6.

CASSEROLE OF GREEN BEANS

1½ pounds green beans,
   stems removed, halved,
   and rinsed in cold water
4 tablespoons vegetable fat
   (except coconut oil)
4 tablespoons flour
2½ cups nonfat milk
1½ cups grated mild
   cheddar cheese

Grating of nutmeg
Salt
Freshly ground black pepper
1 cup bread crumbs,
   toasted in 2 tablespoons
   vegetable fat (except
   coconut oil) (optional)
Paprika

In soup kettle, bring to a rolling boil several quarts of salted water. / Into it, plunge the beans, / leave them uncovered. / After the water has returned to the boil, cook the beans for 12 minutes, or until they are just crisp-tender. / (The age of the beans will determine their cooking time.) / Refresh them in cold water; drain and reserve. / In a large saucepan, melt the fat and in it, over gentle heat, cook the flour for a few minutes, stirring. / Gradually add the milk, stirring constantly, / then add the cheese, stirring until it is melted. / Season the sauce to taste. / Gently fold the beans into the sauce. / Arrange the mixture in a greased ovenproof serving dish. / Prepare the bread crumbs. / (At this point you may stop and continue later.) / Spread the bread crumbs evenly over the beans. / Add a sprinkling of paprika. / Bake the beans at 350 degrees for 15 minutes. / Or until the dish is well heated and the crumbs begin to brown. ● Serves 6.

SALADS . . . .

Recipe submitted by Margaret (Mrs. Arnold) Coffey, Bedford, Virginia

LAYERED SALAD

1 head lettuce or 2/3 of
   a rectangular baking
   dish filled
¾ cup chopped green pepper
1 cup chopped celery
1 cup chopped onion
1 small can green peas

1 cup mayonnaise
1 tablespoon sugar
1 cup grated mild cheddar
   cheese
2 slices bacon, cooked
   and crumbled

Layer first five ingredients, one on top of the other. / Spread mayonnaise on top. / Sprinkle with sugar and grated cheese / and finally sprinkle with crumbled bacon. / Cover salad and leave in refrigerator over night or at least 6 hours. ● Serves 4.

PINEAPPLE AND CREAM CHEESE SALAD

6 slices pineapple
1 cup cream cheese
Purple grape-juice

French dressing*
Lettuce leaves

Work enough grape-juice into the cream cheese to soften it so that it can be made into balls with the hands or with butter paddles. / Place a slice of pineapple on a lettuce leaf, / put a cheese ball on top and pour grape-juice and French dressing over all. ●Serves 3.

SPINACH SALAD

1 pint spinach
2 hard-cooked eggs

French dressing*

Wash spinach carefully. / Select only thick, tender leaves (save others and stems for cooking). / If too large, tear to size. / Shake off excess water. / Chop whites and yolks of eggs separately and turn into bowl with leaves. / Moisten with tart French dressing. / Any mild-flavored vegetable may be added for variation. ●Serves 2.

TOMATO AND LETTUCE SALAD

3 tomatoes
Lettuce leaves

6 tablespoons Italian dressing*

Scald the tomatoes, / remove the skins and chill. / Just before serving time, cut them in halves, crosswise, and place one piece, with the outside upward, on each serving plate with one or two leaves of white, crisp lettuce underneath. / Pour over each portion a tablespoon of Italian dressing. ●Serves 3.

CUCUMBER JELLY SALAD

2 cups grated cucumber
Salt and paprika
2 tablespoons vinegar
1 tablespoon vegetable oil (except coconut oil)
1 teaspoon gelatin

2 teaspoons cold water
6 halves of walnut-meats
Mayonnaise*
Lettuce leaves

Peel cucumbers, removing most of the white as well as the green skin. / Grate enough to give 2 cups and season with salt, paprika, vinegar and oil. / Add gelatin mixed with cold water. / Place over the fire until warm and well mixed. / Do not boil. / In the bottom of an individual mold put a half kernel of walnut, / then pour in the cucumber mixture and when it has cooled, chill. / When ready to serve, turn each mold. ●Serves 4.

CAESAR SALAD

2 cloves garlic, crushed, peeled and finely minced
½ cup peanut or olive oil
½ cup freshly grated Parmesan cheese
¼ cup crumbled blue cheese, preferably Roquefort
1 teaspoon kosher-type salt
½ teaspoon ground white pepper

1 large Romaine, cut washed and thoroughly dried
1 raw egg beaten with a fork
4 teaspoons lemon juice, strained
1 tablespoon Worchestershire sauce

Combine the minced garlic with half of the oil and set aside for at least one hour. / Sprinkle the cheeses, salt, pepper, and remaining oil over the lettuce. / Beat the egg, lemon juice and Worcestershire sauce together. / Pour over the lettuce and toss well. / Just before serving, pour the oil and garlic mixture over the salad. / Serve immediately. ● Serves 6.

BREADS . . . .

Recipes submitted by Geri (Mrs. Clyde F.) Baley, Fredericksburg, Virginia

MOTHER BALEY'S POTATO MUFFINS

1½ cups flour
2 tablespoons sugar
2 teaspoons baking powder
1 teaspoon salt

1½ cups mashed potatoes
1 egg, beaten
2/3 cup non-fat milk

Sift dry ingredients together. / Add the egg to the milk then pour the milk and egg mixture into the sifted dry ingredients and stir until well mixed. / Stir in mashed potatoes and blend thoroughly. / Fill greased muffin pans 2/3 full. / Bake at 350°F. for 30-35 minutes. ● Makes 12 muffins.

BANANA BREAD

1 cup mashed bananas
  (2 large ones)
¼ cup sour milk with 1
  teaspoon soda
1½ cups sugar
2 eggs

1/3 cup vegetable oil
2 cups flour
1 teaspoon vanilla
½ teaspoon salt
½ cup chopped walnuts or
  pecans (optional)

Mix together bananas, milk, sugar and eggs. / Add remaining ingredients. / Knead dough on floured board, and squeeze off dough to place in 1 large and 1 small loaf pan. / Bake at 350° for 1½ hrs. / This freezes nicely and will keep up to to 6 months.

This recipe was submitted by Peggy (Mrs. James) Taaffe, McLean, Virginia

PEGGY'S BLUEBERRY COFFEECAKE

4 eggs, separated
1 cup vegetable fat (except
  coconut oil)
2 cups sugar

2 cups sifted flour
1 tsp. vanilla
1 cup blueberries, drained

Whip egg whites until stiff. / In separate bowl, cream fat and sugar, / add egg yolks one at a time. / Add flour and vanilla. / Fold in egg whites and place in a greased pan 11 x 16 x 1 inches or ring tube pan. / Gently press in fruit. / Bake 35 minutes at 350° in flat pan. / Top while hot with powdered sugar.

RAISIN BREAD

Needs no kneading. Serve this soft-textured, spiced bread warm.

1 cup whole wheat flour
3 to 4 cups unbleached flour
½ cup sugar
1 teaspoon salt
2 packets active dry yeast
1 cup non-fat milk
1/3 cup water

2 tablespoons honey
¼ cup vegetable fat
  (except coconut oil)
1 egg
1¼ cup seedless raisins
2 teaspoons cinnamon
½ teaspoon nutmeg

In a large mixing bowl, combine whole wheat flour, 1 cup of white flour, sugar, salt and yeast. / Put milk, water, honey and fat in a saucepan. / Place over low heat, stirring. / When liquid is almost hot to the touch (120 to 130 degrees), remove from heat. / Gradually add milk mixture to dry ingredients, beating at low speed. / Add egg and beat at medium speed for 2 minutes. / Add 1 cup of white flour, stir in well and beat batter at high speed for 2 minutes. / Stir in enough additional flour to produce a stiff batter. / Cover, let rise in a warm place (80 to 85 degrees) until double in bulk, about 1 hour. / Stir batter down. / With a spoon beat in raisins and spices. / Turn batter into two greased 1-quart casseroles. / Bake immediately at 350 degrees for 40 to 45 minutes. / Remove loaves from casseroles and serve immediately. ● Makes 2 loaves.

BAKING POWDER BISCUIT

2 cups flour
4 teaspoons baking-powder
1 teaspoon salt

2 tablespoons vegetable fat
  (except coconut oil)
¾ cup liquid non-fat milk

Mix dry ingredients and sift twice. / Break fat with tips of fingers, or cut in with two knives. / Add liquid gradually, mixing with a knife until soft dough forms. / It is not always possible to determine the exact amount of liquid due to differences in flours. / Toss on a floured board, / pat and roll lightly to one-inch in thickness. / Shape with a biscuit-cutter. / Bake in hot oven 450° - 460° degrees for twelve to fifteen minutes. ● Makes 12 biscuits.

BASIC ROLL RECIPE

This is the recipe that I have used for years in making breads for the freezer. My family always delights in hot rolls or a brown loaf of bread.

2 cups scalded nonfat milk	6 cups flour (enough to
1½ teaspoons salt	make a smooth, tender
4 tablespoons sugar	dough)
1 yeast cake softened in ¼	4 tablespoons vegetable fat
cup warm water	(except coconut oil)

Note: For whole wheat rolls or cornmeal rolls use 4 cups flour and 2 cups cornmeal or whole wheat flour. If a greater amount of sugar is used the rolls will be sweeter. If a greater amount of fat used, the rolls will be richer and more tender. Not less than two or more than eight tablespoons of sugar or fat should be used, however.

Place yeast in ¼ cup water, add 1 tablespoon of the sugar and allow to soften — water must be warm not hot to allow for yeast activity. / Measure sugar and salt into large mixing bowl. / Scald milk. / Then using low fat milk the milk is ready to use when steam begins to rise. Pour hot milk over sugar and salt in the mixing bowl and stir. / Add the fat, stir, and cover. / Allow to cool until liquid is barely warm. / When mixture is ready, stir, then, add yeast mixture and stir until all ingredients have been mixed thoroughly. / Add flour then stir. / Continue until the liquid becomes dough that you can handle with hands. / Leave on floured surface and knead (push hands into dough). / The more you knead yeast bread the finer the texture, so, knead it as many times to feel dough is light to touch. / A light touch of the fingers to the dough gives a response of soft springy feeling without feeling sticky. / Dough is ready to rise. / Place in greased mixing bowl, dot with fat to keep surface soft / cover with towel and place in warm place. / Allow to rise twice in bulk, time about 1 hour. / When towel has been pushed up by dough it is ready to shape into rolls or loaves. / Grease muffin tins or loaf pans. / Shape dough and allow to rise again twice in bulk. / Then, place in 425 degree oven and bake until brown, about 25 minutes. / Turn out on foil or a rack and allow to cool. / (I turn on foil cut the size to wrap and allow to cool then wrap for freezer.) / This quantity makes 24 clover leaf rolls and 2 loaves. / It will keep in freezer for 6 months.

VARIATIONS OF STANDARD ROLL RECIPE

Plain Rolls — Follow standard roll recipe. When dough is right, cut or tear it into pieces about the size of a small egg or a walnut. Fold the sides under until the top of the roll is perfectly smooth. Brush the top with fat. Place in greased bread tin, on bread sheet or in individual molds. When light, bake in a hot oven (400° - 425°F.).

Cinnamon Rolls—Follow standard roll recipe. When dough is light, roll into a sheet about one-fourth inch thick, spread liberally with melted fat, sprinkle with sugar and cinnamon. Add currants if desired. Roll like jelly-roll. With sharp knife or shears cut slices from the roll and place them an inch apart on a well-greased sheet. When light, bake hot oven (400° - 425°F.) about twenty minutes. When baked, the tops may be brushed with the yolk of egg diluted with a tablespoon of milk and returned to oven to brown.

Clover-Leaf Rolls—Follow standard roll recipe. When light, break dough into small pieces about the size of marbles. Brush with fat and place the three or four of these tiny balls close together in greased muffin rings or pans. When very light, bake about fifteen minutes in hot oven (400° - 425°F.) The success of these rolls depends on having the three balls together equal only as much dough as an ordinary roll would require and letting them rise very light before baking them.

Crescent Rolls—Follow standard roll recipe, adding flour to make a stiffer dough than for most rolls. When light, cut the dough into small pieces the shape of triangles. Brush with fat. Roll each triangle, beginning at the base. Press dough lightly with palm of hand, bringing ends around to form a crescent. Place on tins some distance apart. When light, bake in hot oven (400° - 425°F). Fifteen minutes. Brush with egg yolk mixed with milk and return to oven for browning.

Dinner Rolls—Follow standard roll recipe, using four table-spoons fat, desired amount of sugar and two egg whites. Add one half the flour, beating until smooth, then add the beaten whites of eggs. Add the remainder of the flour, knead lightly and let rise. When light, cut or break dough into rolls the size of walnuts. Shape, place on well-greased pans, one-half to one inch apart, let rise and glaze with white of egg diluted with water. Bake in hot oven (400° - 425°F.).

Finger Rolls—Follow standard roll recipe. When light cut and shape into long pieces about the size and shape of a finger. Place on well-greased pan, brush with melted fat or egg-white. When light, bake in hot oven (400° - 425°F.).

Luncheon Rolls—Follow standard roll recipe using 6 to 8 tablespoons of fat. Add two well-beaten eggs after one half the flour has been added. Add remaining flour and knead. When light shape into small biscuits. Place one inch apart in well-greased pan. When double in bulk, brush with egg-yolk diluted with milk and bake in hot oven (400° - 425°F.).

Parker House Rolls (Pocket-Book Rolls)—Follow standard roll recipe. Four tablespoons each of sugar and fat give excellent results. When light, roll dough one-fourth inch thick. Cut with biscuit cutter, brush each circle with melted fat and crease through the center of each roll with the dull edge of a knife.

Fold each roll over double. Place on well-greased pan one inch apart, brush with melted fat and when very light bake in hot oven (400° - 425°F.).

Twisted Rolls—Follow standard roll recipe. When light, break dough into small pieces and roll out with palm of hand into rolls about seven inches long and one half inch thick, taking an end of each strip between the thumb and forefinger of each hand, twist in opposite directions and bring the ends together. Shape the two ends alike, place one half inch apart on well-greased pans, brush with melted fat or egg yolk diluted with milk. When light, bake in hot oven (400° - 425° F.).

Tea Biscuit—Follow standard roll recipe. When dough is light, roll and cut with biscuit-cutter. Place on well-greased pans one-half inch apart. When light bake in hot oven (400° - 425° F).*

English Muffins—Follow standard roll recipe, making a very soft dough. Knead lightly until smooth and elastic. Work down and when light again roll out with rolling-pin to about one-fourth inch in thickness. Cut in circles. When light, bake on ungreased hot griddle. As soon as they are brown on one side, turn them over. When both sides are browned, bake more slowly until finished. They may be browned on the griddle and then put into the oven to finish baking.

A modification of this recipe may be made by adding only enough flour to make a drop batter. Let it rise until light. Drop batter into large, greased English muffin rings, arranged on a greased baking-sheet. Bake in a hot oven (400° - 425° F.) until nearly done. Turn rings upside down and complete baking.

BREADS ....

FLAKEY PASTRY

1½ cups flour	3 to 4 tablespoons cold
½ teaspoon salt	water
½ cup vegetable fat (except)	
coconut oil)	

Sift flour and salt. / Cut in fat with pastry blender or two knives. / Add water and mix thoroughly, leaving fat in small lumps. / Prick pastry with fork. / Roll lightly, place in pie pan and bake quickly in a hot oven 450°F. for about 15 to 20 minutes. ● Makes 12.

DESSERTS ....

Recipe was submitted by Mary (Mrs. John Carter) Dean, Medical College of Virginia, Richmond

MANDARIN ORANGE FREEZE

2 cups orange flavored	½ cup sugar
yogurt	1/3 cup chopped pecans
2 cups madarin oranges	

Stir yogurt to blend. / Drain mandarin oranges. / Combine yogurt, oranges, sugar, and nuts. / Line muffin pan with paper bake cups. / Spoon in yogurt mixture. / Freeze until firm. / Remove cups from freezer and let stand at room temperature before serving. ● Serves 6-8.

W. MARVIN'S AMBROSIA

3 fresh oranges	½ cup light corn syrup
3 fresh grapefruit	½ cup flaked or fresh
½ small fresh pineapple	coconut, shredded
½ cup orange juice	

Peel and section oranges and grapefruit. / Peel and dice pineapple and mix it with the orange and grapefruit sections. / Combine orange juice and syrup. / Divide fruit mixture into 6 sherbert glasses, / pour juice over fruit and top with coconut. / Other fruits may be added in season. ● Serves 6.

This recipe was submitted by Sue (Mrs. H.A.) Dean, Charlottesville, Virginia

DANIELLE'S FAVORITE CHOCOLATE CAKE

2 cups all-purpose flour	5 eggs
2 cups sugar	1 cup buttermilk plus 1
¾ cup vegetable fat	teaspoon baking soda
(except coconut oil)	3 squares unsweetened
Pinch of salt	chocolate, melted
1 teaspoon vanilla extract	

Sift the flour and sugar. / Cream fat until fluffy. / Slowly add the sugar. / Add salt and vanilla. / Add eggs, one at a time, beating well after each. / Alternately add flour and milk (when soda has been added to buttermilk it should foam). / Lastly pour in the melted chocolate. / Pour into a 15½ x 10½ x 1 inch pan which has been greased, / then lined with waxed paper and greased again. / Bake at 325° about 35 minutes. / Turn out on waxed paper on a board and remove paper. / Cool. / Flip cake over. / Cake can be cut in half and layered with the favorite chocolate icing or cake can be left as a sheet.

CHOCOLATE ICING

6 ounces semi-sweet	½ cup sour cream
chocolate pieces	1 teaspoon vanilla extract
¼ cup vegetable fat	¼ teaspoon salt
(except coconut oil)	3 cups confectioner's sugar

Melt chocolate and fat over hot water; remove. / Blend in sour cream, vanilla, and salt. / Gradually beat in sugar to make frosting a spreading consistency.

Recipe submitted by Fern (Mrs. George) Heller, Englewood, Colorado

FERN'S IMPOSSIBLE PIE

4 eggs, beaten	1¾ cup brown sugar
½ cup flour	2 cups non-fat milk
½ cup coconut	½ cup chopped nuts
½ cup vegetable fat, melted	
(except coconut oil)	

Mix all ingredients together and pour into a greased 9-inch pie plate. / Bake for 35 minutes at 350°F. (It makes its own crust.)
● Serves 6.

Recipe submitted by "Geri" (Mrs. Clyde F.) Baley, Fredericksburg, Virginia

CURRIED PECANS

1 pound pecan halves	2 tablespoons curry powder
½ cup peanut oil	1 tablespoon ginger
½ cup vegetable fat	1 tablespoon chutney sauce
(except coconut oil)	Salt to taste
2 tablespoons brown sugar	

Preheat oven to 350°F. / Place pecans on baking sheet and toast for 10 minutes. / Do not allow the pecans to brown. / Remove from oven, but LEAVE OVEN ON. / Melt fat and oil in a large skillet. / Add sugar, salt, curry powder, and ginger; blend well. / Add pecans to skillet and stir with a wooden spoon until well coated. / Add chutney sauce and mix well. / Place pecans on a paper towel on baking sheet and put in oven. / NOW TURN OFF OVEN. / Let pecans dry out in the oven for about 10 minutes. / Remove from oven; / salt very lightly and store in an airtight container when cool.

Recipe submitted by Elizabeth (Mrs. Winfry) Carter, Newport News, Virginia

CHOCOLATE POUND CAKE

1½ cups vegetable fat	1 tablespoon vanilla
(except coconut oil)	3 cups flour
3 cups sugar	¼ teaspoon salt
5 eggs	½ teaspoon baking powder
1 cup non-fat milk	½ cup cocoa

Cream together fat and sugar, / then add 5 eggs, one at a time, beating after each. / Add milk and vanilla gradually and beat. / Then sift the remaining 4 ingredients together and add to creamed mixture. / Bake in greased, but not floured, tube pan for 1 hour and 20 minutes at 325°F. / Let stand in pan 25 minutes before removing.

If chocolate frosting is desired, use the following:

½ cup vegetable fat (except	4 cups confectioner's sugar
coconut oil)	1 teaspoon vanilla
6 tablespoons non-fat milk	1 cup chopped nuts (optional)
3 tablespoons cocoa	

Mix fat and milk and bring to a boil. / Remove from heat and add sugar, cocoa and vanilla; / beat with a mixer until desired texture is reached.

"BUD'S" DEEP DISH APPLE PIE

8 cups tart, cooking apples, peeled, cored, and sliced (9 medium apples)	1 teaspoon lemon juice
	1 teaspoon ground cinnamon
	½ teaspoon ground nutmeg
1 cup sugar	1/8 teaspoon ground cloves
3 tablespoons cognac or brandy (if desired)	2 tablespoons vegetable fat (except coconut oil)
1 teaspoon finely shredded lemon peel	Make pastry for 2 pie shells. See recipe page

Combine apples, sugar, cognac, lemon peel, lemon juice, and spices; / turn into a 9x1½ inch round baking pan which has been lined with pastry. / Dot with fat. / Fit pastry over fruit mixture; / turn edges under, fluting edge to seal it to pan. / Brush top of pastry with milk. / Sprinkle with a little cinnamon, if desired. / Prick holes in top of crust with fork for escape of steam. / Bake in 425° oven for 15 minutes. / Reduce oven to 350°. / Continue baking 45 minutes longer or till pastry is golden. / Variation: May substitute other fruits such as peaches, berries and cherries. / Garnish with rosebud shaped ice milk or soft cheese squeezed through a cake decorator tube. / Serve immediately.

MOTHER CARTER'S APPLESAUCE CAKE

1 cup vegetable fat (except coconut oil)	4 teaspoons soda
	2 teaspoons cinnamon
4 cups applesauce	2 teaspoons nutmeg
2 cups sugar	1 teaspoon cloves
2 cups raisins	1 teaspoon allspice
4 cups flour	

Makes one large cake in an angel food pan or two cakes in 10" tube pan. Grease the bottoms of the pans and line with waxed paper.

In fairly good-sized sauce pan, melt vegetable fat, / add applesauce, sugar, and raisins. / Heat slightly till sugar and fat have melted. / Let this mixture cool and add dry ingredients. / Bake cake in large pan for 1½ hours at 300°F or in small pans for 1 hour at 300°F. Let cool in pans, then remove to keep moist.

LEMON SHERBERT

½ cup lemon juice	1 quart non-fat milk
1½ cups sugar	

*All ingredients should be cold to prevent lemon juice from making the milk curdle. If milk does curdle it may not look as good but it can be used—so don't waste it. / Mix together the lemon juice and sugar. / Add slowly to the milk stirring constantly. / Milk should never be added to lemon juice because of the danger of curdling. / Place mixture in freezer tray or pan and freeze to a mush. / Serve in sherbert dishes. / Garnish each dish with lemon slice and mint leaf. ● Serves 6-8.

BEVERAGES . . . .

PUNCH

Punch is the English rendering of the Hindustani word, "pauch," meaning "five" for the five ingredients: spirits, water, sliced lemons or limes, sugar, and spice. The English got their recipe for their mixed drinks from the Far East, along with tea, ginger root, and spices, along with other items such as muslins and shawls.

The English brought America alcoholic beverages. They became household staples in colonial days. A good drink was regarded as a preventive against fevers. Many of the early rising planters fortified themselves with a starter before making the rounds of the plantation. A gentleman in Virginia who had earned his title and had to set an example of good conduct, would never drink too much since drunkedness would violate the rules of hospitality. Every plantation had a spirits cellar and a cabinet located in the dining room where wines were stored.

Thomas Jefferson is known to have proposed the reduction of duties on wine to avoid the use of whiskey as a substitute. He declared wine a necessity of life.

Today, studies show alcohol consumption on the increase. We should remember that our activity has decreased, therefore, a sedentary lifestyle demands a limited use of alcohol.

CELEBRATION SIPPERS

WINE WELCOMER

2 cups orange juice
1 cup frozen lemonade
concentrate, thawed
1 cup orange liqueur
1 fifth (750 mil) dry white
wine, chilled

3½ cups bottle carbonated
water
Ice

In large pitcher or punch bowl, combine orange juice, lemonade concentrate, orange liqueur, and wine. / To serve add carbonated water and ice to punch; stir. / Garnish with orange slices. ● Serves 20.

ISLAND FRUIT PUNCH

3¾ cups pears
1½ cups frozen lemonade
concentrate, thawed
3 cups unsweetened pineapple
juice

2 cups water
3½ cups lemon-lime
carbonated beverage

Serves 24.

MOTHER'S RECIPE FOR PUNCH

This recipe is one that Mother (Mrs. Christopher Carter) uses each time she has the church circle. The circle members like it and request the recipe when it is her turn for the meeting.

1 cup sugar
4 cups water
¼ cup tea leaves
3 cups orange juice
1 cup lemon juice

3 cups pineapple juice
1½ quarts gingerale
2 quarts orange sherbet
(or as desired)

Mix sugar and 1 cup water water and boil 7 minutes. / Add an additional 3 cups boiling water. / When cooled to just below boiling add tea leaves and allow to steap. / Add juices. / Place in refrigerator in covered container until ready to serve. / When ready to serve pour into punch bowl. / Add gingerale and orange sherbet. Serve. ● Serves 24.

CRANBERRY PUNCH

1 quart fresh cranberries
1 quart water
1 cup sugar
5 whole cloves
1 teaspoon grated lemon
rind

1 teaspoon grated orange
rind
2 tablespoons lemon juice
1 quart apple juice
Thin slices of orange

Cook cranberries and water in a covered kettle until skins pop. / Puree berries; add sugar, cloves, rinds. / Stir thoroughly. / Chill. / Add the lemon and apple juice and stir to blend. / Serve immediately. / Garnish with thin slices of oranges. ● Serves 30. A great holiday punch.

HOT SPICED PUNCH

1 quart apple cider
3 sticks cinnamon
4 tablespoons lemon juice

1 teaspoon nutmeg
1 teaspoon whole cloves

Simmer cider, cinnamon sticks, and lemon juice for 15 minutes. / Put nutmeg and cloves in a small cheesecloth bag and place in simmering cider long enough to give it the taste desired. ● Serves 8-10.

OUR SPECIAL HOT SPICED TEA

¼ cup loose orange pekoe
tea or 6 tea bags
2 quarts water
2 cups lemonade (frozen
reconstituted)

2 cups orange juice (frozen
reconstituted)
2 cups sugar
Cloves
Cinnamon

Heat water to just below boiling. / Place in tea ball with loose tea or tea bags. / Allow to steep. / Tea should be strong. / Remove tea ball or bags. / Place back over heat. / Add sugar and stir. / Then, add lemonade and orange juice. / Heat to below boiling. / Turn off heat. / Add cloves and cinnamon. / Ready to serve. / Tea may be stored in refrigerator and quantity heated as needed. / Keep tightly covered. / Great to have on hand when guests come. ● Serves 24.

AFTERWORD

Can We Continue to Risk the Lives of Our Children, the Future Generations, by Continuing our Apathy and Ignorance about the Importance of Good Nutrition for Good Health?

Since we have all the modern technologies to give us a bountiful food supply, all the advantages of scientific knowledge as to how to produce, distribute, and use a wide variety of foods, and all the abilities to apply them throughout the United States we should be the healthiest and happiest people in the world.

The world has for many years now looked to the United States for the creativity to provide an example to other nations of good and productive living. But in many instances *we have allowed the environment of the rapid pace of today, with its restrictive confirmity, to deny us the right to eat properly.* The increasing health problems resulting from this was cause for concern by the U.S. Senate Select Committee on Nutrition and Human Needs, which developed the new Dietary Goals.

Can we afford to do less than act on the basis of our best knowledge and best abilities by following those goals as preventive health? Would we want to wait until the laboratories have proven all scientific facts rather than use what we know at present *to reduce* the *risk of health problems today?* The answer to these questions rests with the administrators of each Federal, state and local agency; health organizations; volunteer organizations and individuals who have the responsibilities for promoting good health throughout communities. Their efforts, finally, come down to the family and to the individual.

I believe the decision whether to follow the Dietary Goals or to neglect them *will determine the health of tomorrow's citizens.* Are we to remain at the mercy of disease treatments or shall we organize a national effort to prevent disease? *Can we continue to risk the lives of our children, the future generations, by continuing our apathy and ignorance about the importance of good nutrition for good health?*

Unless we act, neither shall we nor our children be healthy. And certainly, America can then lay not claim to be a model to other nations of a healthy people.

—*M. C. D.*

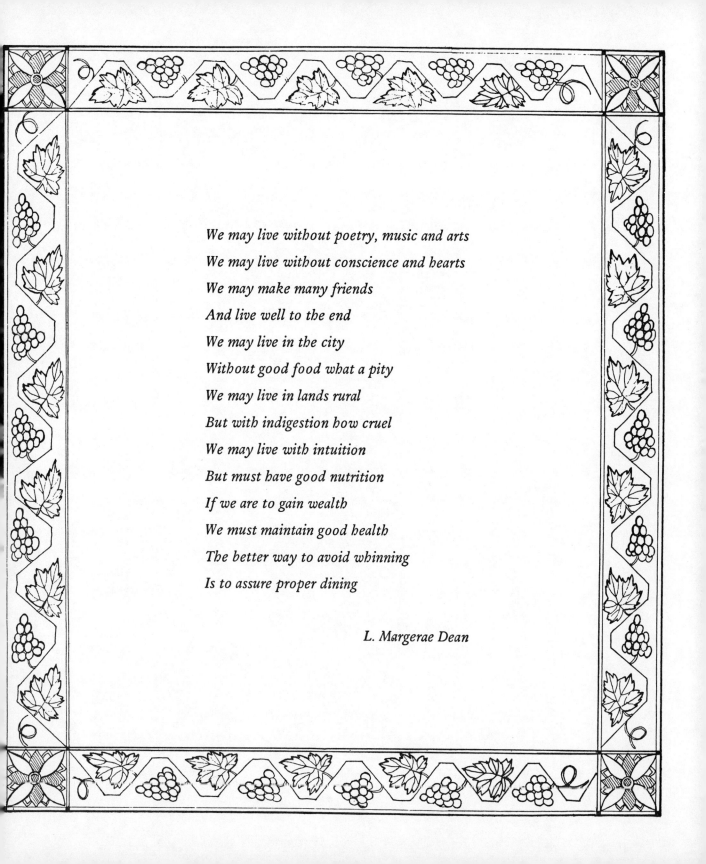

We may live without poetry, music and arts

We may live without conscience and hearts

We may make many friends

And live well to the end

We may live in the city

Without good food what a pity

We may live in lands rural

But with indigestion how cruel

We may live with intuition

But must have good nutrition

If we are to gain wealth

We must maintain good health

The better way to avoid whinning

Is to assure proper dining

L. Margerae Dean

95th Congress }
1st Session }   COMMITTEE PRINT

DIETARY GOALS FOR THE UNITED STATES

SECOND EDITION

PREPARED BY THE STAFF OF THE

SELECT COMMITTEE ON NUTRITION
AND HUMAN NEEDS
UNITED STATES SENATE

SELECT COMMITTEE ON NUTRITION AND HUMAN NEEDS

GEORGE McGOVERN. South Dakota, *Chairman*

EDWARD M. KENNEDY, Massachusetts   CHARLES H. PERCY, Illinois
HUBERT H. HUMPHREY, Minnesota   ROBERT DOLE, Kansas
PATRICK J. LEAHY, Vermont   RICHARD S. SCHWEIKER, Pennsylvania
EDWARD ZORINSKY, Nebraska

ALAN J. STONE, *Staff Director*
MARSHALL L. MATZ, *General Counsel*

(II)

DECEMBER 1977

Printed for the use of the Select Committee on Nutrition
and Human Needs

U.S. GOVERNMENT PRINTING OFFICE

98-364 O   WASHINGTON : 1977

For sale by the Superintendent of Documents, U.S. Government Printing Office
Washington, D.C. 20402 Stock No. 052-070-04376-8

FOREWORD

The purpose of this report is to point out that the eating patterns of this century represent as critical a public health concern as any now before us.

We must acknowledge and recognize that the public is confused about what to eat to maximize health. If we as a Government want to reduce health costs and maximize the quality of life for all Americans, we have an obligation to provide practical guides to the individual consumer as well as set national dietary goals for the country as a whole.

These recommendations, based on current scientific evidence, provide guidance for making personal decisions about one's diet. They are not a legislative initiative. Rather, they simply provide nutrition knowledge with which Americans can begin to take responsibility for maintaining their health and reducing their risk of illness.

As with the first edition, this second edition of "Dietary Goals" is a continuation of a process for which the Select Committee hopes the nutrition community, both within the Government and outside, will take over responsibility.

In addition to thanking the Select Committee staff and the original four consultants who have continued to advise the Select Committee on this report—Drs. Mark Hegsted, Philip Lee, Sheldon Margen and Beverly Winikoff—I want to thank Dr. George Bray for his special work on the new obesity goal, and Dr. Lenora Moragne, R.D.

GEORGE McGOVERN, *Chairman.*

CONTENTS

SUPPLEMENTAL FOREWORD BY SENATORS PERCY, SCHWEIKER, AND ZORINSKY

In my Foreword to the first edition of "Dietary Goals for the United States," I stated that Government and industry have a responsibility to respond to the findings of the report. They have done just that. The response has been vigorous and constructive. The original "Dietary Goals" report, though controversial, has helped focus public and professional attention on the need for continuous assessment of the current state of the art in the nutrition field. Furthermore, the report has stimulated debate and research on unresolved issues, and has helped us progress toward the formulation of a national nutrition policy based on sound dietary practices.

The second edition of "Dietary Goals," the product of commendable staff work, greatly improves upon earlier efforts by refining some of the original dietary goals, by adding sections on obesity and alcohol consumption and by more fully representing the scientific controversies which exist both with respect to the setting of dietary guidelines and to the substance of the goals themselves. I am most grateful for the help we have received in connection with this edition. I have long believed in the merits of dietary moderation, maintaining ideal body weight and avoiding excess, especially so called empty calories. To me this emphasis, taken together with regular physical exercise, are as sound public health measures as I know.

Despite the many improvements reflected in this second edition, however, I have serious reservations about certain aspects of the report. After hearing additional testimony from witnesses, discussing these goals with a number of experts and reading rather convincing correspondence from a variety of informed sources, I have become increasingly aware of the lack of consensus among nutrition scientists and other health professionals regarding (1) the question of whether advocating a specific restriction of dietary cholesterol intake to the general public is warranted at this time, (2) the question of what would be the demonstrable benefits to the individual and the general public, especially in regard to coronary heart disease, from implementing the dietary practices recommended in this report and (3) the accuracy of some of the goals and recommendations given the inadequacy of current food intake data.

The record clearly reflects extreme diversity of scientific opinion on these questions. Many such conflicting opinions are included in the Committee's recent publication, "Dietary Goals for the United States—Supplemental Views." Since it is possible that this diversity might be overlooked simply because few people will be able to take the time to read through the voluminous (869 pages) "Supplemental Views" publication, I have selected a few opinions representative of both viewpoints on the issues in controversy.

On the question of whether or not a restriction of dietary cholesterol intake for the general populace is a wise thing to recommend at this time, the Inter-Society Commission for Heart Disease Resources (1972), the American Heart Association (1973), and several other expert panels suggest a reduction of dietary cholesterol to less than 300 mg per day.

Yet, in October 1977 the Canadian Department of National Health and Welfare reversed its earlier position and concluded in a National Dietary Position that:

> Evidence is mounting that dietary cholesterol may not be important to the great majority of people. . . . Thus, a diet restricted in cholesterol would not be necessary for the general population.

A similar conclusion was drawn in 1974 by the Committee on Medical Aspects of Food in its report to Great Britain's Department of Health and Social Security.

Between these points of view are groups such as the New Zealand Heart Foundation which recommends a range of daily cholesterol intake, the maximum of which roughly equals the current average American intake.

Because of these divergent viewpoints, it is clear that science has not progressed to the point where we can recommend to the general public that cholesterol intake be limited to a specified amount. The variances between different individuals are simply too great.

A similar divergence of scientific opinion on the question of whether dietary change can help the heart illustrates that science can not yet verify with any certainty that coronary heart disease will be prevented or delayed by the diet recommended in this report.

For example, Dr. Jeremiah Stamler, chairman of the Department of Preventive Medicine, Northwestern School of Medicine, strongly believes thousands of premature coronary heart disease deaths can "probably be prevented annually through dietary change." However, Dr. E. H. Ahrens, Jr., Professor of Medicine at Rockefeller University, told the Select Committee in March:

> Advice to the public on changing its dietary habits in hope of reducing the rate of new events of coronary heart disease is premature, hence unwise.

The same polarity is evidenced when one compares the view of William Kannel, Framingham Heart Study's Director, that Dietary Goals "could have a substantial effect in reducing" coronary heart disease, with the opinion of Vanderbilt University's Dr. George Mann that "no diet therapy has been shown effective for the prevention or treatment" of that disease.

The American Medical Association in an April 18, 1977, letter to the Nutrition Committee states:

> The evidence for assuming that benefits to be derived from the adoption of such universal dietary goals as set forth in the report is not conclusive and . . . potential for harmful effects . . . would occur through adoption of the proposed national goals.

This impressive lack of agreement among scientists on the efficacy of dietary change was also noted by the National Heart, Blood and Lung Institute's Dr. Robert Levy, when he observed that there are "bona fide scientific people coming out on both sides of the issue," and by

Health Undersecretary Theodore Cooper's remarks last year to the Committee that a "great deal more nutrition work (is needed) . . . before one can speak with greater certainty concerning large-scale application" of dietary change. Because of this continuing debate, I feel great care must be taken to accurately inform the public about the benefits of the diet proposed in this report.

In fact, because I recognize many will read or hear only about the Dietary Goals and Food Selection pages (pp. 4 and 5) of this Second Edition, I feel the American public would be in a better position to exercise freedom of dietary choice if it were stated in bold print on the Goals and Food Selection pages that *the value of dietary change remains controversial and that science cannot at this time insure that an altered diet will provide improved protection from certain killer diseases such as heart disease and cancer.*

Finally, I want to emphasize the limitations, acknowledged in this edition, in setting goals and food selection recommendations on the basis of food disappearance data, because of the difference between disappearance data, household food consumption data and intake data, which are discussed in the Preface. These data were used because they are the best available at this time. However, in some cases they may not accurately reflect actual food intake. For example, the recommendations to reduce animal fat intake from the present level shown by food disappearance data must be viewed with some reservation because food disappearance data does not adjust for fat loss from retail preparation of meat, fat trimming before and after cooking, fat lo during cooking and tablewaste. The same case could be made f vegetable fat because many vegetable oils used in cooking are d carded and not consumed. Better food intake information, expect shortly, may produce more reliable and perhaps altered recommend tions.

In conclusion, I recognize the desirability of providing dieta guidance to the public and in helping the consumer become more r sponsible for his every day health status. In my judgment, howeve the best way to do this is to fully inform the public not only abo what is known, but also about what remains controversial regardin cholesterol, the benefits of dietary change, and the reliability of curre food intake data. Only then, will it be possible for the individual co sumer to respond optimally to the Dietary Goals in this report.

After the Nutrition Committee staff is transferred to the Sena Agriculture Committee's Subcommittee on Nutrition, I hope they wi in cooperation with the Human Resources Subcommittee on Healt and Scientific Research continue to review the science and revise Di tary Goals in order that we may continue to progress toward the fo mulation of national dietary guidelines based on sound dietar practices.

CHARLES H. PERCY,
Ranking Minority Member.
RICHARD SCHWEIKER.
EDWARD ZORINSKY.

SUPPLEMENTAL FOREWORD BY SENATOR DOLE

I wish to underscore the importance of the initiative taken by the Select Committee in the field of human nutrition. More than ever I am coming to believe that preventive medicine in the long run will prove to be the cheapest, most desirable route to good health, maximum productivity and lowered medical and health costs for the consumer and the taxpayer.

Our initiatives, of course, mark only the beginning of a broad scale involvement in nutrition. Indeed, because absolute answers for preventing today's leading killer diseases remain largely unknown, I am encouraged that our work will continue under the Nutrition Subcommittee of the Senate Agriculture, Nutrition and Forestry Committee.

I am also encouraged that under the Food and Agriculture Act of 1977, which I supported, human nutrition research and education will become matters of high priority at the USDA. Of special importance the act's promotion of better information on human nutrition research requirements, nutrient composition of foods, and factors, affecting food selection. With better information in these areas, the effort we have made thus far will be of increased benefit.

As I reflect on past hearings, personal readings, and discussions about nutrition with staff and constituents alike, I am concerned about certain gaps in our knowledge. For example, more precise information is needed about what people really eat. The question of the exact amounts and kinds of foods Americans consume suffers from an absence of highly refined research tools. The Goals report recommends a reduction in overall fat consumption from approximately 40 percent of energy intake or total calories to 30 percent from fat; and goes on to suggest that this recommendation be met by a mix of lean meats, fish, and poultry.

In the Preface a range of 27 to 33 percent energy intake from fat is recommended. Review of research, including the 15 expert panels appearing on page 75 of the Report suggest a goal of 25 to 35 percent intake from fat.

I am pleased that the second edition deletes language from the first edition recommending "eat less meat" and is not meant to recommend a reduction in intake of nutritious protein foods.

Information about our current level of food intake, including fat are arrived at from USDA "food disappearance data." As this Report states, this guide to food consumption may not be the most accurate research approach, but it is the best data base available at this time. In lieu of this I feel that in the future we need to examine carefully the exact numbers and ranges that we have chosen for the "Dietary Goals." Values presented here should be used as a basis for further consideration and discussion.

Finally I would like to note that the relationship of cholesterol and lipoproteins is a very recent example of how nutrition research can uncover important correlations between diet and health that had previously not been known. We need to examine this lipoprotein concept more thoroughly and expand such basic research. Such research may help clarify the relationship of ingested cholesterol to plasma cholesterol and thereby improve protection against heart disease.

I am confident that this second edition of "Dietary Goals" is indicative of the need for long-term, coordinated research to provide more appropriate and adequate information with which our citizens may assess their particular diets and take individual steps to improve them.

In the future I would like to see the Subcommittee on Nutrition and the Congress support the following:
— Oversight hearings on the implementation of research authorities of the Food and Agriculture Act of 1977.
— Assistance in improving the data base from which dietary goals are developed, especially in the areas of food actually eaten by individuals instead of household intake or commodity disappearance.
— Investigation into on-going research into trace elements, their food sources, and their necessity for health body functions and longevity.
— The significance of high density lipoproteins, their relation to cholesterol, and how this information correlates with what we currently know about risk factors for heart disease.
— Methods for identifying high risk people who are most likely to benefit from following special diet guidelines in order to maintain their health and prevent disease.
— Effectiveness of current government and non-government efforts to inform people about appropriate diets and to motivate people to select such diets.

I add these remarks to highlight the fact that while much remains unknown or controversial in matters of diet and health, much can and is being done to define and resolve the issues before us and to generate and communicate to the American public the information it needs to select a healthy diet. In the interim, interpretation of the "Dietary Goals" should be carefully assessed according to individual needs and desires.

ROBERT DOLE.

[Press Conference, Friday, January 14, 1977, Room 457, Dirksen Senate Office Building]

STATEMENT OF SENATOR GEORGE McGOVERN ON THE PUBLICATION OF DIETARY GOALS FOR THE UNITED STATES

Good morning.

The purpose of this press conference is to release a Nutrition Committee study entitled *Dietary Goals for the United States*, and to explain why we need such a report.

I should note from the outset that this is the first comprehensive statement by any branch of the Federal Government on risk factors in the American diet.

The simple fact is that our diets have changed radically within the last 50 years, with great and often very harmful effects on our health. These dietary changes represent as great a threat to public health as smoking. Too much fat, too much sugar or salt, can be and are linked directly to heart disease, cancer, obesity, and stroke, among other killer diseases. In all, six of the ten leading causes of death in the United States have been linked to our diet.

Those of us within Government have an obligation to acknowledge this. The public wants some guidance, wants to know the truth, and hopefully today we can lay the cornerstone for the building of better health for all Americans, through better nutrition.

Last year every man, woman and child in the United States consumed 125 pounds of fat, and 100 pounds of sugar. As you can see from our displays, that's a formidable quantity of fat and sugar.

The consumption of soft drinks has more than doubled since 1960—displacing milk as the second most consumed beverage. In 1975, we drank on the average of 295, 12 oz. cans of soda.

In the early 1900's, almost 40 percent of our caloric intake came from fruit, vegetables and grain products. Today only a little more than 20 percent of calories comes from these sources.

My hope is that this report will perform a function similar to that of the Surgeon General's Report on Smoking. Since that report, we haven't eliminated the hazards of smoking, nor have people stopped smoking because of it. But the cigarette industry has modified its products to reduce risk factors, and many people who would otherwise be smoking have stopped because of it.

The same progress can and must be made in matters of nutritional health, and this report sets forth the necessary plan of action:

1. Six basic goals are set for changes in our national diet;

2. Simple buying guides are recommended to help consumers attain these goals; and

3. Recommendations are also made for action within Government and industry to better maximize nutritional health.

I hope this report will be useful to millions of Americans. In addition to providing simple and meaningful guidance in matters of diet, it should also encourage all those involved with growing, preparing, and processing food to give new consideration to the impact of their decisions on the nation's health. There needs to be less confusion about what to eat and how our diet affects us.

With me this morning are three of the country's leading thinkers in the area of nutritional health. They have very graciously assisted the staff of the Select Committee in the preparation of this report. They will explain in greater detail its purpose and goals.

First, Dr. Mark Hegsted, Professor of Nutrition from the Harvard School of Public Health. Dr. Hegsted has a long and distinguished career in science, bringing conscience as well as great expertise to his work. Dr. Hegsted has worked very closely and patiently with the committee staff on this report, devoting many hours to review and counseling. He feels very strongly about the need for public education in nutrition and the need to alert the public to the consequences of our dietary trends. He will discuss these trends and their connection with our most killing diseases.

Following his presentation, Dr. Beverly Winikoff of the Rockefeller Foundation will discuss the changes necessary in food marketing and advertising practices if the consumer is to make more healthful food choices. Dr. Winikoff, who with Dr. Hegsted and Dr. Lee testified at our hearings in July, has also been extremely helpful in assisting the committee staff in preparing this report.

Dr. Philip Lee, the Director of the Health Policy Program at the University of California in San Francico, and and a former Assistant Secretary for Health, will conclude our presentation with a discussion of the costs of our current dietary trends. Dr. Lee has also consulted with the committee staff on this report and has offered much encouragement.

Before Dr. Hegsted begins, I would also like to note that the staff has also received valuable assistance from Dr. Sheldon Margen, nutritionist with the University of California in Berkeley, who is traveling outside the country today.

I want to thank each of these people personally for their help and their spirted concern for the public interest.

The Committee will continue its investigation into the connection between diet and health on February 1 and 2, when hearings will be held concentrating on problems of diet and heart disease and obesity.

After the presentation today we will be glad to answer questions.

[Press Conference, Friday, January 14, 1977, Room 457, Dirksen Senate Office Building]

STATEMENT OF DR. D. M. HEGSTED, PROFESSOR OF NUTRITION, HARVARD SCHOOL OF PUBLIC HEALTH, BOSTON, MASS.

The diet of the American people has become increasingly rich—rich in meat, other sources of saturated fat and cholesterol, and in sugar. There will be people who will contest this statement. It has been pointed out repeatedly that total sugar use has remained relatively constant for a number of years. We would emphasize, however, that our total food consumption has fallen even though we still eat too much relative to our needs. Thus, the proportion of the total diet contributed by fatty and cholesterol-rich foods and by refined foods has risen. We might be better able to tolerate this diet if we were much more active physically, but we are a sedentary people.

It should be emphasized that this diet which affluent people generally consume is everywhere associated with a similar disease pattern—high rates of ischemic heart disease, certain forms of cancer, diabetes, and obesity. These are the major causes of death and disability in the United States. These so-called degenerative diseases obviously become more important now that infectious diseases are, relatively speaking, under good control. I wish to emphasize that these diseases undoubtedly have a complex etiology. It is not correct, strictly speaking, to say that they are caused by malnutrition but rather that an inappropriate diet contributes to their causation. Our genetic make-up contributes—not all people are equally susceptible. Yet those who are genetically susceptible, most of us, are those who would profit most from an appropriate diet. Diet is one of the things that we can change if we want to.

There will undoubtedly be many people who will say we have not proven our point; we have not demonstrated that the dietary modifications we recommend will yield the dividends expected. We would point out to those people that the diet we eat today was not planned or developed for any particular purpose. It is a happenstance related to our affluence, the productivity of our farmers and the activities of our food industry. The risks associated with eating this diet are demonstrably large. The question to be asked, therefore, is not why should we change our diet but why not? What are the risks associated with eating less meat, less fat, less saturated fat, less cholesterol, less sugar, less salt, and more fruits, vegetables, unsaturated fat and cereal products—especially whole grain cereals. There are none that can be identified and important benefits can be expected.

Ischemic heart disease, cancer, diabetes and hypertension are the diseases that kill us. They are epidemic in our population. We cannot afford to temporize. We have an obligation to inform the public of the current state of knowledge and to assist the public in making the correct food choices. To do less is to avoid our responsibility.

[Press Conference, Friday, January 14, 1977, Room 457, Dirksen Senate Office Building]

STATEMENT OF DR. BEVERLY WINIKOFF, ROCKEFELLER FOUNDATION, NEW YORK, N.Y.

What are the implications of these dietary goals?

The fact that the goals can be stated in nutritional terms first and then mirrored in a set of behavioral changes impels a closer look at why Americans eat the way they do. What people eat is affected not only by what scientists know, or by what doctors tell them, or even by what they themselves understand. It is affected by Government decisions in the area of agricultural policy, economic and tax policy, export and import policy, and involves questions of good production, transportation, processing, marketing, consumer choice, income and education, as well as food availability and palatability. Nutrition, then, is the end result of pushes and pulls in many directions, a response to the multiple forces creating the "national nutrition environment."

Even "personal dietary preferences" are not immutable but interact with other forces in the environment and are influenced by them. People learn the patterns of their diet not only from the family and its sociocultural background, but from what is available in the marketplace and what is promoted both formally through advertising and informally through general availability in schools, restaurants, supermarkets, work places, airports, and so forth.

It is generally recognized with regard to the overall economic climate that both what the Government does do and what it does not do shape the arena in which other forces interact. This is also true with regard to nutrition. In determining the parameters of the socioeconomic system, Government also determines the nature of the national buffet. Government policy, then, must be made with full awareness of this responsibility.

It is increasingly obvious that if new knowledge is to result in new behaviors then people must be able to act, without undue obstacles, in accordance with the information that they learn. The problem of education for health as it has been practiced is that it has been in isolation, not to say oblivion, of the real pressures, expectations, and norms of society which mold and constrain individual behavior. There must be some coordination between what people are taught to do and what they can do. Part of the responsibility for this coordination rests with the Government's evaluation and coordination of its own activities. Effective education must be accompanied by Government policies which make it easier, indeed likely, that an individual will change his or her lifestyle in accordance with the information offered.

At present, we see a situation in which the opposite is often the case. Nutrition and health education are offered at the same time as barrages of commercials for soft drinks, sugary snacks, high-fat foods, cigarettes and alcohol. We put candy machines in our schools, serve high-fat lunches to our children, and place cigarette machines in our work places. The American marketplace provides easy access to sweet soft drinks, high-sugar cereals, candies, cakes, and high-fat beef, and more difficult access to foods likely to improve national nutritional health.

This trend can be reversed by specific agricultural policies, pricing policies, and marketing policies, as well as the recommendations outlined in these "Dietary Goals for the United States."

In general, Americans have quite accurate perceptions of sound nutritional principles, as was demonstrated recently by a Harris poll conducted for the Mount Sinai Hospital in Chicago. However, people do lack understanding of the consequences of nutrition-related diseases. There is a widespread and unfounded confidence in the ability of medical science to cure or mitigate the effects of such diseases once they occur. Appropriate public education must emphasize the unfortunate but clear limitations of current medical practice in curing the common killing diseases. Once hypertension, diabetes, arteriosclerosis of heart disease are manifest, there is, in reality, very little that medical science can do to return a patient to normal physiological function. As awareness of this limitation increases, the importance of prevention will become all the more obvious.

But prevention is not possible solely through medical intervention. It is the responsibility of government at all levels to take the initiative in creating for Americans an appropriate nutritional atmosphere—one conducive to improvement in the health and quality of life of the American people.

98-364 O - 78 - 2

[Press Conference, Friday, January 14, 1977, Room 457, Dirksen Senate Office Building]

STATEMENT OF DR. PHILIP LEE, PROFESSOR OF SOCIAL MEDICINE AND DIRECTOR, HEALTH POLICY PROGRAM, UNIVERSITY OF CALIFORNIA, SAN FRANCISCO, CALIF.

The publication of *Dietary Goals for the United States* by the Senate Select Committee on Nutrition and Human Needs is a major step forward in the development of a rational national health policy. The public health problems related to what we eat are pointed out in *Dietary Goals*. More important, the steps that can and should be taken by individuals, families, educators, health professions, industry and government are made clear.

As a Nation we have come to believe that medicine and medical technology can solve our major health problems. The role of such important factors as diet in cancer and heart disease has long been obscured by the emphasis on the conquest of these diseases through the miracles of modern medicine. Treatment not prevention, has been the order of the day.

The problems can never be solved merely by more and more medical care. The health of individuals and the health of the population is determined by a variety of biological (host), behavioral, sociocultural and environmental factors. None of these is more important than the food we eat. This simple fact and the importance of diet in health and disease is clearly recognized in *Dietary Goals for the United States*.

The Senate Select Committee on Nutrition and Human Needs has made four recommendations to encourage the achievement of the very sound dietary goals incorporated in the report. These are:

1. a large scale public nutrition education program involving the schools, food assistance programs, the Extension Service of the Department of Agriculture and the mass media;

2. mandatory food labeling for all foods;

3. the development of improved food processing methods for institutional and home use; and

4. expanded federal support for research in human nutrition.

It is important that *Dietary Goals for the United States* be made widely available because it is the only publication of its kind and it will be an invaluable resource for parents, school teachers, public health nurses, health educators, nutritionists, physicians and others who are involved in providing people with information about the food they eat.

The recommendations, if acted upon promptly by the Congress, can help individuals, families and those responsible for institutional food services (schools, hospitals) be better informed about the consequences of present dietary habits and practices. Moreover, they provide a practical guide for action to improve the unhealthy situation that exists.

The effective implementation of the Senate Select Committee recommendations and the proposed dietary goals could have profound health and economic benefits. Not only would many people lead longer and healthier lives but the reduced burden of illness during the working lives of men and women would reduce the cost of medical care and increase productivity.

What can be done to assure sustained and effective action on these recommendations? First, the Congress can act to appropriate the needed funds for the proposed programs. In some instances, such as mandatory food labeling, it must also enact the authorizing legislation. Second, the new Secretaries of Agriculture and Health, Education, and Welfare can act as soon as they take office to create a joint policy committee to address the issues raised by the Senate Select Committee and provide a means to assure that health considerations will no longer take a back seat to economic considerations in our food and agriculture policies. Finally, our greatest bulwark against the interests that have helped to create the present problems is an informed public.

281

PREFACE

Dietary Goals for the United States—Second Edition is intended to update and elaborate upon *Dietary Goals for the United States*,[1] published in February 1977. This edition, like the first, is written primarily for use by consumers. It represents the Senate Select Committee on Nutrition and Human Needs' best judgment as to prudent dietary recommendations based on current scientific knowledge.

Since the publication of the 1st Edition of *Dietary Goals for the United States*, the Select Committee has continued to solicit the opinions of many of our leading experts on human nutrition, as well as concerned health and industry groups. Numerous comments were received. With the issuance of this edition, the Select Committee further addresses the on-going scientific controversies which exist, both with respect to the setting of dietary guidelines, and the substance of the *Dietary Goals*.

The actual comments received ranged from the general to the specific, and have been printed in full either in hearing records or in *Dietary Goals for the United States—Supplemental Views*.[2] Many of the points raised are discussed in this Preface.

THE SELECT COMMITTEE AND DIETARY GOALS

The Senate Select Committee on Nutrition and Human Needs came into existence in 1968 as a bridge between the food and farm interests in the Agriculture Committee, and the health, welfare, and research interests in the then Labor and Public Welfare Committee. It was provided with oversight responsibilities in nutrition which it actively pursued through investigations, hearings, reports, and the drafting of legislation. The legislation was then sent to the appropriate standing Committee for consideration, and in most cases, eventual passage.

In the early years, the Select Committee focused its attention on programs designed to eliminate hunger, as this was the most pressing nutrition concern. But during those years, more and more evidence was building to provide a basis on which the Select Committee could expand to its full scope—the investigation and oversight of nutrition as it relates to the health of all Americans.

Two years ago, the Select Committee began to respond to the growing need expressed by consumers, researchers and health professionals to address the accumulation of scientific data linking diet and many of the Nation's major killer diseases. Issues other than hunger required attention. Both sides of malnutrition—overconsumption as well as underconsumption—demanded evaluation.

In expanding the scope of its work, the Select Committee more clearly recognized the necessity of trying to reduce the Nation's staggering medical care costs by promoting health maintenance and preventive medicine. In examining the problem of medical care cost inflation, the Select Committee concluded that improved nutrition was a key part of the solution.

Furthermore, a concerted action to improve the Nation's health through better nutrition was viewed as a means to fill the policy vacuum which was keeping the Nation from redressing the balance between curative and preventive medicine.

Members of the medical care industry and of Government had been studying how best to address this imbalance. In Canada, some direction was provided when the Minister of Health, Marc LaLonde, issued a document in 1974 entitled, *A New Perspective on the Health of Canadians*.[3] This report acknowledged and analyzed the need for greater emphasis on preventive health care measures, in conjunction with the necessity of greater self-reliance and conservation by the Canadian people. The issuance of the LaLonde report presented a common ground for discussion on how to proceed with the new direction Canada had set for itself.

In a similar way, *Dietary Goals for the United States* provided a potential catalyst for action and guidelines everyone could address, whether they agreed on its substance or not.

The 2nd Edition of *Dietary Goals for the United States* continues to provide a common ground for discussion, and a basis for considering changes required to improve our food and health systems.

And, although not specifically addressed in this report, there are also potentially enormous non-health benefits to be gained by following a basically prudent diet, and by asserting more overall control over our health. For example, approximately one-fifth of the energy consumed in the United States goes into food production and processing. Perhaps the kind of basic prudent dietary recommendations made in this report will help to provide not only a framework for reducing dietary risk but also for more prudent use of energy.

Food production and processing is America's number one industry and medical care ranks number three. Nutrition is the common link between the two. Nutrition is a spectrum which runs from food production at one end to health at the other.

By recognizing this connection, this report has helped to begin process of weaving into whole cloth many separate threads. Hopefully, as one result, nutrition will become a major priority of this Nation's agriculture policy. Demands for better nutrition could bring halt to the expansion and/or use of less nutritious or so-called "empty calorie" or "junk" foods in the American diet, as well as make nutrition the rallying point of public demands for *better* health, as opposed to *more* medical care. Human nutrition research may become the

[1] Dietary Goals for the United States, February 1977, U.S. Government Printing Office, Washington, D.C., Stock No. 052-070-03913-2, Price—95¢.
[2] Dietary Goals for the United States—Supplemental Views, November 1977, U.S. Government Printing Office, Washington, D.C., Stock No. 052-070-04294-0, Price—$5.75.
[3] A New Perspective on the Health of Canadians, a working document, April 1974, Marc LaLonde, Minister of National Health and Welfare, Government of Canada.

utting edge in many areas of bio-medical science. Most importantly, utrition knowledge will become a means by which Americans can egin to take responsibility for maintaining their health and reducng their risk of illness.

RISK FACTORS, DIET AND HEALTH

The Concept

The objective of this report, improved health through informed diet selection by every American, is best served if the reader fully nderstands the idea of "risk factors," and what this phrase means in erms of diet and health.

In general, "risk factors" refers to specific characteristics—age, lifetyle, diet, income, habits such as smoking or excessive use of alcohol, r even where people live or work— that are associated with a higher han average incidence of a specific health problem. Risk factors are sually identified by nutritionists. statisticians, epidemiologists, and hose health professionals who look carefully at the reports describing he incidence of various diseases in various population groups. If it s determined that one group of people who have something in common lso have a higher incidence of a certain disease, they begin to study he possibility that the common factor among these people may either ause, or help cause, the disease.

Risk factors, therefore, are warning flags. They suggest that, if a haracteristic describes a person, the chances are greater that he or she may now or in the future have the same health problem of the other eople who have the same characteristic, be it a habit, an age, or a ietary pattern.

However, the existence of risk factors among a group of people can ot tell us about the specific fate of any one person within that group. Risk factors can only tell us the probability of an event occurring. As result, altering a risk factor or group of risk factors changes the robability of an event occurring. but does not guarantee for a specific ndividual that an event will or will not occur to him or her.

Finally, on the one hand, there are some risk factors that a person as no control over—age, sex, and genetics or diseases that are common n their family. On the other are those controllable risk factors such s smoking, exercising, abusing alcoholic beverages, regularly brushng one's teeth, maintaining a reasonable pattern of work and rest, nd, of course, selecting the most appropriate diet.

Specificity of Risk Factors

It is important to know which risk factors are associated with which pecific health problems. In some cases, several risk factors are associted with one disease. For instance, smoking, lack of exercise, diet nd several other characteristics are considered risk factors for heart lisease. On the other hand, one risk factor may be associated with everal diseases. For example, obesity is associated with an increased isk of heart disease, the severity of hypertension, and makes it much nore difficult for a diabetic to control the ups and downs of his/her lood glucose and related problems. The following diagram illustrates he interrelationship of some risk factors associated with heart disease.

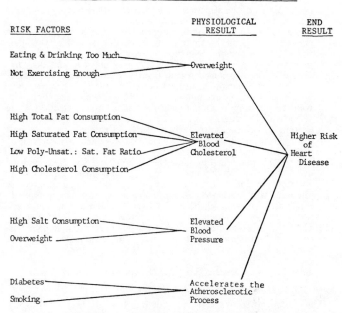

Some Risk Factors Associated with Heart Disease

TARGETING AND VARIATIONS AMONG PEOPLE

The specific goals in this report provide dietary guidelines for the general population. However, each person differs with respect to energy needs, and the thousands of food products available differ in their nutrient and energy value. Nutrient requirements differ during certain periods of the normal life cycle, as during the growth and development of children, and during pregnancy and lactation. They also differ among different sex and age groups.

Targeting the food recommendations for specific age groups with special needs, is only partially addressed in this edition of *Dietary Goals*. For example, the low-fat dairy products recommendation should not be applied to young children.

Also, persons with physical and/or mental ailments who have reason to believe that they should not follow guidelines for the general population should consult with a health professional having expertise in nutrition, regarding their individual case.

The reader will be in a better position to use the *Dietary Goals* for planning his or her own diet if the following is kept in mind:

(1) Foods are made up of various combinations or "natural packages" of macro-nutrients and micro-nutrients. Macro-nutrients are proteins, carbohydrates, fats and alcohol. Energy (which is

measured in calories) is provided by macro-nutrients. Micro-nutrients are vitamins and minerals. These are needed to release the energy of macro-nutrients so that they can be used for the body. Micro-nutrients are also needed for other purposes such as maintaining the body's normal functions.

(2) The amount of energy-producing macro-nutrients that a person should eat depends on the amount of energy needed by that person's body. A person needs more energy if he or she is active and gets a lot of exercise than if he or she is inactive and does not exercise. Another consideration regarding how much of the macro-nutrients a person should eat is that people who want to gain weight should consume more macro-nutrients whereas people who want to lose weight should consume less macro-nutrients.

(3) The amount of energy provided by a food depends on how much protein (4 calories/gm), carbohydrates (4 calories/gm), fats (9 calories/gm) and/or alcohol (7 calories/gm) are in a serving of that food.

(4) The proper place in the diet—the amount and the frequency of use—of a food for any one person depends on many factors including: that individual's need for energy, and specific vitamins or minerals, which is based primarily on age, sex and energy expenditure; that person's health and lifestyle; and the nutrient composition of other foods that make up that person's total diet.

(5) The appropriateness of a food for any one person also depends on personal factors such as taste preference, financial means, religious persuasion, family traditions, and other personal values.

RECOMMENDED DIETARY ALLOWANCES AND THE DIETARY GOALS

Setting Recommended Dietary Allowances

The concept of setting dietary guidelines has been well established since 1943 when the Food and Nutrition Board of the National Academy of Sciences (NAS, FNB) set forth "Recommended Dietary Allowances" (RDA)[4] for the first time. The RDA, which focus on micronutrients, protein and total energy in the diet, are now in their eighth edition and were most recently revised in 1974. As stated in that edition:

> The Recommended Dietary Allowances are the levels of intake of essential nutrients considered, in the judgment of the Food and Nutrition Board on the basis of available scientific knowledge, to be adequate to meet the known nutritional needs of practically all healthy persons.

The RDA are continually up-dated and published with the objective of providing standards for good nutrition, and to encourage the development of food use practices by the American people that will allow for maximum dividends in the maintenance and promotion of health. The RDA have come to serve as a guide in such areas as the interpretation of food consumption records, the establishment of standards for public assistance programs, the evaluation of the ade-

quacy of food supplies in meeting natural nutrient needs, and the [es]tablishment of guidelines for nutrition labeling of foods.

The Food and Nutrition Board realizes and acknowledges that present knowledge of nutritional needs is incomplete, and that human requirements for many nutrients have not been established. [In] fact, since the essentiality of many nutrients is still unknown, t[hey] recommend that a person should obtain his or her nutrients from [as] varied a selection of foods as is practicable. In addition, the RD[A] should not be confused with requirements, because differences in nutrient requirements of individuals that derive from differences [in] their genetic make-up are ordinarily unknown. Finally, the RDA a[re] intakes of nutrients that meet the needs of healthy people, and do [not] take into account special needs arising from infections, metabolic d[is]orders, chronic diseases, or other abnormalities that require spec[ial] dietary treatment.

Setting Dietary Goals

Setting *Dietary Goals* extends the concept of the "Recommend[ed] Dietary Allowances" to include macro-nutrients, as well as sodi[um] and cholesterol. By having dietary guidance for both micro- a[nd] macro-nutrients, the American people will be in an even better positi[on] to develop food use practices that will increase the probability [of] maximum dividends in the maintenance and promotion of health.

The *Dietary Goals* are stated in terms of specific levels. Howeve[r,] each level represents a conclusion based on the scientific evidence a[nd] the levels recommended by the thirteen panels of scientific exper[ts] whose recommendations are summarized in Appendix B. Therefo[re,] each specific level should be considered as the center of a range. T[he] ranges are:

Total Carbohydrate (55–61%)
  Complex Carbohydrates and "Naturally Occurring" [5] Suga[rs] (45–51%)
  Refined and Processed [5] Sugars (8–12%)
Total Fat (27–33%)
  Poly-unsaturated (8–12%)
  Mono-unsaturated (8–12%)
  Saturated (8–12%)
Protein (10–14%)
Cholesterol (250–350 mg)
Salt (4–6 gms)

Finally, because changing one's dietary pattern is normally a slo[w] process of adjustment, the *Dietary Goals* should initially be viewed [as] indicating a direction and general magnitude for the change recom[-] mended. Once the *Dietary Goals* are achieved, one must approach foo[d] consumption as an average to be reached over a period of a few day[s] and, therefore, not expect to consume each day the exact recommende[d] proportion of calories from fats, carbohydrates and protein, or th[e] exact amount of salt and cholesterol.

[5] "Naturally occurring" sugars are those which are indigenous to a food, as opposed [to] refined (cane and beet) and processed (corn sugar, syrups, molasses and honey) suga[rs] which may be added to a food product.

[4] *Recommended Dietary Allowances*, 8th Ed., 1974, Committee on Interpretation of the Recommended Dietary Allowances, Food and Nutrition Board, National Research Council, National Academy of Sciences, Washington, D.C.

Differences Between the RDA and the Dietary Goals

There is a major distinction between the RDA and the *Dietary Goals*. The RDA are determined from basic research on animals and metabolic studies in humans which examine the particular micro-nutrients presently considered to be essential to normal human development. Because of the current state of nutrition research, nutritionists have greater confidence in their conclusions concerning micro-nutrients than in their observations about macro-nutrients.

The *Dietary Goals*, which primarily examine macro-nutrients, are derived from basic research on animals, metabolic studies and clinical trials with humans, and epidemiological investigations. In addition, and unlike the RDA, the *Dietary Goals* depend on using food consumption patterns from one or more of three data bases which include:

1) Food Disappearance: Food that disappears into civilian food consumption, sometimes referred to as the U.S. per capita food supply. The data are collected annually by the Economic Research Service of the United States Department of Agriculture (USDA). The nutritive value of these amounts of foods is estimated by the Agricultural Research Service of USDA.

2) Household Food Consumption: These food consumption data are collected every ten years or so from representative samples of households across the country by the Agricultural Research Service. These data are food used by households over a seven-day period in terms of food brought into the kitchen—as purchased, or obtained from home gardens, or as gift or pay. Nutritive values of these amounts of foods are estimated and compared to the RDA's for family members.

3) Food Intake or Food Actually Eaten by Individuals: These data are usually collected by recall methods for a day or a period of a few days. They include amounts of food eaten at home and away from home.

The percentages of the energy provided by the macro-nutrients (fat, protein and carbohydrate) in the current American diet, as depicted in the first and second editions of *Dietary Goals for the United States*, are based on 1974 food disappearance data from USDA.

Food disappearance was chosen as the best data base available, because the alternative, the most recent USDA Household Food Consumption Survey, was completed over ten years ago. While there is debate within nutrition circles as to which survey method is most accurate, clearly food disappearance, food purchased for use in the home and food in-take data are all interrelated, and have been found to be comparable with respect to the percent of caloric intake from carbohydrates, fats and protein.

To be as accurate and helpful as possible for the user it is important that the Dietary Goals be based on the data which most closely reflects actual food intake. Therefore, in the future serious consideration should be given to altering the dietary guidelines to reflect either the 1977–78 USDA Household Food Consumption Survey data,[6] or the

Health and Nutrition Examination Survey (HANES) food intake data,[7] whose analyses have not yet been completed.

THE FIRST EDITION OF DIETARY GOALS FOR THE UNITED STATES

The First Edition of *Dietary Goals* was drafted in response to an ominous fact pattern which associates certain dietary patterns and factors with six of the ten leading causes of death. The first two hearings in July 1976 in the "Diet Related to Killer Diseases" series ("Diet and Preventive Medicine" and "Diet and Cancer")[8] helped make the Select Committee more aware of a very sobering epidemiological information base. The following represent some of the epidemiological observations presented at the Diet and Cancer hearing:

- Deaths from colon and breast cancer are uncommon in countries with diets low in animal and dairy fats;
- Groups whose diets are low in fat and high in dietary fiber have much lower rates of cancers of the colon, rectum, breast and uterus than comparable groups of Americans who consume more fat and less dietary fiber;
- Japanese who migrate to the United States and change to a Western diet from their traditional Japanese diet which contains little animal fat and almost no dairy products, dramatically increase their incidence of breast and colon cancer;
- Compared with persons of normal weight, obese people have a higher risk of developing cancer, especially cancers of the uterus, breast, and gall bladder.

The first witness in the "Diet Related to Killer Diseases" series, Dr. Ted Cooper, then Assistant Secretary for Health, HEW, told the Committee that:

> While scientists do not yet agree on the specific causal relationships, evidence is mounting and there appears to be general agreement that the kinds and amounts of food and beverages we consume and the style of living common in our generally affluent, sedentary society may be the major factors associated with the cause of cancer, cardiovascular disease, and other chronic illnesses.

He agreed that malnutrition in the United States is associated with six of the ten leading causes of death, including heart disease, some cancers, stroke and hypertension, arteriosclerosis, diabetes, and cirrhosis of the liver.

Dr. Gio Gori, Deputy Director of the National Cancer Institute, told the Committee that:

> In the United States the number of cancer cases a year that appear to be related to diet are estimated to be 40 percent of the total incidence for males and about 60 percent of the total incidence for females. The forms of cancer that appear to be dependent on nutrition as shown by epidemio-

---

[6] Published data unavailable until 1979.

[7] Dietary Intake Findings, United States, 1971–74. DHEW No. (HRA) 77–1647. Series 11, No. 22. U.S. Government Printing Office, July 1977. Stock No. 017–022–00564–6.
[8] "Diet Related to Killer Diseases," July 27 and 28, 1976. U.S. Government Printing Office, Washington, D.C., Stock No. 052–070–03872–1, Price $3.40.

logic studies include: Stomach, liver, breast, prostate, large intestine, small intestine, and colon. There are other forms of cancer for which evidence is being collected, but as yet, strong evidence is not available.

Again, I want to emphasize we are not saying that there is a direct relationship between diet and cancer. We do have strong clues that dietary factors play a preponderant role in the development of these tumors.

Dr. Ernst L. Wynder, President and Medical Director of the American Health Foundation in New York, agreed. He testified:

> Breast cancer, the biggest killer of all cancers in women, has a geographic distribution similar to that of colon cancer and is also associated worldwide with the consumption of a high fat diet. Again, the disease is relatively rare in Japan, but increases among Japanese migrants to the United States. Like colon cancer, it is relatively uncommon among Puerto Ricans who have a relatively low intake of cholesterol and fat in their diet.

The Select Committee reviewed a wide variety of scientific data and testimony in developing the recommended guidelines. The information received came from dietitians, nutritionists, research scientists, and the highest health officials of this country. In addition, consideration was given to recommendations of various professional panels in the United States and other countries, which are summarized in Appendix B.

Finally, during the report's development the Select Committee continually consulted with nutritionists, including Dr. Mark Hegsted who was the first president of the National Nutrition Consortium and a past president of the Food and Nutrition Board of the National Academy of Sciences; and health policymakers, including Dr. Philip Lee who was the first Assistant Secretary for Health, HEW.

THE SECOND EDITION OF DIETARY GOALS FOR THE UNITED STATES

As the first publication by the Federal Government to set guidelines for the macro-nutrients in our diet, this report has generated a great deal of interest, debate, and even controversy among consumers, scientists, and industry representatives.

Two industries—meat and egg producers—requested additional hearings to express their views. These were held on March 24 [9] and July 26 [10] respectively.

In addition, the National Live Stock and Meat Board sent the Select Committee the names of 24 experts, "whose professional backgrounds and experience in recent years suggest intimate knowledge of the fact, fallacies and controversy which surround the concepts or hypotheses

of diet as a precursor to atherosclerosis and other of the degenerative diseases in America and elsewhere." Their responses and others solicited by the Select Committee were immediately sought, and those received are printed in their entirety in *Dietary Goals for the United States—Supplemental Views.*[11]

Also, since the release of the 1st Edition, Senator Kennedy, Chairman of the Subcommittee on Health and Scientific Research, released a survey conducted by Dr. Kaare Norum of the University of Oslo involving over 200 scientists from 23 countries, on the relationship between diet and health. The survey, reported in the Journal of the American Medical Association, June 13, 1977, found that 99.9 percent believed that there is a connection between diet and the development of heart disease, with 91.9 percent believing that our knowledge in this area is sufficient to recommend a moderate change in diet. Specifically the scientists recommended, in order of priority:

1. Fewer total calories.
2. Less fat.
3. Less saturated fat.
4. Less cholesterol.
5. More poly-unsaturated fat.
6. Less sugar.
7. Less salt.
8. More fiber.
9. More starchy foods.

It has been correctly pointed out that this kind of "survey" has certain inherent limitations. For example, Dr. David Kritchevsky, in his letter printed in the Supplemental Views report, thought the survey would have been more useful if the respondents had been asked to weigh, on a 1–5 scale, the relative importance of each dietary factor rather than simply indicating whether or not it was associated with heart disease.

However, the findings of this survey do indicate very substantial agreement among nutrition researchers as to the association between diet and heart disease, based on their own research and that of their colleagues as reported in scientific journals. Use of this survey is illustrative of a greater question. That is, at what point should generally agreed upon opinions be shared with the public as scientifically endorsed recommendations. Important advice in this area was given to the Select Committee at the February 1977 heart disease hearing [12] by Dr. Antonio Gotto, Chairman of the Department of Medicine at Baylor College of Medicine, in Houston, Texas:

> I wish to reiterate one extremely important point that is explicitly and implicitly contained in these goals. That point is that medical practice often must be based on the best available existing evidence, even though it falls short of final scientific proof. Certainly all of the scientific evidence concern-

[9] "Diet Related to Killer Diseases, Vol. III. Response to Dietary Goals for the U.S.—Re Meat", March 24, 1977, U.S. Government Printing Office, Washington, D.C., Stock No. 052-070-04277-0, Price $3.
[10] "Diet Related to Killer Diseases, Vol. VI. Response to Dietary Goals for the U.S.—Re Eggs", July 26, 1977, U.S. Government Printing Office, Washington, D.C., Stock No. 050-070-04280-0, Price $2.75.

[11] "Dietary Goals for the United States—Supplemental Views." November 1977, U.S. Government Printing Office, Washington, D.C. Stock No. 052-070-04294-0, Price $5.75.
[12] "Diet Related to Killer Diseases, Vol. II, Part 1, Cardiovascular Disease." February 1977, U.S. Government Printing Office, Washington, D.C., Stock No. 052-070-03987-0, Price $6.15.

ing diet and its relationship to the major killer diseases is not in, but even when much more evidence accumulates from surveys, epidemiological studies and basic research, there will continue to be honest professional disagreement concerning the basic dietary path to good health.

However, because there already is much evidence which points in a general direction and because health problems in our country are now enormously pressing, in my opinion, it is critical to take some action now.

FURTHER EVOLUTION OF DIETARY GOALS

The 1st Edition of *Dietary Goals for the United States* was intended s that first step. This 2nd Edition is a further evolution of a con- inuous, on-going process for which the Select Committee hopes the utrition community will take over responsibility.

The diet we eat today, while loosely tied to the RDA and the concept f four or seven food groups, was not planned or developed for any articular purpose. It isn't the result of a planned policy. The Secre- ary of Agriculture, Robert Bergland, indicated as much when he ecently told the Select Committee:

We think this country must develop a policy around human nutrition, around which we build a food policy for this country and as much of this world as is interested. And in that framework we have to fashion a more rational farm policy. We've been going at it from the wrong end in the past.

Dietary Goals is a report in pursuit of the Secretary of Agriculture's ated ideal. Nutrition and health considerations must be in the fore- ront of the development of this Nation's agriculture and food policy. n accepting such a policy position, instead of ignoring or clouding ne scientific facts in order to prevent any shift in the economic status uo, we must be willing to make economic and market adjustments to eet the scientific requirements that will, or probably will provide mproved health benefits for the Nation.

Since the release of the 1st Edition of *Dietary Goals*, eight more earings have been held in the series, "Diet Related to Killer Diseases." hey are: "Diet and Cardiovascular Disease," [13] "Obesity," [14] "Dietary oals for the U.S.—Re: Meat," [15] "Dietary Fiber and Health," [16] Nutrition: Mental Health and Mental Development," [17] "Dietary oals for the U.S.—Re: Eggs," [18] "Nutrition: Aging and the El-

derly," [19] and "Nutrition at HEW: Policy, Research, and Regulation." [20]

These hearings, which have included dozens of independent re- searchers and numerous governmental health officials, have brought to light more evidence from epidemiological studies, and basic clinical research, and have highlighted further the areas of controversy. For example, Dr. Robert Levy, Director, National Heart, Lung, and Blood Institute, National Institutes of Health, testifying at the February 1977 Diet and Cardiovascular Disease hearing, stated that:

The major question, we might call it the $64 million ques- tion, is . . . whether aggressive treatment of risk factors de- lays or prevents atherosclerosis and its sequelae.

With some of these risk factors we think the answer is in. With cigarette smoking we have shown with prospective and retrospective studies, that there is no doubt that if one stops smoking, one's risk decreases.

With blood pressure, we do not know that treating blood pressure will prevent heart attacks; but we have evidence it will prevent renal failure, heart failure, and stroke; so we treat it aggressively.

With cholesterol, the issue is a little more murky. We have no doubt from the vast amount of epidemiological data avail- able that elevated cholesterol is associated with an increased risk of heart attack, especially some specific types of high cholesterol.

We have no doubt that [blood] cholesterol can be low- ered by diet and/or medication in most patients.

Where the doubt exists is the question of whether lowering [blood] cholesterol will result in a reduced incidence of heart attack; that is still presumptive. It is unproven, but there is a tremendous amount of circumstantial evidence. Not only is there circumstantial epidemiologic data, but there is very exciting animal data. * * * Here * * * is one of many studies that have been done over the last decade with nonhuman pri- mates. It shows that not only can we prevent atherosclerosis from progressing by making dietary changes, but that regres- sion actually occurs. Atherosclerosis will lessen if we lower [blood] cholesterol levels in animals through diet. The prob- lem is we can't do these kinds of studies in man; it is not ethical. * * *

There is no doubt that [blood] cholesterol can be lowered by diet in free-living populations. It can be lowered by 10 to 15 percent.

The problem with all of these [clinical] trials is that none of them have showed a difference in heart attack or death rate in the treated group. Only when soft-end points were used in fact was there any subjective difference, and this was only in studies that were not blinded.

[13] "Diet Related to Killer Diseases, Vol. II, Part 1, Diet and Cardiovascular Disease," ebruary 1, 1977, U.S. Government Printing Office, Washington, D.C., Stock No. 052–070– 3987–6, Price $6.15.
[14] "Diet Related to Killer Diseases, Vol. II, Part 2, Obesity," February 2, 1977, U.S. overnment Printing Office, Washington, D.C., Stock No. 052–070–04275–3, Price $3.25.
[15] "Diet Related to Killer Diseases, Vol. III, Response to Dietary Goals for the U.S.—Re eat." March 24, 1977, U.S. Government Printing Office, Washington, D.C., Stock No. 52–070–04256–1, Price $4.
[16] "Diet Related to Killer Diseases, Vol. IV, Dietary Fiber and Health," March 31, 1977, S. Government Printing Office, Washington, D.C., Stock No. 052–070–04277–0, Price $3.
[17] "Diet Related to Killer Diseases, Vol. V, Nutrition: Mental Health and Mental Develop- ent." June 22, 1977, U.S. Government Printing Office, Washington, D.C., Stock No. 52–070–04278–8, Price $3.75.
[18] "Diet Related to Killer Diseases, Vol. VI, Response to Dietary Goals for the U.S.—Re ggs," July 26, 1977, U.S. Government Printing Office, Washington, D.C., Stock No. 52–070–04280–0, Price $2.75.

[19] "Diet Related to Killer Diseases. Vol. VII. Nutrition: Aging and the Elderly," Septem- ber 23, 1977, U.S. Government Printing Office. Washington, D.C., in press.
[20] "Diet Related to Killer Diseases. Vol. VIII, Nutrition at HEW: Policy, Research and Regulation," October 17, 1977, U.S. Government Printing Office, Washington, D.C., in press.

Does this mean that [blood] cholesterol lowering is not effective [in reducing the risk of heart disease]? We think not. We think it means that investigators up until the early 1970's did not appreciate the difficulty of demonstrating the efficacy of lipid lowering. * * *

We are convinced, as clearly as in this Committee, that prevention is not only the most cost-effective, but the best scientific strategy in our conquest of cardiovascular disease.

Some witnesses have claimed that physical harm could result from the diet modifications recommended in this report. The concern centers on mineral deficiencies which might occur primarily because of the increase in consumption of foods from the complex carbohydrate group. However, after further review, the Select Committee still finds that no physical or mental harm could result from the dietary guidelines recommended for the general public—excluding of course the special nutrient requirements of certain target groups, such as pregnant and lactating women. This matter is discussed further under Goal 2 in the text of the report.

The intense discussion and debate which prompted the issuance of this 2nd Edition are good signs. The sense of immediacy has not lessened, nor has the concern among those charged with developing the Nation's health policy. No better indication of this exists than remarks made by Assistant Secretary of Health, Julius B. Richmond, M.D., who said at our hearing in October, 1977:

> Many experts now believe that we have entered a new era in nutrition, when the lack of essential nutrients no longer is the major nutritional problem facing most American people. Evidence suggests that the major problems of heart disease, hypertension, cancer, diabetes, and other chronic disease are significantly related to diet. Although improved nutrition alone will not prevent these diseases, more attention is being focused on the underlying dietary habits which may be antecedent or contributing causes of these conditions. We view this as a positive sign of the progress that has been made thus far and that undoubtedly will continue. . . . We believe it is essential to convey to the public the current state of knowledge about the potential benefits of modifying dietary habits, without overstating the benefits that could possibly result from the adoption of alternative dietary practices, such as reducing excessive caloric intake and eating less fat, less sugar, and less salt.

ADDITIONS AND CHANGES

New Goal Added

The 2nd Edition of *Dietary Goals* includes a new goal: To avoid overweight, consume only as much energy (calories) as is expended; if overweight, decrease energy intake and increase energy expenditure.

Of all the comments received on *Dietary Goals*, perhaps the one heard most often was that there should be a goal addressing total energy (caloric) consumption. The specific *Dietary Goals* of the 1st Edition were not intended to minimize the importance of monitoring total energy intake.

The alarming prevalence of obesity in the United States is part attributable to the fact that the energy requirements of American have decreased steadily over recent decades. This decline in energy expenditure has not been paralleled by a decline in energy intake. T physical activity of people in the United States is generally consider to be light to sedentary rather than heavy as was true earlier in t century.

Obesity resulting from the over-consumption of calories is a maj risk factor in many killer diseases. Therefore, it is extremely impo tant either to maintain an optimal weight, or to alter one's weight reach an optimal level. Altering one's calorie consumption is not t only way to control weight and thus lessen the risk factors associat with obesity. Exercise can and should play an important and integr role as well. Even if dietary patterns remain the same, the influen of an increasingly sedentary lifestyle may turn what was previous a diet very adequate in calories into one with too many calories.

Finally, in adding this new goal which stresses the risk of bei overweight, the reader should also be aware of an important b much smaller part of the American population which is underweig Although being marginally underweight is apparently not harm and even may be beneficial, underweight may be accompanied vitamin-mineral deficiencies. This possibility is of concern particular among the very young and elderly Americans.

Preschool age children, and pregnant and lactating women, requi special attention to ensure that they receive enough calories, as w as enough protein, vitamins and minerals, for full physical and ment development. Older Americans, whose overall caloric needs are ge erally reduced with age, must be especially attentive about their d in order to prevent any nutrient deficiencies from occuring.

Alcohol

Many comments, including the "Review of Dietary Goals of t United States" published by The Lancet [21] on April 23, 1977, poin out that the *Dietary Goals* would be more helpful if they had tak into account the usage of alcoholic beverages.

As with the monitoring of total energy intake, there was no inte to minimize the intake of alcohol in the diet. The amount of calor obtained from alcohol should be a factor in diet planning. Alcoh which supplies 7 calories per gram, but no vitamins and minerals, a toxic substance that uses other nutrients in the diet in its metaboli process, and excessive alcohol consumption is the primary factor cirrhosis of the liver—the ninth leading killer of Americans. Al recent studies indicate that pregnant women should abstain fr alcohol intake in order to protect the health of the fetus.

Although surveys have rarely calculated alcohol intake, estima can be made on a basis of data similar to USDA "disappearance dat for food. In 1971, the average annual consumption of absolute alcoh from spirits, wine and beer among the drinking-age U.S. populati was 2.6 gallons per person. The energy value of this amount of alcoh (excluding the energy from sugars in some alcoholic beverages) equ an average intake of approximately 210 Calories per person per d

---

[21] An editorial in a British medical journal reprinted in "Dietary Goals for the U.S. Supplemental Views," pp. 1–3.

Alcohol consumption varies among individuals probably more than does the intake of any other energy source. A large percentage of the population abstains from alcohol consumption whereas many persons drink far more than 200 calories of alcohol daily. But on the average, adult females obtain 10 percent of their RDA for calories from alcohol and adult males 7½ percent. In order to acknowledge the intake of alcohol in American diets, footnotes have been added to the chart accompanying the Goals (page 5) to remind readers of the energy contribution of alcoholic beverages.

Goal No. 2

Change: "Increase carbohydrate consumption to account for 55–60 percent of the energy (caloric) intake."

To: "Increase the consumption of complex carbohydrates and 'naturally occurring' sugars from about 28 percent of energy intake to about 48 percent of energy intake."

The intent of this goal is primarily to increase the consumption of complex carbohydrates as indicated in the food selection recommendation, "Increase consumption of fruits, vegetables and whole grains." In addition, "naturally occurring" sugars are obtained from fruits, vegetables and whole grains, as well as from milk products. The wording of the goal has been altered to provide greater accuracy and clarity.

Goal No. 3

Change: "Reduce sugar consumption by about 40 percent to account for about 15 percent of total energy intake."

To: "Reduce the consumption of refined and processed sugars by about 45 percent to account for about 10 percent of total energy intake."

In reviewing the responses pertaining to the sugar recommendation in this report, it was clear to the Select Committee that there needed to be more preciseness provided to the consumer than was available by solely using the generic term, sugar. In particular, while the text described the various sugars, the graph on page 12 in the 1st Edition comparing the current American diet with the recommended dietary goals lumped all sugars together under the generic term sugar.

The new graph (p. 5) will break down the current consumption of 24 percent of total caloric intake from sugars into: (1) 6 percent occurring naturally in fruits, vegetables and milk products; and (2) 18 percent refined (cane and beet) and processed (corn sugar, syrups, molasses and honey).

The recommended dietary goal is adjusted to 10 percent of total caloric intake from refined and processed sugars. The specific amount of sugars occurring naturally in foods that a person consumes will be dependent on his or her selection of foods in the category of complex carbohydrates and "naturally occurring" sugars.

Goal No. 6. Reduce cholesterol consumption to about 300 mg a day

The role of dietary and plasma cholesterol in the development of heart disease has probably received more attention than any other nutritional research issue. Many important findings have resulted from this on-going research effort.

Cholesterol is a fat soluble substance which is only synthesized by animal organisms. It does not supply energy, but is essential for normal cell function, and as a building block for hormones. It is not chemically related to either triglycerides or phospholipids, which are the two important fats from a nutritional point of view (see the text of Goal 5 for further discussion of fats).

The amount of plasma cholesterol,[22] that is the cholesterol in the blood stream, has been shown to be a good indicator of risk of heart disease. That is, the higher one's plasma cholesterol, the higher one's risk of having heart disease. Likewise, the lower one's plasma cholesterol, the lower one's risk of having heart disease.

Research indicates that diets high in cholesterol and/or high in saturated fats raise the total plasma cholesterol level. Conversely, a low cholesterol diet and/or one high in polyunsaturated fat tends to lower total plasma cholesterol.

This research indicates that altering the saturated fat intake has a larger impact on the level of plasma cholesterol than does altering the intake of cholesterol.

In the United States, plasma cholesterol levels are considered normal by many physicians in the range of 200–300 mgs. However, normal is not optimal, nor does it imply any protection from heart disease. In fact, a plasma cholesterol level of 260 mgs or higher carries with it five times the risk for heart disease as compared to a level of 220 mg or lower (see the text of Goal 6 for more information). Only in societies where the level of the plasma cholesterol is under 150 or 160 mgs do we find virtually no deaths from heart disease. Interestingly, babies all over the world have plasma cholesterol levels of about 70–90 mgs at birth.

In examining the complex biochemical mechanisms which cause the development of arterial disease leading to heart attacks and hardening of the arteries scientists discovered that cholesterol deposited in the wall of the artery forms a plaque. These plaques continue to build up in the arteries, reducing the blood flow. This partial or full blockage in the coronary arteries eventually leads to reduced function, incapacity such as severe chest pain (angina pectoris), heart attacks and death.

One of the most significant research concerns has been the investigation of lipoproteins which are the carriers of cholesterol and other fatty substances in the blood stream. Two lipoproteins have been found to be of particular interest: LDL or low density lipoprotein, and HDL or high density lipoprotein.

The level of LDL is directly related to the consumption of dietary cholesterol and fat, and high levels of LDL have been directly correlated with heart dsease.

Whereas LDL is the most common carrier of cholesterol in the blood, HDL carries much less. In addition, HDL appears to be protective with respect to heart disease. That is the higher one's HDL level, the less risk of having heart disease. Furthermore, unlike LDL, the level

---

[22] Plasma cholesterol is replacing serum cholesterol as the preferred method of analyzing cholesterol in the blood stream. However, for the purposes of this report, both terms, as well as blood cholesterol, are used and can be considered interchangeable.

of HDL is not greatly affected by the fat in one's diet; it seems to be altered (increased) by exercise, nicotinic acid and estrogens.

In addition to dietary determinants, there are also metabolic factors. Cholesterol is so essential to human bodily functions that it is naturally synthesized. Most of the plasma cholesterol is synthesized in the liver and to a lesser extent in the intestine. Thus, whether or not we consume dietary cholesterol, the normal human body can and will produce all the cholesterol it requires.

However, because most people consume some dietary cholesterol, there is a feedback regulation of cholesterol synthesis. This biological mechanism inhibits the synthesis of cholesterol in the liver when the dietary intake of cholesterol is increased. Conversely, with a low intake of dietary cholesterol, there is an increase in cholesterol synthesis in the liver.

In trying to better understand the feedback regulation mechanism for cholesterol synthesis, researchers have found that significant alterations in plasma cholesterol can result from dietary modification. Therefore, they have concluded that the feedback mechanism is not completely effective in compensating for the dietary intake of cholesterol.

It is impossible to cover all the cholesterol research findings in this report. In the appendix of the hearing of July 26, 1977, there is an extensive review of the controversy. In addition, much of the 900 pages in the report *Dietary Goals for the United States—Supplementary Views* [23] is addressed to the fat and cholesterol debate.

This report also cannot begin to discuss the many unanswered research questions. Nevertheless, some of the important questions which are currently being investigated include:

(1) Does lowering the plasma cholesterol level through dietary modification prevent or delay heart disease in man?
(2) What is the *exact* relationship between dietary cholesterol and plasma cholesterol?
(3) Does consumption of a low fat (under 20 percent), low animal protein and high complex carbohydrate diet reduce the risks associated with the intake of dietary cholesterol at current American levels?
(4) Is hydrogenation of vegetable oils a factor in the development of heart disease?
(5) How do the various lipoproteins interact, and why does HDL apparently protect against heart disease?

With regard to the cholesterol issue, the Select Committee has received countless comments and questions generally focusing on two areas:

(1) Is the cholesterol recommendation for the general population, or for people at high risk of heart disease?
(2) What does this mean for egg consumption, which is the single largest source of cholesterol in the American diet?

[23] Dietary Goals for the U.S.—Supplemental Views, November 1977, U.S. Government Printing Office, Washington, D.C. Stock No. 052-070-04294-0. Price $5.75.

The 300 mg per day recommendation does not mean eliminating egg consumption. Nor does it imply that one should replace eggs with one of the highly processed egg-substitutes or imitation egg products.

Eggs are an excellent, inexpensive source of protein, vitamins and minerals. The 250 mgs of cholesterol in an average egg, as well as the bulk of the calories, is contained in the yolk. As a result, some researchers advocate using in one's diet only egg whites, which have most of the protein.

Finally, one should view cholesterol as only one component of the total diet. We recommend a general level of cholesterol consumption and leave the ultimate source of that dietary component up to the consumer. Since eggs are only one source of dietary cholesterol, a specific recommendation as to the number of eggs necessary to meet the goal is inappropriate.

Keeping in mind that the risk of heart disease is significantly lower among women until they reach menopause, and that young children and the elderly need particularly good sources of high quality protein, vitamins and minerals, it may be advisable for persons in these groups to include more eggs in their diet—even to the point of easing the cholesterol recommendation in order to increase egg consumption.

It is not possible to say exactly how much to ease the recommendation since no scientific panels have specifically set cholesterol intake levels for population sub-groups. In suggesting that the cholesterol might be eased for young children, pre-menopausal women and the elderly in order to obtain the nutritional benefits of additional eggs, the Select Committee does remain concerned as to what happens when the period of reduced risk is over and possible cumulative effects from the diet take place.

In summary, the Select Committee understands that there is still controversy surrounding the exact relationship of dietary cholesterol to heart disease, and that we must aggressively continue research in order to bring resolution to the current dispute. However, over the last 25 years, there has been a steady and mounting accumulation of basic research and epidemiological evidence which indicates that a high plasma cholesterol level is a major risk factor in heart disease and that dietary cholesterol is one of a number of factors which affects plasma cholesterol. As one result, ten national and international panels have recommended the restriction of dietary cholesterol for the general population (see Appendix B).

This past year, Dr. Robert Levy, Director, National Heart, Lung and Blood Institute, National Institutes of Health, announced that recent surveys suggest that the average American's plasma cholesterol level has dropped five to ten percent since the early 1960's, which may have contributed to the sharp decline in deaths from heart and blood vessel diseases over the last several years.

As public policymakers, the members of the Select Committee cannot ignore the known findings which indicate the high probability that cholesterol intake contributes to the development of cardiovascular disease. The Select Committee cannot ignore the fact that 850,000 mericans die each year from heart and blood vessel disease, that 50 ercent of all deaths are related to cardiovascular illness, which, ther directly or indirectly, costs the Nation over $50 billion annually. eart disease is America's number one killer.

It therefore seems that the only prudent course of action to take in e best interest of the health of the Nation is to recommend that olesterol consumption be reduced to about 300 mg a day.

oal No. 7

Change: "Reduce salt consumption by about 50 to 85 percent to pproximately 3 gms a day."

To: "Limit the intake of sodium by reducing the intake of salt sodium chloride) to about 5 grams a day."

Upon further review of the evidence concerning sodium intake, the elect Committee believes that, while a 3 gram or even a 2 gram dietary oal for salt (sodium chloride) intake is probably justified for a high isk population having hypertension, 5 grams a day is a more appro riate level of salt intake to recommend at this time for the general opulation.

Furthermore, it is important to understand that sodium occurs aturally in foods. Therefore, the daily sodium requirement for the verage person will normally be met without consuming salt or sodium lts, which may be obtained from either processed foods or home food reparation.

ood Selection Suggestion No. 3

Change: "decrease consumption of meat and increase consumption of oultry and fish."

To: "decrease consumption of animal fat, and choose meats, poultry nd fish which will reduce saturated fat intake."

The recommendation in the 1st Edition that consumers "decrease nsumption of meat and increase consumption of poultry and fish," as intended to help implement the goals of reducing overall fat con umption from approximately 40 percent to 30 percent of our energy take, and of reducing saturated fat consumption to account for about) percent of total caloric intake.

PROTEIN

In setting the dietary goal of 30 percent of total calories from fat, e Select Committee examined both the research on fats and on rotein because the majority of fat in the American diet is obtained rough the consumption of foods of animal origin, which are also ır primary source of protein.

In the 1st Edition, the Select Committee neither recommended a de rease in overall protein intake, nor indicated a preference for vege ıble protein over animal protein. In fact, meat, poultry and fish are n excellent source of essential amino acids, vitamins and minerals. Vith respect to minerals, for example, meat is a good source of iron and thus helps to reduce the probability of iron deficiency anemia, a nutritional disorder which can occur among groups such as teenagers and pre-menopausal women.

The Select Committee does not believe that there is sufficient scienti fic evidence to recommend a reduction in overall protein intake. How ever, by following the Report's recommendation to increase the consumption of whole grains, fruits and vegetables, while maintaining the same level of overall protein intake, an alteration in the ratio be tween animal and vegetable proteins will occur.

Some other points also need to be considered. First, the average American eats daily almost twice as much protein as the Food and Nutrition Board of the National Academy of Sciences recommends for meeting the needs of most healthy people. There is no known nutri tional need for our current high level of protein intake.

Second, while the protein level of the American diet, based on USDA disappearance data, has remained at about 12 percent of calories since 1909, the ratio of animal protein to vegetable protein has steadily changed from 1.06 to 2.26. This means that, whereas the per capita level of calories from protein in the American diet in 1909 was 12 per cent, of which 6 percent was of animal origin and 6 percent was of vegetable origin; today, the mix is greater than 8 percent of calories from animal protein and less than 4 percent from vegetable protein.

Third, there is basic research which raises some questions about over all protein intake, as well as the ratio of animal and vegetable pro teins. One series of investigations found that diets that derive their protein from animal sources elevate plasma cholesterol levels to a much greater extent than do diets that derive their protein from vegetable sources. Another line of basic research demonstrated that, in almost all cases, high protein diets are more atherosclerotic than are low pro tein diets. Therefore, two important questions for future consideration are: (1) should protein intake be reduced? and (2) is the ratio of ani mal to vegetable protein important?

FAT

With respect to total fat consumption, there is increasing scientific research that suggests some day a dietary fat intake of 20 percent to 25 percent might be recomemnded; and even less for those people who already have heart disease. The basic research is strongly corroborated by epidemiological studies of populations throughout the world who live quite well on a diet containing as little as 10 percent calories from fat. In summary, the goal of limiting fat consumption to 30 percent of total calories has not been a major point of contention and is derived from the recommendations of expert panels from around the world (see Appendix B).

Along with consuming less animal fat by eating smaller portions of meat, it would also be possible to reduce fat consumption by eating the least fatty cuts of meats, by reducing the fat content of meat, or by some combination of both.

Animal fat is not the only source of saturated fat in the diet. Of the 56 grams of saturated fat consumed per person per day, based on 1977 USDA disappearance data, 16 grams, or 28 percent, are from a vege table source. Hydrogenated vegetable oils, which are found in vegetable shortenings, many margarines and numerous other processed food products, provide the majority of the saturated fats obtained from vegetable sources.

It is important to recognize all the sources of fat in the diet. For example, the fats in meats, chicken, butter, lard, margarine, vegetable shortenings, salad dressings and oils, and home fried foods are visible to the consumer. But there are also fats in the diet which are not apparent, such as those found in fish, ground meats, eggs, milk, cheese, ice cream, nuts, peanut butter, bakery products, potato chips, and many highly processed food products.

In changing to, "decrease consumption of animal fat, and choose meat, poultry and fish which will reduce saturated fat intake," the Select Committee suggests that tables 11, 12, and 13 in the text be especially utilized in order to best implement *Dietary Goals* 4 and 5.

PART I

DIETARY GOALS FOR THE UNITED STATES— SECOND EDITION

INTRODUCTION

During this century, the composition of the average diet in t[he] United States has changed radically. Foods containing complex ca[r]bohydrates and "naturally occurring" [1] sugars—fruit, vegetables a[nd] grain products—which were the mainstay of the diet, now play [a] minority role. At the same time, the consumption of fats and refin[ed] and processed sugars has risen to the point where these two mac[ro]nutrients alone now comprise at least 60 percent of total caloric intak[e,] an increase of 20 percent since the early 1900s. [2]

In the view of doctors and nutritionists consulted by the Sel[ect] Committee, these and other changes in the diet amount to a wave [of] malnutrition—of both over- and under-consumption—that may be [as] profoundly damaging to the Nation's health as the widespread co[n]tagious diseases of the early part of the century.

The over-consumption of foods high in fat, generally, and saturat[ed] fat in particular, as well as cholesterol, refined and processed suga[r,] salt and/or alcohol has been associated with the development of o[ne] or more of six to ten leading causes of death: heart disease, so[me] cancers, stroke and hypertension, diabetes, arteriosclerosis and c[ir]rhosis of the liver. The associations are discussed more fully later [in] this report.

In his testimony at the Select Committee's July 1976 hearings on t[he] relationship of diet to disease, Dr. Mark Hegsted of the Harva[rd] School of Public Health, said:

I wish to stress that there is a great deal of evidence and it continues [to] accumulate, which strongly implicates and, in some instances, proves that [the] major causes of death and disability in the United States are related to [the] diet we eat. I include coronary artery disease which accounts for nearly h[alf] of the deaths in the United States, several of the most important forms of can[cer,] hypertension, diabetes and obesity as well as other chronic diseases.

The over-consumption of food in general, combined with our m[ore] sedentary lifestyle, has become a major public health problem. In tes[ti]mony at the same hearings, Dr. Theodore Cooper, Assistant Secreta[ry] for Health, estimated that about 20 percent of all adults in the Unit[ed]

[1] "Naturally occurring": Sugars which are indigenous to a food, as opposed to refi[ned] (cane and beet) and processed (corn sugar, syrups, molasses and honey) sugars which [may] be added to a food product.
[2] The food supply estimates are based on United States Department of Agriculture d[ata] showing the amounts of food that "disappear" into civilian channels.

States "are overweight to a degree that may interfere with optimal health and longevity."

At the same time, current dietary trends may also be leading to malnutrition through undernourishment. Fats are relatively low in vitamins and minerals, and refined sugar (cane and beet) and most processed sugars have no vitamins and minerals. Consequently, diets with reduced caloric intake to control weight and/or save money, but which are high in fats and refined and processed sugars, may lead to vitamin and mineral deficiencies. As will be discussed later, low-income people may be particularly susceptible to inducements to consume diets high in fats, and refined and processed sugars.

The Department of Health, Education, and Welfare reported that health care expenditures in the United States in Fiscal Year 1976 totaled about $139.4 billion and predicted the cost could exceed $230 billion by Fiscal Year 1980. In testimony before the Select Committee in 1972, Dr. George Briggs, professor of nutrition at the University of California, Berkeley, estimated, based on a study by the Department of Agriculture, that improved nutrition might cut the Nation's health bill by one-third.

More recently, in an October 1977 letter to the Select Committee, Dr. Briggs provided an analysis of the cost of poor nutritional status which contributes to some of the diseases in the United States. The potential annual savings in nutrition related costs, "based on the more conservative end of the range of current scientific opinion," were as follows:

	Billion
Dental diseases	$3
Diabetes	4
Cardiovascular disease	10
Alcohol	20
Digestive diseases	3
Total	$40

It should be noted that this analysis does not include cancer, kidney disease due to mismanagement of hypertension, or the long-term costs associated with low birthweight babies due to maternal malnutrition.

Beyond the monetary savings, it is obvious then that improved nutrition also offers the potential for prevention of vast suffering and loss of productivity and creativity.

One in three men in the United States can be expected to die of heart disease or stroke before age 60 and one in six women. It is estimated that 25 million suffer from high blood pressure and that about 5 million are afflicted by diabetes mellitus.[3]

Given the wide impact on health that has been traced to the dietary trends outlined, it is imperative, as a matter of public health policy, that consumers be provided with dietary guidelines or goals for macro-nutrients that will encourage the most healthful selection of foods.

Based on (1) testimony presented to the Select Committee in the ten days of hearings entitled "Diet Related to Killer Diseases" which began in July 1976 and ended in October 1977; (2) the Select Committee's 1974 National Nutrition Policy hearings; (3) guidelines established by governmental and professional bodies in the United States and at least eight other nations (Appendix B); and (4) a variety of expert opinion, the following Dietary Goals are recommended for the United States. Although genetic and other individual differences among health individuals exist, there is substantial evidence indicating that following these guidelines may be generally beneficial.

---

[3] Statistics from reports and testimony presented to the Select Committee's National Nutrition Policy hearings, June 1974, appearing in National Nutrition Policy Study, 1974, Part 6, June 21, 1974, Heart disease, p. 2633; high blood pressure, p. 2529, diabetes, p. 2523.

U.S. DIETARY GOALS

1. To avoid overweight, consume only as much energy (calories) is expended; if overweight, decrease energy intake and increase energy expenditure. (See pages xxxiii–xxxxiv, 7–10, 15, 38.)
2. Increase the consumption of complex carbohydrates and "naturally occurring" sugars from about 28 percent of energy intake to about 48 percent of energy intake. (See pages xxxv, 11–16.)
3. Reduce the consumption of refined and processed sugars by about 45 percent to account for about 10 percent of total energy intake. (See pages xxxv, 27–33.)
4. Reduce overall fat consumption from approximately 40 percent to about 30 percent of energy intake. (See pages 35–38.)
5. Reduce saturated fat consumption to account for about 10 percent of total energy intake; and balance that with poly-unsaturated and mono-unsaturated fats, which should account for about 10 percent of energy intake each. (See pages 39–41.)
6. Reduce cholesterol consumption to about 300 mg. a day. (See pages xxxv–xxxix, 42, 43.)
7. Limit the intake of sodium by reducing the intake of salt to about 5 gram a day. (Pages xxxix, 49–51.)

The Goals Suggest the Following Changes in Food Selection and Preparation:

1. Increase consumption of fruits and vegetables and whole grains. (See pages 17–26.)
2. Decrease consumption of refined and other processed sugars and foods high in such sugars. (See pages 33, 34.)
3. Decrease consumption of foods high in total fat, and partially replace saturated fats, whether obtained from animal or vegetable sources, with poly-unsaturated fats. (See pages 43–48.)
4. Decrease consumption of animal fat, and choose meats, poultry and fish which will reduce saturated fat intake. (See pages xxxix–xli, 43–48, and use particularly, tables 11–13, pp. 45–48.)
5. Except for young children, substitute low-fat and non-fat milk for whole milk, and low-fat dairy products for high fat dairy products. (See pages 43–48.)
6. Decrease consumption of butterfat, eggs and other high cholesterol sources. Some consideration should be given to easing the cholesterol goal for pre-menopausal women, young children and the elderly in order to obtain the nutritional benefits of eggs in the diet. (See pages xxxvii–xxxix for more details concerning eggs and cholesterol, pp. 43–48.)
7. Decrease consumption of salt and foods high in salt content. (See page 51 and Appendix E.)

Persons with physical and/or mental ailments who have reason to believe that they should not follow guidelines for the general population should consult with a health professional having expertise in nutrition, regarding their individual case.

(4)

Although the Dietary Goals are stated in terms of specific leve[ls] each specific level should be considered as the center of a range (s[ee] p. xxvi in the Preface for details.)

While there may be a tendency to read only the summaries provid[ed] on these two pages, the Select Committee recommends that, wheneve[r] possible, the entire report be read in order to obtain a more comple[te] perspective of the relationship between diet and health.

The question of whether dietary changes alone such as those su[g]gested in these goals can reduce the leading causes of death in t[he] United States remains controversial. Individuals, in exercising fre[e]dom of dietary choice, should recognize that these dietary recomme[n]dations do not *guarantee* improved protection from the killer disease[s.] They do, however, increase the *probability* of improved protection.

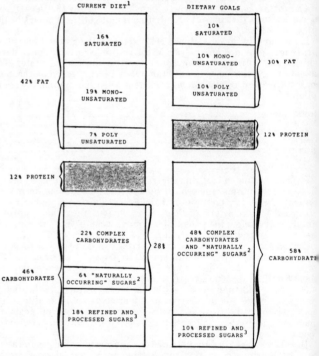

FIGURE 1

[1] These percentages are based on calories from food and nonalcoholic beverages. Alco[hol] adds approximately another 210 calories per day to the average diet of drinking-age Ame[ri]cans.

[2] "Naturally occurring": Sugars which are indigenous to a food, as opposed to refin[ed] (cane and beet) and processed (corn sugar, syrups, molasses and honey) sugars whi[ch] may be added to a food product.

[3] In many ways alcoholic beverages affect the diet in the same way as refined and oth[er] processed sugars. Both add calories (energy) to the total diet but contribute little or [no] vitamins or minerals.

Sources for current diet: *Changes in Nutrients in the U.S. Diet Caused by Alternatio[ns] in Food Intake Patterns.* B. Friend. Agricultural Research Service. U.S. Department [of] Agriculture. 1974. Proportions of saturated versus unsaturated fats based on unpublish[ed] Agricultural Research Service data.

EXPLANATION OF GOALS

GOAL 1. TO AVOID OVERWEIGHT, CONSUME ONLY AS MUCH ENERGY (CALORIES) AS IS EXPENDED; IF OVERWEIGHT, DECREASE ENERGY INTAKE AND INCREASE ENERGY EXPENDITURE

Fifteen million Americans are obese to an extent which seriously raises their risk of ill health. Obesity is associated with the onset and clinical progression of diseases such as hypertension, diabetes mellitus, heart disease and gall bladder disease. It may also modify the quality of one's life.

There is strong evidence suggesting that, for those overweight, the best protection against heart disease is weight reduction. A study by Drs. Franz Ashley and William Kannel, *Relation of Weight Change to Changes in Atherogenic Trains: The Framingham Study*, discussed the importance of obesity on heart disease.

The clinical and preventive implications seem clear. Weight gain is accompanied by atherogenic alterations in blood, lipids, and blood pressure, uric acid and carbohydrate tolerance. It is uncertain whether the nutrient composition of excess calories, derived largely from saturated calories accompanied by cholesterol and simple carbohydrates, or the positive energy balance per se, is important. But whatever the cause, development of ordinary . . . obesity encountered in the general population is associated with excess development of coronary heart disease.

As told to the Committee by Dr. Beverly Winikoff of the Rockefeller Foundation in July 1976, at the first hearing in the "Diet Related to Killer Diseases" series:

With increasing affluence, we have also increased our body weights. Obesity is probably the most common and one of the most serious nutritional problems affecting the American public today.

Over 30 percent of all men between 50–59 are 20 percent overweight, and fully 60 percent are over 10 percent overweight. About one-third of the population is overweight to a degree which has been shown to diminish life expectancy. For unknown reasons, in the United States, this type of malnutrition is a more common burden among the poor than among the more wealthy.

Obesity has the effect of increasing blood cholesterol, blood pressure and blood glucose levels. Through these effects, it is an important risk factor for coronary disease.

Reductions in obesity improve the condition of hypertensives and diabetics, and thereby reduces the risk of heart disease and stroke. Data from the Framingham study examined by Ashley and Kannel in 1973 indicate that each 10 percent reduction in weight in men 35–55 years old would result in about a 20 percent decrease in incidence of coronary disease.

Conversely, each 10 percent increase in weight would result in a 30 percent increase in coronary disease.

In light of the fact that close to 700,000 Americans die of coronary disease every year, the staggering implications of these figures become apparent: if a 20 percent decrease in incidence did occur throughout the population and were reflected in a 20 percent decrease in overall mortality, about 140,000 lives would be saved per year. Since at least one-half the coronary deaths—about one-third of a million—occur before reaching a hospital, prevention is not only cheaper, but clearly more effective than cure.

Dr. Ted Cooper, then Assistant Secretary for Health, concurred:

When I was Director of the National Heart and Lung Institute we instituted several studies in order to find ways to give specific guidance to the public about what kinds of nutritional information would be of particular help in reducing that relationship between the proneness, particularly of the middle-aged American male to coronary artery disease. So I do feel that particularly excessive weight, which is a form of malnutrition, obesity, that is not from a deficiency but an excess or a disbalance of intake, can substantially contribute to coronary artery disease.

We must * * * move much further in utilizing optimal nutrition as a preventive health measure. In many instances our knowledge is already adequate to permit us to utilize education as an important tool to prevent disease and to improve the well-being and longevity of our citizens by fostering more healthful food consumption practices. Here I am particularly referring to obesity, a widespread and most important nutritional disease and a public health problem of constantly growing proportions in the United States. . .

The energy needs of an individual vary from day to day depending upon the amount of physical activity. However, our society is clearly less active than during the early parts of this century, or even just 20 years ago.

As one result, more adult Americans are putting on more body weight and body fat than ever before, and this trend is appearing earlier and more often during childhood and adolescence.

Dr. Ted Van Itallie, Director of the Obesity Research Center, St. Luke's Hospital Center, New York, N.Y., testifying at the February 2, 1977, Obesity hearing, stated that:

The data on weight by height and age of adults reported in 1966 by the National Center for Health Statistics indicate that, in this country, the average weight of men 68 inches tall increases by about 16 pounds between the ages of 21 and 49. For women 64 inches tall, the increment between the ages of 21 and 59 is 27 pounds. . . . In view of the disposition among physicians, actuaries and public health workers to regard increases in body weight after the age of 25 as being undesirable, it is not surprising that the proportion of individuals classified as obese increases markedly with age.

Studies of body composition in subjects within various age categories have demonstrated that the increase in body weight associated with aging is usually due entirely to an increase in body fat content. Indeed, in sedentary men, age 55, the increment in total body fat may be one-third greater than the increment in body weight. It is also worth mentioning that, with advancing age, the proportion of fat in the body increases in sedentary individuals even if body weight does not increase.

At that same hearing, Dr. Johanna Dwyer, Director of the Frances Stern Nutrition Center, New England Medical Center Hospital, Boston, in discussing obesity in childhood and adolescence stated that:

There is some limited evidence that obesity in childhood affects morbidity at least with respect to respiratory illness and that it may give rise to psychological problems, although infant or child mortality does not seem to be affected. In later childhood and adolescence, obesity is associated with a number of handicaps, including physical health, constraints on eating imposed by low energy needs, body image and its effects on sense of worth, social status and future social mobility, college admissions, parent-child relations, and adverse therapogenic effects of misdirected or ineffective treatments. But these are all relatively short range problems. The most important set of difficulties resulting from obesity are more long range in nature and involve their impact on adult health status. Assuming that obesity in early life is likely to continue into adult life, which is a legitimate generalization (although the exact proportions affected by this type of predestination are difficult to arrive at) we must also consider risks adult obesity which may be generated over the longer term. These include creased incidence of heart disease, hypertension, post-surgical complicatio hypoventilation, insulin antagonism, gynecological irregularities and toxemia pregnancy . . .

Although the exact mechanisms leading to obesity are often unclea the fact remains that for an individual to add fat to his body sto requires that he ingest more calories than he is expending in I daily activities. This can occur for several reasons: (1) Because fo intake is excessive; (2) because energy (caloric) expenditure is low than normal; (3) because minimum caloric needs are reduced as peop grow older; or (4) for any combination of these reasons.

Thus, the basic goals which underlie the treatment of obesity ar (1) to decrease energy intake and (2) to increase energy expenditu

GUIDE TO REDUCING ENERGY (CALORIC) INTAKE

The factors which influence eating patterns are complex and divers and the treatments for obesity are almost as numerous as the factor At the February 2, Obesity hearing, George Bray of Los Angel County Harbor General Hospital, in commenting on the success weight loss treatments, said:

What can we say about the long term effectiveness of these various approach to treating the overweight? We have little firm data. We do know that treatme of the overweight individual is often transient. Dr. Mayer has labelled this t "rhythm method of girth control". In long term follow-up studies, it is apparer that every program has some success, but that for most, less than 10 to 20 perce of the individuals who enter a treatment program other than surgery will solv their problems.

The evergrowing list of diets are an affirmation of the fact that no diet y described is by itself a solution to the problem of obesity. The truth of th statement is reflected in the fact that new diets appear yearly, each claiming t be the "ultimate solution." The list of diets include low carbohydrate diets, hig protein diets, high fat diets, and diets which contain mainly a single food. Y there is no substantive argument with the statement that "calories do count" i the development of obesity, and that diet, properly used, is a mainstay in th medical management of overweight people. For unless caloric intake is reduce below caloric needs, the extra calories which have been stored in adipose tissu will not be burned. There is a large and convincing body of information whic shows that if caloric restriction is sufficiently severe, and is maintained for sufficiently long period of time, body weight will decline.

Obesity experts differ as to the reasons for the general failure o many obese people to maintain weight loss. However, the obesit treatments which are the most successful over time tend to modify th total diet in a balanced manner.

The dietary pattern set forth in this report is a balanced approacl that addresses the interrelated nature of all the components whic. make up a total diet. The *Dietary Goals* should be of assistance i achieving success with respect to individual weight loss (as describ in other sections of the report) and reducing the prevalence of obesit in America.

To facilitate the use of the *Dietary Goals* and to ascertain to wha degree one is over optimal weight, we suggest use of Table 1 on page 10

Height	Men		Women	
	Average	Range	Average	Range
10 in.			102	92–119
11 in.			104	94–122
0 in.			107	96–125
1 in.			110	99–128
1 in.	123	112–141	113	102–131
2 in.	127	115–134	116	105–134
3 in.	130	118–148	120	108–138
4 in.	133	121–152	123	111–142
5 in.	136	124–156	128	114–146
6 in.	140	128–161	132	118–150
7 in.	145	132–166	136	122–154
8 in.	149	136–170	140	126–158
9 in.	153	140–174	144	130–163
10 in.	158	144–179	148	134–168
11 in.	162	148–184	512	138–173
0 in.	166	152–189		
1 in.	171	156–194		
2 in.	176	160–199		
3 in.	181	164–204		

[1] Height without shoes, weight without clothes. Adapted from the Table of the Metropolitan Life Insurance Co. (Courtesy the Metropolitan Life Insurance Co.)

GOAL 2. INCREASE THE CONSUMPTION OF COMPLEX CARBOHYDRATES AND "NATURALLY OCCURRING" [1] SUGARS FROM ABOUT 28 PERCENT OF ENERGY INTAKE TO ABOUT 48 PERCENT OF ENERGY INTAKE.

As discussed in the Preface, energy is provided by the carbohydrates, fats, protein and/or alcohol in food. Until the turn of the century, carbohydrates were the principal source of energy in the American diet. Figure 2 shows that since 1910 there has been a decrease in carbohydrate and an increase in fat as energy sources in the U.S. diet. Figure 3 indicates that sugars (simple carbohydrates) have replaced starch (a complex carbohydrate) as the primary form of carbohydrate in the diet. Figure 4 depicts the changes in the consumption of foods containing complex carbohydrates and "naturally occurring" sugars.

FIGURE 2

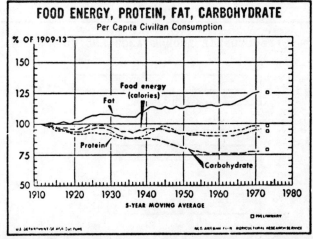

Source: "Changes in Nutrients in the U.S. Diet Caused by Alterations in Food Intake Patterns," B. Friend. Agricultural Research Service. U.S. Department of Agriculture.

There are several possible reasons for the decreasing consumption of foods containing complex carbohydrates. A key factor may be the rise in real income, permitting a movement away from diets high in

[1] "Naturally occurring": Sugars which are indigenous to a food, as opposed to refined (cane and beet) and processed (corn sugar, syrups, molasses and honey), sugars which may be added to a food product.

inexpensive foods, such as greens, beans and whole grains. Another related factor might be the prestige value associated with more expensive foods.

In addition, there is a relatively small amount of advertising of fruits, vegetables and whole grains. This point was raised by Dr. Joan Gussow, chairperson of the Program in Nutrition at Teachers College, Columbia University, at the Select Committee hearings in 1974 on National Nutrition Policy.

> . . . No amount of information about the nutritive or non-nutritive qualities of the foods advertised will compensate for the total imbalance in the nature of the foods advertised on television. The nature of the foods advertised is largely highly processed foods, many of them snack foods, highly sugared, highly salted. . . . We should have advertising of fruits and vegetables. They should be public service announcements selling people on those components of the diet which, in fact, they are not currently being sold on—dairy products, beans and rice and grains, and other forms of protein foods. . . . And all these foods don't get sold because they do not have a high enough mark-up.

FIGURE 3

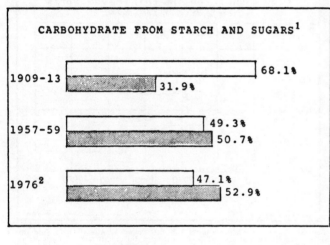

CARBOHYDRATE FROM STARCH AND SUGARS[1]

1909-13	68.1%	31.9%
1957-59	49.3%	50.7%
1976[2]	47.1%	52.9%

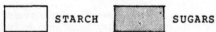

☐ STARCH   ▨ SUGARS

[1] Sugars include: 'naturally occurring' (milk products, vegetables and fruit), syrups, molasses, honey, cane and beet.
[2] Preliminary.

Source: *Nutritional Review*, National Food Situation, CFE (Adm.) 299-9, January 1975. Preliminary data for 1976 unpublished. Agricultural Research Service, U.S. Department of Agriculture.

The emphasis of food advertising is discussed in detail in Part II of this report.

FIGURE 4.—Changes in pounds (per capita, per year) of foods containing complex carbohydrates and "naturally occurring" sugars consumed between 1947–4 and 1976

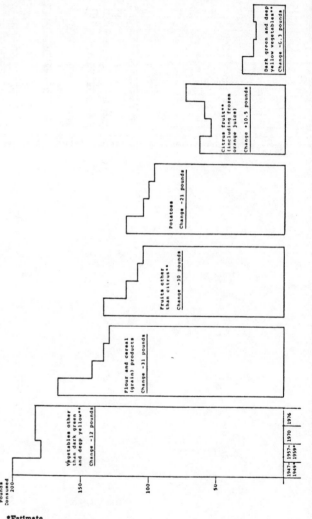

*Estimate.
**Fresh plus processed.

Source: Based on statistics in Nutritional Reviews CFE (Adm.) 299-11, January 19 Agricultural Research Service, U.S. Department of Agriculture.

Heart Disease

The displacement of foods containing complex carbohydrates, and "naturally occurring" sugars—fruit, vegetables and whole grains—may be a danger to health for several reasons. First, there is evidence that diets high in complex carbohydrates may reduce the risk of heart disease. Drs. William E. and Sonja J. Connor, writing in *Present Knowledge in Nutrition*, published in 1976 by the Nutrition Foundation, report:

Most population groups with a low incidence of coronary heart disease consume from 65 percent to 85 percent of their total energy in the form of carbohydrate derived from whole grains (cereals) and tubers (potatoes).

This point is made also by Dr. Jeremiah Stamler, chairman of the Department of Community Health and Preventive Medicine at Northwestern University, in *Atherosclerosis*, a publication designed to educate doctors on the relationship of diet to heart disease. He argues that moderate carbohydrate consumption does not elevate blood triglyceride and cholesterol levels but, in fact, apparently results in reduction in these risk factors. He reports:

My research colleague, Mario Mancini, has demonstrated that blood triglyceride and cholesterol levels are lower in southern Italians than in Britons, Swedes or Swiss despite the fact that their carbohydrate intake is higher—55 to 60 percent of calories instead of 40 to 55 percent—with most of it coming from starch.

Diet makes a difference in cholesterol levels as evidenced by the low levels among southern Italian workingmen who eat very little saturated (animal or dairy) fats, as compared to the upper-income southern Italians, northern Italians and Americans—all of whom eat more saturated fats.

Triglyceride and cholesterol levels usually have nothing to do with population or racial genetics because southern Italians who have emigrated to the United States develop the typical American higher blood levels as they become able to afford the high-saturated fat, high-cholesterol American diet.

In their report, the Connors conclude that:

High carbohydrate diets are quite appropriate for both normal individuals and for most of those with hyperlipidemia (high levels of fat in the blood), provided that the carbohydrate intake is largely derived from grains and tubers, that an energy excess is not consumed and that adiposity does not result. The use of high carbohydrate diets by civilized man has an historical basis, is economically sound and has every implication of causing less, rather than more, disease especially in the coronary heart disease-hyperlipidemia area.

Diabetes

The cause or causes of diabetes are still unknown. However, the handling of the diets for the treatment of diabetes may give some insight on how to prevent diabetes. For example, the Connors also report that the high complex carbohydrate diet is important in the treatment of diabetics because it reduces the threat of atherosclerosis and hyperlipidemia, which are common to diabetics, by lowering cholesterol and saturated fat levels. The Connors note that some diabetics find a high carbohydrate diet also results in improved glucose tolerance; in others insulin requirements have been stabilized.

Dietary Fiber

The dietary fiber which occurs in foods containing complex carbohydrates may also be beneficial. Dietary fiber may be divided generally into two categories, according to Dr. P. J. Van Soest, of the Department of Animal Science at Cornell University, the more mature, less fermentable and digestible bran fiber from grains, and the less mature more fermentable and digestible fiber from fruits and vegetables. It is probable, he says, that both kinds of dietary fiber are important to nutrition, but relatively little is known about the properties of dietary fiber and its role in nutrition.

Dr. Denis P. Burkitt, among the first advocates of the high fiber diet, has postulated that an increase in fiber consumption, preferably natural fiber rather than fiber added to refined products such as white bread, will markedly reduce the incidence of bowel cancer and other diseases, primarily those of the intestine.

Dietary fiber and/or phytate, which occurs in foods that also contain dietary fiber, bind certain minerals (iron, zinc, copper, magnesium, calcium and chromium) and therefore, may reduce their absorption. This possibility and the fact that relatively little is known about the properties of dietary fiber, suggest that an extreme increase in complex carbohydrate consumption should be avoided in order to reduce the possibility of mineral deficiencies or other health problems from occurring. However, if a person consumes a balanced mix of foods when increasing his or her consumption of complex carbohydrates to attain this Dietary Goal, then there appears to be no likelihood of any mineral deficiency or other health problems occurring.

Vitamin and Mineral Sources

Increased consumption of fruit, vegetables and whole grains is also important with respect to supplying adequate amounts of micronutrients, vitamins and minerals. This is particularly important for those who are limiting their food intake to control weight or save money. For many people consumption may be reaching a critical level below which it may be difficult to obtain adequate levels of micro-nutrients from the volumes of food consumed. Under these circumstances, it is essential to eat foods that maximize the potential for consuming a broad range of micro-nutrients.

Fats and refined and processed sugars, the principal macro-nutrients that have displaced complex carbohydrates, are, as Table 2 shows, relatively poor sources of micro-nutrients, particularly in view of the levels of calories they induce.

It is important to note that knowledge of the full range of micro-nutrients has not been developed. For example, inquiry is only beginning into the function of elements such as chromium, selenium, vanadium and others, which appear to have important regulatory functions in and between cells. Furthermore, there is only limited knowledge of human requirements for most nutrients, as shown in Appendix C, prepared by the Department of Agriculture.

Consequently, although vitamin and mineral supplements and nutrient fortification may improve chances for obtaining micro-nutrients, they cannot be seen as substitutes for food. Nor can it be assumed that taking supplements and/or eating fortified foods, while continuing to eat a diet high in fats and refined and processed sugars, will meet one's nutrient needs.

Obesity

Finally, an increase in the consumption of complex carbohydrates is likely to ease the problem of weight control. As suggested above, displacing fats and refined and processed sugars reduces the risk of obesity. Furthermore, the high water content and bulk of fruits and vegetables and bulk of whole grain can bring a longer lasting satisfaction of appetite more quickly than do foods high in fats and refined and processed sugars.

TABLE 2.—NUTRIENT LEVELS IN FATS AND SUGARS

[Nutrients in edible portion of 1 pound of food as purchased]

	Food energy (calories)	Proteins (grams)	Fat (grams)	Carbo-hydrates (grams)	Calcium (milli-grams)	Phos-phorus (milli-grams)	Iron (milli-grams)	Sodium (milli-grams)	Potas-sium (milli-grams)	Vitamin A (I.U.)	Thia-mine (milli-grams)	Ribo-flavin (milli-grams)	Niacin (milli-grams)	Ascorbic acid (milli-grams)
Fats:														
Butter	3,248	2.7	367.0	1.8	91	73	0	4,477	104	15,000	0	0	0	0
Lard	4,091	0	454.0	0	0	0	0			0				0
Cooking and salad oils	4,010	0	454.0	0	0	0	0			0				0
Sugars:														
Beet or cane, brown	1,692	0	0	437.3	386	86	15.4	136	1,560	0	0.05	0.15	0.8	0
Granulated	1,746	0	0	451.3	0	0	.5	5	14	0	0	0	0	0
Powdered	1,746	0	0	451.3	0	0	.5	5	14	0	0	0	0	0
Dextrose crystallized	1,520	0	0	413.0	0	0	Trace							0
Maple	1,579			408.0	649	50	6.4	64	1,098					0
Apple (fresh)	252	.8	2.5	60.5	29	42	1.1	4	459	380	.12	.08	.3	16
Orange (fresh)	180	5.8	1.3	69.6	314	99	3.6	9	880	1,120	.45	.22	2.2	319

Source: U.S. Department of Agriculture, Handbook 8.

1. FRUITS AND VEGETABLES

A Department of Agriculture report published in 1972 found that nutrient availability from fruits and vegetables had declined with increased use of canned, frozen and dried produce and shifts in consumption away from such vegetables as white and sweet potatoes, dark green and yellow vegetables, dry beans and dry peas, and grain products. The report, entitled *Trends in Fresh Fruit and Vegetable Consumption and Their Nutritional Implications*, said:

> The shift from the uses of fresh fruits and vegetables to processed (shown in figure 5), as well as changes in selection among different fruits and vegetables have resulted in some significant trends in nutrients obtained from this food group. The amount of vitamin A obtained from fruits and vegetables has declined 11 percent since 1925–29, and 18 percent since 1947–49. Vitamin B₆ and magnesium declined by nearly 20 percent since 1925–29, while the amount of thiamin obtained from fruits and vegetables declined almost 10 percent.

It appears that increased consumption of fresh fruits and vegetables, particularly the high nutrient forms, would be beneficial for many persons in need of dietary improvement. Educating consumers, particularly those of low income, to the greater advantage of the most economical and most nutritious fruits and vegetables, would offer a great potential for dietary improvement.

FIGURE 5.—Trends in consumption of fresh and processed fruits and vegetables

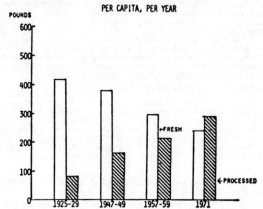

PER CAPITA, PER YEAR

¹ Includes potatoes and sweet potatoes.

Source: "Trends in Fresh Fruit and Vegetable Consumption, Nutritional Qualities of Fresh Fruits and Vegetables," Futura Publishing Co., Mount Kisco, N.Y., 1974.

Although canned and frozen fruits and vegetables are normally processed within hours of harvesting, if fruits and vegetables are used directly from the garden, it is likely that their nutrient content will exceed that of their processed counterparts, as indicated in a report by Dr. Owen Fennema, professor of Food Chemistry at Northwestern University, appearing in *Nutritional Evaluation of Food Processing*.[2] However, he and other experts say that fresh fruits and vegetables in the supermarket may have undergone nutrient-depletion in shipping and storage, and consequently frozen varieties may provide equivalent or better nutritional values. A similar position is taken in *Diet and Exercise*, published by the Swedish government to promote its nutrition and physical fitness program, which says: "Deep frozen and fresh vegetables are of equal value from a nutritional point of view."

On the other hand, it is also true that although considerable knowledge has been gathered about the nutritional impact of freezing, canning and other processing, this knowledge is not held for all nutrients, all foods or all processes. Furthermore, it is important to understand the degree of our ignorance about what constitutes food value. Out of more than 50 known nutrients, Recommended Dietary Allowances have been established for only 17. In addition, there is no definitive evidence that food composition described solely in terms of all known nutrients would be an accurate measure of total food value.

Consequently, it would seem advisable to create at least a balance in the diet between fresh and processed produce. When considering whether to use canned or frozen produce, one should weigh nutritional value, cost, convenience and ingredients such as salt and sugar that are added. While the amount of nutrients, particularly specific vitamins, obtained in the diet from either canned or frozen produce may be relatively small—depending on one's food selection—canned produce is generally thought to have retained less nutrients than frozen or fresh. Of course, to gain the maximum advantage of the nutrients in all three forms of produce requires proper preparation in the home. In addition, it would appear to be prudent to increase consumption of potatoes and dark leafy vegetables because of nutrient content and the varieties of fiber they may offer.

A shift to more use of fresh produce not only offers greater opportunity for micro-nutrient consumption, but increases control over use of food additives. Refined sugars and salt are the two foremost food additives. The health aspects of these additives and non-nutritive additives such as colorings and flavorings, will be discussed later.

Finally, the use of fresh produce also removes food from the processing system in which a sizeable portion of food prices may result from nonfood costs such as packaging, advertising and any added cost that may accrue to imperfect competition in food manufacturing, a condition which has been discussed in a variety of reports including that of the Food Marketing Commission in 1965 and more recently at hearings of the Select Committee in October 1975.

Refinement

Highly-refined fruits and vegetables generally should not be viewed as nutritional equivalents or substitutes for the same food in its fresh form. For example, Table 3 shows that potato chips and dehydrated potatoes should not be thought of as the nutritional equivalent of fresh, baked potatoes. In addition, it is apparent that potato chips carry significantly more fat than the baked or mashed form: potato chips are 40 percent fat compared to 0.1 percent fat in baked potatoes.

Although it would be possible to restore vitamin C and certain other nutrients through fortification, it is doubtful that the numbers and balance of nutrients in the fresh form could ever be duplicated. In addition, it is not known how processing may affect fiber composition.

Several nutritionists and food technologists interviewed in preparation of this report said that the decline in nutrient content in various individual food items may not be important because the nutrients needed for optimal health are likely to be readily available in the great abundance of food in the marketplace.

[2] *Nutritional Evaluation of Food Processing*, 1975. Nutritional Aspects of Food Processing Methods, pp. 11–15; Effects of Freeze-Preservation on Nutrients, pp. 244–288.

It is important to understand, however, that several studies sugges that more than 50 percent of the United States diet undergoes som form of processing before it enters the home.[3] Given the need to maxi mize micro-nutrient availability for those on reduced diets; the nee to ensure adequate nutrient availability to those who do not widel vary their diets; and the need to maximize the nutritional power o the food supply; it would seem prudent not only to increase use o fresh foods but also those undergoing the least processing.

2. GRAIN PRODUCTS

Of the grain products, bread is the most widely consumed (Fig. 6) However, bread consumption has been declining in the United States in part perhaps because it has been viewed, incorrectly, as fattening Bread is of intermediate caloric density, and a relatively good pro tein source. Professor Olaf Mickelsen of Michigan State University reports in *Cereal Foods World*, of July 1975:

> Contrary to what most people think, bread in large amounts is an ideal foo in a weight reducing regimen. Recent work in our laboratory indicates tha slightly overweight young men lost weight in a painless and practically effort less manner when they included 12 slices of bread per day in their program. Tha bread was eaten with their meals. As a result, they became satisfied before the consumed their usual quota of calories. The subjects were admonished to restric those foods that were concentrated sources of energy: otherwise, they were fre to eat as much as they desired. In eight weeks, the average weight loss for each subject was 12.7 pounds.

FIGURE 6

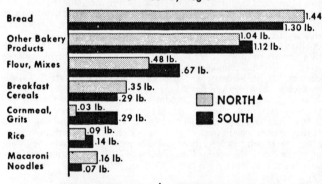

GRAIN PRODUCTS USED PER PERSON
Per Week by Region

Bread — 1.44 lb / 1.30 lb
Other Bakery Products — 1.04 lb / 1.12 lb
Flour, Mixes — .48 lb / .67 lb
Breakfast Cereals — .35 lb / .29 lb
Cornmeal, Grits — .03 lb / .29 lb
Rice — .09 lb / .14 lb
Macaroni Noodles — .16 lb / .07 lb

NORTH▲   SOUTH

QUANTITIES AS PURCHASED   ▲ NORTHEAST, NORTH CENTRAL, WEST
HOUSEHOLDS WITH INCOMES OF $5,000 -9,999 1 WEEK IN SPRING, 1965

U.S. DEPARTMENT OF AGRICULTURE   NEG ARS. 5944-69 (4) AGRICULTURAL RESEARCH SERVICE

[3] *Human Nutrition*, Jean Mayer, 1972. pg. 657. *Total Consumer Buying of Fresh Versu Processed Foods Remains Stable.* Alden C. Manchester. Economic Research Service, U. Department of Agriculture, NFS-144, May 1973 (Unpublished 1975 fizures show tren stable.) *Anticipating Public Policy Issues: Nutrition, Diet, Health and Food Qualit,* Graham T. T. Molitor. Unpublished report prepared for the General Accounting Offic July 1976. pg. 164.

TABLE 3.—NUTRITIVE VALUES FOR VARIOUS FORMS OF POTATOES

Fresh	Grams	Water (percent)	Food energy (calories)	Protein (grams)	Carbo-hydrate (grams)	Fat (grams)	Iron (milligrams)	Thiamin (milligrams)	Riboflavin (milligrams)	Niacin (milligrams)	Vitamin C (milligrams)
Baked (1 potato)	202	75.1	145	4.0	32.8	0.2	1.1	0.15	0.07	2.7	31
Mashed (1 cup, milk added)	210	82.8	137	4.4	27.3	1.5	.8	.17	.11	2.1	21
French fries (10 strips, frozen, oven heated)	78	52.9	172	2.8	26.3	6.6	1.4	.11	.02	2.0	16
Dehydrated:											
(a) Flakes (1 cup, dry form)	45	5.2	164	3.2	37.8	.3	.8	.19	.03	2.4	14
(b) Flakes (1 cup, prepared with milk, water, table fat, salt.)	210	79.3	195	4.0	30.5	6.7	.6	.08	.08	1.9	11
Potato chips (10 chips)	20	1.8	114	1.1	10.0	8.0	.4	.04	.01	1.0	3

1 teaspoon of margarine=5 gms of fat

Source: "Nutritive Value of American Foods in Common Units; Agriculture Handbook No. 456," Agricultural, Research Service. U.S. Department of Agriculture.

Another study by Mickelsen found that 12 young men could obtain 90 to 95 percent of their protein needs from white enriched bread. In some countries bread may contribute as much as 80 percent of protein needs.

There are also arguments, though somewhat less conclusive, suggesting not only that increased bread consumption is warranted but that more whole wheat bread should be eaten. There have been no studies that have found whole wheat flour to be superior nutritionally to white flour when consumed in a normal diet, and surprisingly few studies have even considered the question.

However, whole wheat bread may provide more micro-nutrients and definitely provides more fiber than white bread.

White bread is made from wheat that has undergone a degree of milling that removes large amounts of bran and wheat germ. A report at the 1976 Convention of the American Association of Cereal Chemists [4] estimated that the average milling level in the United States is 76 percent extraction, meaning that about 76 percent of the wheat kernel has been retained. One hundred percent extraction flour is whole wheat flour. Figure 7 shows how various levels of milling affect various micro-nutrients, and Table 4 from an unpublished report by Doris Baker, of the Department of Agriculture, shows the degree to which milling may reduce fiber content.

In bread, as with other foods undergoing processing, there is the danger that, as the degree of processing increases, nutrients, known and unknown, are removed or altered in ways not currently understood.

[4] *Natural Levels of Vitamins and Minerals in Commercially Milled Wheat Flour in the United States and Canada* (Flour Base Line Study for the American Bakers Association Ad Hoc Industry Committee on Fortification of Cereals). Paul J. Mattern, University of Nebraska, chairman of panel presenting report.

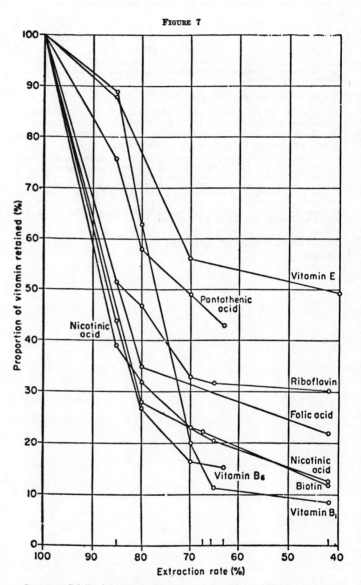

FIGURE 7

COMMENT.—Relation between extraction rate and proportion of total vitamins of the grain retained in flour. (Reproduced from "Wheat in Human Nutrition" (Food and Agriculture Organization, Rome, 1970, p. 90)).

303

TABLE 4.—FIBER CONTENT IN [In grams] WHITE VS. WHOLE WHEAT BREAD

Type bread	Fiber content by various determinations			
	Crude fiber	Acid	Buffered	Neutral
White:				
No. 1	1.3	1.2	8.8	2.8
No. 2	.9	1.5	9.3	2.9
Whole:				
No. 1	2.7	2.8	12.3	6.6
No. 2	2.6	2.6	12.9	5.1
No. 3	3.2	3.1	11.5	7.3

Source: U.S. Department of Agriculture. "Fiber in Wheat Foods," a study presented by Doris Baker at 1976 Convention of the American Association of Cereal Chemists.

Conserving Nutrient Resources

The reduction of milling also acts to conserve food resources, as pointed out in a compendium on bread, prepared for classroom use by Dr. Paul Seib, Associate Professor in the Department of Grain Science and Industry at Kansas State University:

... White bread represents a less efficient use of the nutrients in wheat than whole wheat. If one uses whole wheat flour instead of white flour for every 100 gm. of wheat we gain 30 g. of material containing: (a) 93 kcal. in bread of which 73 percent is digestible energy for a net gain of 63 kcal., and (b) 4.65 g. of protein of which 73 percent is digestible for a net gain of 3.4 g. of protein. Since flour-milling by-products go to animal feeds in the U.S., where they are converted to meat at an efficiency of about 10–25 percent, a loss in energy and protein value is sustained by not eating whole wheat bread.

Even greater conservation of resources might be possible if grains carried a larger share of the protein burden, as they did earlier in the century.

TABLE 5.—NUTRIENT CONTENT OF SELECTED GRAINS

	Water (percent)	Food energy (calories)	Protein (grams)	Fat (grams)	Carbohydrate (grams)	Calcium (milligrams)	Phosphorus (milligrams)	Iron (milligrams)	Sodium (milligrams)	Potassium (milligrams)	Vitamin A (milligrams)	Thiamine (milligrams)	Riboflavin (milligrams)	Niacin (milligrams)	Vitamin C (milligrams)
Whole grain wheat (Hard Red Spring)	13.0	330	14.0	2.2	69.1	36	383	3.1	(3)	370	(0)	0.57	0.12	4.3	(0)
Whole wheat flour (hard wheats)	12.0	333	13.3	2.0	71.0	41	372	3.3	3	370	(0)	.55	.12	4.3	(0)
80 percent extraction wheat flour (hard wheats)	12.0	365	12.0	1.3	74.1	24	191	1.3	2	95	(0)	.26	.07	2.0	(0)
Bread flour enriched (hard wheats)	12.0	365	11.8	1.1	74.7	16	95	[2]2.9	2	95	(0)	[1].44	[1].26	[1]3.5	(0)
Brown rice cooked	70.3	119	2.5	.6	25.5	12	73	.5		70	(0)	.09	.02	1.4	(0)
White rice cooked (enriched)	72.6	109	2.0	.1	24.2	10	28	[2].9	374	28	(0)	[1].11	[3](2)	[1]1.0	(0)
White rice instant cooked (enriched)	72.9	109	2.2	Trace	24.2	3	19	[2].8	273	Trace	(0)	[1].13	[3]2	[1]1.0	(0)
Cornmeal, white or yellow unbolted (whole grain)	12	355	9.2	3.9	73.7	20	256	2.4	(1)	(284)	[4]510	.38	.11	2.0	(0)
Cornmeal, degermed dry enriched	12	364	7.9	1.2	78.4	6	99	[2]2.9	(3)	120	440	[1].44	[1].26	[1]3.5	(0)
Rye (whole grain)	11	334	12.1	1.7	73.4	(38)	376	3.7	(3)	467	(0)	.43	.22	1.6	(0)
Rye flour (light)	11	357	9.4	1.0	77.9	22	185	1.1	(1)	156	(0)	.15	.07	.6	(0)

[1] Based on product with minimum level of enrichment.
[2] Values for iron, thiamin and niacin are based on the minimum levels of enrichment specified in standards of identity.
[3] Riboflavin enrichment standard pending further hearings.
[4] Based on yellow varieties.

Source: Agriculture Handbook 8, U.S. Department of Agriculture, 1963.

Selecting Grain Products

Table 5 compares nutrients offered in various grains and grain products. Table 6, from Frances Moore Lappe's *Diet for a Small Planet*, offers a comparison of costs of grain protein versus other protein sources.

As is apparent in Table 5, the common side-dish rice suffers in processing. The hierarchy of nutrient value in rice, from most to least:

    Brown rice
    Parboiled (converted) rice
    Common white enriched rice
    Instant rice

Hot cooked breakfast cereals are generally less refined and processed and less expensive than ready-to-eat cereals. Of the hot cereals (wheat, rye or oat), whole grained cereals are most nutritious, according to Ruth Fremes and Dr. Zak Sabry in *NutriScore* (Fremes is a Canadian home economist and Sabry headed Nutrition Canada, that nation's recent nutrition survey). Less nutritious are cream of wheat and corn meal. The authors point out also that "infant" and "quick" cat cereals may have less nutrients than their longer-cooking counterparts.

TABLE 6.—Protein cost

Source: Frances Moore Lappe, "Diet for a Small Planet," 1971.

In ready-to-eat cereals, sugar-coated cereals should be avoided, and *NutriScore* explains that granola also offers high caloric intake for the amounts of nutrients available. The book says:

Granola does have *slightly* more protein, calcium, riboflavin and niacin than plain cereals, but the difference is not great enough to make this a special reason for buying it. Its major disadvantages are its high caloric value, its high content, the high saturation of fat in the shredded coconut and its high cost.

Flaked, shredded and puffed cereals may be enriched, but Fremes and Sabry note that many trace elements are not added, nor is fiber, and so, the enriched refined cereal is never as good nutritionally as the wholesome unrefined cereal."

GOAL 3. REDUCE THE CONSUMPTION OF REFINED AND OTHER PROCESSED SUGARS BY ABOUT 45 PERCENT TO ACCOUNT FOR ABOUT, 10 PERCENT OF TOTAL ENERGY INTAKE

Figure 3 (p. 12) from an article by Louise Page and Berta Friend, of the U.S. Department of Agriculture, appearing in "Sugars in Nutrition" published by the Nutrition Foundation, shows that various kinds of sugar accounted for only 32 percent of total carbohydrate consumption in the period 1909 to 1913. However, by 1976, sugars had replaced starch and other complex carbohydrates, as the predominate carbohydrate source. Thus the consumption of all types of sugars has increased from 18 percent of total caloric intake to approximately 24 percent, and the consumption of refined sugar (cane and beet) has increased from 12 percent of total caloric intake to approximately 18 percent. Figure 8 indicates per capita consumption in pounds of refined and processed sugars since 1875, and Table 7 details per capita consumption of caloric sweeteners, 1960–76.

(27)

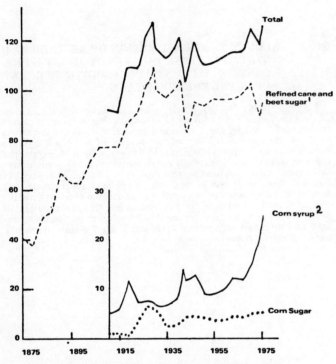

FIGURE 8.—Per capita sugar consumption—United States

[1] Sucrose.
[2] Glucose and frutose.

SOURCES: 1875–1909: U.S. Bureau of Census—*"Historical Statistics of U.S.–Colonial times to 1959."* (1960) p. 187. 1910–1965: USDA Rep. #138 (1968) p. 84. 1966–76: Sugar and Sweetener Report. (May, 1977) p. 31. 1976-preliminary figure.

TABLE 7.—CALORIC SWEETENERS: PER CAPITA U.S. CONSUMPTION, 1960–76 [1]

[In pounds]

Calendar year	Refined cane and beet sugar						Corn sweeteners [2]					Minor caloric [2]			Total caloric
	U.S. grown sugar			Cane sugar		Total	Corn sirup		Dextrose	Total		Honey	Edible sirups	Total	
	Beet sugar	Cane sugar	Total	Imported	Total		High-fructose	Other							
1960	25.2	28.1	53.3	44.0	72.4	97.6	------	8.2	3.4	11.6	1.2	0.8	2.0	111.2
1961	26.1	28.7	54.8	43.0	71.7	97.8	------	8.6	3.4	12.0	1.1	.9	1.9	111.7
1962	23.9	28.0	51.9	45.4	73.4	97.3	------	9.3	3.6	12.9	1.1	.7	2.0	112.2
1963	27.2	27.8	55.0	41.7	56.5	96.7	------	9.9	4.3	14.2	1.1	.7	1.8	112.7
1964	28.4	30.3	58.8	37.9	68.2	96.7	------	10.0	4.1	15.0	1.0	.7	1.7	113.4
1965	28.3	28.6	59.7	38.1	66.2	96.8	------	11.0	4.1	15.4	1.0	.5	1.8	113.7
1966	26.6	29.9	56.5	40.3	69.7	98.2	------	11.9	4.2	16.1	.9	.7	1.4	114.8
1967	27.8	26.5	56.5	41.8	71.2	98.3	------	12.6	4.3	16.9	.9	.6	1.6	115.7
1968	30.1	25.2	54.3	44.7	70.6	99.0	------	13.2	4.5	17.7	1.0	.5	1.6	117.5
1969	31.4	25.0	55.3	45.4	70.5	100.7	------	14.0	4.6	18.6	1.0	.5	1.4	120.0
1970	31.1	25.4	56.4	45.5	71.3	101.9	------	15.6	5.0	20.0	.8	.5	1.5	122.0
1971	30.4	25.8	55.8	48.5	72.4	102.4	------	16.7	4.4	20.9	1.0	.5	1.4	123.8
1972	30.1	25.4	55.3	47.0	71.1	102.8	0.9	16.4	4.9	22.9	1.0	.4	1.3	125.2
1973	24.9	24.0	47.4	46.2	70.5	101.5	1.4	17.7	5.1	24.6	.8	.4		125.8
1974	30.5	24.9	46.5	59.7	96.6		2.7			25.6		.4		122.4
1975 [3]		24.9	55.4	49.5	38.8	96.2	4.7						1.3	122.0
1976 [4]	33.3	23.5	56.8	38.3	61.8	95.1	7.1	17.7	5.1	29.9	1.0	.4	4.1	126.4

[1] U.S. Department of Agriculture, Sugar and Sweetener Report, SSR vol. 2, February 1977.
[2] Dry basis. Recent corn sweetener consumption may be understated due to incomplete data.
[3] Preliminary.
[4] Estimate.

The largest components in the sugars category are refined sugar (cane and beet), which accounts for 14 percent of total calories, and processed sugars (corn sugar, syrups, molasses and honey), which account for 4 percent of total calories. The other 6 percent of total calories consumed as sugar are obtained from fruit, vegetables and milk products.

The greatest impetus for the increased use of sugars apparently has come from the addition of refined sugar (cane and beet) to processed foods. Figure 9, also from the Page/Friend article, shows the dramatic increase in the use of refined sugar added outside the control of the consumer.

Page and Friend report:

Use in processed food products and beverages has increased more than three-fold from nearly 20 to 70 lbs., while household purchase has dropped one-half from a little more than 50 to about 25 lb. Currently, food products and beverages account for more than two-thirds of the refined sugar consumed—70 lb. out of a little over 100 lb. Moreover, beverages now comprise the largest single industry use of refined sugar, accounting for over one-fifth of the total refined sugar in the United States diet, or nearly 23 lb. Furthermore, the amount used in beverages has increased nearly sevenfold since early in the century when 3½ lb./person/year was used in these products. Use of refined sugar in beverages is now second only to household use.

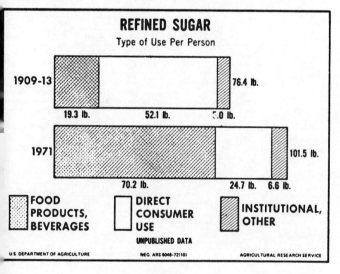

REFINED SUGAR

Type of Use Per Person

1909-13		76.4 lb.
19.3 lb.	52.1 lb.	5.0 lb.
1971		101.5 lb.
70.2 lb.	24.7 lb.	6.6 lb.

☐ FOOD PRODUCTS, BEVERAGES   ☐ DIRECT CONSUMER USE   ☐ INSTITUTIONAL, OTHER

UNPUBLISHED DATA

U.S. DEPARTMENT OF AGRICULTURE   NEG. ARS 6048-72(10)   AGRICULTURAL RESEARCH SERVICE

FIGURE 9

Table 8, provided by Page and Friend, shows changes in refined sugar used in this century.

TABLE 8.—REFINED SUGAR, ESTIMATED PER CAPITA CONSUMPTION BY TYPE OF USE, SELECTED PERIODS, 1909-13 TO 1971 [1]

[In pounds]

Type of use	1909-13	1925-29	1935-39	1947-49	1957-59	1965	1971 (preliminary)
In processed foods:							
Cereal and bakery products	4.5	7.7	9.7	12.9	15.4	15.6	17.6
Confectionery products	6.5	8.0	8.2	9.8	9.6	10.4	11.0
Processed fruits and vegetables [2]	3.0	4.6	4.4	9.0	9.8	9.5	10.4
Dairy products	1.5	2.3	2.4	4.6	4.9	5.3	5.8
Other food products [3]	.3	.7	1.2	1.5	1.7	2.5	2.6
Total food products	15.8	23.4	25.9	37.8	41.4	43.4	47.4
Beverages (largely in soft drinks)	3.5	5.0	5.2	10.6	12.6	16.9	22.8
Total processed food and beverages	19.3	28.4	31.1	48.4	54.0	60.2	70.2
Other food uses:							
Eating and drinking places [4]	4.5	5.7	6.3	7.7	7.3	6.2	5.5
Household [5]	52.1	65.0	58.8	37.4	33.1	28.2	24.7
Institutional and other use [6]	.5	.9	.9	1.3	1.0	1.4	1.1
Total	57.1	71.6	66.0	46.4	41.4	35.8	31.3
Total food use	76.4	100.0	97.1	94.8	95.4	96.0	101.5
Nonfood use [7]	.3	.4	.4	.4	.7	.6	.9
Total consumption	76.7	100.4	97.5	95.2	96.1	96.6	102.4

[1] Prepared by Food Consumption Section, Economic Research Service, U.S. Department of Agriculture.
[2] Canned, bottled, and frozen foods (processed fruit and vegetable products); jams, jellies, and preserves.
[3] Includes miscellaneous food uses such as meat curing, and syrup blending.
[4] Includes hotels, motels, restaurants, cafeterias, and other eating and drinking establishments.
[5] Household use assumed synonymous with deliveries in consumer-sized packages (less than 50 lb).
[6] Largely for military use.
[7] Includes use in pharmaceuticals, tobacco, and other nonfood use.

Source: "Sugars in Nutrition," Levels of Uses of Sugar in the United States, L. Page, B. Friend, 1974.

This increased use of refined sugar is traceable in large part to the desire of food manufacturers to create unique food products with a competitive edge. Just recently, for example, Nabisco introduced an Oreo cookie with double the amount of sugar filling. Robert Buzzell and Robert Nourse in "Product Innovation in Food Processing" report that the addition of sugar to cereal in 1948 was the direct cause of recovery of slumping cereal sales. Since then, the varieties of sweetened cereals have grown dramatically. The profusion of varieties of cereals, soft drinks and other products represent efforts to protect market shares.

Dental Disease

Sugars, particularly foods that contain sticky forms of refined and processed sugars (taffy-like candies, sugar-coated cereals, granolas, raisins and other dried fruits) have been implicated in tooth decay, which may be the most widespread disease related to nutrition. The consumption of sugars can lead to cavities (caries) in children and adults, and gum disease and eventual loss of teeth (periodontal disease) in adults. Dr. Mayer, citing a government survey, said in the *Times* article:

In nations of the Far East, where sugar intake per person per year ranged (at the time) from 12 to 32 pounds, the national averages for decayed, missing or filled teeth in adults 20 to 24 years old ran from 0.9 to 5. By contrast, in South American nations, where sugar intake was high (44 to 88 pounds per person annually) the averages for decayed, missing or filled teeth in the same age group ran from 8.4 to 12.6. As for the United States today, it has been estimated that 98 percent of American children have some tooth decay; by age 55 about half of the population of this country have no teeth.

Nutrient Danger

The most important problem, perhaps, is the danger in displacing complex carbohydrates which are high in micro-nutrients, with refined sugar, which is essentially an energy source offering little other nutritional value. This not only increases the potential for depriving the body of essential micro-nutrients but, noted Dr. Jean Mayer in an article in the "New York Times Magazine" in June 1976, sugar calories may actually increase the body's need for certain vitamins.

(Sugar calories) increase requirements for certain vitamins, like thiamin, which are needed (for the body) to metabolize carbohydrates. They may increase the need for the trace mineral, chromium, as well.

Thus, a greater burden is placed on the other components of the diet to contribute all the necessary nutrients—other foods need to show extraordinary "nutrient density" to compensate for the emptiness of the sugar calories.

Diabetes

The role of refined sugar in the development of diabetes is unclear, largely because the cause or causes of diabetes are still unknown. Many researchers who have been before the Select Committee believe there is no relationship between the level of refined sugar consumption and the occurrence of diabetes.

On the other hand there are a few researchers who believe there is a connection between the increasingly larger proportion of refined sugar calories in the diet and the higher incidence of diabetes. Dr. A. M. Cohen and associates report in "Sugars in Nutrition" that rats with a genetic predisposition to diabetes will develop the disease when exposed to high refined sugar diets and that they can be prevented from contracting it with a sugar-free diet. It is not yet known whether or not some humans may have a genetic tendency comparable to that reported by Dr. Cohen in his rat experiments.

Dr. Mayer noted in an article in the *Los Angeles Times* in October 1975, that several epidemiological studies indicate a connection between high refined sugar use and diabetes. For example, Yemenite Jewish immigrants to Israel had a low incidence of diabetes until they had consumed a Westernized diet high in sugar for several years. However, other simultaneous changes such as an increased energy intake might also have contributed to the increased incidence of diabetes among these Yemenites.

These considerations have led to a number of governmental and professional health organizations in the United States, and other nations, cited earlier, to recommend a general decrease in sugar consumption (Appendix B).

In "Sugars in Nutrition," Dr. Arvid Wretlind, of the Nutrition Unit, Karolinska Institutet, Stockholm, writing about refined sugar usage in Europe, suggests that sugar consumption be reduced to 10 percent of calories.

In Europe there has been, and in some countries still is, a continuous increase in sugar consumption. In some of these countries the sugar content of the diet has reached a level between 15 and 18 percent of calories. The increase in sugar consumption, followed by an increased fat intake will, generally speaking, result in a decreased content of essential nutrients and in a reduced consumption of other foods which contain not only energy but also valuable nutrients. The conclusion is that the amount of sugar in a moderate diet should be moderate. maximum level of 10. cal/percent is proposed.

Reducing the consumption of refined and processed sugars to above 10 percent of caloric intake is an equally reasonable goal for the United States, and would return the consumption of such sugars to a point slightly below that of the early 1900's.

GUIDE TO REDUCING THE INTAKE OF REFINED AND PROCESSED SUGAR

In reviewing ways of cutting the consumption of refined and processed sugars, the most obvious item for general reduction is soft drinks. Total elimination of soft drinks from the diet, for many people, would bring at least half the recommended reduction in the consumption of such sugars.

Soft drink consumption in the United States doubled between 1960 and 1975, rising from 13.6 gallons a year to 27.6, as shown in Table 9 from the Department of Agriculture's "Sugar and Sweetener Report," September 1976. This translates into 221 sixteen-ounce cans and 21.5 pounds of refined and processed sugar a year.

TABLE 9.—SOFT DRINK SALES, PER CAPITA CONSUMPTION AND AMOUNTS AND VALUE OF SUGAR USED MANUFACTURE, 1960-75

	Sales (millions)	Per capita soft drink consumption		Per capita sugar consumption (pounds)	Value su (millio
		16-oz	Gallons		
Year:					
1960	$1,857	109	13.6	11.3	$
1965	3,195	154	19.2	15.2	
1970	5,016	193	24.1	19.2	
1975	9,426	221	27.6	21.5	1,

Source: Sugar and Sweetener Report, vol. 1, No. 8, September 1976 Economic Research Service, U.S. Department Agriculture.

This increase has evidently been made at the expense of increases some more nutritious beverages. As Table 10 shows, between 1962 and 1975, soft drinks became the second most highly consumed beverage displacing milk. Currently, soft drinks compete with coffee for first place.

TABLE 10.—TRENDS IN BEVERAGE CONSUMPTION

[Gallons, per capita, per year]

Beverage	1962 [1]	
Coffee	40.4	3
Milk	25.6	2
Soft drinks	16.8	3
Juices	4.3	

[1] Earliest data available.

Source: Copyright, John C. Maxwell, Jr., Maxwell Associates, Richmond, Va.

Another source of concern is the caffeine in cola soft drinks, which account for about 65 percent of total drink consumption (at least one non-cola also contains caffeine). Medical World News, of January 197 reports that suspected connections between caffeine and ulcers, hea

308

disease and bladder cancer have been investigated but that evidence is not strong enough to cause caffeine to be adjudged a risk factor in these diseases. There have been findings of withdrawal symptoms of headache, nervousness and irritability among subjects deprived of normal coffee doses as well as similar symptoms among those who may have ingested too much caffeine. The report said colas are of special concern since they are the major caffeine source for most children.

(Doctors, particularly pediatricians) have reported signs—including irritability, headaches, and nervousness—of what has come to be known as "caffeinism" among cola-guzzling youngsters whose total caffeine intake (30 mg per 8-oz. can) may be boosted by cocoa or hot chocolate (up to 50 mg per 5-oz. cup) and chocolate bars (25 mg).

Reduction in soft drink consumption also offers the advantage of reducing consumption of non-nutritive additives, colors, flavors, and preservatives.

The second major area for consideration in cutting the consumption of refined and processed sugars is baked goods, reported by Page and Friend to be the second highest source of sugar use. In this area, as in others, home preparation provides greater control over refined and processed sugars, as well as fat use.

Finally, it is important to remember that refined and processed sugars have been added to a wide range of products. Although labeling regulations do not currently require the content of the different sugars to be described, if some kind of sugar (corn syrup, fructose sugar, dextrose, honey, etc.) is listed as one of the first two or three ingredients, then one can reasonably assume that there is a lot of sugar added to the product. As noted earlier, use of fresh food enables greater protection against hidden refined and processed sugars.

GOAL 4. REDUCE OVERALL FAT CONSUMPTION FROM APPROXIMATELY 40 PERCENT TO ABOUT 30 PERCENT OF ENERGY INTAKE

Figures 10 and 11 show the growth in fat consumption in the United States over this century, both in absolute terms and as a percent of calories.

Between the beginning of the century and 1973, the amount of nutrient fat available per person per day rose from about 125 to 156 grams, according to a report by the Agricultural Research Service, *Fat in Today's Food Supply—Level of Use and Sources.* The report noted that this increase is equivalent to about 2½ tablespoons of butter or regular margarine; or a little more than 2 tablespoons a day of vegetable oil; or about 24 pounds a year in nutrient fat.

Discussing the sources of the increase, the report says:

The same foods did not always account for the increase in fat throughout the 60-year period, but for most years salad and cooking oils were the chief contributors. Following salad and cooking oils, dairy products and shortening shared equally in the contribution to the gain in nutrient fat during the first 15 years and margarine, shortening and meat, in that order during the next 40 years. However, in the last seven years, meat provided the largest increase in fat, followed by salad and cooking oils and then by shortening.

The higher fat consumption trends have occurred in other nations as well. Governmental and professional groups in the United States and eight other nations have recommended decreases in total fat consumption. As seen in Appendix B, the intake of total fat ranges from a recommended maximum of 35 percent to as low as 25 percent, which was recommended as the low end of the range by one panel.

One of the principal reasons for reducing the consumption of fat is to make a place in the diet for complex carbohydrates which generally carry higher levels of micro-nutrients than fat without the complications of fat, which are to be discussed.

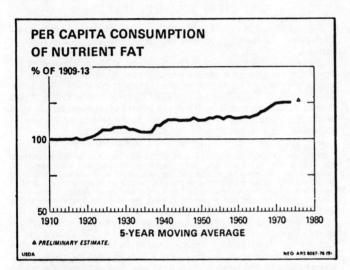

PER CAPITA CONSUMPTION OF NUTRIENT FAT

% OF 1909-13

5-YEAR MOVING AVERAGE

△ PRELIMINARY ESTIMATE.

USDA   NEG· ARS 6067-76 (9)

Source: Handbook of Agricultural Charts, Agricultural Handbook No. 504, U.S. Department of Agriculture, 1976.

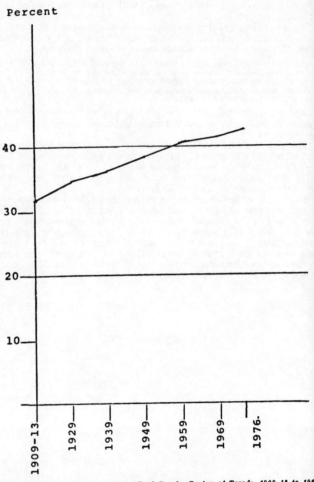

Percent

Source: *Nutrients in United States Food Supply, Review of Trends, 1909-13 to 196...* B. Friend. The American Journal of Clinical Nutrition. Vol. 20, No. 8, August 1967, pp. 907-914. Data after 1965 unpublished, Agricultural Research Service, U.S. Department of Agriculture.

As noted more extensively under Goal 1, obesity is considered a risk factor in: Cardiovascular disease, hypertension (high blood pressure), atherosclerosis, hernia, gallbladder disease, diabetes mellitus, and liver diseases.

With respect to weight control, it should be understood that fat is the most concentrated source of food energy. As pointed out in *Fats in Food and Diet*, published by the U.S. Department of Agriculture, fat supplies 9 calories per gram, whereas alcohol supplies 7 calories per gram, and protein and carbohydrates supply only four calories per gram.

Cancer

In addition to the relationship of fat intake to obesity, and its apparent consequences, there is also evidence suggesting a connection between dietary fat and cancer of the breast and colon. Testifying before the Select Committee in July 1976, Dr. Gio Gori, Deputy Director of the National Cancer Institute, said:

There is * * * a strong correlation between dietary fat intake and incidence of breast cancer and colon cancer. As the dietary intake of fat increases, you have an almost linear increase in the incidence of breast and colon cancer.

And Dr. Gori said:

Colon cancer has also been shown to correlate highly with the consumption of meat, even though it is not clear whether the meat itself or its fat content is the real correlating factor. Mortality rates from colonic cancer are high in the United States, Scotland, and Canada, which are high meat consuming countries; other populations such as in Japan and Chile where meat consumption is low, experience also a low incidence of colon cancer. Seventh Day Adventists and Mormons have a restricted fat and meat intake when compared to other populations living in the same district and, as indicated, they suffer considerably less from some forms of cancer, notably breast and colon.

Dr. Wynder, testifying at the hearing, said that incidence of cancer seems to be related as much to unsaturated as saturated fats. As an example, he cited studies indicating that both types of fat, and cholesterol, may cause increased secretion in the breast of the hormone prolactin and that this secretion may induce tumors. A four-week vegetarian diet in a group of American women resulted in a 40 to 60 percent decrease in prolactin secretion, he said.

The September 10, 1976, *Washington Post* noted that Dr. Bruce K. Armstrong, of Perth Medical Centre, Australia, presented to a conference at Cold Spring Harbor Laboratory in New York a report suggesting that diets high in animal fat might increase the risk of womb cancer.

Dr. Armstrong said principal risk factors included obesity, early onset of puberty, late onset of menopause, a mild case of diabetes and high blood pressure. With respect to high intake of fat, he said it may cause excessive secretion of estrogens that either cause cancer or stimulate other cancer-causing agents. He also discussed findings suggesting that vegetarian women appeared to be at reduced risk, generally experiencing earlier menopause and lower blood pressure than non-vegetarians.

A guide to reducing fat consumption follows the explanations of the saturated fat and cholesterol goals.

GOAL 5. REDUCE SATURATED FAT CONSUMPTION TO ACCOUNT FOR ABOUT 10 PERCENT OF TOTAL ENERGY INTAKE; AND BALANCE THAT WITH POLY-UNSATURATED AND MONO-UNSATURATED FATS, WHICH SHOULD ACCOUNT FOR ABOUT 10 PERCENT OF ENERGY INTAKE EACH

Figure 12, from the Department of Agriculture report, *Fat in Today's Food Supply—Level of Use and Sources*, cited earlier, shows the trends in saturated, oleic (mono-unsaturated) and linoleic (poly-unsaturated fat consumption in this century.

There are a number of fats found in foods, but the important fats from a nutritional perspective are those known as triglycerides and phospholipids. Both of these are composed of a very simple alcohol, and two or three large molecules called fatty acids.

The fatty acids, which are called fats in general discussion, are of three types: (1) saturated, in which all the double bonds are saturated; (2) mono-unsaturated, in which there is one unsaturated double bond; and (3) poly-unsaturated, in which two or more double bonds are unsaturated.

Saturated fats are the main kind of fatty acid made by the animal body. Mono-unsaturated fats are usually made by plants, but some can be made by animals. Poly-unsaturated fats, which are often called essential fatty acids, can only be made by plants, and are needed for normal cell function. The key poly-unsaturated fatty acid is linoleic acid which has two unsaturated bonds in specific locations on the fatty acid. Some other poly-unsaturated fatty acids contain more than two unsaturated double bonds, but they are not essential to normal bodily functions.

Only poly-unsaturated fats lower serum cholesterol. Mono-unsaturated fats have little or no effect on serum cholesterol, and saturated fats elevate serum cholesterol.

The level of saturated fat in the diet is of concern because it has been directly linked to excessive levels of cholesterol in the blood and therefore to an increased risk of heart disease. Feeding studies in animals in the early 1900's linked high cholesterol intake to atherosclerosis. Evidence that cholesterol could affect the same arterial lesions in man came from Scandanavian countries where atherosclerotic diseases appeared to decline during the war years when consumption of calories and animal fat declined.

The correlation between serum cholesterol and heart disease became more clear in the 1950's. As reported by Drs. McGill and Mott in *Present Knowledge in Nutrition*, the Framingham study, mentioned earlier, determined that of all risk factors in heart disease, "the strongest and most consistent risk factor was elevated serum cholesterol concentration. This finding has been confirmed in the U.S. and Western Europe in the past two decades." The authors note that in the early 1950's researchers discovered that serum cholesterol levels were lowered by substituting poly-unsaturated fats for saturated fats.

A twelve-year study of patients in two hospitals in Finland, started in 1958, reinforces this view. During the first six years, the patients in the trial hospital were fed an experimental diet which involved an overall reduction of fats and a reduction of the proportion of saturated fat. For the same time period, the patients in the control hospital were given a normal diet. During the next six years, the two diets were continued, but the two hospitals reversed their experimental roles. In both hospitals the coronary heart disease (CHD) mortality rate was dramatically reduced on the low-fat diet. The overall CHD incidence rate per 1,000 man-years for the experimental diet was 14.4 as opposed to a 33.0 rate experienced by those eating the normal or control diet.

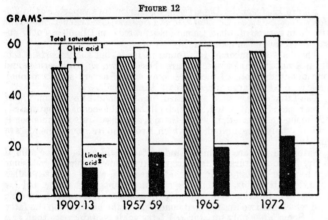

FIGURE 12

FIG. 11. Fatty acids. Per capita civilian consumption. △=preliminary.

[1] Mono-unsaturated.
[2] Poly-unsaturated.

Source: *Fat in Today's Food Supply—Level of Use and Sources.* Journal of the American Oil Chemists' Society, Vol. 51, No. 6, Pages 244–250. 1974.

Dr. Osmo Turpeinen reporting on the Finnish study in *Future Trends in Nutrition and Dietetics*, 1975, summarizes the evidence of the relation between diet and heart disease to date:

As * * * all these studies have dealt with relatively small numbers of subjects and their design of experiment has shown certain shortcomings, these intervention studies may not yet have produced the final, irrefutable proof of the potentiality of dietary prevention of coronary heart disease. Nevertheless, they have furnished at least substantial evidence in favor of the view that a proper re-adjustment of the fatty acid composition and of cholesterol content of our commonly used diets may have considerable preventive effect.

(One of the reasons the results of these tests were inconclusive is that they involved older people who already had developed atherosclerosis. Had tests been instituted earlier, the results might have been more striking.)

The proportion of saturated fat in the diet has declined from about 40 percent of total fat in the early 1900's to about 38 percent in 1975, but the total amount of saturated fat in the average American diet has increased. Concurrently, mono- and poly-unsaturated fat consumption has grown even more quickly. These increases are primarily due to increased use of salad and cooking oils.

In addition, it should be pointed out that saturated fat is obtained from both animal and vegetable sources. According to unpublished 1977 disappearance data from the Consumer and Food Economics institute, ARS, USDA, the per capita consumption of saturated fats breaks down as follows: 72 percent animal sources (40 grams/person, day) and 28 percent vegetable sources (16 grams/person/day).

Although saturated fat as a percentage of total calories may be a declining proportion of total fat consumption, its level, and that of the other fatty acids, remains higher than recommended by the Inter Society Commission for Heart Disease Resources.

Preliminary figures for 1976 indicate that saturated fat currently comprises about 16 percent of total calories, poly-unsaturated fat accounts for about 7 percent and mono-unsaturated, 19 percent. The Commission recommends that daily intake of saturated fat be less than 10 percent of total calories. Up to 10 percent of total calories should be derived from poly-unsaturated fat, with the remaining 10 percent coming from mono-unsaturated fats. The limits conform generally with the recommendations of other U.S. and international agencies (Appendix B), and provide a prudent balance among fat types.

Achieving this balance requires partial substitution of poly-unsaturated for saturated fat and the overall reduction of all fatty acids. A guide to these changes follows discussion of the next goal, reduction of cholesterol.

GOAL 6. REDUCE CHOLESTEROL CONSUMPTION TO ABOUT 300 GRAMS A DAY

There is evidence not only that fat and saturated fat tend to increase serum cholesterol levels but direct consumption of cholesterol does as well.

Dr. McGill and Dr. Mott reported in *Present Knowledge in Nutrition*:

The average American ingests 600 mg. of cholesterol per day, well above the 300 mg. limit below which there is a linear relationship with serum cholesterol. As in the controlled experiments, comparisons among populations with wide ranges of average cholesterol intake show a close relationship between dietary cholesterol and serum cholesterol concentrations. It is now widely accepted that high dietary cholesterol intake is a major determinant of the high cholesterol concentrations found in the U.S. populations as well as in other technically developed countries.

At the Select Committee's heart disease hearing in February 1977, Dr. Antonio Gotto, chairman of the Department of Medicine at Baylor, discussed the relationship between serum cholesterol levels and the risk of heart disease. In particular, Dr. Gotto referred to the following significant findings that he and Dr. Michael DeBakey discovered:

Lipoprotein phenotyping and significance of cholesterol and triglyceride measurements

Dr. Ancel Keys and Dr. E. H. Ahrens and their colleagues as well as other investigators in the 1950's, observed the cholesterol-lowering effect of a diet rich in polyunsaturated fat. Dr. Ahrens and his group also observed that some individuals seemed to develop hyperlipidemia on a high fat diet while others developed hyperlipidemia on a high carbohydrate diet. Such individuals were referred to as having fat-sensitive or carbohydrate-sensitive lipemia, respectively. There was an important advance in methodology in the early 1960's that led to an awakening of interest in lipoproteins. Doctors Fred Hatch and Robert Lees improved the method for separating the plasma lipoproteins on paper electrophoresis.

With this improved methodology, Drs. Donald Frederickson, Robert Levy and Robert Lees at the National Institutes of Health refined the system of electrophoresis and developed it into a means of classifying lipoprotein phenotypes, based on which family or families of the plasma lipoproteins are present in elevated concentrations. This simplified classifications system has popularized measurement of lipoproteins in clinical laboratories and the phenotyping of lipoproteins by physicians in this country and throughout the world. Some of the abnormal lipoprotein phenotypes are associated with inherited lipoprotein disorders. Some are associated primarily with high cholesterol; others with elevated triglyceride and some with both high levels of cholesterol and triglyceride. The type II lipoprotein phenotype, associated with hypercholesterolemia, and type IV phenotype, associated with hypertriglyceridemia, have been reported in a number of studies to have a high frequency of association with premature coronary artery disease. There is still disagreement by medical experts as to the importance of high triglycerides as a risk factor for coronary heart disease. As to relative importance, the level of serum cholesterol appears to carry greater weight as a risk factor than does triglyceride.

One of the problems in using the lipoprotein phenotyping system is that it is based on arbitrary values for concentrations of lipids and lipoproteins for defining the normal from the abnormal in the population. Thus, there is some cutoff value for cholesterol which supposedly separates those with hypercholesterolemia and those with normal cholesterols in the population. The problem with this approach is that except for the small percentage of individuals who have recognized inherited forms of hyperlipidemia, the rest of the population have values of cholesterol and triglycerides that exhibit a normal distribution. There do not appear to be distinct values for either cholesterol or triglyceride which separate the population at risk for coronary heart disease from those who are not at risk.

At the Cardiovascular Center in Houston, we have recently studied 496 patients who were referred for evaluation of chest pain and underwent coronary catheterization for the study of the presence of coronary artery disease. Approximately 100 of the patients did not have significant coronary artery narrowing while the remainder of the patients had at least 25 percent narrowing of one or more of the major coronary arteries. We found that the frequency of coronary heart disease and the extent of disease, as measured by the number of vessels involved, showed a continuous correlation with both serum cholesterol and serum triglyceride concentrations. There was a stronger correlation between these parameters with cholesterol than there was for triglyceride. If the patients were divided in quartiles based on the level of cholesterol or triglyceride or both, that quartile with the lowest lipid levels had the lowest frequency of coronary artery disease. There was a stepwise increase such that the quartile with the highest lipid value had the greatest frequency of coronary artery disease. This extensive study, based on direct measurements of coronary artery artherosclerosis, shows a direct relation between the absolute values of serum cholesterol and triglyceride and a frequency and extent of coronary artery narrowing. *The average serum cholesterol in the patients with coronary artery disease was about 230–235 mg% while only about 200–205 mg% in those without coronary artery disease.*

Many physicians would not consider a cholesterol of 235 mg% as an abnormal value. Such values should not be looked upon as representing safe or acceptable levels of serum cholesterol. Obviously, such a patient can be at risk for developing coronary heart disease. *If we attempted to classify these patients on the basis of lipoprotein phenotype using the currently accepted criteria for such classification, we found virtually no correlation between the phenotype with the frequency or extent of coronary artery narrowing.* Thus the association between serum cholesterol and coronary heart disease tended to be obscured if one adopted current definitions for defining hyperlipidemia. *The levels of cholesterol now used to define hyperlipidemia are most certainly too high and should be looked upon as separating individuals with overt hyperlipidemia.* (Italics supplied by committee.)

Professional and governmental bodies in the United States and other countries have generally recommended that cholesterol intake be decreased to 300 mg. a day or less (Appendix B). Also see the preface for further discussion of cholesterol.

GUIDE TO REDUCING CONSUMPTION OF FAT, SATURATED FAT AND CHOLESTEROL

High levels of fat, saturated fat and cholesterol most often enter our diets in the process of acquisition of animal protein. Consequently, the foregoing recommendations suggest that more of our animal protein needs be satisfied by a mix of lean meats, poultry and fish; and a different balance between vegetable and animal sources of protein will result from increased consumption of fruits, vegetables and whole grains.

The proportion of calories in our diet derived from protein, based on disappearance data, has remained relatively constant in this century at about 12 percent. As noted earlier, prior to increased meat consumption, a greater share of our protein was drawn from vegetable sources, especially grains. Tables 11, 12 and 13 show that, in general, increased use of vegetable source proteins will aid greatly in reducing not only the percentage of calories from fat but levels of saturated fat and cholesterol (only foods of animal origin have significant amounts of cholesterol).

Although the changes just described will assist in approaching the goals outlined, it is necessary also to (1) select foods from within the meat, fish, poultry and vegetable groups that are relatively low in fat, saturated fat and cholesterol; (2) reduce fat use and consumption of foods high in fat; (3) make partial substitution of polyunsaturated fat for saturated fat; (4) trim away visible fat from meats, poultry and fish, and reduce or eliminate the use of fat drippings; and (5) be more aware of the fats in foods such as hamburgers, cheese, ice cream, bakery products and many highly processed foods, that are not always apparent. Tables 11, 12 and 13 provide guidance in these areas.

With respect to overall fat consumption, in using Table 11, it may be useful to follow a strategy of selecting greater numbers of foods that derive 30 percent or less of their calories from fat.

The following excerpt from a presentation by the American Heart Association to the Federal Trade Commission compares consumption goals to commonly used food measures.

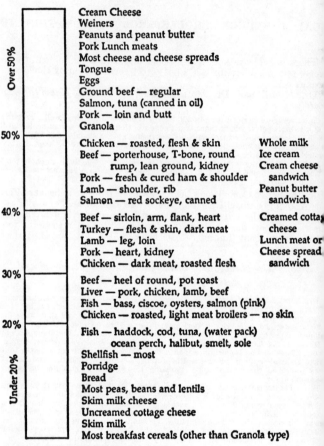

Percentage of Calories from Fat in Foods

Over 50%
Cream Cheese
Weiners
Peanuts and peanut butter
Pork Lunch meats
Most cheese and cheese spreads
Tongue
Eggs
Ground beef — regular
Salmon, tuna (canned in oil)
Pork — loin and butt
Granola

50% – 40%
Chicken — roasted, flesh & skin
Beef — porterhouse, T-bone, round rump, lean ground, kidney
Pork — fresh & cured ham & shoulder
Lamb — shoulder, rib
Salmon — red sockeye, canned

Whole milk
Ice cream
Cream cheese sandwich
Peanut butter sandwich

40% – 30%
Beef — sirloin, arm, flank, heart
Turkey — flesh & skin, dark meat
Lamb — leg, loin
Pork — heart, kidney
Chicken — dark meat, roasted flesh

Creamed cottage cheese
Lunch meat or Cheese spread sandwich

30% – 20%
Beef — heel of round, pot roast
Liver — pork, chicken, lamb, beef
Fish — bass, ciscoe, oysters, salmon (pink)
Chicken — roasted, light meat broilers — no skin

Under 20%
Fish — haddock, cod, tuna, (water pack) ocean perch, halibut, smelt, sole
Shellfish — most
Porridge
Bread
Most peas, beans and lentils
Skim milk cheese
Uncreamed cottage cheese
Skim milk
Most breakfast cereals (other than Granola type)

Source: "NutriScore," Fremes, Sabry, 1976.

314

Food	Total fat	Total saturated	Total monoun-saturated	Total polyun-saturated
Animal fats:				
Chicken	100.0	32.5	45.4	17.6
Lard	100.0	39.6	44.3	11.8
Beef tallow	100.0	48.2	42.3	4.2
Avocado	15.0	2.0	9.0	2.0
Beef products:				
T-bone steak (cooked, broiled—56 percent lean, 44 percent fat)	43.2	18.0	21.1	1.6
Chuck, 5th rib (cooked or braised—69 percent lean, 31 percent fat)	36.7	15.3	17.5	1.5
Brisket (cooked, braised, or pot roasted—69 percent lean; 31 percent fat)	34.8	14.6	16.7	1.4
Wedge and round-bone sirloin steak (cooked or broiled—66 percent lean, 34 percent fat)	32.0	13.3	15.6	1.2
Rump (cooked or roasted—75 percent lean; 25 percent fat)	27.3	11.4	13.1	1.2
Round steak (cooked or broiled—82 percent lean; 18 percent fat)	14.9	6.3	6.9	.7
Cereals and grains:				
Wheat germ	10.9	1.9	1.6	6.6
Oats (puffed, without added ingredients)	5.5	1.0	1.9	2.2
Oats (puffed, with added nutrients, sugar covered)	3.4	.6	1.2	1.4
Barley (whole grain)	2.8	.5	.3	1.3
Domestic buckwheat (dark flour)	2.5	.5	.8	.9
Cornmeal, white or yellow (whole-ground, unbolted)	3.9	.5	.9	2.0
Shredded wheat breakfast cereal	2.5	.4	.4	1.3
Wheat (whole grain, Hard Red Spring)	2.7	.4	.3	1.3
Wheat flakes breakfast cereal	2.4	.4	.3	1.2
Rye (whole grain)	2.2	.3	.2	1.1
Wheat meal breakfast cereal	1.4	.3	.1	.7
Wheat flour, all purpose	1.4	.2	.1	.6
Rice (cooked brown)	.8	.2	.2	.3
Bulgur from Hard Red Winter wheat	1.5	.2	.2	.7
Oatmeal or rolled oats, cooked	1.0	.2	.4	.4
Rye flour	1.4	.2	.1	.6
Cornstarch	.6	.1	.1	.3
Rice (cooked white)	.2	.1	.1	.1
Farina (enriched, regular, cooked)	.2			.1
Corn grits, cooked	.1			.1
Dairy products:				
Nondairy coffee whitener (powder)	35.6	32.6	1.0	
Cream cheese	33.8	21.2	9.4	1.2
Cheddar cheese	32.8	20.2	9.8	.9
Light whipping cream	32.4	20.2	9.6	.9
Muenster cheese	29.8	19.0	8.7	.7
American pasteurized cheese	28.9	18.0	8.5	1.0
Swiss cheese	27.6	17.6	7.7	1.0
Mozzarella cheese	19.4	11.8	5.9	.7
Ricotta cheese (from whole milk)	14.6	9.3	4.1	.4
Vanilla ice cream	12.3	7.7	3.6	.5
Half and half cream	11.7	7.3	3.4	.4
Chocolate chip ice cream	11.0	6.3	2.6	.4
Canned condensed milk (sweetened)	8.7	5.5	2.4	.3
Ice cream sandwich	8.2	4.7	2.6	.5
Cottage cheese (creamed)	4.0	2.6	1.1	.1
Yogurt (from whole milk)	3.4	2.2	.9	.1
Cottage cheese (uncreamed)	.4	.2	.1	
Eggs:				
Fried in margarine	15.9	4.2	7.2	1.9
Scrambled in margarine	12.6	3.7	5.5	1.4
Fresh or frozen	11.3	3.4	4.5	1.4
Fish:				
Eel, American	18.3	4.0	9.0	2.7
Herring, Atlantic	16.4	2.9	9.2	2.4
Mackerel, Atlantic	9.8	2.4	3.6	2.4
Tuna, albacore (canned, light)	6.8	2.3	1.7	1.8
Tuna, albacore (white meat)	6.8	2.1	2.1	3.0
Salmon, sockeye	8.9	1.8	1.5	4.7
Salmon, Atlantic	5.8	1.8	2.7	.5
Carp	6.2	1.3	2.7	1.4
Rainbow trout (United States)	4.5	1.0	1.5	1.4
Striped bass	2.1	.5	.6	.7
Ocean perch	2.5	.4	1.0	.7
Red snapper	1.2	.2	.2	.4
Tuna, skipjack (canned, light)	.8	.2	.2	.2
Halibut, Atlantic	1.1	.2	.2	.4
Cod, Atlantic	.7	.1	.1	.3
Haddock	.7	.1	.1	.2

Food	Total fat	Total saturated	Total monoun-saturated	Total polyun-saturated
Fowl:				
Chicken (broiler fryer, cooked or roasted dark meat)	9.7	2.7	3.2	2.4
Turkey (cooked or roasted dark meat)	5.3	1.6	1.4	1.5
Chicken (broiler/fryer, cooked or roasted light meat)	3.5	1.0	.9	.9
Turkey (cooked or roasted light meat)	2.6	.7	.6	.7
Lamb and veal:				
Shoulder of lamb (cooked or roasted, 74 percent lean; 26 percent fat)	26.9	12.6	11.0	1.6
Leg of lamb (cooked or roasted, 83 percent lean; 17 percent fat)	21.2	9.6	8.5	1.2
Veal foreshank (cooked or stewed, 86 percent lean; 14 percent fat)	10.4	4.4	4.2	.7
Nuts:				
Coconut	35.5	31.2	2.2	.7
Brazil nut	68.2	17.4	22.5	25.4
Peanut butter	52.0	10.0	24.0	15.0
Peanut	49.7	9.4	27.9	15.0
Cashew	45.6	9.2	26.4	7.4
Walnut, English	63.4	6.9	9.9	41.8
Pecan	71.4	6.1	43.1	17.9
Walnut, black	59.6	5.1	10.8	40.8
Almond	53.9	4.3	36.8	10.1
Pork products:				
Bacon	49.0	18.1	22.8	5.4
Sausage, cooked	32.5	11.7	15.1	3.9
Deviled ham, canned	32.3	11.3	15.2	3.5
Liverwurst, braunschweiger, liver sausage	32.5	11.0	15.5	4.1
Bologna	27.5	10.6	13.3	2.1
Pork loin (cooked or roasted, 82 percent lean; 18 percent fat)	28.1	9.8	13.1	3.1
Ham (cooked or roasted, 84 percent lean; 16 percent fat)	22.1	7.8	10.4	2.4
Fresh ham (cooked or roasted, 82 percent lean; 18 percent fat)	20.2	7.1	9.5	2.2
Canadian bacon (cooked and drained)	17.5	5.9	7.9	1.8
Chopped ham luncheon meat	17.4	5.7	8.3	2.2
Canned ham	11.3	4.0	5.3	1.2
Salad and cooking oils:				
Coconut	100.0	86.0	6.0	2.0
Palm	100.0	47.9	38.4	9.3
Cottonseed	100.0	26.1	18.9	50.7
Peanut	100.0	17.0	47.0	31.0
Sesame	100.0	15.2	40.0	40.5
Soybean, hydrogenated	100.0	15.0	23.1	57.6
Olive	100.0	14.2	72.5	9.0
Corn	100.0	12.7	24.7	58.2
Sunflower	100.0	10.2	20.9	63.8
Safflower	100.0	9.4	12.5	73.8
Shellfish:				
Eastern oyster	2.1	.5	.2	.6
Pacific oyster	2.3	.5	.4	.9
Ark shell clam	1.5	.4	.3	.3
Blue crab	1.6	.3	.3	.6
Alaska king crab	1.6	.2	.3	.6
Shrimp	1.2	.2	.2	.5
Scallop	.9	.1		.4
Soups:				
Cream of mushroom (diluted with equal parts of water)	3.9	1.1	.7	.8
Cream of celery (diluted with equal parts of water)	2.3	.6	.5	1.0
Beef with vegetables (diluted with equal parts of water)	.8	.3	.3	
Chicken noodle (diluted with equal parts of water)	1.0	.3	.4	.2
Minestrone (diluted with equal parts of water)	1.1	.2	.3	.5
Vegetable (diluted with equal parts of water)	.9	.2	.3	.4
Clam chowder, Manhattan style (diluted with equal parts of water)	.9	.2	.2	.5
Table spreads:				
Butter	80.1	49.8	23.1	3.0
Margarine (hydrogenated soybean oil, stick)	80.1	14.9	46.5	14.4
Margarine (corn oil, tub)	80.3	14.2	30.4	31.9
Margarine (corn oil, stick)	80.0	14.0	38.7	23.3
Margarine (safflower oil, tub)	81.7	13.4	16.0	48.4
Vegetable fats (household shortening)	100.0	25.0	44.0	26.0

Source: Consumer and Food Economics Institute, U.S. Department of Agriculture, Agricultural Research Service, Hyattsville, Maryland. "Comprehensive Evaluation of Fatty Acids in Foods," Journal of The American Dietetic Association, May 1975; July 1975; August 1975; October 1975; March 1976; April 1976; July 1976; September 1976; November 1976; January 1977; unpublished data on shellfish and margarine.

TABLE 13.—CHOLESTEROL CONTENT OF COMMON MEASURES OF SELECTED FOODS

[In ascending order]

Food	Amount	Cholesterol (milligrams)
Milk, skim, fluid or reconstituted dry	1 cup	5
Cottage cheese, uncreamed	½ cup	7
Mayonnaise, commercial	1 tbsp	10
Lard	do	12
Yogurt, made from fluid and dry nonfat milk, plain or vanilla	Carton (227 gr) [1]	17
Cream, light table	1 fl oz	20
Cottage cheese, creamed	½ cup	24
Cheese, pasteurized, processed American	28 g	(25)
Cheese, pasteurized processed Swiss	28 g	(26)
Cream, half and half	1 cup	26
Ice cream, regular, approximately 10 percent fat	½ cup	27
Cheese, cheddar	1 oz	28
Milk, whole	1 cup	34
Sausage, frankfurter, all meat, cooked	1 frank	34
Butter	1 tbsp	35
Beef and vegetable stew, canned	1 cup	36
Cake, baked from mix, yellow 2 layer, made with eggs, water, chocolate frosting	75 g	36
Oysters, salmon	3 oz, cooked	40
Clams, halibut, tuna	do	55
Chicken, turkey, light meat	do	67
Beef, pork, lobster, chicken, turkey, dark meat	do	75
Lamb, veal, crab	do	85
Tuna, canned in oil, drained solids	184 g	116
Lobster, cooked, meat only	145 g	123
Shrimp	3 oz, cooked	130
Heart, beef	do	230
Egg	1 yolk or 1 egg	250
Liver, beef, calf, hog, lamb	3 oz, cooked	370
Kidney	do	680
Brains	3 oz, raw	>1,700

[1] Estimates in parenthesis imputed.

Source: "Cholesterol Content of Foods," R. M. Feeley, P. E. Criner, and B. K. Watt, J. American Dietetic Association 61:134, 1972.

A relatively small number of foods do contribute a major proportion of the cholesterol and saturated fat in the American diet. For example, in our 1972 report, the Inter-Society Commission for Heart Disease Resources recommended the reduction of dietary cholesterol *to less than 300 mg. per day*. We noted that the average American daily cholesterol intake was approximately 600 mg. per day. A single egg yolk, however, contains 250 mg. cholesterol by itself, nearly the daily allowance. We further recommend *an intake of less than 10 percent of total calories to be obtained from saturated fat*. Assuming a caloric intake of 2,500 calories per day, the average American should take in no more than 250 calories or *less than 27 grams of saturated fat per day*. One cup of whole milk contains 5 grams saturated fat. One cup of ice cream contains 8 grams; six ounces of ham approximately 8 grams. These are very substantial portions of the maximum recommended allowance for a day. Therefore the contribution of *individual foods* to the cholesterol and saturated fat intake in the diet can be highly significant.

Fremes and Sabry point out in *NutriScore* that food labels rarely if ever indicate the type and saturation of fats used in processed foods. They report that the saturated fats, palm oil and coconut oil, are used interchangeably in powdered, frozen or liquid coffee creamers used at home and in restaurants and coffee machines. They say:

> But what of all the other products like chips, convenience spreads and cookies? What oil is in them? We don't know and won't know without some government regulations and industry cooperation. Until it becomes mandatory for maufacturers to declare the type of oil on the labels of foods with vegetable oil listed, we would recommend that you stay away from all commercial snack foods, including potato chips, baked goods, crackers and all mixes. If you must use a whipped topping occasionally, consider this: packaged synthetic toppings are just as saturated as real whipped cream; and real milk or table cream has much less fat than whipped cream or the substitutes.

GOAL 7. LIMIT THE INTAKE OF SODIUM BY REDUCING THE INTAKE OF SALT (SODIUM CHLORIDE) T ABOUT 5 GRAMS/DAY

The primary source of sodium in the American diet is salt (sodium chloride). Salt consumption in the United States is estimated to range from about 6 to 18 grams a day, according to the National Academy of Sciences', Food and Nutrition Board's, Recommended Dietary Allowances." Drs. George Meneely and Harold Battarbee, in "Present Knowledge in Nutrition", suggest, however, that the average human requirement for sodium is probably only about one-fourth of a gram.

Since sodium occurs indigenously in most foods and many sodium salts are added in the processing of foods (see appendix E), the average requirement normally will be achieved without adding salt either in cooking, or at the table. Dr. Meneely and Battarbee cite studies indicating that desire for salt is not a physiological necessity but an acquired taste.

Excessive sweat loss from exercise, heat or fever can lead to significant sodium losses. The following guidelines are taken from the 19__ edition of the "Recommended Dietary Allowances":

> Whenever more than a 4-liter intake of water is required to replace sweat loss, extra sodium chloride (salt) should be provided. The need will vary with sweating in the proportion of 2 g sodium chloride (salt) per liter of extra water loss, and on the order of an extra 7 g/day for persons doing heavy work under hot conditions (Lee, 1964). In unadapted individuals, the need for additional water and salt may be somewhat higher than in fully acclimated persons.

The authors point also to evidence that there is an important balance between sodium and potassium, required for the proper flow of fluids among and through cells. (The Academy describes a requirement for potassium of 2.5 grams a day.) They provide the following Tables 14 and 15 showing the impact of various processing methods on sodium and potassium content, and say:

> Aside from the rather uncertain matter of treks to salt licks, there are no terrestrial mammals except man which add salt to their food. Table 14 which traces the changes in sodium and potassium in 100 g of peas exemplifies the extent to which potassium is depleted and sodium increased during canning and freezing. Peas, drained and before butter and salt are added for serving at table, thus contain 255 times as much sodium as the fresh product and more than half of the potassium is gone. Sodium intake is thereby greatly increased, potassium reduced. The sodium and potassium content of several other foods are shown in Table 15 and Appendix E.

> Consumer purchase of salt has declined somewhat as his use of processed and prepared foods has increased. Sodium intake is more and more determined by the food processors rather than by the individual.

Salt is added to processed food principally as a flavoring agent rather than as a preservative. In some instances it is the primary flavoring agent and may be used to mask other, less appealing, flavors.

Hypertension

Salt has been found to cause an increase in blood pressure, hypertension, among some individuals, but others do not seem genetically susceptible. There is some evidence that imbalance with potassium intake may be a factor in hypertension. Dr. Meneely and Dr. Battarbee estimate that 20 percent of the United States population is susceptible to hypertension and up to 40 percent of older people. They recommend reduction of salt intake as an important countermeasure.

TABLE 14.—CHANGES IN SODIUM AND POTASSIUM CONTENT OF PEAS

Food (100 g edible portion)	Na–(mg)	K–(mg)
Fresh peas	0.9	380
Frozen peas	100.0	160
Canned peas, liquid poured off	230.0	180
Add salt, serve with salted butter	(?)	(?)

TABLE 15.—SODIUM AND POTASSIUM CONTENT OF SEVERAL FOODS

Food (100 g edible portion)	Na–(mg)	K–(mg)
Olives	2,400	55
White bread	507	105
Cornflakes	660	165
Cheddar cheese	700	82
Dried nonfat milk	525	1,335
Bacon	1,770	225
Chipped beef	4,300	200
Smoked ham, raw	2,530	248
Frankfurter	1,100	230
Salami	1,260	302
Canned crabmeat	1,000	110
Canned salmon	540	330

Source: Present Knowledge in Nutrition: Sodium and Potassium, G. Meneely, H. Battarbee, 1976.

Millions of children and youths are moving toward hypertension. Excess dietary sodium is clearly an adverse factor in some, if not in most, people prone to hypertension. The evidence indicates that a systematic effort to reduce dietary sodium chloride intake and increase dietary potassium intake would result in the amelioration of much suffering among those who are prone and would increase both duration and quality of life for many millions of people.

Other Findings

Drs. Meneely and Battarbee, who also describe excessive salt as "noxious per se," report observations of possible connections between high sodium intake and heart disease. Researchers have found that increases in sodium from 4 grams to 24 grams a day in humans altered the ability to clear intravenously administered fat from the bloodstream. Other researchers have found improvement in vascular disease resulting from a decline in salt consumption even when blood pressure failed to decline.

They also report findings of possible connections between high salt intake and changes in levels of gastric acid secretion, stomach cancer and cerebrovascular disease.

Dr. John Brainard, reporting in *Minnesota Medicine*, April, 1976, draws a connection between migraine headaches and salt. Twelve migraine sufferers were advised to avoid all known factors in migraine, such as sodium nitrite and monosodium glutamate, and also sodium chloride by following a salt restriction which entailed "avoiding all salted snack foods, such as pretzels, nuts and potato chips before dinner." Ten out of 12 responded favorably, the report said, with a few saying migraine no longer was a problem. And the report noted:

It has not been appreciated that the sudden salt load of a handful of salted nuts or potato chips, particularly if taken on an empty stomach, can cause a severe migraine six or twelve hours later. The reason for the lag period is not known.

Finally, in *Human Nutrition*, Dr. Jean Mayer warns of hypertension that may develop as a result of high salt intake by children. He reports:

Clinically, it is well known that the tendency for edema to develop in prematurely-born infants is a function of the sodium content of the diet. It has also been demonstrated that a high salt content of the diet increases the likelihood of renal cast formation (an indication of possible kidney damage) in these infants.

Although there is some evidence that increased potassium intake might help offset possible adverse effects of high sodium consumption, the most prudent course appears to be to reduce salt intake to at least the level of 5 gm a day.

GUIDE TO REDUCING SALT CONSUMPTION

The goal of 5 gm of salt a day amounts to about one teaspoon and 2,000 mg of sodium alone (salt is about 40 percent sodium). However, as mentioned earlier, the daily goal will be met for most in the United States without the addition of salt to food or consumption of foods on which the salt is visible, such as pretzels and potato chips.

Furthermore, commonly-used seasoning may also be relatively high in sodium. For example, based on Agriculture Handbook 456, a tablespoon of catsup plus the salt on 10 french fries would result in sodium ingestion of about 370 mg. or about 25 percent of the allowance suggested by the foregoing goal. The same french fries would bring only 2 mg of sodium if served unsalted.

In pursuing a reduced sodium diet as purchased from the current market basket available to the consumer, it may be helpful to review appendix E which lists average sodium and potassium content of common foods.

EFFECTS OF GOALS BEYOND NUTRITIONAL CONCERNS

1. SOCIO-CULTURAL IMPLICATIONS

The social, cultural and psychological significance of food in our lives can scarcely be overestimated. Sharing of food is one of the prime social contacts; provision of food is one of the prime signs of caring. Just as the general meaning of food in our lives should not be underestimated, changes in our eating behavior must not be underestimated in terms of their potential impact on our whole way of life. A substantive discussion of the socio-cultural impact of profound changes in eating habits (both those which have in fact occurred in 20th century America and those recommended here) is beyond the scope of this report. Nevertheless, it is possible to illustrate the growing concern that a diet increasingly dependent on highly processed, highly packaged food, i.e., an increasingly mechanized approach to the provision of food, may have not only potential for negative nutritional effect but also a negative psychological effect.

All of the following examples refer directly only to institutional environments. In such situations it is clear that the tendency toward mechanization of the feeding process is particularly strong—stronger, by far, because of the necessities of institutional management, than the same tendency in the home. Nevertheless, observations on the psychological impact of different kinds of eating environments, made in institutional settings, may be appropriately applied to the home-eating situation when the difference in degree is acknowledged.

In May of 1976, the Washington Post reported on the overhaul of food service practices at the Montgomery County Detention Center in Maryland. Inmates had been fed for five or six years on frozen TV-type meals served in aluminum foil pans. While fed this way, groups of inmates, on a regular weekly basis, threw their trays against the wall in anger. When a switch was made to fresh foods, prepared on the premises by an inmate chef, complaints about the food dropped to "almost nothing."

It is plausible to speculate that feelings about taste and nutrition were not the sole motivators of the inmates' disgust over the way they were being fed. The feeding status quo had been de-humanized and was therefore, de-humanizing. The switch not only improved nutrition (more fresh fruits, vegetables and salads; the option of whole wheat bread; and steps toward reducing sugar intake) and saved money (20 to 30 cents per day per capita), but perhaps even more important, as soon as the frozen dinners were replaced, "morale picked up immediately."

Schools, as another example of an institutional mass-feeding situation in which there is a strong temptation to turn to mass-produced food, are relying increasingly on pre-plated convenience meals and formulated foods. While the children may not have rebelled, many parents and concerned outsiders have objected, and not simply on nutritional grounds. Marian Burros, in a Washington Post article in August of 1976, cited the following general objection to the trend toward using formulated foods to save time and/or money: ". . . such a position ignores the concept that the feeding of children in any school program should be an integral part of their education process and not just something to get out of the way as quickly as possible."

Others have more explicitly described the reasons behind that concept which they feel is being ignored. A Washington Star editorial in June of 1976, praising the work of Mary Goodwin, Montgomery County public health nutritionist, in combating the convenience trend, made the following comments:

> The pleasures of seeing, smelling and tasting food that looks, smells and tastes good, nourish the personality with sensuous experience even as the vitamins and minerals are making their contribution to the growth of bone and muscle. An awareness of real people preparing and serving the foods helps too.
> Which is to say that if you eat enough precooked, frozen, reheated foil-and-plastic packed lunches out of machines, part of you will starve to death. On-site food preparation—most important of all—is, in her (Mary Goodwin's) words "a way of keeping children in contact with the real world rather than a highly mechanized, impersonal one."

Dr. Bruno Bettelheim, a noted child psychiatrist, believes that eating plays a central psychological role in human life, and that in this regard not only what the food is, but also where and how it is served makes a difference. Several quotes from Bettelheim's article, "Food to Nurture the Mind," in the May 1975, School Review, summarize his case. Concerning the general psychological significance of food he says:

> Eating and being fed are intimately connected with our deepest feelings. They are the basic interactions between human beings on which rest all later evaluations of oneself, of the world, and of our relationship to it. Eating experiences condition our entire attitude to the world, not so much because of how nutritious is the food we are given, but because of the feelings and attitudes with which it is given.

Concerning the specific importance of the sharing of food and the effect it has on inter-personal relations, he says:

> The social climate of a mental institution changes immediately if the entire staff, up to the top of the hierarchy, takes its meals with the patients. The fact that patients, staff, and doctors eat together, and eat the same fare, immediately reduced the levels of tension, the potentiality of violent outbreaks. And this not just at mealtime but all during the day and throughout the institution. Nothing is more divisive than when people eat a different fare, in different rooms.

At a time when more and more meals are being taken away from the home, removed from the company of family members, perhaps more consideration should be given to the possibility that this trend is a factor that substantially contributes to the stresses found in modern family life.

Perhaps the most significant statement in Dr. Bettelheim's article is the following:

> The distinction between physical and emotional need, between body and intellect, is, in reality, a false one.

The impact of changed eating patterns in the home as well as in institutions, on our whole way of life is, no doubt, unquantifiable. I may even be indescribable. It is important in examining historical trends in eating habits, and in assessing the need for future changes in eating habits, to remember that we are dealing with an aspect of our lives which is by no means limited to the physical.

2. FOOD BUDGET

A shift to the dietary goals outlined offers potential for significant reduction in food costs. Savings may be achieved through home preparation and through reduction of and substitution for fats, refined and processed sugar and expensive, fatty protein sources.

Table 6, from "Diet for a Small Planet," comparing costs of protein sources, shows that every legume listed and every grain product except one provides the daily protein allowance for less than one dollar, whereas the majority of meat protein sources cost over one dollar a day.

Within the category of grain products, choosing the less processed, more nutritious products may often mean a savings. For instance, in one sampling, brand-name converted rice cost more than 25 percent less than the low-priced store brand of instant rice. Slightly processed hot cereals like oatmeal are generally less expensive than ready-to-eat cereals.

The most dramatic savings made by a reduction in sugar consumption result from cutting back on or eliminating purchases of candy, sweet baked goods, and soft drinks. Costs are also cut when the consumer chooses the unsweetened as opposed to the presweetened version of a particular food item; the prime example is breakfast cereals.

Reducing fat consumption, and particularly consumption of saturated fats, may also yield cost savings in several areas. For example, chicken or turkey, which are lower in saturated fat than meats, may average less than half the price of the beef, pork and lamb cuts. Butter, on a per teaspoon basis, is generally more expensive than even the most costly of the unsaturated vegetable oils. Reduced use of prepared salad dressing, catsup, and sauces can not only cut expenses but reduce fat and/or salt and sugar consumption.

Greater home preparation can also yield savings in some areas as well as greater control over diet composition. A recent study by the Department of Agriculture comparing the costs of various convenience foods with their home-prepared counterparts found that out of 25 meat dishes tested, 21 were more expensive per serving when purchased ready-made. Many of the cost differentials were dramatic. The report said:

The cost of home-prepared batter-dipped chicken was less than one-third that of the convenience products. Both chicken a-la-king frozen in a pouch and canned chicken salad spread, were about 60 percent more expensive per serving. . . . Consumers paid approximately 40 cents more per serving for frozen turkey dinner tetrazzine than for the separate ingredients.

Many will find it impossible to change food preparation patterns drastically. However, it is evident that home-preparation can offer savings as well as nutrition advantages.

CONSUMPTION OF FOOD ADDITIVES

There are more than 1,300 food additives currently approved for use as colors, flavors, preservatives, thickeners and other agents for controlling physical properties of food.

The exact amounts of additives now in use are not known, but more accurate measures may be available after a survey being planned by the Food and Drug Administration for 1977. A study prepared by the FDA in 1976 estimates that the average daily consumption of artificial colors alone among children aged 1 to 5 may be about 60 milligrams and average consumption for children aged 6 to 12 may be about 75 milligrams. The study finds, as shown in Table 16, that the largest single category contributing to artificial coloring consumption among children is beverages.

TABLE 16.—AVERAGE MILLIGRAMS OF ALL FD AND C COLORS IN FOOD INTAKE BY FOOD CATEGORY AMONG TWO GROUPS OF CHILDREN

Food category	Color intake			
	Average diet eaters only (mg), age—		Diets of total age group (mg), age—	
	1-5	6-12	1-5	6-12
Candy and confections	5.2	6.0	0.9	1.2
Beverages	21.1	29.3	8.5	13.6
Dessert powders	18.0	20.7	1.8	1.9
Cereals	8.4	10.6	3.8	4.6
Maraschino cherries		8.4		(¹)
Bakery goods	3.5	5.1	2.5	3.8
Ice cream	2.6	3.6	.8	1.3
Sausage	7.5	9.2	1.6	2.3
Snack food	3.0	3.4	.5	.8
Miscellaneous	48.6	55.4	38.8	46.4
Food with color, less miscellaneous	21.3	30.3	20.5	29.3
Food with color, including miscellaneous	60.0	76.2	59.2	75.5

¹ Less than 0.05 milligrams.

Source: Arletta Beloian, Food and Drug Administration memorandum: Estimates of average, 90th percentile and maximum daily intakes of FD & C artificial food colors in one day's diets among two age groups of children. July 30, 1976.

The food additives now in use are considered safe by the FDA based on varying degrees of testing, review of scientific literature, expert opinion and long-time usage. The most testing, according to an FDA official, has been given to artificial colors, most of which have had animal toxicity testing by the food industry. The FDA will begin in 1977 a re-evaluation of the safety of colors, flavors, and "direct" additives. Artificial flavors have had the least animal testing of the three additive categories.

Although food additives as a category may not justifiably be considered harmful, the varying degrees of testing and quality of testing and the continuing discoveries of apparent connections between certain additives and cancer, and possibly hyperactivity, give justifiable cause to seek to reduce additive consumption to the greatest degree possible.

In NutriScore, Fremes and Sabry suggest that "necessity should be the touchstone for the use of additives." They argue, as do others, that only those additives that serve a necessary function should be permitted in food. They do not define necessary, but it is apparent that necessity most strictly defined has to do with protecting food safety.

There are several additives commonly considered under the heading of preservatives and flavor enhancers that Fremes, Sabry and others classify as unnecessary and possibly a hazard to health.

Nitrates and Nitrites

"NutriScore" comments:

> While these additives are not in themselves harmful, they may combine with other chemicals in food or in the intestine to form nitrosamines, which are known to cause cancer. The advantages of using nitrites in processed foods is that they maintain a pinkish-red color, which makes the meat look fresh and attractive, and they check the growth of bacteria. Some of these bacteria, like botulinum, produce deadly poisons. Government should therefore limit the addition of nitrites to the amount needed to check the growth of botulinum bacteria and no more.

> This has been done in Canada, where the Canadian Health Protection Branch has recently reduced the amounts of nitrates and nitrites allowed in cured and processed meats. Industry, for its part, should find a preservative other than nitrite that will be effective against bacteria, yet will not present a cancer hazard.

BHT and BHA

These chemical preservatives are judged safe by the Food and Drug Administration, but neither is essential. "Nutrition Scoreboard" points out that foods not using the chemicals can be found readily.

Monosodium Glutamate

"NutriScore" recommends against use of foods containing monosodium glutamate, saying it may be associated with headaches, flushes in the head and body and tingling in the spine. The chemical is a flavor enhancer but not a necessary food ingredient. Researchers at Yale University School of Medicine said in a letter to the editor of the November 4, 1974 Journal of the American Medical Association that their studies indicated:

> That MSG offers a hazard to those endangered by excessive sodium intake: its moderate saltiness fails to warn the user about its high sodium content and can therefore lead to increased sodium ingestion.

PART II

RECOMMENDATIONS FOR GOVERNMENTAL ACTION

INTRODUCTION

The dietary trends in the United States described in Part I ha occurred in other nations as well, in several cases prompting gover mental action. In 1968, the medical boards of Finland, Norway ar Sweden published "Medical Viewpoints on the National Diet in Scar dinavian Countries" which recommended:

1. The dietary energy supply should, in many cases, be reduced prevent overweight.

2. The total fat consumption, at present about 40 percent, should I decreased to between 25 and 30 percent of total calories.

3. The use of saturated fat should be lowered, and the consumptic of poly-unsaturated fat should be simultaneously increased.

4. The consumption of sugar and products containing sugar shou be less.

5. The consumption of vegetables, fruits, potatoes, skimmed mil fish, lean meat and cereal products should be increased.

In 1969, the Swedish National Board of Health and Welfare mot vated by "the decidedly negative results of the changed food habi in our country during the last 30–40 years (and) the enormous cos of medical care of disease related to these changes," began a 10-yea campaign to encourage the public to exercise more and alter the diets. Table 17 shows recommended dietary changes.

TABLE 17.—Example of changes desirable in the average consumption of foo in Sweden. The proposed changes are expressed percent of the mean consum tion in 1960.

Food group	
1. Green vegetables, dried peas and beans	+1
2. Fruit	+
3(a). Potatoes	+
(b). Other root vegetables	+1
4. Standard milk	+
5. Meat, fish and eggs	±
6. Flour, meal macaroni for direct consumption	+:
Crispbread and soft bread	+:
7. Fats and oils	—
Other products: sugar, syrup, sweets, etc.	—:

Source: "Activities in Sweden to Improve Dietary Habits," *Nutr. Diet.*, No. 19, p 154–165 (Karger, Basel. 1973).

The impact of Sweden's program has not been completely measure An interview survey conducted in 1974 found that sugar consumptio had declined from 61.5 to 47.8 pounds a year and fresh vegetable co sumption had risen from 31.5 to 44.8 pounds a year. Poultry co umption rose from 3.3 to 8.8 pounds, but potato consumption dropped rom 191.4 to 144.9 pounds. Consumption of certain fruits also eclined.

In addition, the percentage of energy in the diet derived from fats eclined from about 41 percent in 1965 to 38.5 percent in 1974.

In 1975, Norway's ministry of agriculture presented to the nation's egislative body a report on nutrition and food policy which described rends in food consumption such as those in the United States and aid:

The aforementioned unfavorable health tendencies, particularly with respect o cardiovascular disease, as well as the gradual understanding that is being ained of the connection between nutrition and health, make it necessary for ne Government to base itself on the experts' recommendations, issued by the ational Nutrition Council, when planning the Norwegian nutrition and food olicy.

The report noted that the government would therefore take steps o try to reduce total fat intake to 35 percent of energy intake and ompensate by increasing consumption of starchy foods, principally ereals and potatoes. A reduction in sugar consumption is sought as ell as an increase in use of poly-unsaturated fats.

UNITED STATES EXPERIENCE

The United States' most recent experience with governmental diet ounselling occurred during World War II when the government in- ervened to control food prices, and required production of the most utritious foods, as well as attempting to educate the public in prin- iples of nutrition.

The education program, aimed primarily at fighting nutrient de- ciencies, enlisted the aid of the food industry, advertisers and edu- ators and revolved around the Seven Basic Food Groups. After the ar, the Basic Seven concept was simplified to the Basic Four.

The basic food group concept has been criticized for a variety of easons. First, it recommends eating foods in all groupings, but does ot caution about risk factors that may be associated with over-con- imption of the dietary elements outlined in Part I. In addition, ritics have said that the wide variety of choices by grouping does not asure adequate nutrition. It has also been said that: the groupings re not designed to meet current nutrition problems; that they give o much emphasis to animal source products; and that they do not ke ethnic food preferences into adequate consideration.

There was optimism at the close of the war that advances in nutri- on would continue at the wartime pace. However, in a speech in 1948 azel K. Stiebeling, chief of the Bureau of Human Nutrition and ome Economics in the Department of Agriculture, anticipated haz- rds to sound nutritional health for the United States.

We do not yet understand the dynamics of modifying food habits well enough apply . . . laws (of nutrition) in a fully effective way. But we are all aware the bewilderment that household food buyers feel over much of the current lvertising—advertising that attempts to push to the maximum of human ca- city the consumption of every separate commodity—indiscriminately. Surely the education of the public and in the orientation of food production and trade r bettering consumption patterns, we should look at the physiological research, d at the relative economy and usefulness of various foods to serve these needs. d science should speak with one voice in broad over-all terms about food choice d food use. This will have to be done if we are to progress at a pace in keeping th scientific knowledge and potentialities.

THE IMPACT OF TELEVISION FOOD ADVERTISING

Since World War II, the largest expenditure for public information on diet in the United States has been made by the food industry. In 1975, according to Leading National Advertisers, Inc., about $1.15 billion was spent on food advertising, which represents about 28 per- cent of total television advertising spending.

The most recent study to suggest the possible impact of current food advertising on the nation's nutritional health has been prepared by Lynne Masover and Dr. Jeremiah Stamler, of Northwestern Univer- sity Medical School, and presented to the 1976 convention of the American Public Health Association. The study, which analysed the food advertising on four Chicago television stations during the period August 4–10, 1975, reported:

A detailed look at this weekly food advertising time—restaurants excluded— found that the group of non-nutritive beverages was, by far, the single most- advertised food group, capturing approximately two-fifths of time, of which nearly one-third was for wine and beer. Sweets took up about 11 percent of the time; non-nutritive beverages plus sweets—all items low in nutrients and most of them high in calories—commanded an absolute majority of time. Add to these the oils, fats, and margarines, baked goods, snack foods, and relishes, and the proportion of advertising going to low-nutrient, generally high-calorie foods was nearly 70 percent! . . .

Of the restaurants advertised, nearly all were of the limited-menu, fast-food type specializing in foods high in saturated fats and cholesterol.

The study found that only about 25 percent of the time was devoted to "nutritious groups," such as bread, cereal, pasta, meat, fish and sea- food, dairy products, fruits and vegetables, soups and nut products.

More specifically, Table 18 shows that on weekdays during the period of analysis, almost 70 percent of the time devoted to food advertising promoted foods generally high in fat, saturated fat, cholesterol, refined and processed sugars and/or salt. However, only 3 percent of the time was devoted to fruit and vegetables. Of that total, no time was spent for the promotion of fresh vegetables and 0.7 percent was devoted to fresh fruit and juices. Fish, seafood and poultry received about the same advertising exposure as beef, 3.2 percent of the time compared to 3.5 percent for beef.

Table 19 indicates an even less healthful balance of weekend food advertising in which about 85 percent of time is devoted to foods high in fat, saturated fat, cholesterol, refined and processed sugars and/or salt. During the sample weekend period, no advertising time was given to fresh fruit or vegetables.

TABLE 18.—*Total weekday food advertising by food groups on four Chicago Tele- vision stations, August 4–10, 1975 (including local and network advertising)* *

Food group	Percent time of all stations combined
Nonnutritive beverages	37.5
Carbonated (with sugar)	13.2
Carbonated (sugar-free)	2.9
Beer and wine	9.2
Drink mixes	7.2
Coffee and tea	5.0
Grain	17.5

See footnotes at end of table.

TABLE 18.—*Total weekday food advertising by food groups on four Chicago Television stations, August 4–10, 1975 (including local and network advertising)*[*]— Continued

Food group	time of all stations combined
Bread, cereal, and pasta	13.4
Baked goods	4.1
Sugars and sweets	10.3
Candy, frosting, syrups	5.2
Chewing gum (sugar)	2.6
Chewing gum (sugar-free)	1.5
Gelatin, pudding	1.0
Oil, fat, margarine	8.5
Oil, fat, margarine	4.2
Salad dressing	4.3
Food stores	7.0
Food store-item unspecified	4.0
Food store-low fat dairy	1.5
Food store-fresh beef	1.0
Food store-all other	.5
Processed meat, fish, poultry	5.7
Fish, seafood, poultry	3.2
Beef, pork, lamb	2.5
Snack foods	2.9
Potato chips	1.3
Corn chips	.7
All other snack foods	.9
Dairy	3.1
High fat dairy	2.4
Low fat dairy	.7
Relishes, condiments, sauces	2.6
Vegetables	1.3
Processed vegetables, juices	0.9
Fresh vegetables, juices	.0
Processed potato products	.4
Fruit	1.7
Processed fruit, juices	1.0
Fresh fruit, juices	.7
Soup	1.1
Sugar substitutes	.5
Nuts, nut products	.3
Egg substitutes	0
Total	100.0
Total food advertising time (minutes)	751.5

[*]Restaurants and food preparation equipment excluded.

SOURCE: Unpublished thesis material, Lynne Masover, Department of Community Health and Preventive Medicine, Northwestern University Medical School, Chicago, Ill.

TABLE 19.—*Total weekend food advertising by food groups on four Chicago Television stations, August 4–10, 1975 (including local and network advertising)*[*]

Food group	All stations combined
Nonnutritive beverage	51.
Beer and wine	24.
Carbonated (with sugar)	17.
Carbonated (sugar-free)	2.
Drink mixes	4.
Coffee and tea	3.
Grain	19.
Bread, cereal, and pasta	10.
Baked goods	9.
Sugar and sweets	12.
Candy, frosting, syrups	7.
Chewing gum (sugar)	4.
Chewing gum (sugar-free)	1.
Gelatin, pudding	
Oil, fat, and margarine	5.
Oil, fat and margarine	3.
Salad dressing	2.
Snack foods	3.
Corn chips	1.
Potato chips	1.
All other snack foods	1.
Dairy	2.
High fat dairy	1.
Low fat dairy	
Vegetables	1.
Processed vegetables, juice	1
Fresh vegetables	0
Processed potato products	
Relishes, condiments, sauces	1.
Processed meat, fish, poultry	
Fish, seafood, poultry	
Beef, pork, lamb	
Sugar substitutes	0
Eggs and egg substitutes	0
Food store specials	0
Fruit	0
Infant foods	0
Nut products	0
Soup	0
	99.
Total food advertising time (minutes)	100.

[*]Restaurants and food preparation equipment excluded.

SOURCE: Unpublished thesis material, Lynne Masover, Department of Community Health and Preventive Medicine, Northwestern University Medical School, Chicago, Ill.

With respect to restaurant and fast food advertising, not included in the above totals, the percent of total general advertising time devoted to them rose from 2.8 percent on weekdays to 3.2 percent on weekends.

In the report's conclusion, Masover and Stamler said:

When this outlay of food advertising is juxtaposed with what is known about the prevalence in the United States of malnutrition of both the under-nutrition and over-nutrition types, coronary heart disease, hypertension, diabetes, and alcoholic liver cirrhosis, it is reasonable to conclude that on weekdays over 70 percent and on weekends over 85 percent is negatively related to the nation's health needs . . . Television is the primary source of information for the American public today. On the other hand, positive nutrition education from other sources is comparatively miniscule in the country. Thus it is reasonable to infer further that these combined circumstances are significant contributors to the current array of nutrition-related health problems. Therefore it is further reasonable to inquire why food advertising time on television should not be used exclusively to present the viewing audience with good rather than bad food choices?

A report prepared by Richard Manoff for the Ninth International Congress of Nutrition in 1972 suggests that more than 50 percent of the money spent on television food advertising may be negatively related to health. Calculations based on Table 20, provided in his report, indicate that a minimum of 48 percent of the money spent on television food advertising in 1971 went for items that may be generally characterized as high in fat, saturated fat, cholesterol, refined and processed sugar, salt or alcohol. This is a conservative estimate, not including sugared cereals and certain cake mixes, meat products, butter and cheeses that may be high in one or more of the dietary risk factors. In addition, coffee, tea and cocoa are not included in this calculation.

TABLE 20.—U.S. FOOD AND BEVERAGE ADVERTISING EXPENDITURES

[In thousands of dollars]

	1971	
	6-media total [1]	TV
gars, sirups, and jellies	10,125.2	[2] 5,993.2
ortening and oils	39,547.7	[2] 34,498.6
ur and prepared baking mixes	18,580.6	12,603.6
asons, spices, and extracts	6,576.1	[2] 4,363.9
sserts and dessert ingredients	32,361.4	[2] 22,824.3
ndiments, pickles, and relishes	10,785.2	[2] 8,056.3
uces, gravies, dips	13,214.8	[2] 10,986.2
ad dressings and mayonnaise	20,506.1	[2] 15,814.6
scellaneous ingredients	14,753.0	12,639.3
ups	25,608.5	17,028.7
reals	89,144.0	81,645.5
alth and dietary foods	9,893.2	4,047.1
ant foods	3,074.0	2,161.3
stas	25,426.4	21,010.0
pared dinners	27,850.9	22,305.3
k, butter, and eggs	30,358.8	25,622.8
eese	11,170.4	8,651.2
cream and sherbets	4,575.3	[2] 4,195.5
uits and vegetables	36,239.5	24,198.5
ats, poultry, fish	50,131.5	42,631.1
ead and rolls	50,183.2	34,454.8
kes, pies, cookies	24,244.7	[2] 21,189.0
fee, tea, cocoa	82,084.7	75,691.4
it and vegetable juice	23,105.0	19,991.8
ndy, gum, snacks	104,190.2	[2] 98,298.3
t drinks	108,050.4	[2] 96,055.8
er, wine, liquor	231,785.6	[2] 104,712.7
Total food and beverage [3]	1,159,522.6	890,882.4

[1] Total of measured media excluding spot radio.
[2] Used to determine percent advertising that may be negatively related to health.
[3] Including combination copy advertising which is not detailed.

Source: LNA Competitive Brand Cumulative for 1970 and 1971 (4), presented in "Potential Uses of Mass Media in Nutrition Programs," R. K. Manoff, and appearing in the proceedings of the 9th International Congress on Nutrition, Mexico, 1972, vol. 4, pp. 256-277 (Karger, Basel 1975).

It is important to point out that the amounts of advertising for various kinds of foods are not dictated by any overall plan for the achievement of a healthful diet but by needs of various firms at any given moment. Furthermore, those foods most heavily advertised are predominantly processed foods since it is difficult to develop brand loyalties for relatively undifferentiated raw staples.

ADVERTISING AND LOW-INCOME CONSUMERS

It is likely that those most influenced by food advertising are low-income and elderly consumers who are least capable of comprehending written guidance on food selection and least able to make comparisons between foods based on the nutrition labelling and price.

A report quoted by James T. Parker of the Division of Adult Education of the U.S. Office of Education at the Department of Agriculture's 1976 Outlook Conference, found that, with respect to consumer economics, almost 30 percent of the population falls into the lowest category of functional literacy:

In terms of the general knowledge areas, the greatest area of difficulty appears to be consumer economics. Almost 30 percent of the population falls into the lowest level (those adults who function only with difficulty because of their unsatisfactory mastery of the requirements for functional literacy), while one-third of the population is categorized as (those adults who are functional, but not proficient).

This means, the report said, that about 34.7 million adults "function with difficulty" within consumer economics and an additional 39 million "are functional (but not proficient)." As an example, the report noted:

When given pictures of three competing packaged cereals marked by net weight and price, only three out of four respondents identified the cereal which, in the sense of lowest cost per ounce, was the "best buy."

The report finds that the level of general competency decreases as levels of education and income decline. And the report finds ". . . the general trend is that the older the individual, the more likely that he/she is incompetent."

In a test gauging nutrition knowledge, 71 percent correctly selected tuna when asked to choose an item for a high-protein dinner from the list: tuna, macaroni, peaches and spinach. The report shows the lowest percent choosing the correct answer, 60 percent, was in the lowest income grouping, under $5,000 family income. In this group, 26 percent selected spinach, the most often chosen incorrect answer among all groups.

Scores by age grouping were: 18–29 years, 62 percent correct; 30–39 years, 79 percent correct; 40–49 years, 80 percent correct; 50–59 years, 72 percent correct, 60–65 years, 66 percent correct.

In another test related to nutrition, only 56 percent correctly calculated the number of calories in question. Again, the lowest scores fell in the lowest income and highest age groups. In the under-$5000 family income group, only 38 percent achieved the correct answer.

LACK OF NUTRITION INFORMATION

While constantly presented with persuasive messages on the kinds of food to buy, the consumer has had remarkably little information on the nutritional characteristics of the food itself.

Currently, nutrition labelling is voluntary and therefore not available on many food packages. Moreover, labels rarely provide information on the types of fats in food, or amounts of sugar, cholesterol or calories. Food additives are listed for some foods but not others.

In short, the situation is one in which the consumer is under intense pressure to buy certain foods but at the same time is ignorant of some of their most important nutritional characteristics.

The following recommendations are based on the premise that the first step toward improving the nation's health through diet is provision of information that will enable food growers, processors, wholesalers, retailers and consumers to make more healthful food choices.

RECOMMENDATIONS

To encourage the achievement of the foregoing dietary goals, it i recommended:

1. That Congress provide money for a public education program i nutrition based on the foregoing or similar goals. The initial min mum period for the promotion of these dietary goals should be fi years.

Such a campaign should involve the following five functional areas

(1) health and nutrition education in the classroom and caf terias of our schools;

(2) nutrition and health education for school food servic worl·ers;

(3) nutrition education in the federally-funded food assis ance programs;

(4) nutrition education conducted by the Extension Servi of the Department of Agriculture; and

(5) extensive use of television to educate the public in the p tential benefits of following certain dietary goals.

2. That Congress require food labelling for all foods, containing t following information to enable the consumer to make informed con parisons between foods:

(1) percent and type of fats;

(2) percent sugar;

(3) milligrams of cholesterol;

(4) milligrams of salt;

(5) caloric content;

(6) a complete listing of food additives for all foods, inclu ing those now covered by standards of identity; and

(7) nutrition labelling which is currently voluntary.

3. That Congress provide money to the Departments of Agric ture and Health, Education, and Welfare to jointly conduct studi and pilot projects that would develop new techniques in food proces ing and institutional and home meal preparation aimed at reduci risk factors in the diet.

4. That Congress increase funding for human nutrition research the Department of Agriculture in accordance with the plan of t Agricultural Research Service, contained in Appendix D, and th Congress establish a committee for the coordination of human nut tion research undertaken by the Departments of Agriculture a Health, Education, and Welfare.

5. That the Department of Agriculture and Department of Heal Education, and Welfare form a joint committee to periodically co sider the implications of nutritional health concerns on agricultu policy.

BIBLIOGRAPHY

Agricultural Research Service. *Composition of Foods, Agriculture Handbook No. 8.* U.S. Department of Agriculture. December 1963.

Agricultural Research Service. Nutritional Review, National Food Situation, CFE (Adm.) 299–9, January 1975. U.S. Department of Agriculture.

Agricultural Research Service. *Nutritive Value of American Foods, Agriculture Handbook No. 456.* U.S. Department of Agriculture. November 1975.

Agricultural Research Service. Nutritional Review, CFE (Adm.) 299–11, January 1977. U.S. Department of Agriculture.

American Heart Association. *Position on the Federal Trade Commission Proposed Regulations Concerning Fats and Cholesterol in Foods.* Statement presented at Federal Trade Commission hearings on nutritional information in food advertising. 1976.

Ashley, F. W. and Kannel, W. B. *Relation of Weight Change to Changes in Atherogenic Traits: The Framingham Study.* Journal of Chronic Diseases, March 1974.

Aykroyd, W. R.; Doughty, Joyce. *Wheat in Human Nutrition.* Food and Agriculture Organization of the United Nations. Rome, Italy. 1970.

Baker, Doris. *Fiber in Wheat Foods,* unpublished study. Agricultural Research Service, U.S. Department of Agriculture. 1976. (Presented at the 61st Annual Meeting of the American Association of Cereal Chemists.)

Bartoshuk, L. M. and others. *Saltiness of Monosodium Glutamate and Sodium Intake.* (Letter to the editor, Journal of the American Medical Association, Vol. 230. No. 5, November 4, 1974.)

Beloian, Arletta. Food and Drug Administration memorandum: *Estimates of average, 90th percentile and maximum daily intakes of FD & C artificial food colors in one day's diets among two age groups of children.* July 30, 1976.

Bettelheim, Bruno. *Food to Nurture the Mind.* School Review, Vol. 83, May 1975.

Blix, G.; Isaksson, B.; Wretlind, A. *Activities in Sweden to Improve Dietary Habits.* Clinical Nutrition. S. Karger. New York. 1973.

Brainard, John B. *Salt Load as a Trigger for Migraine.* Minnesota Medicine, Vol. 59, April 1976.

Burkitt, Denis P. *The Role of Dietary Fiber.* Nutrition Today. January/February 1976.

Burros, Marian. *Feeding the Inmates.* Washington Post. May 6, 1976.

Burros, Marian. *Kids: Nutrition or Convenience.* Washington Post. August 26, 1977.

Buzzell, Robert D.; Nourse, Robert E. M. *Product Innovation in Food Processing.* Harvard University. Boston. 1967.

Consumer and Food Economics Institute, U.S. Department of Agriculture, Agricultural Research Service, Hyattsville, Maryland. "Comprehensive Evaluation of Fatty Acids in Foods," *Journal of The American Dietetic Association*, May 1975; July 1975; August 1975; October 1975; March 1976; April 1976; July 1976; September 1976; November 1976; January 1977.

Consumer and Food Economics Institute, U.S. Department of Agriculture, Agricultural Research Service, Hyattsville, Maryland. "Comprehensive Evaluation of Fatty Acids in Foods: Shellfish", unpublished.

Department of Health, Education, and Welfare. *Forward Plan for Health FY 1978–82*. Government Printing Office. 1976.

Feeley, R. M.; Criner, P. E. and Watt, B. K. Cholesterol Content of Foods. Journal of the American Dietetic Association. Vol. 61, No. 2, August 1972.

Food and Nutrition Board. *Recommended Dietary Allowances*. National Academy of Sciences. Washington, D.C. 1974.

Fremes, Ruth; Sabry, Zak. *NutriScore*. Methuen/Two Continents Publications. New York. 1976.

Friend, Berta, *Nutrients in United States Food Supply, Review of Trends, 1909–13 to 1965*. The American Journal of Clinical Nutrition. Vol. 20, No. 8, August 1967.

Friend, Berta. *Changes in Nutrients in the U.S. Diet Caused by Alterations in Food Intake Patterns*. Agricultural Research Service, U.S. Department of Agriculture. 1974.

Gray, Fred; Little, Thomas W. *Sugar and Sweetener Report*. Vol. 1, No. 8, September 1976. U.S. Department of Agriculture. Washington, D.C.

Harris, Robert S.; Karmas, Endel, editors. *Nutritional Evaluation of Food Processing*. Avi Publishing Company Inc. Westport, Connecticut. 1975.

Jacobsen, Michael F. *Nutrition Scoreboard*. Avon Books, New York 1974.

Lappe, Frances Moore, *Diet for a Small Planet*. Ballantine Books. New York. 1971.

Leverton, Ruth M. *Fats in Food and Diet*. Agricultural Research Service, U.S. Department of Agriculture, Agriculture Information Bulletin No. 361. 1976.

Manber, Malcolm. *The Medical Effects of Coffee*. Medical World News. Vol. 17, January 1976.

Manchester, Alden C. *Total Consumer Buying of Fresh Versus Processed Food Remains Stable* NFS–144 and unpublished up-dating of this report. Economic Research Service, U.S. Department of Agriculture. 1973.

Manoff, Richard K. *Potential Uses of Mass Media in Nutrition Programs*. Proceedings of the 9th International Nutrition Congress on Nutrition, Mexico, 1972. Karger, Basel. 1975.

Masover, Lyn; Stamler, Jeremiah. *Television Food Commercials: A Positive or Negative Contribution to Nutrition Education?* Paper presented at the American Public Health Association Annual Meeting October 21, 1972.

Mattern, Paul J. panel chairman. Natural Levels of Vitamins and Minerals in Commercially Milled Wheat Flour in the United States and Canada. Report presented at the 61st Annual Meeting of the American Association of Cereal Chemists.

Mayer, Jean. *Human Nutrition*. Charles C. Thomas, Springfield Illinois. 1972.

Mayer, Jean. *Adult diabetes: Sugar of Overweight the Culprit?* Los Angeles Times, October 23, 1975.

Mayer, Jean. *The Bitter Truth About Sugar*. New York Times Magazine, June 20, 1976.

Maxwell, John C. Jr. Statistics provided for Table 11. Maxwell Associates. Richmond, Virginia. 1977.

MEDCOM, Inc. *Atherosclerosis*. New York. 1974.

Mickelsen, Olaf. *The Nutritional Value of Bread*. Cereal Foods World. Vol. 20, No. 7, July 1975.

Mintz, Morton. *Fat Intake Seen Increasing Cancer Risk*. Washington Post, September 10, 1976.

Molitor, Graham T. T. *Anticipating Public Issues: Nutrition, Diet, Health, and Food Quality*. Unpublished report prepared for the General Accounting Office. 1976.

National Board of Health and Welfare, Sweden. *Diet and Exercise*. Stockholm, 1972.

National Commission on Food Marketing. *Food From Farmer to Consumer*. Government Printing Office. 1966.

Northcutt, Norvell, and others. *Adult Functional Competency: A Summary*. University of Texas, Austin. 1975.

Nutrition Foundation, The. *Present Knowledge in Nutrition*. Washington, D.C. 1976.

Rizek, Robert L.; Friend, Berta; Page, Louise. *Fate in Today's Food Supply—Level of Use and Sources*. Journal of the American Oil Chemists' Society. Vol. 51, No. 6, June 1974.

Royal Norwegian Ministry of Agriculture, *Report to the Storting No. 32 (1975–76) on Norwegian Nutrition and Food Policy*. Oslo 1975.

Seib, Paul. *Nutritional Value of Bread*, unpublished classroom compendium. Kansas State University.

Select Committee on Nutrition and Human Needs. Nutrition Education—1972: Part 1—Overview—Consultant's Recommendations December 5, 1972. Government Printing Office.

Select Committee on Nutrition and Human Needs. National Nutrition Policy Study—1974: Part 5—Nutrition and the Consumer, June 20 1974. Government Printing Office.

Select Committee on Nutrition and Human Needs. National Nutrition Policy Study—1974: Part 6A—Appendix to Nutrition and Health June 21, 1974. Government Printing Office.

Select Committee on Nutrition and Human Needs. 1975 Food Price Study, hearings. Part I—Food Prices: The Federal Role, September 30, October 1, 1975. Government Printing Office.

Select Committee on Nutrition and Human Needs. Diet and Killer Diseases hearings. July 27, 28, 1976. Government Printing Office. January 1977.

Senti, F. R. Contribution of Grain Products in U.S. Diets. Talk presented to 67th Annual Meeting of the Millers National Federation, April 28–30, 1969. Agricultural Research Service. U.S. Department of Agriculture.

Sipple, Horace L.; McNutt, Kristen W., editors. *Sugars in Nutrition.* Academic Press. New York. 1974.

Stiebeling, Hazel K. *Some Nutritional Considerations in Long-Range Outlook.* Address presented at the 26th Annual Agricultural Outlook Conference, October 11, 1948. Bureau of Agricultural Economics, U.S. Department of Agriculture.

Traub, Larry G.; Odland, Dianne. *Convenience Foods—1975 Cost Update.* Economic Research Service, U.S. Department of Agriculture. Presented at the National Agricultural Outlook Conference, November 20, 1975.

Turpeinen, O. *Future Trends in Nutrition: Fats and Oils.* Future Trends in Nutrition and Dietetics. S. Karger. New York. 1975.

U.S. Department of Agriculture. *Handbook of Agricultural Charts, Agricultural Handbook No. 504.* 1976.

Vergroesen, A. J. *Physiological Effects of Dietary Linoleic Acid.* Statement presented at Federal Trade Commission hearings on nutritional information in food advertising. 1976.

Washington Star. *Dragons for Lunch* (editorial). June 1, 1976.

Weihrauch, John D.; Brignoli, Carol A., Reeves, James B. III, and Iverson, John L.: *Fatty Acid Composition of Margarines, Processed Fats, and Oils: A New Compilation of Data for Tables of Food Composition.*

White, Philip L.; Selvey, Nancy, editors. *Nutritional Qualities of Fresh Fruits and Vegetables.* Futura Publishing Company. Mount Kisco, New York. 1974.

APPENDIX A

BENEFITS FROM HUMAN NUTRITION RESEARCH

[By C. Edith Weir]

This report is part of a study conducted at the direction of the Agricultural Research Policy Advisory Committee, U.S. Department of Agriculture. A joint task group representing the State Agricultural Experiment Stations and the U.S. Department of Agriculture was assigned the responsibility for making the study. Task group members were:

Dr. Virginia Trotter, co-chairman, dean, College of Home Economics, University of Nebraska; Dr. Steven C. King, co-chairman, associate director, Science and Education Staff, U.S. Department of Agriculture; Dr. Walter L. Fishel, assistant professor, Department of Agriculture and Applied Economics, University of Minnesota; Dr. H. Wayne Bitting, program planning and evaluation staff, Agricultural Research Service, U.S. Department of Agriculture; Dr. C. Edith Weir, Assistant Director, Human Nutrition Research Division, Agricultural Research Service, U.S. Department of Agriculture.

Better health, a longer active lifespan, and greater satisfaction from work, family and leisure time are among the benefits to be obtained from improved diets and nutrition. Advances in nutrition knowledge and its application during recent decades have played a major role in reducing the number of infant and maternal deaths, deaths from infectious diseases, particularly among children, and in extending the productive lifespan and life expectancy. Significant benefits are possible both from new knowledge of nutrient and food needs and from more complete application of existing knowledge. The nature and magnitude of these benefits is estimated in Table 1. Potential benefits may accrue from alleviating nutrition-related health problems, from increased individual performance and satisfactions and increased efficiency in food services. A vast reservoir of health and economical benefits can be made available by research yet to be done on human nutrition.

Major health problems are diet related.—Most all of the health problems underlying the leading causes of death in the United States (Fig. 1) could be modified by improvements in diet. The relationship of diet to these health problems and others is discussed in greater detail later in this report. Death rates for many of these conditions are higher in the U.S. than in other countries of comparable economic development. Expenditures for health care in the U.S. are skyrocketing, accounting for 67.2 billion dollars in 1970—or 7.0 percent. of the entire U.S. gross national product.

The real potential from improved diet is preventive.—Existing evidence is inadequate for estimating potential benefits from improved diets in terms of health. Most nutritionists and clinicians feel that the real

SOURCE. Human Nutrition Research Division, Agricultural Research Service, U.S. Department of Agriculture. Issued August 1971 by Science and Education Staff, United States Department of Agriculture, Washington, D.C.

98–364 O - 78 - 8

327

potential from improved diet is preventative in that it may defer or modify the development of a disease state so that a clinical condition does not develop. The major research thrust, nationwide, has been on the role of diet in treating health problems after they have developed. This approach has had limited success. USDA research emphasis has been placed on food needs of normal, healthy persons and findings from this work have contributed much of the existing knowledge on their dietary requirements.

Benefits would be shared by all.—Benefits from better nutrition, made possible by improved diets, would be available to the entire population. Each age, sex, ethnic, economic, and geographic segment would be benefited. The lower economic and nonwhite population groups would benefit most from effective application of current knowledge.

These savings are only a small part of what might be accomplished for the entire population from research yet to be done. Some of the improvements can be expressed as dollar benefits to individuals or to the nation. The social and personal benefits are harder to quantify and describe. It is difficult to place a dollar figure on the avoidance of pain or the loss of a family member; satisfactions from healthy, emotionally adjusted families; career achievement; and the opportunity to enjoy leisure time.

Major health benefits are long range.—Predictions of the extent to which diet may be involved in the development of various health problems have been based on current knowledge of metabolic pathways of nutrients, but primarily of abnormal metabolic pathways developed by persons in advanced stages of disease. There is little understanding of when or why these metabolic changes take place. The human body is a complex and very adaptive mechanism. For most essential metabolic processes alternate pathways exist which can be utilized in response to physiological, diet, or other stress. Frequently, a series of adjustments take place and the ultimate result does not become apparent for a long time, even years, when a metabolite such as cholesterol accumulates. Early adjustment of diet could prevent the development of undesirable long-range effects. Minor changes in diet and food habits instituted at an early age might well avoid the need for major changes, difficult to adopt later in life.

Regional differences in diet related problems.—The existence of regional differences in the incidence of health problems has been generally recognized and a wide variation in death rates still exists among geographic areas. These differences in death rate may reflect the cumulative effect of chronic low intake levels of some nutrients throughout the lifespan and by successive generations. A number of examples of regional health problems attributable to differences in the nutrient content of food or to dietary pattern could be given. Perhaps the best known is "the goiter belt" where soils and plants were low in iodine and the high incidence and death rate of goiter was reduced when the diet was supplemented with iodine. Another situation existed in some of the southern states where pellagra was a scourge a few decades ago. Corn was the major food protein source for low income families in these areas. The resulting niacin deficiency raised the incidence of pellagra to epidemic proportions.

Migration from the high death rate areas almost always results in a reduction in the death rate, although the improvement never approaches the level achieved by those who were born and continued to live in the low rate areas. Similarly, persons who move from low rate areas into higher rate areas lose part of the advantage. If the death rate for one of the high death rate areas, Wilkes Barre, Pennsylvania, were applied to the entire U.S. population, 140,489 more persons under 65 years would have died per year during the period 1959–61. If the death rate for one of the lower rate areas, Nebraska, had prevailed there would have been 131,634 fewer deaths. The highest death rate areas generally correspond to those where agriculturists have recognized the soil as being depleted for several years. This suggests a possible relationship between submarginal diets and health of succeeding generations.

TABLE 1.—MAGNITUDE OF BENEFITS FROM NUTRITION RESEARCH

Health problem	Magnitude of loss	Potential savings from improved diet
PART A. NUTRITION RELATED HEALTH PROBLEMS		
Heart and vasculatory	Over 1,000,000 deaths in 1967	25-percent reduction.
	Over 5 million people with definite or suspect heart disease in 1960–62	20-percent reduction.
	$31.6 billion in 1962	
Respiratory and infectious	82,000 deaths per year	20 percent fewer incidents.
	246 million incidents in 1967	15–20 percent fewer days lost.
	141 million work-days lost in 1955–66	Do.
	166 million school days lost	$1 million.
	$5 million in medical and hospital costs	$20 million.
	$1 billion in cold remedies and tissues	
Mental health	2.5 percent of population of 5.2 million people are severely or totally disabled. 25 million people have manifest disability.	10 percent fewer disabilities.
Infant mortality and reproduction.	Infant deaths in 1967—79,000	50 percent fewer deaths.
	Infant death rate 22.4 per 1,000	Do.
	Fetal death rate 15.6 per 1,000	Do.
	Maternal death rate 28.0 per 1,000 live births	Do.
	Child death rate (1–4 yrs.) 96.1 per 100,000 in 1964	Reduce rate to 10 per 100,000.
	15 million with congenital birth defects	3 million fewer children with birth defects.
Early aging and lifespan	49.1 percent of population, about 102 million people have one or more chronic impairments.	10 million people without impairments
	People surviving to age 65:	Percent
	White males — 66	1 percent improvement per year to 90 percent surviving.
	Black males — 50	
	White females — 81	
	Black females — 64	
	Life expectancy in years:	
	White males — 67.8	Bring Black expectancy up to to White.
	Black males — 61.1	
	White females — 75.1	
	Black females — 68.2	
Arthritis	16 million people afflicted	8 million people without afflictions.
	27 million work days lost	13.5 million work days.
	500,000 people unemployed	125,000 people employed.
	Annual cost $3.6 billion	$900 million per year.
Dental health	44 million with gingivitis; 23 million with advanced periodontal disease; $6.5 billion public and private expenditures on dentists' services in 1967; 22 million endentulous persons (1 in 8) in 1957; ½ of all people over 55 have no teeth.	50 percent reduction in incidence severity and expenditures.
Diabetes and carbohydrate disorders.	3.9 million overt diabetic; 35,000 deaths in 1967; 79 percent of people over 55 with impaired glucose tolerance.	50 percent of cases avoided or improved.
Osteoporosis	4 million severe cases, 25 percent of women over 40	75 percent reduction.
Obesity	3 million adolescents; 30 to 40 percent of adults; 60 to 70 percent over 40 years.	80 percent reduction in incidence.
Anemia and other nutrient deficiencies.	See improved work efficiency, growth and development, and learning ability.	
Alcoholism	5 million alcoholics; ½ are addicted	33 percent.
	About 24,500 deaths in 1967 caused by alcohol	Do.
	Annual loss over $2 billion from absenteeism, lowered production and accidents.	Do.

TABLE 1.—MAGNITUDE OF BENEFITS FROM NUTRITION RESEARCH—Continued

Health problem	Magnitude of loss	Potential savings from improved diet
esight	48.1 percent, or 86 million people over 3 years wore corrective lenses in 1966; 81,000 become blind every year; $103 million in welfare.	20 percent fewer people blind or with corrective lenses.
smetic	10 percent of women ages 5 or more with vitamin intakes below recommended daily allowances.	
ergies	32 million people (9 percent) are allergic.	20 percent people relieved.
	16 million with hayfever asthma.	
	7–15 million people (3–6 percent) allergic to milk.	90 percent people relieved.
	Over 693 thousand persons (1 in 3,000) allergic to gluten.	Do.
gestive	8,495 thousand work-days lost; 5,013 thousand school-days lost; About 20 million incidents of acute condition annually.	25 percent fewer acute conditions.
	$4.2 billion annual cost; 14 million persons with duodenal ulcers; $5 million annual cost; 4,000 new cases each day.	Over $1 billion in costs.
ney and urinary	55,000 deaths from renal failure; 200,000 with kidney stones.	20 percent reduction in deaths and acute conditions.
scular disorders	200,000 cases.	10 percent reduction in cases.
cer	600,000 persons developed cancer in 1968; 320,000 persons died of cancer in 1968.	20 percent reduction in incidence and deaths.

PART B. INDIVIDUAL SATISFACTIONS INCREASED

roved work efficiency		5 percent increase in on the job productivity.
roved growth and development	113,000 deaths from accident. 324.5 million work-days lost; 51.8 million people needing medical attention and/or restricted activity.	25 percent fewer deaths and work-days lost.
roved learning ability	Over 6.5 million mentally retarded persons with I.Q. below 70; 12 percent of school age children need special education.	Raise I.Q. by 10 points for persons with I.Q. 70–80.

PART C. INCREASED EFFICIENCY IN FOOD SERVICES

roved efficiency in food eparation and menu anning.		Not estimated.
uced losses of nutrients food storage, handling, d preparation.		Do.
roved efficiency in food lection.		Do.
roved efficiency in food ograms.		Do.

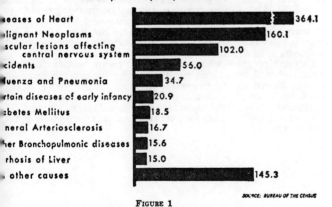

LEADING CAUSES OF DEATH
Rates per 100,000, U.S. 1969

- eases of Heart — 364.1
- lignant Neoplasms — 160.1
- scular lesions affecting central nervous system — 102.0
- cidents — 56.0
- luenza and Pneumonia — 34.7
- rtain diseases of early infancy — 20.9
- abetes Mellitus — 18.5
- neral Arteriosclerosis — 16.7
- her Bronchopulmonic diseases — 15.6
- rhosis of Liver — 15.0
- other causes — 145.3

SOURCE: BUREAU OF THE CENSUS

FIGURE 1

GENERAL POPULATION—RECOMMENDATIONS OF 12 EXPERT COMMITTEES ON DIETARY FAT AND CORONARY HEART DISEASE

Country	Fat content of total calories percent	Increased PUFA (polyunsaturated fatty acids)	PUFA–SAFA ratio (polyunsaturated fatty acids to saturated fatty acids)	Daily dietary cholesterol (milligrams)	Reduction of sugar	Advised labeling of fat content of foods
United States:						
Inter-Soc. Commission for Heart Disease Resources 1970	<35	Yes	1.0	<300		Yes.
American Health Foundation (1972)	35	Yes	1.0	300	Yes	Yes.
						Yes.
American Heart Association (1973)	35	Yes	1.0	300	Yes	Yes.
White House Conference (1973)	35	Yes		300	Yes	Yes.
Norway, Sweden, and Finland, 1968	25–35				Yes	Yes.
United Kingdom:						
DHSS COMA Report (1974)	(1)	No			Yes	
Royal College Physicians & British Cardiac Society (1975)	(2)	Yes		(3)	Yes	
New Zealand:						
Heart Foundation (1971)	35			300–600		
Royal Society (1971)		No		(2)		
Australia:						
Academy of Science (1975)	35	Yes	1.0	<350	Yes	Yes.
Germany: (Federal Republic) (1975)	(1)			300		
The Netherlands (1973)	35	Yes	1.0	250–300	Yes	Yes.

1 Reduce total fat, especially saturated.
2 Toward 35.
3 Reduce.
4 Reduce saturated fat.

Source: "Physiological Effects of Dietary Linoleic Acid," A. J. Vergroesen. Statement prepared for Federal Trade Commission hearing on nutrition information in food advertising, 1976.

HIGH RISK POPULATION—RECOMMENDATIONS OF 6 EXPERT COMMITTEES ON DIETARY FAT AND CORONARY HEART DISEASE

Country	Fat content of total calories (percent)	Increased PUFA (polyunsaturated fatty acids)	PUFA–SAFA ratio (polyunsaturated fatty acids to saturated fatty acids)	Daily dietary cholesterol (milligrams)	Reduction of sugar	Advised labeling of fat content of foods
United States:						
Inter-Soc. Commission for Heart Disease Resources 1970	<35	Yes	1.0	<300		Yes.
American Medical Association (1972)	(1)	Yes		(2)		Yes.
New Zealand:						
Heart Foundation (1971)	35	Yes	1.0	300–600		Yes.
Royal Society (1971)	(1)	Yes		(2)		
Australia:						
National Heart Foundation (1974)	30–35	Yes	1.5	<300	Yes	
International Society of Cardiology (1973)	<30	Yes	>1.0	<300		Yes.

1 Substantial decrease in saturated fat.
2 Reduce.
3 Avoid excess saturated fat.

Source: "Physiological Effects of Dietary Linoleic Acid," A. J. Vergroesen. Statement prepred for Federal Trade Commission hearing on nutrition information in food advertising, 1976.

STATE OF KNOWLEDGE ON NUTRITIONAL REQUIREMENTS

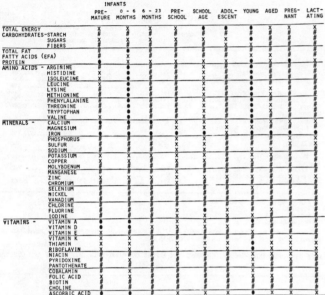

AS OF 1976   # - LITTLE OR NO DATA   X - FRAGMENTARY DATA   ● - SUBSTANTIAL PROGRESS MADE

Nutrition Institute
Agriculture Research Service
United States Department of Agriculture
Beltsville, Maryland 20705

U.S. DEPARTMENT OF AGRICULTURE,
AGRICULTURAL RESEARCH SERVICE,
Washington, D.C., November 12, 1976.

Hon. GEORGE McGOVERN,
Chairman, Select Committee on Nutrition and Human Needs, U.S. Senate, Washington, D.C.

DEAR MR. CHAIRMAN: We welcome the opportunity to respond t your recent request concerning the implementation of a national, com prehensive human nutrition research program under the leadershi of the Agricultural Research Service.

The Department of Agriculture and the Agricultural Researc Service have a comprehensive mandate to perform human nutritio research, including human requirements for nutrients, studies of foo consumption patterns, study of nutrient content of foods and mean of preserving and enhancing its nutrient quality. The Agricultur Research Service ongoing program is funded at a $13 million level.

A significant amount of research has been accomplished in this are but many important questions remain to be answered. For exampl only limited knowledge exists concerning proper diets for humans This was confirmed during recent Congressional Hearings on the rela tionship between diet and disease when the Assistant Secretary fo Health, the nation's top health officer, stated: "While scientists d not yet agree on the specific causal relationships, evidence is mountin and there appears to be general agreement that the kinds and amoun of food and beverages we consume and the style of living common i our generally affluent, sedentary society may be the major factors as sociated with the cause of cancer, cardiovascular disease, and othe chronic illnesses."

The agricultural research community believes that major breal throughs of knowledge can result from an expanded nationally coord nated human nutrition program. Potential savings in terms of huma lives and resources devoted to health care can be immense. Increase knowledge of human requirements for nutrients and how this can b accomplished by changes in crop and animal production practices an food processing techniques can result in increased efficiency in foo consumption patterns. Overall, an expanded nutrition research pro gram can contribute to strengthening the nation's economy and to th well being of its citizens.

National program managers feel that major breakthroughs ca occur and long term needs met by building on research knowledg already known and by concentrating efforts in five major areas o work. Rationale for recommended long-range studies and recurrin additional funding requirements are summarized below:

1. Human requirements for nutrients necessary for optium growt well-being—$66.6 million.

Our dietary guidance for families is hindered by inadequate knowledge about the nutritional needs at different stages of life, and the consequences of inadequate nutrition. This knowledge is needed to guide major USDA feeding programs for groups believed to be at nutritional risk. This research would establish the extent of biological variability for nutrients in individuals differing in age, sex, and genetic background. Many of these population groups have never been studied to quantitate their requirements for a particular nutrient.

2. The nutrient composition of foods and the effects of agricultural practices, handling, food processing and cooking on the nutrients they contain—$11 million.

Nutritional needs must be translated into the foods or food patterns that can best meet these needs. Up-to-date information on the composition of all important foods for the many nutrients required by man is a research goal that requires additional support.

3. Surveillance of nutritional benefits in the evaluation of the USDA food programs—$9.5 million.

The major USDA programs in child nutrition, food stamps for low-income families, and the nutrition education efforts among the hard-to-reach poor need continual surveillance and evaluation in terms of measures of nutritional health of the recipients. Research is needed on the relationship between specific foods in the diet and health.

4. Factors affecting food preferences and food habits—$4.8 million.

The nutrition educator is faced with a problem of helping people to change and improve their nutrition through diet. There is insufficient knowledge about food habits, choice, and motivations. Factors affecting food preference, such as odor, taste, and texture, need increased attention.

5. Techniques and equipment to guide consumers in the selection of food for nutritionally adequate diets in the home or in institutions—$4.7 million.

Guidance of consumers toward nutritionally adequate diets must include research-based knowledge on food management procedures and preparation of foods for the table, to assure retention of both nutritional and eating qualities and to avoid food-borne illness.

National program managers recommend that $60 to $65 million of the proposed $95 million (about 70%) be used to finance research performed by Land-Grant Colleges and other qualified public and private institutions. It is envisioned that the bulk of this research would be performed through the Land-Grant College System.

Estimated funding and distribution of effort in the five categories listed above for the expanded human nutrition program is as follows:

	Intramural Agricultural Research Service		Extramural land-grant and other institutions	
	Amount	Percent	Amount	Percent
	[Dollar amounts in millions]			
Category:				
1	$21.8	70.0	$44.8	70
2	3.1	10.0	6.4	10
3	3.1	10.0	6.4	10
4	1.6	5.1	3.2	5
5	1.5	4.9	3.2	5
Total	31.1	100.0	64.0	100

We appreciate your interest in human nutrition research and hope that the information provided meets your needs. All estimated funding levels are provided for information. They have not had the approval of Department officials or the Office of Management and Budget and should not be considered a request for funds. If I can be of further assistance, please do not hesitate to contact us.

Sincerely,

T. W. EDMINSTER, *Administrator*.

AVERAGE SODIUM AND POTASSIUM CONTENT OF COMMON FOODS [1]

[Weight in grams except as noted]

	Weight (grams)	Sodium (milligrams)	Potassium (milligrams)
Meat, fish or poultry: Cooked without added salt:			
Average	30	33	125
Clams, soft	100	36	239
Clams, hard	100	205	311
Crab, canned	100	1,000	110
Crab, steamed	100	456	271
Flounder	100	237	587
Frankfurters (2)	100	1,100	220
Frozen fish (cod)	100	400	400
Haddock	100	177	348
Kidneys, beef	100	253	324
Lobster, canned	100	210	180
Lobster, fresh	100	325	258
Oysters, raw	100	73	121
Salmon, canned	100	522	349
Salmon, salt-free canned	100	48	391
Scallops, fresh	100	265	476
Shrimp, raw	100	140	220
Shrimp, frozen or canned	100	140	220-312
Sweet breads	100	116	433
Tuna, canned	100	800	240
Tuna, salt-free, canned	100	46	382
Cheese:			
American cheese	30	341	25
Cream cheese	30	75	22
Cottage cheese	30	76	28
Cottage cheese, unsalted	30	6	
Low-sodium cheese (cheddar)	30	3	120
Egg:			
Whole, fresh and frozen (1)	50	61	65
Whites, fresh and frozen	50	73	70
Yolks, fresh	50	26	49
Milk:			
Buttermilk, cultured	120	135	192
Condensed sweetened milk	120	135	377
Evaporated milk, undiluted	120	142	364
Powdered milk. skim	30	160	544
Low-sodium milk, canned	120	6	288
Whole	240	120	346
Yogurt (skim milk)	100	51	143
Vegetables (See p. 82).			
Potato:			
White, baked in skin	100	4	323
White, boiled	100	2	285
Instant, prepared with water, milk, fat.	100	256	290
Sweet (canned solid pack)	100	48	200
Bread and cereal products:			
Breads:			
Bakery white	25	127	26
Bakery, wholewheat	25	132	68
Bakery, rye	25	139	36
Low sodium (local)	25	4	25
Plain muffin	40	132	38
English muffin	57	215	57
A-proten rusk (1)	11	4	5
Graham crackers (2)	14	93	53
Low-sodium crackers (2)	9	10	11
Vanilla wafers (5)	14	35	10
Yeast doughnut	30	70	24
Cake doughnut	35	160	32

See footnotes at end of table.

AVERAGE SODIUM AND POTASSIUM CONTENT OF COMMON FOODS—Continued [1]

[Weight in grams except as noted]

	Weight (grams)	Sodium (milligrams)	Potassium (milligrams)
Bread and cereal products—Continued			
Cereal (dry):			
Kellogg's Corn Flakes	30	282	
Puffed Rice	15	Trace	
Rice Krispies	30	267	
Special K	30	244	
Puffed Wheat	15	Trace	
Shredded Wheat	20	1	
Kellogg's Sugar Frosted Flakes	30	200	
Sugar Pips	30	67	
Bran Flakes	30	118	
Cereal (cooked—without added salt):			
Corn grits—enriched, regular	100	1	
Farina enriched—regular	100	2	
Farina instant cooking	100	7	
Farina quick cooking	100	190	
Oatmeal or Rolled Oats	100	2	
Pettijohn's Wheat.	100	Trace	
Rice	100	5	
Rice, instant	100	Trace	Tr
Wheat, rolled	100	Trace	
Wheatena	100	Trace	
Fat:			
Bacon (1 strip)	7	73	
Butter	5	49	
Margarine	5	49	
Mayonnaise	15	90	
Mayonnaise, low-sodium	15	17	
Low-sodium butter	15	1	
Unsalted margarine (Fleishman's)	5	1	
Vegetable oil	15	0	
Cream:			
Coffee mate	[3] 1	4	
Half-and-half	30	14	
Heavy whipping cream (30 percent)	30	10	
Poly-perx	30		
Sour cream (Sealtest)	30	13	
Table cream (18 percent)	30	13	
Whipped topping	30	4	
Gravy:			
Low sodium (JHH analysis)	30	10	
Regular (JHH analysis)	30	210	
Peanut butter:			
Cellu: Salt free	15	1	
Regular, made with small amounts of added fat and salt	15	91	
Desserts:			
Baked custard (Delmark)	120	128	
D'zerta	120	35	
Gelatin	120	51	
Ice cream (4-oz. cup)	60	23	
Sherbert	60	6	
Water ice	60	Trace	
Cakes:			
All varieties except gingerbread and fruit cakes (both mixes and recipes)	[3] 50	123	
With low-sodium shortening and baking powder	[3] 50	10-20	75
Pies: All varieties except raisin, mince (⅛ of 9-in pie)	[3] 320	375	
Candy:			
Hard candy (1 equals 5 g)	100	32	
Gum drops (8 small equals 10 g)	100	35	
Jelly beans	100	12	
Salt:			
(1 g NaCl—1 packet salt)		400	
(5 g NaCl—1 tsp.)		2,000	
Salt substitutes:			
Diamond Crystal	[4] 500	1	
Co-salt	[4] 500	0	
Adolph's	[4] 500	0	
McCormick's	[4] 500	0	
Morton	[4] 500	0	
Sugar substitutes:			
Saccharine (¼ gr tablet)	1	1	
Sucaryl	[4] 500	0	
Sweet-10	[4] 500	0	
Adolph's	[4] 500	0	
Morton	[4] 500	0	
Diamond Crystal	[4] 500	0	

See footnotes at end of table.

AVERAGE SODIUM AND POTASSIUM CONTENT OF COMMON FOODS—Continued [1]

[Weight in grams except as noted]

	Weight (grams)	Sodium (milligrams)	Potassium (milligrams)
Beverages:			
Beer	100	7	25
Chocolate syrup (2 tsp)	10	5	29
Coca-Cola (JHH analysis)	100	4	1
Coffee, instant (beverage)		1	50
Cranberry juice	100	1	10
Diet Seven-Up	100	10	0
Egg nog, reconstituted	240	250	630
Fresca	100	18	0
Frozen lemonade, reconstituted	100	Trace	16
Gingerale (JHH analysis)	100	6	2
Hot chocolate (Carnation 1 pack—6 oz. water)	100	104	190
Kool-Aid, reconstituted	240	Trace	0
Meritene, reconstituted	240	250	740
Pepsi Cola (JHH analysis)	100	2	4
Royal Crown Cola	100	3	Trace
Seven-Up	100	9	0
Sprite	100	16	0
Tab	100	5	0
Tea, instant (beverage)		Trace	25

[1] Fresh fruits and fruit juices are naturally very low in sodium and thus are not listed individually in this table.
[2] Teaspoon.
[3] Average serving.
[4] Milligrams.

VEGETABLE LISTS

Group I (0–20 mg/100 gm)

NOTE.—Assumes the use of fresh vegetables without salt added in cooking. The amount of salt added to canned and frozen vegetables can vary. Handbook #8 estimates that canned vegetables average 235 mg of sodium/100 gms edible portion. Frozen vegetables range from almost no sodium/100 gms edible portion to as high as 125 mgs of sodium/100 gms. edible portion.

Average 7.4 mg

	Mg Na		Mg Na
Asparagus	7	Mushrooms (raw)	15
Broccoli	12	Mustard green	10
Brussel sprouts	14	Navy beans	7
Cabbage (common)	14	Okra	2
Cauliflower	9	Onions	7
Chicory	7	Parsnips	8
Collards	16	Peas, dried, split (cooked)	13
Corn	2	Peas, green	1
Cow peas	1	Potatoes, baked in skin	4
Cucumbers	6	Potatoes, boiled, pared before cooking	3
Egg plant	1		
Endive	14	Radishes	18
Escarole	14	Rutabagas	4
Green peppers	13	Squash (summer or winter)	1
Kohlrabi	6	String beans	2
Leeks	5	Sweet potato	10
Lentils	3	Tomatoes	4
Lettuce	9	Turnip greens	17
Lima beans (not frozen)	1	Wax beans	2
		Yams	4

Group II (23–60 mg/100 gm)

Average 40 mg

	Mg Na		Mg Na
Artichoke	30	Kale	43
Beets	43	Parsley	45
Black-eyed peas (frozen only)	39	Red cabbage	26
Carrots	33	Spinach	50
Chinese cabbage	23	Turnips	34
Dandelion greens	44	Watercress	52

Group III (75–126 mg/100 gm)

Average 8½ mg

	Mg Na		Mg Na
Beet greens	76	Chard, Swiss	86
Celery	88		

Source: "Composition of foods—raw, processed, prepared." Agricultural Handbook No. 8. U.S. Dept. of Agriculture, Agricultural Research Service, Washington, D.C.: Government Printing Office, 1963.

TABLE I

APPENDICES

COOKING TERMS, METHODS AND SEASONINGS

Au Gratin—*topped with cheese or cheese and crumbs.*
Barbecue—*cooked or served with a highly seasoned sauce.*
Baste—*to moisten with liquid during cooking.*
Bisque—*a rich, thick cream soup.*
Bouillon—*a clear broth.*
Broth—*a thin soup, or the liquid in which food was cooked.*
Casserole—*a combination of foods baked in a dish referred to as a casserole dish.*
Condiments—*relishes, sauces and other accompaniments served with meats, poultry and fish.*
Consomme—*clear soup of two or more meat broths highly seasoned.*
Croquette—*finely cut meat, poultry or fish, shaped, coated and deep fat fried.*
Croutons—*small cubes of bread toasted or lightly browned in fat.*
Curry—*a dish seasoned with curry powder – usually served with a variety of condiments.*
Drippings—*the fat and juices collected in a roasting pan.*

En Brochette—*cooked on a skewer.*
Escalloped or Scalloped—*a combination of foods or foods and a sauce or liquid baked in layers.*
Filet or Fillet—*a boneless, long shaped piece of meat or fish.*
Glazed—*a sweet cooking frequently used on hams.*
Goulash—*a highly seasoned stew.*
Gumbo—*a soup containing okra.*
Parboil—*to partially cook in water.*
Pilau or Pilaf—*rice boiled with meat, poultry or fish and highly seasoned.*
Roux—*a smooth blend of fat and flour used for thickening.*
Stock– *the liquid in which meat or poultry has been cooked.*
Souffle—*a baked dish of finely cut meat, poultry, fish, containing beaten eggs.*
Suet—*the firm white fat of beef.*
Truss—*to fasten together with skewers or string.*

SUBSTITUTES FOR INGREDIENTS

For These	*You May Use These*
1 whole egg, for thickening or baking	2 egg yolks. Or 2½ tablespoons sifted dried whole egg plus 2½ tablespoons water.
1 square (ounce) chocolate	3 tablespoons cocoa plus 1 tablespoon fat.
1 teaspoon sulfate-phosphate baking powder	1½ teaspoons phosphate baking powder. Or 2 teaspoons tartrate baking powder.
1 cup buttermilk or sour milk, for baking	1 cup sweet milk mixed with one of the following: 1 tablespoon vinegar. Or 1 tablespoon lemon juice. Or 1¾ teaspoons cream of tartar.
1 cup fluid whole milk	½ cup evaporated milk plus ½ cup water. Or 1 cup reconstituted dry whole milk. Or 1 cup reconstituted nonfat dry milk plus 2½ teaspoons vegetable fat. (To reconstitute dry milk follow directions on the package.)
1 cup fluid skim milk	1 cup reconstituted nonfat dry milk prepared according to directions on the package.
1 tablespoon flour, for thickening	½ tablespoon cornstarch, potato starch, rice starch, or arrowroot starch. Or 2 teaspoons quick cooking tapioca.
1 cup cake flour, for baking	⅞ cup all-purpose flour.
1 cup all-purpose flour, for baking breads	Up to ½ cup bran, whole-wheat flour, or cornmeal plus enough all-purpose flour to fill cup.

TABLE II

HERB CHART

	Basil	Bay	Marjoram	Oregano	Parsley	Peppermint
Appetizers	Tomato juice, Seafood cocktail	Tomato juice, Aspic		Tomato	Garnish	Fruit cup, Mellon balls, Cranberry juice
Soups	Tomato, Spinach	Stock, Herb bouquet	Spinach, Clam bouillon, Onion	Tomato, Bean	Any Garnish, Herb bouquet	Pea
Fish	Shrimp, Broiled fish, Fillets of fish, Mackerel	Bouillon	Broiled fish, Baked fish, Creamed fish	Stuffing	Any	
Eggs or Cheese	Scrambled eggs, Mock rarebit		Omelette aux fines herbes, Scrambled eggs	Boiled eggs	Creamed eggs, Scrambled eggs	
Meats	Liver, Lamb	Stews, Pot Roast, Shishkebob	Pot roast, Beef, Veal	Lamb, Meat loaf	Lamb, Veal, Steak, Stews	Lamb, Veal
Poultry and Game	Duck	Fricassee, Stews	Creamed chicken, Stuffings	Stuffing	Stuffings, Herb bouquet	
Vegetables	Eggplant, Squash, Tomatoes, Onions	Boiled potatoes, Carrots, Stewed tomatoes	Carrots, Zucchini, Peas, Spinach	Tomatoes, Cabbage, Broccoli	Potatoes, Carrots, Peas	Carrots, New potatoes, Spinach, Zucchini
Salads	Tomato, Mixed green, Sea food	Fish salads, Aspic	Chicken, Mixed green	Tomato aspic, Fish salad	Potato, Fish, Mixed green	Fruit, Coleslaw, Orange, Pear, Mint
Sauces	Tomato, Spaghetti, Orange (for game), Lemon (for fish)	All marinades	White sauce	Spaghetti, Tomato		
Desserts and Beverages	Fruit compote	Custards				Fruit compote, Frostings, Ices, Tea

	Rosemary	Saffron	Sage	Savory	Tarragon	Thyme
Appetizers	Fruit cup		Cottage cheese, Cheese for spread	Vegetable juice cocktail	Fish cocktail, Tomato juice	Tomato juice, Fish cocktails
Soups	Pea, Spinach, Chicken	Fish consomme, Chicken	Cream soup, Chowders	Fish con-somme, Bean	Consomme, Chicken, Tomato	Gumbo, Pea, Clam chowder, Vegetable
Fish	Salmon, Stuffings	Halibut	Stuffings	Broiled fish, Baked fish	Broiled fish, Mock lobster Newburg	Broiled fish, Baked fish
Eggs or Cheese	Scrambled eggs	Scrambled eggs	Cheddar spread, Cottage	Scrambled eggs, Deviled eggs	All egg dishes	Shirred eggs, Cottage cheese
Meats	Lamb, Veal ragout, Beef Stew	Veal	Stews	Veal	Veal	Meat loaf, Veal
Poultry and Game	Turkey, Chicken, Duck	Chicken	Turkey, Stuffings	Chicken, Stuffings	Chicken, Duck	Stuffings, Fricassee
Vegetables	Peas, Spinach, French-fried potatoes	Spanish rice, Rice	Lima beans, Eggplant, Onions, Tomatoes	Beans, Rice, Lentils, Sauerkraut	Salsify, Celery root, Mushrooms, Baked potatoes	Onions, Carrots, Beets
Salads	Fruit	Fish		Mixed green, String bean, Russian	Mixed green, Chicken, Fish	Pickled beets, Tomato, Aspics
Sauces	White sauce, Jelly	Fish sauce		Horse-radish, Fish sauces	Bearmaise	Creole, Herb bouquets
Desserts and Beverages	Fruit compote	Cake Frostings	Sage tea	Stewed pears		

Source: Adapted from the Spice Islands Herb Chart, and printed by permission of Spice Islands Company, South San Francisco, Calif. 335

TABLE III–A

Table of Weights and Measures and Conversion Values

3 teaspoons	=	1 tablespoon
2 tablespoons	=	1 fluid ounce
4 tablespoons	=	¼ cup
8 tablespoons	=	½ cup
16 tablespoons	=	1 cup
2 cups	=	1 pint or 16 fluid ounces
4 cups	=	1 quart
4 quarts	=	1 gallon
4 ounces	=	¼ pound
16 ounces	=	1 pound
1 teaspoon	=	5 cubic centimeters (cc) or 5 grams
1 tablespoon	=	15 cubic centimeters or 15 grams
1 fluid ounce	=	28.5 cubic centimeters (30cc)
1 ounce	=	28.5 grams (or 30 grams in round numbers)
2.2 pounds	=	1 kilogram (1000 grams)
1 pint	=	600 cubic centimeters
3 ounces	=	90 grams or 90 cubic centimeters
3½ ounces	=	100 grams or 100 cubic centimeters
35 fluid ounces (1-3/5 pints)	=	1 liter (1000 cubic centimeters)
1 cup (8 fluid ounces)	=	240 cubic centimeters
1 liter	=	1000 milliliters (ml)
1 gram	=	1000 milligrams (mg)
1 gram	=	1,000,000 micrograms (ug)

 From A.K. Hatfield and P.S. Stanton, *HOW TO HELP YOUR CHILD EAT RIGHT!*, Acropolis Books, Washington, D.C. 20009, 1978, p. 147-148.

TABLE III-B

TABLE OF WEIGHTS AND MEASURES AND CONVERSION VALUES

1 pound butter or margarine	= 4 sticks
	= 2 cups
	= 64 pats or squares
1 stick butter or margarine	= ½ cup
	= 16 pats or squares
1 tablespoon flour	= 1/4 ounce
1 cup flour	= 4-1/2 ounces
4 cups sifted all purpose flour	= 1 pound
4-1/2 cups sifted cake flour	= 1 pound
1 tablespoon sugar	= 3/5 ounce
1 cup sugar	= 10 ounces
2 cups granulated sugar	= 1 pound
2-2/3 cups confectioner's sugar	= 1 pound
2-2/3 cups brown sugar	= 1 pound
1 square of chocolate	= 1 ounce
1 ounce of chocolate	= 1/4 cup cocoa
8 average eggs	= 1 cup
8 to 10 egg whites	= 1 cup
12 to 14 egg yolks	= 1 cup
1 pound of walnuts or pecans in shell	= 1/2 pound shelled

Weight Equivalents

	Milligram	Gram	Kilogram	Grain	Ounce	Pound
1 microgram (mcg)	0.001	0.000001				
1 milligram (mg)	1.	0.001		0.0154		
1 gram (gm)	1,000.	1.	0.001	15.4	0.035	0.0022
1 kilogram (kg)	1,000,000.	1,000.	1.	15,400.	35.2	2.2
1 grain (gr)	64.8	0.065		1.		
1 ounce (oz)		28.3		437.5	1.	0.063
1 pound (lb)		453.6	0.454		16.0	1.

Comparative Temperatures

	Centigrade	Fahrenheit
Boiling water, sea level	100	212
Body temperature	37	98.6
Tropical temperature	30	89
Room temperature, average	20	70
Freezing	0	32

337

TABLE IV

DEFINITIONS

Alcohol — An ingredient in a variety of beverages including beer, wine, mixed or straight drinks. Pure alcohol yields about 7 calories per gram. More than 75% is available in the body.

Calorie — A unit used to express heat or energy value of food.

Carbohydrate — One of three major energy sources in foods.

Cholesterol — A fat-like substance present in blood muscle, liver, brain, and other tissues throughout the body.

Enrichment — The addition of one or more nutrients to a food in order to increase nutritional value.

Fat — One of the three major energy sources in food. Fat yields about 9 calories per gram.

Fiber — An indigestible part of fruits, vegetables, cereals and grain. Fiber is important in the diet as roughage or bulk.

Food Exchange — The measuring of comparable foods in like nutritional value.

Food habit — A pattern of an individual or group serving as a basis for choosing, preparing, and eating food.

Fortification — The addition of one or more food nutrients to a food to "add to" its nutrients content.

Gram — A unit of mass and weight in the metric system. An ounce is 28.25 grams.

Meal Plan — A guide showing the number of food Exchanges to use in each meal and snack to control distribution of calories, carbohydrates, proteins and fats throughout the day.

Mineral — A substance essential in small amounts to build and repair body tissue and/or control functions of the body. Calcium, iron, magnesium, phosphorus, sodium and zinc and other minerals.

Monounsaturated fat — Fat that is neutral in that it neither raises nor lowers blood cholesterol. Olive oil and peanut oil, for example, are monounsaturated.

Nutrient — Substance in food necessary for life. Protein, fats, carbohydrates, minerals, vitamins and water are nutrients.

Polyunsaturated Fat — Fats from vegetable oils such as corn, cotton seed, sunflower, safflower and soybean oil. Oils high in polyunsaturated fats tend to lower the level of cholesterol in the blood.

Protein — One of the three major nutrient groups in foods which contain amino acid that are essential for the life processes. Protein provides about 4 calories per gram.

Saturated fat — Fat that is often hard at room temperature, primarily from animal food products (like butter, lard, meat fat). Saturated fat tends to raise the level of cholesterol in the blood.

Vitamin — Substance essential in small amounts which assist in body processes and functions. This includes vitamins A, D, E, the B complex and C.

TABLE V

HEIGHT-WEIGHT-AGE TABLE FOR BOYS OF SCHOOL AGE*

(Weight is Expressed in Pounds)

HT. INS.	5 YRS.	6 YRS.	7 YRS.	8 YRS.	9 YRS.	10 YRS.	11 YRS.	12 YRS.	13 YRS.	14 YRS.	15 YRS.	16 YRS.	17 YRS.	18 YRS.	19 YRS.	HT. INS.
38	34	34														38
39	35	35														39
40	36	36														40
41	38	38	38													41
42	39	39	39	39												42
43	41	41	41	41												43
44	44	44	44	44												44
45	46	46	46	46	46											45
46	47	48	48	48	48											46
47	49	50	50	50	50	50										47
48		52	53	53	53	53										48
49		55	55	55	55	55	55									49
50		57	58	58	58	58	58	58								50
51			61	61	61	61	61	61								51
52			63	64	64	64	64	64	64							52
53			66	67	67	67	67	67	68							53
54				70	70	70	70	70	71	72						54
55				72	72	73	73	74	74	74						55
56				75	76	77	77	78	78	78	80					56
57					79	80	81	81	82	83	83					57
58					83	84	84	85	85	86	87					58
59						87	88	89	89	90	90	90				59
60						91	92	92	93	94	95	96				60
61							95	96	97	99	100	103	106			61
62							100	101	102	103	104	107	111	116		62
63							105	106	107	108	110	113	118	123	127	63
64								109	111	113	115	117	121	126	130	64
65								114	117	118	120	122	127	131	134	65
66									119	122	125	128	132	136	139	66
67									124	128	130	134	136	139	142	67
68										134	134	137	141	143	147	68
69										137	139	143	146	149	152	69
70										143	144	145	148	151	155	70
71										148	150	151	152	154	159	71
72											153	155	156	158	163	72
73											157	160	162	164	167	73
74											160	164	168	170	171	74

HEIGHT-WEIGHT-AGE TABLE FOR GIRLS OF SCHOOL AGE*

(Weight is Expressed in Pounds)

HT INS.	5 YRS.	6 YRS.	7 YRS.	8 YRS.	9 YRS.	10 YRS.	11 YRS.	12 YRS.	13 YRS.	14 YRS.	15 YRS.	16 YRS.	17 YRS.	18 YRS.	HT. INS.
38	33	33													38
39	34	34													39
40	36	36	36												40
41	37	37	37												41
42	39	39	39												42
43	41	41	41	41											43
44	42	42	42	42											44
45	45	45	45	45	45										45
46	47	47	47	48	48										46
47	49	50	50	50	50	50									47
48		52	52	52	52	53									48
49		54	54	55	55	56	56								49
50		56	56	57	58	59	61	62							50
51			59	60	61	61	63	65							51
52			63	64	64	64	65	67							52
53			66	67	67	68	68	69	71						53
54				69	70	70	71	71	73						54
55				72	74	74	74	75	77	78					55
56					76	78	78	79	81	83					56
57					80	82	82	82	84	88	92				57
58						84	86	86	88	93	96	101			58
59						87	90	90	92	96	100	103	104		59
60						91	95	95	97	101	105	108	109	111	60
61							99	100	101	105	108	112	113	116	61
62							104	105	106	109	113	115	117	118	62
63								110	110	112	116	117	119	120	63
64								114	115	117	119	120	122	123	64
65								118	120	121	122	123	125	126	65
66									124	124	125	128	129	130	66
67									128	130	131	133	133	135	67
68									131	133	135	136	138	138	68
69										135	137	138	140	142	69
70										136	138	140	142	144	70
71										138	140	142	144	145	71

From material prepared by Bird T. Baldwin, Ph.D., Iowa Child Welfare Research Station, State University of Iowa, and Thomas D. Wood, M.D., Columbia University, New York, as cited in Marie V. Krause and Martha A. Hunscher, *Food, Nutrition and Diet Therapy*, Fifth Edition, W. B. Saunders Company, Philadelphia, 1972, p.699.

TABLE VII

DESIRABLE WEIGHTS FOR MEN
(Ages 25 and Over)*

HEIGHT (WITH SHOES, 1-INCH HEELS)		WEIGHT IN POUNDS ACCORDING TO FRAME (IN INDOOR CLOTHING)		
		Small Frame	Medium Frame	Large Frame
Feet	Inches			
5	2	112–120	118–129	126–141
5	3	115–123	121–133	129–144
5	4	118–126	124–136	132–148
5	5	121–129	127–139	135–152
5	6	124–133	130–143	138–156
5	7	128–137	134–147	142–161
5	8	132–141	138–152	147–166
5	9	136–145	142–156	151–170
5	10	140–150	146–160	155–174
5	11	144–154	150–165	159–179
6	0	148–158	154–170	164–184
6	1	152–162	158–175	168–189
6	2	156–167	162–180	173–194
6	3	160–171	167–185	178–199
6	4	164–175	172–190	182–204

*Courtesy of the Metropolitan Life Insurance Company, New York, N.Y. Derived from data of the 1969 Build and Blood Pressure Study, Society of Actuaries.

DESIRABLE WEIGHTS FOR WOMEN
(Ages 25 and Over)*

HEIGHT (WITH SHOES, 2-INCH HEELS)		WEIGHT IN POUNDS ACCORDING TO FRAME (IN INDOOR CLOTHING)		
		Small Frame	Medium Frame	Large Frame
Feet	Inches			
4	10	92– 98	96–107	104–119
4	11	94–101	98–110	106–122
5	0	96–104	101–113	109–125
5	1	99–107	104–116	112–128
5	2	102–110	107–119	115–131
5	3	105–113	110–122	118–134
5	4	108–116	113–126	121–138
5	5	111–119	116–130	125–142
5	6	114–123	120–135	129–146
5	7	118–127	124–139	133–150
5	8	122–131	128–143	137–154
5	9	126–135	132–147	141–158
5	10	130–140	136–151	145–163
5	11	134–144	140–155	149–168
6	0	138–148	144–159	153–173

*Note: for girls between 18 and 25, subtract 1 pound for each year under 25. Courtesy of the Metropolitan Life Insurance Company, New York, N.Y. Derived from data of the 1959 Build and Blood Pressure Study, Society of Actuaries.

From material prepared by Bird T. Baldwin, Ph.D., Iowa Child Welfare Research Station, State University of Iowa, and Thomas D. Wood, M.D., Columbia University, New York, as cited by Marie V. Krause and Martha A. Hunscher, *Food, Nutrition and Diet Therapy*, Fifth Edition, W. B. Saunders Company, Philadelphia, 1972, p. 700.

TABLE VIII-A

FOOD AND NUTRITION BOARD, NATIONAL ACADEMY OF SCIENCES–NATIONAL RESEARCH COUNCIL RECOMMENDED DAILY DIETARY ALLOWANCES,[a] Revised 1974

Designed for the maintenance of good nutrition of practically all healthy people in the U.S.A.

| | Age | Weight | | Height | | Energy | Protein | Fat-Soluble Vitamins | | | |
| | | | | | | | | Vita-min A Activity | | Vita-min D | Vita-min E Activity[e] |
	(years)	(kg)	(lbs)	(cm)	(in)	(kcal)[b]	(g)	(RE)[c]	(IU)	(IU)	(IU)
Infants	0.0–0.5	6	14	60	24	kg × 117	kg × 2.2	420[d]	1,400	400	4
	0.5–1.0	9	20	71	28	kg × 108	kg × 2.0	400	2,000	400	5
Children	1–3	13	28	86	34	1,300	23	400	2,000	400	7
	4–6	20	44	110	44	1,800	30	500	2,500	400	9
	7–10	30	66	135	54	2,400	36	700	3,300	400	10
Males	11–14	44	97	158	63	2,800	44	1,000	5,000	400	12
	15–18	61	134	172	69	3,000	54	1,000	5,000	400	15
	19–22	67	147	172	69	3,000	54	1,000	5,000	400	15
	23–50	70	154	172	69	2,700	56	1,000	5,000		15
	51+	70	154	172	69	2,400	56	1,000	5,000		15
Females	11–14	44	97	155	62	2,400	44	800	4,000	400	12
	15–18	54	119	162	65	2,100	48	800	4,000	400	12
	19–22	58	128	162	65	2,100	46	800	4,000	400	12
	23–50	58	128	162	65	2,000	46	800	4,000		12
	51+	58	128	162	65	1,800	46	800	4,000		12
Pregnant						+300	+30	1,000	5,000	400	15
Lactating						+500	+20	1,200	6,000	400	15

[a] The allowances are intended to provide for individual variations among most normal persons as they live in the United States under usual environmental stresses. Diets should be based on a variety of common foods in order to provide other nutrients for which human requirements have been less well defined. See text for more detailed discussion of allowances and of nutrients not tabulated. See Table I (p. 6) for weights and heights by individual year of age.

[b] Kilojoules (k J) = 4.2 × kcal.

[c] Retinol equivalents.

[d] Assumed to be all as retinol in milk during the first six months of life. All subsequent intakes are assumed to be half as retinol and half as β-carotene when calculated from international

From *Recommended Dietary Allowances*, Eighth Revised Edition, 1974, National Academy of Sciences, Washington, D.C., 1974.

TABLE VIII-B

RECOMMENDED DAILY DIETARY ALLOWANCES,[a] Revised 1974

	Water-Soluble Vitamins							Minerals					
	Ascorbic Acid (mg)	Folacin[f] (µg)	Niacin[g] (mg)	Riboflavin (mg)	Thiamin (mg)	Vitamin B_6 (mg)	Vitamin B_{12} (µg)	Calcium (mg)	Phosphorus (mg)	Iodine (µg)	Iron (mg)	Magnesium (mg)	Zinc (mg)
Infants	35	50	5	0.4	0.3	0.3	0.3	360	240	35	10	60	3
	35	50	8	0.6	0.5	0.4	0.3	540	400	45	15	70	5
Children	40	100	9	0.8	0.7	0.6	1.0	800	800	60	15	150	10
	40	200	12	1.1	0.9	0.9	1.5	800	800	80	10	200	10
	40	300	16	1.2	1.2	1.2	2.0	800	800	110	10	250	10
Males	45	400	18	1.5	1.4	1.6	3.0	1,200	1,200	130	18	350	15
	45	400	20	1.8	1.5	2.0	3.0	1,200	1,200	150	18	400	15
	45	400	20	1.8	1.5	2.0	3.0	800	800	140	10	350	15
	45	400	18	1.6	1.4	2.0	3.0	800	800	130	10	350	15
	45	400	16	1.5	1.2	2.0	3.0	800	800	110	10	350	15
Females	45	400	16	1.3	1.2	1.6	3.0	1,200	1,200	115	18	300	15
	45	400	14	1.4	1.1	2.0	3.0	1,200	1,200	115	18	300	15
	45	400	14	1.4	1.1	2.0	3.0	800	800	100	18	300	15
	45	400	13	1.2	1.0	2.0	3.0	800	800	100	18	300	15
	45	400	12	1.1	1.0	2.0	3.0	800	800	80	10	300	15
Pregnant	60	800	+2	+0.3	+0.3	2.5	4.0	1,200	1,200	125	18+[h]	450	20
Lactating	80	600	+4	+0.5	+0.3	2.5	4.0	1,200	1,200	150	18	450	25

units. As retinol equivalents, three fourths are as retinol and one fourth as β-carotene.

[e] Total vitamin E activity, estimated to be 80 percent as α-tocopherol and 20 percent other tocopherols. See text for variation in allowances.

[f] The folacin allowances refer to dietary sources as determined by *Lactobacillus casei* assay. Pure forms of folacin may be effective in doses less than one fourth of the recommended dietary allowance.

[g] Although allowances are expressed as niacin, it is recognized that on the average 1 mg of niacin is derived from each 60 mg of dietary tryptophan.

[h] This increased requirement cannot be met by ordinary diets; therefore, the use of supplemental iron is recommended.

TABLE IX

*The
digestive
system*

Basal metabolism (Aub-DuBois)

Age (yr)	Kilocalories per hour per square meter body surface	
	Male	Female
10–12	51.5	50.0
12–14	50.0	46.5
14–16	46.0	43.0
16–18	43.0	40.0
18–20	41.0	38.0
20–30	39.5	37.0
30–40	39.5	36.5
40–50	38.5	36.0
50–60	37.5	35.0
60–70	36.5	34.0

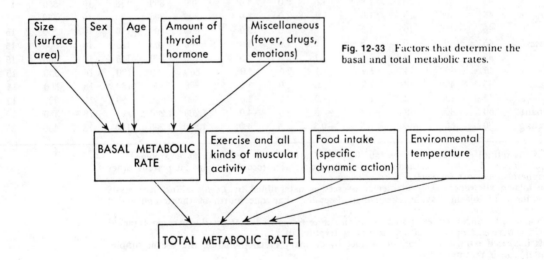

Fig. 12-33 Factors that determine the basal and total metabolic rates.

From Catherine F. Anthony and Norma J. Kolthoff, *Textbook Of Anatomy And Physiology*, Eighth Edition, The C. V. Mosby Company, St. Louis, 1971, p. 431.

TABLE X

ACTIVITY CHART

Numbers Represent Calories Used Per Hour Per Pound of Bodyweight

DENTARY ACTIVITIES, such as: Reading; writing; ting; watching television or movies; listening to the lio; sewing; playing cards; and typing, miscellaneous ficework, and other activities done while sitting that quire little or no arm movement.

eping	0.43	Undressing	0.90
ting	0.65	Ironing	1.00
ting	0.70	Typing	1.00
iting	0.70	Walking, slowly	1.50
essing	0.90		

GHT ACTIVITIES, such as: Preparing and cooking od; doing dishes; dusting; handwashing small articles clothing; ironing; walking slowly; personal care; scellaneous officework and other activities done while nding that require some arm movement; and rapid ing and other activities done while sitting that are re strenuous.

paring food	0.80	Standing at	
ning	0.93	attention	0.74
ficework	1.00	Typing Rapid	0.91
		Standing Relaxed	0.69

DDERATE ACTIVITIES, such as: Making beds; pping and scrubbing; sweeping; light polishing and xing; laundering by machine; light gardening and pentry work; walking moderately fast; other activities e while standing that require moderate arm move-nt; and activities done while sitting that require more rous arm movement.

king moderately		Light Exercise	1.10
ast	1.95	Singing	0.79
pping	1.09	Carpentry work	1.56
ubbing	1.09	Driving automobile	1.10

VIGOROUS ACTIVITIES, such as: Heavy scrubbing and waxing; handwashing large articles of clothing; hanging out clothes; stripping beds; other heavy work; walking fast; bowling; golfing; and gardening.

Walking fast	1.90	Active Exercise	1.88
Bowling	1.85	Walking downstairs	2.36
Bookbinding	1.10	Sawing wood	3.12

STRENUOUS ACTIVITIES, such as: Swimming, playing tennis; running; bicycling; dancing; skiing; and playing football.

Swimming	3.25	Severe Exercise	3.90
Running	3.70	Walking very fast	4.22
Bicycling Moderate	2.50	Walking upstairs	7.18
Dancing	3.80		

Adapted from Charts Energy Expenditures Per Hour Under Different Conditions of Muscular Activity, Macmillan Company, New York.

TABLE XI

CHOLESTEROL CHART

item	100 grams edible portion[2] mg.	Edible portion of 1 pound as purchased (mg.)	Refuse from item as purchased (percent)
Beef, raw	70	270	15
with bone[3]	70	320	0
without bone[3]	> 2,000	> 9,000	0
Brains, raw	> 2,000	> 9,000	0
Butter	250	1,135	0
Caviar or fish roe	> 300	> 1,300	0
Cheese			
cheddar	100	453	0
cottage, creamed	15	70	0
cream	120	545	0
other (25% to 30% fat)	85	385	0
Cheese spread	65	295	0
Chicken, flesh only, raw	60	—	0
Crab			
in shell[3]	125	270	52
meat only[3]	125	565	0
Egg, whole	550	2,200	12
Egg white	0	0	0
Egg yolk			
fresh	1,500	6,800	0
frozen	1,280	5,300	0
dried	2,950	13,380	0
Fish			
steak[3]	70	265	16
filet[3]	70	320	0
Heart, raw	150	680	0
Ice cream	45	205	0
Kidney, raw	375	1,700	0
Lamb, raw			
with bone[2]	70	265	16
without bone[3]	70	320	0
lard and other animal fat	95	430	0
Liver, raw	300	1,360	0
Lobster			
whole[3]	200	235	74
meat only[3]	200	900	0
Margarine			
all vegetable fat	0	0	0
two-thirds animal fat, one-third vegetable fat	65	295	0
Milk			
fluid, whole	11	50	0
dried, whole	85	385	0
fluid, nonfat (skim)	3	15	0
Mutton			
with bone[3]	65	250	16
without bone[3]	65	295	0
Oysters			
in shell[3]	> 200	> 90	90
meat only[2]	> 200	> 900	0
Pork			
with bone[3]	70	260	18
without bone[3]	70	320	0
Shrimp			
in shell[3]	125	390	31
flesh only[3]	125	565	0
Sweetbreads (thymus)	250	1,135	0
Veal			
with bone[3]	90	320	21
without bone[3]	90	410	0

[1] From Watt, B. K., and Merrill, A. L.: Composition of foods —raw, processed, prepared. U.S. Department of Agriculture, Agriculture Handbook, No. 8, December, 1963.
[2] Data apply to 100 grams of edible portion of the item, although it may be purchased with the refuse indicated, and described for implied in the first column.
[3] Designate items that have the same chemical composition for the edible portion but differ in the amount of refuse.

TABLE XII

COMPOSITION OF BEVERAGES—ALCOHOLIC AND CARBONATED NON-ALCOHOLIC PER 100 GRAMS*

	Food Energy	Protein	Carbo-hydrate	Calcium	Phosphorus	Iron	Thiamine	Riboflavin	Niacin
Beverages, alcoholic and carbonated non-alcoholic:									
Alcoholic:									
Beer, alcohol 4.5% by volume (3.6% by weight)	42	.3	3.8	5	30	Trace	Trace	.03	.6
Gin, rum, vodka, whisky:									
80-proof (33.4% alcohol by weight)	231	....	Trace	....	....	....	....	....	....
86-proof (36.0% alcohol by weight)	249	....	Trace	....	....	....	....	....	....
90-proof (37.9% alcohol by weight)	263	....	Trace	....	....	....	....	....	....
94-proof (39.7% alcohol by weight)	275	....	Trace	....	....	....	....	....	....
100-proof (42.5% alcohol by weight)	295	....	Trace	....	....	....	....	....	....
Wines:									
Dessert, alcohol 18.8% by volume (15.3% by weight)	137	.1	7.7	8	....	....	.01	.02	.2
Table, alcohol 12.2% by volume (9.9% by weight)	85	.1	4.2	9	10	.4	Trace	.01	.1
Carbonated, non-alcoholic:									
Carbonated waters:									
Sweetened (quinine sodas)	31	....	8						....
Unsweetened (club sodas)	....	....	....						....
Cola type	39	....	10						....
Cream sodas	43	....	11						....
Fruit-flavored sodas (citrus, cherry, grape, strawberry, Tom Collins mixer, other) (10%-13% sugar)	46	....	12						....
Ginger ale, pale dry and golden	31	....	8						....
Root beer	41	....	10.5						....
Special dietary drinks with artificial sweetener (less than 1 calorie per ounce)	....	....	....						....

* From *Composition of Foods—Raw, Processed, Prepared* (U.S. Department of Agriculture, Agriculture Handbook, No. 8 [December, 1963]).

TABLE XIII

Food Composition Table
Nutritive Value of Edible Part of Foods

Food	Weight g	Weight oz	Approximate measure and description	Calories	Protein g	Fat g	Carbohydrate g	Calcium mg	Iron mg	Vitamin A activity IU	Thiamin mg	Riboflavin mg	Ascorbic acid mg
Apples, raw	150	5.3	1 apple, about 3 per lb	70	tr	tr	18	8	0.4	50	0.04	0.02	3
Apple, baked	130	4.6	1 medium apple, 2½ in dia	120	tr	tr	30	8	0.4	50	0.04	0.02	3
Apple brown betty	115	4.0	½ cup	175	2	4	34	21	0.7	115	0.07	0.05	2
Apple pie (see pies)													
Apple juice (sweet cider)	124	4.3	½ cup, bottled or canned	60	tr	tr	15	8	0.8	—	0.01	0.03	1
Applesauce	128	4.5	½ cup, sweetened, canned	115	tr	tr	31	5	0.7	50	0.03	0.02	2
Apricots, fresh, raw (as purchased)	114	4.0	3 apricots, about 12 per lb	55	1	tr	14	18	0.5	2890	0.03	0.04	10
Apricots, canned	130	4.6	½ cup or 4 medium halves. 2 tbsp juice, syrup pack	110	1	tr	29	14	0.4	2255	0.03	0.03	5
Apricots, dried, stewed	108	3.8	½ cup (scant) or 8 halves 2 tbsp juice, sweetened	135	2	tr	34	26	1.5	2287	tr	0.04	3
Apricot nectar	125	4.4	½ cup (peach, pear, similar values)	70	1	tr	19	12	0.3	1190	0.02	0.02	4
Apricot whip	94	3.3	½ cup made with whipped nonfat dry milk	130	4	tr	30	64	1.2	2342	0.02	0.12	4
Asparagus, green, cooked	73	2.6	½ cup, 1½ to 2 in lengths	15	2	tr	3	15	0.5	655	0.12	0.13	19
Avocado, raw (as purchased)	142	5.0	½ avocado, 3⅛ in diameter, peeled and pitted	185	3	19	7	11	0.7	315	0.12	0.22	15
Bacon, broiled or fried	15	0.5	2 slices, cooked crisp (20 slices per lb, raw)	90	5	8	1	2	0.5	0	0.08	0.05	—
Bacon, Canadian, cooked	43	1.5	3 slices, cooked crisp	100	18	12	tr	13	2.2	0	0.62	0.12	0
Bananas, raw (as purchased)	175	6.1	1 banana, medium size	100	1	tr	26	10	0.8	230	0.06	0.07	12
Bavarian cream	99	3.5	½ cup (orange)	210	2	10	30	27	0.1	627	0.10	0.05	54
Bean sprouts, cooked	63	2.2	½ cup, mung, drained	18	2	tr	4	11	0.6	15	0.06	0.07	4
Beans, snap, green, cooked	63	2.2	½ cup	15	1	tr	4	32	0.4	340	0.05	0.06	8
Beans, lima, immature, cooked	85	2.8	½ cup, green	95	7	1	17	40	2.2	240	0.16	0.09	15
Beans, lima, dry, cooked	144	5.0	¾ cup	195	12	1	37	41	4.2	—	0.19	0.08	—
Beans, pinto, dry, raw	99	3.5	½ cup (Mexican red beans)	350	23	1	64	160	6.9	0	0.65	0.24	2
Beans, red kidney, dry, canned	191	6.7	¾ cup	173	11	1	32	56	3.5	8	0.10	0.08	—
Beans, white, dry, cooked	191	6.7	¾ cup, with tomato sauce and pork	233	12	5	37	104	3.5	248	0.15	0.06	4
Beans, white, dry, canned	196	6.9	¾ cup, with tomato sauce, without pork	233	12	1	45	133	3.9	120	0.14	0.07	4
Beef, corned, canned	85	3.0	3 slices, 3 x 2 x ¼ in	185	22	10	0	17	3.7	20	0.01	0.20	—

From A.K. Hatfield and P.S. Stanton, *HOW TO HELP YOUR CHILD EAT RIGHT!* Acropolis Books, Washington, D.C. 20009, 1978, p. 149-163.

Food	Weight g	Weight oz	Approximate measure and description	Calories	Protein g	Fat g	Carbohydrate g	Calcium mg	Iron mg	Vitamin A activity IU	Thiamin mg	Riboflavin mg	Ascorbic acid mg
Beef, corned hash, canned	85	3.0	½ cup, approximately	155	7	10	9	11	1.7	—	0.01	0.08	—
Beef, dried or chipped	57	2.0	4 thin slices, 4 x 5 in	115	19	4	0	11	2.9	—	0.04	0.18	—
Beef, hamburger, broiled	85	3.0	1 patty, 3 in dia (ground beef, regular)	245	21	17	0	9	2.7	30	0.07	0.18	—
Beef, heart, braised	85	3.0	2 round slices, 2½ in dia, ½ in thick	160	27	5	1	5	5.0	20	0.21	1.04	1
Beef, liver (see liver)													
Beef, loaf (see meat loaf)													
Beef, pot roast, cooked	85	3.0	1 piece, 4 x 3¾ x ½ in	245	23	16	0	10	2.9	30	0.04	0.18	—
Beef, potpie, baked	227	7.9	1 indiv. pie, 4¼ in dia	560	23	33	43	32	4.1	1860	0.25	0.27	7
Beef, roast, oven cooked	85	3.0	2 slices, 6 x 3¼ x ⅛ in relatively lean	165	25	7	0	11	3.2	10	0.06	0.19	—
Beef steak, broiled	85	3.0	1 piece, 3½ x 2 x ¾ in, relatively fat, no bone	330	20	27	0	9	2.5	50	0.05	0.16	—
Beef Stroganoff, cooked	130	4.6	½ cup	250	17	18	6	41	2.6	395	0.12	0.29	2
Beef, tongue, braised	85	3.0	7 slices, 2¼ x 2¼ x ⅛ in	210	18	14	tr	6	1.9	—	0.04	0.25	—
Beets, cooked	85	3.0	½ cup, diced	28	1	tr	6	12	0.5	15	0.03	0.04	5
Beverages, alcoholic, see page 397													
Beverages, cola-type	185	6.5	about ¾ cup, carbonated soft drink	75	0	0	19	—	—	0	0	0	0
Beverages, gingerale	240	8.4	1 cup, carbonated soft drink	75	0	0	19	—	—	0	0	0	0
Biscuits, baking powde	28	1.0	1 biscuit, 2 in dia (enriched flour)	105	2	5	13	34	0.4	tr	0.06	0.06	tr
Blackberries, raw	72	2.5	½ cup	45	1	1	10	23	0.7	145	0.03	0.03	15
Blueberries, raw	70	2.5	½ cup	45	1	1	11	11	0.7	70	0.02	0.04	10
Bluefish, cooked	85	3.0	1 piece, 3½ x 2 x ½ in	135	22	4	0	25	0.6	40	0.09	0.08	—
Bologna (see sausage)													
Bouillon cubes	4	0.1	1 cube, ⅝ in	5	1	tr	tr	—	—	—	—	—	—
Branflakes	26	0.9	¾ cup, 40 percent bran, added thiamin, iron	80	3	1	21	19	9.3	0	0.11	0.05	0
Bread, Boston brown	48	1.7	1 slice, 3 x ¾ in	100	3	1	22	43	0.9	0	0.05	0.03	0
Bread, cracked wheat	25	0.9	1 slice, 18 slices per lb loaf	65	2	1	13	22	0.3	tr	0.03	0.02	tr
Bread, French or Vienna	20	0.7	1 slice, 3¼ x 2 x 1 in (enriched flour)	60	2	1	11	9	0.4	tr	0.06	0.04	tr
Bread, Italian	20	0.7	1 slice, 3¼ x 2 x·1 in (enriched flour)	55	2	tr	11	3	0.4	0	0.06	0.04	0
Bread, raisin	25	0.9	1 slice, 18 slices per lb loaf	65	2	1	13	18	0.3	tr	0.01	0.02	tr
Bread, rye, light	25	0.9	1 slice, 18 slices per lb loaf (⅓ rye, ⅔ wheat)	60	2	tr	13	19	0.4	0	0.05	0.02	0

Food Composition Table (continued)

Food	Approximate measure	Weight (g)	Weight (oz)	Food energy (cal)	Protein (g)	Fat (g)	Carbohydrate (g)	Calcium (mg)	Iron (mg)	Vitamin A (IU)	Thiamin (mg)	Riboflavin (mg)	Ascorbic acid (mg)
Bread, pumpernickel	1 slice, 3¼ x 2 x 1in (dark rye flour)	34	1.2	85	3	0	19	30	0.8	0	0.08	0.05	0
Bread, white	1 slice, 18 slices per lb loaf soft crumb (enriched)	25	0.9	70	2	1	13	21	0.6	tr	0.06	0.05	tr
Bread, white	1 slice, 18 slices per lb loaf soft crumb (unenriched)	25	0.9	70	2	1	13	21	0.2	tr	0.02	0.02	tr
Bread, white	1 slice, 20 slices per lb loaf firm crumb (enriched)	23	0.8	65	2	1	12	22	0.6	tr	0.06	0.05	tr
Bread, white, toasted	1 slice, 18 slices per lb loaf soft crumb (enriched)	22	0.8	70	2	1	13	21	0.6	tr	0.05	0.05	tr
Bread, whole wheat	1 slice, 18 slices per lb loaf firm crumb	25	0.9	60	3	1	12	25	0.8	tr	0.06	0.03	tr
Breadcrumbs	¼ cup, dry, grated	25	0.9	98	3	1	18	31	0.9	tr	0.06	0.08	tr
Broccoli, cooked	½ cup, stalks cut ½ in pieces	78	2.7	20	3	1	4	68	0.6	1940	0.07	0.16	70
Brussels sprouts, cooked	½ cup or 5 medium sprouts	78	2.7	28	4	1	5	25	0.9	405	0.06	0.11	68
Buns (see rolls)													
Butter	1 tbsp or ⅛ stick	14	0.5	100	tr	12	tr	3	0	470	—	—	0
Cabbage, raw	½ cup, finely shredded	45	1.6	10	1	tr	3	22	0.2	60	0.03	0.03	21
Cabbage, cooked	½ cup, cooked short time, little water	73	2.6	15	1	tr	3	32	0.2	95	0.03	0.03	24
Cabbage, Chinese, raw	½ cup, 1 in pieces	38	1.3	5	1	tr	1	16	0.3	55	0.02	0.02	10
Cake, angel food	1 piece (mix), 1/12 of cake, 10-in dia	53	1.9	135	3	tr	32	50	0.2	0	tr	0.06	0
Cake, Boston cream pie	1 piece, 1/12 of pie, 8 in dia (unenriched flour)	69	2.4	210	4	6	34	46	0.3	140	0.02	0.08	tr
Cake, plain, cupcakes	1 cupcake (mix), 2½ in dia, without icing	25	0.9	90	1	3	14	40	0.1	40	0.01	0.03	tr
Cake, plain, cupcakes	1 cupcake (mix), 2½ in dia, with choc. icing	36	1.3	130	2	5	21	47	0.3	60	0.01	0.04	tr
Cake, devil's food	1 piece (mix) 1/16 cake, 9 in dia, 2 layer, choc. icing	69	2.4	235	3	9	40	41	0.6	100	0.02	0.06	tr
Cake, fruit, dark	1 slice, 1/30 loaf, 8 in long (enriched flour)	15	0.5	55	1	2	9	11	0.4	20	0.02	0.02	tr
Cake, pound	1 slice, 2¾ x 3 x ⅝ in (unenriched flour)	30	1.1	140	2	9	14	6	0.2	80	0.01	0.03	0
Cake, sponge	1 piece, 1/12 cake, 10 in dia (unenriched flour)	66	2.3	195	5	4	36	20	0.8	300	0.03	0.09	tr
Cake, white	1 piece (mix) 1/16 cake, 9 in dia, 2 layer, choc. icing	71	2.5	250	3	8	45	70	0.4	40	0.01	0.06	tr
Candy, caramels	4 small	28	1.0	115	1	3	22	42	0.4	tr	0.01	0.05	tr
Candy, chocolate, plain	1 bar, 3¾ x 1½ x ¼ in	28	1.0	145	2	9	16	65	0.3	80	0.02	0.10	tr
Candy, chocolate bar, almond	1 bar, 5⅓ x 1⅞ x ⅓ in	51	1.8	265	4	19	25	102	1.4	70	0.07	0.25	0

Food	Weight g	Weight oz	Approximate measure and description	Calories	Protein g	Fat g	Carbohydrate g	Calcium mg	Iron mg	Vitamin-A activity IU	Thiamin mg	Riboflavin mg	Ascorbic acid mg
Candy, chocolate creams	28	1.0	2 pieces, 1¼ in dia (base) ⅝ in thick	110	1	4	20	—	—	—	—	—	0
Candy, chocolate fudge	28	1.0	1 piece, 1¼ x 1¼ x 1 in	115	1	4	21	22	0.3	tr	0.01	0.03	tr
Candy, hard	28	1.0	6 pieces, 1 in dia ¼ in thick	110	0	tr	28	6	0.5	0	0	0	0
Candy, peanut brittle	28	1.0	1 piece, 3¼ x 2½ x ¼ in	125	2	4	21	11	0.6	10	0.03	0.01	0
Cantaloupes, (as purchased)	385	13.5	½ melon, 5 in dia	60	1	tr	14	27	0.8	6540 (orange fleshed)	0.08	0.06	63
Carrots, raw	50	1.8	1 carrot, 5½ in long or 25 thin strips	20	1	tr	5	18	0.4	5500	0.03	0.03	4
Carrots, raw	55	1.9	½ cup, grated	23	1	tr	6	21	0.4	6050	0.03	0.03	5
Carrots, cooked	73	2.6	½ cup, diced	23	1	tr	5	24	0.5	7610	0.04	0.04	5
Catsup, tomato (see tomato)													
Cauliflower, cooked	60	2.1	½ cup, flower buds	13	2	tr	3	13	0.4	35	0.06	0.05	33
Celery, raw	40	1.4	1 stalk, large outer, 8 in. long	5	tr	tr	2	16	0.1	100	0.01	0.01	4
Celery, raw	50	1.8	½ cup, diced	8	1	tr	2	20	0.2	120	0.02	0.02	5
Cheese, blue	28	1.0	¾ in sector or 3 tbsp (roquefort type)	105	6	9	1	89	0.1	350	0.01	0.17	0
Cheese, cheddar (American)	28	1.0	1 cube, 1⅛ in	115	6	10	2	206	0.3	368	0.02	0.13	0
Cheese, cheddar (American)	7	0.3	1 tbsp, grated	30	2	2	tr	52	0.1	90	tr	0.03	0
Cheese foods, cheddar	28	1.0	2 round slices, 1⅝ in dia, ¼ in thick or 2 tbsp	90	6	6	2	160	0.2	280	tr	0.16	0
Cheese, cottage	61	2.1	¼ cup creamed cottage cheese (made from skim milk)	65	8	3	2	58	0.2	105	0.02	0.15	0
Cheese, cottage	28	1.0	2 tbsp uncreamed cottage cheese (make from skim milk)	25	5	tr	1	26	0.1	tr	0.01	0.08	0
Cheese, cream	16	0.5	1 tbsp	60	1	6	tr	10	tr	250	tr	0.04	0
Cheese, Swiss	28	1.0	1 slice, 7 x 4 x ⅛ in domestic	105	8	8	1	262	0.3	320	tr	0.11	0
Cheese sauce	60	2.1	¼ cup	110	5	9	4	156	0.1	337	0.02	0.14	1
Cheese soufflé	79	2.8	¾ cup	200	10	16	7	210	1.0	826	0.08	0.23	1
Cheesecake	162	5.7	⅒ of cake, 9 in dia	400	15	23	35	128	0.8	958	0.08	0.33	1
Cherries, raw, sweet	130	4.6	1 cup, with stems	80	2	tr	20	26	0.5	130	0.06	0.07	12
Cherries, raw, West Indian	11	0.4	2 medium cherries (acerola)	3	—	—	1	1	—	—	—	0.01	100

Food Composition Table (continued)

Food	Measure	Weight (g)	Food energy (cal)	Protein (g)	Fat (g)	Carbohydrate (g)	Calcium (mg)	Iron (mg)	Vitamin A (IU)	Thiamine (mg)	Riboflavin (mg)	Niacin (mg)	Ascorbic acid (mg)
Chick peas, dry, raw	1/3 cup (garbanzos)	105	380	22	5	64	97	7.5	tr	0.58	0.19	3.7	2
Chicken, broiled	3 slices, flesh only	85	115	20	3	0	8	1.4	80	0.05	0.16	3.0	-
Chicken, canned	1/3 cup, boned meat	85	170	18	10	0	18	1.3	200	0.03	0.11	3.0	3
Chicken, creamed[1]	1/2 cup	99	222	20	12	6	84	1.1	445	0.04	0.20	3.5	1
Chicken, fried	1/2 breast, with bone	94	155	25	5	1	9	1.3	70	0.04	0.17	3.3	-
Chicken, fried	1 drumstick, with bone	59	90	12	4	tr	6	0.9	50	0.03	0.15	2.1	1
Chicken pie (see poultry potpie)													
Chili con carne, canned	3/4 cup, made with beans	188	250	14	11	23	60	3.2	113	0.06	0.14	6.5	-
Chili con carne, canned	3/4 cup, made without beans	191	383	20	29	11	73	2.7	285	0.04	0.23	6.7	-
Chili powder	1 tbsp hot, red peppers, dried, ground	15	50	2	2	8	40	2.3	9750	0.03	0.17	0.5	2
Chili sauce	1 tbsp, mainly tomatoes	17	20	tr	tr	4	3	0.1	240	0.02	0.01	0.6	3
Chocolate, bitter	1 square baking chocolate	28	145	3	15	8	22	1.9	20	0.01	0.07	1.0	0
Chocolate candy (see candy)													
Chocolate-flavored milk	1 cup, choc. milk drink, made with skim milk	250	190	8	6	27	270	0.5	210	0.10	0.40	8.8	3
Chocolate morsels	30 morsels or 1 1/2 tbsp	15	80	1	4	10	5	0.3	tr	tr	tr	0.5	0
Chocolate syrup	2 tbsp	40	80	tr	tr	22	6	0.6	-	-	0.13	1.4	0
Chop suey, cooked	3/4 cup	122	325	7	20	16	43	2.9	85	0.11	0.09	4.3	17
Clams, canned	1/2 cup or 3 medium clams	85	45	7	1	2	47	3.5	-	0.01	0.11	3.0	-
Cocoa, beverage	3/4 cup, made with milk	182	176	6	8	20	215	0.7	293	0.07	0.34	6.3	2
Coconut, fresh	1/4 cup, shredded	33	113	1	12	3	4	0.6	0	0.02	0.01	1.2	1
Coconut, dried	1/4 cup, shredded, sweetened	16	85	2	6	8	3	0.3	0	0.01	0.01	0.6	0
Codfish, dried	1/2 cup	51	190	41	2	0	25	1.8	47	0.04	0.23	1.8	0
Coffee cake	1 piece, frosted 3 x 3 x 1 1/4 in	79	260	4	11	37	25	1.0	40	0.12	0.13	2.8	0
Cole slaw	1/2 cup	60	50	1	4	5	24	0.3	231	0.03	0.03	2.1	25
Cookies, brownies	1 piece, 1 7/8 x 1 7/8 x 5/8 in	26	145	2	9	17	12	0.5	81	0.03	0.04	0.9	-
Cookies, chocolate chip	1 cookie, 2 1/4 in dia	11	60	1	3	7	4	0.2	76	0.01	0.01	0.4	0
Cookies, cocoanut bar chews	1 cookie, 3 x 7/8 x 1/3 in	11	55	tr	2	9	7	0.3	18	0.01	0.01	0.4	0
Cookies, oatmeal	1 cookie, 2 1/8 in dia (raisins and nuts)	11	65	1	1	6	5	0.3	64	0.04	0.02	0.4	0
Cookies, sugar, plain	1 cookie, 2 1/2 in dia	9	40	1	2	6	2	0.1		0.02	0.01	0.3	0
Corn, ear, cooked	1 ear sweet corn, 5 in long	140	70	3	1	16	2	0.5	310 (yellow corn)	0.09	0.08	4.9	7
Corn, sweet, canned	1/2 cup, solids and liquid	128	85	3	tr	20	5	0.5	345 (yellow corn)	0.04	0.06	4.5	7
Corn grits, cooked	2/3 cup, enriched, degermed	163	85	2	tr	18	1	0.5	100 (yellow corn)	0.07	0.05	5.7	0
Corn muffins	1 muffin, 2 3/4 in dia, enriched flour and enriched degermed meal	40	125	3	4	19	42	0.7	120 (yellow corn)	0.08	0.09	1.4	tr

[1]One-half cup of a creamed dish calls for 1/4 cup white sauce and about 1/3 cup of any one of a variety of meats, vegetables, or other foods which may be combined suitably. (See eggs, creamed, and fish, creamed.)

Food	Weight g	Weight oz	Approximate measure and description	Calories	Protein g	Fat g	Carbohydrate g	Calcium mg	Iron mg	Vitamin A activity IU	Thiamin mg	Riboflavin mg	Ascorbic acid mg
Corned beef (see beef)													
Corned beef hash (see beef)													
Cornflakes	33	1.2	1⅓ cup (added nutrients)	133	3	tr	28	5	0.5	0	0.15	0.03	0
Cornmeal, dry	138	4.8	1 cup, white or yellow, enriched, degermed	500	11	2	108	8	4.0	610 (yellow corn)	0.61	0.36	0
Cow peas (see peas)													
Crabmeat, canned	85	3.0	½ cup flakes	85	15	2	1	38	0.7	—	0.07	0.07	—
Crackers, graham	14	0.5	2 medium or 4 small, plain	55	1	1	10	6	0.2	0	0.01	0.03	0
Crackers, saltines	8	0.3	2 crackers, 2 in square	35	1	1	6	2	0.1	0	tr	tr	0
Cranberry juice, canned	125	4.4	½ cup, or small glass, ascorbic acid added	85	tr	tr	21	7	0.4	tr	0.02	0.02	20
Cranberry sauce, canned	69	2.4	¼ cup, strained, sweetened	85	tr	tr	21	4	0.1	13	0.01	0.01	1
Cream, half-and-half	15	0.5	1 tbsp (cream and milk)	20	1	2	1	16	tr	70	tr	0.02	tr
Cream, coffee	15	0.5	1 tbsp, light table cream	30	1	3	1	15	tr	130	tr	0.02	tr
Cream, heavy, whipping	15	0.5	1 tbsp, unwhipped (volume doubled when whipped)	55	tr	6	1	11	tr	230	tr	0.02	tr
Creamer, coffee	2	–	1 tsp powder, imitation cream	10	tr	1	1	1	tr	tr	—	—	—
Cucumber, raw	50	1.8	6 slices, pared, ⅛ in thick	5	tr	tr	2	8	0.2	tr	0.02	0.02	6
Custard, baked	124	4.3	½ cup	143	7	7	14	139	0.5	435	0.05	0.24	1
Dates, pitted	45	1.6	¼ cup or 8 dates	123	1	tr	33	26	1.3	23	0.04	0.04	0
Dessert topping, whipped	11	0.4	2 tbsp (low calorie, with nonfat dry milk)	17	1	–	3	29	–	1	0.01	0.04	1
Doughnuts	32	1.1	1, cake-type, enriched flour	125	1	6	16	13	0.4	30	0.05	0.05	tr
Eggs, raw, boiled, poached	50	1.8	1 whole egg	80	6	6	tr	27	1.1	590	0.05	0.15	0
Egg white, raw	33	1.2	1 egg white	15	4	tr	tr	3	tr	0	tr	0.09	0
Egg yolk, raw	17	0.6	1 egg yolk	60	3	5	tr	24	0.9	580	0.04	0.07	0
Eggs, creamed[1]	113	4.0	½ cup (1 egg in ¼ cup white sauce)	190	9	14	7	103	1.2	928	0.07	0.25	tr
Eggs, fried	54	1.9	1 egg, cooked in 1 tsp fat	115	6	10	tr	28	1.1	590	0.05	0.15	0
Eggs, scrambled	64	2.2	1 egg, with milk and fat	110	7	8	1	51	1.1	690	0.05	0.18	0
Endive, curly, raw (includes escarole)	57	2.0	3 leaves	10	1	tr	2	46	1.0	1870	0.04	0.08	6
Farina, cooked	163	5.7	⅔ cup, quick, enriched	70	2	tr	14	98	0.5	0	0.08	0.05	0
Fats, cooking, lard	13	0.5	1 tbsp solid fat	115	0	13	0	0	0	0	0	0	0
Fats, cooking, vegetable	13	0.5	1 tbsp solid fat	110	0	13	0	0	0	–	0	0	0
Figs, fresh, raw	114	4.0	3 small, 1½ in dia	90	1	tr	23	40	0.7	90	0.07	0.06	2
Figs, dried	21	0.7	1 fig, large, 1 x 2 in	60	1	tr	15	26	0.6	20	0.02	0.02	0

[1]One-half cup of a creamed dish calls for ¼ cup white sauce and about ⅓ cup of any one of a variety of meats, vegetables, or other foods which may be combined suitably. (See chicken, creamed, and fish, creamed.)

Fish (see various kinds of fish)													
Fish, creamed[1]	136	4.8	1/2 cup (tuna, salmon, other, in white sauce)	220	20	13	8	81	0.9	385	0.05	0.18	tr
Fish sticks, cooked	114	4.0	5 sticks, breaded, each 3.8 x 1.0 x 0.5 in	200	19	10	8	13	0.5	—	0.05	0.08	—
Frankfurter, heated	56	2.0	1 frankfurter	170	7	15	1	3	0.8	—	0.08	0.11	—
French toast, fried	79	2.8	1 slice (enriched bread)	180	6	12	14	78	1.0	568	0.09	0.17	tr
Fruit balls, raw	11	0.4	1 ball, 1 in dia (dried apricots, dates, nuts)	45	1	1	8	10	0.4	285	0.02	0.02	tr
Fruit cocktail, canned	.128	4.5	1/2 cup, heavy syrup	98	1	tr	25	12	0.5	180	0.03	0.02	3
Gelatin, dry	7	0.3	1 tbsp, plain (1 envelope)	25	6	tr	0	—	—	—	—	—	—
Gelatin dessert, plain	120	4.2	1/2 cup, ready to eat	70	2	0	17	—	—	—	—	—	—
Gingerbread	63	2.2	1 piece (mix), 1/9 of 8 in square cake	175	2	4	32	57	1.0	tr	0.02	0.06	tr
Grapefruit, white, raw (as purchased)	241	8.4	1/2 med 3-3/4 in dia	45	1	tr	12	19	0.5	10	0.05	0.02	44
Grapefruit, white, canned	125	4.4	1/2 cup, syrup pack	88	1	tr	22	16	0.4	10	0.04	0.02	38
Grapefruit juice, canned	124	4.3	1/2 cup, unsweetened	50	1	tr	12	10	0.5	10	0.04	0.02	42
Grapefruit juice, dehydrated crystals	124	4.3	1/2 cup, or 1 small glass, prepared, ready to serve	50	1	tr	12	11	0.1	10	0.05	0.03	46
Grapes, American type, raw	153	5.4	1 cup or 1 medium bunch (slip skin, as Concord)	65	1	1	15	15	0.4	100	0.05	0.03	3
Grapes, European type, raw	160	5.6	1 cup or 40 grapes (adherent skin, as Tokay)	95	1	tr	25	17	0.6	140	0.07	0.04	6
Grape juice, canned	127	4.4	1/2 cup	83	1	tr	21	14	0.4	—	0.05	0.03	tr
Greens, collards, cooked	95	3.3	1/2 cup	28	3	1	5	145	0.6	5130	0.14	0.19	44
Greens, dandelion, cooked	90	3.2	1/2 cup	30	2	1	6	126	1.6	10,530	0.12	0.15	16
Greens, kale, cooked	55	1.9	1/2 cup, leaves, stems	15	2	1	2	74	0.7	4070	—	—	34
Greens, mustard, cooked	70	2.5	1/2 cup	18	2	1	3	97	1.3	4060	0.06	0.10	34
Greens, spinach, cooked	90	3.2	1/2 cup	20	3	1	3	84 (unavailable)	2.0	7290	0.07	0.13	25
Greens, turnip, cooked	73	2.6	1/2 cup	15	2	tr	3	126	0.8	4135	0.08	0.17	34
Guavas, raw	82	2.8	1 guava	50	1	tr	12	21	0.5	180	0.05	0.03	212
Haddock, fried	85	3.0	1 fillet, 4 x 2-1/2 x 1/2 in	140	17	5	5	34	1.0	—	0.03	0.06	2
Ham, boiled	57	2.0	1 slice, 6-1/4 x 3-3/4 x 1/8 in	135	11	10	0	6	1.6	0	0.25	0.09	—
Ham, cured, roasted	85	3.0	2 slices, 5-1/2 x 3-3/4 x 1/8 in	245	18	19	0	8	2.2	0	0.40	0.16	—
Ham, luncheon, canned	57	2.0	2 tbsp, spiced or unspiced	165	8	14	1	5	1.2	0	0.18	0.12	—
Hamburger (see beef, hamburger)													

[1]One-half cup of a creamed dish calls for 1/4 cup white sauce and about 1/3 cup of any one of a variety of meats, vegetables, or other foods which may be combined suitably. (See chicken, creamed, and eggs, creamed.)

Food	Weight g	Weight oz	Approximate measure and description	Calories	Protein g	Fat g	Carbohydrate g	Calcium mg	Iron mg	Vitamin-A activity IU	Thiamin mg	Riboflavin mg	Ascorbic acid mg
Honey, strained	21	0.7	1 tbsp.	65	tr	0	17	1	0.1	0	tr	0.01	tr
Hot dog (see frankfurter)													
Ice cream, plain	50	1.8	1 container, 3 fluid oz (factory packed)	95	2	5	10	73	0.2	220	0.02	0.11	1
Ice cream, plain brick	71	2.5	1 slice, ⅛ of qt brick	145	3	9	15	87	0.1	370	0.03	0.13	1
Ice milk	66	2.3	½ cup, frozen dessert	100	3	4	15	102	0.1	140	0.04	0.15	1
Jams, jellies, preserves	20	0.7	1 tbsp	55	tr	tr	14	4	0.2	tr	tr	0.01	tr
Kale (see greens)													
Lamb chop, cooked	137	4.8	1 thick chop with bone	400	25	33	0	10	1.5	—	0.14	0.25	—
Lamb, leg, roasted	85	3.0	2 slices, 3 x 3¼ x ⅛ in lean and fat, no bone	235	22	16	0	9	1.4	—	0.13	0.23	—
Lard (see fats, cooking)													
Lemon juice, fresh	15	0.5	1 tbsp	5	tr	tr	1	1	tr	tr	tr	tr	7
Lemonade	248	8.7	1 cup, frozen, sweetened concentrate, diluted	110	tr	tr	28	2	tr	tr	tr	0.02	17
Lentils, dry, cooked	100	3.5	½ cup	120	9	tr	22	12	2.5	200	0.20	0.09	0
Lettuce, headed, raw	454	16.0	1 head, compact, as iceberg, 4¾ in dia	60	4	tr	13	91	2.3	1500	0.29	0.27	29
Lettuce, loose leaf, raw	50	1.8	2 large leaves or 4 small	10	1	tr	2	34	0.7	950	0.03	0.04	9
Lime juice, canned	62	2.2	¼ cup	15	tr	tr	6	6	0.1	5	0.01	0.01	13
Liver, beef, fried	57	2.0	1 slice, 5 x 2 x ⅓ in	130	15	6	3	6	5.0	30,280	0.15	2.37	15
Liver, calf, fried	74	2.6	1 slice, 5 x 2 x ½ in	230	15	15	4	5	9.0	19,130	0.18	2.65	30
Liver, chicken, fried	85	3.0	3 medium livers	235	20	15	5	15	6.4	27,370	0.19	2.11	17
Liver, pork, fried	70	2.5	1 slice, 3¾ x 1¾ x ½ in	225	17	15	3	8	15.3	12,070	0.34	2.53	19
Macaroni, cooked	105	3.7	¾ cup (enriched)	115	4	1	24	6	1.0	0	0.15	0.08	0
Macaroni and cheese, baked	150	5.3	¾ cup (macaroni enriched)	325	13	17	30	272	1.4	645	0.15	0.30	tr
Mackerel, broiled	85	3.0	1 piece	200	19	13	0	5	1.0	450	0.13	0.23	—
Mangoes, raw	198	7.0	1 medium mango	90	1	—	23	12	0.3	8380	0.08	0.07	55
Margarine	14	0.5	1 tbsp or ⅛ stick (fortified with vitamin A)	100	tr	12	tr	3	0	470	—	—	0
Marshmallows	9	0.3	1, 1¼ in dia	25	tr	0	8	2	0.2	0	0	tr	0
Meat and bean stew, cooked	244	8.5	1 cup (Mexican dish)	345	17	16	34	90	4.6	1177	0.37	0.22	59
Meat loaf, beef, baked	77	2.7	1 slice, 3¾ x 2¼ x ¾ in	240	19	17	3	34	2.9	138	0.10	0.21	—
Milk, dry skim, instant	17	0.6	¼ cup powder	61	6	tr	9	220	0.1	5 (unfortified)	0.06	0.30	1
Milk, dry, whole	26	0.9	¼ cup powder	129	7	7	10	234	0.1	290	0.08	0.38	2
Milk, evaporated, canned	126	4.4	½ cup, undiluted, unsweetened	173	9	10	12	318	0.2	405	0.05	0.43	2

Milk, fluid, skim or buttermilk	245	8.6	1 cup (½ pt)	90	9	tr	12	296	0.1	10	0.09	0.44	2
Milk, fluid, whole	244	8.5	1 cup (½ pt) 3.5 percent fat	160	9	9	12	288	0.1	350	0.07	0.41	2
Milk, goat's, fluid	244	8.5	1 cup, whole milk	165	8	10	11	315	0.2	390	0.10	0.27	2
Milk, malted, plain, beverage	353	12.4	1 fountain-size glass (about 1½ cup)	368	17	15	42	476	1.1	885	0.21	0.74	3
Milkshake, chocolate	342	12.0	1 fountain-size glass	420	11	18	58	363	0.9	687	0.12	0.55	4
Molasses, cane, black-strap	20	0.7	1 tbsp, 3rd extraction	45	—	—	11	137	3.2	—	0.02	0.04	—
Molasses, cane, light	20	0.7	1 tbsp, 1st extraction	50	—	—	13	33	0.9	—	0.01	0.01	—
Muffins, plain	40	1.4	1 muffin, 2¾ in dia, enriched white flour	120	3	4	17	42	0.6	40	0.07	0.09	tr
Mushrooms, canned	122	4.3	½ cup, solids and liquid	20	3	tr	3	8	0.6	tr	0.02	0.30	2
Noodles, egg, cooked	120	4.2	¾ cup, enriched	150	5	2	28	12	1.1	83	0.17	0.11	0
Nuts, almonds	36	1.3	¼ cup, shelled	213	7	19	7	83	1.7	0	0.09	0.33	tr
Nuts, cashew, roasted	35	1.2	¼ cup	196	6	16	10	13	1.3	35	0.15	0.09	—
Nuts, peanuts (see peanuts, roasted)													
Nuts, pecan halves	27	0.9	¼ cup	185	3	19	4	20	0.7	35	0.23	0.04	1
Nuts, walnut halves	25	0.9	¼ cup, English or Persian	163	4	16	4	25	0.8	8	0.08	0.03	1
Oatmeal or rolled oats, cooked	160	5.6	⅔ cup, regular or quick cooking	87	3	1	15	15	0.9	0	0.13	0.03	0
Oils, salad or cooking	14	0.5	1 tbsp	125	0	14	0	0	0	—	0	0	0
Okra, cooked	43	1.5	4 pods, 3 x ⅝ in	13	1	tr	3	39	0.2	210	0.06	0.08	9
Olives, green	16	0.6	4 medium or 3 large	15	tr	2	tr	8	0.2	40	—	—	—
Olives, ripe	10	0.4	3 small or 2 large	15	tr	2	tr	9	0.1	10	tr	tr	—
Onion, raw	110	3.9	1 onion, 2½ in dia	40	2	tr	10	30	0.6	40	0.04	0.04	11
Onions, cooked	105	3.7	½ cup or 5 onions, 1¼ in dia	30	2	tr	7	25	0.4	40	0.03	0.03	7
Onions, young, green	50	1.8	6 small, without tops	20	1	tr	5	20	0.3	tr	0.02	0.02	12
Oranges (as purchased)	180	6.3	1 orange, 2⅝ in dia (all commerical varieties)	65	1	tr	16	54	0.5	260	0.13	0.05	66
Orange juice, fresh	124	4.3*	½ cup or 1 small glass (all varieties)	55	1	1	13	14	0.3	250	0.11	0.04	62
Orange juice, canned	125	4.4	½ cup or 1 small glass, unsweetened	60	1	tr	14	13	0.5	250	0.09	0.03	50
Orange juice, frozen concentrate	125	4.4	½ cup or 1 small glass, diluted, ready to serve	60	1	tr	15	13	0.1	275	0.11	0.01	60
Orange juice, dehydrated, crystals	124	4.3	½ cup or 1 small glass, prepared, ready to serve	60	1	tr	14	13	0.3	250	0.10	0.04	55
Oysters, raw	120	4.2	½ cup or 8–10 oysters	80	10	2	4	113	6.6	370	0.17	0.22	—
Oyster stew, milk	230	8.1	1 cup with 3–4 oysters	200	11	12	11	269	3.3	640	0.13	0.41	—
Pancakes, wheat	27	0.9	1 griddle cake, 4 in dia (enriched flour)	60	2	2	9	27	0.4	30	0.05	0.06	tr
Papayas, raw	91	3.2	½ cup in ½ in cubes	35	1	tr	9	18	0.3	1595	0.04	0.04	51
Parsley, raw	4	0.1	1 tbsp chopped	tr	tr	tr	tr	8	0.2	340	tr	0.01	7
Parsnips, cooked	77	2.7	½ cup	50	1	1	12	35	0.5	25	0.06	0.07	8

Food	Weight g	Weight oz	Approximate measure and description	Calories	Protein g	Fat g	Carbohydrate g	Calcium mg	Iron mg	Vitamin A activity IU	Thiamin mg	Riboflavin mg	Ascorbic acid mg
Peaches, raw (as purchased)	114	4.0	1 peach, 2 in dia	35	1	tr	10	9	0.5	1320 (yellow-fleshed)	0.02	0.05	7
Peaches, raw	84	2.9	½ cup, sliced, fresh or frozen	33	1	tr	8	8	0.4	1115 (yellow-fleshed)	0.02	0.04	6
Peaches, canned	129	4.5	½ cup, halves or slices, solids and liquid, syrup-pack	100	1	tr	26	5	0.4	550 (yellow-fleshed)	0.01	0.03	4
Peaches, canned	123	4.3	½ cup, solids, liquid, (water-pack)	38	1	tr	10	5	0.4	550 (yellow-fleshed)	0.01	0.03	4
Peanuts, roasted	36	1.3	¼ cup, halves, salted	210	9	18	7	27	0.8	—	0.12	0.05	0
Peanut butter	32	1.1	2 tbsp	190	8	16	6	18	0.6	—	0.04	0.04	0
Pears, raw (as purchased)	182	6.3	1 pear, 3 x 2½ in dia	100	1	1	25	13	0.5	30	0.04	0.07	7
Pears, canned	117	4.1	2 medium halves with 2 tbsp juice, syrup pack	90	tr	tr	23	6	0.2	tr	0.01	0.02	2
Peas, green, cooked	80	2.8	½ cup	58	5	1	10	19	1.5	430	0.22	0.09	17
Peas, cowpeas, dry, cooked	124	4.3	½ cup, blackeye peas or frijoles	95	7	1	17	21	1.6	10	0.21	0.06	tr
Peas, pigeon, dry, raw	99	3.5	6 tbsp (gandules)	310	22	2	50	140	4.0	169	0.45	0.34	0
Peas, split, dry, cooked	125	4.4	½ cup	145	10	1	26	14	2.1	50	0.19	0.11	—
Peppers, sweet, green, raw	74	2.6	1 medium pod, without stem and seeds; 5 pods per lb	15	1	tr	4	7	0.5	310	0.06	0.06	94
Peppers, sweet, red, raw	60	2.1	1 medium pod, without stem and seeds	20	1	tr	4	8	0.4	2670	0.05	0.05	122
Peppers, green, stuffed	113	4.0	1 medium pepper, cooked with meat stuffing	200	12	14	12	31	1.9	637	0.09	0.14	64
Peppers, hot, red (see chili powder)													
Peppers, pimientos, canned	38	1.3	1 medium pod	10	tr	tr	2	3	0.6	870	0.01	0.02	36
Perch, ocean, fried	85	3.0	1 piece: 4 x 3 x ½ in	195	16	11	6	28	1.1	—	0.08	0.09	—
Persimmons, raw	125	4.4	1 fruit, 2½ in dia. (Japanese)	75	1	tr	20	6	0.4	2740	0.03	0.02	11
Pickle relish	15	0.5	1 tbsp	20	tr	tr	5	3	0.1	—	—	—	—
Pickles, cucumber, bread and butter	42	1.5	6 slices, ¼ x 1½ in dia	30	tr	tr	7	13	0.8	80	0.01	0.02	4
Pickles, cucumber, dill	65	2.3	1 large pickle, 3¾ x 1¼ in	10	1	tr	1	17	0.7	70	tr	0.01	4

Pickles, cucumber, sweet	15	0.5	1 pickle $2\frac{1}{2} \times \frac{3}{4}$ in dia	20	tr	tr	6	2	0.2	10	tr	tr	1
Pie, apple	135	4.7	4-in sector or $\frac{1}{7}$ of pie 9 in dia (unenriched flour)	350	3	15	51	11	0.4	40	0.03	0.03	1
Pie, cherry	135	4.7	4-in sector or $\frac{1}{7}$ of pie, 9 in dia (unenriched flour)	350	4	15	52	19	0.4	590	0.03	0.03	tr
Pie, custard	130	4.6	4-in sector or $\frac{1}{7}$ of pie, 9 in dia (unenriched flour)	285	8	14	30	125	0.8	300	0.07	0.21	0
Pie, lemon meringue	120	4.2	4-in sector or $\frac{1}{7}$ of pie, 9 in dia (unenriched flour)	305	4	12	45	17	0.6	200	0.04	0.10	4
Pie, mince	135	4.7	4-in sector or $\frac{1}{7}$ of pie, 9 in dia (unenriched flour)	365	3	16	56	38	1.4	tr	0.09	0.05	1
Pie, pumpkin	130	4.6	4-in sector or $\frac{1}{7}$ of pie, 9 in dia (unenriched flour)	275	5	15	32	66	0.7	3210	0.04	0.13	tr
Pineapple, raw	70	2.5	$\frac{1}{2}$ cup, diced	38	1	tr	10	12	0.4	50	0.06	0.02	12
Pineapple, canned	122	4.3	1 large or 2 small slices 2 tbsp juice, syrup pack	90	tr	tr	24	13	0.4	50	0.09	0.03	8
Pineapple, crushed	130	4.6	$\frac{1}{2}$ cup, canned syrup pack	100	1	tr	25	15	0.4	60	0.10	0.03	9
Pineapple juice, canned	125	4.4	$\frac{1}{2}$ cup or small glass	68	1	tr	17	19	0.4	60	0.06	0.02	11
Pizza (cheese)	75	2.6	$5\frac{1}{2}$ in sector or $\frac{1}{8}$ of pie, 14 in dia	185	7	6	27	107	0.7	290	0.04	0.12	4
Plantain, green, raw	100	3.5	1 baking banana, 6 in	135	1	—	32	8	0.8	380	0.07	0.04	28
Plums, raw (as purchased)	60	2.1	1 plum, 2 in dia	25	tr	tr	7	7	0.3	140	0.02	0.02	3
Plums, canned	128	4.5	$\frac{1}{2}$ cup or 3 plums with 2 tbsp juice, syrup pack	100	1	tr	27	11	1.1	1485	0.03	0.03	2
Popcorn, popped	9	0.3	1 cup, added oil and salt	40	1	2	5	1	0.2	—	—	0.01	0
Pork chop, cooked	99	3.5	1 chop, trimmed, thick, with bone	260	16	21	0	8	2.2	0	0.63	0.18	—
Pork roast, cooked	85	3.0	2 slices, $5 \times 4 \times \frac{1}{8}$ in	310	21	24	0	9	2.7	0	0.78	0.22	—
Potato chips	20	0.7	10 medium chips, 2 in dia	115	1	8	10	8	0.4	tr	0.04	0.01	3
Potatoes, baked	99	3.5	1 medium potato, about 3 per pound raw	90	3	tr	21	9	0.7	tr	0.10	0.04	20
Potatoes, boiled	122	4.3	1 potato, peeled before boiling	80	2	tr	18	7	0.6	tr	0.11	0.04	20
Potatoes, French-fried	57	2.0	10 pieces, $2 \times \frac{1}{2} \times \frac{1}{2}$ in, cooked in deep fat	155	2	7	20	9	0.7	tr	0.07	0.04	12
Potatoes, mashed	98	3.4	$\frac{1}{2}$ cup (milk, butter added)	95	2	4	12	24	0.4	165	0.08	0.05	9
Poultry pot pie	227	7.9	1 indiv. pie, $4\frac{1}{4}$ in dia (chicken or turkey)	535	23	31	42	68	3.0	3020	0.25	0.26	5
Pretzels	3	0.1	5, $3\frac{1}{8}$ in sticks	10	tr	tr	2	1	tr	0	tr	tr	0
Prunes, dried, cooked	105	3.7	5 medium prunes with 2 tbsp juice, sweetened	160	1	tr	42	21	1.5	733	0.03	0.06	1
Prune juice, canned	128	4.5	$\frac{1}{2}$ cup or small glass	100	1	tr	25	18	5.3	—	0.02	0.02	3
Pudding, chocolate	130	4.6	$\frac{1}{2}$ cup (chocolate blanc mange)	190	6	8	26	158	0.9	211	0.06	0.27	1

Food	Weight g	Weight oz	Approximate measure and description	Calories	Protein g	Fat g	Carbohydrate g	Calcium mg	Iron mg	Vitamin A activity IU	Thiamin mg	Riboflavin mg	Ascorbic acid mg
Pudding, cornstarch	124	4.3	½ cup (plain blanc mange)	140	5	5	20	145	0.1	195	0.04	0.20	1
Pudding, rice with raisins	136	4.8	½ cup (old-fashioned)	300	8	8	52	243	0.8	313	0.10	0.35	3
Pudding, tapioca	74	2.6	½ cup	140	5	5	12	104	0.4	327	0.04	0.19	1
Radishes, raw	40	1.4	4 small	5	tr	tr	1	12	0.4	tr	0.01	0.01	10
Raisins, seedless	10	0.4	1 tbsp pressed down	30	tr	tr	8	7	0.4	2	0.01	0.01	tr
Raspberries, red, raw	62	2.2	½ cup	35	1	1	9	14	0.6	80	0.02	0.06	16
Rhubarb, cooked	136	4.8	½ cup, sugar added	190	1	tr	50	106	0.8	110	0.03	0.08	9
Rice, parboiled, cooked	131	4.6	¾ cup (enriched)	140	3	tr	31	25	1.1	0	0.14	0.02	0
Rice, flakes	30	1.1	1 cup, added nutrients	115	2	tr	26	9	0.5	0	0.10	0.02	0
Rice, puffed	15	0.5	1 cup, added nutrients	60	1	tr	13	3	0.3	0	0.07	0.01	0
Rolls, bagel	55	1.9	1 roll, 3 in dia (egg)	165	6	2	28	9	1.2	30	0.14	0.10	0
Rolls, barbecue bun	40	1.3	1 bun, 3½ in dia (enriched)	120	3	2	21	30	0.8	tr	0.11	0.07	tr
Rolls, hard	52	1.8	1 round roll	160	5	2	31	24	0.4	tr	0.03	0.05	tr
Rolls, sweet, pan	43	1.5	1 roll	135	4	4	21	37	0.3	30	0.03	0.06	tr
Rolls, white, plain	28	1.0	1 commercial pan roll, (enriched flour)	85	2	2	15	21	0.5	tr	0.08	0.05	tr
Rutabagas, cooked	77	2.7	½ cup	25	1	tr	6	43	0.3	270	0.04	0.06	18
Salads[2]													
Salad, chicken	125	4.4	½ cup, with mayonnaise	280	25	19	1	20	1.7	200	0.04	0.15	1
Salad, egg	128	4.5	½ cup, with mayonnaise	190	6	18	1	35	1.3	630	0.06	0.16	1
Salad, fresh fruit	125	4.4	½ cup with French dressing (orange, apple, banana, grapes)	130	—	6	21	25	0.6	154	0.06	0.05	22
Salad, jellied, vegetable	122	4.3	½ cup, no dressing	70	3	—	16	14	0.2	25	0.03	0.02	20
Salad, lettuce	130	4.6	¼ solid head, with French dressing	80	1	6	5	28	0.7	618	0.05	0.10	9
Salad, potato	139	4.9	½ cup with mayonnaise	185	2	12	17	21	0.8	40	0.11	0.05	17
Salad, tomato aspic	119	4.2	½ cup, no dressing	45	5	0	7	12	0.5	1441	0.07	0.05	22
Salad, tuna fish	102	3.6	½ cup, with mayonnaise	250	21	18	1	14	1.2	98	0.04	0.09	1
Salad dressing, blue cheese	15	0.5	1 tbsp	75	1	8	1	12	tr	30	tr	0.02	tr
Salad dressing, boiled	16	0.6	1 tbsp, home made	25	1	2	2	14	0.1	80	0.01	0.03	tr

[2]Only a few common types of salads are listed here. The calorie and nutritive values of any combination of foods in a salad are easily estimated. The ½-cup servings of salads in this table, using mayonnaise, were made with ⅓ cup of the main ingredient, such as chicken, plus 2 tablespoons of a crisp vegetable, such as celery, plus 1 tablespoon of mayonnaise. One tablespoon of French dressing was used in the fruit and lettuce salads. The total calorie yield of a salad may vary greatly depending on the kind and amount of salad dressing added.

359

Food	Weight (g)	Measure	Calories	Protein (g)	Fat (g)	Carbohydrate (g)	Calcium (mg)	Iron (mg)	Vitamin A (IU)	Thiamine (mg)	Riboflavin (mg)	Vitamin C (mg)
Salad dressing, commercial	15	1 tbsp, mayonnaise type	65	tr	6	2	2	tr	30	tr	tr	—
Salad dressing, French	16	1 tbsp	65	tr	6	3	2	0.1	—	—	—	—
Salad dressing, low calorie	26	2 tbsp (cottage cheese, nonfat dry milk, no oil)	17	2	0	2	31	0	18	0.01	0.06	—
Salad dressing, mayonnaise	14	1 tbsp	100	tr	11	tr	3	0.1	40	tr	0.01	—
Salad dressing, thousand island	16	1 tbsp	80	tr	8	3	2	0.1	50	tr	tr	tr
Salmon, boiled or baked	119	1 steak, 4 x 3 x ½ in	200	34	7	tr	—	1.4	—	0.12	0.33	—
Salmon, canned	85	½ cup, pink salmon	120	17	5	0	167 (includes bones)	0.7	60 (pink)	0.03	0.16	—
Salmon loaf	113	½ cup or 1 slice, 4 x 1¼ x 1¼ in	235	29	10	5	43	1.8	332	0.08	0.20	2
Sandwiches[3]												
Sardines, canned oil	57	5 small fish, 3 x 1 x ¼ in	120	13	6	0	248	1.7	127	0.01	0.11	—
Sauce, chocolate	40	2 tbsp	75	1	4	9	32	0.2	87	0.01	0.05	—
Sauce, custard	31	2 tbsp (low calorie, with nonfat dry milk)	45	2	1	7	56	0.2	89	0.02	0.09	—
Sauce, hard	17	1 tbsp	90	—	6	11	1	0	231	0	0	0
Sauce, hollandaise (mock)	26	2 tbsp	75	2	7	3	36	0.2	353	0.02	0.06	1
Sauce, lemon	28	2 tbsp	40	0	1	8	—	—	34	—	—	2
Sauerkraut, canned	118	½ cup, solids and liquid	25	1	tr	5	43	0.6	60	0.04	0.05	17
Sausage, bologna	57	2 slices, 4.1 x 0.1 in	173	7	16	1	4	1.0	—	0.09	0.12	—
Sausage, frankfurters (see frankfurters)												
Sausage, liverwurst	57	3 slices, 2½ in dia, ¼ in thick	150	10	12	1	5	3.1	3260	0.10	0.63	0
Sausage, pork, cooked	26	2 small patties, or links	125	5	11	tr	2	0.6	0	0.21	0.09	—
Sausage, Vienna	16	1 canned sausage, about 2 in long	40	2	3	tr	1	0.3	—	0.01	0.02	—
Shad, baked	85	1 piece, 4 x 3 x ½ in	170	20	10	0	20	0.5	20	0.11	0.22	—
Sherbet, fruit	97	½ cup, orange	130	1	1	30	16	tr	60	0.01	0.03	2
Shrimp, canned	85	½ cup, meat only	100	21	1	1	98	2.6	50	0.01	0.03	—
Syrup, table blends	21	1 tbsp, light and dark	60	0	0	15	9	0.8	0	0	0	0
Soup, bean with pork	250	1 cup, ready to serve (canned)	170	8	6	22	63	2.3	650	0.13	0.08	3

[3]Sandwiches, as such, are not included in this list, but the "makings" are available for any type desired. For example, a simple sandwich might consist of two slices of enriched bread, 2 tablespoons butter, one slice boiled ham, 1 tablespoon mayonnaise, plus two leaves of lettuce. The sum of the calories and of the nutrients gives the total contribution of the sandwich. For salad sandwiches, the procedure is essentially the same. Chicken, egg, or tuna salads, in the measures given in this table, provide the amount of filling needed for a sandwich made with a large bun or two slices of bread.

Food	Weight g	Weight oz	Approximate measure and description	Calories	Protein g	Fat g	Carbohydrate g	Calcium mg	Iron mg	Vitamin A activity IU	Thiamin mg	Riboflavin mg	Ascorbic acid mg
Soup, chicken noodle	250	8.8	1 cup, ready to serve (canned)	65	4	2	8	10	0.5	50	0.02	0.02	tr
Soup, clam chowder	255	8.9	1 cup, ready to serve (canned)	85	2	3	13	36	1.0	920	0.03	0.03	—
Soup, beef broth	240	8.4	1 cup, ready to serve (canned) bouillon, consommé	30	5	0	3	tr	0.5	tr	tr	0.02	—
Soup, cream vegetable	240	8.4	1 cup, ready to serve (canned) tomato, mushroom, other	135	2	10	10	41	0.5	70	0.02	0.12	tr
Soup, minestrone	245	8.6	1 cup, ready to serve (canned)	105	5	3	14	37	1.0	2350	0.07	0.05	—
Soup, tomato	245	8.6	1 cup, ready to serve (canned)	90	2	3	16	15	0.7	1000	0.05	0.05	12
Soup, vegetable	250	8.8	1 cup, ready to serve (canned)	80	3	2	14	20	0.8	3250	0.05	0.02	—
Spaghetti, cooked	105	3.7	¾ cup, enriched	115	4	1	24	8	1.0	0	0.15	0.08	0
Spaghetti, meat balls	186	6.5	¾ cup (in tomato sauce)	250	15	9	30	93	2.8	1193	0.20	0.23	17
Spaghetti, in tomato sauce	188	6.5	¾ cup (with cheese)	200	7	7	28	60	1.7	810	0.18	0.14	10
Spinach (see greens)													
Squash, summer, cooked	105	3.7	½ cup, diced	15	1	tr	4	26	0.4	410	0.05	0.08	11
Squash, winter, baked	103	3.6	½ cup, mashed	65	2	1	16	29	0.8	4305	0.05	0.14	14
Stew, beef and vegetable	176	6.2	¾ cup	160	11	8	11	21	2.1	1733	0.10	0.13	11
Strawberries, raw	75	2.6	½ cup, capped	30	1	1	7	16	0.8	45	0.02	0.05	44
Sugar, brown	14	0.5	1 tbsp, firmly packed	50	0	0	13	12	0.5	0	tr	tr	0
Sugar, granulated	11	0.4	1 tbsp (beet or cane)	40	0	0	11	0	tr	0	0	0	0
Sugar, lump	6	0.2	1 domino, 1⅛ x ¾ x ⅜ in	25	0	0	6	0	tr	0	0	0	0
Sugar, powdered	8	0.3	1 tbsp	30	0	0	8	0	tr	0	0	0	0
Sweet potatoes, baked	110	3.9	1 medium potato, about 6 oz, raw	155	2	1	36	44	1.0	8910	0.10	0.07	24
Sweet potatoes, candied	175	6.1	1 potato, 3½ x 2¼ in	295	2	6	60	65	1.6	11,030	0.10	0.08	17
Tangerine	116	4.1	1 medium 2⅜ in dia	40	1	tr	10	34	0.3	360	0.05	0.02	27
Tartar sauce (see salad dressing, mayonnaise)													
Toast, melba	6	0.2	1 slice, 3¾ x 1¾ in	20	1	tr	4	5	0.1	0	0.01	0.01	0
Tomato, catsup	15	0.5	1 tbsp	15	tr	tr	4	3	0.1	210	0.01	0.01	2
Tomato juice, canned	122	4.3	½ cup or small glass	23	1	tr	5	9	1.1	970	0.06	0.04	20
Tomatoes, raw	200	7.0	1 tomato, about 3 in dia, 2⅛ in high	40	2	4	9	24	0.9	1640	0.11	0.07	42

Food	Measure											
Tomatoes, canned	½ cup	4.2	121	1	1	5	7	0.6	1085	0.06	0.04	21
Topping, whipped	1 tbsp pressurized	0.1	4	tr	1	tr	tr	–	20	–	0	–
Tortillas	1 tortilla, 5 in dia	0.7	20	1	1	10	22	0.4	40 (yellow corn)	0.04	0.01	–
Tuna fish, canned	½ cup, in oil, drained solids	3.0	85	24	7	0	7	1.6	70	0.04	0.10	–
Tuna salad (see salad, tuna fish)												
Turnip greens (see greens)												
Turnips, cooked	½ cup, diced	2.7	78	1	tr	4	27	0.3	tr	0.03	0.04	17
Veal, roast, cooked	2 slices, 3 x 2½ x ¼ in	3.0	85	23	14	0	10	2.9	–	0.11	0.26	–
Veal cutlet, broiled	1 cutlet, 3¾ x 3 x ½ in	3.0	85	23	9	–	9	2.7	–	0.06	0.21	–
Veal cutlet, (breaded) (wiener schnitzel)	2 slices, 2½ x 2½ x ¾ in	4.8	136	26	21	5	37	4.2	295	0.22	0.41	–
Vinegar	1 tbsp	0.5	15	0	–	1	1	0.1	–	–	–	–
Waffles	1 waffle, 7 in dia (enriched flour)	2.6	75	7	7	28	85	1.3	250	0.13	0.19	tr
Watermelon, raw	1 wedge, 4 x 8 in, with rind	32.4	925	2	2	27	30	2.1	2510	0.13	0.13	30
Welsh rarebit	½ cup	4.4	125	19	26	6	534	0.7	1118	0.04	0.40	–
Wheat flour, white	1 cup, enriched, sifted	4.0	115	12	1	88	18	3.3	0	0.51	0.30	0
Wheat flour, white	1 cup, unenriched, sifted	3.9	110	12	1	84	18	0.9	0	0.07	0.05	0
Wheat flour, whole wheat	1 cup, hard wheat	4.2	120	16	2	85	49	4.0	0	0.66	0.14	0
Wheat germ	2 tbsp	0.3	30	2	1	4	6	0.8	0	0.17	0.06	0
Wheat flakes	1 cup, added nutrients	1.1	25	3	tr	24	12	1.3	0	0.19	0.04	0
Wheat, shredded	1 biscuit, 4 x 2¼ in	0.9	25	2	1	20	11	0.9	0	0.06	0.03	0
White sauce (medium)	¼ cup	2.3	65	3	8	6	76	0.1	305	0.03	0.11	tr
Yeast, brewers, dry	1 tbsp	0.3	8	3	tr	3	17	1.4	tr	1.25	0.34	tr
Yeast, compressed	1 1-oz cake	1.0	28	3	tr	3	4	1.4	tr	0.20	0.47	tr
Yeast, dry active	4 ¼-oz packages	1.0	28	12	tr	12	12	4.4	tr	0.69	1.52	tr
Yoghurt	1 cup from partially skimmed milk	8.6	245	8	4	13	294	0.1	170	0.10	0.44	2

TABLE XIV-A

DIABETIC DIETS

Tables of Foods Allowed and Foods to Avoid

For Foods Allowed, see list of exchange in Appendix for measures and equivalents

1. Food Allowed as Desired

Bouillon, broth and consomme (fat free)
Coffee, plain
Flavoring extracts
Gelatin desserts (without sugar or artificial sweeteners)
Tea without sugar
Lemon
Pickles (except sweet)
Sauces (prepared without sugar or oil)
Seaweeds
Seeds
All fresh Fruit Juices
Herbs and Spices

| Chives | Parsley | Salt |
| Garlic | Pepper | Soy Sauce |

Mustard, dry or prepared
Vinegar

2. Milks Allowed

Whole milk
Low fat milk
Non-fat dry milk
Evaporated milk
Buttermilk
Yogurt, plain

3. Vegetables Allowed

Asparagus	Kale
Beansprouts	Lettuce, all kinds
Beet greens	Mushrooms
Broccoli	Okra
Brussels Sprouts	Parsley
Cabbage, head	Radish
Cabbage, celery	Romaine
Cabbage, mustard	Spinach
Cauliflower	Summer Squash
Celery	Sweet potato leaves
Chinese peas	Taro leaves
Cucumber	Tomato, fresh or canned
Eggplant	Tomato Juice
Endive	Turnip
Escarole	Turnip greens
Fern fronds	Vegetable juice
Green beans	Watercress
Green onion	Zucchini
Green pepper	

4. Starchy Vegetables Allowed

Artichoke, medium	Mixed vegetables
Beansprouts, soy	Onion
Beets	Papaya, green
Burdock	Peas
Carrots	Parsnips
Catsup	Pumpkin
Chayote fruit	Rutabaga
Corn	Soybeans, green
Cowpeas, green pods	Squash, winter yellow
Green peas	Water chestnut
Lima beans, green	Yam, bean root
Lotus, root	

5. Fruits Allowed, fresh, cooked, dried, canned or frozen without sugar

Apple	Nectarines
Applesauce	Orange, fresh
Apple juice	Orange juice
Apricots, fresh	Papaya
Apricots, dried	Passion fruit juice
Apricots, canned	Peach, fresh
Banana	Peach, dried
Cherries, canned	Peach, canned
Blueberries	Pear, fresh
Dates	Pear, dried
Figs, fresh	Pear, canned
Figs, dried	Pineapple, fresh
Figs, canned	Pineapple, canned
Fruit cocktail	Pineapple juice
Grapes, fresh	Plums, fresh
Grapes, canned	Plums, canned
Grape juice	Persimmon
Grapefruit, fresh	Pomegranate
Guava, fresh	Prunes, dried
Mandarin oranges	Prune juice
Mango	Raisins
Melon	Strawberries
Cantaloup	Tangerine
Honeydew	
Watermelon	

6. Bread Allowed

Biscuit	Muffin
Bread (white and whole wheat, rye)	Roll
Bun, hamburger or finger roll	Pancake
Cornbread	Waffles
English Muffin	

TABLE XIV–B

DIABETIC DIETS

7. Cereals Allowed
All cooked
Dry puffed or flaked
Shredded wheat

8. Crackers allowed
Graham
Melba toast
Ritz, plain
Ry-Krisp
Saltines
Soda

9. Flour Products Allowed
Cornstarch
Flour
Macaroni, Noodles, Spaghetti
Long rice
Rice

10. Vegetables Allowed
Beans and peas, dried, cooked
Breadfruit
Corn
Corn on Cob
Poi
Popcorn
Potatoes
  White, whole
  White, mashed or baked
  Sweet or Yams
Taro
  Hawaiian
Japanese dasheen

11. Meats Allowed
Cottage cheese, uncreamed
Egg whites
Fish
Cuttlefish
Fishcake, Chinese or Japanese
Canned Abalone, salmon, tuna
Canned Sardines, small in oil, drained
Canned Sardines, large in tomato sauce
Salmon
Squid, fresh or dried
Poultry
  Chicken (skin removed)
    Breast
    Drumsticks
    Thigh
    Wing
  Turkey, sliced, roasted
Veal, lean
Beef, lean
Lamb, lean
Pork, lean
Canadian Bacon

12. Meat Use Sparingly
Cheese
  American, Cheddar, Swiss
Egg
Frankfurter
Bologna
Liverwurst
Vienna Sausage
Duck roast
Shellfish
Clams
Crab
Lobster
Lobster tail
Oysters
Scallops
Shrimp, fresh or frozen
Organ meats
  Heart
  Kidney
  Liver
  Sweetbreads
  Tongue
Milk, whole
Cream, whipping
Macadamia
Nuts
Pork sausages

13. Fats Allowed
Fats, unsaturated
  Vegetable fat, except coconut oil
  Dressings
    French, special
    Italian
    Mayonnaise, special
  Nuts
    Almonds
    Peanuts
    Pecans
    Walnuts
  Oil
    Cottonseed
    Corn
    Safflower
    Sesame
    Soybean
  Olives
  Peanut Butter
  Sunflower seeds

14. Food for Occasional Use
Desserts
  Cake, sponge
  Custard
Doughnuts, plain
Ice Milk
Popsicle
Sherbet

15. Foods to Avoid
Cakes, except sponge
Candy
Cookies
Doughnuts
Fruits in syrup
Fruit punch or fruit ade
Gum
Honey
Jams and Jellies
Molasses
Pies and Pastries
Preserves
Puddings
Soft Drinks
Sugar of all kinds
Sweet rolls
Sweet pickles
Sweet and Sour foods
Sweetened Condensed milk
Syrups

Alcoholic beverages will help add up the calories, however, requires no insulin for metabolism. They should be included in the diet only if allowed by your physician.

TABLE XV–A

FOOD EXCHANGES

Adapted from Food Exchange Lists for Meal Planning, The American Dietetic Association

Food Exchanges are based on the comparable calorie content of foods. Within a food group, an item high in calories is reduced in quantity to equal an item lower in calories. Therefore, if you wish to have something other than 1 cup of orange juice with breakfast, you can refer to the Fruit Exchange List and choose instead one small apple or ½ a banana and know it equals 40 calories.

The purpose of the food exchange list is to allow flexibility in calorie or fat controlled diets.

The food exchanges have been used successfully in treating diabetes by diet alone, and the weight watching person can eat most foods, provided it is in the prescribed amounts.

Milk Exchanges

One Exchange of Milk contains 12 grams of carbohydrate, 8 grams of protein, a trace of fat and 80 calories.

Non-Fat Fortified Milk

Non-fat or skim milk	1 cup
Powdered (non-fat dry, before adding liquid)	1/3 cup
Canned, evaporated—non-fat or skim milk	1/2 cup
Buttermilk made from non-fat milk	1 cup
Yogurt made from non-fat milk (plain, unflavored)	1 cup

Low-Fat Fortified Milk

1% fat fortified milk (omit 1/2 Fat Exchange)	1 cup
2% fat fortified milk (omit 1 Fat Exchange)	1 cup
Yogurt made from 2% fortified milk (plain, unflavored) (omit 1 Fat Exchange)	1 cup

Whole Milk (Omit 2 Fat Exchanges)

Whole milk	1 cup
Canned, evaporated whole milk	1/2 cup
Buttermilk made from whole milk	1 cup
Yogurt made from whole milk (plain, unflavored)	1 cup

Vegetable Exchanges
(All Non-Starchy Vegetables)

One Exchange of Vegetables contains about **5 grams of carbohydrate, 2 grams of protein and 25 calories.** One exchange is 1/2 cup.

Asparagus	Greens:
Bean Sprouts	Mustard
Beets	Spinach
Broccoli	Turnip
Brussels Sprouts	Mushrooms
Cabbage	Okra
Carrots	Onions
Cauliflower	Rhubarb
Celery	Rutabaga
Eggplant	Sauerkraut
Green Pepper	String Beans, green or yellow
Greens:	Summer Squash
Beet	Tomatoes
Chards	Tomato Juice
Collards	Turnips
Dandelion	Vegetable Juice Cocktail
Kale	Zucchini

The following raw vegetables may be used as desired:

Chicory	Lettuce
Chinese Cabbage	Parsley
Endive	Radishes
Escarole	Watercress

Starchy Vegetables are found in the Bread Exchange List.

Fruit Exchanges
(All Fruits and Fruit Juices)

One Exchange of Fruit contains 10 grams of carbohydrate and 40 calories.

Apple	1 small
Apple Juice	1/3 cup
Applesauce (unsweetened)	1/2 cup
Apricots, fresh	2 medium
Apricots, dried	4 halves
Banana	1/2 small
Berries	
Blackberries	1/2 cup
Blueberries	1/2 cup
Raspberries	1/2 cup
Strawberries	3/4 cup
Cherries	10 large
Cider	1/3 cup
Dates	2
Figs, fresh	1
Figs, dried	1
Grapefruit	1/2
Grapefruit Juice	1/2 cup
Grapes	12
Grape Juice	1/4 cup
Mango	1/2 small
Melon	
Cantaloupe	1/4 small
Honeydew	1/8 medium
Watermelon	1 cup
Nectarine	1 small
Orange	1 small
Orange Juice	1/2 cup
Papaya	3/4 cup
Peach	1 medium
Pear	1 small
Persimmon, native	1 medium
Pineapple	1/2 cup
Pineapple Juice	1/3 cup
Plums	2 medium
Prunes	2 medium
Prune Juice	1/4 cup
Raisins	2 tablespoons
Tangerine	1 medium

Cranberries may be used as desired if no sugar is added.

Meat Exchanges
(Lean Meat)

One Exchange of Lean Meat (1 oz.) contains 7 grams of protein, 3 grams of fat and 55 calories.

Beef:	Baby Beef (very lean), Chipped Beef, Chuck, Flank Steak, Tenderloin, Plate Ribs, Plate Skirt Steak, Round (bottom, top), All cuts Rump, Sirloin, Tripe	1 oz.
Lamb:	Leg, Rib, Sirloin, Loin (roast and chops), Shank, Shoulder	1 oz.
Pork:	Leg (Whole Rump, Center Shank), Ham, Smoked (center slices)	1 oz.
Veal:	Leg, Loin, Rib, Shank, Shoulder, Cutlets	1 oz.
Poultry:	Meat without skin of Chicken, Turkey, Cornish Hen, Guinea Hen, Pheasant	1 oz.
Fish:	Any fresh or frozen	1 oz.
	Canned Salmon, Tuna, Mackerel, Crab and Lobster,	1/4 cup
	Clams, Oysters, Scallops, Shrimp,	5 or 1 oz.
	Sardines, drained	3
Cheeses containing less than 5% butterfat		1 oz.
Cottage Cheese, Dry and 2% butterfat		1/4 cup
Dried Beans and Peas (omit 1 Bread Exchange)		1/2 cup

Bread Exchanges
Bread, Cereal and Starchy Vegetables)

One Exchange of Bread contains 15 grams of carbohydrate, 2 grams of protein and 70 calories.

Bread

White (including French and Italian)	1 slice
Whole Wheat	1 slice
Rye or Pumpernickel	1 slice
Raisin	1 slice
Bagel, small	1/2
English Muffin, small	1/2
Plain Roll, bread	1
Frankfurter Roll	1/2
Hauburger Bun	1/2
Dried Bread Crumbs	3 Tbs.
Tortilla, 6"	1

Cereal

Bran Flakes	1/2 cup
Other ready-to-eat unsweetened Cereal	3/4 cup
Puffed Cereal (unfrosted)	1 cup
Cereal (cooked)	1/2 cup
Grits (cooked)	1/2 cup
Rice or Barley (cooked)	1/2 cup
Pasta (cooked), Spaghetti, Noodles, Macaroni	1/2 cup
Popcorn (popped, no fat added)	3 cups
Cornmeal (dry)	2 Tbs.
Flour	2-1/2 Tbs.
Wheat Germ	1/4 cup

Crackers

Arrowroot	3
Graham, 2-1/2" sq.	2
Matzoth, 4" x 6"	1/2
Oyster	20
Pretzels, 3-1/8" long x 1/8" dia.	25
Rye Wafers, 2" x 3-1/2"	3
Saltines	6
Soda, 2-1/2" sq.	4

Dried Beans, Peas and Lentils

Beans, Peas, Lentils (dried and cooked)	1/2 cup

Dried Beans, Peas and Lentils (cont'd)

Baked Beans, no pork (canned)	1/4 cup

Starchy Vegetables

Corn	1/3 cup
Corn on Cob	1 small
Lima Beans	1/2 cup
Parsnips	2/3 cup
Peas, Green (canned or frozen)	1/2 cup
Potato, White	1 small
Potato (mashed)	1/2 cup
Pumpkin	3/4 cup
Winter Squash, Acorn or Butternut	1/2 cup
Yam or Sweet Potato	1/4 cup

Prepared Foods

Biscuit 2" dia. (omit 1 Fat Exchange)	1
Corn Bread, 2" x 2" x 1" (omit 1 Fat Exchange)	1
Corn Muffin, 2" dia. (omit 1 Fat Exchange)	1
Crackers, round butter type (omit 1 Fat Exchange)	5
Muffin, plain small (omit 1 Fat Exchange)	1
Potatoes, French Fried, length 2" to 3-1/2" (omit 1 Fat Exchange)	8
Potato or Corn Chips (omit 2 Fat Exchanges)	15
Pancake, 5" x 1/2" (omit 1 Fat Exchange)	1
Waffle, 5" x 1/2" (omit 1 Fat Exchange)	1

Fat Exchanges

One Exchange of Fat contains 5 grams of fat and 45 calories.

Margarine, soft, tub or stick*	1 teaspoon
Avocado (4" in diameter)**	1/8
Oil Corn, Cottonseed, Safflower, Soy, Sunflower	1 teaspoon
Oil, Olive**	1 teaspoon
Oil, Peanut**	1 teaspoon
Olives**	5 small
Almonds**	10 whole
Pecans**	2 large whole
Peanuts**	
Spanish	20 whole
Virginia	10 whole
Walnuts	6 small
Nuts, other**	6 small
Margarine, regular stick	1 teaspoon
Butter	1 teaspoon
Bacon fat	1 teaspoon
Bacon, crisp	1 strip
Cream, light	2 tablespoons
Cream, sour	2 tablespoons
Cream, heavy	1 tablespoon
Cream Cheese	1 tablespoon
French dressing***	1 tablespoon
Italian dressing***	1 tablespoon
Lard	1 teaspoon
Mayonnaise***	1 teaspoon
Salad dressing, mayonnaise type***	2 teaspoons
Salt Pork	3/4 inch cube

*Make with corn, cottonseed, safflower, soy or sunflower oil only
**Fat content is primarily monounsaturated
***If made with corn, cottonseed, safflower, soy or sunflower oil can be used on fat modified diet.

Adapted from Food Exchange Lists for Meal Planning, The American Dietetic Association.

TABLE XVI

A PANTRY SHELF FOR EMERGENCY MEALS

Soups. Canned soups are a boon for today's busy homemaker. Plan to stock the flavors listed below along with others that are your family's favorites.

Cream of chicken	Tomato
Cream of celery	Consomme
Cream of mushroom	Cheddar cheese

Meats. The many kinds of canned meats offer every homemaker a variety of main dishes for quick and easy meals. Many of them can go into casseroles or provide the basis of sandwich fillings. Plan to stock:

Ham	Prepared meat salads
Chicken (boned as well as	Pressed meat (Spam, etc.)
with dumplings)	Corned beef hash
Potted meats	

Fish. Like canned meat, canned fish can be an invaluable aid when you're confronted with the need to prepare a meal in a minute. You'll want to keep on hand at least one can each of:

Salmon	Shrimp
Tuna fish	Sardines
Lobster	Oysters
Crab	

Fruits. For versatility and good flavor, fruits are difficult to beat. Be certain that your shelf includes:

Fruit cocktail	Applesauce
Peach halves	Fruit juice (These are especially
Pear halves	important since they may substitute for water

Vegetables. For using alone or in combination with other ingredients, these vegetables are essential.

Tomatoes (whole pack, puree,	Asparagus
sauce, and paste(	Beets
Onions (tiny whole)	Beans (limas, baked, green, kidney)
Carrots	Green peas
Corn (both cream and whole kernel)	

Starches. The foods in this group are often used as the basis of in-a-hurry pantry shelf casseroles or as extenders for leftovers. They're invaluable, and you'll want to keep in stock:

Potatoes (instant mashed and	Macaroni
tiny whole)	Noodles (small ones for stroganoff
Rice (both brown and white	and other similar dishes and the
types, quick-cooking)	wider ones used for lasagna)
Spaghetti	

Bread mixes. These are a must for plan-ahead homemakers. Include the following kinds on your emergency shelf:

Biscuit mix	Corn bread mix
Pancake mix	Muffin mix
Pastry mix	

You'll also want to include crackers (soda, fancy round, flavored, snack-type, oyster) and melba toast.

Desserts. The kinds and varieties of mixes available today encourage every homemaker, even when her time is shortest, to finish her meal with a special fillip. Basic emergency dessert supplies include:

Puddings (both instant and canned)	Frosting mix
Cake mix	Cookie mix
Pie fillings	

Miscellaneous. This category includes accompaniments and complementary foods you'll want to keep a handy supply of on your shelf:

Pimentos	Spaghetti and meat balls
Olives	Beef stew
Mushrooms	Beef cubes and chicken cubes
Milk (canned evaporated,	Bread crumbs
powdered)	Lemon juice
Spaghetti sauce mix	Jugs of water (Water storage needs
Gravy mixes	to be replaced once each month.)

REFERENCES

Infants and Preschool Children

Dierks, E. C. and Morse, L. M. *Food Habits and Nutrient Intake of preschool children.* J. Am. Dietet. A. 47:292, 1965.

Foman, S. J. *Infant Nutrition,* Philadelphia: W. B. Saunders, 1967.

Fox, H. M., Fryer, B. A., Lamkin, G. H., Vivian, V. M., and Eppright, E. S. *The North Central regional study of diets of preschool children, Family environment,* J. Home Econ. 62:241,1970.

Nutrition Review: Solid foods in the nutrition of young infants Nutrition Review 25:233, 1967.

Suggested Guidelines for Evaluation of the Nutritional Status of Preschool Children. Rev. Washington, D.C.: U.S. Children Bureau, 1967.

Tepley, L. J. *Nutritional needs of the preschool child.* Nutrition Review, 22:65, 1964.

Willis, N. H. *Basic Infant Nutrition.* Philadelphia: J. B. Lippincott, 1964.

The Family Nutrition

Aykroyd, W. R. *Food for Man,* New York: The MacMillian Co. 1964.

Benedict, Ruth. *The American Family,* Thomas Y. Crowell Co., 1969.

Family Food Buying, USDA Guide for Calculating Food Amounts and Comparing costs, 1977.

Family Food Budgeting, USDA Home and Garden Bull No. 94, 1971.

Galbraith, John K. *The Affluent Society.* Boston, Mass.: Houghton Mifflin Company, 1958.

Kutsky, R. J. *Handbook on Vitamins and Hormones.* New York: Van Nostrand Reinhold Co., 1973.

Leverton, Ruth M. *Food Becomes You.* Ames Iowa State University Press, 1965.

Lowenberg, M. E. and Todhunter, E. N. *Food and Man.* New York: John Wiley and Sons, Inc. 1968.

Stephens, William N. *The Family in Cross-Cultural Perspective.* Holt, Rinehart & Winston, Inc. 1963.

Health

Carter, R. *Your Food and Your Health,* New York: Harper and Row Co., 1964.

Gerard, R. W. *Food for Life* Chicago: University of Chicago Press, 1965.

Krause, M. and Hunscher, M. *Food Nutrition and Diet Therapy,* 5th ed., Philadelphia: W. B. Saunders Co., 1964.

Labruza, Theodore. *Food and Your Well Being.* West Publishing Co., 1977.

Nasser, E. S. *Your Diet, Digestion and Health,* 2nd ed., New York: Barnes and Noble, 1962.

National Health Journal Life and Health. RP-18-25 Nov. 1977.

Nutritional Value of Foods. Rev. USDA Home and Garden Bull. No. 72, 1970.

Rumyon, Thora. *Nutrition for Today.* New York: Harper and Row, 1976.

Webster, Jabus Sutton. *Health for Effective Living,* McGraw Hill Co., 5th ed., 1970.

Williams, Sue R. *Nutrition and Diet Therapy,* 3rd ed., The C. V. Mosby Co., 1977.

Wayler, T. J. and Klien, R. S. *Applied Nutrition,* New York: The MacMillian Co., 1965.

Wilson, E. D., Fisher, K. H. and Fugua, M. E. *Principles of Nutrition,* 3rd ed., New York: John Wiley and Sons, 1966.

Sociological or Cultural

Casiel, J. *Social and Cultural Implications of Food and Food Habits. AM,* J. Public Health, 47:732, 1957.

Lowenberg, M. E. *Socio-Cultural Basis of Food Habits.* Food Tech 24:27, 1970.

Niehoff, A. *Changing Food Habits,* J. Nuti, Educ, 1:10, 1969.

Roundtree, Jili, and Manghan, H. D. *Open Doors to Improve Nutrition: The Family influence on children's food habits; nutrition of school child.* School Lunch J. 19:13, 1965.

Nutrition for Nutritionist and Dietitian

Bogert, L. J., Bridges, G. M. and Calloway, D. H. *Nutrition and Physical Fitness,* Philadelphia: 8th ed., W. B. Saunders Company, 1966.

Brown, E. L. *College students look at the basis for their food habits.* J. Home Econ., 59:784, 1967.

Caldwell, R. C. *Physical properties of foods and their caries-producing potential.* J. dent., Res., 59:1293–1299, 1970.

Carlsson, J. and Egelberg, J. *Effect of diet on early plaque formation in man.* Odont, Rev. 16:112–125, 1965.

Critchly, P. *Effects of food on bacterial metabolic processes.* J. dent. Res., 49:1283–1291, 1970.

Dawes, C. *Effects of diet on salivary secretion and composition.* J. dent. Res. 49:1263–1973, 1970.

Deutsch, R. M. *The Family Guide to Better Food and Better Health,* Des Moines, Iowa: Meredith Corporation, 1971.

Eppright, E., Pattison, M. and Barbour, H. *Teaching Nutrition,* 2nd ed., Ames Iowa: Iowa State University Press, 1963.

Farber, S. M., Wilson, N. L. and Wilson, R. H. L. *Food and Civilization.* A. Symposium, Springfield, Ill: Charles C. Thomas, 1966.

Goodhart, R. S. *Nutrition for You,* New York: E. P. Dutton Company, 1958.

Greisheimer, E. M. and Wiedman, M. P. *Physiology and Anatomy,* 9th ed., Philadelphia: J. B. Lippincott Company, 1972.

Grollman, S. *The Human Body: Its Structure and Function,* 2nd ed., New York: The Macmillian Company, 1969.

Harding, M. G., et al. *Carbohydrates in Foods,* J. A., Diet, Assoc., 46:197, 1965. Leung, W. T. W. *Food Composition Table for Use in Latin America.* Interdepartmental Committee on Nutrition for National Defense, National Institutes of Health, Bethesda, Md. 1961.

Henkin, R. D. *The role of taste in disease and nutrition, sweetness and increased salivary flow.* Borden's Rev. Nutr. Res. 28:71–87, 1967.

Jenner, A. *Social, emotional and cultural influences as related to eating patterns and malnutrition.* Con. Nutr. Notes 24:37, 1968.

Jolliffe, N., et al. *Clinical Nutrition,* 2nd ed., New York: Harper & Row, 1962. (Useful chapters on normal nutrition).

Lamb, M. W. *Food acceptance, a challenge to nutrition education—a review.* J. Nuti. education. 1:20, 1969.

Malm, M. *The role of sugar in modern nutrition.* Marabou symp., Suppl., No. 9; Naringsforsking, argan 17, p. 28, 1973.

Martin, E. A. *Nutrition in Action,* 3rd ed. New York: Holt, Rinehart and Winston, 1971.

McHenry, E. W. *Foods Without Fads.* J. B. Lippincott Company, Philadelphia, 1960.

Niliforuk, G. *Posteruptive effects of nutrition on teeth.* J. dent. Res., 49:1252–1261, 1970.

Orr, M. L. and Watt, B. K. *Amino Acid Content of Foods.* Home Econ. Res., No. 4, Washington, D.C.: U.S. Department of Agriculture, 1957.

Peckham, G. C. *Foundations of Food Preparation,* 2nd ed., The MacMillan Company, 1969.

Pre-School Child Malnutrition. Primary Deterrent to Human Progress. Pub. 1282, Washington, D.C.: National Academy of Sciences—National Research Council, 1966.

371

Robinson, C. H. *Basic Nutrition and Diet Therapy*, 2nd ed., New York: The Macmillan Company, 1970.

Studies No. 11, Food and Agriculture Organization, Rome, 1954 Church, C. F., and Church, H. N. *Food Values of Portions Commonly Used*, 11th ed., Philadelphia: J. B. Lippincott Company, 1970.

Stare, F. J. *Eating for Good Health*. New York: Doubleday, 1964.

Tanzer, J. M. *Sucrose metabolism of Streptococcus mutans: Streptococcus mutans and dental caries*. Proc. Round Table Discussion, 73rd Annual Meeting, Amer. Soc. Microbiol., Nat., Inst. dent., Res. pp. 25–32, 1973.

Taylor, C. M. and Pye, O. F. *Foundations of Nutrition*, 6th ed., New York: The Macmillan Company, 1966.

Taylor, C. M. *Food Values in Shares and Weights*, 2nd ed., New York: The Macmillan Company, 1959.

Watt, B. K. and Merrill, A. L. *Composition of Foods, Raw, Processed, Prepared*. Handbook No. 8, U.S. Department of Agriculture, Washington, D.C., 1963.

Journals
American Journal of Clinical Nutrition
American Journal of Public Health
Annual Review of Biochemistry
British Journal of Nutrition
Chemical Abstracts-Nutrition Division
Food Science
Food Technology
Journal of the American Dietetic Association
Journal of Home Economics
Journal of Laboratory and Clinical Medicine
Journal of Nutrition
Journal of Nutrition Education
Metabolism
Nutrition Abstracts and Reviews
Nutrition Today
Today's Health
Vitamins and Hormones

Weiss, R. L. and Trithart, A. H. *Between meal eating habits and dental caries, Experience in pre-school children*. Amer. J. Publ. Hlth 50:1097–1104, 1960.

White, P. L. *Let's Talk About Food*. Chicago: American Medical Association, 1967.

Wohl, M. G. and Goodhart, R. S. *Modern Nutrition in Health and Disease*, 4th ed., Philadelphia: Lea and Febiger, 1968.

Wright, C. E. *Food Buying*. New York: The Macmillan Company, 1962.

RECIPE INDEX

376

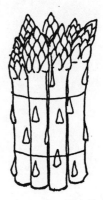

NUTRITION INDEX

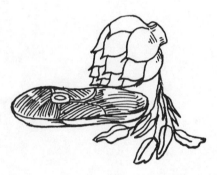